THE DESCENT OF THE GODS

The Collected Edition
General Editors
Henry Summerfield
Colin Smythe

THE DESCENT OF THE GODS

COMPRISING
THE MYSTICAL WRITINGS
OF
G. W. RUSSELL
'A.E.'

Edited
with an introduction and notes
by
Raghavan Iyer
&
Nandini Iyer

COLIN SMYTHE
Gerrards Cross, 1988

This collection copyright © 1988 by the Estate of G.W. Russell
Introduction and notes copyright © 1988 by Raghavan and Nandini Iyer

This collection first published in 1988 by Colin Smythe Limited.
Gerrards Cross, Buckinghamshire
as part 3 of the Collected Works of G.W. Russell – A.E.

British Library Cataloguing in Publication Data

A.E.
 The descent of the gods, comprising the
 mystical writings of G.W. Russell, A.E.
 1. Mysticism
 Rn. George William Russell I. Title
 II. Iyer, Raghavan   III. Iyer, Nandini
 149'.3   BL625

ISBN 0–901072–44–3

Printed in Great Britain
Typeset by Inforum Ltd, Portsmouth
and printed and bound by Billing & Son Ltd.,
Worcester

For
Pico
and all pathfinders

>What we need is that interior tenderness shall be elevated into seership, that what in most is only yearning or blind love shall see clearly its way and hope. To this end we have to observe more intently the nature of the interior life. We find, indeed, that it is not a solitude at all, but dense with multitudinous being: instead of being alone we are in the thronged highways of existence. For our guidance when entering here many words of warning have been uttered, laws have been outlined, and beings full of wonder, terror, and beauty described. Yet there is a spirit in us deeper than our intellectual being which I think of as the Hero in man, who feels the nobility of its place in the midst of all this, and who would fain equal the greatness of perception with deeds as great.
> — A.E.

CONTENTS

PREFACE	xi
INTRODUCTION by Raghavan and Nandini Iyer	
George William Russell – Mystic, Hero and Seer	1
The Mysticisms of A.E.	7
Theosophical Presuppositions and Concepts	12
The Language of the Gods	20
The Trials of the Soul	27
The Interpreters	34
The Gaelic Awakening	40
Fountain of Inspiration	45
Illumination and Seership	54
The Mythic Imagination	61
The Descent of the Gods	67
Testament of Faith in the Future	73
A.E.'s Appeal	76
I. THE LANGUAGE OF THE GODS	
The Candle of Vision	81
Preface	82
Retrospect	83
The Earth Breath	87
The Slave of the Lamp	89
Meditation	91
The Many-Coloured Land	95
Analytic	100
The Mingling of Natures	104
The Memory of Earth	108
Imagination	113
Dreams	118
The Architecture of Dream	123
Have Imaginations Body?	129
Intuition	134
The Language of the Gods	138

Ancient Intuitions	142
Power	146
The Memory of the Spirit	149
Celtic Cosmogony	154
The Celtic Imagination	160
Earth	164
The Speech of the Gods	167
The Element Language	174
Review of R.H. Fitzpatrick's *Lyrics*	187
Review of Charles Johnston's *From the Upanishads*	189
Works and Days	190

II. THE TRIALS OF THE SOUL

The Hour of Twilight (A)	195
The Hour of Twilight (B)	197
The Secret of Power	200
A Priestess of the Woods	203
A Tragedy in the Temple	207
The Meditation of Ananda	210
A Talk by the Euphrates	214
The Cave of Lilith	217
A Strange Awakening	220
The Midnight Blossom	236

III. THE HEAVENLY CITY

The Interpreters	243
At the Dawn of the Kaliyuga	322
'Go Out in Thought'	325
The Hero in Man	328

IV. THE GAELIC AWAKENING

The Legends of Ancient Eire	341
The Mountains	348
On an Irish Hill	350
The Awakening of the Fires	354
Priest or Hero?	362
Chivalry	370
In the Shadow of the Gods	372
An Irish Mystic's Testimony	377
Review of Franz Hartmann's *Among the Gnomes*	383

Contents

V. FOUNTAIN OF INSPIRATION

Song And its Fountains	387
Jagrata, Svapna and Sushupti	454
Concentration	456
Comfort	458
Review of Maurice Maeterlinck's *The Treasure of the Humble*	460
An Eastern Candle of Vision	462
Introduction to *The City Without Walls*, arranged by Margaret Cushing Osgood	464

VI. THE MYTHIC IMAGINATION

The Mask of Apollo	469
The Story of a Star	472
A Doomed City	476
The Mystic Nights' Entertainment	478
The Enchantment of Cuchullain	490
The Childhood of Apollo	515
The Fountains of Youth	518
A Dream of Angus Oge	523
Religion and Love	527

VII. THE DESCENT OF THE GODS

The Avatars	535
The Ascending Cycle	616
Shadow and Substance	619
The Renewal of Youth	622
Self-Reliance	632
Ireland Behind the Veil	635
On the March	641
Transformations	645
The Christ, a review of Dr. Arthur Drews' *The Christ Myth*	648

APPENDIX A: THE THEOSOPHICAL MOVEMENT

Lodges of Magic	653
A Word upon the Objects of the Theosophical Society	657
To the Fellows of the Theosophical Society	659
On the Spur of the Moment	664

To the Editor of *Lucifer*	667
A Basis for Brotherhood	668
W.Q.J.	671
Stand and Serve	672
Word and Theory	674
APPENDIX B: The Return	677
NOTES AND COMMENTARY	687
SELECT BIBLIOGRAPHY	771
GLOSSARY OF TERMS AND NAMES	773
TITLE INDEX	779

PREFACE

George William Russell was continually seeking, in varied ways, to bridge eternity and time. He could also show a shrewd sense of timing, although his writings were ahead of his time. Today there are large numbers of earnest seekers after mystical enlightenment scattered across the globe, who can readily respond to the poignancy and penetration of insight in A.E.'s thought and writing. These can best be appreciated when his work is considered as a whole. Hence the need for bringing together the mystical writings of A.E. within a single collection.

The editors are deeply grateful to Colin Smythe and Henry Summerfield for providing scarce texts and all the support needed to complete the work. William Daniel's unpublished dissertation, 'The Early A.E.: Prose, Poetry, Life: 1867–1905' (Harvard, 1968), has enabled the editors to include three hitherto unrecognized contributions of A.E. An enormous debt of gratitude is owed to Steven Carlson and Elton Hall for considerable research and assistance in tracking down references, unearthing information and assembling materials. Claudia Carlson, Barbara Coster and Susan Ryan cheerfully assumed the onerous task of typing the manuscript.

All those who have helped in preparing this work have found that their love of A.E. has deepened, and they have gained valuable inspiration in daily life. A splendid example of such help may be found in A.E.'s essay 'The Hour of Twilight'. This is an especially suitable time for calm reflection upon the wisdom in which A.E.'s work abounds.

N.R.I.
R.N.I.

Oxford
May 8, 1978

INTRODUCTION
MYSTIC, HERO AND SEER

*Life can only be understood backwards,
but it must be lived forwards.*
                                    Kierkegaard

The contribution of George William Russell (A.E.) to the Irish Renaissance is readily recognized, yet attempts to appraise his literary, artistic and political achievements often obscure rather than reveal his considerable impact and influence. His greatness of soul was enshrined in his calm renunciation of personal goals and single-minded commitment to a life of altruistic service. His artistic endeavours were always ancillary to a continuous mystic quest. A.E.'s mysticism was neither static nor half-hearted. Rooted in an ever-renewed vision, his insights were ripened through action. This process underwent successive phases of development, from youthful ecstasy to a mature and tranquil seership in later life. During his middle years A.E.'s humane faith animated his heroic efforts and social concerns. In the context of Irish nationalism, he felt a strong obligation to test his deeper convictions in the public arena. His profound compassion for all human beings prevented A.E.'s mysticism from becoming purely subjective or self-indulgent. The mystic glimmerings of his youth were nourished through unostentatious love of humanity, and his main aim as a writer was to convey those ideas which might help to restore nobility to the soul's odyssey, even in times of apathy, anomie and despair.

George Russell's upbringing bore little relation to his aspirations and destiny. Born in 1867, his early youth was cramped by a rigid educational system that ran contrary to his generous impulses. He was enrolled in several schools which required him to comply with a restrictive classical and religious training under threat of corporal punishment. He was aggrieved that his schoolmasters were indifferent to the need for any large conception of national identity and purpose. In later years, Russell would refuse to credit his formal education for any of his intellectual attainments. He seems to have been sustained mainly by his private reading of varied literature ranging from fairy stories to romantic novels. When he left school in 1884, he was, by his own account, untrammelled by the least trace of scepticism. Instead, he zealously guarded his desire to discover the alchemist's elixir of life and the philosopher's stone, subjects upon which he read avidly.

From 1884 to 1891 Russell pursued the primary ambition of his youth, that of an artist. He was gifted with a remarkable ability to record his inner life on canvas. To develop his talent he took evening classes at the Metropolitan School of Art in Dublin. He also attended the Royal Hibernian Academy, where he startled teachers and fellow students alike with renderings of his visionary experiences. Spurning the passive imitation of external models, he set himself the task of skilfully representing the powers and presences of his own imagination, and actively drew upon mythic archetypes and ancient landscapes as the stimulus for his creative inspiration. These seven years were marked by an absorbing interest in mystic literature and the inward promptings of his soul. His apprenticeship in art coincided with an event which held the crucial clue to A.E.'s growth as a mystic. While on holiday, walking in the country, he was overcome suddenly by a gust of spiritual illumination which conferred upon him the realization that

> beings were looking in upon me out of the true home of man. . . . The visible world became like a tapestry blown and stirred by the winds behind it. If it would but raise for an instant I knew I would be in Paradise.[1]

He became aware at that moment of another presence within him, a being that had accumulated knowledge over millennia, struggling with its noble and base desires yet affirming its fundamental identity with the Oversoul with which it was destined to re-unite. Russell recognized this as the psyche, a portion of the re-incarnating individuality which existed prior to and outside the body. He later came to think that this greater self was not disparate but closely connected with vast assemblages of beings, which explained the glorious visitations in his own imagination.

In the light of a series of mystical experiences of a similar nature, Russell's entire conception of himself was radically transformed. He became assured that he was not the *persona* that acquaintances

---

1 *The Candle of Vision. The Descent of the Gods*, p. 85. All page references to this volume will be preceded by the word *Descent*. Details of other works cited will be found in the Select Bibliography on pp. 771–72.

associated with his Christian name, but essentially an incorruptible spark of divinity which ensouled his fallible mind. He also discovered that when he attempted to turn his spiritual afflatus into a personal possession, his sense of immortality would immediately dissolve. Such experiences convinced him of two great truths: first of all, that creative gifts should be used in the service of one's fellow-men; and secondly, that one's true mission in life must not be dictated by personal ambition but should assist the purposes for which the psyche had taken on incarnation. It is hardly surprising that the revelation of his mystical nature wrought an overwhelming change in his behaviour. The recalcitrant and puckish schoolboy soon became the shy and diffident young man of his artistic apprenticeship. His silent yet benevolent manner concealed the quickening of a subtle intelligence.

In 1884 George Russell encountered at art school one of the most notable friends he was to make during his life, William Butler Yeats. Their relationship was highly unconventional because they lacked agreement on basic assumptions. Yeats deployed mystical imagery to adorn his verse and to provide a vehicle for aesthetic expression. Russell, on the other hand, saw in his commitment to the spiritual life a sacred resolve to renounce all lesser concerns for the sake of universal welfare. Nonetheless, throughout their lives Russell and Yeats shared a mutual affection as artists and men of letters, and frequently rendered assistance to one another by way of advice and recommendations. They respected each other, but from a distance. During the early years of their friendship Yeats introduced Russell into diverse literary circles in Dublin. There he encountered Charles Johnston, the Orientalist, and others who were interested in ancient religion and philosophy.

Russell became thoroughly preoccupied with the study of these ideas, stimulated especially by *Isis Unveiled* by Helena Petrovna Blavatsky, which was given by a friend. About this time he embarked upon a series of paintings depicting the gradual evolution of primitive forms into the human image within the mind of God. One picture particularly haunted him. Its subject was the archetypal man newly born in Divine Mind. One night as he lay in bed seeking a name for it, he felt a presence beyond his own mind about to speak and it finally whispered to him the name Aön. Several weeks later while searching for an art journal in the Dublin Library, he chanced upon an open book describing the word 'Aeon' and its origin as the name the Gnostics had given to the first beings separated from Deity. He at once had confirmation that his imaginary excursions were more than mere fantasizing. Later he adopted the name Aeon as a *nom de plume*, mistakenly shortened to the initials A.E. by a printer.

A.E.'s intense involvement in mystical studies eventually eclipsed his desire to become an artist and he turned to language and linguistics in an attempt to uncover and express arcane truths. He recorded in verse and allegory his own experiments in the spiritual life, gradually withdrawing from formal academic training to pursue private studies. He would spend months brooding over the divine origin of the letters of the alphabet, hoping to discover the primeval roots of language in a pre-existent Logos. In 1887 he co-authored an article with Charles Johnston entitled 'The Speech of the Gods', which conveyed the fruit of their explorations. By 1890 he had decided that his loyalties to his mystical commitment and to his training as a painter were in conflict. He surrendered his artistic pursuits and dedicated himself wholeheartedly to Theosophy. He accepted employment as a clerk in a draper's shop in Dublin. This work was to give A.E. the economic security he needed during the next seven years to tread the path of self-knowledge.

Theosophy, as a unified system of cosmological, psychological and moral principles, was the vital force that shaped the remainder of A.E.'s life and thought. In the last year of his life he remarked that his true teachers were the founders of the Theosophical Society, H.P. Blavatsky and W.Q. Judge, as well as sages of ancient India whose works, the Upaniṣads, *Bhagavad Gītā* and *Yoga Sūtras*, were made available by the Theosophical Society. From 1890 to 1897 he lived communally with a group of Theosophists who represented the nucleus of the Dublin Lodge. There he lectured regularly on various aspects of Theosophical philosophy. His life settled into a regular routine of study, meditation and work, and he slowly developed the skill necessary to make his naturally altruistic feelings effective both in personal relationships and as an orator and writer whose influence was to extend throughout Ireland and beyond. This probationary period served A.E. well, cultivating the practical side of his nature and bequeathing him a sufficient wisdom in human affairs to blend his ethical ideals and external relations with increasing success. The flights of his youthful mysticism were ripening into compassionate intelligence and mature control. During this period he frequently turned to verse. With the help of Charles A. Weekes, he published a collection of poems entitled *Homeward: Songs by the Way*. He collaborated in founding the magazine *Irish Theosophist* and was a regular contributor to its pages, where lingers some of his most vigorous prose, ranging from lyrical allegories to subtle disquisitions on mystical philosophy and Theosophical metaphysics. Altogether they represent the fruits of the deep study and meditation he had nurtured since youth.

As his efforts at practical altruism expanded, he became increasingly concerned with the fate of the Irish people, sensing that a new epoch in Ireland's political history was imminent and that its entire future as a nation was being decided during his life-time. He helped to infuse a spirit of brotherhood into the emerging polity, holding that Ireland could accomplish a far-reaching spiritual renaissance by returning to its ancestral roots. To this end he fostered the revival of interest in Celtic mythology and folklore and contrasted the native heroism of the ancient Gaelic peoples with the feudal servitude imposed upon them by the Christian Church. His message was unambiguous: Ireland could build a future only on the foundations of its pre-Christian past. As A.E. was a poet, patriot, a practised speaker and very efficient in accounting matters, W.B. Yeats suggested to Sir Horace Plunkett that he be recruited into the Irish Agriculture Organization Society in 1897. With this change A.E. passed permanently from private disciple to public teacher. He dissociated himself from the Theosophical Society which had been sundered by bitter factional disputes and devoted himself to the social welfare of his countrymen. As an officer of the I.A.O.S., he helped to devise a credit system for the impoverished farmers of the Congested Districts of western Ireland. He strove also to bring these farmers together in rural collectives to alleviate their poverty and to instil the ideas of fraternity and mutual assistance which he hoped would be the basis for a new society in the future Irish Free State. Russell's writings during this period are suffused with an heroic fervour. They urge the disinherited to throw off the shackles of economic, political and mental slavery and to reclaim their ancient estate as free men. He constantly pointed to the innate dignity of each human soul as the true foundation of all social reform. In 1905 he became editor and a leading contributor to the *Irish Homestead*, then an organ of the I.A.O.S. His commentaries ranged far beyond agricultural matters, extending to issues of social welfare, politics and Irish culture generally. He inserted an ethical dimension into these endeavours and brought his vast erudition to bear upon the affairs of daily life.

From this time until his death in 1935, his national influence grew as a result of his tireless labours on behalf of a free Irish state. In 1922 he published *The Interpreters*, a political allegory conveying his ideas regarding the reshaping of the civil order along spiritual lines. The avowed aim of the book was to trace politics back to its mystical foundations. *The Candle of Vision*, published in 1918, remains A.E.'s most popular and acclaimed prose work. It is indeed the autobiography of a mystic. It combines richness of insight with a lyrical prose style, captivating in its lucidity and beauty. The tone is at once congenial and penetrating. It stands with other timeless mystical texts as a compelling diary of the inner life, intimate yet accessible. Characteristically, the book is marked by its universal appeal to the intuitions of all men and women. In the later years of his life A.E. continued to write, editing the *Irish Statesman*, a weekly that incorporated the *Irish Homestead*. He began to travel abroad, lecturing on social and cultural topics, urging land reform and aid for the impoverished. He became an international figure, respected for his generosity of spirit and immense knowledge in a variety of practical concerns. His efforts to raise the lot of the common man were indefatigable. His rare ability to blend the qualities of compassion, erudition and heroism in pursuit of a noble cause won him widespread love and admiration.

Throughout his tenure as editor of two influential publications, he composed verse, thus acknowledging the fertility of his variegated imagination. His poetry was always addressed to the unfettered feelings and spiritual perceptions of the common man. Many recognized the authentic accents of a great soul and wrote to him of the profound change his verse had wrought in their lives. As a companion volume to his poetry he published *Song and Its Fountains* in 1932. The book attempted to trace the multitudinous forms of poetic utterance – song, speech and verse – back to their primeval source in divine consciousness. Though little read, this work presents some of A.E.'s mature observations on the nature and function of creativity and its relation to the forms of aesthetic activity. The compression and eloquence of *Song and Its Fountains* place its finest passages on equal footing with *The Candle of Vision*, a work with which it is wholly consonant.

A.E.'s last major work, *The Avatars*, was completed in 1933, two years before he died. As a young man, he had been fired by H.P. Blavatsky's prophecy that a Teacher of Humanity would labour in the latter half of the twentieth century to further the Theosophic impulse initiated in 1875. *The Avatars* is the story of the birth of the religion of cosmic consciousness and human solidarity that would inspire mankind in the future. A.E. admitted that its art was uncertain but hoped that it could give some guidance to those who had read his other books. However limited its reception may have been at the time, it conveys a serene assurance rarely found in modern literature, faithfully echoing the enchanting legends of Krishna.

A.E. died peacefully amidst friends, highly esteemed by a nation to which he had devoted his abundant energies. His accomplishments as a mystic, hero and seer are truly significant, although he sought neither recognition nor praise but merely fulfilment of those ends for which his soul had assumed the sorrows of incarnation. That A.E. was able to translate his inner truth into a sharable reality and give of his own spiritual gifts for the sake of others must stand as his luminous achievement and enduring example.

THE MYSTICISM OF A.E.

The air is full of souls.
Philo Judaeus

From his early youth A.E. belonged to the homeless tribe of mystics. These spiritual exiles inherit the ancient title *mystikós*, from *mystés* – one whose eyes and lips are closed, who has entered into the Mysteries, the sacred verities which can neither be fully articulated nor wholly validated in any language. The unmanifest may be suggested and shrouded by the manifest, and the mystic experiences this through his endeavours to translate his insights 'from the region of things felt to the region of things understood'.[1] The mystic's eyes are necessarily closed to the mundane world inasmuch as they intently and inwardly gaze upon the hidden realm of supersensuous realities. The mystics lips are sealed – even in eloquent speech – because of the unutterable beauty of his beatific experience and the transcendent glow of his transfiguring insight. Authentic mystical awareness is markedly different from the varied forms of fantasy and reverie. Mystical experience is essentially noetic, rooted in the capacity for enlarged comprehension of noumenal truths, rather than the rush of emotion or the randomness of memory. Though the mystic path is etched across the awesome vault of infinite duration, each mystical experience is an event in time, transient, limited by a fragile beginning and a frustrating end. The experience is also episodic in that the temporal and captive consciousness of the individual cannot control it. In the enigmatic language of the Upaniṣads, the *Ātman* – the universal overbrooding Spirit – shows itself to whom it will. Daydreams and fantasy, though they share the wayward charm of evanescent but joyous wonder, do not convey the ethical consequences of a deep mystic experience. In the presence of the magnanimous sweep of the mystic vision, a natural

---

1 'The Hour of Twilight'. *Descent*, p. 195.

self-effacement fuses with a profound sense of self-completion. One becomes a selfless participant in the silent sacrifice of invisible and visible nature, in which each part has clarity and significance in relation to every other part, all sharing the diffused light of an architectonic unity.

The mystic senses the priceless privilege of being alive and the sacredness of breathing; awareness of this sanctified continuity of all life affects his every thought and act, at least during his 'peak experiences'. The fragmentation and discontinuity in consciousness of the vast majority of mankind – gaps between thought and feeling, idea and image, sensibility and sense, belief and knowledge – are integrated in the mystic's self-awareness. Sensing a fundamental continuity within himself, the mystic witnesses an equally vibrant solidarity between individuals. What is possible for one person to discover is possible for another, however adverse conditions may appear. The intense flashes of awareness that the mystic is privileged to enjoy are stepping-stones on the path of awakening most of which are trod in silence.

> Some interpret the spirit with sadness and some with joy, but in this country I think it will always cry out its wild and wondrous story of immortal youth and will lead its votaries to a heaven where they will be drunken with beauty. What is all this? Poetry or fantasy? It has visited thousands in all ages and lands, and from such visions have come all that is most beautiful in poetry or art. These forms inhabited Shelley's luminous cloudland, and they were the models in the Pheidian heart, and they have been with artist, poet and musician since the beginning of the world, and they will be with us until we grow into their beauty and learn from them how to fulfil human destiny, accomplishing our labour which is to make this world into the likeness of the Kingdom of Light.[1]

Within the historical tradition of sages, saints and seers, a few, like St. John of the Cross, St. Teresa, Bernard of Clairvaux, as well as the author of *The Cloud of Unknowing*, speak of actual experiences encountered upon the mystical way. Other sources, such as the writings of A.E., *The Voice of the Silence* and *Light on the Path*, characterize the phases of the mystic path without attention to details of particular experiences. Still other influential thinkers – Plato and Plotinus, Śankara and Eckhart – elaborated the metaphysical framework and philosophical underpinnings of the path

---

1 *The Candle of Vision. Descent*, p. 163.

itself. A.E. presents an account of his haunting visions directly, in works like *The Candle of Vision*, and metaphorically in stories and poems like 'A Strange Awakening' and 'A Priestess of the Woods', interwoven with thoughts on the nature of the universe and man's relation to it. He happily shares his own experiences without any insistence that they should be ours. But he affirms that anyone who wills it can awaken spiritual insight within himself.

> So the lover of Earth obtains his reward, and little by little the veil is lifted of an inexhaustible beauty and majesty. It may be he will be tranced in some spiritual communion, or will find his being overflowing into the being of the elements, or become aware that they are breathing their life into his own. Or Earth may become on an instant all faery to him, and earth and air resound with the music of its invisible people. Or the trees and rocks may waver before his eyes and become transparent, revealing what creatures were hidden from him by the curtain, and he will know as the ancients did of dryad and hamadryad, of genii of wood and mountain. Or earth may suddenly blaze about him with supernatural light in some lonely spot amid the hills, and he will find he stands as the prophet in a place that is holy ground, and he may breathe the intoxicating exhalations as did the sibyls of old. Or his love may hurry him away in dream to share in deeper mysteries, and he may see the palace chambers of nature where the wise ones dwell in secret, looking out over the nations, breathing power into this man's heart or that man's brain, or any who appear to their vision to wear the colour of truth. So gradually the earth lover realises the golden world is all about him in imperishable beauty, and he may pass from the vision to the profounder beauty of being, and know an eternal love is within and around him, pressing upon him and sustaining with infinite tenderness his body, his soul and his spirit.[1]

A.E.'s mysticism emphasizes understanding through love, and in his lifelong effort to elevate his love, he suffuses mystical naturalism with intimations of the rich void throughout and beyond nature. He emphasizes our identity with all nature because he sees the soul in nature and in ourselves. 'The great heart of the earth is full of laughter', one of his characters says. 'Do not put yourselves apart from its joy, for its soul is your soul and its joy is your true being.'[2]

He beholds Deity as both immanent and transcendent.

---

1 *The Candle of Vision. Descent*, pp. 164–65.
2 'A Priestess of the Woods'. *Descent*, p. 205.

The Descent of the Gods

I follow in no faery ways;
I heed no voice of fay or elf;
I in the winter of my days
Rest in the high ancestral self.[1]

As the veil of visible nature is dissolved before the mystic's sight, time itself is seen as an illusion from a metaphysical standpoint. Consciousness is expanded or constricted by its apprehension of time. The mystic senses a vibration prior to visible nature, though insofar as it is expressible, it too has a beginning and an end. His experience is timeless though located in time, and the mystic is hard pressed to describe his crossings between the unmanifest and the manifest. Speaking of the hour of twilight as a metaphor for that time when 'the Mystic shall be at home' and 'more really himself', A.E. calls it 'the hour for memory'.

> Wherever it is spent, whether in the dusky room or walking home through the quiet evening, all things grow strangely softened and united; the magic of the old world reappears. The commonplace streets take on something of the grandeur and solemnity of starlit avenues of Egyptian temples; the public squares in the mingled glow and gloom grow beautiful as the Indian grove where Shakuntala wandered with her maidens; the children chase each other through the dusky shrubberies, as they flee past they look at us with long remembered glances: lulled by the silence, we forget a little while the hard edges of the material and remember that we are *spirits*.[2]

When the horizon set by one's awareness of time is foreshortened, memory is reduced to recent particulars redolent with echoes of childhood remembrance. As that horizon is expanded through a sense of eternity, recollection arises with a profound awareness of mythic time, and the soul gazes within the archaic history of humanity. Soul-memory exhibits natural affinities to strange dreams, insignificant in detail yet suggesting a cosmic drama in which each creature plays an appropriate role. Soul-memory also portrays to waking consciousness what would otherwise be witnessed only in the post-mortem dreamlike state called *devachan*, the realm of the gods. A.E. deeply felt the reality of the Golden Age. Though language forces a contrast between endlessness and clock-time, A.E. could declare: 'I knew the Golden Age was all about me, and it

---

1 'A Priestess of the Woods'. *Descent*, p. 206.
2 'The Hour of Twilight'. *Descent*, p. 195.

was we who had been blind to it but that it had never passed away from the world.'¹

If most individuals see nature as a static created world comprising myriad separate entities, the mystic beholds *natura naturans*, a dynamic process constantly unleashing creative energies. For A.E. the mystical experience is grounded in the commonality of human life.

> For this in truth it seems to me to mean: all knowledge is a revelation of the self to the self, and our deepest comprehension of the seemingly apart divine is also our furthest inroad to self-knowledge; Prometheus, Christ, are in every heart; the story of one is the story of all; the Titan and the Crucified are humanity.²

Precisely because 'Christ is incarnate in all humanity',³ every human being has golden moments and mystical glimpses, yet because 'Prometheus is bound for ever within us',⁴ such moments and glimpses are obliterated in waking life through indulgence, egotism, obsession with results and the concern for salvation. And if these barriers to deeper unity are bypassed without genuine self-transcendence, they become still stronger obstacles: passivity, aggression, fantasy and malign interference in the lives of others. To thread passing moments into a continuous current in life, one must hold firmly to a selfless line of thought and motivation.

> ... these moods, though lit up by intuitions of the true, are too partial, they belong too much to the twilight of the heart, they have too dreamy a temper to serve us well in life. We should wish rather for our thoughts a directness such as belongs to the messengers of the gods, swift, beautiful, flashing presences bent on purposes well understood.⁵

One's mind must be prepared and alert. One needs to identify with the whole of nature so as to become inconspicuous as a *persona*, yet ever vigilant and willing to follow the injunction given in *The Voice of the Silence* – 'Thy Soul has to become as the ripe mango fruit: as soft and sweet as its bright golden pulp for others' woes, as hard as that fruit's stone for thine own throats and sorrows.' A.E.

---

1 *The Candle of Vision. Descent*, p. 86.
2 *The Hero in Man. Descent*, p. 329.
3 *Ibid.*
4 *Ibid.*
5 *Ibid.*, p. 330.

knew only too well that this lay far ahead of contemporary humanity. Yet he perceived a continuity between the mystic's unwavering vision of the Hero in man and everyday experience, through the idea of sacrifice on behalf of the wretched of the earth.

> Now if the aim of the mystic be to fuse into one all moods made separate by time, would not the daily harvesting of wisdom render unnecessary the long Devachanic years? No second harvest could be reaped from fields where the sheaves are already garnered. Thus disregarding the fruits of action, we could work like those who have made the Great Sacrifice, for whom even Nirvana is no resting place. Worlds may awaken in nebulous glory, pass through their phases of self-conscious existence and sink again to sleep, but these tireless workers continue their age-long task of help. Their motive we do not know, but in some secret depth of our being we feel that there could be nothing nobler, and thinking this we have devoted the twilight hour to the understanding of their nature.[1]

A.E. thus linked the highest moments of illuminative insight to our common experience, so that late in life he could look back with a sense of serenity and peace, vindicating his fidelity to his original vow and vision. His ready acceptance of every individual in his own life, seeing the Christos-Prometheus in each, renewed his conviction that we are companions in a kingdom of light which only waits to be discovered.

THEOSOPHICAL PRESUPPOSITIONS AND CONCEPTS

The universe is even as a great temple.
Claude de St. Martin

A.E.'s devotion to Theosophy was based upon a deep apprehension that its central truths were not derived from any ancient or modern sect but represented the accumulated wisdom of the ages, the unrecorded inheritance of humanity. Its vast scheme of cosmic and human evolution furnished him with the symbolic alphabet necessary to interpret his recurrent visions as well as the universal

---

[1] 'The Hour of Twilight'. *Descent*, p. 196.

Theosophical Presuppositions and Concepts 13

framework and metaphysical vocabulary, drawn from many mystics and seers, which enabled him to communicate his own intuitive perceptions. All of A.E.'s mystical writings are enriched by the alchemical flavour of theosophical thought. In approaching his work, it is helpful for the reader to have a broad understanding of theosophical presuppositions and concepts. Theosophy is an integrated system of fundamental verities taught by initiates and adepts across millennia. It is the *Philosophia Perennis*, the philosophy of human perfectibility, the science of spirituality and the religion of responsibility. It is the primeval fount of myriad religious systems as well as the hidden essence and esoteric wisdom of each. Man, an immortal being in his true nature, has been able to preserve this sacred heritage through the sacrificial efforts of enlightened and compassionate individuals or Mahatmas who constitute an ancient Brotherhood. They quietly assist in the ethical evolution and spiritual development of humanity. *Theosophia* is Divine Wisdom, transmitted and verified over aeons by the sages who belong to this secret Brotherhood.

The supreme presupposition of theosophical thought is an eternal substance-principle postulated as the ineffable ground of all being. It is called a substance-principle because it becomes increasingly substantial and differentiated on the plane of manifestation while it essentially remains a homogeneous principle in abstract space and eternal duration. The perceived universe is a complex mirroring of this Unknown Source, all finite conceptions of which are necessarily incomplete. It is the Absolute Negation of all that exists. It is Be-ness or *Sat*, the No-thing of ancient philosophy, the 'Boundless Lir', which A.E. called the Unknown Beginning of Celtic cosmogony. Compared with It, all manifestation is no more than an impermanent illusion or *Māyā*, a kaleidoscopic medium through which the one Reality shows itself in a series of reflections. Spirit and matter are the two facets of this indivisible principle which only seem to be separate during a vast period of cosmic manifestation. They radiate from this transcendent source, yet are not causally related to It, since neither quality nor mode may properly be ascribed to It. They appear periodically on the objective plane as the opposite poles of this Reality, yet they are not inherently separate, but mutually coexist as spirit-matter. In manifestation this substratum differentiates itself into seven planes of increasing density, reaching towards the region of sense-data. Everywhere the root essence of homogeneous substance is the same, transforming itself by minute degrees from the most ethereal to the most gross.

The seven planes of manifestation may be seen as condensations of rarefied matter and also as living streams of intelligences – primordial rays proceeding from an invisible Spiritual Sun. All modes of activity in the Universe are internally guided by powers and potencies arrayed in an almost endless series of hierarchies, each with its exact function and precise scope of action. They are called Dhyān Chohans in the Theosophical scheme and bear many other titles in the rich panoply of religious traditions – Angels, Devas, Gods, Elohim, etc. All these are transmitting agents of cosmic Law (*Rta*) which guides the evolution of each atom on every plane in space, the hierarchies varying enormously in their respective degrees of creative consciousness and monadic intelligence. As an aggregate, this immense host of forces forms the manifesting *Verbum* of an unmanifest Presence, constituting simultaneously the active Mind of the cosmos and its immutable Law. The idea of myriad hierarchies of intelligences animating visible Nature is a vital key to understanding much of A.E.'s mysticism. In his early years his many flashes of intuitive perception revealed multitudes of radiant beings elaborating the interior architecture of matter. This led him to the reverential recognition of a sacred Logos or *Verbum*, which he called the Army of the Voice, operating behind the screen of surface events as the noumenal cause of natural phenomena. His lifelong quest involved the deciphering of the signs of these intelligent forces by following the traces of their effects. He was firmly convinced, as were the medieval theosophists, that the natural world bears the signatures of a divine archetypal world. With proper keys to archaic symbolism, man can read these signatures and recover the lost knowledge which would restore him to a primeval state of gnosis equivalent to that of the Gods. Hence A.E.'s deep absorption in the study of the metaphysical roots of language. He determined that the letters composing the Sanskrit language were the phenomenal expressions of these finer forces and that by understanding them one could discover the root vibration, the ineffable Word reverberating throughout the sentient world of visible Nature.

The theosophical teaching concerning the Great Chain of Being in the supernatural realm continually appears in A.E.'s prose as the inexhaustible fountainhead of aesthetic expression, heroic action and mystic illumination. The Candle of Vision, the Magician of the Beautiful, the Mount of Transfiguration, the Mighty Mother, are all different faces of the Divine Logos. A.E. concluded that the diverse expressions of creativity in the arts, religion and philosophy stem from this common unseen source and that the search for its origin was his hallowed mission as mystic and artist. Even *The Interpreters* may be seen as a bold attempt to reconstitute the City of Man according to the archetypal modes conveyed by the concordant activity of the divine hierarchies. The problem of tracing particulars back to universals was as crucial to A.E.'s art as to his psychology. Theosophy teaches a sevenfold classification of man's inner constitution, corresponding to seven cosmic planes of being. Man is truly a microcosm and miniature copy of the macrocosm. Like the macrocosm, he is divine in essence, a direct radiation from the central Spiritual Sun. As pure spirit, he needs the vestures through which he may experience life on differentiated planes of existence, so that he can become fully conscious of his individual immortality and his indissoluble identity with the whole. He is a complete reflection of the Universe, revealing himself to himself by means of seven differentiations. In his deepest self he is *Ātman*, the universal spirit which is mirrored in his luminous soul or *buddhi*, as these are termed in Sanskrit. *Buddhi* partakes more of spirit than any principle below it and is focussed through *manas* or impersonal intellect, the source of human individuation. These three constitute the imperishable fire in Man, the immortal triad that undertakes an immense pilgrimage through successive incarnations to emerge as an effortlessly self-conscious agent of the divine will.

Below this overbrooding triad is a volatile quaternary of principles drawn from the lower planes of cosmic matter: they are *kāma*, the force of blind passion and chaotic desire shared by man with animal life; *prāṇa*, the life-current energizing the whirling atoms on the objective plane of existence; the astral paradigmatic body (*liṅga śarīra*), the original form around which the physical molecules shape themselves, and hence the model for the physical frame (*sthūla śarīra*.) This quaternary of principles is evanescent and changeable, established for man's use at the time of incarnation and dissolved at death into its primary constituents on their corresponding planes. The real man, the higher triad, recedes from the physical plane to await his next incarnation. The function of each of these sheaths differs from one individual to another according to the level of spiritual development of the incarnated soul. The astral body of the Adept, for example, is of a much higher degree of resilience and purity than that of the average man. In A.E. himself, the sheaths intervening between the spiritual man and the brain-mind were sufficiently transparent that in his body he could receive communications from the overbrooding triad in a relatively lucid manner. As he recounts in *Song and Its Fountains*, man is a compound being simultaneously experiencing two worlds, inner and outer. His present life-experience is but a minute portion of what was witnessed by the immortal individuality in previous incarnations. Thus if man assiduously searches within himself he can recover a vast heritage of knowledge spanning aeons. These memories are locked in mansions of the soul which only ardent desire and strong discipline can penetrate.

The manifold levels of memory are a recurrent theme in A.E.'s account of his visionary experiences. Theosophy teaches that memory is integral to consciousness and that since all matter is alive and conscious, all beings from cells to deities have memory of some type. In man, memory is generally divided into four categories: physical memory, remembrance, recollection and reminiscence. In remembrance, an idea impinges upon the mind from the past by free association; in recollection, the mind deliberately searches it out. Reminiscence, however, is of another order altogether. Called 'soul-memory', it links a human being to his previous lives and assures him that he will live again. In principle, any man or woman may recover the knowledge gained in previous incarnations and maintain continuity with the *sūtrātman*, the thread-soul, the eternal witness to every incarnation. There are also types of memory which are indistinguishable from prophecy, since the more one progresses towards homogeneous and rarefied planes of existence, the more past, present and future collapse into eternal duration, within the boundless perspective of which an entire cycle of manifestation may be surveyed. Such was the level of insight reached by the great seers who recorded their findings in what is known as the *Gupta Vidyā* or Secret Doctrine. A.E. penetrated deeply into the realms of reminiscence, bringing back the fruits of knowledge in previous lives. Greater still was his ability to enter into former and more spiritual epochs of humanity and to make those visions come alive for those who had lost all but a faint intuition of a larger sense of self.

The source and destiny of the soul's inward life is a fundamental teaching of Theosophy and involves the entire scope of evolution. Coeval with the manifestation of the seven worlds of the cosmic plenum is the re-emergence of beings who assume once more the evolutionary pilgrimage after an immense period of rest. The emanation of matter and spirit into the objective plane of existence is but half the cycle. Its return brings all beings and forms to the bosom of absolute darkness. The period of manifestation covering trillions of years is called a *manvantara* and the corresponding period of rest, called *pralaya*, lasts for an equal duration. They are the Days and Nights of Brahmā, which were reckoned with meticulous precision by the ancient Aryans. The whole span of the *manvantara* is governed by the law of periodicity which regulates rates of activity on

Theosophical Presuppositions and Concepts

all planes of Being. This is sometimes spoken of as the 'Great Breath' which preserves the cosmos. Theosophically, the essence of life is motion, growth and expansion of awareness in every atom. Each atom is at its core a monad, an expression of the highest self (*Ātman*), and its vesture is the spiritual soul (*buddhi*). Prior to the monad's emergence in the human family, it undergoes aeons of experience in the lower kingdoms of nature, developing by natural impulse (metempsychosis) until the latent thinking faculty of *manas* is awakened by the sacrificial efforts of beings who have risen far above the human state in *manvantaras* past. They kindle the spark of self-consciousness, making the unconscious monad a true man (*manuṣya*), capable of thought, reflection and deliberate action. The soul embarks upon a long cycle of incarnations in human form to prepare itself for entry into still greater planes of existence.

The evolutionary tide on earth is regulated by the unerring hand of cyclic law. Man passes through a series of Rounds and Races which allow him to assimilate the knowledge of every plane of existence from the most ethereal to the most material. Man's planetary evolution describes a spiral passing from spirit into matter and returning to spirit again with a wholly self-conscious mastery of the process. Each Round is a major evolutionary period lasting many millions of years; each race in turn witnesses the rise and fall of continents, civilizations and nations. An earlier Race than our own, the Lemurian, lived in an idyllic golden age, an epoch ruled by natural religion, universal fraternity and spontaneous devotion to spiritual teachers. Many of the myths regarding an era of childlike purity and unsullied trust in humanity's early flowering preserve the flavour of this period. As man evolved more material vestures, *kāma* or passion tainted his power of thought and inflamed his irrational tendencies. The nightmare tales of Atlantean sorcerers, recounted by A.E. and others, are the heavy heirloom of contemporary humanity. The destruction of Atlantis ushered in the Aryan race of our own epoch. The Indian sages who inaugurated this period are among the torch-bearers for the humanity of our time. One must recognize the sacred role of ancient India as mother and preserver of the spiritual heritage of present humanity in order to grasp the significance of A.E.'s lifelong devotion to classical Indian scriptures. In them, he recognized the authentic voice of the *Verbum*, uncorrupted by time and human ignorance.

Pertinent to A.E.'s work is the Theosophical doctrine of the *yugas*, the cycle of four epochs through which every Race passes, the Golden, Silver, Bronze and Iron Ages. The *yugas* indicate a broad sweep of karmic activity at any point in the life of an individual or collection of individuals. The entire globe may not be undergoing the same age simultaneously nor may any one individual be necessarily in the same state as his social *milieu*. According to Hindu calculations, *Kali Yuga* began over 5,000 years ago and will last altogether for a total of 432,000 years. This dark age is characterized by widespread confusion of roles, inversion of ethical values and enormous suffering owing to spiritual blindness. A.E. celebrated the myth of the Golden Age as extolling the plenitude of man's creative potential. The doctrine of the *yugas* is not deterministic. It merely suggests the relative levels of consciousness which most human beings tend to hold in common. Thus, a Golden Age vibration can be inserted into an Iron Age to ameliorate the collective predicament of mankind. A.E. saw that the Golden Age surrounded human beings as a primordial state of divine consciousness, but their own pride and ignorance precluded its recovery. In the wonder of childhood, in archaic myths, in the sporadic illuminations of great artists, and in mystical visions, A.E. beheld shimmering glimpses of the Golden Age of universal eros, the rightful original estate of humanity. His writings are ensouled by a compassionate concern to elevate the condition of humanity so that it might joyously reclaim its divine inheritance.

The progress of man in harmony with cyclic law is facilitated by a grasp of the doctrines of responsibility and hope, karma and rebirth. These two are fundamental to theosophical thought and unravel many of the riddles of life and nature. They show that every person's life and character are the outcome of previous lives and thought-patterns, that each one is his or her own judge and executioner, and that all rise or fall strictly by their own merits and misdeeds. Nothing is left to chance or accident in life but everything is under the governance of a universal law of ethical causation. Man is essentially a thinker, and all thoughts initiate causes that generate suffering or bliss. The immortal triad endures the mistakes and follies of the turbulent quaternary until such time as it can assume its rightful stature and act freely in consonance with cosmic order and natural law.

As man is constantly projecting a series of thoughts and images, his complete responsibility is irrevocable. He is the centre of any disturbance of universal harmony and the ripples of effects must return to him. This is the law of karma or justice, signifying moral interdependence and human solidarity. A.E. did not see karma as a providential means of divine retribution but rather as a universal current touching those who bore the burden of its effects. This he called the law of spiritual gravitation. He emphasized that the entire

Theosophical Presuppositions and Concepts 19

scope of man's affairs – his environment, friends, family, employment and the like – were all dictated by the needs of the soul. Karma worked on the soul's behalf to provide those opportunities for knowledge and experience which would aid its progress. A.E. expanded this concept to encompass all connections with other human beings of even the most casual kind, seeing them as karmically ordained not for one's own progress but for the sake of those who struggled with the dire limitations of ignorance, poverty or despair. The most moving account of this trial is found in *The Hero in Man*, wherein while walking among the wretched outcasts of Dublin, he rejoices in the conviction that the compassion he feels for each benighted soul will forge a spiritual bond through which he may help them in the future. Karma meant for A.E. a summons to the path of action and duty. As he would not separate his own karma from that of his fellow-men, he determined to devote his life to the remission of the karmic burden of others.

Related to the doctrines of reincarnation and karma are the post-mortem states which all human souls encounter between involuntary births, *kāmaloka* and *devachan*. At death the true self or immortal triad casts off the physical and astral bodies and is released from the thraldom of passions and desires. Its natural tropism to gravitate upwards allows it to enter the rarefied plane of consciousness where its thoughts are carried to culmination, clothed in a finer body suited to that sublime existence. This state, *devachan*, is a period of rest and assimilation between lives and the basis of the popular mythology of heaven. On the other hand, the lower quaternary languishes after death in *kamaloka*, the origin of theological dogmas concerning hell and purgatory. There it dissolves by degrees back into its primary elements at a rate determined by the cohesion given them by the narcissistic personality during life on earth. Inflamed passions and poisonous thoughts sustained for long periods of time charge this entity with a vivid, vicarious and ghoulish existence. This plane of consciousness, termed 'the Astral Light' by Eliphas Levi, is intimately connected with the lives and thoughts of most of mankind. It is the vast slag-heap of nature into which all selfish and evil thoughts are poured and then rebound back to pollute and contaminate human life on earth. A.E. realized that this plane of carnalized thought served to perpetuate the horrors of the Iron Age and condemn man to a state of spiritual darkness. The crucial difference between individuals lies in whether they are enslaved by the Astral Light (the region of psyche) or whether they are capable of rising above it to a calm awareness of the wisdom and compassion latent in their higher nature, the realm of nous.

A.E. repeatedly pointed beyond the region of psychic action to the pristine sphere of noetic awareness called *ākāśa*, from which empyrean individuals could derive the inspiration needed to go forth and inaugurate a Golden Age by laying down the foundations of a regenerated civilization. He extolled the sages, past and present, who had accomplished the arduous transformation of their own natures, overcoming every vice and limitation and perfecting themselves in noetic ideation and sacrificial action. A.E.'s deepest allegiance was to those Mahatmas or hierophants who had renounced everything for the sake of suffering humanity. As a solitary mystic on the ancient path of service, he saluted them as his guides and preceptors and acknowledged their invisible presence behind his modest labours for mankind. These wise beings are the noble trustees of the *Philosophia Perennis* and the compassionate teachers of the human family. The mystical pilgrimage of A.E. was an authentic reflection of their ageless Wisdom.

THE LANGUAGE OF THE GODS

Out of the silence that is peace a resonant voice shall arise.

Light on the Path

'In the beginning was the Word', declare St. John and the Upaniṣads. All existence is a confluence of vibratory motions, from the cosmic to the atomic. Creative speech – Logos, Verbum, the Word – is sound impregnated with the potency of ideation. The primordial and sempiternal sound is like the quiet pulsation of the ocean's depths and the inaudible reverberation hidden within the gentle whisper of the breeze, the joyous dance of the elements and the 'still, sad music of humanity'. When the mind listens to the cacophony of seemingly discontinuous sounds, or speaks a transient tongue which corresponds to evanescent phenomena, it is turned away from its true self out into the world. It perceives an array of discrete entities and separate existences, and constructs for itself an illusory identity. This is the fugitive psyche, the soul that is captive to a temporal succession of images, bound up with likes and dislikes. When the mind turns within, searches for the root of sound in the silence, it retreats and looks to its own ultimate origin. When it engages in deep meditation, it senses a continuity in duration which reflects an eternal wholeness.

The Language of the Gods

Ancient philosophers and mystics held that through this inward turning the mind becomes an awakened nous, a noetic focus which renders universal truths intelligible in relation to everyday experience.

The meditation they urged on us has been explained as 'the inexpressible yearning of the inner man to go out into the infinite'. But that Infinite we would enter is living. It is the ultimate being of us. Meditation is a fiery brooding on that majestical Self. We imagine ourselves into Its vastness. We conceive ourselves as mirroring Its infinitudes, as moving in all things, as living in all beings, in earth, water, air, fire, æther. We try to know as It knows, to live as It lives, to be compassionate as It is compassionate. We equal ourselves to It that we may understand It and become It. We do not kneel to It as slaves, but as Children of the King we lift ourselves up to that Glory, and affirm to ourselves that we are what we imagine. 'What a man thinks, that he is: that is the old secret', said the wise. We have imagined ourselves into this pitiful dream of life. By imagination and will we re-enter true being, becoming that we conceive of.[1]

A.E. was convinced that this vision 'brings its own proof to the spirit',[2] but he was also conscious that criteria for knowing are necessary if the mystical perspective is not to degenerate into mere epistemological relativism. Knowledge-claims may be for many people what Plato called 'true opinion', statements for which they can offer no support outside received tradition or majority convention. For the mystical philosopher, however, knowledge-claims must be validated. Some claims to knowledge may be simply avowals which do not tell us anything about the world or ourselves, but merely report the subjective experiences of another. Other claims to knowledge are pragmatic. Their apparent objectivity is established if they are conclusions which all investigators are likely to reach, or if they are expedient within the contexts in which they are held. Such validation, of course, does not yield timeless truths or any fundamental insight into the structure of the world or the self. Knowledge-claims may also be justified as inferences from other accepted statements, or if they at least do not contradict such statements. As strict inferences, such statements do not add to the sum or significance of knowledge, however much they may spell out what is thought to be known already. Often a statement is offered as true in the belief that it in some way 'corresponds' to the facts. Since

---

1 *The Candle of Vision. Descent*, p. 93.
2 *Ibid.* p. 94.

we commonly assume that we know both the relevant facts and the meanings of statements, this view finds general, if uncritical, acceptance. But specific facts are not easily discerned or interpreted, and the general concept of 'a fact' is obscure, while many statements and even 'statement' are not unambiguous. It can be philosophically frustrating to make precise the notion of 'correspondence' without restricting it to familiar operations.

Our shared language is putatively divided between words which denote sense-objects and words which signify ratiocinative concepts. For the mystic who has experienced the harmonics of invisible nature and intimations of the fount of sound itself, such language seems woefully inadequate to the task of elucidation. A.E. writes of his experience:

> The tinted air glowed before me with intelligible significance like a face, a voice. The visible world became like a tapestry blown and stirred by winds behind it. If it would but raise for an instant I knew I would be in Paradise. Every form of that tapestry appeared to be the work of gods. Every flower was a word, a thought. The grass was speech; the trees were speech, the waters were speech; the winds were speech.[1]

A.E. speaks in company with mystics throughout the ages, and cannot be understood by the simple application of a single criterion for knowledge-claims. We must look to the integrity of the seer and to our own authentic experience to discover whether we are warranted in ascribing truth and meaning to what he says. 'Spiritual moods are difficult to express and cannot be argued over', A.E. avowed, 'but the workings of imagination may well be spoken of, and need precise and minute investigation.'[2] If in meditation one focusses the mind with laser-like precision upon one object, penetrating to its inmost and ineffable core, one is able to trace the roots of existence and simultaneously to unveil the origins of things, witnessing terraces of being from near perfect homogeneity to almost total heterogeneity. This process allows one to discern different levels of causality and intermediate orders of existence.

In his preface to *The Candle of Vision*, A.E. warned the reader:

> When I am in my room looking upon the walls I have painted, I see there reflections of the personal life, but when I look through the windows I see a living nature and landscapes not painted by hands.

---

1 *The Candle of Vision. Descent*, p. 85.
2 *Ibid*. p. 95.

So, too, when I meditate I feel in the images and thoughts which throng about me the reflections of personality, but there are also windows in the soul through which can be seen images created not by human but by the divine imagination. I have tried according to my capacity to report about the divine order and to discriminate between that which was self-begotten fantasy and that which came from a higher sphere.[1]

A.E. found the sifting of the imagination a lonely task to which neither modern psychology nor philosophy gave assistance. 'I surmise', he wrote, 'from my reading of the psychologists who treat of this that they themselves were without this faculty and spoke of it as blind men who would fain draw although without vision.'[2] One untutored in geometry would be foolish to declare a theorem undemonstrated, and more foolish still to pronounce geometry a superstition or aberration of the speculative mind. One must train the mind to comprehend the nature of axioms, rules of inference, geometrical operations and proofs before making judgements. This applies also to the cognitive content of mystical experience.

> We rarely find philosophical writers referring to vision of their own, yet we take them as guides on our mental travelling, though in this world we all would prefer to have knowledge of earth and heaven through the eyes of a child rather than to know them only through the musings of one who was blind, even though his intellect was mighty as Kant's.[3]

For A.E. no laboriously elaborated conventional wisdom can threaten the self-validating authority of direct experience, though unscrutinized experience can be misleading. To his own question, 'What certitude have you that these things you speak of are in any way related to a real world invisible to our eyes?'[4] he replied that he could not fall back upon external authority, even that of other mystic seers. Rather,

> On that path, as an ancient scripture says, to whatsoever place one would travel that place one's own self becomes, and I must try first to uproot false ideas about memory, imagination and vision so that by

---

1 *The Candle of Vision. Descent*, p. 82.
2 *Ibid.*, p. 95.
3 *Ibid.*, p. 151.
4 *Ibid.*, p. 100.

pure reason people may be led out of error and be able to distinguish between that which arises in themselves and that which comes otherwise and which we surmise is a visitor from a far country.[1]

Freed from enslavement to a conventional picture of reality, reason and the self-willed expansion of the range of experience together warrant claims to knowledge for the mystic. His world is not reserved for a unique class of individuals who have special spiritual privileges. While A.E. confesses, 'I perhaps to build on had some little gift of imagination I brought with me into the world', he adds, 'I know others who had no natural vision who acquired this, and by sustaining meditation and by focussing the will to a burning-point, were raised above the narrow life of the body.'[2] Meditation is a deliberate experience undertaken for the purpose of discovery without the burden of pre-established goals or results. What is discovered can then be subjected to reason. As A.E. admits, 'Being an artist and a lover of visible beauty, I was often tempted from the highest meditation to contemplate, not divine being, but the mirage of forms.'[3] Neither the vision nor the layers of delusion are exclusive to him. 'There is nothing uncommon about such visions. It is in the interpretation of them that error arises.'[4]

The crucial test of mystical claims to knowledge lies for A.E. in our innate capacities for self-transformation as thinking beings.

> On the mystic path we create our own light, and at first we struggle blind and baffled, seeing nothing, hearing nothing, unable to think, unable to imagine. We seem deserted by dream, vision or inspiration, and our meditation barren altogether. But let us persist through weeks or months, and sooner or later that stupor disappears. Our faculties readjust themselves, and do the work we will them to do. Never did they do their work so well. The dark caverns of the brain begin to grow luminous. We are creating our own light.[5]

When this disciplined effort is made, we may share with A.E. some inexplicable but recognizable flashes of resplendent insight. We may then readily acknowledge the long lineage of mystic seers and sages.

---

1 *The Candle of Vision. Descent*, p. 100.
2 *Ibid.*, p. 104.
3 *Ibid.*
4 *Ibid.*, p. 101.
5 *Ibid.*, p. 93.

Whether they are Syrian, Greek, Egyptian or Hindu, the writers of the sacred books seem to me as men who had all gazed upon the same august vision and reported of the same divinity.[1]

Then we may distinguish clearly between the psychic images of personal consciousness and the universal noetic vision of mystical awareness. Claims to knowledge will gain a coherence forged by pure reason, a vital correspondence to a world unfolded in lucid insight, and timeless relevance to the spiritual nature of man.

This prospect envisaged by A.E. is articulate because the language in which it is expressed is a distant echo of the Logos in the cosmos, the transcendent Word, and the Soundless Sound. Man, the microcosmic mirror of the macrocosm, elaborates the archetypal patterns of sempiternity in time, patterns which are themselves mystic presentments of the eternal and unknowable.

> For myself I think man is a protean being, within whose unity there is diversity, and there are creatures in the Soul which can inform the images of our memory, or the eternal memory, aye, and speak through them to us in dream, so that we hear their voices, and it is with us in our minute microcosmic fashion even as it was said of the universe that it is a soliloquy of Deity wherein Ain-Soph talks to Ain-Soph.[2]

The core of man's being is consubstantial with the root of nature. No bridge need be built between man and Deity save the bridge of awareness constructed out of unfolding knowledge through meditation.

> We tremble on the verge of the vast halls of the gods where their mighty speech may be heard, their message of radiant will be seen. They speak a universal language not for themselves only but for all. What is poetry but a mingling of some tone of theirs with the sounds that below we utter?[3]

The primordial Word is both primordial light and universal form. The language of the gods is the primary modulation of that light – 'colours beyond the rainbow' and first figures. The Word resounds throughout the abstract medium which is space. The *ākāśa* of the

---

1 *The Candle of Vision. Descent*, p. 151.
2 *Ibid.*, p. 124.
3 'Works and Days'. *Descent*, p. 191.

Hindu philosophers is not a vacuum but rather a homogeneous and supple substance. It receives, transmits and echoes that first speech imprinted upon it, and as sound recrosses sound, a world composed of interlaced vibrations arises, assumes forms and eventually crystallizes in its grosser aspects into the world of ordinary experience. 'So the gods speak to each other across the expanses of ethereal light, breaking the divine silences with words which are deeds.'[1] Mortal speech is a distant derivate of divine speech and must ultimately be traced back to the Word or Verbum. This view of the origin of language, drawn from H.P. Blavatsky's *The Secret Doctrine* and elaborated in A.E.'s imagination, is at variance with the theory that language must be traced back to rudimentary conventions derived from pre-human onomatopoeia. A.E. held that 'we shall expect to discover a spiritual relation between sounds and the various powers, forms and colours and the universe',[2] for 'the roots of human speech are the sound correspondences of powers which in their combination and interaction make up the universe'.[3] To trace the origin of language through discovery of its fundamental structure is to outline the unfoldment of nature from its seed in the abstract Word. In human speech,

> Every root is charged with significance, being the symbol of a force which is itself the fountain of many energies, even as primordial being when manifested rolls itself out into numberless forms, states of energy and consciousness.[4]

A.E. proposed that the first root of language – A – is 'the sound symbol for the self in man and Deity in the cosmos'.[5] Its equivalent in symbolic form is the colourless circle, whose centre is everywhere and whose circumference is nowhere, in the language of Pascal, Nicholas of Cusa and Hermes Trismegistus. 'The old world,' H.P. Blavatsky wrote, 'consistent in its symbolism with its pantheistic intuitions, uniting the visible and invisible Infinitudes into one, represented Deity and its outward VEIL alike – by a circle.'[6] St. John states that 'the Word was with God, and the Word was God.'[7] The second root – R – represents motion, the lines which generate heat – H – and gives rise to the triangle, symbol of life and transfor-

---

1 'Works and Days'. *Descent*, p. 191.
2 'The Speech of the Gods'. *Descent*, p. 167.
3 *The Candle of Vision. Descent*, p. 138.
4 *Ibid.*
5 *Ibid.*
6 H.P. Blavatsky: *The Secret Doctrine*, II, p. 545.
7 *John*, I.1.

mation. As the root sounds proceed from the back of the throat (A) towards the closed lips (M), they represent the increasing involvement of Spirit in material planes, the ultimate dissolution of voiced creations, and the return to stasis (OO). While we can expect to find abstractions at the dawn of speech, in such a view we cannot insist upon empirical demonstrations of A.E.'s order and sequence of sounds. As he knew, the investigation of Indo-European or Aryan roots uncovers abstract conceptions more than particular terms.

> We find for example comparatively few words, such as *bow*, *arrow*, and *tent*, while there are a great many expressing abstract or reflective ideas, like *to shine, to fly, to know, to burn*.[1]

While 'these intuitions in respect of language are to some extent capable of being reasoned or argued over',[2] A.E. recognizes that his own experience was insufficient to warrant complete confidence in specific results or to guarantee an adequate elaboration of recognized correspondences. Pitfalls abound, he conceded, but they should encourage us to take up the pursuit he pioneered, to compare and study on our own.

> I wish here only to give indications and directions of approach to that Divine Mind whose signature is upon us in everything, and whose whole majesty is present in the least thing in nature.[3]

A.E.'s own vision and expression, his compassion and conduct, brought word and deed together in a living example of more divine and primordial speech which is the manifestation of the Word against the background of eternal Silence.

THE TRIALS OF THE SOUL

> *To love and bear; to hope till Hope creates*
> *From its own wreck the thing it contemplates.*
>
> Shelley

When the Ever-Unknowable reflects itself in the process of manifestation, the root substance-principle – the absolute Archaeus –

---

1 'The Speech of the Gods'. *Descent*, p. 168.
2 *The Candle of Vision. Descent*, p. 141.
3 *Ibid.*, p. 143.

unfolds itself as the invisible and visible cosmos in three hypostases. The first may be called Spirit, transcendent and overbrooding; the second, matter, the immanent side of nature; while the third, connecting these two at every point, might be likened materially to electricity and spiritually to mind. This third term is the impersonal intelligence of number and ratio, geometric form and arithmetic progression. The basic triad is present at every level of being, for Spirit expresses itself through matter – like the partially revealed dancer in the Dance of the Seven Veils – while matter lives and is transformed only under the vivifying impulse of Spirit. Both join in innumerable permutations and elaborations of the initial threefold Word, fused in cosmic intelligence (*Mahat*) which is also cosmic law (*Ṛta*). In the sphere of self-consciousness, this triad can be qualitatively defined as Wisdom (*Prajñā*), Compassion (*Karuṇa*) and Intelligence (*Buddhi*). Each depends upon the others for its own level of purity, clarity and activity. The elaboration of the primal Word is the movement from homogeneity to heterogeneity, from subtle to gross, from potential to actual, and from subjective to objective. The creative energy enshrined in the Word is pure *eros*, and its every expression reveals as well as masks its more fundamental nature. Hence every level of being finds light and darkness, the greater and the lesser, knowledge and relative ignorance, in ceaseless contradiction. The urge to manifest is the urge to objectify, to take form, to exist in time, rather than to abide in eternity. At the spiritual level, this impulsion is towards individuation, but at the natal level it is the desire to live as an ego; psycho-physically it is the thirst for life.

The mystic retraces this gestation of consciousness and returns, self-consciously and spiritually awake, to its source. He experiences, understands and controls the avenues leading from personal and individual existence to cosmic and universal consciousness. Self-transformation requires self-knowledge at every stage, a path fraught with dangers. The mystic recognizes that 'knowledge is power' but also knows that power corrupts the unwary. He must make compassion his own. Only then will persistent effort and unremitting vigilance lead to supreme wisdom. A.E. depicted the quest as lying between the darkness of earth and the light of spiritual self-consciousness.

> The Master in each of us draws in and absorbs the rarest and best of experiences, love, self-forgetfulness, aspiration, and out of these distils the subtle essence of wisdom, so that he who struggles in pain for his fellows, when he wakens again on earth is endowed with the

The Trials of the Soul

tradition of that which we call self-sacrifice, but which is in reality the proclamation of our own universal nature.[1]

A.E. knew that this passage was similar to that from the rich silence of dreamless sleep, where all personal consciousness is dissolved, through the veneer of chaotic images in the transition from dreams to the waking state. But self-created enemies lie along the uncharted paths waiting to mislead and destroy the pilgrim who glimpses the golden summit in the distance but ignores the steep ravines and rocky ledges between himself and that glorious height. A.E.'s writings explore both the promise of the mystic venture and the dark distractions which lead down labyrinthine byways.

Ethereal sights may be mistaken for divine intimations, misleading the erratic seer. In the archetypal story 'A Priestess of the Woods', the daughter of a magician learns about the elemental intelligences of nature.

> She saw deeper things also; as a little child, wrapped up in her bearskin, she watched with awe her father engaged in mystic rites; when around him the airy legions gathered from the populous elements, the Spirits he ruled and the Spirits he bowed down before; fleeting nebulous things white as foam coming forth from the great deep who fled away at the waving of his hand; and rarer the great sons of fire.[2]

But her father died before she learned about more than superficial signs and appearances. Her knowledge of the spirits of the earth was sufficient to make her priestess, but she knew nothing of the formless orders and divine principles. In the course of time, her message was reduced to the repeated warning of the dangers of becoming linked to gnomes, sylphs, salamanders and undines. She saw how men utterly enslave themselves to elemental intelligences through seeking worldly delights, and how they bargain away their lives for momentary gain. There is law in nature, and to violate its orders is to call forth recompense. Yet she could teach nothing that confers a greater vision, a larger perspective, a fuller hope.

When a young man passing through the forest heard her compelling discourse to the woodland folk, he took up his lyre and sang:

---

1 'The Hour of Twilight'. *Descent*, p. 195.
2 'A Priestess of the Woods'. *Descent*, p. 203.

> I never heed by waste or wood
> The cry of fay or faery thing
> Who tell of their own solitude;
> Above them all my soul is king.[1]

Though angered by the intrusion, the eyes of the youth 'dazzled the young priestess with the secrecy of joy'.[2] Fearlessly he told her: 'Your priestess speaks but half truths, her eyes have seen but her heart does not know. . . . The great heart of the earth is full of laughter; do not put yourselves apart from its joy, for its soul is your soul and its joy is your true being.'[3] She could not counter his confident affirmation, so she bowed down before it, telling her people, 'His wisdom may be truer; it is more beautiful than the knowledge we inherit.'

Though she maintained her vigils and cleaved to her knowledge, her heart dwelt upon a deeper mystery. Her dominion over nature spirits ebbed, and with it her life. Life is structured by a lesser mystery, and her awakening was accompanied by a release from incarnate life itself. The young priestess, despite her ignorant elemental worship, was pure, and so her heart was touched. Those more travelled on the spiritual path may not find awakening to a deeper life so easy, for their images of the goal may involve conditional aspiration, residual desires for unearthly sensations and incomplete knowledge. The gods have many names and titles, each signifying some level and form of manifestation. The celestial Aphrodite points beyond herself to *Alaya*, compassion absolute, which, like boundless space, encompasses all things arising in it but favours none. She also appears as the terrestrial Venus of Plato's *Symposium*, who satisfies every desire without quenching the endless thirst of desire itself.

In 'A Tragedy in the Temple', Asur entered the service of the Temple of Isthar wherein a friend 'blew to flame the mystic fire which already smouldered within him',[4] but became attracted to her sidereal form.

> 'Brother,' he said, 'I am haunted by a vision, by a child of the stars as lovely as Isthar's self; she visits my dreaming hours, she dazzles me with strange graces, she bewilders with unspeakable longing. Some-

---

1 'A Priestess of the Woods'. *Descent*, p. 204.
2 *Ibid*, p. 205.
3 *Ibid*.
4 'A Tragedy in the Temple'. *Descent*, p. 207.

The Trials of the Soul 31

time, I know, I must go to her, though I perish. When I see her I forget all else and I have will to resist no longer. The vast and lonely inspiration of the desert departs from my thought, she and the jewel-light she lives in blot it out.'[1]

The tendencies and habits of lifetimes do not easily melt away under the heat of religious fervour. As the pilgrim-soul approaches the gateway to the arduous spiritual path, all which must perish in the divine fire precipitates the conflict between the aspirant's will to merge in the universal light and his temporal traits. This fierce struggle has been portrayed as the great battle in the *Bhagavad Gītā*, shown in the Buddha's final contest with Māra before his Enlightenment, and depicted in the *Psalms* as the valley of the shadow of death. Māra-Lilith waits at the entrance to the mystic path to fascinate and terrify the lonely wayfarer. 'At the portal of the "assembling", the King of the Māras, the *Mahā Māra*, stands trying to blind the candidate by the radiance of his "Jewel".'[2]

Asur's friend would not help him, not understanding how the jewel of Māra is formed from all the lurking passions which agitate the dark recesses of worldly consciousness. But in a dream he saw the dreadful prospect:

> The form of Asur moved towards a light streaming from a grotto, I could see within it burning gigantic flowers. On one, as on a throne, a figure of weird and wonderful beauty was seated. I was thrilled with a dreadful horror, I thought of the race of Liliths, and some long forgotten and tragic legends rose up in my memory of these beings whose soul is but a single and terrible passion; whose love too fierce for feebler lives to endure, brings death or madness to men. . . . I saw her in all her terrible beauty. From her head a radiance of feathered flame spread out like the plume of a peacock, it was spotted with gold and green and citron dyes, she raised her arms upwards, her robe, semi-transparent, purple and starred over with a jewel lustre, fell in vaporous folds to her feet like the drift over a waterfall.[3]

For anyone not unconditionally devoted to the diamond light of formless Spirit, this opalescent glamour exercises a fatal fascination.

1 'A Tragedy in the Temple'. *Descent*, p. 208.
2 H.P. Blavatsky: *The Voice of the Silence*, p. 23 fn.
3 'A Tragedy in the Temple'. *Descent*, pp. 208–09.

When his friend next saw Asur, 'his face was as white as the moon, his eyes only reflected the light'.[1]

The dominion of Māra-Lilith is limited to the weakness of human beings. In A.E.'s 'The Cave of Lilith' the temptress tells a sage:

> I, here in my cave between the valley and the height, blind the eyes of all who would pass. Those who by chance go forth to you, come back to me again, and but one in ten thousand passes on. My illusions are sweeter to them than truth. I offer every soul its own shadow. I pay them their own price. I have grown rich, though the simple shepherds of old gave me birth. Men have made me; the mortals have made me immortal. I rose up like a vapour from their first dreams, and every sigh since then and every laugh remains with me. I am made of hopes and fears. The subtle princes lay out their plans of conquest up in my cave, and there the hero dreams, and there the lovers of all time write in flames their history. I am wise, holding all experience, to tempt, to blind, to terrify. None shall pass by.[2]

The sage knows that desire attaches itself to objects which must decay and perish, and that much sorrow ensues. When suffering becomes so intense that it touches the inmost depths, the soul searches for a profounder joy. 'When desire dies the swift and invisible will awakens', the sage replies. Those who have entered the cave of Lilith emerge again, never to go back.

'The Secret of Power' depicts the war within and outside the individual over his destiny. Light and darkness are qualities embodied by beings. In a universe where magic is possible – where Nature's secret operations may be learned – both good and evil magicians exist, and both exert their magnetism on the soul.

> Two figures awful in their power opposed each other; the frail being wavering between them could by putting out its arms have touched them both. It alone wavered, for they were silent, resolute and knit in the conflict of the will; they stirred not a hand nor a foot; there was only a still quivering now and then as of intense effort, but they made no other movement. . . . Here were the culminations of the human, towering images of the good and evil man may aspire to. I looked at the face of the evil adept. His bright red-brown eyes burned with a strange radiance of power; I felt an answering emotion of pride, of personal intoxication, of psychic richness rise up within me

---

1 'A Tragedy in the Temple'. *Descent*, p. 209.
2 'The Cave of Lilith'. *Descent*, p. 217.

The Trials of the Soul

gazing upon him. His face was archetypal; the abstract passion which eluded men in the features of many people I knew, was here declared, exultant, defiant, giantesque; it seemed to leap like fire, to be free. . . . I withdrew my gaze from this face . . . and turned it on the other. An aura of pale soft blue was around this figure through which gleamed an underlight as of universal gold. . . . I caught a glimpse of a face godlike in its calm, terrible in the beauty of a life we know only in dreams, with strength which is the end of the hero's toil, which belongs to the many times martyred soul; yet not far away nor in the past was its power, it was the might of life which exists eternally.[1]

All desire is an aspect of love. In 'A Talk by the Euphrates', Merodach the priest explains:

> There are two kinds of love men know of. There is one which begins with a sudden sharp delight – it dies away into infinite tones of sorrow. There is a love which wakes up amid dead things: it is chill at first, but it takes root, it warms, it expands, it lays hold of universal joys. So the man loves: so the God loves. Those who know this divine love are wise indeed. They love not one or another: they are love itself.[2]

Universal love is the philosopher's stone, reducing all things to their essence because it is consubstantial with *prima materia*, the core of the cosmos. Personal love may soothe but it is partial, while the greater love identifies with and affects every condition. In 'The Meditation of Ananda', the monk comes to feel this love for all creatures flowing through him.

> From his heart he went out to them. Love, a fierce and tender flame, arose; pity, a breath from the vast; sympathy, born of unity. This triple fire sent forth its rays; they surrounded those dark souls; they pervaded them; they beat down oppression.[3]

The divine magic of universal love invisibly affects beings everywhere. Kind acts by others may be sparked by Ananda's love, though unknown to the doers or to him. Magic is a force of nature directed by self-conscious intelligence, and its exercise affects all

---

1 'The Secret of Power'. *Descent*, pp. 201–02.
2 'A Talk by the Euphrates'. *Descent*, p. 216.
3 'The Meditation of Ananda'. *Descent*, p. 211.

nature for better or for ill. As a science, magic requires exact knowledge, but as an art, it must be either wisdom or sorcery. In time this becomes an ultimate question for the soul. Will its sorrows be merged with the sorrows of humanity, as in 'A Strange Awakening', so that the gloom of the world is dispelled by the pristine light of the Spiritual Sun, or will suffering only drive the soul to a ferocious, demonic pride, leading it to join the company of Dostoevsky's Grand Inquisitor?

A.E. saw that one dare not experience joy and hear the whole world cry in pain, that the quest is completed successfully only when one helps to lead others to its goal. 'The Midnight Blossom' expressed this great affirmation:

> 'Brother,' said Varunna, 'here is the hope of the world. Though many seek only for the eternal joy, yet the cry you heard has been heard by great ones who have turned backwards, called by these beseeching voices. The small old path stretching far away leads through many wonderful beings to the place of Brahma. There is the first fountain, the world of beautiful silence, the light which has been undimmed since the beginning of time. But turning backwards from the gate the small old path winds away into the world of men, and it enters every sorrowful heart. This is the way the great ones go.'[1]

THE INTERPRETERS

Ideals must work in practice, otherwise they are not potent.
                                                                Gandhi

Politics seems far removed from mysticism. Mysticism transcends time, whilst politics is preoccupied with the temporal. Mysticism is individual, whereas politics is collective. Politics concerns the welfare of the whole and involves the convergence of particulars which are enormously varied and distinct, demanding precision in the timely application of general ideas. For Plato true politics or statesmanship required skilful blending of the warp and weft of human nature in the light of wisdom. Wisdom is neither casuistry nor technique but an eye for essentials together with an apprehension of

---

1 'The Midnight Blossom'. *Descent*, p. 238.

cosmic law and the Celestial City, and their eternal relevance to limits and possibilities in human affairs. Wisdom is the rainbow bridge between mystical vision and responsibility in the redemptive use of political power. While the mystic is wholly absorbed in his contemplation, the sage is able to frame approximate harmonies on earth and elicit them from others. Skill in action is the mark of the adept who works disinterestedly on behalf of all humanity. He voluntarily leaves the heavenly city of his meditation to lead others to its gates. A.E. dedicated himself to this path of sacrificial action. He sought to democratize the mystical experience and to consecrate its perceived truths with a practical significance in the lives of ordinary men and women.

In *The Interpreters* he seeks the mystical foundations of the political order, connecting metaphysical presuppositions with political ideals and objectives. The cosmic order governing invisible potencies behind material forms is the demiurgic model or matrix within which the physical universe manifests itself. The political realm is a complex compound of higher and lower orders of creation. On the one hand, it generates ultimate questions and universal goals, but on the other it must embody its imperfect formulations in time. Too often the critical ratios between the worlds of eternity and time are forgotten and forms are given disproportionate attention. *The Interpreters* suggests that political systems and human institutions have their hidden basis in cosmology and transcendental law.

The allegory is set at a time in human evolution when material nature has been conquered and a world polity has arisen to channel the energies of the entire race into an exploration of the supernatural roots of energy and power. A despotic technocracy manages global concerns, regulating the moral, intellectual and spiritual lives of individuals. Within this tyrannical order, rebellions periodically erupt. The novel takes as its setting a prison where several revolutionaries await their execution. The dialogue that ensues among them reflects an uncommon state of awareness about the real origins of political roles and social institutions. The participants are the products of a civilization which views the cosmos in terms of three fundamental concepts – Deity is the indissoluble essence of mind, energy and matter. The relations between the points of this triad account for the multiplicity of manifested forms in the universe. Each of the major figures in the story perceives the world from the standpoint of only one of these three aspects. Other characters elaborate these basic notions or present alternative ways of revising or synthesizing them. The nucleus of the work postulates the divine Triad and its partial reflections on earth:

36   The Descent of the Gods

Every one in this age sought for the source and justification of their own activities in that divine element in which matter, energy, and consciousness when analysed disappeared.[1]

These three potencies emanate from the luminous Triad emerging from the Absolute at the dawn of manifestation. Theosophical cosmogenesis teaches that from Spirit or Cosmic. Ideation comes our consciousness; from Cosmic Substance the several vehicles in which that consciousness is individualized and attains to self-consciousness; while *Fohat* or Cosmic Energy is the mysterious link between mind and matter, the animating principle electrifying every atom into life. A.E. referred to this Trinity as the Logos, the Archaeus and the Light of the Logos. In Sanskrit they are known as *Puruṣa, Mūlaprakṛti* and *Daiviprakṛti*. They represent the triple-faced unity of Parabrahm, which is both behind and beyond all cycles of manifestation. As the Triad falls into matter and heterogeneity, its fundamental unity is dispersed among multitudes of beings who recast the universe in one or another of its aspects.

Culain, Lavelle and Heyt are the triad of characters representative of these three evolutionary forces focalized on the human plane. Culain is an acknowledged Socialist who preaches the absolute unity of all in all. He speaks for the Logos, the Universal Spirit which does not particularize but works on behalf of all because it is the highest abstraction of consciousness. Lavelle is a devotee of the Archaeus or radiant matter. This is not ordinary matter as the senses perceive it but rather the pristine essence of Beauty permeating the world of visible nature. Heyt is the spokesman of a higher order of science that has resolved the material world into a substratum of pure energy. As an imperialist mistakenly imprisoned with the rebels, he speaks on behalf of the State's intention to manipulate coercively the operations of mankind in order to augment and apply this knowledge. Because each position signifies only a portion of divine unity, there exists a relative degree of untruth, an insoluble element, in each. The paradox of each position is revealed by Leroy, a sort of philosophical anarchist, who signifies absolute human freedom and the emancipated consciousness that resists reduction into ideologies and systems. His counterpart is Brehon, an aged historian able to connect the divergent points of the dialogue, disentangling truth from the personal prejudice in each.

A.E.'s political vision rests upon a dialectical articulation of each

1 *The Interpreters. Descent*, p. 274.

of the characters as embodying a partial formulation of human experience. Culain is animated by a tender pity and immense love for mankind, similar to those individuals in history who have risen from the masses of oppressed peoples to struggle heroically for human equality and universal welfare. Like Tolstoy or Bakunin, he combines a leonine temperament with a fathomless heart. He concludes one of his eloquent discourses with the declaration:

> I know we can open the soul to that innumerable life so that it can reflect itself in us, and truly we become it, for it is at its root one being, one Heavenly Man manifesting in legions of forms. I am communist and socialist because I believe humanity to be a single being in spite of its myriad forms, faces and eyes, and there is only in it such seeming separation as we find in our own being when it is dramatically sundered in dream. Whatever makes us clutch at the personal, whatever strengthens the illusion of separateness whether it be the possession of wealth, or power over the weak, or fear of the strong, all delay the awakening from this pitiful dream of life by fostering a false egoism.[1]

He is ensouled by the power of the Logos, the moving spirit in history behind the screen of time and transient personalities. A.E. sees him as the mighty architect of humanity's future, laying the foundations of the Heavenly City by promoting fraternity and equality.

Heyt is the ideological antithesis of Culain. Whilst Culain desires to foster the dream of a classless society within every human heart, Heyt wishes to impose it from without. He justifies the arms of the states by arguing for the higher realization of human power they offer. Like Culain he devalues human individuality in the face of collective goals but the future humanity he envisages is devoid of spiritual or intellectual content. It shows servitude and assimilation to some aspect of Cosmic Energy. A.E. drew upon the diverse political systems of his day which advocated a perfection of materialistic science as the basis for Heyt's character. He and the regime he represents have subordinated all individual concerns to the pursuit of power in the name of equality. It was just such mechanistic conformity in social organization that A.E. despised and deemed unacceptable for the humanity of the future.

Although he had some sympathy with the standpoints of each of the characters, Lavelle could be regarded as A.E.'s mouthpiece. He

---

1 *The Interpreters. Descent*, p. 282.

is an acolyte of that Spirit which reveals itself as radiant form, the harmonious evolution of all things towards the beautiful. This principle A.E. referred to elsewhere as the Archaeus or planetary spirit. It is that aspect of Cosmic Mind which individualizes itself in space and time:

> I believe that Wisdom is within the soul to guide it. It is ready at every instant to declare to us the evolutionary purpose. It has planned for us a polity as it has planned for the bee the polity of the hive. . . . We can be conscious co-workers with the spirit of nature. . . . If we think with the Earth spirit our souls become populous with beauty, for we turn the cup of our being to a spring which is always gushing.[1]

Much of Lavelle's account of history and politics points to the expressions of the Archaeus in varied cultures and epochs. He echoes the Theosophical teaching that every great civilization marks the cresting of an evolutionary wave as it circles the globe. As Lavelle, A.E. suggests that Ireland is in a unique position among nations and cultures in that it is still in touch with the primeval radiance of the Archaeus through its mythology and folk-heritage. Mongrel cultures have lost this thread and all foundations upon which to resurrect a higher culture.

Lavelle is the earth spirit which throws itself into innumerable forms as the antagonist of any political system which would dissolve all differences between nations, cultures and individuals in the name of enduring conformity. For him the One becomes the many by virtue of its own superabundance of power. The attempt artificially to straiten Nature's manifold creativity is in Lavelle's and A.E.'s mind a deviation from cosmic law which works through a complex of forces and not as a monolithic agent. He answers both Heyt and Culain by arguing that universal rights must be balanced by individual obligations. The individual is the central concern of A.E.'s political philosophy; the whole is reflected in the part and the great in the small.

Leroy is perhaps the most arcane figure in the novel. He speaks on behalf of the dark angel, the cosmic force that seeks the abolition of forms and outworn ideologies. His character is built upon an abstruse and elaborate metaphysic referred to obliquely in the novel as the 'War in Heaven'. Like the myth of Prometheus, it is a veiled version of ancient accounts of cosmogenesis. It presupposes a perpetual struggle between regeneration and regulation, between

---

1 *The Interpreters. Descent*, p. 266.

free thought and orthodoxy, between spiritual and material creation. The higher powers of solar intelligences are continually at war with the lesser powers attached more intimately to form and stasis. They incarnate into the lower regions to rescue man from his spiritual inertia and bestow upon him the sacred prerogative of creative ideation. Leroy revolts against the passivity induced by all systems of external authority. He stands for the absolute autonomy of the individual and the integrity of the unconditional and indefinable element in every soul:

> Have you never dreamed it might be our own primal will carried us here, that we would not be the slaves of light, and we chose free individual existence full of agony even rather than spiritual passivity. . . . We grow into a myriad wisdom through aeons of pain, and by that wisdom we are higher than seraph or archangel who have not wept as we have nor stayed themselves against the cosmic powers.[1]

The anarchy of Leroy's position is balanced by the calm presence of Brehon, the historian. He resolves the antithetical elements dialectically, sifting the essential from the incidental, reminiscent of Socrates in prison patiently listening to the conflicting opinions of his companions, testing them, discarding the details and bringing together the crucial insights. Brehon's concluding discourse reasserts the unity of thought and experience under the auspices of Cosmic Mind. Each man is an integral ray of Absolute Consciousness, simultaneously allied with oneness and manyness. Man's task is to harmonize and transcend the antipodes of his being, to contemplate that divine Triad of mind, energy and matter exalted above itself and existing in a unity. In Pythagorean language, such a being makes of the Triad a Tetraktys, a triangle of cosmic force with a point in the centre concentrating its focus in and through the enlightened man. A.E. remarks that such beings are complete symbols of the Self-Existent or Solitary of Heaven in whom all qualities inhere and yet who are committed solely to the ethical elevation of the human race. In a striking passage Brehon portrays such a soul:

> when the soul ascends to the spiritual sun a more blinding radiance is emitted from that being. It is the benediction on Earth for yielding to Heaven the things which are Heaven's, and this benediction falls on the path by which the soul had mounted upwards, and it illuminates

[1] *The Interpreters, Descent*, p. 291.

and strengthens what it touches, the power as it flows outward following the chain of thought and mood by which the soul had ascended.[1]

The solar element in man is the true hero in the secret saga of history. It is the spiritual genius latent in every individual which, when stirred by the fires of wisdom, is able to reflect some facet of the Heavenly City, its true ancestral home. Patañjali postulated that the whole universe was created for the sake of the human soul. For A.E. politics bears a similar relationship to man's immortal self. It is an imperfect means to a transcendental end, the repeated channelling of human energies for the enlightenment of the entire race. Its perfectibility is based upon its approximation to that celestial city of divine beings who are attuned to the silent music of the immortal soul.

THE GAELIC AWAKENING

When you know yourselves, you will be known.

Jesus

While most commentators on the Irish Renaissance of the late nineteenth and early twentieth centuries emphasize its literary and artistic achievements, A.E. sought to understand it in the light of universal history. He perceived it not only as a moral force inducing the revaluation of contemporary mores, but also as a vital creative impulse, engendering a new philosophy of man. Aesthetic and political accomplishments were its external ornamentation, compared to the deeper currents of spiritual renewal underlying the movement. A.E.'s participation in this renaissance was guided by an intuitive perception of the invisible causes behind the shadow-play of secular history. He illustrated in *The Interpreters* his conviction that the earth is ensouled by a planetary spirit, a divine Logos honoured in the great religions and mythologies of mankind. Universal history, recorded in archaic symbols and myths, is the ceaseless activity of this moving spirit which manifests itself through *Avatārs* in the greatest human epochs. A.E. recognized the plastic potency of this spirit in the revival of interest in Gaelic mythology and the premonitory yearnings of the Irish people for a new political and social order. Whereas many of his contemporaries viewed this

[1] *The Interpreters. Descent*, pp. 306–7.

resurgence as an opportunity to grasp political power or revivify dying art-forms, A.E. saw it as a portal opening upon a higher world through which eventually the humanity of the future would pass.
   The chief aim of A.E.'s work during this period of awakening was to kindle in the common Irishman an awareness of a spiritual heritage obscured by the repressive institutions of religious orthodoxy. A.E. was convinced that the Catholic Church was the chief despotic force in Ireland's past and present, that its restrictive influence pervaded every aspect of social, economic, political and intellectual life, and that it stultified the creative will and imagination. The Church was the massive barrier to free thought and the cultivation of man's higher faculties, and A.E. felt it as a philosophic certainty that the removal of this barrier would release a great spiritual energy bettering man's condition. He spoke persuasively and persistently of the glory and grandeur of ancient Eire, of the gods and heroes native to the island, and of the Mystery Schools that flourished before the advent of Christianity and Patrick. Though this ancestral vibration was virtually stifled in his time, it could be quickened by those who cherished its vast promise for the future:

> Though to-day none eat of the fruit or drink the purple flood welling from Connla's fountain, I think that the fire which still kindles the Celtic races was flashed into their blood in that magical time, and is our heritage from the Druidic past. It is still here, the magic and mystery; it lingers in the heart of a people to whom their neighbours of another world were frequent visitors.[1]

A.E.'s pronouncements on this theme are to be found in *The Interpreters* and in his articles 'Priest or Hero?' and 'The Awakening of the Fires'. In the first he distinguishes between the emancipated and the imprisoned intellect; in the second he threads together the mythic fragments of Ireland's past to project a grand prophecy for its future. Their appeal is to individual self-regeneration and collective self-determination, an appeal that presages twentieth-century man's search for spiritual values. The confrontation between priest and hero pits dead-letter laws and ritualism against the innate freedom of the human spirit. In Irish legend these antipodal forces of orthodoxy and iconoclasm were represented in the bardic accounts of Ossian's conversations with Patrick. Ossian was a member of the great tribe of heroes called the Fenians, and the son of its paradigm Finn MacCool. The legend recalls that when this brotherhood was

---

[1] 'On an Irish Hill'. *Descent*, p. 351.

in full flower in Ireland, Ossian ventured abroad at the behest of Niam, a daughter of the great god Manannan. After an odyssey of some three hundred years, he returned to his native land, to discover that the tribe of heroes had passed away because St. Patrick had come and permanently established Christianity. Even the forms of men had altered: they seemed as dwarfs compared to the giants of his day. During his labours to help a group of them raise a marble slab, Ossian fell from his horse and, upon touching the earth, became an old man bereft of his former powers. Stranded in his old age, unable to help himself or find food, he was taken home by St. Patrick. Attempting to convert Ossian, Patrick painted in the brightest colours the heaven which might be his if he repented. He similarly described the dark hell in which his old comrades languished. Like Lucifer in *Paradise Lost*, Ossian chose hell, preferring the dignity of heroic rebellion rather than ignoble servitude to an anthropomorphic deity.

In Ossian's firm refusal to submit to the priest's entreaties, A.E. discovered a message and a mission for the people of Ireland. He recognized that the age of heroes was bellicose and that the virtues of love and pity which Jesus exemplified were ennobling. Yet he also realized that imported religious dogmas must necessarily separate a people from the native spirit which overbroods them. He held that the One Life multiplied itself in myriad ways in the world and that enforced doctrinal conformity among different cultures was an insult to the ontological plenty of the cosmos. Whatever good Christianity might have brought was far outweighed by the schism it wrought in the very soul of the Irish people, insisting to them that the heaven-world and godlike men were no longer a part of their natural landscape but removed to an alien abode, the keys to which were in the hands of foreign priests.

> Religion must always be an exotic which makes a far-off land sacred rather than the earth under foot: where the Great Spirit whose home is the vast seems no more a moving glamour in the heavens, a dropping tenderness at twilight, a visionary light on the hills, a voice in man's heart: when the way of life is sought in scrolls or from another's lips.[1]

Yet A.E. felt that Christian priests had committed a much greater injury than alienation from the heaven-world by crippling men's free action with the threat of eternal damnation. A.E. saw this as the

---

1 'Priest or Hero?'. *Descent*, p. 364.

The Gaelic Awakening

worst sort of tyranny, shrinking the ideals of men and perverting the soul's innate awareness of its own divinity. Armed with creedal dogmas, priests could bend the will of an unwary people to serve their narrow purposes. A.E. thought that this unremitting suppression of human energy had over hundreds of years almost extinguished the autonomous and heroic spirit in the Irish people. He resolved to dedicate his powers to the reawakening of soul-force in his countrymen who were spiritually enfeebled by orthodoxy.

For A.E. the critical choice before man was between hero and priest, between the figure representing free thought guided by promptings from within and an oligarchy that preaches cringing obeisance to tyrannical laws imposed from without. This choice was metaphysical and moral, orienting the soul in its mental posture towards the worlds of spirit and matter. From this orientation flowed numerous effects spreading out to encompass every social institution from education to economics. A.E. held that every political revolution must be preceded by an ethical change which springs from individual resolve. True revolution begins with the determination to turn inward, to foreswear all allegiances save those of the mind focussed through the spiritual heart. Until enough individuals are willing to undergo the trials of this path, external revolutions will make little difference since they cannot reach the causal plane of noetic action where man's consciousness is emancipated and his divine destiny won. A.E. himself trod this desolate path, and he fashioned his own heroic character in the heat of trial. He had walked among the hills of Eire where the archaic past whispered to him secrets of the gods and heroes that had passed. In those hours of illumination, he resolved to rekindle the fire of their ancient wisdom, voicing in mellifluous prose the legends they had transmitted. In *The Awakening of the Fires* he suggests that Celtic myths and fables conceal a promise of

> freedom which, though but half recognized, is yet our most precious heritage. We are not yet involved in a social knot which only red revolution can sever; our humanity, the ancient gift of nature to us, is still fresh in our veins: our force is not merely the reverberation of a past, an inevitable momentum started in the long ago but is free for newer life to do what we will with in the coming time.[1]

A.E. saw the liberation that Celtic mythology presaged as arising from a sacred source beyond even the highest of bygone peoples. That fount was wisdom itself, the splendour of the Archaeus which

1 'The Awakening of the Fires'. *Descent*, p. 355.

spoke through its devotees in the earliest races of mankind. The Adepts and Initiates of early epochs, Sons of Wisdom, voluntarily chose to incarnate on earth to instruct infant humanity. Their presence spawned the fabulous tales of gods and heroes walking freely among men in antiquity, teaching the Mysteries, founding great colleges of learning, and subduing the demonic forces later arrayed against them by ungrateful pride-choked spiritual failures. In the filigree of ancient fables there is a unified core of truth and a euhemerized account of the achievements of these noble instructors of infant humanity. The holy vibration they induced in the childhood of the race was never exhausted but periodically renewed, always pointing towards the star of divinity which shone brightly at the dawn of their earthly pilgrimage. Irish mythology is a living tributary of the ocean of ageless wisdom. It is suggested in Theosophical literature that Ireland was settled hundreds of thousands of years ago by peoples fleeing the Atlantean deluge. Towards the close of the civilization built by the Atlanteans, many had turned to sorcery to satisfy their animal appetites and Nature rose up to stem the tide of evil. A flood submerged the continent on which Atlantis had flourished, scattering the peoples yet unstained by sin to the emerging land masses of the future race. They fled to Egypt, the British Isles and the Americas, and founded mighty civilizations wherever they went, preserving the accumulated knowledge of their race. The core of their leadership was always the sacred Brotherhood of Initiates who retained the Universal Wisdom and directed their people in accord with nature's laws. They founded cities and organized the entire gamut of human institutions to prepare men for higher degrees of initiation in the progressive unfoldment of their spiritual natures.

    The transmitters of this great evolutionary current in Celtic prehistory were the Druids, a brotherhood of Magi, adepts in the secret arts who possessed the hidden knowledge of man's past. They handed down these teachings through an oral tradition, and instructed those who proved themselves worthy for initiation into their order. In Celtic legends and myths, only fragments of their knowledge remain, veiled many times over, yet the Gaelic past is permeated by their teaching. The purity and integrity of the Druid doctrine deteriorated over time in accordance with the cyclic laws of nature. Just as the Egyptian Mysteries degenerated into fetishism and ceremonial worship, so too the Celtic Mysteries dissipated into mere phenomenal magic and necromancy. Ghoulish tales of blood sacrifices came from the very nadir of the cycle when the divine impulse had long since retreated even from the inner precincts of their remaining temples. Yet from the edges of their decline to the final extinction of the mystery fires at the advent of Christianity, they authored a final great chapter in Gaelic history.

This period A.E. refers to as the Age of Heroes, when the epic achievements of the warrior spirit were recorded for future generations. The Irish Iliad was enacted then, peopled with the great heroes of the Ulster cycle: Cuchullain, Nuada and Lugh. The last efflorescence of this period is recounted in the Finn cycle, telling of the exploits of Finn MacCool and his tribe of warriors engaged in a struggle with demonic powers from under the sea. In all these tales is found a general commingling of gods and men, as if the portals to the heaven-world were still accessible to the noblest of men and women. A.E. felt that this free traffic between heaven and earth, the divine and the human, had been obstructed by Christianity, yet he hoped that the mantle of knowledge and power worn by the ancient heroes of Ireland could still be recovered by his fellow countrymen. He saw a two-thousand-year cycle of spiritual suppression in the name of Christian orthodoxy passing away, and the emergence of a fresh opportunity to kindle the noetic vibration which had been obscured. A.E. pointed to that hidden promise celebrated by the ancient Druids in their Hymn to the Sun:

> Great Magnet! Thy hidden power
> Draws us ever onward to spaces anew.
> Secret in the earth thy life forces waken
> Stirrings and whispers that the ear cannot hear;
> Later will come birth in the fullness of thy Splendour –
> Now is the time of thy great mystery of nature,
> Now does the cycle in thy great turning blend;
> All that has been shall lend to what comes after,
> All that will come lies hidden in thy promise.[1]

FOUNTAIN OF INSPIRATION

Truth did not come into the world naked, but it came in types and images. The world will not receive it in any other way.
The Gospel of Philip, 67

A.E.'s humility arose from the recognition that his poetic vision

---

[1] *Hermes* (Concord Grove Press, Santa Barbara), May 1977.

evolved from a source beyond ordinary waking consciousness. Eventually, he gained conviction that talent could be brought to an intensity equal to inspiration, but during his youth no such confidence supported his efforts.

> I have condemned myself many times for my lack of persistence and of faith that the genie in the innermost would have given inspiration to complete a narrative which I thought needed too lordly a style for my talent.[1]

The gulf which he saw as separating inspiration from expression did not deter him from searching for the very fount of poetic inspiration. He knew that whatever its basis in the cosmic scheme, it could be discovered only by turning within and struggling through the successive layers of consciousness which at once expressed and concealed it.

A.E. dwelt in the ordinary world, but from his youth he witnessed elemental life and alchemical operations, subliminal patterns and archetypal matrices of pure potentiality. He perceived correspondences between the concrete world of the psycho-physical senses, the invisible 'world of faery', and formless immaterial *potentia*. Memory fades before a deeper recollection of the hidden roots of consciousness and being.

> It is most difficult at first to retrace our way, to remember what we thought or did even an hour before. But if we persist the past surrenders to us and we can race back fleetly over days or months. The sages enjoined this meditation with the intent that we might, where we had been weak, conquer in imagination, kill the dragons which overcame us before and undo what evil we might have done. I found, when I had made this desire for retrospect dominant in meditation, that an impulse had been communicated to everything in my nature to go back to origins. It became of myself as if one of those moving pictures we see in the theatres, where in a few moments a plant bursts into bud, leaf and blossom, had been reversed and I had seen the blossom dwindling into the bud. My moods began to hurry me back to their first fountains. To see our lives over again is to have memories of two lives and intuitions of many others, to discover powers we had not imagined in ourselves who were the real doers of

---

1 *Song and Its Fountains. Descent*, pp. 441–42.

Fountain of Inspiration 47

our deeds, to have the sense that a being, the psyche, was seeking incarnation in the body.[1]

To yearn to undertake the task of uncovering the fountain-source of consciousness and poetry, one must presuppose a common root which nourishes all consciousness and sustains every creative effort. Aristotelian logic cannot allow for the derivation of a fundamental standpoint either from empirical observation or from rationalistic principles. A.E.'s earliest illuminations revealed his basic stance:

> I remember the deep peace which came to me when I had the intuition that Christ, Prometheus, are in every heart, that we all took upon ourselves the burden of the world like the Christ, and were foreseers as Prometheus was of the agony of the labour he undertook, until the chaos is subdued and wrought in some likeness to the image in the divine imagination.[2]

From this perspective, he could 'track song back to its secret fountains' in deeper states of consciousness, in the powers of memory and evocation. The psychological rationale for his experience was known to the ancient sages of the East.

In Europe the greatest intellects have been occupied by speculations upon the laws and aspects of physical nature, while the more spiritual Hindus were absorbed in investigations as to the nature of life itself; by continual aspiration, devotion, introspection and self-analysis, they had acquired vast knowledge of the states of consciousness possible for man to enter upon; they had laid bare the anatomy of the mind, and described the many states that lay between the normal waking condition of man, and that final state of spiritual freedom and unity with BRAHMA, which it was the aim alike of religion and science to bring about.[3]

The three broad divisions of individual consciousness in Hindu psychology are *jāgrat*, waking consciousness; *svapna*, dreaming consciousness (itself divisible into numerous types and levels); and *suṣupti*, deep dreamless sleep. 'Sushupti, the highest, was accounted a spiritual state; here the soul touches vaster centres in the great life and has communion with celestial intelligences.'[4] These states

1 *Song and Its Fountains. Descent*, pp. 391–92.
2 *Ibid.*, p. 443.
3 'Jagrata, Svapna and Sushupti'. *Descent*, p. 454.
4 *Ibid.*

correspond to those planes of consciousness experienced nightly by every human being. By overcoming the discontinuity usually found in passing from one state to another, the mystic sees that all planes of consciousness and being are integrated in an ontological continuum with their highest source. Discontinuity arises from personal consciousness, which edits its memories of the waking state, remembers dreams only vaguely, and is altogether oblivious to dreamless sleep. A.E. grasped the truth that serene continuity of consciousness through all planes could be self-consciously experienced through a concentrated effort of the will. Since consciousness is embodied, memory is a function both of concentration of mind and of refinement of matter.

> Our thoughts and actions in the waking state react upon the dreaming and deep sleep, and our experiences in the latter influence us in the waking state by suggestion and other means. The reason we do not remember what occurs in Svapna and Sushupti is because the astral matter which normally surrounds the thinking principle is not subtle enough to register in its fullness the experience of any one upon the more spiritual planes of consciousness. To increase the responsiveness of this subtle matter we have to practise concentration, and so heighten the vibrations, or in other words to evolve or perfect the astral principle.[1]

Concentration is the prelude and the product of deep meditation, reducing contrasting states of consciousness to their primal and unitary nature. Each stage is evolved slowly in the alembic of the mind.

> Take some idea – the spiritual unity of all things, for example – something which can only be realized by our complete absorption in spiritual nature; let every action be performed in the light of this idea, let it be the subject of reverent thought. If this is persisted in, we will gradually begin to become conscious upon the higher planes, the force of concentration carrying the mind beyond the waking into Svapna and Sushupti.[2]

If the alchemical reduction is persistently applied until all discontinuities in consciousness are dissolved, the unitary condition of consciousness is experienced.

1 'Jagrata, Svapana and Sushupti', *Descent*, p. 455.
2 *Ibid.*

Fountain of Inspiration

Beyond waking, dreaming and deep sleep is Turya. Here there is a complete change of condition; the knowledge formerly sought in the external world is now present *within* the consciousness; the ideations of universal mind are manifest in spiritual intuitions.[1]

The self-conscious movement towards universal and homogeneous consciousness is accompanied by similar transformations of matter; hence, the evolution of nature.

> This harmonious action of all the qualities of our nature, for universal purposes without personal motive, is in *synchronous vibration* with that higher state spoken of. . . . Therefore we are at one with it.[2]

Consciousness can fuse every waking moment into a continuous current of ideation. Return to universal consciousness is the subjective correlate of the downward descent into divided consciousness and heterogeneous materiality for an essential if enigmatic purpose.

> To the question, 'What have we to do with God?' we make answer that we are the children of Deity – bright sparks born in that Divine flame, the spirit in its primal ecstasy reflected in itself the multitudinous powers that throng in space. It was nourished by Divine love, and all that great beauty thrilled through it and quickened it. But from this vision which the spirit had, it passed to climb to still greater heights – it was spiritual, it might attain divinity. The change from the original transcendental state of vision to that other state of *being*, of all-pervading consciousness, could only be accomplished by what is known as the descent into matter where spirit identifies itself with every form of life, and assimilates their essences. This cyclic pilgrimage it undertook, foreseeing pain, but 'preferring free will to passive slavery, intellectual, self-conscious pain, and even torture, "while myriad time shall flow"', to inane, imbecile, instinctual beatitude', foreseeing pain, but knowing that out of it all would come a nobler state of life, a divinity capable of rule, a power to assist in the general evolution of nature.[3]

An original Promethean resolve plunged the soul into the pain of existence on a plane of separation. The world appears to it as

---

1 'Concentration'. *Descent*, p. 456.
2 *Ibid.*, p. 457.
3 'Comfort'. *Descent*, p. 458–59.

capricious and chaotic, but it is 'a chaos whose very disorder is the result of law'.[1] The soul senses a profound, impersonal justice in this law, consonant with its own inner being, and can therefore remain placid even in the most adverse conditions. 'Out of confidence in this justice may spring up immortal hopes; our motives, our faith shall save us.'[2] The spiritual and material aspects of Brahmā – *Brahma Vāc and Brahma Viraj* – are united at every point in the fluid hierarchy of nature. Compassion stems from recognition of this unity of law in one's own being, from thoughts and actions chosen in terms of universal rather than personal principles and desires.

> Above all it is the law of our own being; it is at one with our ancestral self. In all this lies, I think, such consolation as we may take and offer for pain. Those who comprehend, in their resignation, shall become one with themselves: and out of this resignation shall arise will to go forth and fulfil our lofty destiny.[3]

No more than Socrates did A.E. claim to have fully travelled the path to our pristine origin and root being, but the broad range of his mystical experiences convinced him that he had seen ahead. With his assured understanding of the mystic path, he attempted late in life to convey the meaning of his experiences by indicating the source of some of his poetry. *Song and Its Fountains* recalls in maturity 'the character and architecture of the psyche'[4] enthusiastically celebrated in *The Candle of Vision* fourteen years earlier. Tracing each upsurge of creative expression to a primal source, he was certain that the most profound impulsions sprang from origins outside ordinary space and time.

> One after another the desires and idealisms of later life were, in that retrospect, traced back to their fountains. There grew up the vivid sense of a being within me seeking a foothold in the body, trying through intuition and vision to create wisdom there, through poetry to impose its own music upon speech, through action trying to create an ideal society, and I was smitten with penitence because I had so often been opaque to these impulses and in league with satyr or faun in myself for so many of my days.[5]

1 'Comfort'. *Descent*, p. 459.
2 *Ibid*.
3 *Ibid*.
4 *Songs and Its Fountains. Descent*, p. 391.
5 *Ibid.*, p. 394.

Fountain of Inspiration 51

A.E. was aware that worldly desires had not been utterly banished from his consciousness, and that an existential duality persisted. His retrospective meditation drew together the different dimensions of consciousness, unveiling more fundamental levels, only to reveal their root unity. This revelation is complete, sustained and validated only at the highest levels of meditation. The mystic must take care not to accept as final some lower-order recognition which at best consolidates a penetrating but incomplete insight. A.E. found that his friends who were not assiduous in meditation did not trace 'the congregation of desires' back to their source, and, consequently, tended to be bound by some picture of themselves and the universe.

I began to see too in those with whom I was intimate that each had some governing myth, that somewhere in their past, from the first bridal of soul and body, a germinal mood had been born which had grown to dominion over everything else in them.[1]

Moods – a broad concept for A.E., including states of consciousness and the deep feelings which tincture them – are themselves expressions of the partial incarnation of an inner being seeking birth. This is the true man, the Higher Self of every person. Meditation is the delicate art of midwifery which assists in spiritual birth and moral regeneration.

It was such a being I surmised within me, trying to tune the body to be sensitive to its own impulses by a glamour cast upon desire, and also by vision, dream and the illumination of intuition and conscience. They impelled often in such contrary directions these impulses, that I divined a dual nature in the psyche. It was a being in part avidly desirous of life, while another part was cold to this, but was endlessly seeking for the Spirit.[2]

In a universe suffused with intelligence, the psyche emerges from the involvement of mind with some matrix of matter and activity. Psyche is drawn towards the world of increasingly complex forms, images and desires as well as towards an abstract, formless realm. We may sense a duality in our mental nature, and hence in our actions; on the one hand, a crystalline and ethereal beauty which seldom descends below the loftiest level of dreams, on the other, an opalescent and material reflection which barely rises above the

1 *Song and Its Fountains. Descent*, pp. 394–95.
2 *Ibid.*, p. 398.

turba of images. Yet the two are nourished by the same impulse, as the sun and moon shine with the same light. The creative act is the link between these two; poems are oracles of the divine.

A.E. held that these oracles were transmitted through a medium of psychic substance which tinctured the messages. Whether the higher or lower psyche is dominant at any given moment is of utmost importance in discerning the true meaning of the oracle. Desire discolours, while aspiration purifies. But the two may blend in an elusive alloy and 'they are the fortunate who know what dark passion may be hidden by the cheat of loveliness'.[1] So, each thought must be traced to its source.

> Even when we think desire is left behind, on a sudden the desires we thought dead will rise from their grave in our meditation as if they were penitent, looking at us with angelic lips and eyes, and if we yield to their enchantment we may find they have become more terrible than when they were clothed in flesh. When desires die in the body they may reincarnate in the psyche, and may in our heavenward travelling fright us with terror as incubi or succubi.[2]

To raise consciousness towards its origin is also to trace it to the pristine state which was once its natural incarnated condition. Earliest man, like Adam in Eden, had not yet rebelled against passive spirituality, and the dual psyche within him was only potential.

> It is probable that the bad hexameters in which the Oracles of Apollo were delivered in the decadence of the mysteries continued the tradition of a time when the Earth-born waited on the Heaven-born in a rapt awe and the immortals uttered their oracles, a divine speech, through the purity of prophet or priest. No Church today can convince me that it is inspired until the words arising from it even in anger break in a storm of beauty on the ear.[3]

The process of individuation as a prelude to union with the divine demands the elevation of the psyche and the drawing near to spirit in consciousness so that spirit may descend into the world.

> I have found this duality in everything in my life, and I can only

---

1 *Song and Its Fountains. Descent*, p. 405.
2 *Ibid.*
3 *Ibid.*, p.434.

Fountain of Inspiration

surmise some wisdom, above the outworn heart and an eager heart, which understands that we cannot be wholly of this world or wholly of the heavenworld, and we cannot enter that Deity out of which came good and evil, light and darkness, spirit and matter, until our being is neither one or the other, but a fusion of opposites, a unity akin to that Fulness where spirit, desire and substance are raised above themselves and exist in that mystic unity of all things which we call Deity.[1]

Yet paradoxically, as we individuate we become more universal. The *persona* is restricted to particulars, but the individuated being is not identified with it. The immortal soul thinks naturally in terms of self-transcendence and its duty to humanity.

I sometimes think that the whole life of the soul, since it was first outbreathed by Deity, must be a struggle to find or re-create outside itself all that it first had within itself in the Pleroma. The soul fallen outside the divine circle begins to create in fantasy its lost infinitude.[2]

If the soul will not be swept away in endless images, it must trace them to their origins in retrospective meditation.

The soul returns by the way it came from those high spheres to the body to take up its labours in this world. What are its labours? It has to make conquest of this world, become master of the nature which envelops us, until the eternal is conscious in us, and we have made this world into a likeness or harmony with the Kingdom of Light. As our being here becomes transparent to the Light we receive more and more of the true. Intuitions begin to leap up in us every instant, and we receive, according to our capacity, vision, imagination, knowledge of past and future, illuminations about the nature of things, wisdom and poetry. The fountain of all these lies deep within us where the psyche in ceaseless ecstasy responds to the Will that moves the universe and translates the wisdom of that being into the intellectual fires of the Paraclete, and its fiery tongues give the divine signature to our thoughts.[3]

In attaining this high source, at once the divine centre of our being and the core of the noumenal cosmos, we stand upon the Mount of

---

1 *Song and Its Fountains. Descent*, pp. 416–17.
2 *Ibid.*, p. 447.
3 *Ibid.*, pp. 421–22.

54 The Descent of the Gods

Transfiguration. Our thoughts and lives are irradiated with a life beyond temporality and suffused with the divine. We become more than human – fully human – and easily identify with the struggles, sorrows, joys and aspirations of all. We recognize that:

> There is as great a mystery about our least motion as there is about our whole being. We are affected by the whole cosmos. Emanations from most distant planets pour on us and through us. Everything is related to everything else. 'Thou canst not stir a stone without troubling a star.' Let us still life to the utmost quietude, and what we feel in the stillness is pregnant as if there were multitudes in that intensity of loneliness.[1]

Mystic individuation is the eruption of full self-consciousness, universalization through soul-awakening, and altruism is its natural ethic. By emulating that transfigured state in our present condition, by degrees, we pass into it.

Even if we do not come to unity with the spirit there is a great gain from this meditation in which we try by a divine alchemy to transmute the gross into the subtle and pure, for very soon our whole being begins to circle around an invisible sun, and we are drawn more and more to it; and though it may be aeons before we come nigh it, yet we feel as Adam might have felt, the outcast from Paradise, after long penitence, if he had seen faintly flickering through the outer darkness of the world in which he laboured the shining of the lost Eden, and knew it was not altogether lost but was accessible after purification. To have this surety is no light thing.[2]

ILLUMINATION AND SEERSHIP

Not even the light which comes down nearest to the earth from the sun is mixed with anything, nor does it admit dirt and defilement, but remains wholly pure and without stain and free from external influences among all existing things.

Emperor Julian

The logic of a pregenetic unity to the cosmos requires that we affirm

---

1 *Song and Its Fountains. Descent*, p. 449.
2 *Ibid.*, p. 452.

some principle of real or apparent division of aspects, entities or qualities in existence. Metaphysically, this principle is found in the concept of a Triad of divine aspects. Arithmetically, the number one gives the notion of number, two the idea of duplication, and three the concept of elaboration, that is, permutation and combination. Geometrically, the point and the line can generate a triangle, the simplest enclosure of space in a plane. But the idea of rotation – in this case, the rotation of an isosceles triangle about an axis from the apex through the centre of its base – produces the cone or vortex, the origin of three-dimensional space. Ontologically, the Triad implies an inner side (called 'Spirit' by A.E.), an outer side (the material medium of spirit) and a dynamic principle which draws the two together. Theosophically, this third element is sometimes called *Fohat*, the active aspect of spirit from the standpoint of matter, and the energetic aspect of matter from the standpoint of spirit. If effects can never be completely alienated from their causes, the unity present at the advent of existence will be found at every level of its unfoldment, and *a fortiori* the Triad is implicit in everything from a universe to a grain of sand.

The spiritual alchemy of the Renaissance was rooted in the premise that every base metal was essentially gold *ab ovo* made gross by the infusion of a chaotic, derivative, aqueous element – metalline organization obscuring gold's archetypal structure. Transmutation is the process of purifying the base metal of the aqueous element until only the natural gold remains. Alchemists knew well that aurifaction is shadowed by aurifiction, the production of a metallic substance which assumes some of the external characteristics of gold, usually by mixing minute quantities of gold with lesser metal. Along with transmutation, decisive tests for genuineness of results were performed. Moral aurifiction will be exposed on the psychic plane by its fascination with images and on the plane of action by the projection of appearances. Both may contain a golden residuum in a crude alloy, but unless the tests for gold are known, one will as likely seize upon the lesser as the true metal. The concept of transmutation (along with a constellation of interrelated and supporting ideas) can apply *mutatis mutandis* to the cosmos, the psychic nature of man, and the path to illumination. Spiritual alchemy enunciates the view that there is a correspondence between physical and spiritual nature, and a continuous interaction between them.

A.E. perceived the purest spiritual nature within and throughout the grossest material nature. To the extent that a particular permutation of the two natures imposes itself, under law and circumstance, upon our consciousness it becomes real to us. Similarly, the degree of will we apply to a particular level of the interrelated aspects of the Unknowable determines the clarity of appearance which that level must assume. The psyche, as a complex of thought, will and feeling, changes under these internal and external impulses, and each psychic state is strictly correlated with some level of substance. If the senses are instruments of the power of perception, then there are senses for different levels of being and consciousness that can be experienced. The mystic path is the conscious and willing activation of subtler senses so that the psyche may become fully aware of what it always implicitly reflects.

> In that mysterious journeying from time to eternity, where the soul moves on to ever higher planes of its own being, there must be many transformations of the psyche. Something I think goes with it from this world to that other. 'The gods feed upon men.' Something comes back with it from Heaven to Earth. 'The gods nourish us.' There is, I believe, some commerce between this world and that other.[1]

The ascent and descent of the psyche is the illumination of the soul at different levels and interstices. The psyche aspires; the nous inspires.

> As our aspiration is, so is our inspiration. The higher nature takes our fragmentary knowledge, thought, experience, and our aspiration, which is sacrifice, and it is transfigured, made whole and returned to us. What is earth-born is lifted up and perfected, shot through and through with the light of that higher world where the psyche nigh to its divine root imagines the perfection or truth in all things. Much must be lost of that transcendental lucidity and beauty of the heavenly consciousness when the psyche sinks through murky clouds of desire back to the body again. But something returns.[2]

The transient ascents of the psyche are not merely ephemeral events, for the illumination of the psyche works a change in its nature. Repeated *rapprochement* of the psyche with the divine root clarifies its obscuration so that it reflects the higher light more adequately. 'Our inspiration will be as our aspiration.'[3]

---

1 *Song and Its Fountains. Descent*, p. 421.
2 *Ibid.*
3 *Ibid.*, p. 431.

Illumination and Seership

A.E.'s convictions sprang from his own experience and a steadfast concern to make use of the analogies and correspondences which flooded into his awareness. Ordinary waking thought is insufficient to provide the existential and experimental basis for understanding the process of consciousness.

> Intuition, feeling, thought are too swift in their coming and going, too elusive for a decisive argument over their nature. Though they may shake us by what they import, though what they in an instant hint at may be sacred to us, their coming and going are too swift for precise thought about themselves. In normal thought the fusion between inner and outer is so swift that it deceives the most attentive sense into the idea of unity, and we come to believe that there is no other creator of thought than the thinker who resides in the brain, who is with us from moment to moment, and we do not know what rays from how many quarters of the heavens are focussed on the burning point of consciousness.[1]

Unaware of the elemental denizens pervading waking consciousness, much less the specific effects of collective and individual patterns of thought upon ourselves, we cannot discern their nature. In the subjective dream state, however, we make discoveries.

> In dream there is a dramatic sundering of the psyche. One part of us is seer and another is creator. The seer of dream is unconscious of creation. He looks on the forms which appear as he might look on a crowd drawn together by impulses not of his creation. He does not think all this when he dreams, but, when he wakens and remembers, he knows that the creator of dream had a magical power transcending anything which he could do in his waking state. It can project crowds of figures, set them in motion, make them to move with perfect naturalness, and wear the fitting expression for the deeds they do. Yet in the waking state of the dreamer, let him be given canvas, paints and brushes, and he might boggle as a child would over the drawing of a figure. The creator in dream is swift inconceivably. What seems a long dream to the seer of dream often takes place in an instant, and may be caused by sound or touch which wakens him. Transformations, too, take place in dream which suggest a genius to which psychic substance is instantly malleable.[2]

---

1 *Song and Its Fountains, Descent,* pp. 398–99.
2 *Ibid.*

The psyche, when released through withdrawal from the constraints of concrete matter, operates upon a subtle material medium commensurate with itself. Psychic substance readily takes the impress of intellect and the psyche witnesses instant presentments and elaborations. The seer is unaware of doing anything, and therefore one suspects a superior intelligent force operating in this medium.

> The seer in dreams is apart from the creator. It is not unreasonable to surmise an intellectual creator able to work magically upon psychic substance. Sometimes, indeed, at the apex of dream I have almost surprised the creator of it peering in upon me as if it desired by these miracles to allure me to discovery of itself. In the exploration of dream we acquire some knowledge of the workings of that mysterious psyche. And at times in the making of poetry I have been able to discover the true creator of the poem withdrawn far within from the waking consciousness. The poem seemed like an oracle delivered to the waking self from some dweller or genie in the innermost.[1]

A.E. knew from his Theosophical studies that at least seven kinds of dreams could be distinguished, and that the dreams he frequently experienced intimated a higher awareness than he found readily accessible.

> Whence come vision and high imagination? I think they come from a centre of consciousness behind the sphere of dream. Here I pass from experience to rely on intuition and the wisdom of others. It is to the seers who wrote the Upanishads I turn for illumination. They speak of four states of the soul – waking, dreaming, deep sleep and spirit waking – the last a state in which the spirit is unsleeping in its ecstasy of infinite vision.[2]

The last state – *turīya* – is outside the order of the other three, and is that in which Spirit is at once seer and creator, and where seeing is the activity of shedding the light that is the *prima materia* of creation. Since all four states are implicit at every level of consciousness, the perceptive mystery of creation is present in every dream. When the psyche is unobscured by preconception and fascination, it is illuminated and hence becomes the seer – a condition more readily recognized in the dream state than in either waking consciousness

---

1 *Song and Its Fountains. Descent*, p. 400.
2 *Ibid.*, p. 420.

Illumination and Seership

or deep and traceless sleep. The seer in the psyche cannot see the creator precisely because it is that creator itself. Since its activity is less pellucid than pure spirit, it is the channel of both seership and creation.

Poetry can emerge from states of varying illumination because this light of conscious awareness is also the sound of understanding. *The Voice of the Silence* addresses one who has become a master of *samādhi* – the state of faultless vision – in terms of light and sound.

> And now, Lanoo, thou art the doer and the witness, the radiator and the radiation, Light in the Sound and the Sound in the Light.[1]

When this sovereign state of consciousness free from all change and interruption is reached, the treatise declares:

> Behold! thou hast become the Light, thou hast become the Sound, thou art thy Master and thy God. Thou art THYSELF the object of thy search: the VOICE unbroken, that resounds throughout eternities, exempt from change, from sin exempt, the Seven Sounds in one, THE VOICE OF THE SILENCE.[2]

A.E. never claimed to achieve in consciousness such irreversible and transcendent heights. But he touched chords in the psyche which evoked deep spiritual resonances and gave meaning to the Upaniṣadic teaching.

> But for a moment I understood what power might be in sound or incantation. It made me understand a little those mystics who speak of travelling up a Jacob's Ladder of Sound to the Logos, the fountain of all melody. I found later if meditation on the Spirit is prolonged and profound enough we enter on a state where our being is musical, not a music heard without but felt within as if the soul itself had become music, or had drawn nigh to the ray of the Logos, the Master Singer, and was for that instant part of its multitudinous song.[3]

Like Socrates, who taught the way to beauty itself by recounting the words of Diotima, A.E. took sufficient steps on the Path of Infinite Promise to be able to affirm it with confidence.

---

1 H.P. Blavatsky: *The Voice of the Silence*, p. 22.
2 *Ibid.*, pp. 23–4.
3 *Song and Its Fountains. Descent*, p. 428.

The Descent of the Gods

> I am a far exile from that great glory, and can but peer through a dusky transparency to a greater light than the light of day. That greater light shines behind and through the psyche. It is the light of spirit which transcends the psyche as the psyche in its own world transcends the terrestrial ego. The psyche has a dual nature, for in part it is earth-bound, and in part it clings to the ancient spirit. . . . While I could comprehend a little about the nature of the psyche, I could not apprehend at all the spirit which transcends the soul, for, as the seers said of it, it is eternal, invisible and universal. Yet because it is universal we are haunted by it in every motion of mind. It is at the end of every way. It is present in sunlight.[1]

A.E.'s 'meditations were all intent on the discovery of the nature of soul and spirit',[2] and his own poetic singing constituted an array of oracles from the psyche – partial, eclipsed by external trappings of phrase and circumstance, and bound by limited vision.

> Yet they themselves may pay reverence to the voices of conscience or of intuition which also are oracles out of undiscovered depths in their own being, and intuition and conscience may utter themselves in song as well as in fugitive illuminations of mind, heart or will.[3]

A.E.'s consciousness, focussed by a profound philosophical and psychological framework, could import glimpses of pure and undiffused light from loftier realms.

> Just as the needle-point of a nerve in the eye is sensitive to light from the whole of the heavens spread above us, so at moments we feel that all knowledge is within us. But we have not yet evolved mind to be the perfect instrument to mirror universal mind as the eye mirrors infinitudes of light and darkness. But out of that centre in us through which all the threads of the universe are drawn there may come at times flashes of supernature.[4]

Within the aurifiction of his varied visions and dreams, retold in *The Candle of Vision* and *Song and Its Fountains* and refracted in every poem and story, A.E. perceived the possibilities of the

---

1 *Song and Its Fountains. Descent*, p. 443.
2 *Ibid.*, p. 429.
3 *Ibid.*
4 *Ibid.*, p. 449.

aurifaction of true seership and touched that great work within the laboratory of his own endeavours.

Yet there are enchanted moments when we have vision, however distant, of the divinities who uphold the universe. It is true we are at an immense distance from their greatness, and see them as a shepherd boy far away among his hills might see the glittering of the army of a great king, and he is awed by the majesty and bows low at the vision of greatness, and dreams over it when the army is past and he turns to his humble task with his sheep. So remotely is it I have apprehended splendours overshadowing my insignificance. They stand over all of us.[1]

Perhaps more important than the content of his visions is his method for achieving an elusive transforming awareness.

I do not think we shall ever come to truth otherwise than by such gropings in the cave of the soul, when with shut eyes we are in a dim illuminated darkness, and seek through transient transparencies to peer into the profundities of being.[2]

THE MYTHIC IMAGINATION

Transcendent Beings move variously over the earth.

Plotinus

Contemporary exegesis of world mythology stresses the comparative study of mythological figures and symbols rather than the process of myth-making itself. Speculation on the meaning of myths is indeed hazardous, as psycho-social interpretations raise more questions than they answer. The entire field is shrouded in a mist of confusion that cannot be dispelled without an empathic understanding of the myth-maker and the myth-making faculty. Plausible commentaries on obscure mythologies often say more about their commentators than ancient man. The problem of deciphering myth fundamentally demands a conceptual reversal by which we assume

---

[1] *Song and Its Fountains. Descent*, p. 429.
[2] *Ibid.*, pp. 428–29.

fact in the place customarily assigned to metaphor. Mythologizing was sometimes a secret code instead of a fanciful pastime, as it ascribed archetypal significance to the events and memories of human life. Modern man has largely lost this mythic imagination through psychological materialism and uncritical faith in crude conceptions of the empirical sciences. When the capacity to generate or understand myth is eclipsed, myths are hastily recast in the modes of thought most familiar and acceptable – psychological, sociological and historical. The beam of mythological truth is distorted and dispersed by the smug prejudices of scholiasts. The implications inferred are neither exhaustive nor authentic. Myths conveyed to ancient seers some sort of unified cosmology, psychology and meta-ethics. Even now they could serve as portals to a world inconceivably richer, grander and more magnanimous than reductionist theories of interpretation would suggest.

As a young man A.E. discovered that admission into this wondrous world was not through scholarship but by seership. Consciousness is the vast bridge from immediate concerns to the remote past. His visionary experiences in the Irish hills convinced him that the cosmic powers which distant bards intimated in their legends are ever present to the inner eye. By the proper use of this interior faculty, mythological secrets may be deciphered. A.E.'s own explorations enabled him to catch glimpses of a realm of reality behind the curtain of time beckoning the unfiltered imagination:

> There is within us a little space through which all the threads of the universe are drawn; and, surrounding that incomprehensible centre, the mind of man sometimes catches glimpses of things which are true only in those glimpses; when we record them the true has vanished, and a shadowy story, – such as this – alone remains. Yet, perhaps, the time is not altogether wasted in considering legends like these, for they reveal, though but in phantasy and symbol, a greatness we are heirs to, a destiny which is ours though it be yet far away.[1]

Mystics and seers see time as a limitation to be surmounted by meditation. It is an illusion produced by the succession of our states of consciousness. The stilling of the compulsive flow of thought allows the mystic to dissolve the illusory self. He rises to a plane of awareness that is timeless, relative to the restless mind trapped in the discontinuities of sense perception. Medieval alchemists, like the ancient Hindus, taught that the rarefied realm of pure thought

---

1 'The Story of A Star'. *Descent*, p. 475.

The Mythic Imagination 63

gives access to the sequence of human evolution as well as a coherent knowledge of the cosmic forces regulating its progress. They postulated a homogeneous realm of radiant matter pervading space, the *ākāśa* or *Mysterium Magnum*, the universal medium upon which are impressed vast assemblages of thought-forms emanating from the Cosmic Mind, as well as the record of their interaction with human consciousness on earth. It is both the true source of creation and a permanent repository of everything created. The astral realm is composed of many layers and grades of subtle matter, from the most ethereal to that which is barely beyond the purview of the physical senses. At its highest level it is an *ākāśic* potency reflecting the untrammelled ideation of the Divine Mind, while at its lowest it is the register of the worst thoughts and acts thrown off by human beings. The radical difference between these two poles suggests a firm basis for discriminating true vision from mere fantasy, mythic imagination from mediumistic delusion.

The subtler realm of the *ākāśa* or celestial light is noetic in nature and accessible through the deepest contemplation. Access to this realm requires the complete withdrawal of consciousness from the seductive plane of sense perception, wherein the limitations are greatest. Between this tangible plane of the senses and the heights of *ākāśic* awareness lie the sub-regions of the Astral Light which can induce and inflame the most dire deceptions. This 'red mid-region', as A.E. called it, is a composite of unexpended animal desire, disintegrating shells discarded by immortal souls and the most odious thought-forms engendered by human fantasy. Matter on this plane is in a critical state, inherently unstable and turbid. Desires are quickened and pleasures intensified. The mystic must pass through this region speedily before succumbing to its temptations, symbolized in Tibetan texts by luxuriant blossoms beneath which lurk coiled serpents. The increasing prevalence of degenerate mediums and deluded mystics testifies to the nefarious influence of this region in inverting and perverting all higher aspirations. The perception of formless spiritual essences characterizes the higher imagination and is only gained by directing consciousness effortlessly beyond the plane of psychic distortion. This is the fruit of lifetimes of training involving mental purification and spiritual discipline.

A.E. recognized in his reveries and spontaneous excursions into subjective planes that control is easily surrendered out of obsessive fascination with entrancing images. The acute danger of self-deception in such experiences led him to seek the advice of his wise friend, W.Q. Judge, who counselled him to exercise greater command over his thoughts and to meditate on universal themes. In later years A.E. would recommend that every earnest student of the occult should study one of the great philosophies of mankind as an antidote to wasteful and chaotic fantasizing. For him, the higher planes of the Astral Light, those closest to the pure ākāśa, contained 'the great picture gallery of Eternity' wherein one could enter safely and return to earth with a clear if incomplete recollection of the visit. Even if clouded by the muddled memories of earth-life, one could thread together these fragments of spiritual reminiscence and establish a permanent bond in one's consciousness with the sacred inheritance of humanity. The essential power of the mythic imagination is the capacity to collapse at will the limitations of one's epoch and freely perceive the trans-temporal processes of invisible nature.

I tried to pierce through the great veil of nature, and feel the life that quickened it within. I tried to comprehend the birth and growth of planets, and to do this I rose spiritually, and passed beyond the earth's confines into that seeming void which is the matrix where they germinate.[1]

Mythology is not merely a recollection of extraordinary events, but also points to the plane of perception on which those events occur. If one cannot rise in consciousness to the reality of myth, then one is unable to interpret its symbols correctly. The mythic imagination does not deny the material world but rather includes it in a much vaster cosmos wherein sense perception is the least significant type of experience. The exploration of myth requires a radical transformation of consciousness. The mythic form never disintegrates but abides as a latent stimulus to creative potential. Myth spontaneously appears without author or title, contrivance or calculation, as the universal Logos speaking through receptive individuals. A.E. knew that men may be visited by its numen in their dreams, insights and memories, but to live within its sanctuary requires a complete subjugation of the personal ego together with an increasing identification with the whole of nature. The release of the mythic imagination results from the fusion of self-forgetfulness with heightened self-awareness.

However sublime the archetypal realm may be, A.E. sensed that greater mansions of being lay beyond it. Theosophically, myth is a record of intelligences still tied to form or *rūpa*. By its very nature it

1 'The Story of A Star'. *Descent*, pp. 472–73.

is an authentic but still imperfect account of an ultimately partless and formless reality. The Spiritual Sun cannot be known through its creations, but must be directly experienced in meditation and then traced throughout the stream of its emanations. This beatific vision, comparable to the prisoner's direct gaze into the sun in Plato's allegory, distinguishes the self-governed sage from the mystic. A.E. readily recognized that he had not yet attained to this exalted state.

> They tell in sacred story of those the spirit took to itself who had the infinite vision. I never came nigh that infinitude, but because I sought for it I was often happy and content knowing it was all about me.[1]

The limitless vision exemplified by Śiva, seated on snowy Mount Kailas, is the apotheosis of the mythic imagination. It represents that terrace of enlightenment where man is not only a shining mirror to the creative ideation of Cosmic Mind but also a prime agent in its perpetual activity. He joins the Demiurgic Hierophants who turn the wheel of evolutionary law. His meditation is a benevolent current of noetic energy, an active conduit between divine and human worlds. He is a master of *kriyaśakti*, effortlessly creating forms from his sovereign imagination. Such beings are the source and subject of all great myths, although they have risen above the realm of forms. These are the elect of the human race and the unacknowledged authors of the pioneering arts, sciences and mythologies of mankind. Fragments of their wisdom are strewn in the fables of all cultures, differing only in the symbols and veils through which they disseminate eternal verities.

Celtic cosmogony had been spawned by Irish (Druidic) Adepts aeons ago. In their hoary legends we find the traces of a lost wisdom, an ancient cosmogony. The One gives birth to man, imaging within itself boundless fields of ineffable light which become more shadowy and dim as they recede further from the source. Through these fields rays of luminous intelligences shoot forth and fall from the celestial city to earth. The memory of that past always remains, and the fallen god, the divine ray in human form, preserves the knowledge of that heavenly sojourn in fable and legend. In Ireland, the central characters in this long pilgrimage are the Tuatha de Danaan, the gods who settled the sacred isle of Eire after conquering the gigantic races of the Fomorians. These chthonic forces are identifiable as the Atlanteans of antiquity, persons who had grown

---

1 *Song and Its Fountains. Descent*, pp. 443–44.

powerful through sorcery (see *A Doomed City*). The de Danaans who subdued them were men who had transformed themselves into gods by magical or Druidical power. As A.E. writes:

> They were preëminently magi become immortal by strength of will and knowledge. Superhuman in power and beauty, they raised themselves above nature; they played with the elements; they moved with ease in the air.[1]

They were those who had risen to supernal heights of knowledge and power in previous periods of evolution. They were distinct from the lesser gods who were nature-spirits or secondary intelligences having little to do with expanding frontiers of human consciousness.

The reign of the de Danaans was co-extensive with the cycle of the Golden Age. This vibration, A.E. felt, resonated more deeply than any other throughout the Irish countryside. Tir-na-noge is the mystical name of the land of the immortals, embodying a state of sublime awareness which could be experienced by children, poets, and those of humble heart and pure perception. Romantic poets spoke in impassioned tones of the awful loveliness of a world lying just beyond the circumference of the terrene sphere. More than a vision, it was an assured prophecy concerning a future humanity which would establish wise sovereignty over itself and bring sweet concord to all of nature.

> These mysteries, all that they led to, all that they promised for the spirit of man, are opening to-day for us in clear light, their fabulous distance lessens and we hail these kingly ideals with as intense a trust and with more joy, perhaps, than they did who were born in those purple hours, because we are emerging from centuries indescribably meagre and squalid in their thought, and every new revelation has for us the sweetness of sunlight to one after the tears and sorrow of a prison-house.[2]

The withdrawal of the immortals from their earthly habitation at the close of the Golden Age was a prelude to a final flowering of the Celtic peoples. This period, called the Age of Heroes, records the fabulous exploits of the mystic warriors of the Red Branch like Cuchullain, Connla and Conchobar, who freely discoursed with their presiding deities. They were followed by the heroes of the Finn

1 'The Legends of Ancient Eire'. *Descent*, p. 342.
2 'The Fountains of Youth'. *Descent*, p. 520.

cycle: Finn MacCool and the Fenians. Their legends have persevered through millennia and still inspire movements for social reform in contemporary Ireland. The Gaelic tales speak of the protecting hand the native gods extend over Eire, gods who have not passed away but merely retreated to crypts in the hills or secret sanctuaries far removed from human sight. There they await the new cycle, and with it the ancient wisdom. The stirring of the mythic imagination is a premonition of that splendid resurgence.

THE DESCENT OF THE GODS

The Magus marries earth to heaven.
Pico della Mirandola

Belief in the coming of an *Avatār* was common among A.E.'s compatriots in the Theosophical Society at the end of the nineteenth century. Some years later A.E. found this faith transfigured in a dream in which he saw a divine hero returning to assist the Irish people. So great was the intensity of this dream that one of his sons is said to have approached him that night asking 'What was *the* light?' For A.E. nothing was more sacred than the coming of an *Avatār*, the descent of Deity into the world. The *Avatār* exemplifies the consummation of the mystic's path, and extends the rainbow bridge between heaven and earth upon which the visionary becomes Vision itself. From this crowning vision springs the sacrificial desire to return to earthly life so as to give reality to the prospect of universal enlightenment.

A.E.'s *The Avatārs* is an unparalleled portrait of heavenly Saviours. A futurist fantasy, it completes the allegory of *The Interpreters*, at the close of which the circle of idealistic revolutionaries faced execution at the hands of the State while the political fate of the nation was being decided in a general uprising. In *The Avatars* it transpires that the State has maintained its control in the cities but yielded the rural areas to migratory groups who are harbingers of a new civilization. Their numbers increase as a wave of spiritual regeneration sweeps across the countryside, but in the city spiritual hunger grows though material wants are satisfied. The *Avatārs* appear in the country to galvanize the mystical aspirations of the seekers and to lay the foundations of a spiritual culture which will displace the materialistic values of a despotic regime. The divine pair of *Avatārs*, Aodh and Aoife, do not appear directly in the book. What is intimated is the transformation in consciousness that they initiate in a group of companions – an artist, a philosopher, a poet, a recluse (like Wordsworth's Solitary) and a few friends in a rocky retreat in western Ireland.

A.E. was as concerned with the descent of the gods as with the moral elevation of men. He sensed that only the spiritually vigilant could recognize and profit from the presence of an *Avatār*. The concept of *Avatār* is one of the most recondite in the philosophy of religion. As Jesus declares in *The Gospel According to Thomas*,

> If the Flesh
> Came into Being for the sake
> Of the Spirit, that is
> A Mystery. But if
> The Spirit came into Being
> For the sake of the Body,
> That is a wondrous Miracle.
> How did such great wealth
> Make its home, I wonder,
> In such poverty?[1]

He alludes to the mystery that Spirit should choose to become other than itself for the sake of that other – the body, a sacrificial act which cannot be understood in mundane terms. The *Word* made flesh is incomprehensible to men because it is the supererogatory act of an intelligence greater than man's. It is the prerogative of beings who have wholly transcended the circle of delusion, decay and death, who have travelled beyond even the realm of ethereal forms into the infinitudes of undivided Being. According to Eastern teachings, the magnanimous minds and hearts that attain to this exalted state are exempt from involuntary incarnation and may enjoy the blissful repose of *Nirvāṇa* or unconditioned consciousness. But there have always been those noble souls who have renounced this beatific peace to return across the ocean of incarnated existence to aid human beings in approaching supreme enlightenment. In performing this renunciation, 'the Great Sacrifice', they freely accept the limitations of those to whom they have come. Their compassionate descent represents the ideal of unconditioned love unintelligible to those bound down by the evanescent allegiances of an egocentric world.

Theosophically, the *Avatār* is the descent of Spirit into Matter for the sake of the progressive elevation of the latter to the state

---

[1] *The Gospel According to Thomas*, Stanza 29.

The Descent of the Gods

of self-conscious godhood. Without the sacrifices of these selfless exemplars, evolution towards perfectibility could not proceed and the innate impulse of all beings to aspire upwards would be aborted. This is the deeper significance of the Promethean myth. Had not Prometheus sacrificed himself, the human race would have continued to be enslaved by Zeus. Threats to the spiritual survival of man were real possibilities at critical points in human evolution. The race of man may not have been destroyed physically, yet the compassionate intervention of wise teachers at decisive moments enhanced the effective potential for human beings to rise above ignorance and fear and touch the radiance of hidden mental and spiritual fires. Such has been the sacred work of the *Avatārs* that recorded history has celebrated, saviours such as Krishna, Buddha and Jesus. They come for all humanity to rekindle the flame of spiritual aspiration in the secret heart.

The *Avatār* cannot be comprehended from below. By its very nature, the exemplification can only be apprehended by attaining the level of impersonality it represents. In this enlarged perspective, enlightenment is an ever-present possibility for each human being. Were it not so, we could neither contemplate the prospect nor consider the means to its attainment. *Avatārs* have taught why the human soul is dual in nature, at once demonic and divine. The latency of the immortal spark in the individual soul is the embryo of enlightenment, known also as *bodhicitta*, the seed of Wisdom. To the mind submerged in the dichotomies of incarnated existence, the germinating spiritual seed appears twofold: as the ascent of the soul to the Divine and as the descent of the Divine into the world. Spiritual aspiration is the channel through which a luminous intelligence may work for the welfare of all. As the pre-Socratics often repeated, the way up and the way down are the same. Each man is potentially a Buddha. Christhood is a divine archetype towards which all human growth aspires with differing degrees of self-consciousness. The extent to which a person has approached or is seeking this demonstrated ideal is his true measure as a human being.

There are myriad avenues for the Logos to incarnate in the world. Indeed every pure act of sacrifice is a drawing down of the *Avatār*-light. Each pain endured in the effort to transcend oneself for the sake of others cleanses a channel through which higher energy may flow, and A.E.'s humanized notion of *Avatār* draws upon this esoteric truth. *The Avatārs* portrays them not as those exalted beings mentioned in canonical texts, but rather as a highly evolved type of man who has won a self-validating assurance of his divinity and a supreme sense of the fullness of his being. This is undoubtedly a restricted use of the term *Avatār*, but it does serve to highlight the universal possibilities for human growth. Above all, A.E.'s *Avatārs* come to influence folk behaviour, to establish patterns of communion and celebration, and to serve as microcosmic models for the future:

> You must not think of gods or avatars as fountains only of theological piety. In the ancient world any around whom nations pivoted to new destinies were regarded as avatars. . . . They are, I fancy, more like poets who live their own lordly imaginations. It is not an incredible speculation that one of these divine poets has taken a body in this world. . . . The Avatar awakens these [his forerunners] to full consciousness and indicates their final goal. The purpose of an Avatar is to reveal the spiritual character of a race to itself.[1]

Avatārs are the creative geniuses of the human race, as well as the compassionate heroes and enlightened leaders who have decisively affected the destiny of cultures. They may not be wholly enlightened, but they constitute a type of higher humanity – a fraternity of beings who have fully awakened to their divine nature and who employ their wisdom to better the conditions of others. They work to influence the lives of countless generations and to make accessible to all the spiritual current they set in motion.

An *Avatār* transmits some fundamental truth to an epoch and initiates a new cycle of inner growth. The resounding vibration released by the *Avatār* provides the keynote for the epoch he inaugurates. Thus Krishna came to teach a philosophy of joy and love to a humanity about to descend into the darkness of the Iron Age or Kali Yuga. A.E.'s Aodh and Aoife similarly seek to propagate the Krishna vibration amidst the grim tyranny and oppression exerted by the State. They bequeath the vision of a new humanity conscious of its divine kinship with all of nature. They transmute the everyday relationships between human beings, enabling the qualities of fidelity, altruism and civility to arise spontaneously as the basis of a spiritual culture:

> By the presence of these two the days had been coloured with a rich wonder. . . . Then came stories of men and women raised above themselves in some transfiguration so that they saw each other in some shining way in moonlit dances in forest glades, in dances which

1 *The Avators, Descent*, pp. 541, 542–43.

The Descent of the Gods 71

had been taught them by the mystic visitors. . . . In their enchantment they were god and goddess to each other.[1]

Most of the *Avatār*'s work is always invisible and hidden. A.E.'s *Avatārs* accomplish nothing stupendous on the physical plane, but we recognize them by their subtle influence, by the institutional germs they have begotten and by the lives they have changed. They themselves appear and withdraw almost without trace. Their origins and destiny are shrouded, yet for those who momentarily shared their vision the world is totally transformed. They endow their disciples with the power to promulgate their message of joy and freedom to those who are spiritually deprived. A.E. was aware that the gift of divine Wisdom was so potent that the presence of one enlightened man could gently start a soul-revolution on a global scale. In this sense *The Avatars* was less a fantasy than a dramatization of the cycle of descent of the Fraternity of Sages, the Brotherhood of Bodhisattvas. In the fourteenth century the Tibetan reformer Tsong-Kha-Pa initiated a septenary centennial movement which would signal the spread of a spiritual impulse during the last quarter of each forthcoming century. These impulsions would be focussed through the noble work of disguised emissaries of the Brotherhood. As a young man A.E. had witnessed the tidal wave initiated by H.P.Blavatsky and W.Q.Judge, and for the rest of his life he sought to prepare for the next great impulsion. He wrote in 1897:

> Avatars, kingly souls once on earth, and now again returning with the wisdom of a greater day and the world-spirit urgent within their wills. I seem to see in this confused transition period a plan whereto all is tending; a true social state with divine dynasties and solar heroes at its head, like those who ruled Egypt in its mystic beginning. Already spirits with such imperial instincts begin to appear amongst us, laying a deeper foundation for the spiritual revolution . . . we have become expectant.[2]

As the impulsion of the nineteenth century drew to a close, A.E. became increasingly concerned that careless speculation about teachers and *Avatārs* was disproportionate to the willingness of students to assimilate and apply the teachings as aids to self-transformation. In his articles 'Shadows and Substance' and

1 *The Avatars. Descent*, p. 584.
2 'On the March'. *Descent*, p. 643.

'Self-Reliance', he warns that incessant talk on spiritual matters is useless and even harmful if the ethical requirements of the philosophy are not enacted in daily life. He counselled that the failures of his fellows lay in their wish to use the magical powers of the soul without having first grasped the indivisible nature of the Self. The student must fit himself to the teacher and not the other way around. Indeed, one's faulty attempts to externalize a convenient image of the teacher would be the greatest barrier to ever finding one. A.E. knew that access to teachers was not arbitrary, but wholly dependent upon the efforts of the disciple. He recognized that the student was drawn to the Master by a law of spiritual gravitation – spiritual qualities attract by magnetic affinity. A person who has sufficiently developed within himself the marks of an unprejudiced mind, a pure heart and an ardent desire for wisdom will be naturally drawn to the true exemplar of these excellences.

No one should seek a teacher for instant salvation. Masters come to train disciples in the intelligent service of humanity, not to relieve the burdens of those who refuse to exercise their own powers of choice and self-determination. A.E. knew that one must earn discipleship and that this in itself is an arduous task. But he insisted that anything less might mean a disastrous fall into delusive speculation which could prevent the aspirant from ever finding wise teachers. He recognized that though access to them was never easy, it is aided by devoted study of their teachings. As a man thinks, so shall he be. The power to pursue and incarnate spiritual ideals is coeval with the soul's assumption of a human form. One's thought and ideation determine one's destiny. They constitute both the cause of imprisonment and the means of liberation from the darkness of ignorance and servitude.

> 'What a man thinks, that he is: That is the old secret.' In this self-conception lies the secret of life, the way of escape and return. We have imagined ourselves into littleness, darkness and feebleness. We must imagine ourselves into greatness.[1]

For this reason, the earliest *Avatār* in recorded history – Lord Krishna – descended amidst humanity on the eve of the Iron Age to show the spiritual attributes of the Sage. In his second discourse to Arjuna in the *Bhagavad Gītā*, he offers a portrait of an enlightened being, confirmed in self-knowledge.

1 'The Renewal of Youth'. *Descent*, p. 627–28.

Testament of Faith in the Future

A man is said to be confirmed in spiritual knowledge when he forsaketh every desire which entereth into his heart, and of himself is happy and content in the Self through the Self. His mind is undisturbed in adversity; he is happy and contented in prosperity, and he is a stranger to anxiety, fear and anger.[1]

Implicit is the idea that contemplation of these qualities by anyone mired in illusion will emancipate the mind and confer upon it the pattern of its own growth. A.E. knew that discriminating the essence of spirituality from its formal expression was a prerequisite for enlightenment. *The Avatars* sought to give the aroma of the awakened soul 'a local habitation and a name', thereby testifying to the perfectibility of man. This was the consummation of A.E.'s mission as an artist and his legacy to those who wished to prepare themselves mentally for the coming of the new Teacher.

TESTAMENT OF FAITH IN THE FUTURE

The future enters into us, in order to transform itself in us long before it happens.

Rilke

The prophetic aspect of A.E.'s work has long been submerged under the mass of contributions he made to the social concerns of his day. The latter half of his life was largely devoted to the application of his creative talents in practical contexts. His notable success in agricultural and political reform as well as commercial organization somewhat obscured his profound concern for the future. Yet all his writings show a deep sense of futurity, conveyed more by intimation than declaration. His penetrating vision was interwoven with a progressive view of time. Understanding the cyclic nature of evolution, he saw his work as foreshadowing an epoch greater than his own. As Krishna taught, disengagement from the fruits of actions is the surest way to surmount temporal barriers and the divisions of past, present and future. It frees perception from an obsessive

---

1 *Bhagavad Gita* (Judge Trans.). Chap. II.

attention to the narrow margins of contemporaneous time and allows self-definition to occur within the broader context of human evolution. A.E.'s discipline in self-transcendence gave him the capacity to rise above the parochial limitations of the Victorian Age so as to view human history from the universal standpoint of the immortal soul. From his trans-historical perspective he recognized that events in a particular epoch are meaningful only if they sustain the knowledge acquired by previous generations and transmit their distilled wisdom to future generations. He consciously nurtured the unapprehended seed of the future within the bounded pastures of his own epoch.

Time need not be seen as a gulf permanently separating an individual from the entire sweep of evolution. In majestic vision A.E. witnessed the mythic fires that had burned in previous ages, and he confirmed through his own meditations what sages had taught for aeons: that time is a fiction of the consciousness of the personal man which remembers and forgets life after life. The immortal individuality, in contrast to the ephemeral *persona*, carries an essential record of the actions of the soul through numerous lives. By aligning himself with this overbrooding intelligence, A.E. was able to recover some of the knowledge acquired in previous lives. He saw that history could not be characterized, even for provisional purposes, as the linear march of progress from a superstitious past to an enlightened present. Such notions, which are questioned today, were common in A.E.'s time. In the Theosophical conception of history, which A.E. found thoroughly compatible with his own intuitions, time is seasonal and periodic, with cycles of expansion balanced by periods of stasis or withdrawal. In Plato's words, time is the moving image of Eternity. The motion of the image is properly grasped in terms of cycles, spirals and revolutions. Theosophical teaching divides the long process of human evolution into seven periods. Through the first three and a half, spirit gradually descends into matter, human form materializes, and the intellect eclipses the psycho-spiritual faculties. In the latter three and a half periods, form slowly etherealizes and humanity rises by degrees from random cerebration to a more creative spiritual consciousness. Early and later periods of evolution correspond to each other, such that initial conditions are recapitulated on higher planes with heightened self-awareness. The first is related by analogy to the seventh, the sixth to the second, and the fifth (our own) is related to the third. *The Secret Doctrine* states:

   . . . we are approaching the time when the pendulum of evolution will direct its swing decidedly upwards, bringing Humanity back on a parallel line with the primitive Third Root Race in spirituality.[1]

The memory of the Third Root Race, when all mankind lived in a paradisaic state of purity, permeates A.E.'s writings. He wrote in 'The Ascending Cycle':

> there will be existing on the earth, about the close of [the] Fifth Race, conditions in some ways corresponding with those prevailing when the Third Race men began their evolution. Though this period may be yet distant hundreds of thousands of years, still it is of interest to forecast that future as far as may be, for the future is concealed in the present, and is the outcome of forces working today.[2]

A.E. saw the Theosophical Movement as a pioneering effort to insert the natural and non-sectarian spirituality of the Third Root Race into the divisive and acquisitive age in which he lived. Initiating a noetic and compassionate current in the lives of those burdened by the ideological misconceptions of centuries, it foreshadowed the dawning of a new age of collective spiritual consciousness. Since A.E. viewed his own time as critical in facilitating the global rebirth silently gestating, his later work cannot be comprehended without some recognition of his hopes for the future.

> The Theosophical Society was started to form the nucleus of a universal brotherhood of humanity, and its trend is towards this ideal. May we not justifiably suppose that we are witnessing to-day in this movement the birth of a new race corresponding to the divine Initiators of the Third, a race which shall in its inner life be truly a 'Wondrous Being'. I think we will perform our truest service to the Society by regarding it in this way as an actual entity whose baby years and mystical childhood we should foster. . . . To achieve this we should continually keep in mind this sense of unity; striving also to rise in meditation until we sense in the vastness the beating of those innumerable hearts glowing with heroic purpose: we should try to humanize our mysticism.[3]

This passage shows A.E.'s understanding of timing, the hyphen between learning and wisdom. Since man is in essence a free agent, he can act decisively from the standpoint of eternity yet within temporal limits. The humanizing of mysticism means a mental

1 H.P. Blavatsky: *The Secret Doctrine*, I, pp. 224–5.
2 'The Ascending Cycle'. *Descent*, p. 616.
3 *Ibid.*, pp. 617–18.

fusion of the temporal and transcendental realms to elevate the prospect from which human beings may survey their own lives. A.E. trusted that by expanding the temporal vistas of consciousness, people would confer purpose upon their lives and raise the evolutionary curve of the race. A.E.'s view of the future was Promethean. His political and social efforts sought to enrich present possibilities of action, and to provide a fertile field in which spiritual values may take root.

We should see at the end of the Kaliyuga a new brotherhood formed from those who have risen out of material life and aims, who have conquered self, who have been purified by suffering, who have acquired strength and wisdom, and who have wakened up to the old magical perception of their unity in true Being.[1]

A.E.'S APPEAL

To live to benefit mankind is the first step.
The Voice of the Silence

The simplicity of A.E.'s poetic style veils the intensity of search which his stories convey. His essays fuse philosophical and psychological insight into a wisdom that sprang from his inmost experience and ever used such experience as its touchstone. His mystical writings are suffused with integrity and authenticity. He did not claim to know the mysteries of superior and inferior worlds, much less of the archetypal cosmos and the indivisible One beyond it, but he could affirm that wonder is ubiquitous. His vibrant feeling for humanity and his eloquent visions were channelled towards ennobling conceptions by his dispassionate reflection. He knew that few would share his own perception of the many-layered world, yet his settled conviction that he had but participated in the common human inheritance prevented him from consolidating any sense of uniqueness. His symbols remain light, airy and natural, unlike the artful symbolism of Yeats or the complex elaborations of Charles Williams. His gentle nature and unaffected humility kept him free from the strident concerns of many of his Gaelic contemporaries.

---

1 'The Ascending Cycle'. *Descent*, p. 617.

A.E.'s alliance with the mystical tradition of Theosophy was born of personal experience, and its metaphysical thought provided him with a basis from which to comprehend his own quest. His life corroborated the truths which he sensed. His framework for intellectual apprehension confirmed the quiet conviction of his heart, and the deepest awareness of his innermost being was continuous with the dictates of practical action. A.E.'s extensive support of the co-operative movement, for example, was a direct application of his fervent faith in the ultimate unity of life and the brotherhood of man. He recognized that hectic social involvements, however worthy, tend to erode the inner life unless it is continually renewed by meditation. Far from justifying an antinomian withdrawal from the predicament of humanity, he saw this need as establishing the ideal of a sagely fusion of wisdom and method. His writings, like his life, are shaded precisely between innocence and quaintness. His whole being reflected a rich integration in which sublimation became an alchemical process. The pull of sensual experience was felt but remained apart from eros. The discovery that consciousness can be elevated beyond illusion, with its pain and deception, afforded A.E. the strength to return to the search for meaning with greater fearlessness and a deeper understanding of human fellowship. To the present generation which seeks mystical experience through every conceivable formula, from postures to drugs, from a facile naturalism to a numbing hedonism, A.E.'s calm lack of concern to escape is a gentle but firm reminder that the fruit of insight is heightened responsibility. To live in an evolving cosmos is imaginatively to insert all life into one's consciousness. Should one live as a grasping creature, whose self-consciousness only intensifies the pain of a ruthless struggle for existence, or as a godlike master of blind nature?

A.E. offers a third possibility: the human being as almoner of the divine. When the mystic's experience is dispassionately assimilated by his intellect, it establishes principles of thought and action which at once instruct and alleviate. Goodwill is not an empty notion. A.E. does not advocate any particular path in his writings, nor does he suggest that the reader accompany him on any interior adventure. His own understanding led him to think that the unity of all souls with the Oversoul gave them essentially similar maps, but he also believed that the byways and topological details were the results of many lives of experience, heights touched and mistakes made. To go the way A.E. went is to make a solitary journey within. A.E. accepted reincarnation as a clue to the present circumstances of human beings, individually and collectively. Spiritual unity derives from metaphysical homogeneity, and cannot be expressed in the material realm by any mechanical doctrine of equality. It demands compassion in judgement, justice in action and affirmation of possibilities in principle. In his own life A.E. sought the transcendental in consciousness while confronting the daily round and common task.

His artistic endeavours are intensely personal, though hardly self-centred, and while his writings may not be cast in a language we can comfortably use in an atmosphere of violent cynicism and turgid self-analysis, they can be appreciated by anyone who learns to sit quietly and not be threatened by other voices. For those who find the rubble of contemporary life remote from the diamonds that lurk beneath it, A.E. plays resonant cosmopolitan chords on the Gaelic mythos. Finding no fundamental differences between past and present, East and West, high and low, he infuses his reader with an optimism devoid of exaggeration. A.E. saw the Hero in Man amidst the sordid conditions of human existence. To do so requires gentleness of mind and clarity of heart. He exemplified what it is to be both mystic and cosmopolitan, a man of culture and a man beyond culture, a hero who knows his ignorance, a solitary for whom all are brothers and nothing human is alien.

I. THE LANGUAGE OF THE GODS

THE CANDLE OF VISION[1]

TO
JAMES STEPHENS
BEST OF COMPANIONS

PREFACE

When I am in my room looking upon the walls I have painted I see there reflections of the personal life, but when I look through the windows I see a living nature and landscapes not painted by hands. So, too, when I meditate I feel in the images and thoughts which throng about me the reflections of personality, but there are also windows in the soul through which can be seen images created not by human but by the divine imagination.[2] I have tried according to my capacity to report about the divine order and to discriminate between that which was self-begotten fantasy and that which came from a higher sphere. These retrospects and meditations are the efforts of an artist and poet to relate his own vision to the vision of the seers and writers of the sacred books, and to discover what element of truth lay in those imaginations.

A.E.

RETROSPECT

I had travelled all day and was tired, but I could not rest by the hearth in the cottage on the hill. My heart was beating with too great an excitement. After my year in the city I felt like a child who wickedly stays from home through a long day, and who returns frightened and penitent at nightfall, wondering whether it will be received with forgiveness by its mother. Would the Mother[3] of us all receive me again as one of her children? Would the winds with wandering voices be as before the evangelists of her love? Or would I feel like an outcast amid the mountains, the dark valleys and the shining lakes? I knew if benediction came how it would come. I would sit among the rocks with shut eyes, waiting humbly as one waits in the antechambers of the mighty, and if the invisible ones chose me as companion they would begin with a soft breathing of their intimacies, creeping on me with shadowy affection like children who steal nigh to the bowed head and suddenly whisper fondness in the ear before it has even heard a footfall. So I stole out of the cottage and over the dark ridges to the place of rocks, and sat down, and let the coolness of the night chill and still the fiery dust in the brain. I waited trembling for the faintest touch, the shyest breathing of the Everlasting within my soul, the sign of reception and forgiveness. I knew it would come. I could not so desire what was not my own, and what is our own we cannot lose. Desire is hidden identity.[4] The darkness drew me heavenward. From the hill the plains beneath slipped away grown vast and vague, remote and still. I seemed alone with immensity, and there came at last that melting of the divine darkness into the life within me for which I prayed. Yes, I still belonged, however humbly, to the heavenly household. I was not outcast. Still, though by a thread fine as that by which a spider hangs from the rafters,[5] my being was suspended from the habitations of eternity. I longed to throw my arms about the hills, to meet with kisses the lips of the seraph wind. I felt the gaiety of childhood springing up through weariness and age, for to come into contact with that which is eternally young is to have that childhood of the spirit it must attain ere it can be moulded by the Magician of the Beautiful[6] and enter the House of Many Mansions.[7]

I had not always this intimacy with nature. I never felt a light in childhood which faded in manhood into the common light of day, nor do I believe that childhood is any nearer than age to this being. If it were so what would the spirit have to hope for after youth was gone? I was not conscious in my boyhood of any heaven lying about me.[8] I lived in the city, and the hills from which aid was to come to me were only a far flush of blue on the horizon. Yet I was drawn to them, and as years passed and legs grew longer I came nearer and nearer until at last one day I found myself on the green hillside. I came to play with other boys, but years were yet to pass before the familiar places grew strange once more and the mountains dense with fiery forms and awful as Sinai.

While the child is still in its mother's arms it is nourished by her, yet it does not know it is a mother which feeds it. It knows later in whose bosom it has lain. As the mother nourishes the body so the Mighty Mother[9] nourishes the soul. Yet there are but few who pay reverence where reverence is due, and that is because this benign deity is like a mother who indulges the fancies of her children. With some she imparts life to their own thoughts. Others she endows with the vision of her own heart. Even of these last some love in silence, being afraid to speak of the majesty which smiled on them, and others deceived think with pride: 'This vision is my own.'

I was like these last for a long time. I was aged about sixteen or seventeen years, when I, the slackest and least ideal of boys, with my life already made dark by those desires of body and heart with which we so soon learn to taint our youth, became aware of a mysterious life quickening within my life. Looking back I know not of anything in friendship, anything I had read, to call this forth. It was, I thought, self-begotten. I began to be astonished with myself, for, walking along country roads, intense and passionate imaginations of another world, of an interior nature began to overpower me. They were like strangers who suddenly enter a house, who brush aside the doorkeeper, and who will not be denied. Soon I knew they were the rightful owners and heirs of the house of the body, and the doorkeeper was only one who was for a time in charge, who had neglected his duty, and who had pretended to ownership. The boy who existed before was an alien. He hid himself when the pilgrim of eternity[10] took up his abode in the dwelling. Yet, whenever the true owner was absent, the sly creature reappeared and boasted himself as master once more.

That being from a distant country who took possession of the

The Candle of Vision: Retrospect

house began to speak in a language difficult to translate. I was tormented by limitations of understanding. Somewhere about me I knew there were comrades who were speaking to me, but I could not know what they said. As I walked in the evening down the lanes scented by the honeysuckle my senses were expectant of some unveiling about to take place, I felt that beings were looking in upon me out of the true home of man. They seemed to be saying to each other of us, 'Soon they will awaken; soon they will come to us again,' and for a moment I almost seemed to mix with their eternity. The tinted air glowed before me with intelligible significance like a face, a voice. The visible world became like a tapestry[11] blown and stirred by winds behind it. If it would but raise for an instant I knew I would be in Paradise. Every form on that tapestry appeared to be the work of gods. Every flower was a word, a thought. The grass was speech; the trees were speech; the waters were speech; the winds were speech. They were the Army of the Voice[12] marching on to conquest and dominion over the spirit; and I listened with my whole being, and then these apparitions would fade away and I would be the mean and miserable boy once more. So might one have felt who had been servant of the prophet, and had seen him go up in the fiery chariot,[13] and the world had no more light or certitude in it with that passing. I knew these visitations for what they were and named them truly in my fantasy, for writing then in the first verses of mine which still seem to me to be poetry, I said of the earth that we and all things were her dreams:

> She is rapt in dreams divine.
> As her clouds of beauty pass
> On our glowing hearts they shine,
> Mirrored there as in a glass.
>
> Earth, whose dreams are we and they,
> With her deep heart's gladness fills
> All our human lips can say
> Or the dawn-fired singer trills.

Yet such is human nature that I still felt vanity as if this vision was mine, and I acted like one who comes across the treasure-house of a king, and spends the treasure as if it were his own. We may indeed have a personal wisdom, but spiritual vision is not to speak of as ours any more than we can say at the rising of the sun: 'This glory is mine.'[14] By the sudden uprising of such vanities in the midst of vision I was often outcast, and found myself in an instant like those warriors of Irish legend, who had come upon a lordly house and feasted there and slept, and when they woke they were on the barren hillside, and the Faed Fia was drawn about that lordly house. Yet though the imagination apprehended truly that this beauty was not mine, and hailed it by its heavenly name, for some years my heart was proud, for as the beauty sank into memory it seemed to become a personal possession, and I said 'I imagined this' when I should humbly have said, 'The curtain was a little lifted that I might see.'[15] But the day was to come when I could not deny the Mighty Mother the reverence due, when I was indeed to know by what being I had been nourished, and to be made sweet and mad as a lover with the consciousness of her intermingling spirit.

The sages of old found that at the close of intense meditation their being was drawn into union with that which they contemplated. All desire tends to bring about unity with the object adored,[16] and this is no less true of spiritual and elemental than of bodily desire; and I, with my imagination more and more drawn to adore an ideal nature, was tending to that vital contact in which what at first was apprehended in fantasy would become the most real of all things. When that certitude came I felt as Dante might have felt after conceiving of Beatrice close at his side and in the Happy World, if, after believing it a dream, half hoping that it might hereafter be a reality, that beloved face before his imagination grew suddenly intense, vivid and splendidly shining, and he knew beyond all doubt that her spirit was truly in that form, and had descended to dwell in it, and would be with him for evermore. So did I feel one warm summer day lying idly on the hillside, not then thinking of anything but the sunlight, and how sweet it was to drowse there, when, suddenly, I felt a fiery heart throb, and knew it was personal and intimate, and started with every sense dilated and intent, and turned inwards, and I heard first a music as of bells going away, away into that wondrous underland whither, as legend relates, the Danaan gods withdrew; and then the heart of the hills was opened to me, and I knew there was no hill for those who were there, and they were unconscious of the ponderous mountain piled above the palaces of light, and the winds were sparkling and diamond clear, yet full of colour as an opal, as they glittered through the valley, and I knew the Golden Age[17] was all about me, and it was we who had been blind to it but that it had never passed away from the world.[18]

THE EARTH BREATH

After that awakening earth began more and more to bewitch me, and to lure me to her heart with honied entreaty. I could not escape from it even in that busy office where I sat during week-days with little heaps of paper mounting up before me moment by frenzied moment. An interval of inactivity and I would be aware of that sweet eternal presence overshadowing me. I was an exile from living nature but she yet visited me. Her ambassadors were visions that made me part of themselves. Through the hot fœtid air of the gaslit room I could see the feverish faces, the quick people flitting about, and hear the voices; and then room, faces and voices would be gone, and I would be living in the Mother's being in some pure, remote, elemental region of hers. Instead of the dingy office there would be a sky of rarest amethyst; a snow-cold bloom of cloud; high up in the divine wilderness, solitary, a star; all rapt, breathless and still; rapt the seraph princes of wind and wave and fire, for it was the hour when the King, an invisible presence, moved through His dominions and Nature knew and was hushed at the presence of her Lord. Once, suddenly, I found myself on some remote plain or steppe, and heard unearthly chimes pealing passionately from I know not what far steeples.[19] The earth-breath streamed from the furrows to the glowing heavens. Overhead the birds flew round and round crying their incomprehensible cries, as if they were maddened, and knew not where to nestle, and had dreams of some more enraptured rest in a diviner home. I could see a ploughman lifting himself from his obscure toil and stand with lit eyes as if he too had been fire-smitten and was caught into heaven as I was, and knew for that moment he was a god. And then I would lapse out of vision and ecstasy, and hear the voices, and see again through the quivering of the hot air the feverish faces, and seem to myself to be cast out of the spirit. I could hardly bear after thinking of these things, for I felt I was trapped in some obscure hell. You, too, trapped with me, dear kindly people, who never said a harsh word to the forgetful boy. You, too, I knew, had your revelations. I remember one day how that clerk with wrinkled face, blinking eyes and grizzly beard, who never seemed, apart from his work, to have interests other than his pipe and paper, surprised me by telling me that the previous midnight he waked in his sleep, and some self of him was striding to and fro in the moonlight in an avenue mighty with gigantic images; and that dream self he had surprised had seemed to himself unearthly in wisdom and power. What had he done to be so high in one sphere and so petty in another? Others I could tell of, too, who had their moment of awe when the spirit made its ancient claim on them. But none were so happy or so unhappy as I was. I was happy at times because the divine world which had meant nothing to my childhood was becoming a reality to manhood: and I knew it was not a dream, for comrades in vision soon came to me, they who could see as I saw, and hear as I heard, and there were some who had gone deeper into that being than I have ever travelled. I was more miserable than my work-a-day companions, because the very intensity of vision made the recoil more unendurable. It was an agony of darkness and oblivion, wherein I seemed like those who in nightmare are buried in caverns so deep beneath the roots of the world that there is no hope of escape, for the way out is unknown, and the way to them is forgotten by those who walk in light. In those black hours the universe, a gigantic presence, seemed at war with me. I was condemned, I thought, to be this speck of minute life because of some sin committed in remote ages, I and those with me. We were all lost children of the stars. Everything that suggested our high original being, a shaft of glory from the far fire in the heavens spearing the gloom of the office, the blue twilight deepening through the panes until it was rich with starry dust, the sunny clouds careering high over the city, these things would stir pangs of painful remembrance and my eyes would suddenly grow blind and wet. Sometimes, too, I would rebel and plot in my obscurity, and remember moments when the will in me seemed to be a titanic power, and my spirit would brood upon ways of escape and ascent to its native regions, as those fallen angels in Milton's tremendous narrative rose up from torture, and conspired to tear the throne from Him. And then all that would appear to me to be futile as a speck of dust trying to stay itself against the typhoon, and the last door would close upon me and leave me more hopeless than before.

THE SLAVE OF THE LAMP

Because I was a creature of many imaginings and of rapid alternations of mood out of all that there came to me assurance of a truth, of all truths most inspiring to one in despair in the Iron Age[20] and lost amid the undergrowths of being. I became aware of a swift echo or response to my own moods in circumstance which had seemed hitherto immutable in its indifference. I found every intense imagination, every new adventure of the intellect endowed with magnetic power to attract to it its own kin.[21] Will and desire were as the enchanter's wand of fable, and they drew to themselves their own affinities.[22] Around a pure atom of crystal all the atoms of the element in solution gather, and in like manner one person after another emerged out of the mass, betraying their close affinity to my moods as they were engendered. I met these people seemingly by accident along country roads, or I entered into conversation with strangers and found they were intimates of the spirit. I could prophesy from the uprising of new moods in myself that I, without search, would soon meet people of a certain character, and so I met them. Even inanimate things were under the sway of these affinities. They yielded up to me what they had specially for my eyes. I have glanced in passing at a book left open by some one in a library, and the words first seen thrilled me, for they confirmed a knowledge lately attained in vision. At another time a book taken down idly from a shelf opened at a sentence quoted from a Upanishad, scriptures then to me unknown, and this sent my heart flying eastwards because it was the answer to a spiritual problem I had been brooding over an hour before. It was hardly a week after my first awakening that I began to meet those who were to be my lifelong comrades on the quest, and who were, like myself, in a boyhood troubled by the spirit. I had just attempted to write in verse when I met a boy[23] whose voice was soon to be the most beautiful voice in Irish literature. I sought none of these out because I had heard of them and surmised a kinship. The concurrence of our personalities seemed mysterious and controlled by some law of spiritual gravitation, like that which in the chemistry of nature makes one molecule fly to another. I remember the exultation with which I realized about life that, as Heraclitus has said, it was in a flux, and that in all its flowings there was meaning and law; that I could not lose what was my own; I need not seek, for what was my own would come to me; if any passed it was because they were no longer mine. One buried in a dungeon for many years could not have hailed sunshine, the sweet-smelling earth, and the long hidden infinitude of the skies more joyously than I the melting of that which had seemed immutable. It is those who live and grow swiftly, and who continually compare what is without with what is within, who have this certainty. Those who do not change see no change and recognise no law. He who has followed even in secrecy many lights of the spirit can see one by one the answering torches gleam. When I was made certain about this I accepted what befell with resignation. I knew that all I met was part of myself and that what I could not comprehend was related by affinity to some yet unrealized forces in my being. We have within us the Lamp of the World;[24] and Nature, the genie, is Slave of the Lamp, and must fashion life about us as we fashion it within ourselves.[25] What we are alone has power. We may give up the outward personal struggle and ambition, and if we leave all to the Law[26] all that is rightly ours will be paid. Man becomes truly the Superman[27] when he has this proud consciousness. No matter where he may be, in what seeming obscurity, he is still the King, still master of his fate, and circumstance reels about him or is still as he, in the solitude of his spirit, is mighty or is humble. We are indeed most miserable when we dream we have no power over circumstance, and I account it the highest wisdom to know this of the living universe that there is no destiny in it other than that we make for ourselves.[28] How the spirit is kindled, how it feels its power, when, outwardly quiet, it can see the coming and going of life, as it dilates within itself or is still! Then do we move in miracle and wonder. Then does the universe appear to us as it did to the Indian sage who said that to him who was perfect in meditation all rivers were sacred as the Ganges and all speech was holy.

MEDITATION

There is no personal virtue in me other than this that I followed a path[29] all may travel but on which few do journey. It is a path within ourselves where the feet first falter in shadow and darkness but which is later made gay by heavenly light. As one who has travelled a little on that way and who has had some far-off vision of the Many-Coloured Land, if I tell what I know, and how I came to see most clearly, I may give hope to those who would fain believe in that world the seers spake of, but who cannot understand the language written by those who had seen that beauty of old, or who may have thought the ancient scriptures but a record of extravagant desires. None need special gifts or genius. Gifts! There are no gifts.[30] For all that is ours we have paid the price. There is nothing we aspire to for which we cannot barter some spiritual merchandise of our own. Genius![31] There is no stinting of this by the Keeper of the Treasure House. It is not bestowed but is won. Yon man of heavy soul might if he willed play on the lyre of Apollo,[32] that drunkard be god-intoxicated. Powers are not bestowed by caprice on any. The formulae the chemist illustrates, making exposition before his students, are not more certainly verifiable than the formulae of that alchemy by which what is gross in us may be transmuted into ethereal fires. Our religions make promises to be fulfilled beyond the grave because they have no knowledge now to be put to the test, but the ancients spake of a divine vision to be attained while we are yet in the body. The religion which does not cry out: 'I am to-day verifiable as that water wets or that fire burns. Test me that ye can become as gods.' Mistrust it. Its messengers are prophets of the darkness. As we sink deeper into the Iron Age we are met by the mighty devils of state and empire lurking in the abyss, claiming the soul for their own, moulding it to their image, to be verily their own creature and not heaven's. We need a power in ourselves that can confront these mighty powers. Though I am blind I have had moments of sight. Though I have sinned I have been on the path. Though I am feeble I have seen the way to power. I sought out ways to make more securely my own those magical lights that dawned and faded within me. I wished to evoke them at will and be master of my vision, and I was taught to do this which is as old as human life. Day after day, at times where none might interfere, and where none through love or other cause were allowed to interfere, I set myself to attain mastery over the will.[33] I would choose some mental object, an abstraction of form, and strive to hold my mind fixed on it in unwavering concentration, so that not for a moment, not for an instant, would the concentration slacken.[34] It is an exercise this, a training for higher adventures of the soul. It is no light labour. The ploughman's cleaving the furrows, is easier by far. Five minutes of this effort will at first leave us trembling as at the close of a laborious day. It is then we realize how little of life has been our own, and how much a response to sensation, a drifting on the tide of desire. The rumour of revolt, the spirit would escape its thraldom, runs through the body. Empires do not send legions so swiftly to frustrate revolt as all that is mortal in us hurries along nerve, artery, and every highway of the body to beset the soul.[35] The beautiful face of one we love, more alluring than life, glows before us to enchant us from our task. Old sins, enmities, vanities and desires beleaguer and beseech us. If we do not heed them then they change, they seem to be with us, they open up vistas of all we and they will do, when this new power we strive for is attained. If we are tempted down that vista we find with shame after an hour of vain musing that we were lured away, had deserted our task and forgotten that stern fixity of the will we set out to achieve. Let us persevere in our daily ritual and the turmoil increases; our whole being becomes vitalized, the bad as well as the good. The heat of this fervent concentration acts like fire under a pot, and everything in our being boils up madly.[36] We learn our own hitherto unknown character. We did not know we could feel such fierce desires, never imagined such passionate enmities as now awaken. We have created in ourselves a centre of power and grow real to ourselves.[37] It is dangerous, too, for we have flung ourselves into the eternal conflict between spirit and matter, and find ourselves where the battle is hottest, where the foemen are locked in a death struggle. We are in grips with mightier powers than we had before conceived of. What man is there who thinks he has self-control? He stands in the shallow waters, nor has gone into the great deep, nor been tossed at the mercy of the waves. Let him rouse the arcane powers in himself, and he will feel like one who has let loose the avalanche.[38] None would live through that turmoil if the will were the only power in ourselves we could invoke, for the will is neither good nor bad but is power only, and it vitalizes good or bad indifferently.[39] If that were all our labour would bring us, not closer to divine being, but only to a dilation of the personality. But the ancients who taught us to gain this intensity taught it but as preliminary to a meditation which would not waver and would be full of power. The meditation they urged on us has been explained as 'the inexpressible yearning of the inner man to go out into the infinite.' But that Infinite we would enter is living. It is the ultimate being of us.[40] Meditation is a fiery brooding on that majestical Self.[41] We imagine ourselves into Its vastness. We conceive ourselves as mirroring Its infinitudes, as moving in all things, as living in all beings, in earth, water, air, fire, aether. We try to know as It knows, to live as It lives, to be compassionate as It is compassionate. We equal ourselves to It that we may understand It and become It. We do not kneel to It as slaves, but as Children of the King we lift ourselves up to that Glory, and affirm to ourselves that we are what we imagine. 'What a man thinks, that he is: that is the old secret,'[42] said the wise. We have imagined ourselves into this pitiful dream of life. By imagination and will we re-enter true being, becoming that we conceive of. On that path of fiery brooding I entered. At first all was stupor. I felt as one who steps out of day into the colourless night of a cavern, and that was because I had suddenly reversed the habitual motions of life. We live normally seeing through the eyes, hearing through the ears, stirred by the senses, moved by bodily powers, and receiving only such spiritual knowledge as may pass through a momentary purity of our being. On the mystic path we create our own light,[43] and at first we struggle blind and baffled, seeing nothing, hearing nothing, unable to think, unable to imagine. We seem deserted by dream, vision or inspiration, and our meditation barren altogether.[44] But let us persist through weeks or months, and sooner or later that stupor disappears. Our faculties readjust themselves, and do the work we will them to do. Never did they do their work so well. The dark caverns of the brain being to grow luminous. We are creating our own light. By heat of will and aspiration we are transmuting what is gross in the subtle aethers through which the mind works.[45] As the dark bar of metal begins to glow, at first redly, and then at white heat, or as ice melts and is alternately fluid, vapour, gas, and at last a radiant energy, so do these aethers become purified and alchemically changed into luminous essences, and they make a new vesture for the soul,[46] and link us to mid-world or heavenward where they too have their true home. How quick the mind is now! How vivid is the imagination! We are lifted above the tumult of the body. The heat of the blood disappears below us. We draw nigher to ourselves. The heart longs for the hour of meditation and hurries to it; and, when it comes, we rise within ourselves as a diver too long under seas rises to breathe the air, to see the light. We have invoked the God and we are answered according to old promise.[47] As our aspiration so is our inspiration.[48] We imagine It as Love and what a love enfolds us. We conceive of It as Might and we take power from that Majesty. We dream of It as Beauty and the Magician of the Beautiful appears everywhere at Its miraculous art, and the multitudinous lovely creatures of Its thought are busy moulding nature and life in their image, and all are hurrying, hurrying to the Golden World. This vision brings its own proof to the spirit, but words cannot declare or explain it. We must go back to lower levels and turn to that which has form from that which is bodiless.

THE MANY-COLOURED LAND

I have always been curious about the psychology of my own vision as desirous of imparting it, and I wish in this book to relate the efforts of an artist and poet to discover what truth lay in his own imaginations. I have brooded longer over the nature of imagination than I have lingered over the canvas where I tried to rebuild my vision. Spiritual moods are difficult to express and cannot be argued over, but the workings of imagination may well be spoken of, and need precise and minute investigation. I surmise from my reading of the psychologists who treat of this that they themselves were without this faculty and spoke of it as blind men who would fain draw although without vision. We are overcome when we read *Prometheus Unbound*, but who, as he reads, flings off the enchantment to ponder in what state was the soul of Shelley in that ecstasy of swift creation. Who has questioned the artist to whom the forms of his thought are vivid as the forms of nature? Artist and poet have rarely been curious about the processes of their own minds. Yet it is reasonable to assume that the highest ecstasy and vision are conditioned by law and attainable by all,[49] and this might be argued as of more importance even than the message of the seers. I attribute to that unwavering meditation and fiery concentration of will a growing luminousness in my brain as if I had unsealed in the body a fountain of interior light. Normally we close our eyes on a cloudy gloom through which vague forms struggle sometimes into definiteness. But the luminous quality gradually became normal in me,[50] and at times in meditation there broke in on me an almost intolerable lustre of light, pure and shining faces, dazzling processions of figures, most ancient, ancient places and peoples, and landscapes lovely as the lost Eden. These appeared at first to have no more relation to myself than images from a street without one sees reflected in a glass; but at times meditation prolonged itself into spheres which were radiant with actuality. Once, drawn by some inner impulse to meditate at an unusual hour, I found quick oblivion of the body. The blood and heat of the brain ebbed from me as an island fades in the mists behind a swift vessel fleeting into light. The ways were open within. I rose through myself and suddenly felt as if I had awakened from dream. Where was I? In what city? Here were hills crowned with glittering temples, and the ways, so far as I could see, were thronged with most beautiful people, swaying as if shaken by some ecstasy running through all as if the Dark Hidden Father[51] was breathing rapturous life within His children. Did I wear to them an aspect like their own? Was I visible to them as a new-comer in their land of lovely light? I could not know, but those nigh me flowed towards me with outstretched hands. I saw eyes with a beautiful flame of love in them looking into mine. But I could stay no longer for something below drew me down and I was again an exile from light.[52]

There came through meditation a more powerful orientation of my being as if to a hidden sun,[53] and my thoughts turned more and more to the spiritual life of Earth. All the needles of being pointed to it. I felt instinctively that all I saw in vision was part of the life of Earth which is a court where there are many starry palaces. There the Planetary Spirit was King,[54] and that Spirit manifesting through the substance of Earth, the Mighty Mother, was, I felt, the being I groped after as God. The love I had for nature as garment of that deity grew deeper. That which was my own came to me as it comes to all men. That which claimed me drew me to itself. I had my days and nights of freedom. How often did I start in the sunshine of a Sabbath morning, setting my face to the hills, feeling somewhat uncertain as a lover who draws nigh to a beauty he adores,[55] who sometimes will yield everything to him and sometimes is silent and will only endure his presence. I did not know what would happen to me, but I was always expectant, and walked up to the mountains as to the throne of God. Step by step there fell from me the passions and fears of the week-day, until, as I reached the hillside and lay on the grassy slope with shut eyes, I was bare of all but desire for the Eternal. I was once more the child close to the Mother. She rewarded me by lifting for me a little the veil which hides her true face. To those high souls who know their kinship the veil is lifted, her face is revealed, and her face is like a bride's. Petty as was my everyday life, with the fears and timidities which abnormal sensitiveness begets, in those moments of vision I understood instinctively the high mood they must keep who would walk with the highest; and who with that divine face glimmering before him could do aught but adore!

There is an instinct which stills the lips which would speak of mysteries whose day for revelation has not drawn nigh.[56] The little I

The Candle of Vision: The Many-Coloured Land   97

know of these I shall not speak of. It is always lawful to speak of that higher wisdom which relates our spiritual being to that multitudinous unity which is God and Nature and Man. The only justification for speech from me, rather than from others whose knowledge is more profound, is that the matching of words to thoughts is an art I have practised more. What I say may convey more of truth, as the skilled artist, painting a scene which he views for the first time, may yet suggest more beauty and enchantment than the habitual dweller, unskilled in art, who may yet know the valley he loves so intimately that he could walk blindfold from end to end.

I do not wish to write a book of wonders, but rather to bring thought back to that Being whom the ancient seers worshipped as Deity. I believe that most of what was said of God was in reality said of that Spirit whose body is Earth.[57] I must in some fashion indicate the nature of the visions which led me to believe with Plato that the earth is not at all what the geographers suppose it to be,[58] and that we live like frogs at the bottom of a marsh knowing nothing of that Many-Coloured Earth which is superior to this we know, yet related to it as soul to body. On that Many-Coloured Earth, he tells us, live a divine folk, and there are temples wherein the gods do truly dwell, and I wish to convey, so far as words may, how some apparitions of that ancient beauty came to me in wood or on hillside or by the shores of the western sea.

Sometimes lying on the hillside with the eyes of the body shut as in sleep I could see valleys and hills, lustrous as a jewel, where all was self-shining, the colours brighter and purer, yet making a softer harmony together than the colours of the world I know. The winds sparkled as they blew hither and thither, yet far distances were clear through that glowing air. What was far off was precise as what was near, and the will to see hurried me to what I desired. There, too, in that land I saw fountains as of luminous mist jetting from some hidden heart of power, and shining folk[59] who passed into those fountains inhaled them and drew life from the magical air. They were, I believe, those who in the ancient world gave birth to legends of nymph and dryad.[60] Their perfectness was like the perfectness of a flower, a beauty which had never, it seemed, been broken by act of the individualized will which with us makes possible a choice between good and evil, and the marring of the mould of natural beauty. More beautiful than we they yet seemed less than human, and I surmised I had more thoughts in a moment than they through many of their days. Sometimes I wondered had they individualized life at all,[61] for they moved as if in some orchestration of their being. If one looked up, all looked up. If one moved to breathe the magical airs from the fountains, many bent in rhythm. I wondered were their thoughts all another's, one who lived within them, guardian or oversoul to their tribe? Like these were my first visions of super-nature, not spiritual nor of any high import, not in any way so high as those transcendental moments of awe, when almost without vision the Divine Darkness[62] seemed to breathe within the spirit. But I was curious about these forms, and often lured away by them from the highest meditation; for I was dazzled like a child who escapes from a dark alley in one of our cities of great sorrow where its life has been spent, and who comes for the first time upon some rich garden beyond the city where the air is weighted with scent of lilac or rose, and the eyes are made gay with colour. Such a beauty begins to glow on us as we journey towards Deity, even as earth grows brighter as we journey from the gloomy pole to lands of the sun; and I would cry out to our humanity, sinking deeper into the Iron Age, that the Golden World[63] is all about us and that beauty is open to all, and none are shut out from it who will turn to it and seek for it.

As the will grew more intense, the longing for the ancestral self more passionate, there came glimpses of more rapturous life in the being of Earth. Once I lay on the sand dunes by the western sea. The air seemed filled with melody.[64] The motion of the wind made a continuous musical vibration. Now and then the silvery sound of bells broke on my ear.[65] I saw nothing for a time. Then there was an intensity of light before my eyes like the flashing of sunlight through a crystal. It widened like the opening of a gate and I saw the light was streaming from the heart of a glowing figure. Its body was pervaded with light as if sunfire rather than blood ran through its limbs. Light streams flowed from it. It moved over me along the winds, carrying a harp, and there was a circling of golden hair that swept across the strings. Birds flew about it, and over the brows was a fiery plumage as of wings of outspread flame. On the face was an ecstasy of beauty and immortal youth. There were others, a lordly folk, and they passed by on the wind as if they knew me not or the earth I lived on. When I came back to myself my own world seemed grey and devoid of light though the summer sun was hot upon the sands.

One other vision I will tell because it bears on things the ancients taught us, and on what I have to write in later pages. Where I saw this I will not say. There was a hall vaster than any cathedral, with pillars that seemed built out of living and trembling opal, or from some starry substances which shone with every colour, the colours of eve and dawn. A golden air glowed in this place, and high between the pillars were thrones which faded, glow by glow, to the

The Candle of Vision: The Many-Coloured Land

end of the vast hall. On them sat the Divine Kings.[66] They were fire-crested. I saw the crest of the dragon on one, and there was another plumed with brilliant fires that jetted forth like feathers of flame. They sat shining and starlike, mute as statues, more colossal than Egyptian images of their gods, and at the end of the hall was a higher throne on which sat one greater than the rest. A light like the sun glowed behind him. Below on the floor of the hall lay a dark figure as if in trance, and two of the Divine Kings made motions with their hands about it over head and body. I saw where their hands waved how sparkles of fire like the flashing of jewels broke out. There rose out of that dark body a figure as tall, as glorious, as shining as those seated on the thrones. As he woke to the hall he became aware of his divine kin, and he lifted up his hands in greeting. He had returned from his pilgrimage through darkness, but now an initiate, a master in the heavenly guild. While he gazed on them the tall golden figures from their thrones leaped up, they too with hands uplifted in greeting, and they passed from me and faded swiftly in the great glory behind the throne.

ANALYTIC

Before I may write more of that supernature which rises, a tower of heaven, above the depths where we move, I know I must try to solve some of the doubts and perplexities which come to most who hear of things they have not heard or seen for their own part. They will say, 'You are an artist and have painted such things. We know you have imagination which creates images vividly. You are a poet, and it is the art of your tribe to gild for us the thoughts you have, the emotions you feel, so that what moods are common with us you attire richly till they walk like kings. But what certainty have you that it is not all fancy, and the visions you speak of were not born in the cloudy hollows of your brain, and are not glorified memories of things you have first seen with the sensual eye, and which were afterwards refashioned in memory? What certitude have you that these things you speak of are in any way related to a real world invisible to our eyes?' To solve these doubts I must not fall back on authority, or appeal for trust. It will avail nothing to say that others have seen such things and have with me looked upon them, we speaking of them together as people who see the same scene, who refer as they speak to rocks, waters and trees, knowing these are a common vision. It would be true if I said this, but it would avail me nothing in my desire that you should go hopefully on the way I would have you journey. On that path, as an ancient scripture says, to whatsoever place one would travel that place one's own self becomes, and I must try first to uproot false ideas about memory, imagination and vision so that by pure reason[67] people may be led out of error and be able to distinguish between that which arises in themselves and that which comes otherwise and which we surmise is a visitor from a far country. I too in boyhood had the idea so commonly held that the pictures of imagination are old memories refashioned. I first doubted this as a child when, lying on my bed, there came a sudden illumination of my brain, and pictures moved before my inner eyes like the coloured moving pictures we see in the theatre. I saw, I remember, a sunlit hillside which seemed close to me. There were huge grey boulders strewn about. Beyond this hill-slope I could see far distant mountains, pale blue through the sparkling air. While I looked, giants in brazen armour clambered swiftly up the hillside, swinging clubs which had spiked balls of brass held by a chain at the end. They glittered in the sun as they ran up and past me. Motion, light, shadow, colour were perfect as things seen passing before the physical eyes.[68] Then the illumination in my brain ceased, the picture vanished, and I was startled, for I had seen no hillside like that, no distant mountains, no giants in brazen armour in picture or theatre, and I began a speculation which soon ended because childhood keeps no prolonged meditation. I may take this as a type of vision common to most people. Either when they sit in darkness, or with closed eyes, or as they drift into sleep or awaken from sleep, they pass through strange cities, float in the air, roam through woods, have adventures with people who are not the people they meet every day. There is nothing uncommon about such visions. It is in the interpretation of them that error arises. People pass them by too easily saying, 'It is imagination,' as if imagination were as easily explained as a problem in Euclid, and was not a mystery, and as if every moving picture in the brain did not need such minute investigation as Darwin gave to earthworms. I was asked to believe that giants, armour, hillside and sunny distance so appeared in my brain because I had seen men who might be enlarged to giants, pictures of armour with which they could be clothed by fancy, brass with which the armour could be coloured. Any rocks might be multiplied and enlarged from memory by imagination to form a hillside, and any sky of sunny blue would make my distance. How plausible for a second! How unthinkable after a momentary consideration! I know I could hardly, if you gave me a hundred thousand pictures of heads, by cutting them up and pasting them together, make a fresh face which would appear authentic in its tints and shadows, and it would be a work of infinite labour. But these faces of vision are not still. They move. They have life and expression. The sunlight casts authentic moving shadows on the ground. What is it combines with such miraculous skill the things seen, taking a tint here, a fragment of form there, which uses the colours and forms of memory as a palette to paint such masterpieces? It has been said, 'Every man is a Shakespeare in his dreams.' The dreamer of landscape is more than a Turner, because he makes his trees to bend before the wind and his clouds to fleet across the sky. The waking brain does not do this. It is unconscious of creation. To say we refashion memories is to surmise in the subconscious nature a marvellous artist, to whom all that we have ever seen with the physical eyes is present at once, and as clay in the hands of a divine potter, and it is such swift creation too that it rivals the works of the Lord. Well, I am not one of those who deny that the Kingdom of Heaven is within us or that the King is also in His Heaven. We need not deny that and yet hold that vision comes otherwise. Nor can be it denied that vision is often so radiant and precise, for experience affirms that it is, and hundreds of artists, and indeed people who are not artists at all, will tell you how clearly they see in their dreams. But for those who hold that visions such as I and many others have had are only the refashioning of memory, and there is nothing mysterious about them, I say try to think out tint by tint, form by form, how these could be recombined, and, for whatever marvel I would have you believe, you will have substituted something just as marvellous but not so credible.[69] Not that it is incredible to think that the spirit in man is Creator, for all the prophets and seers of the world have told us that, but the common psychological explanation is not acceptable, because we know that forms can appear in the brain which were transferred by will from one person to another. When we know that, when we know this inner eye[70] can see the form in another's mind, we must regard it as indicating an immense possibility of vision on that plane. We then ask ourselves concerning all these strange cities and landscapes of dream, all these impish faces which flout at us when we are drowsy, all these visions living and moving in our minds, whether they too came, not by way of the physical senses transformed in memory, but came like the image thought transferred, or by obscure ways reflected from spheres above us, from the lives of others and the visions of others. If we brood on this we will come to think the old explanation is untenable and will address ourselves with wonder and hope to the exploration of this strange country within ourselves, and will try to find out its limits, and whether from image or vision long pondered over we may not reach to their original being.

I think few of our psychologists have had imagination themselves. They have busy brains, and, as an Eastern proverb says, 'The broken water surface reflects only broken images.' They see too feebly to make what they see a wonder to themselves. They discuss the mode of imagination as people might discuss art, who had never seen painting or sculpture. One writer talks about light being a vibration, and the vibration affecting the eye and passing along the nerves until it is stored up in the brain cells. The vibration is, it appears, stayed or fixed there. Yet I know that every movement of mine, the words I speak, the circulation of my blood, cause every molecule in my body to vibrate. How is this vibration in the cells unaffected? It must remain unaffected in their hypothesis, for I can recall the original scene, can discuss it, can after years resummon it again and find the image clear as at first. I refer to it in thought and it remains unchanged. The physical explanation of memory itself breaks down even as the material explanation of imagination breaks down. Can an unchanging vibration be retained when the substance which holds the vibration is itself subject to continual movement? The moment we close our eyes and are alone with our thoughts and the pictures of dream, we are alone with mystery and miracle. Or are we alone? Are we secure there from intrusion? Are we not nearer the thronged highways of existence where gods, demons, men and goblins all are psychical visitors. I will not speak here of high things because I am trying to argue with people who see no wonder in anything, and dismiss all high things with a silly phrase as fancy or imagination or hallucination. But I know from questioning many people that it is common with them before they sleep to see faces, while their eyes are closed, and they are, as they think, alone. These faces are sometimes the faces of imps who frown at them, put out their tongues at them, grin or gibber. Sometimes not a face but a figure, or figures, will be seen which, like the faces, seem endowed with life. To call this imagination or fancy is to explain nothing because the explanation is not explained. The more one concentrates on these most trivial mental apparitions, the more certain do we feel they have a life of their own, and that our brain is as full of living creatures as our body is thronged with tiny cells, each a life, or as the blood may swarm with bacteria.[71] I draw attention to the mystery in obvious and common things, and ask that they be explained and not slurred over as if no explanation were necessary. I ask the doubters of my vision to penetrate a little into the mystery of their own thoughts and dreams before they cry out against me, who for many years travelled far and came upon lovely and inhabited regions to which I would also lead them. I know that my brain is a court where many living creatures throng, and I am never alone in it. You, too, can know that if you heighten the imagination and intensify the will. The darkness in you will begin to glow, and you will see clearly, and you will know that what you thought was but a mosaic of memories is rather the froth of a gigantic ocean of life, breaking on the shores of matter, casting up its own flotsam to mingle with the life of the shores it breaks on. If you will light your lamp you can gaze far over that ocean and even embark on it. Sitting in your chair you can travel farther than even Columbus travelled and to lordlier worlds than his eyes had rested on. Are you not tired of surfaces? Come with me and we will bathe in the Fountains of Youth. I can point you the way to El Dorado.[72]

THE MINGLING OF NATURES

To move a single step we must have power. To see we must be exalted. Not to be lost in vision we must learn the geography of the spirit[73] and the many mansions in the being of the Father. If we concentrate we shall have power. If we meditate we shall lift ourselves above the dark environment of the brain. The inner shall become richer and more magical to us than the outer which has held us so long. How may I allure to this meditation those who see only by the light of day; who, when their eyes are shut, are as cave-dwellers living in a blackness beneath the hills?[74] The cave of the body can be lit up.[75] If we explore it we shall there find lights by which the lights of day are made dim. I perhaps to build on had some little gift of imagination I brought with me into the world, but I know others who had no natural vision who acquired this, and by sustained meditation and by focussing the will to a burning-point, were raised above the narrow life of the body. Being an artist and a lover of visible beauty, I was often tempted from the highest meditation to contemplate, not divine being, but the mirage of forms. Yet because I was so bewitched and was curious about all I saw, I was made certain that the images which populate the brain have not always been there, nor are refashioned from things seen. I know that with the pictures of memory mingle pictures which come to us, sometimes from the minds of others, sometimes are glimpses of distant countries, sometimes are reflections of happenings in regions invisible to the outer eyes; and as meditation grows more exalted, the forms traceable to memory tend to disappear and we have access to a memory greater than our own, the treasure-house of august memories in the innumerable being of Earth.[76] When minute analysis is made of images in the brain, those foolish fables about memory and imagination no longer affect those who begin this quest, and we see how many streams are tributary to our life. All I have said may be proved by any as curious about things of the mind as I was, if they will but light the candle on their forehead[77] and examine the denizens in the brain. They will find that their sphere is

The Candle of Vision: The Mingling of Natures 105

populous with the innermost thoughts of others, and will more and more be led by wonder and awe to believe that we and all things swim in an aether of deity,[78] and that the least motion of our minds is incomprehensible except in memory of this: 'In Him we live and move and have our being.'[79] Analysis of the simplest mental apparition will lead us often to stay ourselves on that thought. Once in an idle interval in my work I sat with my face pressed in my hands, and in that dimness pictures began flickering in my brain. I saw a little dark shop, the counter before me, and behind it an old man fumbling with some papers, a man so old that his motions had lost swiftness and precision. Deeper in the store was a girl, red-haired, with grey watchful eyes fixed on the old man. I saw that to enter the shop one must take two steps downwards from a cobbled pavement without. I questioned a young man, my office companion, who then was writing a letter, and I found that what I had seen was his father's shop. All my imaginations – the old man, his yellow-white beard, his fumbling movements, the watchful girl, her colour, the steps, the cobbled pavement – were not imaginations of mine in any true sense, for while I was in a vacant mood my companion had been thinking of his home, and his brain was populous with quickened memories, and they invaded my own mind, and when I made question I found their origin.[80] But how many thousand times are we invaded by such images and there is no speculation over them? Possibly I might have made use of such things in my art. I might have made a tale about the old man and girl. But if I had done so, if other characters had appeared in my tale who seemed just as living, where would they have come from? Would I have again been drawing upon the reservoir of my companion's memories? The vision of the girl and old man may in reality have been but a little part of the images with which my brain was flooded. Did I then see all, or might not other images in the same series emerge at some later time and the connection be lost? If I had written a tale and had imagined an inner room, an old mother, an absent son, a family trouble, might I not all the while be still adventuring in another's life? While we think we are imagining a character we may, so marvellous are the hidden ways, be really interpreting a being actually existing, brought into psychic contact with us by some affinity of sentiment or soul.

I brooded once upon a friend not then knowing where he was, and soon I seemed to myself to be walking in the night. Nigh me was the Sphinx,[81] and, more remote, a dim pyramid. Months later my friend came to Ireland. I found he had been in Egypt at the time I had thought of him. He could not recollect the precise day, but had while there spent a night beside the great monuments. I did not see him in vision, but I seemed to be walking there in the night. Why did the angle of vision change as with one moving about? Did I see through his eyes? Or did I see, as in the other incident, images reflected from his sphere to my own? Where does this vision end? What are its limitations? Would we, fully come to ourselves, be like those beings in the Apocalypse full of eyes within and without? Would we, in the fulness of power, act through many men and speak through many voices? Were Shakespeare and the great masters unconscious magi, blind visionaries, feeling and comprehending a life they could not see, or who, if they saw, thought it was their own creation.[82] We must ask ourselves these questions, for, when our lamp is lit, we find the house of our being has many chambers, and creatures live there who come and go, and we must ask whether they have the right to be in our house;[83] and there are corridors there leading into the hearts of others, and windows which open into eternity, and we hardly can tell where our own being ends and another begins, or if there is any end to our being. If we brood with love upon this myriad unity, following the meditation ordained by Buddha[84] for the brothers of his order, to let our minds pervade the whole wide world with heart of love, we come more and more to permeate, or to be pervaded by the lives of others. We are haunted by unknown comrades in many moods, whose naked souls pass through ours, and reveal themselves to us in an unforgettable instant, and we know them as we hardly know those who are the daily comrades of our heart, who, however intimate, are hidden from us by the husk of the body. As the inner life grows richer we beget more of these affinities. We wonder what relation with them is rightly ours. Do we affect them by a sympathy unknown to them as they move us by a revelation more intimate than could be uttered by words? We discover in ourselves a new sense. By touch with the soul we understand. We realize how profound was that ancient wisdom which told us when we were perfected in concentration we could gain full comprehension of anything we wished by intent brooding.[85] I never attained that perfectness of concentration, but I saw the possibilities in moments of electric intensity of will when I summoned out of the past a knowledge I desired. How is this knowledge possible? Is there a centre within us through which all threads of the universe are drawn, a spiritual atom which mirrors the spiritual infinitudes even as the eye is a mirror of the external heavens?[86] There is not a pinpoint in visible space which does not contain a microcosm of heaven and earth.[87] We know that, for nowhere we do move where the eye does not receive its vision of infinity. Is it only in the visible world, this condensation of the infinite in the atomic, and not also in the soul and again in the spirit? What would the soul in its perfection mirror? Would it reflect within itself the myriad life of humanity? Would the spirit mirror the heavens, and the imaginations of the Divine Mind well up within it in mystic and transcendental ideations? Or do they already mirror each their own world, and is all knowledge already within us, and is our need but for wisdom to create the links between portions of a single being, dramatically sundered by illusion as the soul is in dream?[88] Is not the gathering of the will and the fiery brooding to this end, and are the glimpses we get of supernature caused but by the momentary uplifting of an eye, by which, when it is fully awakened, we dead shall be raised?

THE MEMORY OF EARTH

We experience the romance and delight of voyaging upon uncharted seas when the imagination is released from the foolish notion that the images seen in reverie and dream are merely the images of memory refashioned; and in tracking to their originals the forms seen in vision we discover for them a varied ancestry, as that some come from the minds of others, and of some we cannot surmise another origin than that they are portions of the memory of Earth which is accessible to us. We soon grow to think our memory but a portion of that eternal memory[89] and that we in our lives are gathering an innumerable experience for a mightier being than our own. The more vividly we see with the inner eye the more swiftly do we come to this conviction. Those who see vaguely are satisfied with vague explanations which those who see vividly at once reject as inadequate. How are we to explain what has happened to many, and oftentimes to myself, that when we sit amid ancient ruins or in old houses they renew their life for us? I waited for a friend inside a ruined chapel and while there a phantasm of its ancient uses came vividly before me. In front of the altar I saw a little crowd kneeling, most prominent a woman in a red robe, all pious and emotionally intent. A man stood behind these leaning by the wall as if too proud to kneel. An old man in ecclesiastical robes, abbot or bishop, stood, a crozier in one hand, while the other was uplifted in blessing or in emphasis of his words. Behind the cleric a boy carried a vessel, and the lad's face was vain with self-importance. I saw all this suddenly as if I was contemporary and was elder in the world by many centuries. I could surmise the emotional abandon of the red-robed lady, the proud indifference of the man who stood with his head but slightly bent, the vanity of the young boy as servitor in the ceremony, just as in a church to-day we feel the varied mood of those present. Anything may cause such pictures to rise in vivid illumination before us, a sentence in a book, a word, or contact with some object.[90] I have brooded over the grassy mounds which are all that remain of the duns in which our Gaelic ancestors lived, and they

The Candle of Vision: The Memory of Earth 109

builded themselves up again for me so that I looked on what seemed an earlier civilization, saw the people, noted their dresses, the colours of natural wool, saffron or blue, how rough like our own homespuns they were; even such details were visible as that the men cut meat at table with knives and passed it to the lips with their fingers. This is not, I am convinced, what people call imagination, an interior creation in response to a natural curiosity about past ages. It is an act of vision, a perception of images already existing breathed on some ethereal medium[91] which in no way differs from the medium which holds for us our memories; and the reperception of an image in memory which is personal to us in no way differs as a psychical act from the perception of images in the memory of Earth. The same power of seeing is turned upon things of the same character and substance. It is not only rocks and ruins which infect us with such visions. A word in a book when one is sensitive may do this also. I sought in a classical dictionary for information about some myth. What else on the page my eye caught I could not say, but something there made two thousand years to vanish. I was looking at the garden of a house in some ancient city. From the house into the garden fluttered two girls, one in purple and the other in a green robe, and they, in a dance of excitement, ran to the garden wall and looked beyond it to the right. There a street rose high to a hill where there was a pillared building. I could see through blinding sunlight a crowd swaying down the street drawing nigh the house, and the two girls were as excited as girls might be to-day if king or queen were entering their city. This instant uprising of images following a glance at a page cannot be explained as the refashioning of the pictures of memory. The time which elapsed after the page was closed and the apparition in the brain was a quarter of a minute or less. One can only surmise that pictures so vividly coloured, so full of motion and sparkle as are moving pictures in the theatres were not an instantaneous creation by some magical artist within us, but were evoked out of a vaster memory than the personal, that the Grecian names my eye had caught had the power of symbols which evoke their affinities, and the picture of the excited girls and the shining procession was in some fashion, I know not how, connected with what I had read. We cannot pass by the uprising of these images with some vague phrase about suggestion or imagination and shirk further inquiry. If with the physical eye twenty-five years ago a man had seen a winged aeroplane amid the clouds it had roused him to a tumult of speculation and inquiry. But if the same picture had been seen in the mind it would speedily have been buried as mere fancy. There would have been no speculation, though what appears within us might well be deemed more important than what appears without us. Every tint, tone, shape, light or shade in an interior image must have intelligible cause as the wires, planes, engines and propellers of the aeroplane have.[92] We must infer, when the image is clear and precise, an original of which this is the reflection. Whence or when were the originals of the pictures we see in dream or reverie? There must be originals; and, if we are forced to dismiss as unthinkable any process by which the pictures of our personal memory could unconsciously be reshaped into new pictures which appear in themselves authentic copies of originals, which move, have light, colour, form, shade such as nature would bestow, then we are led to believe that memory is an attribute of all living creatures and of Earth also, the greatest living creature we know, and that she carries with her, and it is accessible to us, all her long history, cities far gone behind time, empires which are dust, or are buried with sunken continents beneath the waters. The beauty for which men perished is still shining; Helen is there in her Troy, and Deirdre wears the beauty which blasted the Red Branch. No ancient lore has perished. Earth retains for herself and her children what her children might in passion have destroyed, and it is still in the realm of the Ever Living to be seen by the mystic adventurer. We argue that this memory must be universal, for there is nowhere we go where Earth does not breathe fragments from her ancient story to the meditative spirit. These memories gild the desert air where once the proud and golden races had been and had passed away, and they haunt the rocks and mountains where the Druids[93] evoked their skiey and subterrene deities. The laws by which this history is made accessible to us seem to be the same as those which make our own learning swift to our service. When we begin thought or discussion on some subject we soon find ourselves thronged with memories ready for use. Everything in us related by affinity to the central thought seems to be mobilized;[94] and in meditation those alien pictures we see, not the pictures of memory, but strange scenes, cities, beings and happenings, are, if we study them, all found to be in some relation to our mood. If our will is powerful enough and if by concentration and aspiration we have made the gloom in the brain to glow, we can evoke out of the memory of earth images of whatsoever we desire. These earth memories come to us in various ways. When we are passive,[95] and the ethereal medium which is the keeper of such images, not broken up by thought, is like clear glass or calm water, then there is often a glowing of colour and form upon it, and there is what may be a reflection from some earth memory connected with the place we move in or it may be we have direct vision of that memory. Meditation again evokes images and pictures which are akin to its subject and our mood and serve in illustration of it. Once, when I was considering the play of arcane forces in the body, a book appeared before me, a coloured symbol on each page. I saw the book was magical, for while I looked on one of these the symbol vanished from the page, and the outline of a human body appeared, and then there came an interior revelation of that, and there was a shining of forces and a flashing of fires, rose, gold, azure and silver along the spinal column,[96] and these flowed up into the brain where they struck upon a little ball that was like white sunfire for brilliancy,[97] and they flashed out of that again in a pulsation as of wings on each side of the head; and then the page darkened, and the changing series closed with the Caduceus of Mercury[98] and contained only a symbol once more.

Such pictures come without conscious effort of will, but are clearly evoked by it. Lastly, but more rarely with me, because the electric intensity of will[99] required was hard to attain, I was able at times to evoke deliberately out of the memory of nature pictures of persons or things long past in time, but of which I desired knowledge. I regret now, while I was young and my energies yet uncoiled, that I did not practise this art of evocation more in regard to matters where knowledge might be regarded as of spiritual value; but I was like a child who discovers a whole set of fresh toys, and plays with one after the other, and I was interested in all that came to me, and was too often content to be the servant of my vision and not its master.[100] It was an excitement of spirit for one born in a little country town in Ireland to find the circle of being widened so that life seemed to dilate into a paradise of beautiful memories, and to reach to past ages and to mix with the eternal consciousness of Earth, and when we come on what is new we pause to contemplate it,[101] and do not hurry to the end of our journey. The instances of earth memories given here are trivial in themselves, and they are chosen, not because they are in any way wonderful, but rather because they are like things many people see, and so they may more readily follow my argument. The fact that Earth holds such memories is itself important, for once we discover this imperishable tablet, we are led to speculate whether in the future a training in seership might not lead to a revolution in human knowledge. It is a world where we may easily get lost,[102] and spend hours in futile vision with no more gain than if one looked for long hours at the dust. For those to whom in their spiritual evolution these apparitions arise I would say: try to become the master of your vision, and seek for and evoke the greatest of earth memories, not those things which only satisfy curiosity, but those which uplift and inspire, and give us a vision of our own greatness; and the noblest of all Earth's memories is the august ritual of the ancient mysteries, where the mortal, amid scenes of unimaginable grandeur, was disrobed of his mortality and made of the company of the gods.

IMAGINATION

In all I have related hitherto imagination was not present but only vision. These are too often referred to as identical, and in what I have written I have tried to make clear the distinction. If beyond my window I see amid the manifolded hills a river winding ablaze with light, nobody speaks of what is seen as a thing imagined, and if I look out of a window of the soul and see more marvels of shining and shadow, neither is this an act of imagination, which is indeed a higher thing than vision, and a much rarer thing, for in the act of imagination that which is hidden in being, as the Son in the bosom of the Father, is made manifest and a transfiguration takes place like that we imagine in the Spirit when it willed, 'Let there be light.'[103] Imagination[104] is not a vision of something which already exists, and which in itself must be unchanged by the act of seeing, but by imagination what exists in latency or essence is out-realized and is given a form in thought, and we can contemplate with full consciousness that which hitherto had been unrevealed, or only intuitionally surmised. In imagination there is a revelation of the self to the self, and a definite change in being, as there is in a vapour when a spark ignites it and it becomes an inflammation in the air. Here images appear in consciousness which we may refer definitely to an internal creator,[105] with power to use or remould pre-existing forms, and endow them with life, motion and voice. We infer this because dream and vision sometimes assume a symbolic character and a significance which is personal to us. They tell us plainly, 'For you only we exist', and we cannot conceive of what is seen as being a reflection of life in any sphere. In exploring the ancestry of the symbolic vision we draw nigh to that clouded majesty we divine in the depths of our being, and which is heard normally in intuition and conscience,[106] but which now reveals character in its manifestation as the artist in his work. I had a gay adventure when I was a boy at the beginning of my mental travelling, when I met, not a lion, but a symbolic vision in the path. I had read somewhere of one whose dreams made a continuous story from night to night, and I was excited at this and wondered whether I too could not build up life for myself in a fairyland of my own creation, and be the lord of this in dream, and offset the petty circumstance of daily life with the beauty of a realm in which I would be king. I bent myself to this, walking about the country roads at night in the darkness, building up in fantasy the country of sleep. I remember some of my gorgeous fancies. My dream-world was self-shining. Light was born in everything there at dawn, and faded into a coloured gloom at eve, and if I walked across my lawns in darkness the grasses stirred by my feet would waken to vivid colour and glimmer behind me in a trail of green fire; or if a bird was disturbed at night in my shadowy woods it became a winged jewel of blue, rose, gold and white, and the leaves tipped by its wings would blaze in flakes of emerald flame, and there were flocks of wild birds that my shouts would call forth to light with glittering plumage the monstrous dusk of the heavens. Many other fancies I had which I now forget, and some of them were intuitions about the Many-Coloured Land. After I had conceived this world, one night in a fury of effort I willed that it should be my habitation in dream. But of all my dreams I remember only two. In the first I saw a mass of pale clouds, and on them was perched a little ape clutching at the misty substance with its fingers and trying to fashion it to some form. It looked from its work every now and then at something beyond and below the clouds, and I came closer in my dream and saw that what the ape was watching was our earth which spun below in space,[107] and it was trying to model a sphere of mist in mimicry of that which spun past it. While I was intent, this grotesque sculptor turned suddenly, looking at me with an extraordinary grimace which said clearly as words could say, 'That is what you are trying to do,' and then I was whirled away again and I was the tiniest figure in vast mid-air, and before me was a gigantic gate which seemed lofty as the skies, and a shadowy figure filled the doorway and barred my passage. That is all I can remember, and I am forced by dreams like this to conclude there is a creator of such dreams within us,[108] for I cannot suppose that anywhere in space or time a little ape sat on a cloud and tried to fashion it into planetary form. The creator of that vision was transcendent to the waking self and to the self which experienced the dream, for neither self took conscious part in the creation.[109] The creator of that vision was seer into my consciousness in waking and in sleep, for what of the vision I remember was half a scorn of my effort and half a warning that my ambition was against natural law. The creator of that vision could combine forms and endow them with motion and life for the vision was intellectual and penetrated me with its meaning. Is it irrational to assume so much, or that the vision indicated a peculiar character in its creator, and that the ironic mood was not alien to it nor even humour? I am rather thankful to surmise this of a self which waves away so many of our dreams and joys, and which seems in some moods to be remote from the normal and terrible as the angel with the flaming sword pointing every way to guard the Tree of Life. In this dream some self of me, higher in the tower of our being which reaches up to the heavens, made objective manifestations of its thought; but there were moments when it seemed itself to descend, wrapping its memories of heaven about it like a cloth, and to enter the body, and I knew it as more truly myself than that which began in my mother's womb, and that it was antecedent to anything which had body in the world.[110] Here I must return to those imaginations I had walking about the country roads as a boy, and select from these, as I have done from vision, things upon which the reason may be brought to bear. It is more difficult, for when there is divine visitation the mortal is made dark and blind with glory and, in its fiery fusion with the spirit, reason is abased or bewildered or spreads too feeble a net to capture Leviathan,[111] for often we cannot after translate to ourselves in memory what the spirit said, though every faculty is eager to gather what is left after the visitation even as the rabble in eastern legend scramble to pick up the gold showered in the passing of the king. By the time I was seventeen or eighteen my brain began to flicker with vivid images. I tried to paint these, and began with much enthusiasm a series of pictures which were to illustrate the history of man from his birth in the Divine Mind[112] where he glimmered first in the darkness of chaos in vague and monstrous forms growing ever nigher to the human, to men beasts and men birds, until at last the most perfect form, the divine idea of man, was born in space.[113] I traced its descent into matter, its conflict with the elements, and finally the series ended in a pessimistic fancy where one of our descendants millions of years hence, a minute philosopher, a creature less than three inches in height, sat on one of our gigantic skulls and watched the skies ruining back into their original chaos and the stars falling from their thrones on the height.[114] Most of these pictures were only the fancies of a boy, but in considering one of the series I began to feel myself in alliance with a deeper consciousness, and that was when I was trying to imagine the apparition in the Divine Mind of the idea of the Heavenly Man.[115] Something ancient and eternal seemed to breathe through my fancies. I was blinded then by intensity of feeling to the demerits of the picture, but I was excited in an extraordinary way over what I had done, and I lay awake long into the night brooding over it. I asked myself what legend I would write under the picture. Something beyond reason held me, and I felt like one who is in a dark room and hears the breathing of another creature, and himself waits breathless for its utterance, and I struggled to understand what wished to be said, and at last, while I was preternaturally dilated and intent, something whispered to me, 'Call it the Birth of Aeon.'[116] The word 'Aeon' thrilled me, for it seemed to evoke by association of ideas, moods and memories most ancient, out of some ancestral life where they lay hidden; and I think it was the following day that, still meditative and clinging to the word as a lover clings to the name of the beloved, a myth incarnated in me, the story of an Aeon, one of the first starry emanations of Deity, one pre-eminent in the highest heavens, so nigh to Deity and so high in pride that he would be not less than a god himself and would endure no dominion over him save the law of his own will. This Aeon[117] of my imagination revolted against heaven and left its courts, descending into the depths where it mirrored itself in chaos, weaving out of the wild elements a mansion for its spirit. That mansion was our earth and that Aeon was the God of our world. This myth incarnated in me as a boy walking along the country roads in Armagh. I returned to Dublin after a fortnight and it was a day or two after that I sent into the Library at Leinster House and asked for an art journal. I stood by a table while the attendant searched for the volume. There was a book lying open there. My eye rested on it. It was a dictionary of religions, I think, for the first word my eye caught was 'Aeon' and it was explained as a word used by the Gnostics[118] to designate the first created beings. I trembled through my body. At that time I knew nothing of mystical literature and indeed little of any literature except such tales as a boy reads, and the imaginations which had begun to overwhelm me were to me then nothing but mere imaginations, and were personal and unrelated in my mind with any conception of truth, or idea that the imagination could lay hold of truth. I trembled because I was certain I had never heard the word before, and there rushed into my mind the thought of pre-existence[119] and that this was memory of the past. I went away hurriedly that I might think by myself, but my thoughts drove me back again soon, and I asked the librarian who were the Gnostics and if there was a book which gave an account of their ideas. He referred me to a volume of Neander's *Church History*,[119a] and there, in the section dealing with the Sabaeans, I found the myth of the proud Aeon who mirrored himself in chaos and became the lord of our world. I believed then, and still believe, that the immortal in us has memory of all its wisdom,[120] or, as Keats puts it in one of his letters,[121] there is an ancestral wisdom in man

The Candle of Vision: Imagination

and we can if we wish drink that old wine of heaven. This memory of the spirit is the real basis of imagination, and when it speaks to us we feel truly inspired and a mightier creature than ourselves speaks through us. I remember how pure, holy and beautiful these imaginations seemed, how they came like crystal water sweeping aside the muddy current of my life, and the astonishment I felt, I who was almost inarticulate, to find sentences which seemed noble and full of melody sounding in my brain as if another and greater than I had spoken them; and how strange it was also a little later to write without effort verse, which some people still think has beauty, while I could hardly, because my reason had then no mastery over the materials of thought, pen a prose sentence intelligently. I am convinced that all poetry is, as Emerson said,[122] first written in the heavens, that is, it is conceived by a self deeper than appears in normal life, and when it speaks to us or tells us its ancient story we taste of eternity and drink the Soma juice,[123] the elixir of immortality.

DREAMS[124]

I had discovered through such dreams as that of the satirical ape that there is One who is vigilant through the sleep of the body,[125] and I was led by other dreams to assume that in the heart of sleep there is an intellectual being moving in a world of its own and using transcendental energies. Most of the dreams we remember are chaotic, and these seem often to be determined in character by the accident which brings about our waking.[126] Chaotic as these are, they are full of wonder and miracle, for in the space of a second, almost before a voice has reached the ear of the sleeper or a hand has touched him, some magical engineer has flung a bridge of wild incident over which the spirit races from deep own-being unto outward being. Never when awake could we pack into a second of vivid imagination the myriad incidents that the artificer of dream can create to bring us from the being we remember not back to the dream of life. This magical swiftness of creation in dream has been noted by many, and those who have had experience of even the most nightmare happenings before waking must be led to surmise that within that blankness we call sleep there is a consciousness in unsleeping vigilance, and this being, which is unsleeping while the body sleeps, excites us to a curiosity as wild as ever led adventurer across uncharted seas. The ancient seers made earth world, mid-world and heaven world synonyms for three states of consciousness, waking, dreaming and deep sleep.[127] But the dream state of the soul moving in the mid-world of which they spoke is an intellectual state, and its character is not easily to be guessed from that chaos of fancies we ordinarily remember and call our dreams; and which I think are not true dreams at all but rather a transitional state on the borderland, like to the froth on the ocean fringes, where there are buffetings of air, churnings of sand, water and weed, while beyond is the pure deep. I had but slight experience of that loftier life in dream which to others I know was truer life than waking. But none can speak truly of the dreams or imaginations of others, but only of what themselves have known. In intensest meditation I think we encroach on that state which to the waking brain is veiled by sleep and is normally a blank,[128] for in the highest dreams of which I retained memory I was on a plane of being identical with that reached in the apex of meditation and had perceptions of a similar order of things. The black curtain of unconsciousness which drapes the chambers of the brain in sleep, once, for an instant, was magically lifted for me, and I had a glimpse of the high adventures of the unsleeping soul. I found myself floating on the luminous night in a body lighter than air and charged with power, buoyed up above a mountainous region. Beneath me was a wrinkled dusk like the crater of some huge volcano. There were others with me, people with airy glittering bodies, all, like myself, intent on a being mightier than our own. A breath of power poured upward from below as from a fountain, or as if from here some sidereal river flowed out to the country of the stars. We hovered over the fountain from which came that invisible breath filling us with delight and power. While we hung intent there came the apparition of a vast and glowing orb of light[129] like the radiance about a god, and of those glittering ones some flung themselves into that sphere of light, and were absorbed in it: and it faded away, ebbing from us as if it had been a living galleon come to the hither side of being but for a moment, to carry with it those who might go to the heaven world to be partakers of the divine nature and live in their parent Flame.[130] I could not cross with that Charon,[131] and I remembered no more, for the curtain of darkness which was magically lifted was again dropped over the chambers of the brain. But when I woke I was murmuring to myself, as if in interpretation, the words of the Apostle, 'We all with open face beholding as in a glass the glory of the Lord are changed unto the same image from glory to glory,'[132] and I knew there were many at that mystery who would wake up again outcasts of Heaven,[133] and the God of this world would obliterate memory so that they would never know they had kept tryst with the Kabiri.[134]

Once before, not in dream but in meditation, there had broken in upon me such a light from the secret places; and I saw through earth as though a transparency to one of these centres of power, 'fountains of Hecate'[135] as they are called in the Chaldaic oracles, and which are in the being of earth, even as in ourselves there are fiery centres undiscovered by the anatomist where thought is born or the will leaps up in flame.[136] And then, and in the dream I have just told, and in that other vision of the heavenly city where I found myself among the shining ones, there seemed to be little of personal fantasy as there was in the dream of the ape, but I seemed to myself to be moving in a real nature which others also have moved in, and which was perhaps the sphere known also to that spiritual geographer who assured Socrates of a many-coloured earth above this with temples wherein the gods do truly dwell. I do not wish now to urge this but only to draw the deductions any psychologist analysing dream might draw from dreams not mystical in character. I may liken myself in my perception of that dream to a man in a dark hall so utterly lightless, so soundless, that nothing reaches him; and then the door is suddenly flung open, and he sees a crowd hurrying by, and then the door is closed and he is again in darkness. Such a man seeing through the door a procession of people in the streets knows they had a life before they came nigh the door and after they passed the door; and he is not foolish if he speculates on this and how they gathered and for what purpose. So I am justified, I think, in assuming that there was some psychic action[137] in priority to my moment of conciousness. I must seek intellectual causes for events which have logical structure and coherency: I cannot assume that the sudden consciousness of being in the air was absolutely the beginning of that episode any more than I can imagine a flower suddenly appearing without plant or root or prior growth,[138] nor can I think that blind motions of the brain, in blank unconsciousness of what they tend to, suddenly flame into a consciousness instinct with wild beauty. To assume that would be a freak in reasoning. I might with as much wisdom assume that if in the darkness I took my little son's box of alphabetical bricks, and scattered them about blindly, when the light was turned on I might find that the letters composed a noble sentence. I can reasonably take either of two possibilities, one being that the dream was self-created fantasy only, and the other that it was the mirroring in the brain of an experience of soul in a real sphere of being. But whether we assume one or other we postulate an unsleeping consciousness within ourselves while the brain is asleep:[139] and that unsleeping creature was either the creator of the dream or the actor in a real event. Who is that unsleeping creature? Is it the same being who daily inhabits the brain? Does it rise up when the body sinks on the couch? Has it a dual life as we have when waking, when half our consciousness is of an external nature and half of subjective emotions and thoughts? Are part of our dreams internal fantasy and part perceptions of an external sphere of being? If I assume that the soul was an actor in a real event which was mirrored in the brain, why did I remember only one moment of the adventure? To see any being means that we are on the same plane. I see you who are physical because I also have bodily life. If I see an elemental being or a heavenly being it means that some part of me is on the same plane of being or

The Candle of Vision: Dreams 121

substance.[140] Had I by meditation and concentration evolved in myself some element akin to that breathed upward from the mystic fountain, and when the soul inhaled this fiery essence a rapport began between free soul and slumbering body, the circuit was complete, and sleeping and unsleeping being became one? On that hypothesis there were journeyings of the soul before and after the moment remembered, but the action in priority and in succession I could not remember because there was as yet no kinship in the brain to the mood of the unsleeping soul or to the deed it did. If the soul is an actor in deep sleep, seeing, hearing and moving in a world of real energies, then we are justified in assuming a psychic body within the physical, for to see, to hear, to move are functions of an organism however ethereal.[141] Is it the shining of the Psyche we perceive within ourselves when through aspiration the body becomes filled with interior light and consciousness is steeped in a brilliancy of many colours while the eyes are closed?[142] Are we then like the half-evolved dragon-fly who catches with the first cracking of its sheath a glimpse of its own gorgeous plumage? Was it this body the prophet spoke of when he said, 'Thou hast been in Eden the Garden of God: every precious stone was thy covering . . . thou wast upon the holy mountains of God: thou hast walked up and down amid the stones of fire?'[142a] And was this spiritual life lost to man because his heart was lifted up because of his beauty, and wisdom was corrupted by reason of its own brightness?

If we brood over the alternative that the dream was self-begotton fantasy, no less must we make obeisance to the dreamer of dreams. Who is this who flashes on the inner eye landscapes as living as those we see in nature? The winds blow cool upon the body in dream: the dew is on the grass: the clouds fleet over the sky: we float in air and see all things from an angle of vision of which on waking we have no experience: we move in unknown cities and hurry on secret missions. It matters not whether our dream is a grotesque, the same marvellous faculty of swift creation is in it. We are astonished at nightmare happenings no less than at the lordliest vision, for we divine in the creation of both the same magical power. I cannot but think the gnat to be as marvellous as the Bird of Paradise, and these twain no less marvellous than the seraphim. The Master of Life[143] is in all, and I am as excited with wonder at the creative genius shown in the wildest dream as in the most exalted vision. Not by any power I understand are these images created: but the power which creates them is, I surmise, a mightier self of ours, and yet our slave for purposes of its own.[144] I feel its presence in all I do, think or imagine. It waits on my will. It is in the instant and marvellous marshalling of memories when I speak or write. Out of the myriad chambers of the soul where they lie in latency, an hundred or a thousand memories rise up, words, deeds, happenings, trivial or mighty, the material for thought or speech waiting in due order for use. They sink back silently and are again ready: at the least desire of the will they fly up to consciousness more swiftly than iron filings to the magnet. If I am wakened suddenly I surmise again that it is that enchanter who builds miraculously a bridge of incident to carry me from deep being to outward being. When thought or imagination is present in me, ideas or images appear on the surface of consciousness, and though I call them my thoughts, my imaginations, they are already formed when I become aware of them. The Indian sage Sankara[145] says by reason of the presence of the highest Self in us, the mind in us is moved as if moved by another than ourselves. Upon its presence depend all motions of body and soul. Could I embrace even the outer infinitude with the eye of the body, if it did not preside over the sense of sight, infinitude interpreting infinitude? It seems to wait on us as indifferently and as swiftly when the will in us is evil as when it is good. It will conjure up for us images of animalism and lust at the call of desire. It might speak of itself as the Lord spoke of Himself to the prophet: 'From me spring forth good and evil.'[146] But if we evoke it for evil it answers with fading power, and we soon are unable to evoke it for good, for the evil we have called forth works for our feebleness and extinction.[147] Or is there another and evil genie,[148] a dark effigy of the higher also waiting on us as slave of our desires? I do not know. Was it of the higher it was said, 'Ask, and ye shall receive. Seek, and ye shall find. Knock, and it shall be opened to you'?[149] Can we by searching find out its ways? Can we come to an identity of ourselves with it? Again I do not know, but the more I ponder over this unsleeping being, the more do I feel astonished as Aladdin with lamp or ring, who had but to touch the talisman and a legion of genii were ready to work his will, to build up for him marvellous palaces in the twinkling of an eye, and to ransack for him the treasure-houses of eternity.

THE ARCHITECTURE OF DREAM

I have failed in my purpose if I have not made it clear that in the actual architecture of dream and vision there is a mystery which is not explained by speaking of suppressed desire or sex or any of those springs which modern psychologists surmise are released in dream. A mood may attract its affinities but it does not create what it attracts, and between anger and a definite vision of conflict there is a gulf as mysterious as there was between Aladdin's desire and the building of his marvellous palace. I desire a house, but desire does not build it. I design a house, but every line is drawn with full consciousness, and when I give the plan to the builder every brick is placed with full consciousness by the masons. No coherent architecture in city or dream arises magically by some unreason which translates bodiless desire into organic form. However swift the succession may be, in that second of time between desire and its visionary embodiment or fulfilment there must be space for intellectual labour, the construction of forms or the choice of forms, and the endowing of them with motion. A second to my brain is too brief a fragment of time for more than sight, but I must believe that to a more intense consciousness, which is co-worker with mine, that second may suffice for a glimpse into some pleroma of form for the selection of these and the unrolling of a vast pageantry. Something there is, a creature within me, behind whose swiftness I falter a hopeless laggard, for it may be a traveller through the Archaeus[150] and back again with the merchandise of its travel before my pulse has beaten twice. As an artist who has laboured slowly at the creation of pictures I assert that the forms of dream or vision if self-created require a conscious artist to arrange them, a magician to endow them with life, and that the process is intellectual, that is, it is conscious on some plane of being, though that self which sits in the gate of the body does not know what powers or dignitaries meet in the inner palace chambers of the soul.[151] When we have dreams of flying and see all things from an angle of vision of which we never could have experience in waking, we know that to speak of the moving pictures of dream as memories or unconscious recombinations of things seen when waking, is to speak without subtlety or intellectual comprehension. I criticise the figures I see in dream or vision exactly as I would the figures in a painting. Even if I see a figure in dream I have seen when waking, if the figure acts in a manner differing from its action when seen with the physical eye, if it now walks when it then sat, or looks down where before it looked up, and if these motions in dream appear authentic so that face and form have the proper light and shade and the anatomies are undistorted, that dream change in the figure of memory is itself a most perplexing thing. We must suppose that memory as memory is as fixed in its way as a sun-picture is fixed or as the attitude of a statue is fixed. If it fades it should be by loss of precision and not into other equally precise but different forms and gestures. Now we could not without cracks or distorting of anatomies or complete remodelling change the pose of a statue even if it was modelled in some easily malleable substance; and the plastic change from stillness to motion in a figure, which we presume to be a memory, is wonderful when we think of it, as wonderful as if the little Tanagra in clay upon my shelf should change from its cast solidity and walk up and down before me. For myself I think man is a protean being,[152] within whose unity there is diversity, and there are creatures in the soul which can inform the images of our memory, or the eternal memory, aye, and speak through them to us in dream, so that we hear their voices, and it is with us in our minute microcosmic fashion even as it was said of the universe that it is a soliloquy of Deity wherein Ain-Soph talks to Ain-Soph.[153]

We can make such general speculations about all pictures moving before the inner eye, and it is always worth while investigating the anatomy of vision and to be intent on what appears to us, for if we have intentness we have memory. A mental picture which at first had yielded nothing to us may be followed by others which indicate a relation to the earliest in the series so that they seem like pages read at different times from the same book. When I was young I haunted the mountains much, finding in the high air vision became richer and more luminous. I have there watched for hours shining landscape and figures in endless procession, trying to discover in these some significance other than mere beauty. Once on the hillside I seemed to slip from to-day into some remote yesterday of earth. There was the same valley below me, but now it was deepening into evening and the skies were towering up through one blue heaven to another. There was a battle in the valley and men reeled darkly hither and thither. I remember one warrior about whom the

The Candle of Vision: The Architecture of Dream   125

battle was thickest, for a silver star flickered above his helmet through the dusk. But this I soon forgot for I was impelled to look upwards, and there above me was an airship[154] glittering with light. It halted above the valley while a man, grey-bearded, very majestic, his robes all starred and jewelled, bent over and looked down upon the battle. The pause was but for an instant, and then the lights flashed more brilliantly, some luminous mist was jetted upon the air from many tubes below the boat, and it soared and passed beyond the mountain, and it was followed by another and yet others, all glittering with lights, and they climbed the air over the hill and were soon lost amid the other lights of heaven. It must be a quarter of a century ago since I saw this vision which I remember clearly because I painted the ship, and it must, I think, be about five or six years after that a second vision in the same series startled me. I was again on the high places, and this time the apparition in the mystical air was so close that if I could have stretched out a hand from this world to that I could have clutched the aerial voyager as it swept by me. A young man was steering the boat, his black hair blown back from his brows, his face pale and resolute, his head bent, his eyes intent on his wheel: and beside him sat a woman, a rose-coloured shawl speckled with golden threads drawn over her head, around her shoulders, across her bosom and folded arms. Her face was proud as a queen's and I long remembered that face for its pride, stillness and beauty. I thought at the moment it was some image in the eternal memory of a civilization more remote than Atlantis[155] and I cried out in my heart in a passion of regret for romance passed away from the world, not knowing that the world's great age was again returning[156] and that soon we were to swim once more beneath the epic skies. After that at different times and places I saw other such aerial wanderers, and this I noted, that all such visions had a character in keeping with each other, that they were never mixed up with modernity, that they had the peculiarities by which we recognize civilizations as distinct from each other, Chinese from Greek or Egyptian from Hindu. They were the stuff out of which romance is made, and if I had been a story-teller like our great Standish O'Grady I might have made without questioning a wonder tale of the air, legendary or futurist, but I have always had as much of the philosophic as the artistic interest in what people call imagination, and I have thought that many artists and poets gave to art or romance what would have had an equal if not a greater interest as psychology. I began to ask myself where in the three times or in what realm of space these ships were launched. Was it ages ago in some actual workshop in an extinct civilization, and were these but images in the eternal memory?[157] Or were they launched by my own spirit from some magical arsenal of being, and, if so, with what intent? Or were they images of things yet to be in the world, begotten in that eternal mind where past, present and future coexist,[158] and from which they stray into the imagination of scientist, engineer or poet to be out-realized in discovery, mechanism or song? I find it impossible to decide. Sometimes I even speculate on a world interpenetrating ours where another sun is glowing, and other stars are shining over other woods, mountains, rivers and another race of beings.[159] And I know not why it should not be so. We are forced into such speculations when we become certain that no power in us of which we are conscious is concerned in the creation of such visionary forms. If these ships were launched so marvellously upon the visionary air by some transcendent artisan of the spirit they must have been built for some purpose and for what? I was not an engineer intent on aerial flight, but this is, I think, notable that at the moment of vision I seemed to myself to understand the mechanism of these airships, and I felt, if I could have stepped out of this century into that visionary barque, I could have taken the wheel and steered it confidently on to its destiny. I knew that the closing of a tube at one side of the bow would force the ship to steer in that direction, because the force jetted from the parallel tube on the other side, no longer balanced by an equal emission of power, operated to bring about the change. There is an interest in speculating about this impression of knowledge for it might indicate some complicity of the subconscious mind with the vision which startled the eye. That knowledge may have been poured on the one while seeing was granted to the other. If the vision was imagination, that is if the airship was launched from my own spirit, I must have been in council with the architect, perhaps in deep sleep. If I suppose it was imagination I am justified in trying by every means to reach with full consciousness to the arsenal where such wonders are wrought. I cannot be content to accept it as imagination and not try to meet the architect. As for these visions of airships and for many others I have been unable to place them even speculatively in any world or any century, and it must be so with the imaginations of many other people. But I think that when we begin speculation about these things it is the beginning of our wakening from the dream of life.

I have suggested that images of things to be may come into our sphere out of a being where time does not exist. I have had myself no definite proof as yet that any vision I saw was prophetic, and only one which suggested itself as such to me, and this was so remarkable that I put it on record, because if it was prophetic its significance

The Candle of Vision: The Architecture of Dream 127

may become apparent later on. I was meditating about twenty-one years ago in a little room, and my meditation was suddenly broken by a series of pictures which flashed before me with the swiftness of moving pictures in a theatre. They had no relation I could discover to the subject of my meditation, and were interpolated into it then perhaps, because in a tense state of concentration when the brain becomes luminous it is easier to bring to consciousness what has to be brought.[160] I was at the time much more interested in the politics of eternity than in the politics of my own country, and would not have missed an hour of my passionate meditation on the spirit to have witnessed the most dramatic spectacle in any of our national movements. In this meditation I was brought to a wooded valley beyond which was a mountain, and between heaven and earth over the valley was a vast figure aureoled with light, and it descended from that circle of light and assumed human shape, and stood before me and looked at me. The face of this figure was broad and noble in type, beardless and dark-haired. It was in its breadth akin to the face of the young Napoleon, and I would refer both to a common archetype. This being looked at me and vanished, and was instantly replaced by another vision, and this second vision was of a woman with a blue cloak around her shoulders, who came into a room and lifted a young child upon her lap, and from all Ireland rays of light converged on that child. Then this disappeared and was on the instant followed by another picture in the series; and here I was brought from Ireland to look on the coronation throne at Westminster, and there sat on it a figure of empire which grew weary and let fall the sceptre from its fingers, and itself then drooped and fell and disappeared from the famous seat. And after that in swift succession came another scene, and a gigantic figure, wild and distraught, beating a drum, stalked up and down, and wherever its feet fell there were sparks and the swirling of flame and black smoke upwards as from burning cities. It was like the Red Swineherd of legend which beat men into an insane frenzy; and when that distraught figure vanished I saw the whole of Ireland lit up from mountain to sea, spreading its rays to the heavens as in the vision which Brigid the seeress saw and told to Patrick. All I could make of that sequence was that some child of destiny, around whom the future of Ireland was to pivot, was born then or to be born, and that it was to be an avatar[161] was symbolized by the descent of the first figure from the sky, and that before that high destiny was to be accomplished the power of empire was to be weakened, and there was to be one more tragic episode in Irish history. Whether this is truth or fantasy time alone can tell. No drums that have since beaten in this land seem to me to be mad enough to be foretold of in that wild drumming. What can I say of such a vision but that it impressed me to forgetfulness of analysis, for what it said was more important than any philosophy of its manner. I have tried to reason over it with myself, as I would with a sequence of another character, to deduce from a sequence better than could be done from a single vision, valid reasons for believing that there must be a conscious intellect somewhere behind the sequence. But I cannot reason over it. I only know that I look everywhere in the face of youth, in the aspect of every new notability, hoping before I die to recognise the broad-browed avatar of my vision.

HAVE IMAGINATIONS BODY?

In the literature of science I read of marvellously delicate instruments devised to make clear to the intellect the mode of operation of forces invisible to the eye, how Alpha rays, Gamma rays, or the vibrations in metal or plant are measured, and I sigh for some device to aid the intellect in solving difficult problems of psychology. I ask myself how may I ascertain with a precision of knowledge which would convince others whether the figures of vision, imagination or dream are two or three dimensional. The figures cast on the screen in a theatre are on the flat, but have all the illusion of motion, distance, shadow, light and form. The figures of human memory I am content to accept as being in two dimensions. They are imprinted by waves of light on the retina, and cast upon some screen in the brain. But I am forced by my own experience and that of others to believe that nature has a memory, and that it is accessible to us. But this memory cannot be recorded as ours through bodily organs of sight or hearing, nor can imagination make clear to me how any medium could exist in nature which would reflect upon itself as a mirror reflects, or as human vision reflects, an impression intelligible to us of what is passing.[162] If there were such a medium, acting as a mirror to nature or life, and retaining the impression, it must be universal as the supposed aether of the scientist; and how could impressions on this medium intelligible to us be focussed as the vibrations of light are through the needle-point of the eye to record a single view-point? In our visions of the memory of nature we see undistorted figures. If we could imagine the whole body to be sensitive to light, as is that single point in the brain on which the optic nerves converge, what kind of vision would we have? The earth under foot, objects right, left, above and below, would all clamour in various monstrous shapes for attention. The feet would see from one angle, the hands from another, back and front would confuse us; so I cannot imagine the recording power in nature as reflecting like a mirror, and retaining and recording the impressions. But we have another mode of memory in ourselves which might suggest the mode of memory in nature, that by which our subjective life is recorded. Mood, thought, passion, ecstasy, all are preserved for us, can be summoned up and re-created. How is this memory maintained? Are we continuously casting off by way of emanation an image of ourselves instant by instant, infinitesimally delicate but yet complete?[163] Is every motion of mind and body preserved so that a complete facsimile, an effigy in three dimensions, exists of every moment in our being.[164] Is the memory of nature like that? Is it by a continuous emanation of itself it preserves for itself its own history? Does this hypothesis lay too heavy a burden on the substance of the universe as we know it? I do not like to use arguments the validity of which I am not myself able to establish. But I might recall that an eminent thinker in science, Balfour Stewart, supposed of the aether[165] that there was a continual transference of energy to it from the visible universe, and that this stored-up energy might form the basis of an immortal memory for man and nature.[166] The conception did not lay too heavy a burden on matter as he imagined it. But what is matter? Is it not pregnant every atom of it with the infinite?[167] Even in visible nature does not every minutest point of space reflect as a microcosm the macrocosm of earth and heaven?[168] This minute point of space occupied by my eye as I stand on the mountain has poured into it endless vistas of manifolded mountains, vales, woods, cities, glittering seas, clouds and an infinite blueness. Wherever I move, whether by rays or waves of light, from the farthest star to the nearest leaf with its complexity of vein and tint, there comes to that pin-point of space, the eye, a multitudinous vision. If every pin-point of external space is dense yet not blind with immensity, what more miracle of subtlety, of ethereal delicacy, could be affirmed of matter and be denied because it strains belief? In that acorn which lies at my feet there is a tiny cell which has in it a memory of the oak from the beginning of earth, and a power coiled in it which can beget from itself the full majestic being of the oak.[169] From that tiny fountain by some miracle can spring another cell, and cell after cell will be born, will go on dividing, begetting, building up from each other unnumbered myriads of cells, all controlled by some mysterious power latent in the first,[170] so that in an hundred years they will, obeying the plan of the tiny architect, have built up 'the green-robed senators of mighty woods.'[171] There is nothing incredible in the assumption that every cell in the body is wrapped about with myriad memories.[172] He who attributes least mystery to matter is furthest from truth, and he nighest who conjectures the Absolute to be present in fullness of being in the atom. If I am reproached for the

The Candle of Vision: Have Imaginations Body? 131

supposition that the soul of earth preserves memory of itself by casting off instant by instant enduring images of its multitudinous life, I am only saying of nature in its fullness what visible nature is doing in its own fashion without cessation. What problem of mind, vision, imagination or dream do I solve by this hypothesis? I have been perplexed as an artist by the obedience of the figures of imagination to suggestion from myself. Let me illustrate my perplexity. I imagine a group of white-robed Arabs standing on a sandy hillock and they seem of such a noble dignity that I desire to paint them. With a restlessness akin to that which makes a portrait-painter arrange and rearrange his sitter, until he gets the pose which satisfies him, I say to myself, 'I wish they would raise their arms above their heads,' and at the suggestion all the figures in my vision raise their hands as if in salutation of the dawn. I see other figures in imagination which attract me as compositions. There may be a figure sitting down and I think it would compose better if it was turned in another direction, and that figure will obey my suggestion, not always, but at times it will; and again and again when I who paint almost entirely from what is called imagination, and who never use models, watch a figure in my vision it will change its motions as I will it. Now this is to me amazing. The invention and actual drawing of the intricate pattern of light and shade involved by the lifting of the hands of my imaginary Arabs would be considerable. My brain does not by any swift action foresee in detail the pictorial consequences involved by the lifting of arms, but yet by a single wish, a simple mental suggestion, the intricate changes are made in the figures of imagination as they would be if real Arabs stood before me and raised their hands at my call. If I ask a crowd of people to whom I speak to change their position so that they may the better hear me I am not astonished at the infinite complexity of the change I bring about, because I realize that the will in each one has mastery over the form by some miracle, and the message runs along nerve and muscle, and the simple wish brings about the complex change. But how do I lay hold of the figures in dream or imagination? By what miracle does the simple wish bring about the complex changes? It may now be seen why I asked for some means by which I might ascertain whether the forms in dream or imagination are two or three dimensional. If they are on the flat, if they are human memories merely, vibrations of stored-up sunlight fixed in some way in the brain as a photograph is fixed, the alteration of these by a simple wish involves incredibilities. I find Freud, referring to a dream he had, saying carelessly that it was made up by a combination of memories, but yet the architecture of the dream seemed to

The Descent of the Gods

be coherent and not a patchwork. It had motion of its own. Wonderful, indeed, that the wonder of what was written about so easily was not seen! How could we imagine even the mightiest conscious artistic intelligence, with seership into all the memories of a life, taking the vibrations which constituted this hand, and adjusting them to the vibrations which made that other arm, or even taking the vibrations which registered a complete figure and amending these so that the figure moved with different gestures from the first gestures recorded as memory? If such a picture was made up even from life-size images it would be a patchwork and the patches would show everywhere. But the dream figure or the figure of imagination will walk about with authentic motions and undistorted anatomies. Does not the effort to imagine such recombinations even by the mightiest conscious intellect involve incredibilities? At least it is so with the artist who watches form with a critical eye. How much greater the incredibility if we suppose there was no conscious artist, but that all this authentic imagery of imagination or dream came together without an intelligence to guide it? But how do we better matters if we assume that the figures in dream or imagination are three dimensional, and that they have actual body and organization however ethereal, delicate or subtle? If they are shadows or effigies emanated from living organisms, and are complete in their phantasmal nature within and without it is possible to imagine life laying hold of them. It is conceivable that the will may direct their motions even as at a word of command soldiers will turn and march. That is why I suggest that the memory of nature may be by way of emanation or shadow of life and form, and why when we see such images they are not the monstrous complexities they would be if they were reflections on some universal aether spread everywhere taking colour from everything at every possible angle and remaining two dimensional. The hypothesis that everything in nature, every living being, is a continuous fountain of phantasmal effigies of itself would explain the way in which ruins build up their antique life to the eye of the seer, so that he sees the people of a thousand years ago in their cities which are now desolate, and the dark-skinned merchants unrolling their bales in the market, and this is why they appear as some one has said, 'thinking the thought and performing the deed.' If we have access to such memories, and if they have organism within as well as without, can we not imagine will or desire of ours constraining them? Can we not imagine such forms swept into the vortex of a dreaming soul swayed by the sea of passion in which they exist and acting according to suggestion? And if we suppose that a deeper being of ours has wider vision than the waking conscious-

The Candle of Vision: Have Imaginations Body? 133

ness, and can use the memories, not only of this plane of being, but of the forms peculiar to mid-world and heaven-world,[173] this might help to solve some of the perplexities aroused in those who are intent and vigilant observers of their own dreams and imaginations. Continually in my analysis of the figures I see I am forced to follow them beyond the transitory life I know and to speculate upon the being of the Ever Living. I think there is no half-way house between the spiritual and the material where the intellect can dwell; and if we find we have our being in a universal life we must alter our values,[174] change all our ideas until they depend upon and are in harmony with that sole cause of all that is.

INTUITION

That sense of a divinity ever present in act or thought my words do not communicate. The ecstatic, half-articulate, with broken words, can make us feel the kingdom of heaven is within him.[175] I choose words with reverence but speak from recollection, and one day does not utter to another its own wisdom. Our highest moments in life are often those of which we hold thereafter the vaguest memories. We may have a momentary illumination yet retain almost as little of its reality as ocean keeps the track of a great vessel which went over its waters. I remember incidents rather than moods, vision more than ecstasy. How can I now, passed away from myself and long at other labours, speak of what I felt in those years when thought was turned to the spirit, and no duty had as yet constrained me to equal outward effort? I came to feel akin to those ancestors of the Aryan[176] in remote spiritual dawns when Earth first extended its consciousness into humanity. In that primal ecstasy and golden age was born that grand spiritual tradition which still remains embodied in Veda[177] and Upanishad, in Persian and Egyptian myth, and which trails glimmering with colour and romance over our own Celtic legends. I had but a faint glow of that which to the ancestors was full light. I could not enter that Radiance they entered yet Earth seemed to me bathed in an aether of Deity. I felt at times as one raised from the dead,[178] made virginal and pure, who renews exquisite intimacies with the divine companions, with Earth, Water, Air and Fire.[179] To breathe was to inhale magical elixirs. To touch Earth was to feel the influx of power as with one who had touched the mantle of the Lord.[180] Thought, from whatever it set out, for ever led to the heavenly city. But these feelings are inommunicable. We have no words to express a thousand distinctions clear to the spiritual sense. If I tell of my exaltation to another, who has not felt this himself, it is explicable to that person as the joy in perfect health, and he translates into lower terms what is the speech of the gods to men.[181]

I began writing desirous to picture things definitely to the intellect and to speak only of that over which there could be reason and

The Candle of Vision: Intuition 135

argument, but I have often been indefinite as when I said in an earlier chapter that earth seemed an utterance of gods,[182] 'Every flower was a thought. The trees were speech. The grass was speech. The winds were speech. The waters were speech.' But what does that convey? Many feel ecstasy at the sight of beautiful natural objects, and it might be said it does not interpret emotion precisely to make a facile reference to a divine world. I believe of nature that it is a manifestation of Deity, and that, because we are partakers in the divine nature, all we see has affinity with us; and though now we are as children who look upon letters before they have learned to read, to the illuminated spirit its own being is clearly manifested in the universe even as I recognize my thought in the words I write. Everything in nature has intellectual significance, and relation as utterance to the Thought out of which the universe was born,[183] and we, whose minds were made in its image, who are the microcosm of the macrocosm, have in ourselves the key to unlock the meaning of that utterance. Because of these affinities the spirit swiftly by intuition can interpret nature to itself even as our humanity instinctively comprehends the character betrayed by the curve of lips or the mood which lurks within haunting eyes. We react in numberless ways to that myriad nature about us and within us, but we retain for ourselves the secret of our response, and for lack of words speak to others of these things only in generalities. I desire to be precise, and having searched memory for some instance of that divine speech made intelligible to myself which I could translate into words which might make it intelligible to others, I recollected something which may at least be understood if not accepted. It was the alphabet of the language of the gods.[184]

This was a definite exercise of intuition undertaken in order to evolve intellectual order out of a chaos of impressions and to discover the innate affinities of sound with idea, element, force, colour and form.[185] I found as the inner being developed it used a symbolism of its own. Sounds, forms and colours, which had an established significance in the complicated artifice of our external intercourse with each other, took on new meanings in the spirit as if it spoke a language of its own[186] and wished to impart it to the infant Psyche.[187] If these new meanings did not gradually reveal an intellectual character, to pursue this meditation, to encourage the association of new ideas with old symbols would be to encourage madness. Indeed the partial uprising of such ideas, the fact that a person associates a vowel with certain colour[188] or a colour with a definite emotion is regarded by some as indicating incomplete sanity. I tried to light the candle on my forehead[189] to peer into every darkness in the belief that the external universe of nature had no more exquisite architecture than the internal universe of being, and that the light could only reveal some lordlier chambers of the soul, and whatever speech the inhabitant used must be fitting for its own sphere, so I became a pupil of the spirit and tried as a child to learn the alphabet at the knees of the gods.[190]

I was led first to brood upon the elements of human speech by that whisper of the word 'Aeon' out of the darkness, for among the many thoughts I had at the time came the thought that speech may originally have been intuitive.[191] I discarded the idea with regard to that word, but the general speculation remained with me, and I recurred to it again and again, and began brooding upon the significance of separate letters, and had related many letters to abstractions or elements,[192] when once again, seemingly by chance, I took down a book from a shelf. It was a volume of the Upanishads, and it opened at a page where my eye caught this: 'From that Self came the air, from air fire, from fire water, from water earth.' I quote from a distant memory but the words are, I think, close enough. What excited me was that I had already discovered what I thought were the sound equivalents for the self, motion, fire, water and earth; and the order of the cosmic evolution of the elements suggested in the passage quoted led me to consider whether there was any intellectual sequence in the human sound equivalents of elements and ideas. I then began to rearrange the roots of speech in their natural order from throat sounds, through dental to labials,[193] from A which begins to be recognizable in the throat to M in the utterance of which the lips are closed. An intellectual sequence of ideas became apparent. This encouraged me to try and complete the correspondences arrived at intuitively. I was never able to do this. Several sounds failed, however I brooded upon them, to suggest their intellectual affinities, and I can only detail my partial discoveries and indicate where harmonies may be found between my own intuitions about language and the roots of speech and in what primitive literature are intuitions akin to my own.

In trying to arrive at the affinities of sound with thought I took letter after letter, brooding upon them, murmuring them again and again, and watching intensely every sensation in consciousness, every colour, form or idea which seemed evoked by the utterance. No doubt the sanity of the boy who walked about the roads at night more than thirty years ago murmuring letters to himself with the reverence of a mystic murmuring the Ineffable Name[194] might have been questioned by any one who knew that he was trying to put himself in the place of his Aryan ancestors, and to find as they might

The Candle of Vision: Intuition 137

have found the original names for earth, air, water, fire, the forces and elements of the nature which was all about them. Even as in the myth in Genesis beings were named by the earliest man,[195] so I invited the Heavenly Man[196] to renew for me that first speech, and to name the elements as they were by those who looked up at the sky, and cried out the name of the fire in the sky from a God-given intuition.[197]

THE LANGUAGE OF THE GODS

If I interpreted rightly that dweller in the mind, the true roots of human speech are vowels and consonants, each with affinity to idea, force, colour and form, the veriest abstractions of these, but by their union into words expressing more complex notions, as atoms and molecules by their union form the components of the chemist.[198] It is difficult to discover single words of abstract significance to represent adequately the ideas associated with these rudiments of speech. Every root is charged with significance,[199] being the symbol of a force which is itself the fountain of many energies, even as primordial being when manifested rolls itself out into numberless forms, states of energy and consciousness. The roots of human speech are the sound correspondences of powers which in their combination and interaction make up the universe.[200] The mind of man is made in the image of Deity, and the elements of speech are related to the powers in his mind and through it to the being of the Oversoul.[201]

These true roots of language are few, alphabet and roots being identical. The first root is A,[203] the sound symbol for the self in man and Deity in the cosmos. Its form equivalent is the circle ○.[203] The second root is R, representing motion. Its colour correspondence is red, and its form symbol is the line .

Motion engenders heat,[204] and the third root following the order from throat sounds to labials is H, the sound correspondence of Heat. Its symbol is the triangle Δ, and it has affinity with the colour orange.

Motion and heat are the begetters of Fire, the sound equivalent of which is the root L, which in form is symbolized by lines radiating from a point as in this figure λ. L is fire, light or radiation, and it is followed in the series of roots by Y which symbolizes the reaction in nature against that radiation of energy. It is the sound equivalent of binding, concentration or condensation. Matter in the cosmos is obeying the law of gravitation and gathering into fire-mists preliminary to its knotting into suns and planets.[205] The colour affinity is yellow. In man it is will which focuses energy and concentrates it to a

The Candle of Vision: The Language of the Gods 139

burning-point for the accomplishing of desire. Its form symbol is ᘐ [206] representing a vortex or spiral movement inward,[207] opposing in this the expansion or radiation implied in the root L.

The root which follows Y is W, the sound symbol of liquidity or water. Its form is semilunar, ᴗ, and I think its colour is green.

We have now descended to earth and with this descent comes dualism,[208] and henceforth all the roots have companion roots. Primordial substance has lost its ethereal character and has settled into a solid or static condition. The two roots which express this are G and K; G is the symbol of earth, as K is of mineral, rock, crystal or hardness of any kind. I could discover with no certainty any colour affinities for either of these roots, and about the forms I am also uncertain though I was moved to relate G with the square □ and K with the square crossed by a diagonal ⟁.

The twin roots next in the series are S and Z, and I can find no better words to indicate the significance of the first than impregnation, inbreathing or insouling. We have reached in evolution the stage when the one life breaks into myriads of lives, which on earth finds its correspondence in the genesis of the cell. Z represents the multiplication, division or begetting of organism from organism. It is the out-breathing or bringing to birth of the seed which is sown. The form symbol of S is, I think, O, and of Z ⊕. I discovered no colour affinities for either.

The duality of roots succeeding this is TH and SH. The first is the sound equivalent of growth, expansion or swelling,[209] and its twin root represents that state where the limit of growth in a particular form is reached[210] and a scattering or dissolution of its elements takes place. In the vegetable world we might find an illustration in the growth and decay of a plant.

After these twain come the duality of T and D. I found great difficulty in discovering words to express the abstractions related to these. Yet in meditating on them with reference to the T, I was continually haunted by the idea of individual action, movement or initiative, and I believe it refers to that state when life divorced from its old interior unity with the source of life, and, confined in a form, begins in its imagination of itself to be an ego, is in a state of outgoing, acts and looks outward, touches and tastes,[211] while D represents the reverse side of that, its reaction or absorption inward to silence, sleep, immobility, abeyance. The form symbol T is + and ⌒ vaguely suggested itself to me as the symbol of D.

There is a parallelism between T and TH as there is between D and SH,T representing movement of the thing by itself while TH represents growth or expansion merely, while D represents the more subjective sinking of a thing into abeyance of its powers as SH represents the external resolving of an organism into its elements.

For the dualism of roots J and TCH my intuition failed utterly to discover correlations, and when I had placed the roots in their correct sequence and endeavoured by intellect and reason to arrive at the logical significance these two might have in the series of sounds, I could never satisfy myself that I had come nigh to any true affinity, so I pass these by.

The roots which follow are V and F, of which the first refers to life in water, to all that swims, while F is related to what lives in air and flies. I am doubtful about the form symbols, but colour affinities began here again, and blue suggested itself to me as the correspondence,[212] while the twin roots which come after them, P and B, are related to indigo, the dark blue.

Life has now reached the human stage, is divided into sexes, and P is the sound symbol for life masculine or paternity, while B represents feminine life or maternity.

The series closes with N and M.[213] The first of these represents continuance of being, immortality if you will, while the last root, in the utterance of which the lips are closed, has the sense of finality, it is the close, limit, measure, end or death of things. Their colour affinities are with violet. In all there are twenty-one consonants which with the vowels make up the divine roots of speech.

The vowels are the sound symbols of consciousness in seven moods or states,[214] while the consonants represent states of matter and modes of energy.

I despair of any attempt to differentiate from each other the seven states of consciousness represented by the vowels. How shall I make clear the difference between A where consciousness in man or cosmos begins manifestation, utterance or limitation of itself, and OO[215] where consciousness is returning into itself, breaking from the limitation of form and becoming limitless once more; or E when it has become passional, or I where it has become egoistic, actively intellectual or reasoning, or O where it has become intuitional. Our psychology gives me no names for these states, but the vowel root always represents consciousness, and, in its union with the consonant root, modifies or defines its significance, doing that again as it precedes or follows it. I once held more completely than I do now an interior apprehension of the significance of all, and I might perhaps, if I had concentrated more intently, have completed more fully the correspondences with idea, colour and form. But life attracts us in too many ways, and when I was young and most sensitive and intuitional I did not realise the importance of what I was attempting to do.

The Candle of Vision: The Language of the Gods 141

This so far as I know is the only considered effort made by any one to ascertain the value of intuition as a faculty by using it in reference to matters where the intellect was useless but where the results attained by intuition could be judged by the reason. Intuition is a faculty of which many speak with veneration, but it seems rarely to be evoked consciously,[216] and, if it is witness to a knower in man,[217] it surely needs testing and use like any other faculty. I have exercised intuition with respect to many other matters and with inward conviction of the certainty of truth arrived at in this way, but they were matters relating to consciousness and were not by their nature easily subject to ratification by the reason. These intuitions in respect of language are to some extent capable of being reasoned or argued over, and I submit them for consideration by others whose study of the literature, learning and language of the ancients may give them special authority.

ANCIENT INTUITIONS

Even where I had a certitude that my attribution of element, form or colour to a root was right I have never thought this exhausted the range of its affinities in our manifold being. I went but a little way within myself, but felt that greater powers awaited discovery within us, powers whose shadowy skirts flicker on the surface of consciousness but with motion so impalpable that we leave them nameless.[218] The root I relate to light may have correspondence also with another power which is to the dark divinity of being what light is to the visible world. I have never thought that the languages spoken by men had all their origin in one intuitional speech. There may have been many beginnings in that undiscoverable antiquity. But I believe that one, or perhaps several, among the early races, more spiritual than the rest, was prompted by intuition, while others may have developed speech in any of the ways suggested by biologists and scholars. The genius of some races leads them to seek for light within as the genius of others leads them to go outward.[219] I imagine a group of the ancestors lit up from within, endowed with the primal blessings of youth and ecstasy,[220] the strings of their being not frayed as ours are, nor their God-endowed faculties abused, still exquisitely sensitive, feeling those kinships and affinities with the elements which are revealed in the sacred literature of the Aryan, and naming these affinities from an impulse springing up within. I can imagine the spirit struggling outwards making of element, colour, form or sound a mirror, on which, outside itself, it would find symbols of all that was pent within itself, and so gradually becoming self-conscious in the material nature in which it was embodied, but which was still effigy or shadow of a divine original.[221] I can imagine them looking up at the fire in the sky, and calling out 'El' if it was the light they adored, or if they rejoiced in the heat and light together they would name it 'Hel'. Or if they saw death, and felt it as the stillness or ending of motion or breath, they would say 'Mor.'[222] Or if the fire acting on the water made it boil, they would instinctively combine the sound equivalents of water and fire, and 'Wal' would be the

The Candle of Vision: Ancient Intuitions 143

symbol. If the fire of life was kindled in the body to generate its kind, the sound symbol would be 'Lub.' When the axe was used to cut, its hardness would prompt the use of the hard or metallic affinity in sound, and 'Ak' would be to cut or pierce. One extension of meaning after another would rapidly increase the wealth of significance, and recombinations of roots the power of expression. The root 'M' with its sense of finality would suggest 'Mi' to diminish, and as to measure a thing is to go to its ends, 'Ma'[223] would also mean to measure, and as to think a thing is to measure it, 'Ma'[224] would also come to be associated with thinking. I had nearly all my correspondences vividly in mind before I inquired of friends more learned than myself what were the reputed origins of human speech, and in what books I could find whatever knowledge there was, and then I came upon the Aryan roots; and there I thought and still think are to be found many evidences in corroboration of my intuitions. There are pitfalls for one who has no pretensions to scholarship in tracking words to their origins, and it is a labour for the future in conjunction with one more learned than myself to elucidate these intuitions in regard to the roots, and to go more fully into the psychology which led to rapid extension of meanings until words were created, which at first sight seem to have no relation to the root values. I still believe I can see in the Aryan roots an intelligence struggling outward from itself to recognize its own affinities in sound. But I wish here only to give indications and directions of approach to that Divine Mind whose signature is upon us in everything,[225] and whose whole majesty is present in the least thing in nature. I have written enough to enable those who are curious to exercise their intuitions or analytic faculty in conjunction with their scholarship, to test the worth of my intuitions. Intuition must be used in these correspondences, for the art of using them is not altogether discoverable by the intellect.[226] I hope also that my partial illumination will be completed, corrected or verified by others.

A second line of investigation I suggest is the study of some harmony of primitive alphabets, such as that compiled by Forster, and, after arranging the letters in their natural order from throat sounds of labials,[227] to see if there is not much to lead us to suppose that there was an original alphabet, where the form equivalents of sound proceeded in an orderly way from the circle through the line, the triangle and the other forms I have indicated. Perhaps the true correspondences were retained as an esoteric secret by the wisest, because there may have been in them the key to mysteries only to be entrusted to those many times tested before the secret of the use of power was disclosed.[228] And again I would suggest a study of that science of divine correspondences which is embodied in mystical Indian literature. The correspondences of form, colour or force with letters given there are not always in agreement with my own. Sometimes as in the Bagavadgita where Krishna, the Self of the Manifested Universe, says, 'I am the A among letters,'[229] I find agreement. In other works like the Shivagama there is partial agreement as where it says, 'Meditate upon the fire force with R as its symbol, as being triangular and red.' The colour and the letter are here in harmony with my own intuitions, but the form is not, and I am more inclined to believe my own intuition to be true because I find in so many of the primitive alphabets the form symbol of R is the line coming out of a circle. The water force is given in the same book a semilunar form as correspondence, but its sound symbol is given as V and not W. The earth force is given as quadrangular in form as I imagine it, but the colour is yellow. I have not investigated the consonants in their attribution to the nervous system given in such books. I have no doubt that in a remoter antiquity the roots of language were regarded as sacred, and when chanted every letter was supposed to stir into motion or evoke some subtle force in the body. Tone and word combined we know will thrill the nervous system, and this is specially so with lovers of music and persons whose virgin sensitiveness of feeling has never been blunted by excess. A word chanted or sung will start the wild fires leaping in the body, like hounds which hear their master calling them by name, and to those whose aspiration heavenward has purified their being there comes at last a moment when at the calling of the Ineffable Name the Holy Breath rises as a flame and the shadow man goes forth to become one with the ancestral self.

What is obvious in that ancient literature is the belief in a complete circle of correspondences between every root sound in the human voice and elements, forms and colours, and that the alphabet was sacred in character.[230] Intuitions which modern psychologists regard as evidence of decadence are found present in the literature of antiquity. The attributions sometimes are the same as mine; sometimes they differ, but they suggest the same theory of a harmony of microcosm with macrocosm, and it is carried out so that every centre in the body is named by the name of a divine power.[231] It is only by a spiritual science we can recover identity, renew and make conscious these affinities. Life had other labours for me from which I could not escape, and I had not for long the leisure in which to reknit the ties between myself and the ancestral being. But while I still had leisure I experienced those meltings of the external into intelligible meanings. The form of a flower long brooded upon

The Candle of Vision: Ancient Intuitions 145

would translate itself into energies,[232] and these would resolve themselves finally into states of consciousness, intelligible to me while I experienced them, but too remote from the normal for words to tell their story. I may have strayed for a moment into that Garden of the Divine Mind where, as it is said in Genesis, 'He made every flower before it was in the field and every herb before it grew.'[233] My failure to find words to express what I experienced made me concentrate more intensely upon the relation of form and colour to consciousness in the hope that analysis might make intellectual exposition possible. I do not wish to linger too long on the analysis made. The message of nature is more important than the symbols used to convey it, and, in detailing these correspondences, I feel rather as one who reading Shelley's 'Hymn of Pan' ignored all that ecstasy and spoke merely of spelling or verse structure. But why do I say that? The works of the Magician of the Beautiful[234] are not like ours and in the least fragment His artistry is no less present than in the stars. We may enter the infinite through the minute no less than through contemplation of the vast.[235] I thought in that early ecstasy of mine when I found how near to us was the King in His Beauty that I could learn to read that marvellous writing on the screen of Nature and teach it to others; and, as a child first learns its letters with difficulty, but after a time leaps to the understanding of their combination, and later, without care for letters or words, follows out the thought alone; so I thought the letters of the divine utterance might be taught and the spirit in man would leap by intuition to the thought of the Spirit making that utterance. For all that vast ambition I have not even a complete alphabet to show, much less one single illustration of how to read the letters of nature in their myriad intricacies of form, colour and sound in the world we live in. But I believe that vision has been attained by the seers, and we shall all at some time attain it, and, as is said in the Divine Shepherd of Hermes,[236] it shall meet us everywhere, plain and easy, walking or resting, waking or sleeping, 'for there is nothing which is not the image of God.'

POWER

I have spoken of a training of the will, but have not indicated the spring of power in our being, nor dilated on those moments when we feel a Titanic energy lurks within us ready to our summons as the familiar spirit to the call of the enchanter. If we have not power we are nothing and must remain outcasts of the Heavens.[237] We must be perfect as the Father is perfect.[238] If in the being of the Ancient of Days[239] there is power, as there is wisdom and beauty, we must liken ourselves to that being, partake, as our nature will permit, of its power, or we can never enter it. The Kingdom is taken by violence. The easier life becomes in our civilizations, the remoter we are from nature, the more does power ebb away from most of us. It ebbs away for all but those who never relax the will but sustain it hour by hour. We even grow to dread the powerful person because we feel how phantasmal before power are beauty and wisdom, and indeed there is no true beauty or wisdom which is not allied with strength. For one who cultivates will in himself there are thousands who cultivate the intellect or follow after beauty, and that is because the intellect can walk easily on the level places, while at first every exercise of the will is laborious as the lift is to the climber of a precipice. Few are those who come to that fullness of power where the will becomes a fountain within them perpetually springing up self-fed,[240] and who feel like the mountain lovers who know that it is easier to tread on the hilltops than to walk on the low and level roads. Because in our ordered life power is continually ebbing away from us, nature, which abhors a vacuum in our being, is perpetually breaking up our civilizations by wars or internal conflicts, so that stripped of our ease, in battle, through struggle and sacrifice, we may grow into power again; and this must continue until we tread the royal road,[241] and cultivate power in our being as we cultivate beauty or intellect. Those who have in themselves the highest power, who are miracle-workers, the Buddhas and the Christs,[242] are also the teachers of peace, and they may well be so having themselves attained mastery of the Fire.[243]

The Candle of Vision: Power

It is because it is so laborious to cultivate the will we find in literature endless analysis of passion and thought, but rarely do we find one writing as if he felt the powers leaping up in his body as the thronged thoughts leap up in the brain. I was never able to recognize that harmony of powers spoken of by the ancients as inhabiting the house of the body, lurking in nerve-centre or plexus, or distinguish their functions, but I began to feel, after long efforts at concentration and mastery of the will, the beginning of an awakening of the fires,[244] and at times there came partial perception of the relation of these forces to centres in the psychic body. I could feel them in myself; and sometimes see them, or the vibration or light of them, about others who were seekers with myself for this knowledge; so that the body of a powerful person would appear to be throwing out light in radiation from head or heart, or plumes of fire would rise above the head jetting from fountains within,[245] apparitions like wings of fire, plumes or feathers of flame, or dragon-like crests, many-coloured. Once at the apex of intensest meditation I awoke that fire in myself of which the ancients have written, and it ran up like lightning along the spinal cord,[246] and my body rocked with the power of it, and I seemed to myself to be standing in a fountain of flame, and there were fiery pulsations as of wings about my head, and a musical sound not unlike the clashing of cymbals with every pulsation;[247] and if I had remembered the ancient wisdom I might have opened that eye[248] which searches infinitude. But I remembered only, in a half terror of the power I had awakened, the danger of misdirection of the energy, for such was the sensation of power that I seemed to myself to have opened the seal of a cosmic fountain, so I remained contemplative and was not the resolute guider of the fire.[249] And indeed this rousing of the fire is full of peril; and woe to him who awakens it before he has purified his being into selflessness, for it will turn downward and vitalize his darker passions and awaken strange frenzies and inextinguishable desires. The turning earthward of that heaven-born power is the sin against the Holy Breath,[250] for that fire which leaps upon us in the ecstasy of contemplation of Deity is the Holy Breath, the power which can carry us from Earth to Heaven. It is normally known to man only in procreation, but its higher and mightier uses are unknown to him. Even though in our scriptures it is said of it that it gives to this man vision or the discerning of spirits, and to that poetry or eloquence, and to another healing and magical powers,[251] it remains for most a myth of the theologians, and is not mentioned by any of our psychologists though it is the fountain out of which is born all other powers in the body and is the sustainer of all our faculties. Normally I found this power in myself, not leaping up Titanically as if it would storm the heavens, but a steady light in the brain, 'the candle upon the forehead,'[252] and it was revealed in ecstasy of thought or power in speech, and in a continuous welling up from within myself of intellectual energy, vision or imagination. It is the afflatus of the poet or musician. As an ancient scripture says of it, 'The Illuminator is the inspirer of the poet, the jeweller, the chiseller and all who work in the arts.' It is the Promethean fire,[253] and only by mastery of this power will man be able to ascend to the ancestral Paradise. Again and again I would warn all who read of the danger of awakening it, and again and again I would say that without this power we are as nothing. We shall never scale the Heavens, and religions, be they ever so holy, will never open the gates to us, unless we are able mightily to open them for ourselves and enter as the strong spirit who cannot be denied. This power might cry of itself to us:

> My kinsmen are they, beauty, wisdom, love;
> But without me are none may dare to climb
> To the Ancestral Light that glows above
>   Its mirrored lights in Time.
>
> King have I been and foe in ages past.
> None may escape me. I am foe until
> There shall be for the spirit forged at last
>   The high unshakable will.
>
> Fear, I will rend you. Love, I make you strong.
> Wed with my might the beautiful and wise.
> We shall go forth at last, a Titan throng,
>   To storm His Paradise.

THE MEMORY OF THE SPIRIT

Hy Brazil, Ildathach, the lands of Immortal Youth which flush with magic the dreams of childhood, for most sink soon below far horizons and do not again arise. For around childhood gather the wizards of the darkness and they baptize it and change its imagination of itself as in the Arabian tales of enchantment men were changed by sorcerers who cried, 'Be thou beast or bird.' So by the black art of education[254] is the imagination of life about itself changed, and one will think he is a worm in the sight of Heaven, he who is but a god in exile, and another of the Children of the King[255] will believe that he is the offspring of animals. What palaces they were born in, what dominions they are rightly heir to, are concealed from them as in the fairy tale the stolen prince lives obscurely among the swineherds. Yet at times men do not remember, in dream and in the deeps of sleep, they still wear sceptre and diadem and partake of the banquet of the gods.[256] The gods are still living. They are our brothers. They await us. They beckon us to come up to them and sit upon equal thrones. To those who cry out against romance I would say, You yourself are romance. You are the lost prince herding obscurely among the swine.[257] The romance of your spirit is the most marvellous of stories. Your wanderings have been greater than those of Ulysses.[258] You have been Bird of Paradise and free of immensity, and you have been outcast and wingless, huddled under the rocks and despairing of the Heavens. If you will but awaken the inner sight, Hy Brazil, Ildathach, all the lands of Immortal Youth will build themselves up anew for you no longer as fantasy but in vivid actuality. Earth will become magical and sweet as ever. You will be drunken with beauty. You may see the fiery eyes of the Cyclops wandering over the mountains and hear the Bell Branch shaken, the sound that summons the spirit home. From long pondering I have come to believe in the eternity of the spirit and that it is an inhabitant of many spheres, for I know not how otherwise I can interpret to myself the myriad images that as memories or imaginations cling to it, following it into the body as birds follow the leader in the migratory flock. Looking back on that other life which began to dominate this there are a thousand things I cannot understand except I believe that for myself and for all of us there has been an eternity of being and that many spheres are open to us. If these images are not earth-born, from what land, Elfland, Heaven-world or God-world, do they come? I have chosen but a few images out of many to explain why I think our dreams and visions come often in all completeness into our sphere out of other spheres of being and are not built up from memories of earth. Looking back upon that other life through the vistas of memory I see breaking in upon the images of this world forms of I know not what antiquity. I walk out of strange cities steeped in the jewel glow and gloom of evening, or sail in galleys over the silvery waves of the antique ocean. I reside in tents, or in palace chambers, go abroad in chariots, meditate in cyclopean buildings, am worshipper of the Earth gods upon the mountains, lie tranced in Egyptian crypts, or brush with naked body through the long sunlit grasses of the prairies. Endlessly the procession of varying forms goes back into remote yesterdays of the world. How do these self-conceptions spring up? How are they clothed with the state of ancient civilizations? If when I perceived them they were the newest things in the world, and the images were minted that instant by the imagination, out of what treasury of design came the fitting scenery, the always varied buildings, garments and setting of wood, plain or mountain? Are they not rather, I ask myself, memories of the spirit incarnated many times? And if so, again I ask myself is it only on earth there has been this long ancestry of self?[259] For there is another self in me which seemed to know not the world but revealed itself to the listening bodily life in cosmic myths, in remote legends of the Children of Darkness and the Children of Light,[260] and of the revolt against heaven. And another self seemed to bring with it vision or memory of elemental beings, the shining creatures of water and wood,[261] or who break out in opalescent colour from the rocks or hold their court beneath the ponderous hills. And there was another self which was akin to the gloomy world of the shades,[262] but recoiled shuddering from them. And there was yet another self which sought out after wisdom, and all these other selves and their wisdom and memories were but tributary to it.[263] The gates of sleep too were often thronged with fleeting presences as I sank into unconsciousness, or was outcast from that innermost being when waking, and I saw but for an instant back into the profundity, and at times it appeared to the imagination as the gate of Eden:

The Candle of Vision: The Memory of the Spirit

With dreadful faces thronged and fiery arms.

Out of what sphere came that being taller and mightier than human, whose body seemed wrought out of flame and whose eyes had the stillness of an immortal, and who seemed to gaze at me out of eternity as I waked in the night.[264] It was so lofty and above humanity that I seemed to myself to be less than an insect, though something in me cried out to it in brotherhood, and I knew not whether I had fallen from its height, or was a lost comrade lagging far behind in time who should have been equal and companion but was too feeble to rise to such majesty. I know that I have not been alone in such imaginations for there are few whose intent will has tried to scale the Heavens who have not been met by messages from the gods who are the fountains of this shadowy beauty, and who are, I think, ourselves beyond this mirage of time and space by which we are enchanted. I have spoken to others, seekers like myself upon this quest, and recognize identity of vision and experience. But I have not been able to devote to every mental image the thought which might make its meaning or origin intelligible. We cannot do that for the forms we see move continuously in visible nature, for we pass them by thinking intensely but of a few of them. But our psychology must take account of every experience of the soul.[265] I have not found in latter-day philosophical writers the explanation of my own experiences, and I think that is because there has been an over-development of intellect and few have cultivated vision, and without that we have not got the first data for fruitful speculation. We rarely find philosophical writers referring to vision of their own, yet we take them as guides on our mental travelling, though in this world we all would prefer to have knowledge of earth and heaven through the eyes of a child rather than to know them only through the musings of one who was blind, even though his intellect was mighty as Kant's.

It is only when I turn to the literature of vision and intuition, to the sacred books and to half sacred tradition, to the poets and seers, that I find a grandiose conception of nature in which every spiritual experience is provided for. I have not entered the paradises they entered but what little I know finds its place in the universe of their vision. Whether they are Syrian, Greek, Egyptian or Hindu, the writers of the sacred books seem to me as men who had all gazed upon the same august vision and reported of the same divinity. Even in our own Gaelic wonder tales I often find a vision which is, I think, authentic, and we can, I believe, learn from these voyages to the Heaven-world more of the geography of the spirit and the many mansions in the being of the Father than we can from the greatest of our sightless philosophers. The Earth-world, Mid-world, Heaven-world and God-world spoken of in the Indian scriptures[266] are worlds our Gaelic ancestors had also knowledge of. When Cormac enters the Heaven-world and is told by those who inhabit it, 'Whenever we imagine the fields to be sown they are sown. Whenever we imagine the fields to be reaped they are reaped,' he saw the same world as the seer who wrote in the marvellous Upanishad:[267] 'There are no chariots there or roads for chariots. The soul makes for itself chariots and roads for chariots. There are no joys or rejoicings there. The soul makes for itself joys and rejoicings. For the spirit of man is creator.' The visionaries of the future will finally justify the visionaries of the past. I do not feel that my knowledge is great enough to do this, nor have I been able to steal from a life made busy by other labours enough time or enough thought even to use in the best way the little I know. I would like to vindicate my predecessors in Ireland and correlate my own vision and the vision of my friends with the vision of those who went before us, for I think when we discard the past and its vision we are like men who, half-way up a mountain, decide foolishly to attempt the ascent from another side of the hill and so continually lose the height which was gained. Our Gaelic ancestors had the gift of seership, and I had thought at one time to reconstruct from the ancient literature the vision of the universe they had, a labour which might be done by any who had vision of his own and who was versed in the comparative study of the religions of the past, and so make intelligible to those who live here to-day the thought of their forefathers, and enable them to begin anew the meditation towards divine things so often broken up in our unhappy history. All literature tends to produce a sacred book by an evolution of thought of the highest minds building one upon another. A literature so continually imaginative, visionary and beautiful as the Gaelic would, I do not doubt, have culminated in some magnificent expression of the spirit if life had not been drawn from central depths to surfaces by continuous invasions.[268] I think that meditation is beginning anew, and the powers which were present to the ancestors are establishing again their dominion over the spirit. To some there come startling flashes of vision, and others feel a hand of power touching them thrust out from a hidden world. Whether they know it or not they are the servants of gods who speak or act through them and make them the messengers of their will. I have written down some of my own thoughts and experiences that others may be encouraged to believe that by imagination they can lay hold of truth; and as something

The Candle of Vision: The Memory of the Spirit   153

must be written about the geography of the spirit by way of guidance to those who rise within themselves in meditation I will try briefly to reconstruct the Celtic vision of Heaven and Earth as I believe it was known to the Druids and bardic seers. Let no one who requires authority read what I have written for I will give none.[269] If the spirit of the reader does not bear witness to truth he will not be convinced even though a Whitley Stokes rose up to verify the written word. Let it be accepted by others as a romantic invention or attribution of divine powers to certain names to make more coherent the confusion of Celtic myth.

CELTIC COSMOGONY

[I]*

['Not yet lost is their power to quicken, to exalt, to purify; still they live and reign, and shall reign'. – The Flight of the Eagle.

[It is a land where if you lie on the earth it must be whispering to you; and its whisper is sweeter than the promise of beloved lips. The voice we hear is not different from or less beautiful than the voice heard by the druid warriors and poets when the Danaan race were their gods and companions in ancient Ireland. We hear more feebly because we are a feebler race; not nourished like those children of the sun on heroic deeds, nor stirred by promises of an immortality of beauty; and we turn our thoughts rather to past generations, and build up again in imagination their ancient world, and do not ourselves dream of leaving the earth behind as Connla, Ossian and the mystic adventurers who found their hearts' desire in enchanted isles beyond the waters of faery. The very name of faery suggests only fable; and as for the gods they are outcast of the last philosophies of nature. Man thought it nobler to believe in only one God. It is true there is one God, whom alone we may worship; but is the nature He has made nobler in men's eyes because they have denied the divinity of His children and their invisible presence on the earth? Is life happier, more moral, or more spiritual, now that no radiant harper causes the tears of spring, or the summer's joy, or the winter's sleep by his music, because love has no longer a divine birth and is not awakened by the Birds of Angus? Does the peace in our hearts seem more assured because it rests on our own strength, which is but of an hour, and is not part of the hymn of peace entering

---

* The original article, entitled 'The Children of Lir', appeared in the 8 March 1902 issue of *The United Irishman*. It contained an extra section at the beginning which is given here in square brackets. A short passage at its end also appears at the end of 'The Memory of the Spirit'.

The Candle of Vision: Celtic Cosmogony

the heart of every victor in the eternal battle, which the queen-mother of the gods still sings, as at Moytura, soothing the troubled world?

> Peace up to Heaven;
> Heaven down to Earth;
> Earth under Heaven,
> Strength in everyone.

[It may be because Ireland is so full of memorials of an extraordinary past, but I think it is because behind the veil these things still endure, that everything seems possible here. I would feel no surprise if I saw the fiery eyes of the Cyclops wandering over the mountains, or heard the call of the Sidhe or the bell-branch shaken that summons the spirit home . . . There is always a sense expectant of some unveiling about to take place, a feeling as we roam at evening down the lanes scented by the honey-suckle that beings are looking in upon us out of the true home of man. While we pace on, isolated in our sad and proud musing, they seem to be saying of us: 'Soon they will awaken. Soon they will come to us again,' and we pause and look around, smitten through by some ancient sweetness, or memory of a pure life-dawn before passion and sin began. Sometimes, too, come startling flashes of vision, or a man may feel a hand of power touching him, thrust out from a hidden world; and his will is no longer his own, and that man is henceforth led through life as Israel of old by the awful cloudy pillar wherein was the Lord. Whether he knows it or not, he is the servant of gods who speak through him the message of their will. There are many memorable figures in our history who seem to betray, by the very blindness of a passionate adherence to a cause or an idea, that they were led by a power not their own. The end is known only to the guiding mind; though it may be there is no appointed event, but only the revelation of character through hero and reformer. The gods are not often concerned with material events. They build themselves eternal empires in the mind through beauty, wisdom, or pity: and so, reading today the story of Cuculain, we do pay reverence by the exaltation of our spirits to the great divinity, Lu the sun-god, who overshadowed the hero.

[I am mindful that these names which once acted like a spell in the secret places of the soul are now no longer powerful. They appear in poetry and romance, but do not mingle in solemn hours, or twilight reveries, or shine at the far end of dream. They do not interpret moods, but require themselves an interpreter; and here I propose, not with any idea of finality of fulness, and without pretence of scholarship, to speak of Druid Ireland, its gods and its mysteries. Let no one who requires authority read what I have written, for I will give none. If the spirit of the reader does not bear witness to truth he will not be convinced even though a Whitley Stokes rose up to verify the written word. Let it be accepted as a romantic invention, or attribution of divine powers to certain names to make more coherent to the writer the confusion of Celtic myth.]

[II]

In the beginning was the boundless Lir,[270] an infinite depth, an invisible divinity, neither dark nor light, in whom were all things past and to be. There at the close of a divine day, time being ended, and the Nuts of Knowledge harvested, the gods partake of the Feast of Age and drink from a secret fountain. Their being there is neither life nor death nor sleep nor dream, but all are wondrously wrought together. They lie in the bosom of Lir, cradled in the same peace, those who hereafter shall meet in love or war in hate. The Great Father and the Mother of the Gods mingle together and Heaven and Earth are lost, being one in the Infinite Lir.

Of Lir but little may be affirmed, and nothing can be revealed.[271] In trance alone the seer might divine beyond his ultimate version this being.[272] It is a breath with many voices which cannot speak in one tone, but utters itself through multitudes.[273] It is beyond the gods[274] and if they were to reveal it, it could only be through their own departure and a return to the primeval silences.[275] But in this is the root of existence from which spring the sacred Hazel[276] whose branches are the gods: and as the mystic night trembles into dawn, its leaves and its blossoms and its starry fruit burgeon simultaneously and are shed over the waters of space. An image of futurity has arisen in the divine imagination: and Sinan, who is also Dana, the Great Mother and Spirit of Nature, grows thirsty to receive its imprint on her bosom, and to bear again her offspring of stars and starry beings. Then the first fountain is opened and seven streams issue like seven fiery whirlwinds,[277] and Sinan is carried away and mingled with the torrent, and when the force of the torrent is broken, Sinan also meets death.

What other names Connla's Well and the Sacred Hazel have in Celtic tradition may be discovered later, but here, without reference to names, which only bewilder until their significance is made known, it is better to explain with less of symbol this Celtic Cosmogenesis.

The Cande of Vision: Celtic Cosmogony 157

We have first of all Lir, an infinite being, neither spirit nor energy nor substance, but rather the spiritual form of these,[278] in which all the divine powers, raised above themselves, exist in a mystic union or trance. This is the night of the gods[279] from which Mananan first awakens, the most spiritual divinity known to the ancient Gael, being the Gaelic equivalent of that Spirit which breathed on the face of the waters.[280] He is the root of existence from which springs the Sacred Hazel, the symbol of life ramifying everywhere: and the forms of this life are conceived first by Mananan, the divine imagination. It throws itself into seven forms or divinities,[281] the branches of the Hazel; and these again break out endlessly into leaves and blossoms and fruit, into myriads of divine beings, the archetypes and ancestral begetters of those spirits who are the Children of Lir. All these are first in the Divine Darkness and are unrevealed, and Mananan is still the unuttered Word, and is in that state the Chaldaic oracle of Proclus saith of the Divine Mind: 'It had not yet gone forth, but abode in the Paternal Depth, and in the adytum of god-nourished Silence.' But Mananan, while one in essence with the Paternal Lir, is yet, as the divine imagination, a separate being to whom, thus brooding, Lir seems apart, or covered over with a veil,[282] and this aspect of Lir, a mirage which begins to cover over true being,[283] is Dana,[284] the Hibernian Mother of the Gods, or Sinan in the antique Dinnshenchus, deity first viewed externally, and therefore seeming to partake of the nature of substance, and, as the primal form of matter, the Spirit of Nature. Mananan alone of all the gods exist in the inner side of this spirit,[285] and therefore it is called his mantle, which, flung over man or god, wraps them from the gaze of embodied beings. His mantle, the Faed Fia, has many equivalents in other mythologies. It is the Aether[286] within which Zeus runs invisibly, and the Akasa[287] through which Brahm sings his eternal utterance of joy. The mantle of Mananan, the Aether, the Akasa, were all associated with Sound as a creative power, for to the mystic imagination of the past the world was upsung into being; and what other thought inspired the apostle who wrote, 'In the beginning was the Word'?[288]

Out of the Divine Darkness Mananan has arisen, a brooding twilight before dawn,[289] in which the cloud images of the gods are thronging. But there is still in Lir an immense deep of being, an emotional life too vast, too spiritual, too remote to speak of, for the words we use to-day cannot tell its story. It is the love yet unbreathed,[290] and yet not love, but rather a hidden unutterable tenderness, or joy, or the potency of these, which awakens as the image of the divine imagination is reflected in the being of the

Mother, and then it rushes forth to embrace it. The Fountain beneath the Hazel has broken. Creation is astir. The Many are proceeding from the One. An energy or love or eternal desire has gone forth which seeks through a myriad forms of illusion[291] for the infinite being it has left. It is Angus the Young,[292] an eternal joy becoming love, a love changing into desire, and leading on to earthly passion[293] and forgetfulness of its own divinity.[294] The eternal joy becomes love when it has first merged itself in form and images of a divine beauty dance before it and lure it afar.[295] This is the first manifested world, the Tirnanoge or World of Immortal Youth. The love is changed into desire as it is drawn deeper into nature, and this desire builds up the Mid-world or World of the Waters.[296] And, lastly, as it lays hold of the earthly symbol of its desire it becomes on Earth that passion which is spiritual death.[297] In another sense Angus may be described as the passing into activity of a power latent in Lir, working through the divine imagination, impressing its ideations on nature in its spiritual state,[298] and thereby causing its myriad transformations. It is the fountain in which every energy has its birth,[299] from the power which lays the foundations of the world, down through love and every form of desire to chemical affinity, just as Mananan[300] is the root of all conscious life, from the imperial being of the gods down to the consciousness in the ant or amoeba. So is Dana[301] also the basis of every material form from the imperishable body of the immortals to the transitory husk of the gnat. As this divinity emerges from its primordial state of ecstatic tenderness or joy in Lir, its divided rays, incarnate in form, enter upon a threefold life of spiritual love, of desire, and the dark shadow of love; and these three states have for themselves three worlds into which they have transformed the primal nature of Dana: a World of Immortal Youth: a Mid-world where everything changes with desire: and which is called from its fluctuations the World of Waters: and lastly, the Earth-world where matter has assumed that solid form when it appears inanimate or dead. The force of the fountain which whirled Sinan away has been spent and Sinan has met death.

The conception of Angus as an all-pervading divinity who first connects being with non-being seems removed by many aeons of thought from that beautiful golden-haired youth who plays on the tympan surrounded by singing birds. But the golden-haired Angus of the bards has a relation to the earlier Eros, for in the mysteries of the Druids all the gods sent bright witnesses of their boundless being, who sat enthroned in the palaces of the Sidhe, and pointed

The Candle of Vision: Celtic Cosmogony

the way to the Land of Promise to the man who dared become more than man.

But what in reality is Angus and what is Dana, and how can they be made real to us? They will not be gained by much reading of the legendary tales, for they are already with us. A child sits on the grass and the sunlight falls about it. It is lulled by the soft colour. It grows dreamy, a dreaminess filled with a vague excitement. It feels a pleasure, a keen magnetic joy at the touch of earth: or it lays its head in a silent tenderness nigh a mother or sister, its mood impelling it to grow nearer to something it loves. That tenderness in the big dreamy heart of childhood is Angus, and the mother-love it divines is Dana; and the form which these all-pervading divinities take in the heart of the child and the mother, on the one side desire, on the other a profound tenderness or pity, are nearest of all the moods of earth to the first Love and the Mighty Mother, and through them the divine may be vaguely understood. If the desire remains pure, through innocence, or by reason of wisdom, it becomes in the grown being a constant preoccupation with spiritual things, or in words I have quoted before where it is better said, 'The inexpressible yearning of the inner man to go out into the infinite.'

Of Dana, the Hibernian Mother of the gods, I have already said she is the first spiritual form of matter, and therefore Beauty. As every being emerges out of her womb clothed with form, she is the Mighty Mother,[302] and as mother of all she is that divine compassion which exists beyond and is the final arbiter of the justice of the gods.[303] Her heart will be in ours when ours forgive.

THE CELTIC IMAGINATION

Other names might be used in this Celtic cosmogenesis and the Dagda stand for Lir, Boan for Dana, Fintan for Mananan, and others again might be interchangeable with these. Even as the generations follow one another in time, each looking upon the same unchanging nature as the ancestors but naming it by other names, so in antiquity races were invaded by others who came with a cosmogony the same in all essentials, but for differences of language and name, as that of the people invaded. After centuries there comes a blending of cultures and a subsidence into legend, bringing about a bewildering mosaic of mythology. The unity of primeval vision is broken up in the prism of literature.[304] Deities grow in number in the popular imagination and coexist there, who in truth, if their spiritual ancestry was known, were but varying names for one divine being.[305] There are several mythologies in Irish legend the figures of which are made contemporary with each other by the later poets, and while it might be of interest to scholars to disentangle these and relate each deity to its proper cycle, only the vision of the universe which underlay them all is of real importance. That spiritual Overworld our Gaelic ancestors beheld was in essentials the same as the Overworld revealed in the sacred books; and in the wonder tales of the Gael we find a great secular corroboration of sacred literature and of half-sacred philosophy such as Plato utters through the lips of Socrates.[306] Earth, Mid-world, Heaven-world and the great deep of deity they knew as they are expounded in the Upanishads.[307] We can discern the same vision in the Apostle whose beginning of things was in the fulness of being out of which arose the Christos or divine imagination,[308] in which, as it went forth on its cyclic labours, life or the Holy Breath was born, or became in it, and these again shine and work in the darkness of earth. And when St. Paul speaks of a third heaven we divine he had risen to the world of the Christos and was there initiated into mysteries of which it was not lawful to speak.[309] In the sacred books there is a profounder life than there is in secular literature where there is vision indeed, but in the sacred books there is the being. The mind in retrospect, meditation and aspiration needs guidance; and this spiritual architecture of Earth-world, with Mid-world, Heaven-world and God-world rising above it, made my own vision so far as it went intelligible to me, for my disconnected glimpses of supernature seemed to find a place in that architecture of the heavens.[310] In earlier pages I described my first visions of other planes, and the beings there, how some were shining and how others were a lordlier folk lit up from within as if a sun was hidden in the heart; and in my retrospect of vision I find all I saw falling into two categories which I think correspond to the Mid-world and World of Immortal Youth of the ancestors. My vision into the highest of these spheres was rare, and only once did consciousness for a moment follow vision and I seemed myself to be in the world I contemplated. At other times I was like one who cannot enter the gardens of a palace, but who gazes distantly through gates on their beauty, and sees people of a higher order than himself moving in a world enchanting to his eyes. I did see in some sphere interpenetrated with this beings in an ecstasy of radiance, colour and sound, lovers who seemed enraptured with their happiness, as they tell in old story of lovers on the plains of Moy Mell, and to me they seemed like some who had lived in Earth in ancient days and who now were in the happy world. And I saw, without being able to explain to myself their relation to that exalted humanity, beings such as the ancient poets described, a divine folk[311] who I think never were human but were those spoken of as the Sidhe. I did not see enough to enable me to speak with any certainty about their life, and I do not know that it would serve any useful purpose to detail visions which remain bewildering to myself. Into the lowest of these two spheres I saw with more frequency, but was able to understand but little of what I saw. I will tell one or two visions out of many. I was drawn to meditate beside a deep pool amid woods. It was a place charged with psychic life, and was regarded with some awe by the people who lived near. As I gazed into the dark waters[312] consciousness seemed to sink beneath them and I found myself in another world. It was more luminous than this, and I found one there who seemed like an elemental king. He was seated on a throne, and I saw that a lustrous air rose up as from a fountain beneath the seat and his breathing of it gave him power. The figure was of a brilliant blue and gold opalescence,[313] and the breast, as with many of the higher beings, was shining, and a golden light seemed to pervade the whole body and to shine through its silvery blueness. The tribe he ruled were smaller than himself, and these I saw descending on the right of the throne, their shining dimmed to a kind of greyness, and each one as it came before the throne bent forward and pressed its lips upon the heart of the king, and in an instant at the touch it became flushed with life and it shot up plumed and radiant, and there was a continuous descent on one side of grey elementals[314] and on the other side a continuous ascent of radiant figures, and I know not what it meant. And at another time I saw one of these lesser beings flying as a messenger out of the heart of one greater, and I saw a return to the heart and the vanishing of the lesser in the greater, and I know not what it meant. And at another time I was astonished, for I saw rising out of deep water seven shining and silvery figures,[315] and three on one side and three on another side and one beneath, they held uplifted hands on the hilt of a gigantic sword of quivering flame, and they waved that mighty sword in air and sank again beneath the waters. And after that seven others rose up and they held a great spear, and it they pointed skywards and sank below; and after that arose two carrying a cauldron, and, when they had vanished, one solitary figure arose and it held in its hands a great and glittering stone; and why these beautiful beings should bring forth the four precious symbols of the Tuatha de Danaan I do not know, for that Mid-world, as Usheen travelling to Tirnanoge saw, is full of strange and beautiful forms appearing and vanishing ever about the mystic adventurer, and there are to be seen many beings such as the bards told of: beings riding like Lir or Mananan upon winged steeds, or surrounded like Angus Oge with many-coloured birds, and why these images of beauty and mystery should be there I do not know, but they entered into the imagination of poets in the past and have entered into the imagination of others who are still living. I can only surmise that they were given the names of Mananan, Angus, Dana or Lir because they were mouthpieces of the bodiless deities[316] and perhaps sitting on high thrones represented these at the Druidic mysteries, and when the mortal came to be made immortal[317] they spoke to him each out of their peculiar wisdom. In myself as in others I know they awakened ecstasy. To one who lay on the mound which is called the Brugh on the Boyne a form like that the bards speak of Angus appeared, and it cried: 'Can you not see me? Can you not hear me? I come from the Land of Immortal Youth.'[318] And I, though I could not be certain of speech, found the wild words flying up to my brain interpreting my own vision of the god, and it seemed to be crying to me: 'Oh, see our sun is dawning for us, ever dawning, with ever youthful and triumphant voices. Your sun is but a smoky shadow: ours the ruddy and eternal glow.[319] Your fire is far away, but ours within our hearts is ever living[320] and through wood

The Candle of Vision: The Celtic Imagination 163

and wave is ever dawning on adoring eyes. My birds from purple fiery plumage shed the light of lights. Their kisses wake the love that never dies and leads through death to me. My love shall be in thine when love is sacrifice.' I do not believe that either to myself or my friend were such words spoken, but the whole being is lifted up in vision and overmastered, and the words that came flying upward in consciousness perhaps represent our sudden harmony with a life which is beyond ourselves, we in our words interpreting the life of the spirit. Some interpret the spirit with sadness and some with joy, but in this country I think it will always cry out its wild and wondrous story of immortal youth and will lead its votaries to a heaven where they will be drunken with beauty. What is all this? Poetry or fantasy? It has visited thousands in all ages and lands, and from such visions have come all that is most beautiful in poetry or art. These forms inhabited Shelley's luminous cloudland,[321] and they were the models in the Pheidian heart, and they have been with artist, poet and musician since the beginning of the world, and they will be with us until we grow into their beauty and learn from them how to fulfil human destiny, accomplishing our labour which is to make this world into the likeness of the Kingdom of Light.[322]

EARTH

I think of earth as the floor of a cathedral where altar and Presence are everywhere.[323] This reverence came to me as a boy listening to the voice of birds one coloured evening in summer,[324] when suddenly birds and trees and grass and tinted air and myself seemed but one mood or companionship, and I felt a certitude that the same spirit was in all. A little breaking of the barriers and being would mingle with being.[325] Whitman writes of the earth that it is rude and incomprehensible at first. 'But I swear to you,' he cries, 'that there are divine things well hidden.' Yet they are not so concealed that the lover may not discover them, and to the lover nature reveals herself like a shy maiden who is slowly drawn to one who adores her at a distance,[326] and who is first acknowledged by a lifting of the veil, a long-remembered glance, a glimmering smile, and at last comes speech and the mingling of life with life. So the lover of Earth obtains his reward, and little by little the veil is lifted of an inexhaustible beauty and majesty. It may be he will be tranced in some spiritual communion, or will find his being overflowing into the being of the elements, or become aware that they are breathing their life into his own. Or Earth may become on an instant all faery to him, and earth and air resound with the music of its invisible people. Or the trees and rocks may waver before his eyes and become transparent, revealing what creatures were hidden from him by the curtain, and he will know as the ancients did of dryad and hamadryad, of genii of wood and mountain. Or earth may suddenly blaze about him with supernatural light in some lonely spot amid the hills, and he will find he stands as the prophet in a place that is holy ground, and he may breathe the intoxicating exhalations as did the sibyls of old.[327] Or his love may hurry him away in dream to share in deeper mysteries,[328] and he may see the palace chambers of nature where the wise ones dwell in secret, looking out over the nations,[329] breathing power into this man's heart or that man's brain, on any who appear to their vision to wear the colour of truth.[330] So gradually the earth lover realizes the golden world is all about him in imperishable beauty,[331] and he may pass from the vision to the profounder beauty of being,[332] and know an eternal love is within and around him, pressing upon him and sustaining with infinite tenderness his body, his soul and his spirit.

I have obscured the vision of that being by dilating too much on what was curious, but I desired to draw others to this meditation, if by reasoning it were possible to free the intellect from its own fetters, so that the imagination might go forth, as Blake says, 'in uncurbed glory.' So I stayed the vision which might have been art, or the ecstasy which might have been poetry, and asked of them rather to lead me back to the ancestral fountain from which they issued.[333]

I think by this meditation we can renew for ourselves the magic and beauty of Earth, and understand the meaning of things in the sacred books which had grown dim. We have so passed away from vital contact with divine powers that they have become for most names for the veriest abstractions, and those who read do not know that the Mighty Mother is that Earth on which they tread and whose holy substance they call common clay; or that the Paraclete[334] is the strength of our being, the power which binds atom to atom and Earth to Heaven: or that the Christos is the Magician of the Beautiful[335] and that it is not only the Architect of the God-world but is that in us which sees beauty, creates beauty, and it is verily wisdom in us and is our deepest self; or that the Father is the fountain of substance and power and wisdom, and that we could not lift an eyelash but that we have our being in Him. When we turn from books to living nature we begin to understand the ancient wisdom, and it is no longer an abstraction, for the Great Spirit whose home is in the vast becomes for us a moving glamour in the heavens, a dropping tenderness at twilight, a visionary light in the hills, a voice in the heart, the Earth underfoot becomes sacred, and the air we breathe is like wine poured out for us by some heavenly cupbearer.[336]

As we grow intimate with earth we realize what sweet and august things await humanity when it goes back to that forgotten mother.[337] Who would be ambitious, who would wish to fling a name like Caesar's in the air, if he saw what thrones and majesties awaited the heavenly adventurer? Who would hate if he could see beneath the husk of the body the spirit which is obscured and imprisoned there,[338] and how it was brother to his own spirit and all were children of the King? Who would weary of nature or think it a solitude once the veil had been lifted for him, once he had seen that great glory? Would they not long all of them for the coming of that divine hour in the twilights of time, when out of rock, mountain, water, tree, bird, beast or man the seraph spirits of all that live shall emerge realizing their kinship, and all together, fierce things made gentle, and timid things made bold, and small made great, shall return to the Father Being and be made one in Its infinitudes?[339]

When we attain this vision nature will melt magically before our eyes, and powers that seem dreadful,[340] things that seemed abhorrent in her, will reveal themselves as brothers and allies. Until then she is unmoved by our conflicts and will carry on her ceaseless labours.

> No sign is made while empires pass.
> The flowers and stars are still His care,
> The constellations hid in grass,
> The golden miracles in air.
>
> Life in an instant will be rent
> When death is glittering, blind and wild,
> The Heavenly Brooding is intent
> To that last instant on Its child.
>
> It breathes the glow in brain and heart.
> Life is made magical. Until
> Body and spirit are apart
> The Everlasting works Its will.
>
> In that wild orchid that your feet
> In their next falling shall destroy,
> Minute and passionate and sweet,
> The Mighty Master holds His joy.
>
> Though the crushed jewels droop and fade
> The Artist's labours will not cease,
> And from the ruins shall be made
> Some yet more lovely masterpiece.[341]

The end of *The Candle of Vision.*

THE SPEECH OF THE GODS[1]*

The Theosophical doctrine, while endorsing many of the views of the Darwanian system of evolution, has so supplemented that doctrine with another – that of man's spiritual descent or downward evolution from the planetary spirits – as to alter entirely the view to be taken of man's character, constitution and dignity in the universe. Of man's various powers, perceptions and potencies, some belong to the arc ascending from the *monera*, some to the arc descending from the divine and spiritual ancestors.[2]

That the Aryan tongue,[3] the language of the intuitional Fifth Race, belongs to the latter category and is man's inheritance from the planetary spirits, we hope to be able to show.

Philological research has demonstrated that the Indo-European or Aryan languages are reducible to a few hundred primitive roots, from which all subsequent stages and variations of language are by various modes of combination derived. In these days of enlightenment, when man is brought into unpleasant proximity with several very disagreeable poor relations, it is interesting to all mankind, and especially to the Aryan nations, to trace exactly the source from which our ancestor – the Aryan, not the ape – derived his few hundred primitive roots, for in their source and character we have a measure of his mind, a finger-post pointing either heavenwards to man's divine progenitors, or ape-wards to the prognathous and hairy chimpanzee.

On the one hand we shall expect to discover a spiritual relation between sounds and the various powers, forms and colours and the universe,[4] the value of which was intuitionally perceived by the earliest Aryans; on the other, we shall look to find the echoes of the grunts and squeals of our poor relation perched on a tree-branch mumbling his acorns.

Roots, say the theorists, were at first either a matter of convention, or were formed by imitating the sounds of nature, and by

---

* See note on p. 174 for A.E.'s complaint about the misprints in this text.

exclamations and interjections. The chief objection to the first theory (which indeed was never very seriously defended) is that contrary to hypothesis the Aryan roots, as a whole, do not express the wants and notions of such a primitive people as we were led to postulate. We find for example comparatively few words, such as *bow, arrow,* and *tent,* while there are a great many expressing abstract or reflective ideas, like *to shine, to fly, to know, to burn.* The second also is all very well *as a theory,* but at the first rude contact with fact it collapses. We find very few words which could possibly be formed according to its principles, and this for the simple reason that there are no distinctive sounds in nature accompanying the majority of the ideas expressed in these Aryan roots.

The theory which we put forward, on the other hand, is that sounds have by nature a spiritual or innate relation with various colours, forms or qualities,[5] and that the Aryan roots were formed with a clear intuitional perception of this fact. It is probable that the process of their formation was instinctive and unconscious, rather than intentional and deliberate.

To make the theory more clear, we may say that it appears to us that the entities on each plane have a spiritual relation to the entities on the other planes. A particular sound, for instance, corresponds to some one colour, to some one taste, to some one odour, and to some one simple figure or form. In order to connect the Aryan roots, or, to speak more correctly, the sounds of the Aryan roots with their values on the other planes, – thus showing their origin to be spiritual and intuitional – it will be necessary to analyse the chief sounds used in this branch of human speech, and to assign to them their spiritual values; and having discovered these values to apply them to the Aryan roots or to the words of any early language akin to the Aryan. It will be seen that besides the values to be assigned to them intuitionally, a parallel series of values will be discovered arising from physiological reasons,[6] such as the position of the organs of speech while pronouncing them; but it must in all cases be borne in mind that the intuitive is the primary meaning, though reasons for it cannot, from its very nature, be stated argumentatively; in most cases, therefore, physiological reason alone will be given. For the convenience of those unacquainted with Sanskrit phonetics, we shall adhere as far as possible to the English alphabet.

To begin with B and M (pronounced *bă* and *ăm*), if we analyse their character and difference from other sounds and from each other, we find that with the exception P (pă) a slight variant of B, they are the only sounds which require the complete closure of the mouth for their formation. Whether it be preceded or followed by a

The Speech of the Gods

vowel, B cannot be correctly pronounced without first closing the lips and then opening them. It is evident therefore that as Bă is the only sound which is made by the bursting forth of the breath from closed lips, it is more suited than any other to express 'the beginning of life,' or 'life.' M differs from B in this, that it is made not by the breath coming from the just opened lips, but by closing them and stopping the breath completely for a time, then the breath finds an outlet by its upper channel, the nose. Taking these facts into consideration, we perceive that it should mean something extreme, like 'end', 'height' or 'death,' or, more fully, the stoppage of the life energy and its transfer to a different channel. (We may here remark that this value agrees with the characteristics of Siva, in the mystic syllable Om, or Aum, representing Brahman the Creator, Vishnu the preserver, and Siva the destroyer and regenerator).[7] It is a similar sound to M, but differs from it in this, that the stoppage of the breath, before its transfer to the upper outlet, is incomplete. It means 'continuance' or change without any real end. P is a variation of the sound for life, its significance is less though similar, it means 'formation of a part,' 'division,' or 'smallness'. The principal characteristic of V is its indefiniteness, it means 'vagueness.' F, its companion sound, means 'airiness' or 'lightness,' it would refer to floating or flying objects. The harshest of the primary sounds is J (jă), its meaning therefore to accord with this peculiarity must be 'matter,' 'heaviness,' or 'earth' (as one of the five objective elements).[8] The hard sharp sound of K (kă), at once defines its meaning – 'hardness,' 'sharpness,' or 'brilliancy.' The analogous sound of G (gă) means 'smoothness,' or 'reflection.' The Brahmanical doctrine of emanations teaches, as is well known, that absolute spirit, or Parabrahm[9] (the great underlying reality of the universe), by its expansive activity[10] created the First and Eternal emanation of the Logos, or Spirit; from this was produced the second emanation of ether, the astral light of the Kabbalists, corresponding to akâsa; from the ether was produced the element of light or fire; from fire was produced air; from air was produced water; from water was produced earth;[11] from earth was produced the vegetable kingdom; from the vegetable kingdom were produced animals, from animals man.

Here we find that earth is, as it were, the turning point to which downward evolution reaches, and from which upward evolution begins.[12] It is a remarkable and significant fact, but none the less a fact, that, if we take the liquid semi-vowel or ethereal series of sounds, and classify them in the order they come in the throat and mouth, their intuitional or spiritual values in this order will correspond accurately to the order of the elements in this Kabbalistic doctrine of emanations.

The first of these ethereal sounds A[13] (pronounced like the â in atma,) is the first sound of the human voice formed farthest within the throat, and the breath necessary to form all other sounds must pass from the A, the value of A therefore is 'God,' the 'first cause' or the 'self'. The next sound of this series is R (âr, as in for), from its peculiar fulness and undefinable sound, its meaning is 'wind,' 'breath,' 'movement' or 'spirit;' it is the spirit which, in the words of Genesis, 'Brooded upon the face of the waters,' and is the first emanation of the A or God; after R comes the sound of H (hay) the sound for 'heat', the five elements in one aspect. Next comes L (el) the spiritual value of which is 'light'. The other aspect of the fire emanation, Y (yea) the sound succeeding L, means 'compression' or 'the drawing together of things;' the next sound of this peculiar class is W (way), the sound for 'water'; marking the two limits of the circular space enclosed by the pronunciation of this sound are the two sounds of Jă and Kă, representing the quality of material solidity of the next emanation, the earth, which thus issues from the centre of the water element.

> Let the waters be gathered together
> And let the dry land appear,

says the cosmogony in Genesis. The ethereal or semi-vowel carry us down the earth element, which is, as we have seen, the turning point of evolution. These ethereal sounds represent the objective and supersensual planes, whose peculiar types of being have been called the fire, air and water elementals. When we reach the earth and the objective kingdoms, we come again to hard sounds. Proceeding outwards from the earth we get the sound of *Ith* which means 'growth' or 'expansion': with this sound came the emanation or evolution of vegetable life – to use the words of Genesis.

> The earth brought forth herbs.

After Ith comes the sound of F and B, representing the kingdom of birds, fishes and animals and the crowning evolution of man.

Close on the heels of life, follows death, represented by the sound of M.

Let us compare this with the Upanishad.

> From that self (Brahan) sprang ether, (or spirit.)
> From ether sprang air; (expansion and heat.)
> From air sprang fire; (light or colour.)
> From fire, water; from water, earth;
> From earth, herbs; from herbs, food; from food, man.[14]

Here we have exactly the order we have arrived at by taking the spiritual values of the sounds as they occur in the human throat and mouth, A, – god; R, – spirit; H, – heat; L, – light; W, – water; K, – hardness; J, – earth; Ith, – growth; B, – life; M, – death.

A few more sounds may be added. S, formed by a rapid series of sibilations, means 'number.' D means 'descent' or 'falling;' T 'ascent.'

We will now try how far we may be enabled with the key obtained to comprehend the intellectual and spiritual life of our ancestors. Nothing remains in writing which tells of their wisdom; but no historian could have taken the measure of it so exactly as it is recorded in the bare roots which have come down to us. The traditions about these men might be untrustworthy and enlarged upon by the imagination of those who related them; but their words contain a history which cannot be otherwise than true, because they were intuitive.

It will be found that the examples given are of words of the very simplest class, referring to actions, thoughts and things, the most likely to be first expressed in this newly developed faculty of intuitive speech. We think that almost all the roots which do not seem to be intuitive were formed by a conventional agreement to regard one of these early words as applicable to several different things, for example, K, hardness or sharpness, was used in forming the intuitive word 'Ak,' 'to pierce into,' 'Ak,' 'to see,' was evidently a result of this primary meaning.

It is easy to see what God meant to the old Assyrians, El, the light; Bel, their sun-god, seems to mean 'he who lives in light,' life and light are joined to express this idea. Aer, God of the atmosphere, was another Assyrian god, he was also called Vul, which is equivalent to Jupiter Tonans. Vul probably means 'light of the sky,' here being used to represent the indefinite air. Ahiah, 'I am that I am,' the name which was uttered from the burning bush, is intuitive, being formed by a double pronunciation of the word for the self or God. Pal, the Assyrian word for 'time' or 'year,' would mean division of light; Pu, month, should mean a division. Mul, star, means 'high light,' M being used here to express something extreme. To the Aryan race death had the meaning, the 'end of movement' or of the 'breath.' Mar, containing the sounds for end and movement. Ur, sky,[15] would mean 'wide air,' as 'Oo' means 'width' and R, air. The root An, endless, is intuitive, also Pu, threshed or purified, P being used here to express division. Ku, to sharpen, is a word of the same class as Ak, to pierce. In Kar, to make, there are combined the sounds for hardness and movement;

in Taks, to hew, the sounds for, to raise, hardness and number, the S, referring to what is hewn away or divided. In Mak, to pound, to macerate, there is the suggestion of ending with something hard. The united sounds of hardness and falling are in Kad, to fall; and of division and hardness in Pak, to come, and Pik, to cut. The letters which form Skap, to chop, mean to cut and divide things. Other words of the same class are Sak and Skar. In Sa, to sow, the prevailing idea seems to have been number. Swid, to sweat, has the sounds for number, water and rolling down. Possibly the idea of Swa, to toss, was taken from seeing things tossed about upon the waves as Fath, to spread out, may have been from observation of the aërial growth of tree branches. Swal, to boil up, is clearly intuitive, as well as Wam, to spit out. Other intuitive words are Yu, to bind, and Yas, to gird. Wa, meant to bind, either because it was observed that water acted as a girdle to all things or through some confusion of meaning between it and Y. It may be observed here that sometimes there is an interchange of meanings between a sound and the one preceding or following it; sometimes L has the meaning of R, or H of L, or Y of W, or G of K.

S and W are joined into one word in Siw, to bind, the idea expressed being the binding together of things. It has been used with the intuitive value attached to it in Flu, to fly, swim, or float. The Sanskrit Rasu, origin intuitively considered, would mean the movement of things, and the Assyrian, Ris, beginning, seems to have the same idea embodied in it. The root Al, to burn, is intuitive, but the light seems to have suggested the word rather than the heat. Knowledge is the reflection in the mind of what is passing in the world, Gnu, to know,[16] is a combination of the sounds for reflection and combination. Than, thinness, would seem to be the result of long continued growth. Gol, a very common word for late, means 'reflection of light,' and the glistening appearance of ice probably suggested a word, to freeze, Gal; a word of the same class is Gea, to glow. Tar, to pass over, has sounds of which the intuitive value seems to be 'ascent through air.' Thu, to swell, to be strong, and Fath, to fly, are examples of the use of Ith.

As it would only be tedious to go on giving examples, after the theory and the method of applying it for the purpose of elucidating the meaning and origin of the roots has been made sufficiently clear, we will add a few more only; they are; Su, to generate, to produce; Cuk, to shine, Mu, to shut up, to enclose; Mi, to go; Bu, to be, to grow; Bars, to carry; Kant, to cut; An, to breathe; Spark, to scatter; Da, to distribute; and Greek, Go, the earth. A little thought will show at once what idea was intended to be embodied in these words.

The Speech of the Gods

Reflecting on the extreme sensibility to sound which this intuitive race possessed, a sensibility which enabled them to find words exactly suited to express the spreading of tree branches and the boiling of water, we cannot help wondering, were they similarly affected by sounds external to themselves, and whether the call of birds or the hoarser cries of animals conveyed any meaning to their ear. The words which they employed to express colour, though, naturally enough, lesser evidence remains of this, show that, for every hue they could find a note of corresponding value on the plane of sound,[17] R and M answering respectively to red and violet, and each letter between to some shade of colour ranging from one to the other of the two mentioned. A study of the forms used in the primeval alphabets, and as symbols, would show that they recognized something more in nature than mere matter, that the tracing of flower and leaf, and the starry arch of heaven, and all beautiful things, were full to them of deep spiritual significance, which the more intellectual scientists of our time cannot see, though they weigh and analyse and examine ever so much. If this essay could persuade even one of them to develop the most god-like faculty man possesses – intuition, – its purpose would be fulfilled.

C. JOHNSTON, F. T. S.
GEO. RUSSELL.

THE ELEMENT LANGUAGE[1]

Note: In an article which appeared in the *Theosophist*, Dec. 1887, I had attempted, with the assistance of my friend Mr. Chas Johnston, to put forward some of the ideas which form the subject matter of this paper. Owing to the numerous misprints which rendered it unintelligible I have felt it necessary to altogether re-write it. G.W.R.

In a chapter in the *Secret Doctrine* dealing with the origin of language, H.P. Blavatsky makes some statements which are quoted here and which should be borne well in mind in considering what follows. 'The Second Race had a "Sound Language," to wit, *chant-like* sounds composed of vowels alone.' From this developed 'monosyllabic speech which was the vowel parent, so to speak, of the monosyllabic languages mixed with hard consonants still in use among the yellow races which are known to the anthropologist. These linguistic characteristics developed into the agglutinative languages. . . . The inflectional speech, the root of the Sanskrit, was the first language (now the *mystery tongue* of the Initiates) of the Fifth Race.'[2]

The nature of that language has not been disclosed along with other teaching concerning the evolution of the race, but like many other secrets the details of which are still preserved by the Initiates, it is implied in what has already been revealed. The application to speech of the abstract formula of evolution which they have put forward should result in its discovery, for the clue lies in correspondences;[3] know the nature of any one thing perfectly, learn its genesis, development and consummation, and you have the key to all the mysteries of nature. The microosm mirrors the macrocosm. But, before applying this key, it is well to glean whatever hints have been given, so that there may be less chance of going astray in our application. First, we gather from the Secret Doctrine that the sounds of the human voice are correlated with forces, colours, numbers and forms.[4] '*Every letter has its occult meaning*, the vowels especially contain the most occult and formidable potencies.' (*s.d.*, I. 94.) and again it is said 'The magic of the ancient priests consisted in those days in addressing *their gods in their own language*. The speech of the men of earth cannot reach the Lords, each must be addressed in the language of his respective element' – is a sentence which will be shown pregnant with meaning. *'The book of rules'* cited adds as an explanation of the nature of that *element*-language: 'It is composed of *Sounds,* not words; of sounds, numbers and figures. He who knows how to blend the three, will call forth the response of the superintending Power' (the regent-god of the specific element needed). Thus this 'language is that of *incantations* or of MANTRAS,[5] as they are called in India, sound being *the most potent and effectual magic agent, and the first of the keys which opens the door of communication between mortals and immortals* (S.D., I. 464).

From these quotations it will be seen that the occult teachings as to speech are directly at variance with the theories of many philologists and evolutionists. A first speech which was like song[6] – another and more developed speech which is held sacred – an esoteric side to speech in which the elements of our conventional languages (*i.e.* the letters) are so arranged that speech becomes potent enough to guide the elements, and human speech becomes the speech of the gods – there is no kinship between this ideal language and the ejaculations and mimicry which so many hold to be the root and beginning of it. Yet those who wish to defend their right to hold the occult teaching have little to fear from the champions of these theories; they need not at all possess any deep scholarship or linguistic attainment; the most cursory view of the roots of primitive speech, so far as they have been collected, will show that they contain few or no sounds of a character which would bear out either the onomatopoetic or interjectional theories. The vast majority of the roots of the Aryan language express abstract ideas, they rarely indicate the particular actions which would be capable of being suggested by any mimicry possible to the human voice. I have selected at random from a list of roots their English equivalents, in order to show the character of the roots and to make clearer the difficulty of holding such views. The abstract nature of the ideas, relating to actions and things which often have no attendant sound in nature, will indicate what I mean. What possible sounds could mimic the sense of 'to move, to shine, to gain, to flow, to burn, to blow, to live, to possess, to cover, to fall, to praise, to think'? In fact the most abstract of all seem the most primitive for we find them most fruitful in combination to form other words. I hope to show this clearly later on. It is unnecessary to discuss the claims of the interjectional theory, as it is only a theory, and there are few roots for which we could infer even a remote origin of this nature. The great objection to the theory that speech was originally a matter of convention and mutual agreement is the scarcity of words among the roots which express the wants of primitive man. As it is, a wisdom within or beyond the Aryan led him to construct in these roots with their abstract significance an ideal foundation from which a great language could be developed. However as the exponents of rival theories have demolished each other's arguments, without anyone having established a clear case for himself, it is not necessary here to do more than indicate these theories and how they may be met.

In putting forward a hypothesis more in accord with the doctrine of the spiritual origin of man, and in harmony with those occult ideas concerning speech already quoted, I stand in a rather unusual position, as I have to confess my ignorance of any of these primitive languages. I am rather inclined, however, to regard this on the whole as an advantage for the following reasons. I think primitive man (the early Aryan) chose his words by a certain intuition which recognized an *innate correspondence between the thought and the symbol*. Pari passu with the growing complexity of civilization language lost its spiritual character, 'it fell into matter,' to use H.P. Blavatsky's expression; as the conventional words necessary to define artificial products grew in number, in the memory of these words the spontaneity of speech was lost, and that faculty became atrophied which enabled man to arrange with psychic rapidity ever new combinations of sounds to express emotion and thought. Believing then that speech was originally intuitive, and that it only needs introspection and a careful analysis of the sounds of the human voice, to recover the faculty and correspondences between these sounds and forces, colours, forms, etc., it will be seen why I do not regard my ignorance of these languages as altogether a drawback. The correspondences necessarily had to be evolved out of my inner consciousness, and in doing this no aid could be derived from the Aryan roots as they now stand. In the meaning attached to *each letter* is to be found the key to the meaning and origin of roots; but the value of each sound separately could never be discovered by an examination of them in their combination, though their value and purpose in combination to form words might be evident enough once the significance of the letters is shewn. Any lack of knowledge then is only a disadvantage in this, that it limits the area from which to choose illustrations. I have felt it necessary to preface what I have to say with this confession, to show exactly the position in which I stand. The correspondences between sounds and forces were first evolved, and an examination of the Aryan roots proved the key capable of application.

It is advisable at this point to consider how correspondences arose between things seemingly so diverse as sounds, forms, colours, and forces. It is evident that they could only come about through the existence of a common and primal cause reflecting itself everywhere in different elements and various forms of life. This primal unity lies at the root of all occult philosophy and science; the One becomes Many; the ideas latent in Universal Mind[7] are thrown outwards into manifestation. In the *Bhagavad-Gita* (chap.IV) Krishna declares: 'even though myself unborn, of changeless essence, and the lord of all existence, yet in presiding over nature – which is mine – I am born but through my own *maya,* the mystic power of self-ideation, the eternal thought in the eternal mind.'[8] 'I establish the universe with a single portion of myself and remain separate;' he says later on, and in so presiding he becomes the cause of the appearance of the different qualities.[9] 'I am the taste in water, the light in the sun and moon, the mystic syllable OM in all the Vedas, sound in space, the masculine essence in men, the sweet smell in the earth, the brightness in the fire' &c.[10] Pouring forth then from one fountain we should expect to find correspondences running everywhere throughout nature; we should expect to find all these things capable of correlation. Coëxistent with manifestation arise the ideas of time and space, and these qualities, attributes or forces, which are latent and unified in the germinal thought, undergo a dual transformation; they appear successively in time, and what we call evolution progresses through Kalpa after Kalpa[11] and Manvantara after Manvantara:[12] the moods which dominate these periods incarnate in matter, which undergoes endless transformations and takes upon itself all forms in embodying these states of consciousness.

The order in which these powers manifest is declared in the Purânas,[13] Upanishads[14] and Tantric[15] works. It is that abstract formula of evolution which we can apply alike to the great and little things in nature. This may be stated in many ways, but to put it briefly, there is at first one divine Substance-Principle, Flame, Motion or the Great Breath; from this emanate the elements Akasa, ether, fire, air, water and earth;[16] the spiritual quality becoming gradually lessened in these as they are further removed from their divine source; this is the descent into matter, the lowest rung of manifestation. 'Having consolidated itself in its last principle as gross matter, it revolves around itself and informs with the seventh emanation of the last, the first and lowest element.' (*S.D.*, I. 297) This involution of the higher into the lower urges life upwards through the mineral, vegetable, animal and human kingdoms, until it culminates in spirituality and self consciousness. It is not necessary here to go more into detail, it is enough to say that the elements in nature being as passive qualities, their ethereal nature becomes gross, then positive and finally spiritual, and this abstract formula holds good for everything in nature. These changes which take place in the universe are repeated in man its microcosm, the cosmic force which acts upon matter and builds up systems of suns and planets, working in him repeats itself and builds up a complex organism which corresponds and is correlated with its cosmic counterpart. The individual spirit Purusha[17] dwells in the heart of every creature, its powers ray forth everywhere; they pervade the different principles or vehicles; they act through the organs of sense; they play upon the different plexuses;[18] every principle and organ being specialized as the vehicle for a particular force or state of consciousness.[19] All the sounds we can utter have their significance; they express moods; they create forms; they arouse to active life within ourselves spiritual and psychic forces which are centred in various parts of the body. Hence the whole organism of man is woven through and through with such correspondences; our thoughts, emotions, sensations, the forces we use, colours and sounds acting on different planes are all correlated among themselves,[20] and are also connected with the forces evolving in greater nature, those universal planes of being which are everywhere present about us, in which we live and move. We find such correspondences form the subject matter of many Upanishads and other occult treatises; for example in Yajnavalkyasamhita, a treatise on Yoga philosophy, we find the sound 'Ra' associated with the element of fire, Tejas Tatwa, with the God Rudra, with a centre in the body just below the heart. Other books add, as correspondences of Tejas Tatwa, that its colour is red, its taste is hot, its form is a triangle and its force is expansion. The correspondences given in different treatises often vary; but what we can gather with certainty is that there must have existed a complete science of the subject: the correlation of sound with such things, once understood, is the key which explains, not only the magic potency of sound, but also the construction of those roots which remain as relics of the primitive Aryan speech.

The thinking principle in man, having experience of nature through its vehicles, the subtle, astral[21] and gross physical bodies, translates these sensations into its own set of correspondences: this principle in man, called the Manas,[22] is associated with the element of âkâsa, whose property is sound; the Manas moves about in the âkâsa, and so all ideas which enter into the mind awaken their correspondences and are immediately mirrored in sound. Let us take as an instance the perception of the colour *red;* this communicated to the mind would set up a vibration causing a sound to be thrown outwards in mental manifestation, and in this way the impulse would arise to utter the letter R, the correspondence of this colour. This Manasic principle in man, the real Ego, is eternal in its nature; it exists before and after the body, something accruing to it from each incarnation; and so, because there is present in the body of man this long-travelled soul, bearing with it traces of its eternal past, these letters which are the elements of its speech have impressed on them a correspondence not only with the forces natural to its transitory surroundings, but also with that vaster evolution of nature in which it has taken part. These correspondences next claim our attention.

The correspondences here suggested do not I think at all exhaust the possible significance of any of the letters. Every sound ought to have a septenary relation to the planes of consciousness, and the differentiations of life, force and matter on each. Complete mastery of these would enable the knower to guide the various currents of force, and to control the elemental beings who live on the astral planes, for these respond, we are told, 'when the exact scale of being to which they belong is vibrated, whether it be that of colour, form, sound or whatever else,' (*Path*, May 1886). These higher interpretations I am unable to give; it requires the deeper being to know the deeper meaning. Those here appended may prove suggestive: I do not claim any finality or authority for them, but they may be interesting to students of the occult Upanishads where the mystic power of sound is continually dwelt upon.

The best method of arranging the letters is to begin with A and conclude with M or OO:[23] between these lie all the other letters, and their successive order is determined by their spiritual or material quality. Following A we get letters with an ethereal or liquid sound, such as R, H, L or Y;[24] they become gradually harsher as they pass from the A, following the order of nature in this. Half way we get letters like K, J, TCHAY, S, or ISH; then they become softer, and the labials, like F, B and M, have something of the musical quality of the earlier sounds. If we arrange them in this manner, it will be found to approximate very closely to the actual order in which the sounds arise in the process of formation. We begin then with

A   This represents God, creative force, the Self, the I, the beginning or first cause. 'Among letters I am the vowel A,' says Krishna in the *Bhagavad*.[25] It is without colour, number of form.

R   This is motion, air, breath or spirit; it is also abstract desire, and here we find the teaching of the Rig-Veda in harmony. 'Desire first arose in It which was the primal germ of mind, and which sages, searching with their intellect, have discovered in their hearts to be the bond which connects Entity with non-Entity.'[26] The corresponding colour of this letter is Red.

H (*hay*) and L   Motion awakens Heat and Light which correspond respectively to H and L. That primordial ocean of being, says the *Book of Dzyan*,[27] was 'fire and heat and motion;' which are explained as the noumenal essences of these material manifestations. The colour of H is orange, of L yellow. L also conveys the sense of radiation.

Y (*yea*)   This letter signifies condensation, drawing together, the force of attraction, affinity. Matter at the stage of evolution to which this refers is gaseous, nebulous, or ethereal: the fire-mists in space gather together to become worlds.[28] The colour of Y is green.

W (*way*)   Water is the next element in manifestation: in cosmic evolution it is spoken of as chaos, the great Deep; its colour, I think, is indigo. After this stage the elements no longer manifest singly, but in pairs, or with a dual aspect.[29]

G (*gay*) and K   Reflection and Hardness; matter becomes crystalline or metallic: the corresponding colour is blue.

S and Z   A further differentiation; matter is atomic: the abstract significance of number or seed is attached to these letters: their colour is violet.

J and T*chay*   Earth and gross Substance: this is the lowest point in evolution; the worlds have now condensed into solid matter. The colour of these letters is orange.

N and N*g*   Some new forces begin to work here; the corresponding sounds have, I think, the meaning of continuation and transformation or change: these new forces propel evolution in the upward or ascending arc: their colour is yellow.

D and T   The colour of these letters is red. The involution of the higher forces into the lower forms alluded to before now begins. D represents this infusion of life into matter; it is descent and involution, death or forgetfulness, perhaps, for a time to the incarnating power. T is evolution, the upward movement generating life; the imprisoned energies surge outwards and vegetation begins.

I*th* and I*sh*   These correspond respectively to growth or expansion and vegetation; the earth, as Genesis puts it, 'puts forth grass and herbs and trees yielding fruit.' The colour of these letters is green.

B and P   After the flora the fauna.[30] B is Life or Being, animal and human. Humanity appears; B is masculine, P feminine. P has also a meaning of division, differentiation or production, which may refer to maternity. The colour here is blue.

F and V   The colour is violet. Evolution moves still upwards, entering the ethereal planes once more. Lightness and vastness are the characteristics of this stage: we begin to permeate with part of our nature the higher spheres of being and reach the consummation in the last stage, represented by

M   which has many meanings;[31] it is thought, it is the end or death to the personality, it is the Receiver into which all flows, it is also the Symbol of maternity in a universal sense, it has this meaning when the life impulse (which is always represented by a vowel) follows it, as in 'ma.' It is the Pralaya of the worlds; the lips close as it is uttered. Its colour is indigo.

O   The last vowel sound symbolizes abstract space, the spirit assumes once more the garment of primordial matter; it is the Nirvana of eastern philosophy.[32]

I will now try to show how the abstract significance of these sounds reveals a deeper meaning in the roots of Aryan language than philologists generally allow. Prof. Max Müller says in the introduction to *Biographies of Words*. 'Of ultimates in the sense of primary elements of language, we can never hope to know anything,' and he also asserts that the roots are incapable of further analysis. I will endeavour now to show that this further analysis can be made.

I should not be understood to say that all the so-called roots can be made to yield a secret meaning when analysed. Philologists are not all agreed as to what constitutes a root, or what words are roots, and in this general uncertainty it should not be expected that these correspondences, which as I have said are not complete, will apply in every instance. There are many other things which add to the difficulty; a root is often found to have very many different meanings; some of these may have arisen in the manner I suggest, and many more are derived from the primary meanings and are therefore not intuitive at all. The intuition will have to be exercised to discover what sensations would likely be awakened by the perception of an action or object; or if the root has an abstract significance, the thought must be analysed in order to discover its essential elements. I described previously the manner in which I thought a single sensation, the perception of the colour Red, would suggest its correspondence in sound, the letter R. Where the idea is more complex, a combination of two, three or four sounds are necessary to express it, but they all originate in the same way. The reader who desires to prove the truth of the theory here put forward can adopt either of two methods; he can apply the correspondences to the roots, or he may try for himself to create words expressing simple, elemental ideas by combining the necessary letters; and then, if he turns to the roots, he will probably find that many of the words he has created in this way were actually used long ago, and this practice will enable him more easily to understand in what sense, or on what plane, any particular letter should be taken. I think it probable that in the Sacred Language before mentioned, this could at once have been recognized by a difference in the intonation of the voice. This may have been a survival to some extent of the chanting which was the distinguishing characteristic of the speech of the Second Race. (*Secret Doctrine*, II. 198) In the written language it is not easily possible to discover this without much thought, unless endeavour has previously been made to re-awaken the faculty of intuitive speech, which we formerly possessed and which became atrophied.[33]

It is not possible here to go into the analysis of the roots at much length: I can only illustrate the method which will be found to apply more surely where the roots express most elemental conceptions. Let us take as example the root, *Wal*, to boil. Boiling is brought about by the action of fire upon water, and here we find the letters W, water, and L, light or fire, united. In *War*, to well up as a spring, the sounds for water and motion are combined. A similar idea is expressed in *Wat*, to well out; the abstract significance of T, which is to evolve, come forth or appear, being here applied to a special action. A good method to follow in order to understand how the pure abstract meaning of a letter may be applied in many different ways, is to take some of the roots in which any one letter is prominent and then compare them. Let us take D. It has an abstract relation to involution or infusion; it may be viewed in two ways, either as positive or negative, as the exertion of force or the reception of force. Now I think if we compare the following roots a similarity of action will be found to underlie them all. *Id*, to swell; *Ad*, to eat; *Da*, to give;[34] *Dhu*, to put; *Da*, to bind; *Ad*, to smell; *Du*, to enter; *Da*, to suck.

I am not here going exhaustively to analyse the roots, as this is not an essay upon philology, but an attempt to make clear some of the mysteries of sound; those who wish to study this side of the subject more fully can study with this light the primitive languages. A few more examples must suffice. The root, *Mar*, to die,[35] may be variously interpreted as the end of motion, the cessation of breath, or the withdrawal of spirit, R being expressive of what on various planes is motion, spirit, air and breath. In *Bur*, to be active, life and movement are combined: in *Gla*, to glow, reflection and light; the same idea is in *Gol*, a lake. We find combined in *Kar* to grind,

The Element Language 183

hardness and motion: in *Thah*, to generate, expansion and heat; in *Pak*, to comb, division and hardness, the suggestion being division with some hard object; the same idea is in *Pik*, to cut. In *Pis*, to pound, the letters for division and matter in its molecular state are combined: in *Fath*, to fly, lightness and expansion: in *Yas*, to gird, drawing together and number; in *Rab*, to be vehement, energy and life; in *Rip*, to break, energy and division. In *Yudh*, to fight, the meaning suggested may be, coming together to destroy. Without further analysis the reader will be able to detect the relation which the abstractions corresponding to each letter bear to the defined application in the following words. *Ak*, to be sharp; *Ank*, to bend; *Idh*, to kindle; *Ar*, to move; *Al*, to burn; *Ka*, to sharpen; *Har*, to burn; *Ku*, to hew; *Sa*, to produce; *Gal*, to be yellow or green; *Ghar*, to be yellow or green; *Thak*, to thaw; *Tar*, to go through; *Thu*, to swell; *Dak*, to bite; *Nak*, to perish; *Pa*, to nourish, to feed; *Par*, to spare; *Pi*, to swell, to be fat; *Pu*, to purify; *Pu*, to beget; *Pau*, little; *Put*, to swell out; *Flu*, to fly, to float; *Bar*, to carry; *Bhu*, to be, to become; *Bla*, to blow as a flower; *Ma*, to think; *Mak*, to pound; *Mi*, to diminish; *Mu*, to shut up, to enclose; *Yas*, to seethe, to ferment; *Yu*, to bind together, to mix; *Yuk*, to yoke, to join; *Ra*, to love; *Rik*, to furrow; *Luh*, to shine; *Rud*, to redden, to be red; *Lub*, to lust; *Lu*, to cast off from; *Wag*, to be moist; *Wam*, to spit out; *So*, to sow, to scatter; *Sak*, to cut, to cleave; *Su*, to generate; *Swa*, to toss; *Swal*, to boil up; *Ska*, to cut; *Skap*, to hew; *Sniw*, to snow; *Spew*, to spit out; *Swid*, to sweat; etc. An analysis of some sacred words and the names of Deities may now prove interesting.

It has been said that before we can properly understand the character of any deity we would have to know the meaning and the numbers attached to each letter in the name,[36] for in this way the powers and functions of the various gods were indicated. If we take as examples names familiar to everyone, *Brahma, Vishnu*, and *Rudra*, the three aspects of Parabrahm in manifestation,[37] and analyse them in the same way as the roots, they will be found to yield up their essential meaning. From the union of *B*, life, *R*, breath, and *Ma*, the producer, I would translate *Brahma* as 'the creative breath of life.'[38] *Vishnu* similarly analysed is the power that 'pervades, expands, and preserves;'[39] I infer this from the union of *V*, whose force is pervasion, *Sh*, expansion, and *N*, continuation. *Rudra* is 'the breath that absorbs the breath.'[40] *Aum* is the most sacred name of all names;[41] it is held to symbolize the action of the Great Breath from its dawn to its close: it is the beginning, *A*, the middle, *U*, and the close *M*. It is also an affirmation of the relation of our spiritual nature to that universal Deity whose aspects are *Brahma, Vishnu*, and *Rudra*. I shall have more to say of the occult power of this word later on. Taken in conjunction with two other words, it is 'the threefold designation of the Supreme Being.' *Om Tat Sat*[42] has a significance referable to a still higher aspect of Deity than that other Trinity; the *Om* here signifies that it is the All; *Tat* that it is self-existent or self-evolved; I think the repetition of the *T* in *Tat* gives it this meaning: *Sat* would signify that in it are contained the seeds of all manifestation. H.P. Blavatsky translates this word as Be-ness,[43] which seems to be another way of expressing the same idea. The mystic incantation familiar to all students of the Upanishads, *'Om, Bhur, Om, Bhuvar, Om, Svar,'* is an assertion of the existence of the Divine Self in all the three worlds or *Lokas*.[44] *Loka* is generally translated as a place; the letters suggest to me that a place or world is only a hardening or crystallization of Fire or Light. In *Bhur Loka* the crystallization of the primordial element of Fire leaves only one principle active, the life principle generally called *Prana*. *Bhur Loka* then is the place where life is active; we have *B*, life, and *R*, movement, to suggest this. In the word *Bhuvar* a new letter, *V*, is inserted: this letter, as I have said, corresponds to the Astral World, so that *Bhuvar Loka* is the place where both the Astral and Life principles are active. It is more difficult to translate *Svar Loka:* there is some significance attached here to the letter *S*, which I cannot grasp. It might mean that this world contains the germs of Astral life; but this does not appear sufficiently distinctive, *Svar Loka* is generally known as *Devachan*, and the whole incantation would mean that the Deity is present throughout the Pranic,[45] Astral,[46] and Devachanic[47] worlds. It is interesting to note what is said in the Glossary by H.P.B., about these three words (p. 367); they are said to be 'lit by and born of fire,' and to possess creative powers. The repetition of them with the proper accent should awaken in the occultist the powers which correspond to the three worlds. I think by these examples that the student will be able to get closer to the true significance of incantation; those who understand the occult meaning of the colours attached to the letters will be able to penetrate deeper than others into these mysteries.

I may here say something about the general philosophy of incantation. There is said to be in nature a homogeneous sound or tone which everywhere stirs up the molecules into activity.[48] This is the 'Word' which St. John says was in the beginning (the plane of causation);[49] in another sense it is the Akasa of occult science, the element of sound, it is the Pythagorean 'music of the spheres.' The universe is built up, moulded and sustained by this element which is everywhere present, though inaudible by most men at this stage of evolution. It is not sound by the physical ears, but deep in the heart sometimes may be heard 'the mystic sounds of the Akasic heights.'[50] The word *Aum* represents this homogeneous sound, it stirs up a power which is latent in it called the *Yagna*.[51] The Glossary says that this 'is one of the forms of Akasa within which the mystic word calls it into existence:' it is a bridge by means of which the soul can cross over to the world of the Immortals. It is this which is alluded to in the *Nada-Bindu Upanishad*. 'The mind becoming insensible to the external impressions, becomes one with the sound, as milk with water, and then becomes rapidly absorbed in *chidakas* (the Akasa where consciousness pervades). The sound . . . serves the purpose of a lure to the ocean waves of *Chitta* (mind) . . . the serpent of *Chitta* through listening to the *Nada* is entirely absorbed in it, and becoming unconscious of everything concentrates itself on the sound.' We may quote further from another Upanishad. 'Having left behind the body, the organs and objects of sense, and having seized the bow whose stick is fortitude and whose string is asceticism, and having killed with the arrow of freedom from egoism the first guardian, . . . he crosses by means of the boat Om to the other side of the ether within the heart, and when the ether is revealed he enters slowly, as a miner seeking minerals enters a mine, into the hall of Brahman. . . . Thenceforth, pure, clean, tranquil, breathless, endless, imperishable, firm, unborn, and independent, he stands in his own greatness, and having seen the Self standing in his own greatness, he looks at the wheel of the world.'[52]

Let no one think that this is all, and that the mere repetition of words will do anything except injure those who attempt the use of these methods without further knowledge.[53] It has been said (*Path*, April 1887) that Charity, Devotion, and the like virtues are structural necessities in the nature of the man who would make this attempt. We cannot, unless the whole nature has been purified by long service and sacrifice, and elevated into a mood at once full of reverence and intense will, become sensitive to the subtle powers possessed by the spiritual soul.

What is here said about the *Aum* which is the name of our own God, and the way in which it draws forth the hidden power will serve to illustrate the method in using other words. The *Thara-Sara Upanishad* of *Sukla-Yajur Veda* says 'Through *Om* is Brahma produced; through *Na* is Vishnu produced; through *Ma* is Rudra produced, etc.' All these are names of gods; they correspond to forces in man and nature, in their use the two are united, and the man mounts upwards to the Immortals.

I have been forced to compress what I had to say in these articles,

I have only been able to suggest rather than put forward ideas, for my own knowledge of these correspondences is very incomplete. As far as I know the subject has been untouched hitherto, and this must be my excuse for the meagre nature of the information given. I hope later on to treat of the relation of sound and colour to form and to show how these correspondences will enable us to understand the language which the gods speak to us through flowers, trees, and natural forms. I hope also to be able to show that it was a knowledge of the relation of sound to form which dictated the form of the letters in many primaeval alphabets.

G.W.R.

REVIEW[1]

Lyrics, by R.H. Fitzpatrick. [London: W. Stewart and Co.]

While one race sinks into night another renews its dawn. The *Celtic Twilight* is the morning-time and the singing of birds is prophetic of the new day. We have had to welcome of late years one sweet singer after another, and now comes a volume of lyrics which has that transcendental note which is peculiar to our younger writers. It is full of the mystery and commingling of the human and the divine soul:

> Hail, thou living spirit!
> Whose deep organ blown
> By lips that more inherit
> Than all music known;
> Art is but the echo of thy mysterious tone.

These lyrics, I imagine, have been wrought in solitary wanderings, in which the forms and shows of things and human hopes and fears have been brooded upon until the intensity of contemplation has allied them with that soul of Nature in which the poet finds the fulfilment of all dreams and ideals. And in this refining back to an Over-Soul there is no suggestion of the student of academic philosophy, no over-wrought intellectualism. Such references arise naturally out of his thought and illuminate it. One can imagine how such lyrics were engendered:

> I stood and twirled a feathered stalk,
> Or drank the clover's honey sap,
> Happiest without talk.

> The summer tidal waves of night
> Slowly in silence rippled in;
> They steeped the feet of blazing light,
> And hushed day's harsher din.

This aloofness from conflict, if it has hindered him from fully accepting and justifying life, the highest wisdom of the poet, has still its compensations. He has felt the manifold meaning of the voices through whose unconsciousness Nature speaks, the songs of birds, the aerial romance and intermingling of light and shadow, and has vision of the true proportion of things in that conflict he has turned his back on:

> 'All things sip,
> And sip at life; but Time for ever drains
> The ever-filling cup in rivalship,
> And wipes the generations from his lip,
> While Art looks down from his serene domains.'

Æ

REVIEW[1]

From the Upanishads. By Charles Johnston. [Whaley: Dublin. 1896.]

We trust we are guilty of no indiscretion in saying that Prof. Max Müller has written to the author of these renderings of the Indian books of wisdom as follows:

'I hope your extracts may help to rouse a wider interest in what is, to my mind, a unique literature, and by no means appreciated as it deserves to be – in fact, hardly discovered as yet. I daresay you have found some passages in which you differ from my translation. Some verses cannot be rendered faithfully, the thoughts and words are too far away from us. We must do the best we can, and that is all I can say for myself.'

The ideal translation should make the same impression as the original did on its first readers or hearers; should bring us into their mood, and make us feel as they did. Who will venture to say that this or that translation can do so fully, for in the Upanishads, where, after sympathy and intuition are exercised to the full, we still feel the profound old wisdom towering above us, like great, dim arches rising up into the twilight, while the stately music of the verse or measured prose resounds like the deep voice of an organ. Yet a translation, in a spirit of earnestness and fullest sympathy – the ideal the present rendering seeks to follow – cannot but kindle in us something of that light which gives the Upanishads their singular worth, lifting us up into the eternal shining, or, rather, opening our eyes to the light that shines through all the world; showing us the Self everlasting that gleams to us out of the eyes of our fellow-men.

WORKS AND DAYS[1]

When we were boys with what anxiety we watched for the rare smile on the master's face ere we preferred a request for some favour, a holiday or early release. There was wisdom in that. As we grow up we act more or less consciously upon intuitions as to time and place. My companion, I shall not invite you to a merrymaking when a bitter moment befalls you and the flame of life sinks into ashes in your heart; nor yet, however true and trusted, will I confide to you what inward revelations of the mysteries I may have while I sense in you a momentary outwardness. The gifts of the heart are too sacred to be laid before a closed door. Your mood, I know, will pass, and to-morrow we shall have this bond between us. I wait, for it can be said but once: I cannot commune magically twice on the same theme with you. I do not propose we should be opportunists, nor lay down a formula; but to be skilful in action we must work with and comprehend the ebb and flow of power. Mystery and gloom, dark blue and starshine, doubt and feebleness alternate with the clear and shining, opal skies and sunglow, heroic ardor and the exultation of power. Ever varying, prismatic and fleeting, the days go by and the secret of change eludes us here. I bend the bow of thought at a mark and it is already gone. I lay the shaft aside and while unprepared the quarry again fleets by. We have to seek elsewhere for the source of that power which momentarily overflows into our world and transforms it with its enchantment.

On the motions of an inner sphere, we are told, all things here depend; on spheres of the less evanescent which, in their turn, are enclosed in spheres of the real, whose solemn chariot movements again are guided by the inflexible will of Fire.[2] In all of these we have part. This dim consciousness which burns in my brain is not all of myself. Behind me it widens out and upward into God. I feel in some other world it shines with purer light: in some sphere more divine than this it has a larger day and a deeper rest. That day of the inner self illuminates many of our mortal days; its night leaves many of them dark. And so the One Ray expanding lives in many vestures.³ It is last of all the King-Self⁴ who wakes at the dawn of ages, whose day is the day of Brahma, whose rest is his rest.⁵ Here is the clue to cyclic change, to the individual feebleness and power, the gloom of one epoch and the glory of another. The Bright Fortnight, the Northern Sun, Light and Flame name the days of other spheres, and wandering on from day to day man may at last reach the end of his journey.⁶ You would pass from rapidly revolving day and night to where the mystical sunlight streams. The way lies through yourself and the portals open as the inner day expands. Who is there who has not felt in some way or other the rhythmic recurrence of light within? We were weary of life, baffled, ready to forswear endeavor, when half insensibly a change comes over us; we doubt no more but do joyfully our work; we renew the sweet magical affinities with nature: out of a heart more laden with love we think and act; our meditations prolong themselves into the shining wonderful life of soul; we tremble on the verge of the vast halls of the gods where their mighty speech may be heard, their message of radiant will be seen. They speak a universal language not for themselves only but for all. What is poetry but a mingling of some tone of theirs with the sounds that below we utter? What is love but a breath of their very being? Their every mood has colours beyond the rainbow; every thought rings in far-heard melody. So the gods speak to each other across the expanses of ethereal light, breaking the divine silences with words which are deeds. So, too, they speak to the soul. Mystics of all time have tried to express it, likening it to peals of faery bells, the singing of enchanted birds, the clanging of silver cymbals, the organ voices of wind and water blent together – but in vain, in vain. Perhaps in this there is a danger, for the true is realized in being and not in perception. The gods are ourselves beyond the changes of time which harass and vex us here. They do not demand adoration but an equal will to bind us consciously in unity with themselves. The heresy of separateness cuts us asunder in these enraptured moments; but when thrilled by the deepest breath, when the silent, unseen, uncomprehended takes possession of thee, think 'Thou art That,'⁷ and something of thee will abide for ever in It. All thought not based on this is a weaving of new bonds, of illusions more difficult to break; it begets only more passionate longing and pain.

Still we must learn to know the hidden ways, to use the luminous rivers for the commerce of thought. Our Druid forefathers began their magical operations on the sixth day of the new moon, taking the Bright Fortnight at its flood-time. In these hours of expansion what we think has more force, more freedom, more electric and penetrating power. We find too, if we have co-workers, that we draw from a common fountain, the same impulse visits us and them. What one possesses all become possessed of; and something of the same unity and harmony arises between us here as exists for all time between us in the worlds above. While the currents circulate we are to see to it that they part from us no less pure than they came. To this dawn of an inner day may in some measure be traced the sudden inspirations of movements, such as we lately feel, not all due to the abrupt descent into our midst of a new messenger, for the Elder Brothers[8] work with law and foresee when nature, time, and the awakening souls of men will aid them. Much may now be done. On whosoever accepts, acknowledges and does the will of the Light in these awakenings the die and image of divinity is more firmly set, his thought grows more consciously into the being of the presiding god. Yet not while seeking for ourselves can we lay hold of final truths, for then what we perceive we retain but in thought and memory. The Highest is a motion, a breath. We become it only in the imparting. It is in all, for all and goes out to all. It will not be restrained in a narrow basin, but through the free-giver it freely flows. There are throngs innumerable who await this gift. Can we let this most ancient light which again returns to us be felt by them only as a vague emotion, a little peace of uncertain duration, a passing sweetness of the heart? Can we not do something to allay the sorrow of the world? My brothers, the time of opportunity has come. One day in the long-marshalled line of endless days has dawned for our race, and the buried treasure-houses in the bosom of the deep have been opened to endow it with more light, to fill it with more power. The divine ascetics stand with torches lit before the temple of wisdom. Those who are nigh them have caught the fire and offer to us in turn to light the torch, the blazing torch of soul. Let us accept the gift and pass it on, pointing out the prime givers. We shall see in time the eager races of men starting on their pilgrimage of return and facing the light. So in the mystical past the call of light was seen on the sacred hills; the rays were spread and gathered; and returning with them the initiate-children were buried in the Father-Flame.

Æ.

II. THE TRIALS OF THE SOUL

THE HOUR OF TWILIGHT[1] (A)

For the future we intend that at this hour the Mystic shall be at home, less metaphysical and scientific than is his wont, but more really himself. It is customary at this hour, before the lamps are brought in, to give way a little and dream, letting all the tender fancies day suppresses rise up in our minds.[2] Wherever it is spent, whether in the dusky room or walking home through the blue evening, all things grow strangely softened and united; the magic of the old world reappears. The commonplace streets take on something of the grandeur and solemnity of starlit avenues of Egyptian temples; the public squares in the mingled glow and gloom grow beautiful as the Indian grove where Shakuntala wandered with her maidens;[3] the children chase each other through the dusky shrubberies, as they flee past they look at us with long remembered glances: lulled by the silence, we forget a little while the hard edges of the material and remember that we are *spirits*.

Now is the hour for memory, the time to call in and make more securely our own all stray and beautiful ideas that visited us during the day, and which might otherwise be forgotten. We should draw them in from the region of things felt to the region of things understood; in a focus burning with beauty and pure with truth we should bind them, for from the thoughts thus gathered in something accrues to the consciousness;[4] on the morrow a change impalpable but real has taken place in our being, we see beauty and truth through everything.

It is in like manner in Devachan,[5] between the darkness of earth and the light of spiritual self-consciousness, that the Master in each of us draws in and absorbs the rarest and best of experiences, love, self-forgetfulness, aspiration, and out of these distils the subtle essence of wisdom, so that he who struggles in pain for his fellows, when he wakens again on earth is endowed with the tradition of that which we call self sacrifice, but which is in reality the proclamation of our own universal nature. There are yet vaster correspondences, for so also we are told, when the seven worlds are withdrawn,[6] the great calm Shepherd of the Ages draws his misty hordes together in the glimmering twilights of eternity, and as they are penned within the awful Fold, the rays long separate are bound into one,[7] and life, and joy, and beauty disappear, to emerge again after rest unspeakable on the morning of a New Day.

Now if the aim of the mystic be to fuse into one all moods made separate by time, would not the daily harvesting of wisdom render unnecessary the long Devachanic years?[8] No second harvest could be reaped from fields where the sheaves are already garnered. Thus disregarding the fruits of action,[9] we could work like those who have made the Great Sacrifice, for whom even Nirvana is no resting place.[10] Worlds may awaken in nebulous glory, pass through their phases of self-conscious existence and sink again to sleep, but these tireless workers continue their age-long task of help. Their motive we do not know, but in some secret depth of our being we feel that there could be nothing nobler, and thinking this we have devoted the twilight hour to the understanding of their nature.[11]

THE HOUR OF TWILIGHT[1] (B)

There are dreams which may be history or may be allegory. There is in them nothing grotesque, nothing which could mar the feeling of authenticity, the sense of the actual occurrence of the dream incident. The faces and figures perceived have the light shade and expression which seems quite proper to the wonderworld in which the eye of the inner man has vision; and yet the story may be read as a parable of spiritual truth like some myth of ancient scripture. Long ago I had many such dreams, and having lately become a student of such things, I have felt an interest in recalling the more curious and memorable of these early visions.

The nebulous mid-region between waking and unconsciousness was the haunt of many strange figures, reflections perhaps from that true life led during sleep by the immortal man. Among these figures two awoke the strangest feelings of interest. One was an old man with long grey hair and beard, whose grey-blue eyes had an expression of secret and inscrutable wisdom; I felt an instinctive reverence for this figure, so expressive of spiritual nobility, and it became associated in my mind with all aspiration and mystical thought. The other figure was that of a young girl. These two appeared again and again in my visions; the old man always as instructor, the girl always as companion. I have here written down one of these adventures, leaving it to the reader to judge whether it is purely symbolical, or whether the incidents related actually took place, and were out-realized from latency by the power of the Master within.[2]

With the girl as my companion I left an inland valley and walked towards the sea. It was evening when we reached it and the tide was far out. The sands glimmered away for miles on each side of us; we walked outwards through the dim coloured twilight. I was silent; a strange ecstasy slowly took possession of me, as if drop by drop an unutterable life was falling within; the fever grew intense, then unbearable as it communicated itself to the body; with a wild cry I began to spin about, whirling round and round in ever increasing delirium. Some secretness was in the air; I was called forth by the powers of invisible nature and in a swoon I fell. I rose again with sudden memory, but my body was lying upon the sands; with a curious indifference I saw that the tide was on the turn and the child was unable to remove the insensible form beyond its reach; I saw her sit down beside it and place the head upon her lap; she sat there quietly waiting, while all about her little by little the wave of the Indian sea began to ripple inwards, and overhead the early stars began softly to glow.

After this I forgot completely the child and the peril of the waters, I began to be conscious of the presence of a new world. All around me currents were flowing, in whose waves danced innumerable lives; diaphanous forms glided about, a nebulous sparkle was everywhere apparent; faces as of men in dreams glimmered on me, or unconsciously their forms drifted past, and now and then a face looked sternly upon me with a questioning glance. I was not to remain long in this misty region, again I felt the internal impulse and internally I was translated into a sphere of more pervading beauty and light; and here with more majesty and clearness than I had observed before was the old man of my dreams.

I had thought of him as old but there was an indescribable youth pervading the face with its ancient beauty, and then I knew it was neither age nor youth, it was *eternalness.* The calm light of thought played over features clear cut as a statue's, and an inner luminousness shone through the rose of his face and his silver hair. There were others about but of them I had no distinct vision.

He said, 'You who have lived and wandered through our own peculiar valleys look backwards now and learn the alchemy of thought.' He touched me with his hand and I became aware of the power of these strange beings. I felt how they had waited in patience, how they had worked and willed in silence; from them as from a fountain went forth peace; to them as to the stars rose up unconsciously the aspirations of men, the dumb animal cravings, the tendrils of the flowers. I saw how in the valley where I lived, where naught had hindered, their presence had drawn forth in luxuriance all dim and hidden beauty, a rarer and purer atmosphere recalled the radiant life of men in the golden dawn of the earth.

With wider vision I saw how far withdrawn from strife they had stilled the tumults of nations; I saw how hearing far within the voices, spiritual, remote, which called, the mighty princes of the earth descended from their thrones becoming greater than princes; under this silent influence the terrible chieftains flung open the doors of their dungeons that they themselves might become free, and all these joined in that hymn which the quietude of earth makes to sound in the ears of the gods. – Overpowered I turned round, the eyes of light were fixed upon me.

'Do you now understand?'

'I do not understand,' I replied. 'I see that the light and the beauty and the power that enters the darkness of the world comes from these high regions; but I do not know how the light enters, nor how beauty is born, I do not know the secret of power.'

'You must become as one of us,' he answered.

I bowed my head until it touched his breast; I felt my life was being drawn from me, but before consciousness utterly departed and was swallowed up in that larger life, I learned something of the secret of their being; I lived within the minds of men, but their thoughts were not my thoughts; I hung like a crown over everything, yet age was no nearer than childhood to the grasp of my sceptre and sorrow was far away when it wept for my going, and very far was joy when it woke at my light; yet I was the lure that led them on; I was at the end of all ways, and I was also in the sweet voice that cried 'return;' and I had learned how spiritual life is *one* in all things, when infinite vistas and greater depths received me, and I went into that darkness out of which no memory can ever return.

Æ.

THE SECRET OF POWER[1]

It is not merely because it is extraordinary that I wish to tell you this story. I think mere weirdness, grotesque or unusual character, are not sufficient reasons for making public incidents in which there is an element of the superhuman. The world, in spite of its desire to understand the nature of the occult, is sick of and refuses to listen to stories of apparitions which betray no spiritual character or reveal no spiritual law. The incident here related is burned into my mind and life, not because of its dramatic intensity or personal character, but because it was a revelation of the *secret of power,* a secret which the wise in good and the wise in evil alike have knowledge of.

My friend Felix was strangely disturbed; not only were his material affairs unsettled, but he was also passing through a crisis in his spiritual life. Two paths were open before him; On one side lay the dazzling mystery of passion; on the other 'the small old path' held out its secret and spiritual allurements. I had hope that he would choose the latter, and as I was keenly interested in his decision, I invested the struggle going on in his mind with something of universal significance, seeing in it a symbol of the strife between 'light and darkness which are the world's eternal ways.' He came in late one evening. I saw at once by the dim light that there was something strange in his manner. I spoke to him in enquiry; he answered me in a harsh dry voice quite foreign to his usual manner. 'Oh, I am not going to trouble myself any more, I will let things take their course.' This seemed the one idea in his mind, the one thing he understood clearly was that things were to take their own course; he failed to grasp the significance of any other idea or its relative importance. He answered 'Aye, indeed,' with every appearance of interest and eagerness to some trivial remark about the weather, and was quite unconcerned about another and most important matter which should have interested him deeply. I soon saw what had happened; his mind, in which forces so evenly balanced had fought so strenuously, had become utterly wearied out and could work no longer. A flash of old intuition illumined it at last, – it was not wise to strive with such bitterness over life, – therefore he said to me in memory of this intuition, 'I am going to let things take their course.' A larger tribunal would decide; he had appealed unto Caesar. I sent him up to his room and tried to quiet his fever by magnetization with some success. He fell asleep, and as I was rather weary myself I retired soon after.

This was the vision of the night. It was surely in the room, I was lying on my bed, and yet space opened on every side with pale, clear light. A slight wavering figure caught my eye, a figure that swayed to and fro; I was struck with its utter feebleness, yet I understood it was its own will or some quality of its nature which determined that palpitating movement towards the poles between which it swung. What were they? I became silent as night and thought no more.

Two figures awful in their power opposed each other; the frail being wavering between them could by putting out its arms have touched them both. It alone wavered, for they were silent, resolute and knit in the conflict of will; they stirred not a hand nor a foot; there was only a still quivering now and then as of intense effort, but they made no other movement. Their heads were bent forward slightly, their arms folded, their bodies straight, rigid, and inclined slightly backwards from each other like two spokes of a gigantic wheel. What were they, these figures? I knew not, and yet gazing upon them, thought which took no words to clothe itself mutely read their meaning. Here were the culminations of the human, towering images of the good and evil man may aspire to. I looked at the face of the evil adept.[2] His bright red-brown eyes burned with a strange radiance of power; I felt an answering emotion of pride, of personal intoxication, of psychic richness rise up within me gazing upon him. His face was archetypal; the abstract passion which eluded me in the features of many people I knew, was here declared, exultant, defiant, giantesque; it seemed to leap like fire, to be free. In this face I was close to the legendary past, to the hopeless worlds where men were martyred by stony kings, where prayer was hopeless, where pity was none. I traced a resemblance to many of the great Destroyers in history whose features have been preserved, Napoleon, Ramases and a hundred others, named and nameless, the long line of those who were crowned and sceptered in cruelty. His strength was in human weakness, I saw this, for space and the hearts of men were bare before me. Out of space there flowed to him a stream half invisible of red; it nourished that rich radiant energy of passion; it flowed from men as they walked and brooded in loneliness, or as they tossed in sleep. I withdrew my gaze from this face which awoke in me a lurid sense accompaniment, and turned it on the other. An aura of pale soft blue was around this figure through which gleamed an underlight as of universal gold.[3] The vision was already dim and departing, but I caught a glimpse of a face godlike in its calm, terrible in the beauty of a life we know only in dreams, with strength which is the end of the hero's toil, which belongs to the many times martyred soul; yet not far away nor in the past was its power, it was the might of life which exists eternally. I understood how easy it would have been for this one to have ended the conflict, to have gained a material victory by its power, but this would not have touched on or furthered its spiritual ends. Only its real being had force to attract that real being which was shrouded in the wavering figure. This truth the adept of darkness knew also and therefore he intensified within the sense of pride and passionate personality. Therefore they stirred not a hand nor a foot while under the stimulus of their presence culminated the good and evil in the life which had appealed to a higher tribunal to decide. Then this figure wavering between the two moved forward and touched with its hand the Son of Light. All at once the scene and actors vanished, and the eye that saw them was closed, I was alone with darkness and a hurricane of thoughts.

Strange and powerful figures! I knew your secret of strength, it is only *to be,* nature quickened by your presence leaps up in response. I knew no less the freedom of that human soul, for your power only revealed its unmanifest nature,[4] it but precipitated experience. I knew that although the gods and cosmic powers may war over us for ever, it is we alone declare them victors or vanquished.

For the rest the vision of that night was prophetic, and the feet of my friend are now set on that way which was the innermost impulse of his soul.

Æ

A PRIESTESS OF THE WOODS[1]

Here is a legend whispered to me, the land or time I cannot tell, it may have been in the old Atlantean days. There were vast woods and a young priestess ruled them; she presided at the festivals and sacrificed at the altar for the people, interceding with the spirits of fire, water air and earth, that the harvest might not be burned up, nor drenched with the floods, nor torn by storms and that the blight might not fall upon it, which things the elemental spirits sometimes brought about. This woodland sovereignty was her heritage from her father who was a mighty magician before her. Around her young days floated the faery presences;[2] she knew them as other children know the flowers having neither fear nor wonder for them. She saw deeper things also; as a little child, wrapped up in her bearskin, she watched with awe her father engaged in mystic rites; when around him the airy legions gathered from the populous elements, the spirits he ruled and the spirits he bowed down before; fleeting nebulous things white as foam coming forth from the great deep who fled away at the waving of his hand; and rarer the great sons of fire, bright and transparent as glass, who though near seemed yet far away and were still and swift as the figures that glance in a crystal. So the child grew up full of mystery; her thoughts were not the thoughts of the people about her, nor their affections her affections. It seemed as if the elf-things or beings carved by the thought of the magician, pushed aside by his strong will and falling away from him, entering into the child became part of her, linking her to the elemental beings who live in the star-soul that glows within the earth. Her father told her such things as she asked, but he died while she was yet young and she knew not his aim, what man is, or what is his destiny; but she knew the ways of every order of spirit that goes about clad in a form, how some were to be dreaded and some to be loved; By reason of this knowledge she succeeded as priestess to the shrine, and held the sway of beauty and youth, of wisdom and mystery over the people dwelling in the woods.[3]

It was the evening of the autumn festival, the open grassy space before the altar was crowded with figures, hunters with their feathered heads; shepherds, those who toil in the fields, the old and hoary were gathered around.

The young priestess stood up before them; she was pale from vigil, and the sunlight coming through the misty evening air fell upon her swaying arms and her dress with its curious embroidery of peacock's feathers; the dark hollows of her eyes were alight and as she spoke inspiration came to her; her voice rose and fell, commanding, warning, whispering, beseeching; its strange rich music flooded the woods and pierced through and through with awe the hearts of those who listened. She spoke of the mysteries of that unseen nature; how man is watched and ringed round with hosts who war upon him, who wither up his joys by their breath; she spoke of the gnomes who rise up in the woodland paths with damp arms grasping from their earthy bed.

'Dreadful' she said 'are the elementals who live in the hidden waters: they rule the dreaming heart; their curse is forgetfulness; they lull man to fatal rest, with drowsy fingers feeling to put out his fire of life. But most of all, dread the powers that move in air; their nature is desire unquenchable; their destiny is – never to be fulfilled – never to be at peace: they roam hither and thither like the winds they guide; they usurp dominion over the passionate and tender soul, but they love not in our way; where they dwell the heart is a madness and the feet are filled with a hurrying fever, and night has no sleep and day holds no joy in its sunlit cup. Listen not to their whisper; they wither and burn up the body with their fire; the beauty they offer is smitten through and through with unappeasable anguish.' She paused for a moment; her terrible breath had hardly ceased to thrill them, when another voice was heard singing; its note was gay and triumphant, it broke the spell of fear upon the people,

> I never heed by waste or wood
>   The cry of fay or faery thing
> Who tell of their own solitude;
>   Above them all my soul is king.
>
> The royal robe as king I wear
>   Trails all along the fields of light;
> Its silent blue and silver bear
>   For gems the starry dust of night.
>
> The breath of joy unceasingly
>   Waves to and fro its folds star-lit,
> And far beyond earth's misery
>   I live and breathe the joy of it.

A Priestess of the Woods

The priestess advanced from the altar, her eyes sought for the singer; when she came to the centre of the opening she paused and waited silently. Almost immediately a young man carrying a small lyre stepped out of the crowd and stood before her: he did not seem older than the priestess; he stood unconcerned though her dark eyes blazed at the intrusion; he met her gaze fearlessly; his eyes looked into hers – in this way all proud spirits do battle. Her eyes were black with almost a purple tinge, eyes that had looked into the dark ways of nature; his were bronze, and a golden tinge, a mystic opulence of vitality seemed to dance in their depths; they dazzled the young priestess with the secrecy of joy; her eyes fell for a moment. He turned round and cried out, 'Your priestess speaks but half truths, her eyes have seen but her heart does not know. Life is not terrible but is full of joy. Listen to me. I passed by while she spake, and I saw that a fear lay upon every man, and you shivered thinking of your homeward path, fearful as rabbits of the unseen things, and forgetful how you have laughed at death facing the monsters who crush down the forests. Do you not know that you are greater than all these spirits before whom you bow in dread: your life springs from a deeper source. Answer me, priestess, where go the fire-spirits when winter seizes the world?'

'Into the Fire-King they go, they dream in his heart.' She half chanted, the passion of her speech not yet fallen away from her. 'And where go the fires of men when they depart?' She was silent; then he continued half in scorn, 'Your priestess is the priestess of ghouls and fays rather than a priestess of men; her wisdom is not for you; the spirits that haunt the elements are hostile because they see you full of fear; do not dread them and their hatred will vanish. The great heart of the earth is full of laughter, do not put yourselves apart from its joy, for its soul is your soul and its joy is your true being.'[4]

He turned and passed through the crowd; the priestess made a motion as if she would have stayed him, then she drew herself up proudly and refrained. They heard his voice again singing as he passed into the darkening woods,

> The spirits to the fire-king throng
> Each in the winter of his day:
> And all who listen to their song
> Follow them after in that way.
>
> They seek the heart-hold of the king,
> They build within his halls of fire,
> Their dreams flash like the peacock's wing,
> They glow with sun-hues of desire.

> I follow in no faery ways;
>   I heed no voice of fay or elf;
>   I in the winter of my days
>   Rest in the high ancestral self.

The rites interrupted by the stranger did not continue much longer; the priestess concluded her words of warning; she did not try to remove the impression created by the poet's song, she only said, 'His wisdom may be truer; it is more beautiful than the knowledge we inherit.'

The days passed on; autumn died into winter, spring came again and summer, and the seasons which brought change to the earth brought change to the young priestess. She sought no longer to hold sway over the elemental tribes, and her empire over them departed: the song of the poet rang for ever in her ears; its proud assertion of kingship and joy in the radiance of a deeper life haunted her like truth; but such a life seemed unattainable by her and a deep sadness rested in her heart. The wood-people often saw her sitting in the evening where the sunlight fell along the pool, waving slowly its azure and amethyst, sparkling and flashing in crystal and gold, melting as if a phantom Bird of Paradise were fading away: her dark head was bowed in melancholy and all that great beauty flamed and died away unheeded. After a time she rose up and moved about, she spoke more frequently to the people who had not dared to question her, she grew into a more human softness, they feared her less and loved her more; but she ceased not from her passionate vigils and her step faltered and her cheek paled, and her eager spirit took flight when the diamond glow of winter broke out over the world. The poet came again in the summer; they told him of the change they could not understand, but he fathomed the depths of this wild nature, and half in gladness, half in sorrow, he carved an epitaph over her tomb near the altar,

> Where is the priestess of this shrine,
>   And by what place does she adore?
> The woodland haunt below the pine
>   Now hears her whisper nevermore.
>
> Ah, wrapped in her own beauty now
>   She dreams a dream that shall not cease;
> Priestess, to her own soul to bow
>   Is hers in everlasting peace.

Æ.

A TRAGEDY IN THE TEMPLE[1]

I have often thought with sadness over the fate of that comrade. That so ardent and heroic a spirit, so much chivalry and generosity should meet such a horrible fate, has often made me wonder if there is any purpose in this tangled being of ours; I have hated life and the gods as I thought of it. What brought him out of those great deserts where his youth was spent, where his soul grew vast knowing only of two changes, the blaze of day and night the purifier, blue, mysterious, ecstatic with starry being? Were not these enough for him? Could the fire of the altar inspire more? Could he be initiated deeper in the chambers of the temple than in those great and lonely places where God and man are alone together? This was my doing; resting in his tent when I crossed the desert, I had spoken to him of that old wisdom which the priests of the inner temple keep and hand down from one to the other; I blew to flame the mystic fire which already smouldered within him, and filled with the vast ambition of God, he left his tribe and entered the priesthood as neophyte in the Temple of Isthar, below Ninevah.

I had sometimes to journey thither bearing messages from our high priest, and so as time passed my friendship with Asur grew deep. That last evening when I sat with him on the terrace that roofed the temple, he was more silent than I had known him before to be; we had generally so many things to speak of; for he told me all his dreams, such vague titanic impulses as the soul has in the fresh first years of its awakening, when no experience hinders with memory its flights of aspiration, and no anguish has made it wise. But that evening there was, I thought, something missing; a curious feverishness seemed to have replaced the cool and hardy purity of manner which was natural to him; his eyes had a strange glow, fitful and eager; I saw by the starlight how restless his fingers were, they intertwined, twisted, and writhed in and out.

We sat long in the rich night together; then he drew nearer to me and leaned his head near my shoulder; he began to whisper incoherently a wild and passionate tale; the man's soul was being tempted.

'Brother' he said, 'I am haunted by a vision, by a child of the stars as lovely as Isthar's self; she visits my dreaming hours, she dazzles me with strange graces, she bewilders with unspeakable longing. Sometime, I know, I must go to her, though I perish. When I see her I forget all else and I have will to resist no longer. The vast and lonely inspiration of the desert departs from my thought, she and the jewel-light she lives in blot it out. The thought of her thrills me like fire. Brother give me help, ere I go mad or die; she draws me away from earth and I shall end my days amid strange things, a starry destiny amid starry races.'

I was not then wise in these things, I did not know the terrible dangers that lurk in the hidden ways in which the soul travels. 'This' I said 'is some delusion. You have brooded over a fancy until it has become living; you have filled your creation with your own passion and it lingers and tempts you; even if it were real, it is folly to think of it, we must close our hearts to passion if we would attain the power and wisdom of Gods.'

He shook his head, I could not realize or understand him. Perhaps if I had known all and could have warned him, it would have been in vain; perhaps the soul must work out its own purification in experience and learn truth and wisdom through being. Once more he became silent and restless. I had to bid him farewell as I was to depart on the morrow, but he was present in my thoughts and I could not sleep because of him; I felt oppressed with the weight of some doom about to fall. To escape from this feeling I rose in adoration to Hea; I tried to enter into the light of that Wisdom; a sudden heart-throb of warning drew me back; I thought of Asur instinctively, and thinking of him his image flashed on me. He moved as if in trance through the glassy waves of those cosmic waters which everywhere lave and permeate the worlds, and in which our earth is but a subaqueous mound. His head was bowed, his form dilated to heroic stature, as if he conceived of himself as some great thing or as moving to some high destiny; and this shadow which was the house of his dreaming soul grew brilliant with the passionate hues of his thought; some power beyond him drew him forth. I felt the fever and heat of this inner sphere like a delirious breath blow fiercely about me; there was a phosphorescence of hot and lurid colours. The form of Asur moved towards a light streaming from a grotto, I could see within it burning gigantic flowers. On one, as on a throne, a figure of weird and wonderful beauty was seated. I was thrilled with a dreadful horror, I thought of the race of Liliths,[2] and some long forgotten and tragic legends rose up in my memory of these beings whose soul is but a single and terrible passion; whose love too fierce for feebler lives to endure, brings death or madness to men. I tried to warn, to awaken him from the spell; my will-call aroused him; he turned, recognized me and hesitated; then this figure that lured him rose to her full height; I saw her in all her terrible beauty. From her head a radiance of feathered flame spread out like the plume of a peacock, it was spotted with gold and green and citron dyes, she raised her arms upwards, her robe, semi-transparent, purple and starred over with a jewel lustre, fell in vaporous folds to her feet like the drift over a waterfall. She turned her head with a sudden bird-like movement, her strange eyes looked into mine with a prolonged and snaky glance; I saw her move her arms hither and thither, and the waves of this inner ocean began to darken and gather about me, to ripple though me with feverish motion. I fell into a swoon and remembered nothing more.

I was awakened before dawn, those with whom I was to cross the desert were about to start and I could remain no longer. I wrote hurriedly to Asur a message full of warning and entreaty and set out on my return journey full of evil forebodings. Some months after I had again to visit this temple; it was evening when I arrived; after I had delivered the message with which I was charged, I asked for Asur. The priest to whom I spoke did not answer me. He led me in silence up to the terrace that overlooked the desolate eastern desert. The moon was looming white upon the verge, the world was trembling with heat, the winged bulls along the walls shone with a dull glow through the sultry air. The priest pointed to the far end of the terrace. A figure was seated looking out over the desert, his robes were motionless as if their wrinkles were carved of stone, his hands lay on his knees, I walked up to him; I called his name; he did not stir. I came nearer and put my face close to his, it was as white as the moon, his eyes only reflected the light. I turned away from him sick to the very heart.

Æ.

THE MEDITATION OF ANANDA[1]

Ananda rose from his seat under the banyan tree. He passed his hand unsteadily over his brow. Throughout the day the young ascetic had been plunged in profound meditation; and now, returning from heaven to earth, he was bewildered like one who awakens in darkness and knows not where he is. All day long before his inner eye burned the light of the Lokas,[2] until he was wearied and exhausted with their splendours; space glowed like a diamond with intolerable lustre, and there was no end to the dazzling procession of figures. He had seen the fiery dreams of the dead in heaven. He had been tormented by the music of celestial singers, whose choral song reflected in its ripples the rhythmic pulse of being. He saw how these orbs were held within luminous orbs of wider circuit; and vaster and vaster grew the vistas, until at last, a mere speck of life, he bore the burden of innumerable worlds. Seeking for Brahma, he found only the great illusion as infinite as Brahma's being.

If these things were shadows, the earth and the forests he returned to, viewed at evening, seemed still more unreal, the mere dusky flutter of a moth's wings in space, so filmy and evanescent that if he had sunk as through transparent aether into the void, it would not have been wonderful.

Ananda, still half entranced, turned homeward. As he treaded the dim alleys he noticed not the flaming eyes which regarded him from the gloom; the serpents rustling amid the undergrowth; the lizards, fireflies, insects, and the innumerable lives of which the Indian forest was rumorous; they also were but shadows. He paused near the village, hearing the sound of human voices, of children at play. He felt a pity for these tiny beings, who struggled and shouted, rolling over each other in ecstasies of joy. The great illusion had indeed devoured them, before whose spirits the Devas themselves once were worshippers. Then, close beside him, he heard a voice, whose low tone of reverence soothed him; it was akin to his own nature, and it awakened him fully. A little crowd of five or six people were listening silently to an old man who read from a

The Meditation of Ananda

palm-leaf manuscript. Ananda knew by the orange-coloured robes of the old man that here was a brother of the new faith, and he paused with the others. What was his illusion? The old man lifted his head for a moment as the ascetic came closer, and then continued as before. He was reading 'The Legend of the Great King of Glory,' and Ananda listened while the story was told of the Wonderful Wheel, the Elephant Treasure, the Lake and Palace of Righteousness, and of the meditation, how *the Great King of Glory entered the golden chamber, and set himself down on the silver couch, and he let his mind pervade one quarter of the world with thoughts of love; and so the second quarter, and so the third, and so the fourth. And thus the whole wide world, above, below, around, and everywhere, did he continue to pervade with heart of Love, far reaching, grown great, and beyond measure.*[3]

When the old man had ended Ananda went back into the forest. He had found the secret of the true, how the Vision could be left behind and the Being entered. Another legend rose in his mind, a faery legend of righteousness expanding and filling the universe, a vision beautiful and full of old enchantment, and his heart sang within him. He seated himself again under the banyan tree. He rose up in soul. He saw before him images long forgotten of those who suffer in the sorrowful earth. He saw the desolation and loneliness of old age, the insults of the captive, the misery of the leper and outcast, the chill horror and darkness of life in a dungeon. He drank in all their sorrow. From his heart he went out to them. Love, a fierce and tender flame, arose; pity, a breath from the vast; sympathy, born of unity. This triple fire sent forth its rays; they surrounded those dark souls; they pervaded them; they beat down oppression.

* * *

While Ananda, with spiritual magic,[4] sent forth the healing powers through the four quarters of the world, far away at that moment a king sat enthroned in his hall. A captive was bound before him – bound, but proud, defiant, unconquerable of soul. There was silence in the hall until the king spake the doom and torture for this ancient enemy.

The king spake: 'I had thought to do some fierce thing to thee and so end thy days, my enemy. But I remember now, with sorrow, the great wrongs we have done to each other, and the hearts made sore by our hatred. I shall do no more wrong to thee; thou art free to depart. Do what thou wilt. I will make restitution to thee as far as may be for thy ruined state.'

Then the soul which no might could conquer was conquered utterly – the knees of the captive were bowed and his pride was overcome. 'My brother,' he said, and could say no more.

* * *

To watch for years a little narrow slit high up in a dark cell, so high that he could not reach up and look out, and there to see daily the change from blue to dark in the sky, had withered a prisoner's soul. The bitter tears came no more, hardly even sorrow, only a dull, dead feeling. But that day a great groan burst from him. He heard outside the laugh of a child who was playing and gathering flowers under the high, grey walls. Then it all came over him – the divine things missed, the light, the glory, and the beauty that the earth puts forth for her children. The narrow slit was darkened, and half of a little bronze face appeard.

'Who are you down there in the darkness who sigh so? Are you all alone there? For so many years! Ah, poor man! I would come down to you if I could, but I will sit here and talk to you for a while. Here are flowers for you,' and a little arm showered them in by handfuls until the room was full of the intoxicating fragrance of summer. Day after day the child came, and the dull heart entered once more into the great human love.

* * *

At twilight, by a deep and wide river, an old woman sat alone, dreamy and full of memories. The lights of the swift passing boats and the light of the stars were just as in childhood and the old love-time. Old, feeble, it was time for her to hurry away from the place which changed not with her sorrow.

'Do you see our old neighbour there?' said Ayesha to her lover. 'They say she was once as beautiful as you would make me think I now am. How lonely she must be! Let us come near and speak to her,' and the lover went gladly. Though they spoke to each other rather than to her, yet something of the past, which never dies when love, the immortal, has pervaded it, rose up again as she heard their voices. She smiled, thinking of years of burning beauty.

* * *

The Meditation of Ananda

A teacher, accompanied by his disciples, was passing by the wayside where a leper sat.

The teacher said: 'Here is our brother, whom we may not touch, but he need not be shut out from truth. We may sit down where he can listen.'

He sat on the wayside near the leper, and his disciples stood around him. He spoke words full of love, kindliness, and pity – the eternal truths which make the soul grow full of sweetness and youth. A small, old spot began to glow in the heart of the leper, and the tears ran down his blighted face.

* * *

All these were the deeds of Ananda the ascetic, and the Watcher[5] who was over him from all eternity made a great stride towards that soul.

1893.

A TALK BY THE EUPHRATES[1]

Priest Merodach walked with me at evening along the banks of the great river.

'You feel despondent now,' he said, 'but this was inevitable. You looked for a result equal to your inspiration. You must learn to be content with that alone. Finally an inspiration will come for every moment, and in every action a divine fire reveal itself.'

'I feel hopeless now. Why is this? Wish and will are not less strong than before.'

'Because you looked for a result beyond yourself, and, attached to external things, your mind drew to itself subtle essences of earth which clouded it. But there is more in it than that. Nature has a rhythm, and that part of us which is compounded of her elements shares in it. You were taught that nature is for ever becoming: the first emanation in the great deep is wisdom: wisdom changes into desire, and an unutterable yearning to go outward darkens the primeval beauty. Lastly, the elements arise, blind, dark, troubled. Nature in them imagines herself into forgetfulness. This rhythm repeats itself in man: a moment of inspiration – wise and clear, we determine; then we are seized with a great desire which impels us to action; the hero, the poet, the lover, all alike listen to the music of life, and then endeavour to express its meaning in word or deed; coming in contact with nature, its lethal influence drowses them; so baffled and forgetful, they wonder where the God is. To these in some moment the old inspiration returns, the universe is as magical and sweet as ever, a new impulse is given, and so they revolve, perverting and using each one in his own way, the cosmic rhythm.'

'Merodach, what you say seems truth, and leaving aside the cosmic rhythm, which I do not comprehend, define again for me the three states.'

'You cannot really understand the little apart from the great; but, applying this to your own case, you remember you had a strange experience, a God seemed to awaken within you. This passed away; you halted a little while, full of strange longing, eager for the great;

A Talk by the Euphrates

yet you looked without on the hither side of that first moment, and in this second period, which is interchange and transition, your longing drew to you those subtle material essences I spoke of, which, like vapour surrounding, dull and bewilder the mind with strange phantasies of form and sensation. Every time we think with longing of any object, these essences flow to us out of the invisible spheres and steep us with the dew of matter: then we forget the great, we sleep, we are dead or despondent as you are despondent.'

I sighed as I listened. A watchfulness over momentary desires was the first step; I had thought of the tasks of the hero as leading upwards to the Gods, but this sleepless intensity of will working within itself demanded a still greater endurance. I neared my destination; I paused and looked round; a sudden temptation assailed me; the world was fair enough to live in. Why should I toil after the far-off glory? Babylon seemed full of mystery, its temples and palaces steeped in the jewel glow and gloom of evening. In far-up heights of misty magnificence the plates of gold on the temples rayed back the dying light: in the deepening vault a starry sparkle began: an immense hum arose from leagues of populous streets: the scents of many gardens by the river came over me: I was lulled by the plash of fountains. Closer I heard voices and a voice I loved: I listened as a song came

> 'Tell me, youthful lover, whether
> Love is joy or woe?
> Are they gay or sad together
> On that way who go?'

A voice answered back

> 'Radiant as a sunlit feather,
> Pure and proud they go;
> With the lion look together
> Glad their faces show.'

My sadness departed; I would be among them shortly, and would walk and whisper amid those rich gardens where beautiful idleness was always dreaming. Merodach looked at me.

'You will find these thoughts will hinder you much,' he said.

'You mean –' I hesitated, half-bewildered, half-amazed. 'I say that a thought such as that which flamed about you just now, driving your sadness away, will recur again when next you are despondent, and so you will accustom yourself to find relief on the great quest by returning to an old habit of the heart, renewing what should be laid aside. This desire of men and women for each other is the strongest tie among the many which bind us: it is the most difficult of all to overcome. The great ones of the earth have passed that way themselves with tears.'

'But surely, Merodach, you cannot condemn what I may say is so much a part of our nature – of all nature.'

'I did not condemn it, when I said it is the strongest tie that binds us here: it is sin only for those who seek for freedom.'

'Merodach, must we then give up love?'

'There are two kinds of love men know of. There is one which begins with a sudden sharp delight – it dies away into infinite tones of sorrow. There is a love which wakes up amid dead things: it is chill at first, but it takes root, it warms, it expands, it lays hold of universal joys. So the man loves: so the God loves. Those who know this divine love are wise indeed. They love not one or another: they are love itself. Think well over this: power alone is not the attribute of the Gods; there are no such fearful spectres in that great companionship. And now, farewell, we shall meet again.'

I watched his departing figure, and then I went on my own way. I longed for that wisdom, which they only acquire who toil, and strive, and suffer; but I was full of a rich life which longed for excitement and fulfilment, and in that great Babylon sin did not declare itself in its true nature, but was still clouded over by the mantle of primeval beauty.

Æ.

THE CAVE OF LILITH[1]

Out of her cave came the ancient Lilith; Lilith the wise; Lilith the enchantress. There ran a little path outside her dwelling; it wound away among the mountains and glittering peaks, and before the door one of the Wise Ones walked to and fro. Out of her cave came Lilith, scornful of his solitude, exultant in her wisdom, flaunting her shining and magical beauty.

'Still alone, star gazer! Is thy wisdom of no avail? Thou hast yet to learn that I am more powerful, knowing the ways of error, than you who know the ways of truth.'

The Wise One heeded her not, but walked to and fro. His eyes were turned to the distant peaks, the abode of his brothers. The starlight fell about him; a sweet air came down the mountain path, fluttering his white robe; he did not cease from his steady musing. Lilith wavered in her cave like a mist rising between rocks. Her raiment was violet, with silvery gleams. Her face was dim, and over her head rayed a shadowy diadem, like that which a man imagines over the head of his beloved: and one looking closer at her face would have seen that this was the crown he reached out to; that the eyes burnt with his own longing; that the lips were parted to yield to the secret wishes of his heart.

'Tell me, for I would know, why do you wait so long? I, here in my cave between the valley and the height, blind the eyes of all who would pass. Those who by chance go forth to you, come back to me again, and but one in ten thousand passes on. My illusions are sweeter to them than truth. I offer every soul its own shadow. I pay them their own price. I have grown rich, though the simple shepherds of old gave me birth. Men have made me; the mortals have made me immortal. I rose up like a vapour from their first dreams, and every sigh since then and every laugh remains with me. I am made up of hopes and fears.[2] The subtle princes lay out their plans of conquest in my cave, and there the hero dreams, and there the lovers of all time write in flame their history. I am wise, holding all experience, to tempt, to blind, to terrify. None shall pass by.[3]

Why, therefore, dost thou wait?'

The Wise One looked at her, and she shrank back a little, and a little her silver and violet faded, but out of her cave her voice still sounded:

'The stars and the starry crown are not yours alone to offer, and every promise you make I make also. I offer the good and the bad indifferently. The lover, the poet, the mystic, and all who would drink of the first fountain, I delude with my mirage. I was the Beatrice who led Dante upwards: the gloom was in me, and the glory was mine also, and he went not out of my cave. The stars and the shining of heaven were illusions of the infinite I wove about him. I captured his soul with the shadow of space; a nutshell would have contained the film. I smote on the dim heart-chords the manifold music of being. God is sweeter in the human than the human in God. Therefore he rested in me.'

She paused a little, and then went on: 'There is that fantastic fellow who slipped by me. Could your wisdom not retain him? He returned to me full of anguish, and I wound my arms round him like a fair melancholy; and now his sadness is as sweet to him as hope was before his fall. Listen to his song!' She paused again. A voice came up from the depths chanting a sad knowledge:

> What of all the will to do?
>   It has vanished long ago,
> For a dream-shaft pierced it through
>   From the Unknown Archer's bow.
>
> What of all the soul to think?
>   Some one offered it a cup
> Filled with a diviner drink,
>   And the flame has burned it up.
>
> What of all the hope to climb?
>   Only in the self we grope
> To the misty end of time,
>   Truth has put an end to hope.
>
> What of all the heart to love?
>   Sadder than for will or soul,
> No light lured it on above:
>   Love has found itself the whole.

'Is it not pitiful? I pity only those who pity themselves. Yet he is mine more surely than ever. This is the end of human wisdom. How shall he now escape? What shall draw him up?'

'His will shall awaken,' said the Wise One. 'I do not sorrow over him, for long is the darkness before the spirit is born. He learns in your caves not to see, not to hear, not to think, for very anguish flying your illusions.'

'Sorrow is a great bond,' Lilith said.

'It is a bond to the object of sorrow. He weeps what thou canst never give him, a life never breathed in thee. He shall come forth, and thou shalt not see him at the time of passing. When desire dies the swift and invisible will awakens. He shall go forth; and one by one the dwellers in your caves will awaken and pass onward. This small old path will be trodden by generation after generation. Thou, too, O shining Lilith, shalt follow, not as mistress, but as handmaiden.'

'I will weave spells,' Lilith cried. 'They shall never pass me. I will drug them with the sweetest poison. They shall rest drowsily and content as of old. Were they not giants long ago, mighty men and heroes? I overcame them with young enchantment. Shall they pass by feeble and longing for bygone joys, for the sins of their proud exultant youth, while I have grown into a myriad wisdom?'

The Wise One walked to and fro as before, and there was silence; and I saw that with steady will he pierced the tumultuous gloom of the cave, and a spirit awoke here and there from its dream. And I thought I saw that Sad Singer become filled with a new longing for true being, and that the illusions of good and evil fell from him, and that he came at last to the knees of the Wise One to learn the supreme truth. In the misty midnight I heard these three voices – the Sad Singer, the Enchantress Lilith, and the Wise One. From the Sad Singer I learned that thought of itself leads nowhere, but blows the perfume from every flower, and cuts the flower from every tree, and hews down every tree from the valley, and in the end goes to and fro in waste places – gnawing itself in a last hunger. I learned from Lilith that we weave our own enchantment and bind ourselves with our own imagination. To think of the true as beyond us or to love the symbol of being is to darken the path to wisdom, and to debar us from eternal beauty. From the Wise One I learned that the truest wisdom is to wait, to work, and to will in secret. Those who are voiceless to-day, to-morrow shall be eloquent, and the earth shall hear them and her children salute them. Of these three truths the hardest to learn is the silent will. Let us seek for the highest truth.

1894.

A STRANGE AWAKENING[1]

CHAPTER I.

That we are living in the Dark Age we all know, yet we do not realize half its darkness. We endure physical and moral suffering; but, fortunately or unfortunately, we are oblivious of the sorrow of all sorrows – the Spiritual Tragedy. Such a rust has come over the pure and ancient spirit of life, that the sceptre and the diadem and the starry sway we held are unremembered; and if anyone speaks of these things he is looked at strangely with blank eyes, or with eyes that suspect madness. I do not know whether to call him great, or pity him, who feels such anguish; for although it is the true agony of the crucifixion, it is only gods who are so martyred. With these rare souls memory is not born: life flows on, and they with it go on in dreams: they are lulled by lights, flowers, stars, colours, and sweet odours, and are sheltered awhile from heaven and hell; then in some moment the bubble bursts, and the god awakens and knows himself, and he rises again with giant strength to conquer; or else he succumbs, and the waves of Lethe, perhaps in mercy, blot out his brief knowledge.

I knew such an one many years ago, and I tell of him because I know of no deeper proof of the existence of a diviner nature than that man's story. Arthur Harvey, as I have heard people describe him, in his early years was gentle, shy, and given to much dreaming. He was taken from school early, came up from the country to the city, and was put to business. He possessed the apathy and unresisting nature characteristic of so many spiritual people, and which is found notably among the natives of India; so he took his daily confinement at first as a matter of course, though glad enough when it was over, and the keen sweet air blew about him in spring or summer evenings, and the earth looked visionary, steeped in dew and lovely colour, and his soul grew rich with strange memories and psychic sensations. And so day-by-day he might have gone on with the alternation of work and dream, and the soul in its imaginings

220

A Strange Awakening

might never have known of the labours of the mind, each working by habit in its accustomed hour, but for an incident which took place about two years after his going to business.

One morning his manager said: 'Harvey, take this letter; deliver it, and wait for an answer.' He started up eagerly, glad for the unwonted freedom from his desk. At the door, as he went out, the whole blinding glory of the sunlight was dashed on him. He looked up. Ah! what spaces illimitable of lustrous blue. How far off! How mighty! He felt suddenly faint, small, mean, and feeble. His limbs trembled under him: he shrank from the notice of men as he went on his way. Vastness, such as this, breaking in upon the eye that had followed the point of the pen, unnerved him: he felt a bitter self-contempt. What place had he amid these huge energies? The city deafened him as with one shout: the tread of the multitude; the mob of vehicles; glitter and shadow; rattle, roar, and dust; the black smoke curled in the air; higher up the snowy and brilliant clouds, which the tall winds bore along; all were but the intricate and wondrous workings of a single monstrous personality; a rival in the universe who had absorbed and wrested from him his own divine dower. Out of him; out of him; the power – the free, the fearless – whirled in play, and drove the suns and stars in their orbits, and sped the earth through light and shadow. Out of him; out of him; never to be reconquered; never to be regained. The exultant laugh of the day; the flame of summer; the gigantic winds careering over the city; the far-off divine things filled him with unutterable despair. What was he amid it all? A spark decaying in its socket; a little hot dust clinging together.

He found himself in a small square; he sat down on a bench; his brain burning, his eyes unseeing.

'Oh! my, what's he piping over?' jeered a grotesque voice, and a small figure disappeared, turning somersaults among the bushes.

'Poor young man! perhaps he is ill. Are you not well, sir?' asked a sympathetic nurse.

He started up, brought to himself, and muttering something unintelligible, continued his journey through the city. The terrible influence departed, and a new change came over him. The laugh of the urchin rankled in his mind: he hated notice: there must be something absurd or out of the common in his appearance to invoke it. He knew suddenly that there was a gulf between him and the people he lived among. They were vivid, actual, suited to their places. How he envied them! Then the whole superficies of his mind became filled with a desire to conceal this difference. He recalled the various characteristics of those who worked along with him.

One knew all topical songs, slang and phrases; another affected a smartness in dress; a third discussed theatres with semi-professional knowledge. Harvey, however, could never have entered the world, or lived in it, if he had first to pass through the portals of such ideas! He delivered his letter; he was wearied out, and as he returned he noticed neither sky nor sunlight, and the hurrying multitudes were indifferent and without character. He passed through them; his mind dull like theirs; a mere machine to guide rapid footsteps.

That evening, a clerk named Whittaker, a little his senior in the office, was struck by Harvey's curious and delicate face.

'I say, Harvey,' he said, 'how do you spend your evenings?'

Harvey flushed a little at the unwonted interest.

'I take long walks,' he said.

'Do you read much?'

'A little.'

'Do you go to the theatre?'

'No.'

'Never?'

'Never.'

'Whew! what a queer fellow! No clubs, classes, music-halls – anything of that sort, eh?'

'No,' said Harvey, a little bitterly, 'I know nothing, nobody; I am always alone.'

'What an extraordinary life! Why, you are out of the universe completely, I say,' he added, 'come along with me this evening. I will initiate you a little. You know you must learn your profession as a human being.'

His manner was very kindly, still Harvey was so shy that he would have found some excuse, but for that chance expression, 'out of the universe.' Was not this apartness the very thing he had just been bitterly feeling? While he hesitated and stammered in his awkwardness, the other said: 'There, no excuses! You need not go to your lodgings for tea. Come along with me.'

They went off together through the darkening streets. One cheerful and irreverent, brimful of remark or criticism; the other silent, his usual dreaminess was modified, but had not departed, and once, gazing up through the clear, dark blue, where the stars were shining, he had a momentary sense as if he were suspended from them by a fine invisible thread, as a spider hung from her roof; suspended from on high, where the pure and ancient aether flamed around the habitations of eternity; and below and about him, the thoughts of demons, the smoke, darkness, horror and anguish of the pit.

CHAPTER II

I cannot tell all the steps by which the young soul came forth from its clouds and dreams, but must hurry over the years. This single incident of his boyhood I have told to mark the character and tendency of his development; spirituality made self-conscious only in departing; life, a falling from ideals which grew greater, more beautiful and luminous as the possibility of realizing them died away. But this ebbtide of the inner life was not regular and incessant, but rather after the fashion of waves which retreat surely indeed, but returning again and again, seem for moments to regain almost more than their past altitude. His life was a series of such falls and such awakenings. Every new experience which drew his soul from its quietude brought with it a revelation of a spiritual past, in which, as it now seemed, he had been living unconsciously. Every new experience which enriched his mind seemed to leave his soul more barren. The pathetic anguish of these moments had little of the moral element, which was dormant and uncultivated rather than perverted. He did not ponder over their moral aspect, for he shared the superficial dislike to the ethical, which we often see in purely artistic natures, who cannot endure the entrance of restraint or pain upon their beauty. His greatest lack was the companionship of fine men or noble women. He had shot up far beyond the reach of those whom he knew, and wanting this companionship he grew into a cynical or sensuous way of regarding them. He began to write: he had acquired the faculty of vigorous expression by means of such emotions as were engendered in his loose way of living. His productions at this time were tinged with a mystical voluptuousness which was the other pole to his inner secret and spiritual being. The double strain upon his energies, which daily work and nightly study with mental productiveness involved, acted injuriously upon his health, and after a year he became so delicate that he could carry on neither one nor other of his avocations without an interval of complete rest. Obtaining leave from his employers, he went back for a period of six weeks to the village where he had been born. Here in the early summer and sunshine his health rapidly improved; his mind even more than his body drank deep draughts of life, and here more than at any period in his life, did his imagination begin to deal with mighty things, and probe into the secret mysteries of life, and here passed into his consciousness, visions of the cosmic romance, the starry dynasties, the long descended line by which the human spirit passed from empire; he began to comprehend dimly by what decadence from starry state the soul of man is ushered into the great visible life. These things came to him not clearly as ideas, but rather as shadowy and shining visions thrown across the air of dawn or twilight as he moved about.

Not alone did this opulence of spiritual life make him happy, another cause conspired with it to this end. He had met a nature somewhat akin to his own: Olive Rayne, the woman of his life.

As the days passed over he grew eager not to lose any chance of speech with her, and but two days before his departure he walked to the village hoping to see her. Down the quiet English lane in the evening he passed with the rapid feet that bear onward unquiet or feverish thought. The clear fresh air communicated delight to him; the fields grown dim, the voice of the cuckoo, the moon like a yellow globe cut in the blue, the cattle like great red shadows driven homeward with much unnecessary clamour by the children; all these flashed in upon him and became part of him: readymade accessories and backgrounds to his dreams, their quietness stilled and soothed the troubled beauty of passion. His pace lessened as he came near the village, half wondering what would serve as excuse for visits following one so soon upon the other. Chance served as excuse. He saw her grey dress, her firm upright figure coming out from among the lilac bushes at the gate of her father's house. She saw Harvey coming towards her and waited for him with a pleasant smile. Harvey, accustomed to introspect and ideal imaginings, here encountered no shock gazing upon the external. Some last light of day reflected upward from the white gate-post, irradiated her face, and touched with gold the delicate brown hair, the nostrils, lips, chin, and the lilac at her throat. Her features were clear-cut, flawless; the expression exquisitely grave and pure; the large grey eyes had that steady glow which shows a firm and undisturbed will. In some undefinable way he found himself thinking of the vague objects of his dreams, delicate and subtle things, dew, starlight, and transparencies rose up by some affinity. He rejected them – not those – then a strong warrior with a look of pity on his face appeared and disappeared: all this quick as a flash before she spoke.

'I am going doctoring,' she said. 'Old nurse Winder is ill, and my father will not be back until late.' Mr. Rayne was the country doctor.

'May I go with you?' he asked.

'Oh, yes, why not? But I have first to call at two or three places on the way.'

He went with her. He was full of wonder at her. How could she come out of her own world of aspiration and mystic religion and show such perfect familiarity, ease and interest in dealing with these sordid village complaints, moral and physical? Harvey was a man who disliked things like these which did not touch his sense of beauty. He could not speak to these people as she did: he could not

A Strange Awakening   225

sympathize with them. The pain of the old woman made him shrink into himself almost with more disgust than pity. While Olive was bending over her tenderly and compassionately, he tried to imagine what it was inspired such actions and such self-forgetfulness. Almost it seemed for a moment to him as if some hidden will in the universe would not let beauty rest in its own sphere, but bowed it down among sorrows continually. He felt a feeling of relief as they came out again into the night.

It was a night of miracle and wonder. Withdrawn far aloft into fairy altitudes, the stars danced with a gaiety which was more tremendous and solemn than any repose. The night was wrought out of a profusion of delicate fires. The grass, trees, and fields glowed with the dusky colours of rich pottery. Everywhere silence; everywhere the exultant breathing of life, subtle, universal, penetrating. Into the charmed heart fell the enchantment we call ancient, though the days have no fellows, nor will ever have any. Harvey, filled up with this wonder, turned to his companion.

'See how the Magician of the Beautiful blows with his mystic breath upon the world! How tremulous the lights are; what stillness! How it banishes the memory of pain!'

'Can you forget pain so easily? I hardly noticed the night – it is wonderful indeed. But the anguish it covers and enfolds everywhere I cannot forget.'

'I could not bear to think of pain at any time, still less while these miracles are over and around us. You seem to me almost to seek pain like a lover. I cannot understand you. How can you bear the ugly, the mean, the sordid – the anguish which you meet. You – so beautiful?'

'Can you not understand?' she said, almost impetuously. 'Have you never felt pity as universal as the light that floods the world? To me a pity seems to come dropping, dropping, dropping from that old sky, upon the earth and its anguish. God is not indifferent. Love eternal encircles us. Its wishes are for our redemption. Its movements are like the ripples starting from the rim of a pond that overcome the outgoing ripples and restore all to peace.'

'But what is pain if there is this love?' asked Harvey.

'Ah, how can I answer you? Yet I think it is the triumph of love pushing back sin and rebellion. The cry of this old nature being overcome is pain. And this is universal, and goes on everywhere, though we cannot comprehend it; and so, when we yield to this divine love, and accept the change, we find in pain a secret sweetness. It is the first thrill that heralds an immense dawn.'

'But why do you say it is universal? Is not that a frightful thought?'

'If God is the same yesterday, to-day, and to-morrow, then the life of Christ on earth was a symbol – must be a symbol – of what endures for ever: the Light and Darkness for ever in conflict: a crucifixion in eternity.'

This belief, so terrible, so pathetic, so strange, coming from this young girl affected Harvey profoundly. He did not reject it. The firmness and surety of her utterance, the moral purity of her character appealed to him who felt his own lack of clear belief and heroic purpose. Like all spiritual people, he assimilated easily the spiritual moods of those whom he came into contact with. Coming from her, the moral, pathetic, and Christian doctrine had that element of beauty which made it blend with his ideal paganism. As he went homewards he pondered over her words, her life, her thoughts. He began to find an inexpressible beauty in her pity, as a feeling welling up from unknown depths, out of the ancient heart of things. Filled with this pity he could overcome his dislike of pain and go forth as the strong warrior of his momentary vision. He found himself repeating again and again her words: 'We find in pain a secret sweetness – a secret sweetness – a secret sweetness.' If he could only find it, what might he not dare, to what might he not attain? And revolving all these things upon his restless pillow, there came over him one of those mystic moods I have spoken of: wandering among dim originals, half in dream and half in trance, there was unfolded within him this ancient legend of the soul:

There was a great Gloom and a great Glory in nature, and the legions of darkness and the glorious hosts were at war perpetually with one another. Then the Ancient of Days, who holds all this within himself, moved the Gloom and the Glory together: the Sons of the Bright Fire he sent into the darkness, and the children of Darkness he brought unto the gates of the day. And in the new life formed out of the union of these two, pain, self-conscious, became touched with a spiritual beauty, and those who were of the Hosts of Beauty wore each one a Crown of Thorns upon the brow.

CHAPTER III

Harvey rose up early; as he walked to and fro in the white dawn, he found the answers to every question in his mind: they rose up with a sweet and joyful spontaneity. Life became filled with happiest meaning: a light from behind the veil fell upon the things he had before disliked, and in this new light, pain, sorrow, and the old moralities were invested with a significance undreamt of before. In admitting into his own mind Olive Rayne's ideas, he removed something of their austerity: what he himself rejected, seen in her, added another and peculiar interest to the saintly ideal of her which he had formed. She had once said, peace and rest were inconceivable while there existed strife and suffering in nature. Nowhere could there be found refuge; drawing near unto the divine, this pain only became wider, more intense, almost insufferable, feeling and assimilating the vastness of divine sorrow brooding over the unreclaimed deep. This pity, this consciousness of pain, not her own, filling her own, filling her life, marked her out from everyone he knew. She seemed to him as one consecrated.[2] Then this lover in his mystic passion passed in the contemplation of his well-beloved from the earthly to the invisible soul. He saw behind and around her, a form unseen by others; a form, spiritual, pathetic, of unimaginable beauty, on which the eternal powers kept watch, which they nourished with their own life, and on which they inflicted their own pain. This form was crowned, but with a keen-pointed radiance from which there fell a shadowy dropping. As he walked to and fro in the white dawn he made for her a song, and inscribed it

TO ONE CONSECRATED

Your paths were all unknown to us:
We were so far away from you,
We mixed in thought your spirit thus –
With whiteness, stars of gold, and dew.

The mighty mother nourished you:
Her breath blew from her mystic bowers:
Their elfin glimmer floated through
The pureness of your shadowy hours.

The mighty mother made you wise;
Gave love that clears the hidden ways:
Her glooms were glory to your eyes;
Her darkness but the Fount of Days.

She made all gentleness in you,
And beauty radiant as the morn's:
She made our joy in yours, then threw
Upon your head a crown of thorns.

Your eyes are filled with tender light,
For those whose eyes are dim with tears;
They see your brow is crowned and bright,
But not its ring of wounding spears.

We can imagine no discomfiture while the heavenly light shines through us. Harvey, though he thought with humility of his past as impotent and ignoble in respect of action, felt with his rich vivid consciousness that he was capable of entering into her subtlest emotions. He could not think of the future without her; he could not give up the hope of drawing nigh with her to those mysteries of life which haunted them both. His thought, companioned by her, went ranging down many a mystic year. He began to see strange possibilities, flashes as of old power, divine magic to which all the world responded, and so on till the thought trembled in vistas ending in a haze of flame. Meanwhile, around him was summer: gladness and youth were in his heart, and so he went on dreaming – forecasting for the earth and its people a future which belongs only to the spiritual soul – dreaming of happy years even as a child dreams.

Later on that evening, while Olive was sitting in her garden, Dr. Rayne came out and handed her a bundle of magazines.

'There are some things in these which may interest you, Olive,' he said; 'Young Harvey writes for them, I understand. I looked over one or two. They are too mystical for me. You will hardly find them mystical enough.'

She took the papers from him without much interest, and laid them beside her on the seat. After a time she took them up. As she read her brows began to knit, and her face grew cold. These verses were full of that mystical voluptuousness which I said characterized Harvey's earlier productions; all his rich imagination was employed to centre interest upon moments of half-sensual sensations; the imagery was used in such a way that nature seemed to aid and abet the emotion; out of the heart of things, out of wild enchantment and eternal revelry shot forth into the lives of men the fires of passion. Nothing could be more unlike the Christ-soul which she worshipped as underlying the universe, and on which she had reliance.

'He does not feel pity; he does not understand love,' she murmured. She felt a cold anger arise; she who had pity for most things felt that a lie had been uttered defiling the most sacred things in the Holy of Holies, the things upon which her life depended. She could never understand Harvey, although he had been included in the general kindliness with which she treated all who came near her; but here he seemed revealed, almost vaunting an inspiration from the passionate powers who carry on their ancient war against the Most High.

The lights were now beginning to fade about her in the quiet garden when the gate opened, and someone came down the path. It was Harvey. In the gloom he did not notice that her usual smile was

A Strange Awakening 229

lacking, and besides he was too rapt in his own purpose. He hesitated for a moment, then spoke.

'Olive,' he said tremulously, 'as I came down the lanes to say goodbye to you my heart rebelled. I could not bear the thought: Olive, I have learned so many things from you; your words have meant so much to me that I have taken them as the words of God. Before I knew you I shrank from pain; I wandered in search of a false beauty. I see now the purpose of life – to carry on the old heroic battle for the true; to give the consolation of beauty to suffering; to become so pure that through us may pass that divine pity which I never knew until you spoke, and then I saw it was the root of all life, and there was nothing behind it – such magic your words have. My heart was glad this morning for joy at this truth, and I saw in it the power which would transfigure the earth. Yet all this hope has come to me through you; I half hold it still through you. To part from you now – it seems to me would be like turning away from the guardian of the heavenly gateway. I know I have but little to bring you. I must make all my plea how much you are to me when I ask can you love me.'

She had hardly heard a word of all he said. She was only conscious that he was speaking of love. What love? Had he not written of it? It would have emptied Heaven into the pit. She turned and faced him, speaking coldly and deliberately:

'You could speak of love to me, and write and think of it like this!' She placed her hand on the unfortunate magazines. Harvey followed the movement of her arm. He took the papers up, then suddenly saw all as she turned and walked away, – what the passion of these poems must have seemed to her. What had he been in her presence that could teach her otherwise? Only a doubter and a questioner. In a dreadful moment his past rose up before him, dreamy, weak, sensual. His conscience smote him through and through. He could find no word to say. Self-condemned, he moved blindly to the gate and went out. He hardly knew what he was doing. Before him the pale dry road wound its way into the twilight amid the hedges and cottages. Phantasmal children came and went. There seemed some madness in all they were doing. Why did he not hear their voices? They ran round and round; there should have been cries or laughter or some such thing. Then suddenly something seemed to push him forward, and he went on blankly and walked down the lane. In that tragic moment his soul seemed to have deserted him, leaving only a half-animal consciousness. With dull attention he wondered at the muffled sound of his feet upon the dusty road, and the little puffs of smoke that shot out before them. Every now and then something would throb fiercely for an instant and be subdued. He went on and on. His path lay across some fields. He stopped by force of habit and turned aside from the road. Again the same fierce throb. In a wild instant he struggled for recollection and self-mastery, and then the smothered soul rushed out of the clouds that oppressed it. Memories of hope and shame: the morning gladness of his heart: the brilliant and spiritual imaginations that inspired him: their sudden ending: the degradation and drudgery of the life he was to return to on the morrow: all rose up in tumultuous conflict. A feeling of anguish that was elemental and not of the moment filled him. Drifting and vacillating nature – he saw himself as in a boat borne along by currents that carried him, now near isles of beauty, and then whirled him away from their vanishing glory into gloomy gulfs and cataracts that went down into blackness. He was master neither of joy nor sorrow. Without will; unpractical; with sensitiveness which made joy a delirium and gloom a very hell; the days he went forward to stretched out iron hands to bind him to the deadly dull and commonplace. These vistas, intolerable and hopeless, overcame him. He threw himself down in his despair. Around his head pressed the cool grasses wet with dew. Strange and narrow, the boundary between heaven and hell! All around him, stricken with the fever of life, that Power which made both light and darkness, inscrutable in its workings, was singing silently the lovely carol of the flowers.

CHAPTER IV.

Little heaps of paper activities piled themselves up, were added to, diminished, and added to again, all the day long before Harvey at his desk. He had returned to his work: there was an unusual press of business, and night after night he was detained long beyond the usual hours. The iron hand which he had foreseen was laid upon him: it robbed him even of his right to sorrow, the time to grieve. But within him at moments stirred memories of the past, poignant anguish and fierce rebellion. With him everything transformed itself finally into ideal images and aspects, and it was not so much the memory of an incident which stung him as the elemental sense of pain in life itself. He felt that he was debarred from a heritage of spiritual life which he could not define even to himself. The rare rays of light that slanted through the dusty air of the office, mystic gold fallen through inconceivable distances from the pure primeval places, wakened in him an unutterable longing: he felt a choking in his throat as he looked. Often, at night, too, lifting his tired eyes

A Strange Awakening

from the pages flaring beneath the bright gas jet, he could see the blueness deepen rich with its ancient clouds of starry dust. What pain it was to him, Child of the Stars, to watch from that horrible prison-house, the face of all faces, immemorial quiet, passivity and peace, though over it a million tremors fled and chased each other throughout the shadowy night! What pain it was to let the eyes fall low and see about him the pale and feverish faces looking ghostly through the hot, fetid, animal, and flickering air!

His work over, out into the night he would drag himself wearily – out into the night anywhere; but there no more than within could he escape from that power which haunted him with mighty memories, the scourge which the Infinite wields. Nature has no refuge for those in whom the fire of spirit has been kindled: earth has no glory for which it does not know a greater glory. As Harvey passed down the long streets, twinkling with their myriad lights fading into blue and misty distances, there rose up before him in the visionary air solemn rows of sphinxes in serried array, and starlit pyramids and temples – greatness long dead, a dream that mocked the hives around him, hoarding the sad small generations of humanity dwindling away from beauty. Gone was the pure and pale splendour of the primeval skies and the lustre of the first-born of stars. But even this memory, which linked him in imagination to the ideal past, was not always his: he was weighted, like all his race, with an animal consciousness which cried out fiercely for its proper life, which thirsted for sensation, and was full of lust and anger. The darkness was not only about him, but in him, and struggled there for mastery. It threw up forms of meanness and horrible temptations which clouded over his soul; their promise was forgetfulness; they seemed to say: 'Satisfy us, and your infinite longing shall die away; to be of clay is very dull and comfortable; it is the common lot.'

One night, filled with this intolerable pain, as he passed through the streets he yielded to the temptation to kill out this torturing consciousness: he accosted one of the women of the streets and walked away with her. She was full of light prattle, and chattered on and on. Harvey answered her not a word; he was set on his stony purpose. Child of the Stars! what had he to do with these things? He sought only his soul's annihilation. Something in this terrible silence communicated itself to his companion. She looked at his face in the light of a lamp; it was white, locked and rigid. Child of the Stars, no less, though long forgetful, she shuddered at this association. She recoiled from him crying out 'You brute – you brute!' and then fled away. The unhappy man turned homeward and sat in his lonely room with stupid, staring eyes, fixed on darkness and vacancy until the pale green light of dawn began to creep in upon him. Into this fevered and anguished existence no light had yet come. Drunken with wretchedness, Harvey could not or would not think; and the implacable spirit which followed him deepened and quickened still more the current of his being, and the GLOOM and the GLORY of his dream moved still nearer to each other. Mighty and mysterious spirit, thou who crownest pain with beauty, and by whom the mighty are bowed down from their seats, under thy guidance, for such a crowning and for such agony, were coiled together the living streams of evil and good, so that at last the man might know himself – the soul – not as other than Thee!

The ways by which he was brought to that moment were unremembered; the sensations and thoughts and moods which culminated in the fire of self-consciousness could be retraced but vaguely. He had gone out of the city one Sunday, and lying down in the fields under the trees, for a time he grew forgetful of misery. He went once more into the world of dreams. He, or the creature of his imagination, some shadow of himself, lived in and roamed through antique forests where the wonderful days were unbroken by sense of sorrow. Childhood shared in an all-pervading exultation; through the pulses of youth ran the fiery energy that quickened the world; and this shadow of the dreamer dwelling amid the forests grew gradually into a consciousness of a fiery life upon which the surface forms were but films: he entered this kingdom of fire; its life became his life; he knew the secret ways to the sun, and the sunny secrets living in the golden world. 'It was I, myself,' rushed into Harvey's mind: 'It was I. Ah, how long ago!' Then for the first time, his visions, dreams and imaginations became real to him, as memories of a spirit travelling through time and space. Looking backwards, he could nowhere find in the small and commonplace surroundings of his life anything which could have suggested or given birth to these vivid pictures and ideas. They began to move about swiftly in his mind and arrange themselves in order. He seemed to himself to have fallen downwards through a long series of lines of ever-lessening beauty – fallen downwards from the mansions of eternity into this truckling and hideous life. As Harvey walked homewards through the streets, some power must have guided his steps, for he saw or knew nothing of what was about him. With the sense of the reality of his imaginations came an energy he had never before felt: his soul took complete possession of him: he knew, though degraded, that he was a spirit. Then, in that supreme moment, gathered about him the memories of light and darkness, and they became the lips through which eternal powers spake to him in a tongue unlike the speech of men. The spirit of light was behind the visions of mystical beauty; the spirit of darkness arrayed itself in the desires of clay. These powers began to war within him: he heard voices as of Titans talking.

The spirit of light spake within him and said – 'Arouse now, and be thou my voice in this dead land. There are many things to be spoken and sung – of dead language the music and significance, old world philosophies; you will be the singer of the sweetest songs; stories wilder and stranger than any yet will I tell you – deeds forgotten of the vaporous and dreamy prime.'

The voice came yet again closer, full of sweet promise, with magical utterance floating around him. He became old – inconceivably old and young together. He was astonished in the wonders of the primal world. Chaos with tremendous agencies, serpentine powers, strange men-beasts and men-birds, the crude first thoughts of awakening nature was before him; from inconceivable heights of starlike purity he surveyed it; he went forth from glory; he descended and did battle; he warred with behemoth, with the flying serpents and the monstrous creeping things. With the Lords of Air he descended and conquered; he dwelt in a new land, a world of light, where all things were of light, where the trees put forth leaves of living green, where the rose would blossom into a rose of light and the lily into a white radiance, and over the vast of gleaming plains and through the depths of luminous forests, the dreaming rivers would roll in liquid and silver flame. Often he joined in the mad dance upon the highlands, whirling round and round until the dark grass awoke fiery with rings of green under the feet. And so, on and on through endless transformations he passed, and he saw how the first world of dark elements crept in upon the world of beauty, clothing it around with grossness and veiling its fires; and the dark spirits entered by subtle ways into the spheres of the spirits of light, and became as a mist over memory and a chain upon speed; the earth groaned with the anguish. Then this voice cried within him – 'Come forth; come out of it; come out, oh king, to the ancestral spheres, to the untroubled spiritual life. Out of the furnace, for it leaves you dust. Come away, oh king, to old dominion and celestial sway; come out to the antique glory!'

Then another voice from below laughed at the madness. Full of scorn it spake, 'You, born of clay, a ruler of stars! Pitiful toiler with the pen, feeble and weary body, what shall make of you a spirit?' Harvey thrust away this hateful voice. From his soul came the impulse to go to other lands, to wander for ever and ever under the star-rich skies, to be a watcher of the dawn and eve, to live in forest places or on sun-nurtured plains, to merge himself once more in the fiery soul hidden within. But the mocking voice would not be stifled, showing him how absurd and ridiculous it was 'to become a vagabond,' so the voice said, and finally to die in the workhouse. So the eternal spirit in him, God's essence, conscious of its past brotherhood, with the morning stars, the White Æons, in its prisonhouse writhed with the meanness, till at last he cried, 'I will struggle no longer; it is only agony of spirit to aspire here at all; I will sit and wait till the deep darkness has vanished.'

But the instruction was not yet complete; he had learned the primal place of spirit; he had yet to learn its nature. He began to think with strange sadness over the hopes of the world, the young children. He saw them in his vision grow up, bear the burden in silence or ignorance; he saw how they joined in dragging onward that huge sphinx which men call civilization; there was no time for loitering amid the beautiful, for if one paused it was but to be trampled by the feet of the many who could not stay or rest, and the wheels of the image ground that soul into nothingness. He felt every pain almost in an anguish of sympathy. Helpless to aid, to his lips came that cry to another which immemorial usage has made intuitive in men. But It is high and calm above all appeal; to It the cries from all the sorrowing stars sound but as one great music; lying in the infinite fields of heaven, from the united feelings of many universes It draws only a vast and passionless knowledge, without distinction of pleasure or pain. From the universal which moves not and aids not, Harvey in his agony turned away. He himself could fly from the struggle; thinking of what far place or state to find peace, he found it true in his own being that nowhere could the soul find rest while there was still pain or misery in the world. He could imagine no place or state where these cries of pain would not reach him; he could imagine no heaven where the sad memory would not haunt him and burn him. He knew then that the nature of the soul was love eternal; he knew that if he fled away a divine compassion would compel him to renew his brotherhood with the stricken and suffering; and what was best forever to do was to fight out the fight in the darkness. There was a long silence in Harvey's soul; then with almost a solemn joy he began to realize at last the truth of he himself – the soul. The fight was over; the GLOOM and the GLORY were linked together, and one inseparably. Harvey was full of a sense of quietness, as if a dew fell from unseen places on him with soothing and healing power. He looked around. He was at the door of his lodgings. The tall narrow houses with their dull red hues rose up about him; from their chimneys went up still higher the dark smoke; but behind its nebulous wavering the stars were yet; they broke through the smoke with white lustre. Harvey looked at them for a moment, and went in strangely comforted.

THE MIDNIGHT BLOSSOM[1]

'Arhans are born at midnight hour, together with the holy flower that opes and blooms in darkness.'

–From an Eastern Scripture.[2]

We stood together at the door of our hut. We could see through the gathering gloom where our sheep and goats were cropping the sweet grass on the side of the hill. We were full of drowsy content as they were. We had naught to mar our happiness, neither memory nor unrest for the future. We lingered on while the vast twilight encircled us; we were one with its dewy stillness. The lustre of the early stars first broke in upon our dreaming: we looked up and around. The yellow constellations began to sing their choral hymn together. As the night deepened they came out swiftly from their hiding-places in depths of still and unfathomable blue – they hung in burning clusters, they advanced in multitudes that dazzled. The shadowy shining of night was strewn all over with nebulous dust of silver, with long mists of gold, with jewels of glittering green. We felt how fit a place the earth was to live on, with these nightly glories over us, with silence and coolness upon our lawns and lakes after the consuming day. Valmika, Kedar, Ananda, and I watched together. Through the rich gloom we could see far distant forests and lights, the lights of village and city in King Suddhodana's realm.

'Brothers,' said Valmika, 'how good it is to be here and not yonder in the city, where they know not peace, even in sleep.'

'Yonder and yonder,' said Kedar, 'I saw the inner air full of a red glow where they were busy in toiling and strife. It seemed to reach up to me. I could not breathe. I climbed the hill at dawn to laugh where the snows were, and the sun is as white as they are white.'

'But, brothers, if we went down among them and told them how happy we were, and how the flowers grow on the hillside, they would surely come up and leave all sorrow. They cannot know or they would come.' Ananda was a mere child though so tall for his years.

'They would not come,' said Kedar; 'all their joy is to haggle and hoard. When Siva[3] blows upon them with angry breath they will lament, or when the demons in fierce hunger devour them.'

'It is good to be here,' repeated Valmika, drowsily, 'to mind the flocks and be at rest, and to hear the wise Varunna speak when he comes among us.'

I was silent. I knew better than they that busy city which glowed beyond the dark forests. I had lived there until, grown sick and weary, I had gone back to my brothers on the hillside. I wondered, would life, indeed, go on ceaselessly until it ended in the pain of the world. I said within myself: 'O mighty Brahma,[4] on the outermost verges of thy dream are our lives. Thou old invisible, how faintly through our hearts comes the sound of thy song, the light of thy glory!' Full of yearning to rise and return, I strove to hear in my heart the music Anahata,[5] spoken of in our sacred scrolls. There was silence, and then I thought I heard sounds, not glad, a myriad murmur. As I listened they deepened; they grew into passionate prayer and appeal and tears, as if the cry of the long-forgotten souls of men went echoing through empty chambers. My eyes filled with tears, for it seemed world-wide and to sigh from out many ages, long agone, to be and yet to be.

'Ananda! Ananda! Where is the boy running to?' cried Valmika. Ananda had vanished in the gloom. We heard his glad laugh below, and then another voice speaking. The tall figure of Varunna loomed up presently. Ananda held his hand, and danced beside him. We knew the Yogi, and bowed reverently before him. We could see by the starlight his simple robe of white. I could trace clearly every feature of the grave and beautiful face and radiant eyes. I saw not by the starlight, but by a silvery radiance which rayed a little way into the blackness around the dark hair and face. Valmika, as elder, first spoke:

'Holy sir, be welcome. Will you come in and rest?'

'I cannot stay now. I must pass over the mountains ere dawn; but you may come a little way with me – such of you as will.'

We assented gladly, Kedar and I. Valmika remained. Then Ananda prayed to go. We bade him stay, fearing for him the labour of climbing and the chill of the snows. But Varunna said: 'Let the child come. He is hardy, and will not tire if he holds my hand.'

So we set out together, and faced the highlands that rose and rose above us. We knew the way well, even at night. We waited in silence for Varunna to speak; but for nigh an hour we mounted without words, save for Ananda's shouts of delight and wonder at the heavens spread above and the valleys that lay behind us. Then I grew hungry for an answer to my thoughts, and I spake:

'Master, Valmika was saying, ere you came, how good it was to be here rather than in the city, where they are full of strife. And Kedar thought their lives would flow on into fiery pain, and no speech would avail. Ananda, speaking as a child, indeed, said if one went down among them they would listen to his story of the happy life. But, Master, do not many speak and interpret the sacred writings, and how few are they who lay to heart the word of the gods! They seem, indeed, to go on through desire into pain, and even here upon the hills we are not free, for Kedar felt the hot glow of their passion, and I heard in my heart their sobs of despair. Master, it was terrible, for they seemed to come from the wide earth over, and out of ages far away.'

'In the child's words is the truth,' said Varunna, 'for it is better to aid even in sorrow than to withdraw from pain to a happy solitude. Yet only the knowers of Brahma can interpret the sacred writings truly, and it is well to be free ere we speak of freedom. Then we have power and many hearken.'

'But who would leave joy for sorrow? And who, being one with Brahma, would return to give counsel?'

'Brother,' said Varunna, 'here is the hope of the world. Though many seek only for the eternal joy, yet the cry you heard has been heard by great ones who have turned backwards, called by these beseeching voices. The small old path stretching far away leads through many wonderful beings to the place of Brahma. There is the first fountain, the world of beautiful silence, the light which has been undimmed since the beginning of time. But turning backwards from the gate the small old path winds away into the world of men, and it enters every sorrowful heart. This is the way the great ones[6] go. They turn with the path from the door of Brahma. They move along its myriad ways, and overcome pain with compassion. After many conquered worlds, after many races of purified and uplifted men, they go to a greater than Brahma. In these, though few, is the hope of the world. These are the heroes for whose returning the earth puts forth her signal fires, and the Devas[7] sing their hymns of welcome.'

We paused where the plateau widened out. There was scarce a ripple in the chill air. In quietness the snows glistened, a light reflected from the crores of stars that swung with glittering motion above us. We could hear the immense heart-beat of the world in the stillness. We had thoughts that went ranging through the heavens, not sad, but full of solemn hope.

'Brothers! Master! look! The wonderful thing! And another, and yet another!' we heard Ananda calling. We looked and saw the holy blossom, the midnight flower. Oh, may the earth again put forth such beauty. It grew up from the snows with leaves of delicate crystal. A nimbus encircled each radiant bloom, a halo pale yet lustrous. I bowed over it in awe; and I heard Varunna say, 'The earth indeed puts forth her signal fires, and the Devas sing their hymn. Listen!' We heard a music as of beautiful thoughts moving along the high places of the earth, full of infinite love and hope and yearning.

'Be glad now, for one is born who has chosen the greater way. Kedar, Narayan, Ananda, farewell! Nay, no farther. It is a long way to return, and the child will tire.'

He went on and passed from our sight. But we did not return. We remained long, long in silence, looking at the sacred flower.

* * *

Vow, taken long ago, be strong in our hearts to-day. Here, where the pain is fiercer, to rest is more sweet. Here, where beauty dies away, it is more joy to be lulled in dream. Here, the good, the true, our hope seem but a madness born of ancient pain. Out of rest, dream, or despair may we arise, and go the way the great ones go.

1894.

III. THE HEAVENLY CITY

THE INTERPRETERS[1]

TO
STEPHEN MACKENNA
FOR THE DELIGHT I HAVE
IN HIS NOBLE TRANSLATION OF PLOTINUS

PREFACE

I have been intimate with some who risked and with some who lost life for causes to which they were devoted, and came to understand that with many the political images in imagination were but the psychic body of spiritual ideas. Behind the open argument lurked a spiritual mood which was the true decider of destiny. Nations conceive of themselves as guided or sustained by a divine wisdom, and I have wondered in what manner impulse might flow from Heaven to Earth. Out of my meditation on this came *The Interpreters*. Those who take part in the symposium suppose of the universe that it is a spiritual being, and they inquire what relation the politics of Time may have to the politics of Eternity. Their varying faiths have been held by many ancients and by some who are modern, but the symposium has been laid in a future century so that ideals over which there is conflict to-day might be discussed divested of passion and apart from transient circumstance. I was not interested in the creation of characters but in tracking political moods back to spiritual origins, and *The Interpreters* may be taken as a symposium between scattered portions of one nature dramatically sundered as the soul is in dream.

A.E.

I

On an evening in the late autumn a young man was hurrying though the lit crowded streets of his city, his mind but dimly aware of his fellow-citizens, for he was raised above himself by the adventure on which he was bent, and what had been familiar seemed now remote as the body is to the soul in spiritual exaltation. Because the high purpose seeks the companionship of high things, he paused awhile, looking beyond the dark roofs, where, over horizons of murky citron, the air glowed through regions of passionate green to a blue abyss becoming momentarily more fathomless. Never to his eyes had that vision appeared so beautiful, trembling from one exquisite transience of colour to another. Tall pillars crested with a ruby glow marked the airways, and their dark lines and lights sank westward over the city. On each side the freighted galleons, winged shapes of dusk and glitter, roared overhead, whirring up swiftly from the horizon or fading with all their glitter into the green west. Not these hurrying lights his eye sought, but those changeless lights which have watched earth from its beginnings. Some cosmic emotion made him feel akin with those heavenly lights. A world empire was in trouble. A nation long restless under its rule had resurrected ancient hopes, and this young man with many others was bent on a violent assertion of its right to freedom. His imagination had long passed beyond fear of death. But, having in thought cast life aside, life strangely had become richly augmented. He seemed to himself a being of fire dwelling in a body of air, so intense with feeling, so light his limbs. In that mood the people in the streets, on his own level yesterday, appeared faint as shadows; but as compensation a new multitudinous life sprang up within him as if all those who had his hope and were with him in his deed had come to a mystic unity in the spirit. In this dilation of consciousness he felt the gods were with him, and it was then he looked up at the stars, feeling in an instant of vision that he was comrade with them and with all god-inspired life, and they, with earth and its people, were sustained and directed by one inflexible cosmic will. He felt it strange he had not realized before how high was the enterprise to which he had been led by a study of the history and culture of his nation. He moved confidently as a warrior of antiquity with whom Athene or Hera went invisibly to battle. He was a poet, and because his soul was a treasure-house stored with the thoughts of the great who lived before him, he interpreted his own emotions as his more uneducated comrades never could have done, they whose action was instinctive, and whose minds were not subtle enough to discern the immortal mingling with their moods, and who would perhaps have lost enthusiasm if they had been told what purposes Nature had with them, and to what event, aeons away, they were being led, and that this heroic enterprise of their life was but an hour's incident in a cyclic pilgrimage.

As he crossed an open square there came a roar which shook the air. An orange flame spurted athwart the dusky citron of the sky, and after that clouds of smoke, ruddily obscure, began to pile themselves up gigantically in the higher blue of night. He gazed at this uprising of flame as the Israelites of old might have looked on the cloud and the fire which mantled the Shepherd of their host, for this was the signal that at the other end of the city the revolt had begun. Yet his body shivered, for the intelligence in it which stood sentinel guarding its mortality knew that this conflagration began a struggle in which itself might perish, and which for it would be the end of all. That mute appeal was unheeded, for the will of the young man was like a drawn bow, and life the arrow ready to be sped by the will. He experienced the terrible joy of life which has been emancipated. The spirit of man had risen from the grave which was fear, was emerging from that narrow prison cell like the sky-reaching genie from the little copper vessel in the tale of Arabian enchantment. Like a god it was laying hands on the powers of storm and commotion. Life had broken its moulds. It was no longer static but fluid, a river moving to some ocean. He watched the ruddily glowing smoke hungrily. Underneath it he imagined faces pale and bright. There were comrades, fearless, wilful, laughing, intoxicated as he was himself, breaking the iron law of the Iron Age.[2] After centuries of frustrated effort the nation, long dominated by an alien power which seemed immutable, had a resurrection. It would join the great procession of states, of beings mightier than man created by man. It would become like Egypt, Assyria, Greece or Rome. The genius of multitudes would unite to give it spiritual greatness. Thoughts like these thronged the brain of the young man as he moved closer to the great building which he and others had planned to take by surprise. The moment arranged drew nigh. Hundreds of men were mysteriously gathering, loitering with intent, gazing at the distant illumination in the sky yet all the time nearing the gate of the arsenal. What had brought about that orchestration of life? They were united in the deed. Were they really united in soul? Was the same mood in the heart of that sombre concentrated workman as in the imaginative poet or that sharp-featured cynical journalist? Were they all raised above themselves by the same aspiration? Here were men hardly able to restrain themselves from action, which was their life. Here were thinkers drawn by some agony of conscience which bade them leave the fireside and the intimate lives about it, trusting their young to a destiny which, had they thought over it, had ever seemed heedless of life. Had each one his own dream which he believed his nation would fulfil? Or was there a Wisdom moving all for purposes of its own? Was there an inexorable war waged by the gods upon humanity, shattering its peace, never allowing it to rest, shepherding the host from cycle to cycle until it had grown to power and those divine enemies became its kinsmen? Of what lay beneath that gathering the poet, for all his imagination, knew little, for he was so blinded by his own impulse that he imputed it to those who moved with him, that crowd which grew ever thicker, casting furtive glances at each other, at those they did not recognize, who might be agents of the power they sought to overthrow. Every heart heard its own beating. Here were resolute men who would act. Then the hour struck from a tall spire, bell after bell tolling slowly as if it symbolized the beating of the heart of the nation. On the instant men everywhere put on their sleeves the scarf which revealed all to each other. Those hitherto only known to the leaders of their groups could now recognize their comrades. Weapons of all kinds were drawn forth. Voices rang out sternly in command, and the crowd, a river of fiery life, surged through the open gate of the arsenal.

II

We waken from dream, from a nightmare in which we fought with demons, to find the body cold, clammy, and trembling, but all recollection of that dark agony is soon lost beyond recall. The body still shudders but knows not why. Our ascents to Heaven, our descents into Hell, lay too high or too heavy a burden upon the soul for memory. It cannot mirror them for more than an instant, and they melt dreamlike from consciousness. Of the physical conflict in the arsenal the poet remembered little. It was blurred to his intellect by excess of energy or passion as objects are blurred to the eye by excess of light. He came back to himself at last crowded into a corner with a group of his surviving comrades cut off from escape. Here at least the revolution had failed. Empires are like those beings in the Apocalypse full of eyes within and without. One of these eyes had discovered a detail of the conspiracy and the open gate of the arsenal was a trap. Another of these apocalyptic eyes overlooked them searching for persons of power among the rebels. They were taken one by one as a finger pointed them out. The poet was of these. He was led by his guards up many steps and along many dim-lit corridors and was halted at last by a door about which armed men stood sentinel. He was thrust within and the door was locked behind him. He was greeted by a tumult of gay and exalted voices. It was a spiritual gaiety. The voices had the exaltation of those who had been engaged in a death struggle not so much with others as with themselves and had been conquerors. They could not have explained why they were so gay. They were prisoners and defeated. Some of them were wounded. On the morrow they might be standing with their backs to a wall taking a wild farewell of the sky, drinking greedily the last drop in the cup of life before a voice called on the executioners to fire. The exaltation was secret and of the spirit, for all conflicts are at the last between soul and body, and here the soul had triumphed; the immortal in each one had made a great stride to conscious dwelling within them and it was sustaining them with its own lavish power. Outwardly they were but men who had not failed each other however they had failed in their enterprise. Their gaze on each other was frank and affectionate. The young poet was hailed uproariously by those who knew him. Others who had heard of him gazed on him with pride.

'All here for Valhalla!'

'I also am a traveller,' said the newcomer.

'They will never allow you to go, Lavelle. You might be admitted. There will be no lingering over our fate. Hell was built for such rascals as we are.'

'Hush, fools, we may be out before day-break. Does that sound like a city subdued?'

The room was reddening in a glow from without. There was a rattle increasing in intensity, not in one place but over the city. Then came a sinister noise like a sabre of sound swishing through the air and deeper and more tremendous notes boomed from further distances.

'See! see!' cried one. 'The air lights have gone out.'

They crowded to the windows. The towering poles which had lifted up their red lamps through the dusk to guide the night journeying airships were now lightless and darkly silhouetted against glowing masses of smoke. The airships were scattering, flying wildly, like winged dragons on some fabulous adventure who had met a volcano in eruption on their path. Some had ascended, their lights scintillating remotely in the higher darkness, while others in lower levels flashed flame-coloured against the blue, their wings gilded with fire from the glowing city below.

'They must come down! They will be ours! There were men ready to rush the boats. They cannot risk passage east or west with the ways unlighted!'

Rumours started mysteriously among the prisoners. Some one had heard or surmised something, and in the fever of feeling it grew in a moment, like a phantasmal tree created by the magic of a faquir, to be of gigantic import. This rumour dwindled to give place to others more exciting. The poet soon turned away, gazing through a window at the spectacle of the night which never tired him. Imagination was at work. It created huge figures of gods seated on the mountains that lay around the city, figures still as if cast in gold, with immense pondering brows bent downward, waiting, perhaps, for god folk to rise up from men folk out of that furnace into which so many had cast themselves as a sacrifice.

'You should feel proud as Helen looking over the ruins of Troy.'

An intense gutteral voice was in his ear. Lavelle turned round and saw a pallid face with beaked nose, lips thick but not sensual, humorous rather, even mocking, quick moving black eyes like polished ebony, bushy grey brows and hair, every feature carved and etched by mind, the head large on a shrunken body. It was the writer he had seen in the crowd, Leroy, a notoriety, in whose work fantastical humour hardly disguised the agony of the idealist without faith in society. There existed between himself and the poet that attraction which opposites have for each other. His feeling for Lavelle was friendly, almost tender. He looked sorrowfully upon the face of the young poet so unlike his own, upon a noble beauty whose invisible sculptors were ecstasy, ardour, and the music of murmured or chanted speech.

'Why?'

'Why, who created the spirit of this revolt? Who led the people to quit the beer which gives peace, to drink the heady wine of imagination? Who ransacked the past and revived the traditions of the nation? Who but you found in the fairy tales of its infancy the basis of a future civilization? The wine has gone to peoples' heads. What are they doing? Thinking they are building a heaven on earth while they are fighting like devils!'

'Ah!' said the poet. 'I wish it were true. But you know how little high traditions move the people.'

'It may be so with them but not with the leaders. The people may not guess the thoughts that move the mightier of their kind but they follow all the same. And the leaders are aglow from a phosphorescence engendered in the brains of poets like you, or imaginative historians like Brehon. What is it they are led by in the end but a fragile thought; a coloured dream; a thing of air!'

'No! no!' said Lavelle impetuously. 'It is not unreal. Heaven is in the kindled spirit of man. How do you come to be here yourself? Are you not with us? For what but a dream do you cast away life?'

'Oh,' said the other, 'I am an anarchist and I wish to be free, and also my Dark Angel told me there was nothing real in my character and I wished to test it.'

'What did you find in yourself?'

'Nothing! More foam on wilder waters! But who is this?'

The door had opened again, and a man, by attire, manner, and voice evidently a personage, was pushed in backwards protesting vehemently of his innocence, that he was not a rebel, that he hated them, when an ungentle thrust from the weapon of his guard cut short speech from him, and he was propelled from the doorway into the room.

'You can explain all that to-morrow,' said a surly voice, evidently sceptical that the prisoner could explain the circumstance which caused his arrest. The door was again closed. The newcomer turned to face the curious and not too friendly faces of the prisoners.

'You are the fanatics who have upset the city! I hope there will not be one of you alive to-morrow night!'

'Sir,' said Leroy, 'I do not know how you came to be here, but I am sure it is not your good angel who inspires you to speak as you do. There are some here who might insist on your escape through the window, and the distance from the window to the pavement is exactly the distance from life to death.'

'I think I know who this is,' said another prisoner. Then turning to the last arrival he asked, 'Why did they take you? You are not of us.'

The newcomer was quieting, his agitation overcome by the coolness of those about him. He had picked up a coloured scarf in the street, missing the owner who was hurrying on, and he was still holding it when he was arrested by a patrol. The scarf was worn by those active in the revolt. One of the prisoners whispered to Leroy it was more likely the arrest was made because of the prisoner's personal likeness to one of their own leaders. The newcomer mentioned his name, Heyt, the autocrat of one of those great economic federations which dominated state policy and whose operations had created deep bitterness among the revolting people. The name was greeted with roars of laughter. The patrol had arrested a pillar of state.

'The guilty on both sides in the same prison!' cried Leroy. 'I never believed Deity had any attributes but I must now endow it with the attribute of humour. Sir,' he said, turning to Heyt. 'If you should be shot before me to-morrow you may die with the consolation that your death has shaken a sceptic in his unbelief.'

Heyt, whose features had assumed the expression of haughtiness which seemed habitual to them, looked disdainfully at Leroy and made no reply. He sat down on a bench which ran along by the wall, ignoring his fellow-prisoners who also ignored him as an unlikely source of information about the progress of the revolt. The excitement began to dwindle, a more solemn mood to replace the gaiety and to turn their thoughts to that other world, in which, had they known it, they already existed, entering it in all hours of intense and deeper being. Even to the heaven lit spirit of the saint the prospect of death and the transit from familiar things induces solemnity of feeling, though the heart has the certitude that there is the heart's desire. These for the most part had taken little thought of that morrow or what spiritual raiment might be put on them, but they remembered the popular persistent talk about death and judgement, and they began to speculate among themselves upon such things as men who knew their stay here may be short and who must think of their further travelling. Leroy with his back to them listened irritably to their anticipations of death and after. Looking out through a window he began whistling softly and savagely to himself. That men who were in revolt against the conventions of this world should accept the conventions of the next world, which to him were even more objectionable, angered him so that he could hardly trust himself to speech.

III

It is rarely that a single mood stays long with those who believe they are nigh to death. A horde of thoughts and feelings rush from the subconscious as if they knew how little time remained for them to prove themselves. There is swift reaction. Leroy's desperate mood soon passed, his ironic humour kindled by the desire of a prisoner for consolation by a priest of his church.

'Do you really believe his blessing will secure you welcome in the

Kingdom of Heaven?' he said. 'My Dark Angel tells me there has been very little difference between his ideas of religion and the churches' for a very long time, so little, indeed, that his master was thinking of quietly dropping his old title and calling himself God. Myself I hold the substitution was effected centuries ago and was quite unnoticed. Everything went on as before. The princes of religion sat undisturbed upon episcopal thrones. I think,' he added grimly, 'their long and faithful services to their new master merit sympathetic consideration from the Judge of all the world.'

The prisoners gathered laughing around Leroy. His resolute spirit dominated the rest as resolute spirits do all men in time of peril. They began to even their mood to his.

'Come, tell us all about it! What is to be our fate? Will there be another court-martial in Heaven when we are despatched here?'

'What are we guilty of before Heaven? What relation have the politics of time to the politics of eternity? Are we concerned with the battles of beasts in the jungle, or the pursuit and flight under the waters? If there are beings above us, not of our order, how do we offend them? Do we throw Heaven into disorder when we revolt against tyranny here? I do not think the ridgepole of the universe is so fragile as to be shaken by our rubbing ourselves against it.'

'I think,' said Lavelle, 'that Heaven and Earth must be a unity, and that men are often Heaven inspired, and that ideas descend on us from a divine world, and they must finally make a conquest of Earth and draw us into a conscious unity with the Heavens. If the universe is a spiritual being, everything finally must be in harmony with it, and wild creatures, the elements even, undergo a transfiguration, fierce things becoming gentle, and –'

'The shark becoming vegetarian,' interrupted Leroy. 'O Lavelle, Lavelle, you are the imperialist of idealism. When you had remade the nation in your own image you would impose the law of your being upon the world. Even the fishes would be swept into your net. How wise was the Chinese sage who said "when a man begins to reform the world I perceive there will be no end to it." There would be no place in your universe for an individualist like myself. I would be a gnat irritating its spiritual body.'

'You may laugh at the marriage of Heaven and Earth,' Lavelle spoke again. 'But there is a power behind ideas. I remember what a dispirited group met to discuss the revolt, what a burden lay upon every heart. Yet when we decided to act for the nation what a magical transformation took place! How joyful everyone became! They were gay and laughed and cried as if it was resurrection morn. What was the source of that joy? By what alchemy was the chill made fiery? I felt glowing as if Heaven had lifted me up to itself. What was that but the power of an idea? You felt it yourself. Is there one even here who would wish now to withdraw? Would we not all prefer death with our nation fighting against the rule of the iron powers?'

'No, no, not one of us repents,' cried the prisoners.

'I prefer to be here, it is true,' said Leroy. 'But I cannot convince myself that I am not a fool. It is ludicrous to me to feel heroic irrational emotions welling up in me overturning reason. It is doubtless heredity. Some remote ancestor of mine ought to be executed in my place.'

'No, no, Leroy. The heroic is the deep reality in you and all of us. It is translucent to spirit and the will of Heaven is seen in its actions.'

'Are our actions then all Heaven inspired? If I am anything I am an anarchist. I would break up tyrannies because I am a lover of liberty. I wish to be free to come and go, to do or not to do, to think as I will, to speak as I will. You would have your nation free that it might come under another domination, that there might be but one cultural mood in it. You want an orchestration of life so that every one in the nation may have the same character and their works make one harmony. There is Rian, who is an artist. I think he is with us truly because the state does not create beauty. I found him in a rage cursing the last imperial edifice in our city. It was designed by a blockhead, he said, to house blockheads whose work it would be to make the whole nation into blockheads. Men ought to revolt against a state which imposes a dull ugliness upon us all our lives. Was not that so, Rian?' Leroy said to a young man who was listening to the talk.

'Well, it helped to bring me here anyhow,' said Rian, smiling.

'Rian is fighting for beauty. Between himself and Heaven that is his motive. He is a creature of aesthetic passions. Put power into his hands and he would arrest people for wearing inharmonious colours in the streets. Our great Culain is a socialist. He has an economic ideal while you have a cultural ideal. I think every one who is with us turned different faces to Heaven in their prayers. Does Heaven accept them all? Are all these conflicting ideals in the cosmic plan? If it approves everything it designs nothing. I am sure too that there are those fighting against us who believe their empire is a manifestation of the Absolute, and they are filled with as pure a glow as you are.'

'Do you really believe, Leroy, that the same quality of inspiration can exist in opposites?'

'Well, the opposites at least are willing to pay for their inspiration in the same coin of life as you are. Is it not better to base your case simply on obvious right than to bring in a mystical theory of nationality? Every people to-day fights in the name of God. The ancients were more logical. They had tribal deities. But you, my dear Lavelle, while you are satisfied with your tribe on earth, claim that all Heaven is with you. In one of the old tales of our people it is told of two heroes that they paused and embraced in the midst of their conflict. They saw noble things in each other. Life was a game to be played nobly as indeed you play it; but if you insist on Heaven as the ally of your race you can only suppose that the forces of Hell are behind your antagonist, and then there is an end of chivalry. You cannot weep over the fallen. You can only curse them as that old savage Dante denied pity to the spirit that uprose out of the miry pool in the Inferno.'

'But you have too subtle a mind to believe the soul of man is completely isolated, is a being by itself and receives no light except from the sun, stars, and lamp-posts.'

'We exist, it is true, in some miraculous being which bathes us, but I do not know whether it does not lend itself to my whimsies, whether it is not a mirror of our being rather than we of it. When I dream I create like a God, but I know my dreams spring out of my desires. Though they seem to melt into infinity I know that infinity is an illusion in the hollow of my brain. I dreamed a few nights ago that I saw God, really an august being, moving on His rolling throne through His dominions contemplating His children the stars. He came close to our earth, but had to skip back very quickly, so high up were the shells bursting, and the anti-aircraft guns were taking no chances with suspicious luminosities. He called me and asked "What is the trouble here?" and I said, "Lord, it is a spiritual conflict." "That interests me. Tell me all about it," and I explained that the people of the earth were at war to decide whether they would receive their culture from such organs of public opinion as "The Horn of Empire" or "The Clarion of the People," and old God looked at me and looked through me, and He burst out laughing, and He laughed and laughed until the aether began rocking, and on the waves of the aether the stars went dancing and scintillating, tossing up and down in the wildest gymnastics, like corks on wild waters. I pretended to be amused also, but I really could not see what the joke was about. Then I awoke hearing people laughing uncontrollably below my window, and it was that laughter caused the dream. It was a miraculous creation in a second, but I know it sprang out of my humour. You, if you dreamed, would see a vision so beautiful that you would imagine it was a vision of Paradise, but it would be no less of yourself than my fantasy. That magical element which bathes us would have made itself for you a mirror with the illusion of infinite reality, just as it made itself a theatre and supplied the properties to stage my ironic imagination. Perhaps that miraculous element which creates illusions in us with such swiftness may be God, and It may like a joke about Itself. Now neither you nor Rian would admit my fantasy was a divine revelation, though it was swift, coherent, and complete, in fact as much a miracle as any vision of Ezekiel.'

'I'll admit it. There is character and originality in it,' said the artist.

'I would not despair, if I had time, of proving your imagination an extension of the imagination of our ancestors,' laughed Lavelle.

Leroy placed his hand affectionately on the shoulder of the poet. He was an older man than any there, more master of himself, and he was talking deliberately to lead a reaction of mood to the normal after the fierce excitement of the struggle in which they had been captured. Leroy and Lavelle were men who lived by intellect and imagination, and to the last their outlook would be intellectual rather than bodily; but there were some of the prisoners who were realists and who had no interest in metaphysical discussion, and these had been watching with passionate interest everything in the city which could be seen from the high windows from which they gazed. There came a shout from these, and all hurried to the windows of the great room to see what new action was taking place in the drama in whose yet unfolded finale their fate was hidden.

IV

Lavelle gazing from the high window saw at first only the restless and ruddy glimmering of fire and shadow over the city. But looking up he saw the vision which had excited his companions. The guardians of empire had sent a summons for aircraft to overawe the revolting people, and they were coming, a blazing caravan travelling across the limitless desert of the sky. Not Babylon nor Luxor to overawe the denizens of their cities ever created in the squat magnificence of their palaces such images of power as these dragons of the air which drew up from far horizons. Irresistible and disdainful as eagles of a tumult of earth-crawling mice, they floated with all their lights displayed that the city might know what might over-hung it. The air everywhere was vibrant from the deep purring of their engines, and it shook as Heaven might have shaken at the opening of the seals in the Apocalypse. The heart felt strained dreading, not individual doom, but the annihilation of cities and races. The conflict below was now too interknit for action, but the ships floated high up like palaces of gods built on some mountain slope of night, minatory to those who gazed and who knew not at what instant the glow of life might be extinguished in an obliterating rain from the sky. From these aerial cruisers[3] the high admirals of empire overawed the subject peoples. There was nothing which could oppose them in the underworld. Their crews were apart from the earth dwelling races, made distinct by the ecstasy of the high air they breathed, by a culture and poetry of their own fully intelligible only to the air-dwellers. Lifted up by pride and united by a spirit which seemed almost a new manifestation of cosmic consciousness, they regarded themselves less as servants of the empire than as acting under a mandate from Heaven to keep the peace of the world. Their vision of earth was wide and etherealized, for there were no frontiers to the realm they travelled in. Their isolation begot dreams disdainful of the differences between races. A world empire was the only politic which harmonized with their mood, and they were ruthless in suppression of revolt in territories whose people remembered an ancient sovereignty over themselves.[4] Nothing exasperates the spirit in man more than power which seems unconquerable and which makes impotent all protest. One of the prisoners cursed bitterly. But with Lavelle, the poet in him made him for an instant almost traitor to his nation, stirred as he was by that vision of the culmination of human power soaring above the planet. The problem of the interpretation of cosmic consciousness raised by Leroy recurred to him. Was his sense of an infinity in his emotion a criterion of truth, or was that antiquity true that might indicated right? Did the long overflow of power through centuries into the organism of empire reveal a harmony with cosmic purpose? Or was that vast being in which all life germinated as indifferent to the creatures which became in it as the night which enveloped the passionate city in an even calm? The thinkers of his time had divined an all-pervading element by which life seemed to be manifested.[5] By it everything was born. Thought and desire by it were translated into deed and energy. It lay between the seed and the corn, between the germ and the fulfilled being. It seemed to vitalize the good and the bad indifferently. As a child equally pleased by flower or glittering serpent, so this omnipotent child seemed to delight equally in bringing to birth monstrous and beautiful forms in nature.[6] That miraculous element withheld itself from nothing which desired manifestation in nature or man. To some, like the poet, it gave the vision of beauty, and to others, to those who floated so high in the aether, it gave almost an omnipotence of power. He felt how frail were his dreams for such a battle as he was engaged in; as frail as clouds cast aside like smoke from the prow of an aerial cruiser. Turning away with bitterness in his heart he was aware of Leroy by his side.

'Leroy,' he said, 'I understand the stories of men who sold themselves to a devil. There are powers which seem as if they would be overcome only by supernatural power. What forces can we summon up to deliver us from these?'

'Well by our death we may become supernatural beings ourselves, and so assail our conquerors with legions of spirits. The primitive believed he absorbed the spirit of the savage he killed and added its force to his own, which perhaps meant that he felt the foe within himself fighting beyond death. Most of our comrades are quite savage enough to continue fighting in that way.'

'Leroy, I can find no comfort in fantasies. Can you, in the evolution of world forces, foresee what may bring about the downfall of power such as we see yonder in the sky? We could not submit to it. We took the only way we knew. We die and go out. Yet I feel there must be a way even in this world by which right may find its appropriate might. If there be no way we are only struggling against the nature of things.'

'I think a revolt so widespread in the world must shake them even up yonder in their heaven, and I do not believe the influence of the dead on the living is altogether a fantasy. The victors in great wars have always been spiritually defeated by the conquered. Rome came to be dominated by Greek culture, and in the world war some centuries ago the last vengeance of the dying German Empire on its conquerors was to imprint on them its own characteristics. Your poetry and Brehon's History will be favourite studies in imperial circles in a few years.'

The poet smiled but faintly. He was one of those who suffer on behalf of their nation that agony which others feel over personal misfortunes. He pursued his meditation dreamily. Why did the Earth spirit inspire so many millions of its children in such contrary ways? Could a cosmic plan be divined amid these opposites? Had Earth any dream of a culmination of her humanity, or was there some trouble in the heavenly house, a division of purpose among gods? He might himself soon be absorbed into that being, and in the light of that new dawn of consciousness his thoughts were less about his own race and its immediate problems than about ultimates. He might have pursued this obscure meditation further, only the door opened, and two figures appeared in the doorway, their faces dark and undistinguishable against the light beyond. They were thrust in by the guards and the door again closed. Out of the shadow one of the newcomers, a huge figure of a man, came forward. The red light through a window fell upon him and a cry of dismay broke from the prisoners. 'Oh, it is Culain! Culain!' and they crowded about the man by whose influence the workers of the nation had been brought to take part in the revolt.

V

The figure which emerged from the shadowy into the red air was massive, noble, and simple. It might have stood for an adept of labour or avatar of the Earth spirit[7] incarnated in some grand labourer to inspire the workers by a new imagination of society. To the workers this Culain appeared an almost superhuman type of themselves, a clear utterer of what in them was inarticulate. That deep, slow, thrilling voice myriads had listened to as the voice of their own souls. It affected Lavelle strangely as it came, the one thing firm and tranquil, out of the excited mass of prisoners. Every figure in that group was momentarily changing in a moth-like flickering from pale to dark caused by the leaping of flame or rolling of smoky clouds over the city. Everything appeared unreal, the room itself, face, limb, body, mass, all that the imagination normally rested upon as solid seemed vague and thin as dream. Only that deep voice seemed real as if it was the undisturbed voice of immortality.

'No! No!' that deep voice was saying. 'It is not over. It is only beginning. It is an earth movement. All that will topple from the sky before it is over.' And he waved a hand towards the glittering menace in the air.

'But we have no sky craft of our own!'

'If the roots deny sap the leaves fall from the tree. They have the air now but we have the earth. We are not using violence. We deny labour. Every tributary which fed them with power ceases to flow from today. For a while they may rain death, but they must descend and be as we are.'

'I wish I could believe that,' cried one. 'But their power comes from sources beyond our control.'

'This is not a revolt of two or three nations. It is a revolt of humanity.[8] To you it may be a rebellion of your nation. To us it is a revolution. The workers of the world have dreamed towards this for centuries. They are organized and know now their own power and their own hearts. They wish nations to be free, but they wish more to

The Interpreters

be free themselves. We would not be in this struggle merely to exchange world masters for nation masters. The workers will have no master except their own collective will. All who have tried to raise humanity from above have only pressed more weightily on those below. Those who are beneath life alone can raise life. Tomorrow no ships will leave harbour. No waggons will carry on land. The air will soon be empty. The armies will starve if they fight. Our terms of peace are the surrender of the world to the workers of the world.'

Here indeed was vaster trouble than the prisoners had planned, or imagined possible, though they might have known that never did one wild power awaken in the world but its kinsmen followed fast as the wild riders follow one another in the vision of St. John.

'It is a new tyranny,' muttered Leroy.

'I am with it,' cried Rian the artist. 'We will make something out of this old world after all. Culain, I will design the most wonderful cities for you if we ever get out of this. We will build palaces for everybody. I have always hated designing houses for the rich. It seemed like the sin of simony, selling beautiful imaginations for money. We artists built first for the gods and we did our best work for them. Since then we have built for the Caesars, the aristocracies, and the oligarchies, and our work was worse with every change of masters. To work for the world will be like working for the gods again.'

'The more masters you have the worse will it be,' growled Leroy.

'Cannot you see the majestic things harmony of effort makes possible, old grumbler that you are?' said Rian. 'I have looked at the remains of the Parthenon, and have sat for days brooding over the ruins of temples in Egypt. The people who saw such beauty and magnificence must have been proud and uplifted in heart. However mean their original nature they lived in an atmosphere of greatness. That divine architecture must have coloured their thought as a sunset makes everything in harmony with its own light. If the empire had created beauty I might have been with it. I am afraid I could always be bribed by fairy gold. But it cannot create. It can only suppress. It multiplies images of stupidity everywhere. Beauty is flying from the grey cities and the mean streets where people live out their lives. If this continues humanity will grow grey and ugly as the world it lives in. We will forget what beauty means. It will be a word with lost meanings like the Etruscan inscriptions. You are frightened at the idea of any kind of state as a mouse is of a trap. Such oppression as we live under I will revolt against with you. But I have imagination of a state of another character. You are so much an individualist that you speak as if every man was a distinct species of being by himself, that no harmonious action was possible, and we were all as apart in character from each other as the lion is from the tiger.'

'We are really much more distinct from each other than animals of different species are,' Leroy retorted. 'One law for the lion and the tiger would not be oppression. They have the same appetites. The lion and the tiger go one path to the pool to drink and to the same covert to stalk the same prey. Our souls drink from a pool deeper and wider than ocean. You and I see different eternities. We have the universe to roam in imagination. It is our virtue to be infinitely varied. The worst tyranny is uniformity.'

'Do you conceive of that being within you as indefinite in character and purpose?' a quiet voice behind Leroy made question. Lavelle, Rian, and Leroy turned. They saw a tall, slightly stooping man, white-haired, a face aquiline and eager, the dark eyes with fire in them which turned from one to another indicating unabated intellectual vigour. It was the prisoner who had entered behind Culain, but who had been overlooked in the excitement caused by the entrance of so notable a personality. The name of the newcomer was familiar to all, but Lavelle alone recognized the historian of the nation. 'How do you come to be here, sir?' he asked. 'You were not in our councils, though you are the father of us all.'

'Well, since you young men made a bible of my history, our rulers seem to think it is better I should be out of the way while the trouble you created continues.'

'People think the state obtains information by incredibly secret methods,' said Leroy. 'I believe it occupies itself in an incredibly unintelligent study of popular journals. It is sufficient for it to find a name there associated with a thing to warrant arrest. But after all it only anticipates. If its prisoners are not guilty before arrest they are ready to join any conspiracy afterwards.'

'I shall not regret my loss of liberty,' said the newcomer. 'I am sure I would hear nothing so interesting without these walls as I shall hear within them.'

Fifty years before, when national sentiment appeared almost extinct, Brehon, then a young man, proposed to himself to write the history of his country, and in the labour of twenty years he had unveiled so extraordinary a past, so rich a literature in a language almost forgotten, that his work became an object of passionate study by his countrymen, and what had been intended almost as a funeral oration or panegyric over a dead nation had the effect of rekindling it, and it came forth young and living from its grave. The historian had been followed by creative writers like Lavelle, in whom the submerged river of nationality again welled up shining and life-giving. The youth of the nation bathed in it, washing from their souls the grime of empire, its mechanical ideals, and the characterless culture it had imposed on them. But after this history had appeared the historian seemed to take no interest in the great movement he had inspired. He became absorbed in more abstruse studies, the nature of which was known to but few among his countrymen.

'I have for a long time thought revolutions spring from other than the ostensible causes to which they are attributed, though these may seem adequate. Even in the moments I have been here I have heard reference to principles which are not commonly discussed. You,' said the historian, addressing Leroy, 'were explaining some political ideal as being an extension of a spiritual concept.'

'Oh, if the people fighting without there had only known the ideas Lavelle and Leroy discuss among themselves, there would have been no revolt,' said Rian. 'They would not have understood what their leaders were talking about. The room before you came in was less like a prison for rebels than an academy of philosophers discussing what relation the politics of time had to the politics of eternity.'

'Could we not continue that discussion and try to discover whether political emotions are not in reality spiritual emotions?' asked the historian. 'The poets and lovers before Plato traced the divine ancestry of love, and other emotions have been related by the mystics to divine originals. Yet political emotions, which are as profound as any, and are powerful enough to draw the lover away from love, are not made sacred by association with an Oversoul.[9] Historical and objective origins are attributed to passions deep and absorbing as those evoked by great religions. We shall not sleep here tonight, I fancy; and how could we employ the hours better than by each telling as between himself and Heaven what imagination about society brought him to consider his imagination more important than life?'

'As between myself and Heaven,' said Rian, 'I believe I desired passionately to build the palaces and cities of dream here on the earth, and I wanted the prophets of beauty like Lavelle to prepare the way in people's souls. I never peered inside myself except to search for unearthly compounds of stone and mortar. But Lavelle and Leroy have probed deeper things in their being. Lavelle will tell us what brought him from dream to action. We cannot spend the night better. Tell us, Lavelle, how the national idea turned a poet into a fighter. You were moved, I know, by impulses you never uttered to the crowds you inspired. I suspect you talked, like Moses, to gods upon the mountains.'

VI

'Where else,' answered Lavelle, 'but on lone earth or mountain come inspiration, and how but by divine visitations, whisperings and breathings from the dark were nations inspired? Every race, Greek, Egyptian, Hindu, or Judaean, whose culture moves us deeply, looked back to divine origins. My belief in such inspirations has, I confess, been more to me than the thoughts about the nation I have shared with others. But I do not know if I can make clear reasons for my belief in an oversoul guiding and inspiring our people. You will agree, I think, that we do not bring about revolutions because of the few people we may know personally. We do so because of the millions we do not know. And I think it is true also that we are stirred less by the ideas we make clear to ourselves than by the myriad uncomprehended ideas and forces which pour on us and through us, which are hardly intelligible to ourselves, which we cannot rationalize, but which give us impulse, direction, and the sensation of fullness of being.'

'I guess what you mean,' said Rian. 'I rarely designed a building without imagination creating a city in harmony with it; and from this piling up of fanciful cities in the imagination comes the inspiration for the single house.'

'Do you see the buildings in your imaginary city clearly?' asked Lavelle.

'I do in part. Sometimes I can see the sun shining on architrave, carving, or pillar, casting clear-cut shadows. This I think strange and wonder how it all was born in me. I often feel a mere craftsman employed by a supernatural architect to carry out a few of his prodigal designs.'[10]

'You believe,' Brehon asked of Lavelle, 'these intuitions about the nation have their origin in a being which has an organic life of its own, just as the half-perceived buildings of imagination with him give the sense they are really complete like a city in the heavens before he becomes aware of them?'

'Yes, I think that is a parallel. But Rian, for all his vision of cities, would find it difficult to draw in detail one after another the buildings he surmises in that architectural atmosphere around the one building he concentrates on. It is no less difficult for me to give substance to a multitude of feelings, which, if I pass them through a filter of words, will not sound like planetary murmurs, though I feel they come out of the soul of the world. I will try, however, to isolate some of these moods and interpret them. I feel it is easier now to do this because here we are, it may be, in the antechamber of death where unrealities are rare visitors. Here I find the thoughts I shared with others fade in power and the spiritual concept of nationality alone remains with me.'

'I think we shall have some light on the problem how theocratic states were born,' said Leroy. 'Lavelle is an antique.'

'It is a long history, beginning when I was a boy,' said the poet, who accepted the ironical comment of his friend with good nature. 'You remember, Rian, our holiday among the mountains? One day you wished to climb to the top of the hill, and I would not, and you went on and for hours I was alone. But as I lay on the hillside I was no longer solitary, but smitten through and through with another being, and I knew it was the earth, and it was living, and its life was mingling with my own. Some majesty was shining on me all the day, nodding at me behind the veil of light and air, or playing hide and seek within the shade, or it was in me as a spirit beseeching love from my own. It seemed older than life, yet younger and nigher to me than my own boyhood. I lay there drenched in the light, and all the while imagination, as a cloud which wanders between the Earth and Heaven, was wandering between my transience and some immortal youth. I can remember that magical day. I can see the white sun blinding the sky, and light in dazzling cataracts outpoured and foam from cloud to cloud, and the earth glow beneath an ocean of light with purple shaded valleys, and lakes that mirrored back the burning air, and woods vaporous as clouds along the hills, and jutting crags, and mountains hewn in pearl, all lustrous as dream images and all remote as dream. Earth had suffused its body with its soul, and I lay on the mountain side clinging to it in a passion. When Rian came down I heard his voice beside me as from an immense distance calling me back to myself; and I was irritated by his coming for I wanted to be alone with that spirit which had found me.'[11]

'Oh, I know,' groaned Leroy. 'If nature catches the soul young it is lost to humanity.'

'No, no, the Earth spirit does not draw us aside from life. How could that which is father and mother of us all lead us to err from the law of our being?'

'The earth may be our mother,' retorted Leroy, 'but I am sure it is not our father. We get intellect from something beyond planets or sun.'

'Be quiet, Leroy,' said Rian, 'we will hear your reasons for revolution later. I am sure they will be the maddest of all, though

Lavelle's political thinking appears to me to begin in very abstract regions.'

'No, there are the true realities,' cried the poet. 'Abstractions begin when we get away from the Earth spirit which has begotten us. Out of it have come plant, animal and man – all real things. Do plant and animal arrange their own evolution? Does the flower dream its own colour and scent? Does the bee devise its own wings or the polity of the hive? Are we less exempt from that dominion over our ways? Since I was born some wisdom, never sleeping though I slept, was in me, and cell by cell I was fashioned and woven together and over my making I had no control. We dwell in the house of the body, but its perfection and intricate life are the work of a wisdom which never relaxes dominion over a single cell. I believe that wisdom is within the soul to guide it. It is ready at every instant to declare to us the evolutionary purpose. It has planned for us a polity as it has planned for the bee the polity of the hive. We are higher than plant or animal. We can be conscious co-workers with the spirit of nature. We fall into unreal fantasy or thin abstraction when we think apart from it. We are empty as a vessel turned downward which fills itself only with air. If we think with the Earth spirit our souls become populous with beauty, for we turn the cup of our being to a spring which is always gushing.'

'The Earth spirit speaks with one voice to you on your mountain and with another voice to some solitary in a desert in Araby.'

'The Earth spirit throws itself into innumerable forms of life,' answered Lavelle. 'Did you expect it to make its children all of one pattern? For every race its own culture. Every great civilisation, I think, had a deity behind it, or a divine shepherd[12] who guided it on some plan in the cosmic imagination. "Behold," said an ancient oracle, "how the Heavens glitter with intellectual sections." These are archetypal images we follow dimly in our evolution.'

'How do you conceive of these powers as affecting civilizations?'

'I believe they incarnate in the race: more in the group than in the individual; and they tend to bring about an orchestration of the genius of the race to make manifest in time their portion of eternal beauty. So arises that unity of character which existed in the civilization of Egypt or Attica, where art, architecture, and literature were in such harmony that all that is best seems almost the creation of one myriad-minded artist.'

'But,' said the indefatigable Leroy, 'your world spirit does not merely inspire variety of civilization in Greece, Egypt, or China, it inspires individuals in the same country to work in contrary directions. How do you distinguish among varieties of national ideals those which have the divine signature from the rest? How do you thus distinguish your inspirations from those of my Dark Angel?' It was as a Dark Angel Leroy wrote his fantasies.

'It is difficult to answer you,' said Lavelle, 'and if there was a general certainty in human thought I might be regarded as foolish to risk life because of momentary illuminations. But to all of us life is a mystery, and we are like Columbus who was encouraged to venture further on the untravelled seas because he saw a single leafy branch floating on the water. We likewise dare all things if we hear a horn blown from some height of being and remember that some who lived before us reported that they too heard that horn. We have control over the work of our hands but little over the working of the soul. But yet we must yield to it, for without it we have nothing. You or I may write something and others will say of it that there is a mastery over our art; or Rian may design a building all will applaud for its beauty; but the fountains of thought or vision are not under our control. If vision ceased suddenly with you or me how could we regain it? If ideas did not well up spontaneously from some deep none of us would know how to trap them, so far beyond conscious life is the true begetter of thought or vision. We would appear to ourselves to have no real being but for the continuity of character of the ideas which well up within us. Because of this continuity and harmony we infer some being out of which they arise. I have come by a roundabout way to answer your question. As it is by the continuity of character in our ideas we infer a soul in ourselves, so it is by continuity and harmony of inspiration in a race we distinguish those inspirations which come from the national genius from ideas which are personal. I came but slowly myself to see these distinctions, for many years passed before imagination and feeling passed into vision and I began to see in that interior light figures which enchanted me with their beauty. These were at first mythological in character and I could not connect them with anything in the world. Then I read the history of our nation, and I was excited by that tale which began among the gods, and from history I turned to literature, and it was then I knew the forms I had seen in vision had been present to the ancestors thousands of years ago, and ever since they had been in the imagination of the poets. I felt the continuity of national inspiration, that the same light was cast upon generation after generation just as the lamp in that high window casts a steadfast glow and shape on the smoke which hurries past,' and he pointed to the ruddy coilings of smoke which flowed by a high building beyond the square.

'What do you mean when you describe forms as mythological in character?'

'There are certain figures which appear continually in our literature, spoken of as a divine folk, apparitions of light taller than human, riding on winged horses, or shining musicians circled by dazzling birds, or queens bearing branches with blossoms of light or fruit from the world of immortal youth, all moving in a divine aether. These were messengers of the gods and through these came about that marriage of Heaven and Earth in our literature which made it for long centuries seem almost the utterance of a single voice. These divine visitations have been the dominant influence in our literature so that our poets have sung of their country as the shadow of Heaven. The hills were sacred, the woods were sacred, and holy too were the lakes and rivers because of that eternal beauty which was seen behind them as the flame is seen within the lamp. Political thought with us too has been more inspired by the national culture than by the economic needs which almost completely inspire political activity elsewhere. But why should I try to convince you of the reality of national character? Has it not been noted by all who come to us? If we had not been restrained by alien power from control over our own destiny we would have manifested the national genius in a civilization of our own and it would have been moulded nearer to the divine polity. While all can see the unity of mood and character I am perhaps alone among you here, though not alone in the nation, in believing it comes from the soul of the world. Such beliefs are perhaps above proof, though we may know the truth after to-morrow's sun has set, falling back into that fountain from which we came.'

VII

'I fail to see Leroy a harmonious bee in the divine hive,' said Rian slyly glancing at that personality. 'I remember a temple wall in Egypt all solemn with immemorial forms, and some ribald ancient had scrawled a comic crocodile upon it. Leroy would be a creator of comic crocodiles in your scheme of things, Lavelle. I am trying to imagine him the slave of the inner light. But–' he broke off laughing.

The other was intellectually indignant. 'I am the slave of the inner light,' he said. 'But I do not wish to be the slave of the inner Lavelle. I do not know why you delight to see everywhere the echo of a single mood. I take joy in Lavelle's imagination, in yours, and in all free imagination, but you desire to impose your dream on others. I, if I met a man with imagination like my own, would turn my back on him. I believe the emanations of all creatures are poisonous to themselves.'

'Well, I am with Lavelle. There could be no place for my art in the world without the aid of others. Architects by themselves do not build cities. Nor would we continue imagining a beauty which could never be manifested. This must also be true of statesmen. They could not go on with the noble labour of civilisation unless there was to be harmonious effort among many to bring it about.'

'An idea may be heaven inspired, but is the will to enforce it by violence part of the inspiration?' the historian asked of Lavelle.

'Every idea which arises in the heaven world of consciousness must ally itself with an appropriate force if it is to be born in this world.[13] When we devise anything for ourselves our thought allies itself with force to move the body, and in carrying out what we devise we must often suppress energies and passions which would impel the body to contrary action. So the national genius, if it is to move the body politic, must ally itself with force to overbear what is hostile to it. How else can right find its appropriate might? How could national genius create a civilization if an alien power controls the economic and cultural activities of the people, if it substitutes in youth a mongrel culture for the national culture? How but by force can the nation free itself from a power which has taken the sceptre from it, which has killed its noblest children and broken up its laws? Now, being in peril, it would force us to fight for it, to fight for the power which enslaves us. So,' added Lavelle bitterly, 'might a man who had violated a woman, on the ground of this enforced intimacy expect the woman to sacrifice herself for him ever afterwards.'

'You spoke of a mongrel culture. Did you mean an alien culture only, or had you another meaning? Do you contend for the superiority of the culture of our nation over the culture of all other races?'

'Could we argue for the superiority of poet over musician and having decided this ask poet or musician to express themselves in the superior art? No, we realize that natural aptitudes are not interchangeable, and each person must of biological or spiritual necessity practise the art for which he is fitted. If there be a true national culture it is best for the nation. It associates what is manifested with what is yet unmanifested in the soul of the country, and tends to draw down from heaven to earth a complete embodiment of the divine idea. I feel it to be true about poetry that it is born in the dream consciousness and made perfect there before it enters the waking consciousness. If a verse or even a line I think beautiful sounds in my brain, I know that by brooding upon it I can draw down the complete poem. I think in the same way when we brood on what is beautiful in the dream of the ancestors we attract out of the deeps of being all beauty which is akin to it.[14] But to argue about the abstract superiority of cultures would be to enter upon a futile controversy like an argument between ants and bees over their civilizations, as if those who had the worst of the argument could change their species.'

'Yet there are no biological distinctions between men such as divide ants from bees. The literature of other races we understand as we do our own. Nothing which is human can be alien to humanity.'

'We can draw inspiration from other races, but their culture can never be a substitute for our own,' said Lavelle. 'The wisdom of others is full of danger, for we may lose what is ours and break up our natural mould of mind. A Chaldaean oracle uttered a warning against changing the ancient names of evocation in a country because such had a power affixed to them by the mind of the Father. A national culture evokes by association of ideas a thousand moods which an alien culture, however noble, cannot evoke because the symbols and forces referred to are not always present in us. If all wisdom was acquired from without it might be politic for us to make our culture cosmopolitan. But I believe our best wisdom does not come from without, but arises in the soul and is an emanation from the earth spirit, a voice speaking directly to us dwellers in this land. We are among the few races still remaining on earth whose traditions run back to the gods and the divine origin of things. There have been men in every generation who have seen through earth as through a coloured transparency into the world of which this is a shadow. Hence it comes that our land, the earth underfoot, is holy ground. In the earliest mythological tales the sacred mountains, lakes, and rivers are named. And why were they sacred? Because there, as on Sinai, men spake with divinities; or, starting hence, they were visitors to the Country of Immortal Youth, and returning reported of it that it was not far off but near and it was accessible to all of us. Even where the literature is unread something of the tradition remains with the peasant, and at times he has vision so that he sees in waste places the blaze of supernatural palaces, and people look out upon him with eyes which are brighter than human. He broods on such things, and in dream he visits the world he broods on, and there arises from this a commingling of natures, and a certainty about spiritual things, and the soul follows a true path and is not led into the maya of abstractions.[15] I know there are few now who travel on the primeval highways of being, and they have become tangled byways for most, and are rarely travelled, but still the way to those who walk in light is known and I would preserve what remains of knowledge so that we may continue to draw from our own well of wisdom. In countries where they have lost the primeval consciousness of unity with the earth spirit they either have no mythology and cosmogony and thought is materialistic, or else they go to Greek or Jew for their spiritual culture. So distant lands are made sacred, but not the air they breathe; not the earth underfoot. A culture so created has rarely deep roots, for it is derivative, and nobody can climb into heaven by its aid, and it is of such cultures I spoke as mongrel. We find something false even in the greatest masterpieces of such literature. We admire the grandiose style of Milton, but feel his Heaven-world is rootless and unreal and not very noble phantasy. We wander in such literature into many palaces of the soul where there are no windows looking out into eternity, and their beauty at last becomes a weariness to us, for we seem for ever to be imprisoned in personal phantasy, and we come to think there is nothing but individual life and the race drops out of the divine procession.'

'The roots of your being seem remote from humanity, Lavelle, though I have heard you move crowds as deeply as Culain. Your heart, I think, you use only on public occasions, but privately its temperature seems a little Arctic.'

'Were we not to discuss our ideals as between ourselves and Heaven and the relation of our politics to the politics of eternity?' Lavelle defended himself. 'I have tried to make clear to you where I think the Spirit breathed in the deeps of my being and what ideas of our destiny arose in me. I do not think I am unconcerned about the quality of human life. Why am I here? Why did I take a part in this revolt? I saw a spiritual culture being extinguished and a materialistic and ignoble culture being imposed on us to the degradation of human life. I believe humanity divine at its root. Out of this root comes beauty, intellect, imagination, and will. Out of this was born everything we adore in humanity. The heroes of our own race, all those we hold in our memory, had this half divine character. They were transparent to spirit. Though I believe with the apostle if we find the Kingdom of Heaven within ourselves everything else will come to us, yet if I had to build up a social order and could not wait for the slow evolution I would begin it with consideration for the poorest first and I would have Culain as my architect.'

The Socialist Leader, a huge figure half hidden in shadow, had been listening with head bent as if brooding doubtfully over ideas remote from his own but which came by long detours to a sudden harmony in action. He lifted up his head as if he was about to speak, but out of the silence which followed Lavelle's words there came a disdainful voice.

'All this is very well in poetry. Our wives and daughters may read such things in pretty books. But what a basis for world politic! Such imaginations as these may allure romantic boys and girls, but Nature does not endow them with vitality. The tribal communities are gone behind time irrevocably and are like fossils in human memory.'

The prisoners peered into the shadow. The voice came from Heyt, the president of the great air federation who had been so strangely thrust into their company. The world state was here to defend itself from its rebels.

VIII

The disdainful voice went on, 'You are intellectuals, in your political thinking like those mathematicians who pursue the elements beyond aether into mathematical space, and when their calculations are worked out are unable to find the material analogue of the result. You have lost relation to the body politic, and political thinking apart from an organism is futile. The intention of Nature is seen in the forms it creates and not in the dreams of its creatures. The kid which hears a lion roaring may desire limbs of a colossus and a neck powerful to toss like the rhinoceros, but does Nature therefore enlarge its stature? You cry out against the world state which Nature has made like the lion, but the will of the world soul is seen in the organisms it endows with power. The might of an organism is a measure of its rightness, for no organism could grow to power through centuries maintaining itself against the evolutionary purpose. The upholding of a regional ideal is like the display of a ruined house inhabited by a few shadowy ghosts. If Nature was with your thought it would have bestowed power on it, but the world soul has decreed the world state.'[16]

'That decree,' an angry voice protested, 'if it ever was made, is now annulled in this city and over the world,' and there was a clamour of prisoners repudiating Heyt's interpretation of cosmic purpose.

'Our discussion would be unprofitable,' said the historian finally, 'if it became merely controversial as to the outcome of the present conflict. Our fellow-prisoner was explaining why as between himself and Heaven he is for a world empire. Should we not listen to him also, for, if fire falls on this city from the sky ships, he may be a

The Interpreters

fellow-traveller with us to the great Original, and I think myself in every dream and hope of man there is some story of the glory of that King.'

'Well,' said Leroy, 'I am ready to hear any politic discussed. It would be one of the finest ironies of life if he converted any, and they were brought out to die for the nation having just become initiates of the empire. Go on, sir,' he said to Heyt. 'I represent individual as you collective humanity. Perhaps our extremes may meet.'

'How does this power enter the organism of empire?' the historian asked of the imperialist. 'An avalanche gathers power as it slides down the mountain, and a man may gather power momentarily from the summoning up of the baser passions of his nature. You will admit power may be generated in many ways, but you, in your use of the word, implied purpose and an overflow from the world soul.'

'I find the design of Nature in the organisms which have birth in it, and from the energy which fills them I divine their future development,' Heyt made answer. 'The power I spoke of does not lie in the generation of mechanical force but in the minds which organize control. Nor do I think the intellectual power which comprehends natural law and uses cosmic forces low in the scale of human faculties. There are many with such wisdom in the service of the world state. Why? Because their science has revealed to them the unity of law and the harmony of power which make the universe a solidarity, and their politic is to make this unity self-conscious in humanity. Minds with this idea leap to each other as atoms of the same element leap to each other in the chemistry of nature. I felt what I believe to be cosmic consciousness stirring in myself and others when organizing unity of control in the many fleets which had roamed the air. Before that each had brought into an element with no frontiers petty ideas of nationality born in regions bounded by hill, river or sea. What place has nationality in the limitless sky, and yet the little nations, if permitted, would proclaim territorial rights in the aether up to the infinite. The cosmic consciousness manifests in the world state and to it these tribal distinctions are invisible.'

'If you get at a sufficient distance from Earth,' said the ironical Leroy, 'it also will disappear and need not be considered. At present altitudes only humanity is invisible.'

'Humanity has heights and depths which are invisible to each other. It is possible the heights may seem inhuman to the depths,' retorted Heyt, equally ironical.

Leroy persisted, 'Lavelle interprets cosmic consciousness in a sense contrary to you. I think you both err. I heard a street orator zealous for souls interpreting cosmic consciousness in his own fashion: "In that last dreadful day," he cried, "God will flout at you. He will point His finger at you. He will say, 'Ha! ha!' You had your chance. You would not take it. Now you will go to Hell!" You and Lavelle are more dignified. You do not create Deity in the image of the corner boy. But are you less anthropomorphic in your conceptions? You justify the moulding of humanity to your will by imperialism in the Heavens. I believe in the intensive cultivation of human life and think the cosmic purpose is seen in the will of myself and others to be individual and free. The cosmic consciousness I conceive to be an autocracy gradually resolving itself into a democracy of free spirits. You would make me the slave of a light I do not see, a law I do not know. How is cosmic consciousness to be recognized when it can be so variously interpreted?'

'The interpretation,' said Heyt, 'which is most in consonance with Nature has first claim to consideration. To men of science the universe is demonstrably under the dominion of unalterable and inflexible law. And it can be sustained in argument that apprehension of that law is the only light of cosmic consciousness in man. I perceive you hold democractic ideas, but where in Nature do you find traces of democracy to justify you in surmising it in supernature? Do you suppose the heavenly host is a democracy and planetary affairs are arranged in council as with men in some petty commune? If you think so argue out with the mathematicians.'

Every one in this age sought for the source and justification of their own activities in that divine element in which matter, energy, and consciousness when analysed disappeared. It was an era of arcane speculation, for science and philosophy had become esoteric after the visible universe had been ransacked and the secret of its being had eluded the thinkers. Heyt was high in the councils of the world state. On such men as upon deities converged all the forces of protest, and to them also came all that was to be said in support of state policy by the thinkers who, as priesthoods have always done, supported established authority. The prisoners were irritated by his tone as of one speaking from an immense height, who could with difficulty discern the ideas stirring in the world beneath him. But the historian in his endeavour to relate political moods to their spiritual ancestry went on.

'To perceive law in Nature does not of necessity lead to the conception of a world state. Where do you get natural or supernatural justification for your denial of freedom of evolution to so many millions? On what truth do you rely to balance all that curbing of life?'

'On the unity of Nature,' was Heyt's answer. 'Has not our science tracked the elements back to one primordial substance, and the forces operating in Nature to one fountain?[17] Our science in its theory and practice is based on these conceptions. Our politic in its theory and practice rests also on these fundamental unities. Through the world state humanity moves upwards to its source and becomes conscious of its own majesty.'

'It is the begetter of very bad art,' interrupted Rian. 'I refuse to believe there can be truth in the spirit which does not create beauty.'

'When the building is well built we may think about the decoration.'

'Beauty is not decoration. If it is not in the design, if it is not laid with the foundation stone, it will never be in the completed edifice. Where there is no beauty there is no spiritual authority. You shall not rule us with that story until the words you cry even in wrath break in a foam of beauty on the ear.'

'Possibly,' said Heyt scornfully, 'you are mourning so much over the ruins which must be removed that the design of the world state is to you invisible. I have no doubt the scrub which withers under the shadow of a great tree can see no shapeliness in the strength which pushes it aside and denies it sunlight. But the decay beneath fertilizes the forest. Nature works the material into higher forms. The world state will absorb its romantics and transmute emotion into wisdom. The change of phase is inevitable as the change from childhood to manhood.'

'How can the state be an organism in the sense that I am?' cried Leroy. 'Is there anything affecting simultaneously its disconnected cells? With us the cells are knit and thrill together. In what sense other than mere metaphor is the world state an organism at all?'

'The state is a true organism because its units exist in an element which is the vehicle of emotion and thought, so that the units vibrate together. Have you never seen an orator by his magic make one creature, of which he is head and heart, out of a thousand people? Is that unity only brought about by the words he utters? Do we not know that as water is stained ruby by wine his passion colours the element which bathes his audience so that they vibrate in unison. This is an internal or psychic unity, and by this they become for the moment as much one being as you are. The orator creates a temporary unity. The state creates an enduring unity. Every state begins with some powerful personality more absorbent than others of the element which is the source of power, and he gathers myriads about him as an atom of crystal flung into a bath draws to itself the atoms of that element in solution. The organism so created continues until a higher phase of consciousness is reached, and humanity instinctively turns and regroups itself about the higher power, realizing a profounder consciousness in the contact. Human evolution is the eternal revealing of the Self to the selves. In the ancient world the state had the character of the most powerful person in it. The state gradually becomes impersonal through science and the comprehension of Nature whose energies are becoming self-conscious in humanity. Science now sits in the seat of Caesar. It is sustained in power because through it life rises from ignorance to wisdom and it clings to the revealer. I do not think your revolution will shake the unity of powerful minds which control human destiny through the world state. Your ideas are weeds growing in the fields of being and they must be uprooted like weeds.'

Heyt paused for a moment and there was a certain grandeur about him as he continued:

'I know that I am part of an organism lit up by a cosmic consciousness which shall rule the world. Humanity has yet to be born from the world egg but it shall be born by the stirring of cosmic consciousness through all its units. It shall control the elements and extend its dominion illimitably through Nature.'

'He will next threaten to subdue the Ruler of Heaven!' cried Leroy, fascinated in spite of himself.

'Yes,' said Heyt turning on him, 'we may storm His Paradise!'

IX

'With such ideas,' said Leroy gaily, 'you will hardly be welcome in the Kingdom of Heaven. Though I would myself cast out from that majesty all souls who would wriggle in as worms and miserable sinners, insulting Heaven by their abasement before it. Here you are an enchanting companion. In prison you enlarge our imagination. But you imprison our minds when you are free. It is true the orator may make a myriad replica of his own passion out of those who listen to him. But that does not prove he is right or they are not fools. The state may create a more long enduring unity of mood among millions but it does not prove that they are not being dehumanized. They become fractional elements in an organism rather than complete beings. The more scientifically efficient is the organism you create the more does it dominate the units and remake them in its own image, and when has the mass ever risen to the level of the individual? Though there be one thousand millions in your world state does it in its totality equal one Shakespeare? I am with Lavelle in the struggle for national freedom, and if the nation wins I shall fight in it for the freedom of the local community and for the greatest richness and variety in life. Prove to me that your world state is a human organism, that the law of its being is the law of my being: let your multitude in action give me the inspiration I receive when solitary, and I will consider it.'

'The culture of the individual! What is that but images and shadows of happenings in mighty states?' retorted Heyt. 'The very words you utter are sparks smitten from the anvil of civilization, and there has been no civilization apart from the highly organized state. You speak of the law of your being. Do you know what is the law of your being? You would probably have denied thirty years ago the being you are to-day. Is there any law for you which is not the law of my being and of all being? Only egomania demands consideration apart from the species. You speak as if the individual mind could be a mirror of infinity.'

'It can,' said Leroy calmly.

'It cannot be the channel of infinite power,' said the other. 'If the Absolute could have manifested itself and become self-conscious in an individual would it have created multitudes? The individual will is not a magnet powerful enough to attract the mighty forces which are becoming self-conscious in humanity. Without these energies operating in the human mind it would be in a state of arrested development – be unable to transmute its vision into being.'

'What,' asked the old historian, 'is the nature of the power you speak of and how is it to be discerned apart from the individual energies we are endowed with?'

'The energy of universal mind, the fountain of all the energies in Nature,' was Heyt's reply. 'It is this we discern in the highest human intelligences and they are conscious of direction. In the great laboratories of the state men seem at first to be absorbed in special studies, but, when they confer later, they find their special labours were only contributory to great discoveries made in common and all had unconsciously worked to one end. We have come to believe every energy and element in nature has intellectual guidance, and the human mind can enter into relation with the mind in Nature. We are passing beyond the stage where scientist or inventor harnessed Nature energies to a mechanism and tapped them for power. We are nearing the possibility of direct intellectual control of these Nature energies through a growing comprehension of their relation to their own intellectual guiders.'[18]

'It is not science sits in the seat of the Caesars,' cried Leroy, 'but the magicians. We are coming back in a spiral of three thousand years to the rule of magician and astrologer!'

'The ancients,' said Lavelle, 'comprehended and used spiritual powers, but your science only uses material energies. The ancients attained to a divine vision and saw beauty in its very essence where you only lay hold of some force like electricity.'[19]

'If they indeed attained such a vision of the universe,' said Heyt, 'it may have come by uniting their consciousness with the very force you despise. I believe this mighty force through all its correlations and manifestations to be guided by intelligence, and that intelligence is the artificer of the universe, of planet and atom, of state and individual alike. The more we understand its operations the more does it enter into consciousness, and the cosmic will reinforces our own. We attain our fullest life by becoming its slaves, for we can have no real being setting ourselves against the cosmic will.'

'You conceive then of cosmic mind shaping world history, acting by its intellectual energy on us through a hierarchy of powers and intelligences, and using the world state as its vehicle because it has widest ramifications?' Brehon asked of Heyt.

'Yes. You may so state it.'

'The design is to endow humanity with power transmitted from higher to lower?'

'Yes.'

'Of course as it is all Heaven inspired it is blasphemy of any of us to question the wisdom of the interpreters of Heaven,' cried Leroy raging. 'We know earth history even if we do not know heavenly history. A union of economic federations first strangle national life, then they become international and create world councils and at last dominate everything. Then they discover divine justification for autocratic rule. It is all in the cosmic plan! You concentrate power in the hands of a few and assert you are endowing all humanity with power and intellect.'

'Intellect in any organism must act from some centre,' said the imperialist. 'I have not asserted the evolution of society is complete. The body of a child is first animated by childish passions. The being of the grown thinker finally is thrilled by the majesty of law. Humanity as a whole will finally absorb and be moved by those powers which are now the heritage of a few. The power passes from mind to mind linking them by a common impulse or will. If there is revolt against the law the power will overcome it or break it. An allegory of this you may find in the tale of the master who made a feast and invited all to it. When they would not come he sent out into the highways and byways and compelled them with an iron hand. The freedom you conceive of is a chimera. You were born without your consent being asked. Your body, as another here has said, is shaped by a power beyond yourself and you are in it as in a prison. Only in a little nook in your brain you nourish a fantastic conception of freedom, while every cell in your body, the air you breathe, the sounds you hear, the vision of Nature you behold stir you with impulses beyond your control.'

'I am not certain that I did not, like Ulysses in the Platonic myth,[20] choose my own body,' said Leroy, 'or that through the labour of ages my spirit did not learn how to build it. And I am certain it is not for another to dictate to me thought or action.'

'You claim too much for the individual from the universe.'

'You see too little of humanity for a ruler. It is easy for you to be slave to your own imagination, and you think it easy for others to be slave to the same imagination, but your world state will be broken upon myriads of wills as rooted in eternity as your own, as passionate for freedom as mine.'

'I believe,' said Lavelle, 'it will be broken by the national will because it tries to blot out the past of nations and would substitute an arid and inhuman science for the infinitely varied cultures which had enriched the world. You train men to run a machine efficiently but they cannot guide their own souls. When the labour of their day is over there is a riot of uncultivated senses, Walpurgis nights where everything that is obscene or vulgar meets undisciplined by any memory of beauty. I count it the greatest of tragedies for a man that he should suddenly lose memory so that he could not recollect what songs were sung about his cradle, or the dreams of his youth, or for what ideal he had laboured. And your ideals have brought on many nations the greatest of spiritual tragedies, for they lose memory of their past and do not see the way they came and by what unnumbered dreams they were led. They lose the beauty of poetry, the ennobling influence of heroic story; and the cavalcades which set out thousands of years before miss their destiny and wander without spiritual guidance in a desert of vulgarity. We have rediscovered our ancient history, language, and literature, our treasure-house or paradise of beautiful memories, and we resume the pilgrimage to our own goal. Other nations with us revolt against the domination your world state would impose on them. The river of national life though submerged for a while rises up again. The momentum of a thousand ages, the character and the deep life created cannot be destroyed in a generation.'

'The future is as living in eternity as the past,' said Heyt. 'It is destiny you oppose. Your revolt will not succeed. Too many myriads have been liberated from the tyranny of the past and the narrow prison cells of its cultures which were but the heaping up of fantastic and personal conceptions. The wisdom of Nature which science reveals constitutes a true intellectual culture which knits the whole earth together in a brotherhood with universal Nature. Humanity can now speak one language. Will it return to the past – put on itself the ancient fetters of frontiers, tariffs, and languages which hindered it from a realization of its myriad unity? I do not think so. Break, if you can, us who brought about a world unity, but you will find you can only continue our work. You must pursue the science of power which has made the skies as native to us as earth to our ancestors, which made unending airways in great spaces, and thronged them with a life which but for us had crawled beneath, or had its movements limited by regional rights. You speak of beauty as if it had perished because of our science, but what beauty ever glimmered in the imagination to equal the vision of earth made possible by our art? You can leave this city at dawn and see the sun set in the valley of Kashmir at night, and you can, if you will, picnic meanwhile on the Mountains of the Moon. Oh, yes! to do this we trampled on a thousand prejudices, but we created a magnificence of power earth has not before known. You see above you in air those who keep watch and ward for the world state. At a word they could destroy this city. If they were destroyed a thousand more could darken the day overhead for you or illuminate your night. What power can you invoke mighty enough to overcome that power?'

'It will be overcome by pity,' came in answer the voice of Culain.

X

'The power of empire,' said the Socialist, 'does not descend from any sky god, but is earth born and sucked up from human depths where millions pay tribute in labour and pain. You breathe the magnificence, but do not feel the agony out of which it is born. Pity for that human agony has grown until it has become mightier than empire, and has marshalled against it armies that are numberless. There are two among you here who find inspiration outside the circle of human life for the deeds they do. But I believe humanity itself is its own absolute, and within itself are its own fountains of beauty and power. Its destiny is to realize its own nature and the unity inherent in that being, not a unity imposed from without. It cannot acknowledge as above its own the beauty of another being, or allow another power to dominate it. You look outside humanity. I look within it and find its profoundest impulse is to itself. Lavelle as a boy began to dream about Heaven and Earth. I as a child began a long meditation about human life, for I was born in a city of many millions, in the dark heart of it where the sunlight was grey before it lit our faces, and the air before we inhaled it had travelled through long leagues of pollution. I lived in a tenement crowded with necessitous life, in an abyss where most had come to the very end of all, where there was nothing more to be feared and there was that peace in pain. It was there I found pity lay at the root of our profoundest being and there was a secret joy in self-forgetfulness. My first thought beyond myself came because of an old woman who wept a quarter of an hour or so before she died being unable to rise and give help to another. That self-forgetfulness when the self was passing from life seemed to me to be wonderful. I have read poets who sung of fabulous and magic things, of starbright, clear, immortal drops of life, and how whoso drinks of that elixir has never fear of death, nor sickness comes, nor anything which wounds. But the life which forgets itself turns to its true immortality, and in that turning there is a deeper life than the poets have fabled. The immortality they imagined was but a shadow.'

'Oh, it is true, Culain,' cried the poet, 'it is true, that was the deepest life. We follow too much after shadows for their beauty. But we do so thinking we will become what we contemplate.'

'Take care, Lavelle, lest you be dragged out of yourself by your virtues as other people are by their vices,' Leroy warned the poet. 'Culain exalts pity over beauty or strength. He would lead you by that star into his fold. You will find his humanity has one soul with a single idea which is to sacrifice the many to the One. To sacrifice life! That would be easy! But to sacrifice the self! To do that is to oppose nature, whose purpose is to bring innumerable personalities into being. It was the labour of ages to bring us to be ourselves and it is no duty of ours to hurry away from ourselves.'

'To think like that is also to mistake shadow for substance,' Culain went on. 'You dream you have a rich life when you only have a multitude of ideas. To think is not to live. I believe it is true we become what we brood on, and if it be true, then only an image of life can give us life. On what should we brood but upon humanity, the only life we know? I too have sat on the mountains. The Earth there did not whisper to me of a life of its own: but with closed eyes as I sat there came up before me images and scenes of human life, not as external things, but as souls they entered into and burned my very soul, and I comprehended and felt agonies, aspirations, doubts, despairs, and striving. I saw in my vision that these souls were brighter as they turned from themselves, and their shining darkened as they clutched at the personal, and I knew the shining came because they were rising to their fount. That this vision was of realities I know, for afterwards I met some I knew first when in an illumined deep of brooding. I know we can open the soul to that innumerable life so that it can reflect itself in us, and truly we become it, for it is at its root one being, one Heavenly Man[21] manifesting in legions of forms. I am communist and socialist because I believe humanity to be a single being in spite of its myriad forms, faces, and eyes, and there is only in it such seeming separation as we find in our own being when it is dramatically sundered in dream. Whatever makes us clutch at the personal, whatever strengthens the illusion of separateness,[22] whether it be the possession of wealth, or power over the weak, or fear of the strong, all delay the awakening from this pitiful dream of life by fostering a false egoism.'

'You know, Culain,' Leroy spoke earnestly, 'that I love your mind and heart. You have vision but it is of a life so innumerable that it can only be revealed in the simplest of generalizations. You say humanity is one being, and you would build on that formula a social order for the whole earth, a social order where everybody possesses everything, and nobody has anything, and the infinite complexities of human nature are constrained into one mould of thought. You have vision and you see infinitude, but you cannot give your vision to those who will build up your communist state. Your organization will be to them an opaque idea, an end in itself, not an avenue to the soul. Life by it will be constrained and limited, and there will be unspeakable cruelty to the souls of men. The greater the organization you build the more must it be governed by regulation and formula. It will force on humanity an iron brotherhood, a brotherhood of force not of affection, and that would be the deepest of the human hells! You offer your candle of vision to the blind. But what use can it be to the blind except as a bludgeon?'

'All this,' said Heyt, 'would merely result in a spineless society dominated by vague emotionalism. In every vital organism there must be an element of power. A grandiose conception of society is a worthy aspiration. Love will follow the swift and strong but will not make itself its own ideal. Nothing is sufficient for itself, not even humanity. It must still enlarge its boundaries, because if it feeds on itself it will get thin and weedy like herds where there is too much inbreeding.'

'I too think an imagination which is over humanity is engaged in its moulding,' said the poet. 'Culain, you admit no influence from Nature, though we come out of its womb, nay, are still in its womb. That Nature in which we are bathed is our real nurse. It is she who moulds us in clans yet in infinite variety. When we surrender ourselves to her how full of life we feel! She transmits to her lovers her own power of making beauty and whatever is done by those who live nigh to her is lovely. When men live too long in great cities the cord which connects them with the mother being is cut, and what becomes then is misshapen. The works of art conceived in cities are first hectic with the colours of decay, and, last, there is nothing which has not erred in every line from its natural beauty.'

There was a friendship born of ancient enmity of ideals between Leroy and Culain, and the latter may have considered it useless renewing a controversy already plumbed to its depth between them, for he began a commentary on Heyt's conception of power.

'What is power? To be able to move life as we desire? We call a ruler powerful who at a word can fill the sky with armadas. But what is it moves the ruler? An emotion? a passion? or a vanity? And those armadas which leap into air at his will – what is the link between them and their ruler but an emotion? Such power at its root is only a unity of sentiment or feeling among many. What is it has made a hundred million of workers withdraw labour from the world state? Can you arouse a deeper feeling than pity to compel them to renew their labours? I think too that as all human power arises from feeling or desire so the forces in Nature if we had knowledge of their mode of motion are also moved by some desire. Is there a chemist in your laboratories who could deny that the affinity between atom and atom was not an affinity of life with life rather than a destiny inherent in the mechanism of their structure?'

'The will in itself is power,' said Heyt. 'The will is the self, the king principle in our being, and it orders all other emotions.'

'In the heroic tales of our people,' said Lavelle, 'one story is more famous than the rest which tells how an aristocracy of lordly warriors was rent asunder by pity for a beauty which had been bowed to sorrow by their kind. Beauty itself exercises the most sovereign power over the soul and the will bends before it. There is a divine beauty which is overlord of our being.'

'The beauty in humanity is inherent in it,' Culain replied. 'As the beauty of a flower is hidden in the seed cell so the beauty of humanity flows from its ancestral self, a mightier Adam or Heavenly Man.'

'Do you conceive of that oversoul to humanity as conscious of its unity with its children?' asked Brehon, 'or is its consciousness of its unity now lost as we in dream are divided up into This and That and Thou and I, and while we dream have not the sense that the dramatis personae are but one character?'

'I cannot say I know,' answered Culain. 'I can only say I believe, and yet I feel that that which upholds belief has knowledge. I can argue here and make the plea for a communist state so logical that it is without flaw, and it needs in this world for its completeness no argument drawn from a deeper life. Yet for myself I elect to be socialist not merely because logic and justice unite in the theory, but because of a vision which is incomplete, but which weighs more heavily with me than the most perfect logic. By faith only can I complete the segment I perceive of the vaster circle of human life which includes the Heavenly Man. I know it to be true indeed that soul can have vision of soul, not seeing only as the eyes see, but feeling the being of another as we feel the passion of our own hearts. Because of this the ancient Buddha commanded his followers to meditate with love and sympathy on life in the four quarters of the world. This I have done for many years, and there broke in upon that meditation, intimate and poignant, the sense of myriads of lives, and I saw and felt them as portion of myself, and they burned my very soul.'

He paused for a while as if he hesitated to reveal himself further, but continued in his slow speech: 'Once at the height of vision, overwhelmed with that intermingled life, I cried out in my heart to know its hope and way and end, and in my vision these myriad souls became transfigured, and all, even the darkest of them, I saw as gods, all shining and ancient with youth; and a fire which was within them all seemed to consume them and draw them into itself and they fled into it and disappeared or were melted in darkness and rapture into that Ancestral Self.'

XI

'Why do you speak of pity as the profoundest emotion in such a being?' asked the historian.

'There are no words but pity or compassion[23] to indicate likeness to that feeling which indeed is not so much pity as an emotion of infinite desire, or the yearning rather of a life limited and divided from itself for the being it has lost, and which should be as much itself as the beatings of the heart. As between myself and Heaven it was the intuition of the unity of humanity which led me to become communist. Wherever in history any were born with that knowledge life near to them reflected it as in a glowing glass, and there was no fierce thought of thine and mine. What was the polity of those who listened to Christ or Buddha? Had they not all things in common? They forbade warfare, for they would not have the spirit at enmity with that which was intimately itself, and they would overcome hatred by love. Those who are with me do not arm. We separate ourselves from a social order which is oppressive. We deny it the strength of labour, and when that is denied the old social order with its passionate possessive instincts must crumble. On its ruins we will build a new social order restoring the world to humanity. No one in the new earth will have private property in the earth. There will be nothing to make men feel they have interests distinct from the being of which they are part.'

'I do not believe,' said Leroy, 'if you put devils in Paradise they become angels. If there are any heavens they must be holy only because of things which are imagined there, not because the streets are as fabled of gold or the gates of precious stones. A man may gain his soul by giving up the world, but if his share of the world is taken from him by force it by no means follows his soul will be paid him as compensation. I am sceptical about all methods of achieving spiritual ends by material means. You say there will be nothing in the new social order to make men feel they have interests distinct from the being of which they are part. You will never create such a world. A man can be a glutton upon a crust of bread as well as upon a Neronian banquet, and if he has not great material possessions his vanity will glut itself upon the shapeliness of his nose, or his ideas, or anything else which is his.'

'If we bring about the ownership of the world by the people of the world, by the race, not by individuals, such a change is itself evidence the inner attitude of the soul has changed,' answered Culain. 'The spiritual change comes and must come before the material change. If it had not come the will of the workers would not have been set upon this polity. The collective will acts in this way because its hidden throne is upon this interior unity.'

'You believe then,' asked the historian, 'that in some region of our being we are conscious of unity with that myriad life? Our being here you say is dramatically sundered as it is in dream. Is there any sphere where this dream does not dominate the spirit?'

'I believe,' said Culain, 'in sleep and death we go back to ourselves, and the meanest of us here is there as a god. There have been men at all times who have known this to be true. A great religion based its psychology upon the unity of the soul with all other life in that state which is dreamless sleep to us. In one of its scriptures we are told of a sage who found an outcast sleeping by the roadside, and he hailed that outcast by heavenly names, "Thou great one, clad in the shining! King!" and of that outcast he said, so high was his being in sleep he was then like a king moving among his dominions. From that high being men come forth every morning to take up and renew their cyclic labour, which is to make the mightier Adam conscious in all its children, and they of it as their oversoul and very self.'

'You think the unity inherent in deepest being must at last become conscious in our life here and express itself in a social order and polity in harmony with itself?'

'I believe we are evolving to a state where the individual life will reflect in itself the entire being of humanity. The heart will attain its own infinitude of feeling as our eyes have already attained their own infinitude of seeing. They reflect the external universe with its multitudinous forms. The soul will reflect the internal world of multitudinous life. When it has attained this consciousness the polity of earth must be transfigured. Who then would grasp at sceptre or crown or possessions for a self which he knows to be unreal?'

'I do not understand,' said a prisoner who had listened with puzzled face to the symposium.

'Never mind, Rudd,' said Leroy kindly. 'Nothing Culain has said need affect your faith in your leader. It only means his communism is more absolute than any one had ever imagined, and if he has his way nobody will be able to call his soul his own.'

'All this,' persisted that prisoner obstinately, 'seems to be less our concern than the churches. The priests can tell me about God and the next world, if I want to know about them. I expect my leader to tell me how this world is to be made fit to live in. I do not like the mixing of religion with politic.'

'The God you heard about in the churches died a very long time ago,' said Leroy. 'It is centuries since His voice was able to be heard even in a whisper in the sanctuary. It came to pass that spirit fell into matter while matter was ascending to spirit. That means, my dear Rudd, that if you want to understand business in its most subtle forms you must now go to the churches. If on the other hand you wish to understand heavenly things you must now consult the politicals.'

'I do not understand,' repeated Rudd.

'Well, if Culain's ideas are true you only need to fall asleep to understand everything. Here are two who are now like kings moving among their dominions,' said Leroy pointing to some prisoners stretched asleep upon the floor. He gazed on them with a kind of exasperated admiration.

'I do not know whether I should praise them for their courage or depise them for their indifference to living. Here are the last exquisite drops in the cup of life and they turn down the cup. I never enjoyed life more intensely. It is worth while to take Death as a companion because it brings out all that is most alive in Life. "Oh," he cried, "there are some people out there who are living intensely." '

A thunder as of some vast concussion in the city smote on their ears. It was followed by a flare which made momentarily a wild illumination in the room. The faces of the prisoners gleamed in a magic moonlight of many colours. The sleepers awoke. All hurried to the windows. The lofty night was pierced by a thousand circling rays. The airships were searching the dark above and below, and the revolving beams made each appear the fiery hub of a wheel whose vast spokes rayed out to some remote and incalculable circumference, and these were the chariots of gods rolling across the sky. One of the rays rested on a little mist overhead. It surmised something sinister within it. There was a vibration in the air as if a brazen gong had been beaten, and at that signal all the rays converged on that mist. Something fell from the cloud. One of the great airships blazed out as if stricken by fire and it dropped within the city. A fountain of flame leaped up where it fell, and there was another fierce illumination of the room and of the staring faces of the watchers at the windows, who all, breathless and still, were intent on the spectacle in the sky. Those aerial cruisers, hitherto floating slumberously over the city, were now in wild activity. Rising to that higher dark where their enemy had been hidden they became hunters of the heavens. For that solitary airship of the rebels there was no escape. Soon it dropped like a falling star. There came a sigh as of pent-up breath escaping, and then Rian broke the silence.

'Oh! that was heroic, that deed of our comrades. With that little ship to lie up there waiting for these giants and for death! That fall! My heart went dropping with them. Oh, what was life to them in those ten tragic seconds!'

'I wonder,' said Leroy, 'did consciousness fly from the centre to the circumference, from earth to heaven? Or did everything in their being race to the centre in a mad concentration on the self that was to perish?'

'All physical combats are a nightmare,' Culain said, 'hate, despair, terror, every emotion called into being suck the soul down and further away from heavenly being.'

'No, no, it cannot be so with these,' cried Lavelle. "Death was a terror sunken below far horizons ere they rose on that adventure. The self had already perished for they had abandoned themselves to the genius of their race and it was captain of their souls. The last of life they knew was the rapture of sacrifice.'

'I would like such an exit,' said Leroy. 'Oh, from all that would crowd on me I think I would know myself truly. While we live a thought hardly lights the brain ere it vanishes. Our emotions have but warmed the heart and they go. They all hide in caves, and we can be conscious of but the minutest fraction of our being at any one time, never the whole being. I think if I took part in such an adventure the whole populace of thoughts and feelings would rush out of their caves and I could be my entire self if but for a few seconds. Perhaps if they put an end to me to-morrow I may have such an instant looking down a rifle before it is fired. I would not lose it. What I fear is that these airships will wreck the city, and I may go out without a moment to arouse the habitants of my being so that they may all answer the call and I may know myself in death.'

XII

'What an epicure of the spirit!' cried Rian. 'The feasts of Heliogabalus are pale images of gluttony set by this desire to swallow life in an instant. I hope if I am shot I will not see rising all at once before me the cities I might have builded. The one thing which might make death bitter would be the thought such imaginations never could be realized.'

'You like the others want to externalise yourself, I want to internalise and be myself fully. The end of life is to be, not to do. If your desire is to act all that is infinite in you will try to drag others out of themselves to aid you in your labours. You will try to build the world in your own image and there will be no freedom. The world can only be free when men are content in themselves and each draws from his own fountain.'

'Many people,' urged Lavelle, 'are born under one star and are kinsmen of each other in the spirit and find themselves most truly when they follow together that single light.'

But Leroy would admit nothing which subdued the individual to the group idea.

'When you speak of people following one star all that means is that they are weak enough to surrender their individuality to some more powerful than themselves. Every man must be original or be nothing. Who is interested in the followers of greatness? Were there any Christians worth thinking about after Christ? If we remember any it was because they revealed something in their spirit which was not in the original gospel. No life inspires us because it is like another life. I was once indeed converted to a church, but it was in a dream. I saw a procession in a squalid street in the core of some grimy city, and a venerable old man was there being consecrated as prince of his church. He was adjudged by it most Christlike; and the highest dignity it could confer on him was to name him prince; to give him a garret in those squalid streets so that he might live among the poorest like his Master. In that church of a dream all the priestly work done by archbishops and other dignitaries was intrusted to the newly consecrated for it was only business. The profound science of the soul was not for youth. I remember in my dream cheering that old man with the tears streaming down my cheeks, and then I awoke and knew it was only a dream and could never happen in life. Though the church endured for an hundred thousand years it would never produce another Christ. I do not believe a second Christ could ever inspire the world as the first did, for time has no story which inspires us when told a second time. The great spiritual clans, the great national clans, all try to cast humanity into a single mould. I am against the state as I am against a state religion. Nature in the infancy of the spirit may have been behind the religions and the nationalities; it may have been in them as the spirit of the hive. But in far ages the time came, I think, when some unknown god whispered to man, "Now, you yourself, my darling, must create yourself by your own efforts. The universe is before you. Its powers are yours. Take whatever you can." We are to reverse the ancient process by which Saturn devoured his children. It is for the children now to devour Saturn, and absorb the universe into themselves individually. The universe is infinite and there can be infinitely varied personalities. If there are differences of character among you it is in spite of yourselves. You are all jealous in demanding adhesion to national dogma, imperial dogma, or social dogma, and you imprison the soul in little cubicles of thought, the soul which might have grown into a myriad wisdom.'

'Oh, now!' Rian managed to interrupt the torrent of speech, 'you need not be so indignantly individual. I remember a few years ago you had built a civilisation in your own head, and wanted us all to come into it. You were proud of it as Nebuchadnezzar when he walked on the roof of his palace and cried out, "Is not this great Babylon that I have built?" '

'Yes, but I learned wisdom like Nebuchadnezzar. My Dark Angel told me the truth about that myth. The great King found the Babylon he created was only the shadow of himself, and he felt solitary as the man who sees replicas of his own face in a thousand mirrors, and he retired to the simple life. I escaped from the coils of the net. I live and feed myself on an acre of ground, but I am free and have the universe to roam in thought. I measure men by the magnificence of their imagination, not by the height of their cities.'

'What is the universe to roam in if the spirit never meets its own kinsmen?' cried Lavelle.

'Do you really so love to meet your spiritual kinsmen?' asked Leroy slyly. 'I never found you so happy or animated with them as with Culain or myself. You liked us because of our unlikeness. Confess, dear Lavelle, you were tired of your followers. They never enlarged the boundaries of your spirit but only multiplied ideas you were already familiar with. Should not that lassitude have filled you with terror at the thought that your enterprise might succeed and millions of many coloured characters be dimmed to one tone?'

'I do not admit the lassitude,' said Lavelle, smiling, 'nor the terrible character of the uniformity of thought you surmise among my friends.'

'Oh, I do not deny minor variations. You permit variety in the little things but not in the great. The dogma of the nation dominates everything and obscures the end of being. You are like people who can only look out on the world through a single keyhole!'

'You know,' said Lavelle, 'I do not think national character or culture is imposed on men from without by other men, but in their highest form or spirit are the extension of divine consciousness into the human.[24] You will not agree with me in this, but you will admit there must be identities of thought or culture among those who live in the same region, or else chaos or mere anarchy, not in your sense but in the physical, will follow.'

'Oh, yes, we preserve language which is necessary for communication of thought as light is for perception of form. But I do not agree that there need be more in common between the souls of men than the spirit of kindness which reconciles all things otherwise incompatible.'

Here the historian interposed. 'You said something a little while ago inferring an original unity for all living things. You spoke of the universe as an autocracy gradually resolving itself into a democracy of free spirits. Can these spirits divest themselves altogether of any relation to that being of which they are emanations? What is the relation? You use language which pre-supposes identity and yet you affirm separateness. If there be any dependence of your being upon heavenly being you must surmise that relation for the rest of humanity. And if there be a link of identity of consciousness in some plane of being this naturally would express itself in life. Do you assume any relation between Heaven and your spirit?'

'You may think of me as a rebel angel,' answered Leroy. 'I am in revolt against Heaven.'

XIII

'I am not averse to Heaven. I confess an artist's longing to see the fabled palaces, the gates of precious stones, and the streets of gold which some rail at. What is amiss with Heaven? Is the government oppressive?' asked Rian, laughing.

'Leroy is lapsing into fantasy,' said Lavelle. 'His Dark Angel will not allow him to be long serious.'

'Fantasy!' cried Leroy, 'when I utter the thing I hold to be most true, when I reveal myself most, you think I am not serious! I am rebel against the Heaven to which in imagination you are slaves. You all rest on divine powers to which humanity must be subservient. Yet it was to escape from their dominion over the spirit I verily believe a migration set in from Heaven to Earth. You assume it was in the divine plan. Have you never dreamed it might be our own primal will carried us here, that we would not be the slaves of light, and we chose free individual existence full of agony even rather than spiritual passivity. Do you remember to Dante, overwhelmed in Paradise, Beatrice speaking?

>What overmasters thee
>A virtue is from which naught shields itself.

When we gaze at the sun we are blinded to all else. What could the spirit be in Heaven but a mirror of that glory? There would be nothing for it but vision and it could have no being of its own. What wisdom could there be for those who are pure by birthright, who have not suffered or struggled nor willed in freedom their own destiny. We grow into a myriad wisdom through aeons of pain, and by that wisdom we are higher than seraph or archangel who have not wept as we have nor stayed themselves against the cosmic powers. You read the scriptures of the world but forget that the seers who revealed the architecture of Heaven told us to fly from Heaven, and that the highest was not there, and it seduced by its sweetness. Aeons ago the spirit of man revolted against Heaven, but it has forgotten its primal will. Heaven through the religions and philosophies and through statecraft renews its lordship over the soul so that in all that is done it defers to some divine power. Yet we have in ourselves the seed of something higher than the Heaven you worship.'

'The extremes have met!' cried Rian. 'The representatives of individuals as of collective humanity both dream of storming the Heavens.'

'That was the one thrilling thought expressed here,' answered Leroy. 'But he will never storm the Heavens with an army of slaves. The more the world state dominates humanity the more is the will of the individual made incapable of powerful effort.'

'The will grows stronger by self-suppression than in self-assertion,' said Heyt. 'In the first case it truly overcomes something. In the other desire is mistaken for will, and the man is most driven when he most thinks he is the driver.'

'That,' said Leroy, 'is one of those subtleties which can be uttered in a sentence but which need hours for their refutation. I will say no more than this that the truth of it depends upon what self is suppressed. I hold your statecraft would suppress manifestation of the deep inner being of man, and when that is overlaid, when you have submission to the world state, there must creep into society that stagnation which is the precursor of death. Whether it be you or Lavelle or Culain achieves the harmony of society individuality must be weakened, and the will lose that diamond hardness which can only be maintained by continuous effort never relaxed for a single instant. If the will be relaxed the powers we should oppose sweep like a tide over the soul and carry it away. We are then like one who has rowed against the stream but who rests on his oars and drifts back and loses all he has gained. I have purchased freedom at a great price, warring against all those who would draw me into an unintellectual harmony with themselves. I give no allegiance to the principles you speak of as the divine beauty or power or soul. If I am swayed by any deity it is some unknown god.'

'Your unknown god is suspiciously like the ancient devil,' said Rian.

'What was the ancient devil but some still earlier deity, some rebel of the Heavens who whispered freedom to the spirit of man; who against all external rule urged on it still to persist, still to defy, still to obey the orders of another captain, that Dweller in the Innermost whose least whisper sounds louder than all the cries of men?'

'Well,' said Rian, 'it is heroic to defy the universe. I admire even if I cannot follow. For all your prickles, Leroy, you are sweet at heart, and I wonder how all this was born with you. Had you a vision on a hill like Lavelle? or did you like Culain find your heart the council chamber where humanity met?'

'We all develop from the first contact of the spirit with the body, and the governing myth in my life was a dream which was born in me as a child. I believe it came from the same primeval consciousness from which welled up the Promethean myth, the legend of Lucifer and the wars in Heaven and many another myth of revolt, that mood in which the many eternally break from the One. In that dream I was one of the Children of Light dwelling in Paradise. Outside that circle were the Children of Darkness[25] whom we know not but they were rumoured to us as dreadful and abhorrent; and in my dream I wandered away from that Paradise into lonely and interstellar spaces, and I was there overshadowed by some dark divine presence, and I know it was one of the Host of Darkness and I trembled. But it whispered gently, "We of the Darkness are more ancient than you of the Light," and of many other things it said I recall this only, "When most you rebel against the known God the lips of the unknown God are tenderest upon your forehead." That, without then understanding, I remembered when I awoke, but because it was the first visitation of the spirit it became powerful in memory and everything in the conscious mind gathered about it, and at last I think that Dark Angel became my soul.'

'From such fragile and gentle dreams what mighty movements in the human mind begin!' the wondering Rian mused aloud. 'Lavelle hears a whisper from the Earth-spirit in his native land, and it becomes at last a sacred land to him, and he fights as desperately to keep it inviolate as the ancient Jews fought for their holy city. Culain saw some one die who had forgotten she had a self, and he began to remake the world in her image. You hear a voice in dream which hints of something higher than Heaven, and you become the most potent scatterer of revolt against all that men worship. Yes, I can see from the foundation stone how grew up the whole architecture of your thought. Talk of beauty leading us by a single hair! Here is a world in revolt, and three who have each a multitude of followers themselves follow phantoms that none other but themselves may see! O, earth whisper! dream of the heart! Dark Angel! who visited these in childhood, do you know what a storm you have created in the world? I revolt against the evil I see and I would replace it with a civilisation and social order I see no less clearly in the mind. In the civilisation Lavelle advocates, or in the social order Culain would establish, I see how the means provide a bulwark against the end to which they would lead us. The common mind of humanity can assert itself in council and need go no further. But to what anarchy of life would not your philosophy bring us!'

'I never asserted,' said Leroy, 'because I protested against human law that the universe itself was without law. If we are true to the law of our being Nature provides the balance. Let us all be individual, myriad-minded, godlike, acting from our own wills and our own centres, and will Nature therefore be upset? No, the law will adjust everything and bring about a harmony of diversities. Lavelle, Culain, and Heyt want to do Nature's work by providing a harmony of identities. I think it was old Plotinus who said that when each utters its own voice all are brought into accord by universal law. So I have absolute faith that if we are ourselves fully we do not become enemies but see more fully the beauty in each other's eyes.'

XIV

A silence followed during which Rian watched that prisoner of puzzled countenance who could not understand Culain, and whose expression indicated that now less than ever could he relate the politics of time to the politics of eternity. The sullen eyes, knit brow, and impatient feet grinding on the floor, betrayed the anger of one at home in practical action who finds himself trapped in a web of incomprehensible abstractions. The artist nature in Rian, sensitive to moods, feared some outbreak of exasperated common mentality, and he turned to the historian.

'Sir, I do not know whether in the long silence since the completion of your history you have passed from the self which was in that book; whether you have grown apart in soul from the nation you did so much to raise from oblivion, and whether we now seem to you to be vain necromancers in our endeavour to continue its life. I feel myself as if the earth was no longer firm under my feet. All these political ideas which inspire my comrades appear to be but the psychic body of ideas descended from heaven, but which have no companionship with each other when they dwell in our minds. Is there some warfare too in the heavenly house? Yet the stars yonder and this earth we trouble, which are celestial bodies, keep their places and seem to have no feuds like ours. You who are older than any here, who have feasted more richly than any upon the wisdom of the world, can you effect any reconcilement? Here are men who have made themselves formidable by the imagination and intellect they brought to bear on the rights of the individual, or the constitution of society and the state, who have many followers to whom they have spoken in the language the commonalty understand, but what allures themselves is something they cannot rationalize, something frailer than the laughter of Helen before which kingdoms faded away. I begin to wonder whether all desperate wars in history were not really fought to enable some fugitive beauty to endure in human thought. These magicians who have enchanted others, do they weave about their own spirits an enchantment no more real than the blossoms of illusion which flicker under the hands of an eastern juggler? I cannot believe as they believe. I can divine a nobler order in the world as a sculptor divined his statue in the unshapen marble. But it is this world suggests its own perfection to me, not another world which would have us fashion this in its own image. I confess I am frightened to think how lightly this earth, so solid to my imagination, weighs with these comrades of mine, so that if the faintest breathing from another nature falls on the scales, this earth with all its state, cities, and history, tilts up as if the earth scale was freighted with nothing.'

'I think,' answered the historian, 'there is some reconcilement of these ideas in my own being, for they have entered it, and are in friendly unison; but I could not now formulate in any completeness a conception of cosmic being in which such varied or contrary impulses are harmonized. Nor do I think, even with years of pondering over a choice of words befitting our imagination, could words ever represent, to one who has no direct vision or intuition of his own, what the words signify. I utter the word "spirit" or "beauty", and in my own being these words are symbols of emotion, moods, memories, powers, intricate and intermingled, and so it is with almost everything we give name to. No single mental process, except perhaps the mathematical, has ever been adequately translated into an external symbolism. Speech is not like a mirror which reflects fully the form before it; but in speech things, which by their nature are innumerable and endless, are indicated by brief symbols. For speech to convey true meanings there must be clairaudience in the hearing. Those who have spoken here have spoken intuitively and without the laborious processes of logic. I also will say what I imagine in regard to these things, evoking in my mind images and powers, and trusting to the intuition with which you have apprehended each other to see what is in my being also. It may help us to a reconcilement if we remember our infinitely varied human nature when analysed is a simple trinity of qualities. Whatever we do, think, feel, or imagine, whether about ourselves or the cosmos, we think in terms of these three fundamentals, which are matter, energy, and spirit. We can surmise beyond these nothing except that transcendental state where all raised above themselves exist in the mystic unity we call Deity.[26] In themselves they are as mysterious as Deity, and when we ponder upon them they allure us to regions where they become dark and blind with glory; so that the solid rock, melted and transfigured into its ultimate essence, becomes primordial substance and is the garment of Deity or mirror of its being, and, therefore, that ancient beauty which is the archetype of all other transitory beauty. The powers which shepherd the elements our science and intuition tell us spring from one cosmic fountain. This is true also of the powers we ourselves use, for some who have passed through the Arcana where the will has its throne found it rooted in the inflexible and intellectual power which sustains the universe. Consciousness also prolongs itself in meditation and ecstasy into a vaster being, as Culain has said, and we do not know whether there is any end to our being. All that is substance in us aspires to the ancestral beauty. All that is power in us desires to become invincible. All that is consciousness longs for fulness of being. These aspirations have moulded philosophies and religions as with Plato and Plotinus who conceived of Deity as beauty in its very essence. There were Indian sages who taught that the will when concentrated had a mastery which extended from the atomic to the infinite, and, in union with the divine will, gave man almost an omnipotence of power.[27] Other religions again led the soul to the fount of being and said to it, "Thou art That." I think these desires express themselves no less in the symbolism of politics, so that when one or another quality is predominant in men or races their polity tends to create that world order in which the predominant spiritual quality will have freest play.'

The historian was interrupted by Rian who said, 'But the spiritual bases of four political theories have been discussed by us, and your trinity of qualities omits to find an ancestry for one of these. Is it Leroy's anarchic ideas that have no spiritual foundation?'

To this Brehon replied, 'If we can imagine this trinity exalted above itself and existing in a unity, so also can we imagine natures so balanced that they may be said to be more complete symbols of the Self-existent or Solitary of the Heavens[28] in whom all qualities inhere. Such men tend to be self-sufficing and to assert absolute kingship over their own being. They exist in increasing numbers; and the philosophy of anarchy which they profess from being the most despised of political theories has in three hundred years become one of the most powerful. That has come not only because the right or justice of the individual, which appeals to the highly evolved soul, is asserted, but also, I think, because the creation of great individuals is the intent of Nature, which it has been said exists for the purposes of soul. The external law imposed by the greatest of states must finally give way before the instinct for self-rule which alone is consonant with the dignity and divinity of man. Though these are travelling on the true path I do not think they will attain their full stature until they comprehend the spiritual foundations on which other political theories rest, and can build on them as do the devotees of beauty or love or power.'

XV

'I can understand Lavelle, Leroy, or Culain stirred by the spirit, but the mass of men seem immovable as rock by that wind,' said Rian. 'I know when I see Lavelle walking down the street he may be treading heavenly pavements, and that Culain sees souls not bodies, but most men walk on concrete pavements and are themselves but animated matter. They nurse some dream of power for their party or profit for themselves, and these desires converge on the state, and so the world is made which we are trying to unmake. I can see when humanity is in a state of flux, as it now is, how men with imagination spiritually quickened could create new moulds into which the molten humanity may pour itself. But you suggest the spiritual powers at all times influence the world order, whereas I think those so influenced are few, and hardly in a thousand years is the multitude melted into a spiritual mood. If the divine nature is so interwoven with our humanity it conceals itself marvellously from our eyes.'

'Our philosophy supposes the universe to be a spiritual being,' answered Brehon, 'and if it be so the least creature which becomes in it cannot escape infection from that which is its own original. The most subtle analysis of consciousness brings us to the apostle who said "In Him we live and move and have our being." We find that miraculous or transcendental element involved in the swift creation which takes place in dream, in the instant and marvellous harmonizing of consciousness with the perpetually varying infinitude of nature, and minute analysis leads us step by step to the realization that the least motion of body or soul involves this transcendental element. Nor do we merely exist in this divine nature. It exists also in us, and I think men ever follow a spiritual light even when they seem to be most turned away from it. When we analyse their desires, even those which seem gross, we find what allures them is some beauty or majesty mirrored in this from a loftier nature. So the lustful man is tormented by an inversion of the holy spirit or creative fire. The drunkard thirsts for fulness of being as the god-intoxicated do. Vanity in us is an echo of the consciousness of beauty in the artificer of the cosmos, while hate is the dark descendant of that wisdom which is perpetually regenerating the universe. Even those lost and hopeless who pursue their desires to spiritual death are still seeking spiritual life. They follow a gleam mistakenly as we may imagine light-demented moths dashing themselves at a moon on water. As in their private lusts men still follow something in its essence universal, so too in their imaginations about society are they allured by images and shadows of their own hidden divinity.'

'They are all God-inspired then?' Rian interposed doubtfully. 'But how is it if all depend on the One we are here in conflict with each other?'

'I think it might be truer to say of men that they are God-animated rather than God-guided. Yet in a sense it would be true to say that of them also. It is not necessary to infer because there are contraries here there must be discord in the heavens. We do not assume Nature is at strife with itself when there is storm or earthquake, for we know the elements from atom to mass are subject to a law from which none can escape, for it inheres in the being of nature which maintains through its myriad transformations music and balance in itself. We can imagine our own antagonisms also harmonized in the being in which they exist and that too by a law from which there is no escape. The law at last makes us conscious of itself and we discover where it constrains us and where there is freedom. In this sense if we equate Deity with law we may be said to be God-guided. We are free of abyss or height, but if we descend to the depths the spiritual powers desert us, as in the Chaldaean myth of the descent of Ishtar the goddess at every gate was bereft of some symbol, and sceptre or diadem or robe or girdle or sandals were taken from her until at last she entered the Underworld naked and shorn of divinity. That was a myth of the soul. To us too as we rise from the depths the spiritual powers return as to Ishtar at the gate of every sphere was restored some of her regalia, until entering through the Everlasting gate she was once more crowned and Queen of Heaven. I do not think there can be finality for us in politic, even in theory, because man is a still evolving being not yet come to his fulness. A change of mood, and what he held to be precious yesterday is no longer so to him and, unregretful, he lets it slip behind time. Every high imagination of man is the opening for him of some door to the divine world and there, like Ishtar, he takes on some new attribute. He may have a vision of beauty or feel the majesty of law, or the love which links the Everliving together; and as he sees or feels he imagines a world

The Interpreters

order in harmony. As his aspiration is so is his inspiration. He becomes maker of beauty, revealer of law, avatar of power, dispenser of justice, or seer of the heart. Whatever he has apprehended of the divine nature he wishes that to prevail on earth.'

'We cannot live truly by mimicry of things either seen or conceived,' interposed Leroy. 'It is life itself we ought to exalt. All this would reduce us to some kind of logical existence in which the premiss was not within us but without. If we are to live truly it must be by inward impulse.'

'Why do we not walk out of this prison?' answered Brehon. 'Because there are walls all about us and a closed door. If there is immutable law the soul must take cognisance of it. Yet, if we consider truly, what is any vision of beauty but the lighting up in us of some lordlier chamber of the soul than it has hitherto inhabited? The apprehension of law is but the growth in ourselves of a profounder self-consciousness. The mighty is apprehended only by the mighty, and no dew of pity ever seemed to fall from the sky save on those who themselves were tender of heart. The universe perpetually echoes back to us our own attributes, and our furthest reaching out to understanding of the nature which envelops us is our deepest comprehension of our own being. The universe exists for the soul not the soul for the universe. We cannot imagine a transformation of the Absolute which could have meaning to itself,[29] but for the spark wandering in the immensity of that being we can imagine endless progress from atomic to infinite life. They are wise who study the architecture of the cosmos, for the heaven and the heaven of heavens were builded for us, and that majesty is but the mirror in which we become conscious of our own magnificence. I do not think as you do that recognition of the divine powers will take sceptre or crown from the spirit of man, for all meditation ends at last with the thinker, and he finds he is what he has himself conceived. The poet Blake said:

> It is impossible for thought,
> A greater than itself to know.

So too the Indian seers of old brought the soul by a thousand pathways to the divine world, but never allowed it to fall down or to worship divine being as beyond it, but whispered it in the ecstasy of contemplation "Thou art immortal. Thou art that." '[30]

'But where are you now leading us?' cried Rian. 'It is a long way from world polity to spiritual ultimates!'

'But that is where all these as they have revealed themselves are tending. All their politic is but a groping through the symbols of earth to the Kingdom of Heaven. They are all citizens of that Kingdom and they drink in imagination from the same fountain. Politic is a profane science only because it has not yet discovered it has its roots in sacred or spiritual things and must deal with them.'

'Shall we find this Kingdom on earth?' asked Rian, 'or must we adventure into another world? Must we take the Kingdom by violence? I can understand the logic of fighting on earth but if we are truly seeking for the Kingdom of Heaven can we gain it by conquest?'

XVI

'If we accept the idea of a divine humanity brought to harmony in some remote Golden Age, how can this better us to-day?' asked Lavelle. 'Must we not still fight for the good we are assured of? I believe the ideals for which men are not ready to die soon perish, for they have not drawn nourishment from what is immortal in them. If we do not throw life into the scale we are outweighed by those who are ready for this sacrifice. If we become philosophical onlookers our nation, its culture and ideals, perish, being undefended, and an unresisted materialism takes its place. The world becomes less lovely by what is actually beautiful fading out of human life, not dying nobly, as it might, overcome by a superior beauty. The incarnate love came not with peace but a sword. It does not speak only with the Holy Breath[31] but has in its armoury death and the strong weapons of the other immortals. We cannot put on the ideals of other peoples or future ages as a garment. It is better to remain unbroken to the last, and I count it as noble to fight God's battles as to keep His peace.'

'I do not advocate philosophical indifference, for I believe we can be fighters in the spirit and use immortal powers,' the old man answered the poet. 'In the divine economy nothing is lost, for the spiritual nature exerts always an influence equal to the intensity of its being. You desire things which can only be a possession of the spirit, but you yet act as if they were material possessions which might be lost or stolen. This may be because you have not yet come to understand the laws of that being in which all spiritual adventures take place. I do not think any one can lose what is his own save by descent from the sphere where the things loved have their natural life. I believe spiritual ideals, except for the few who can maintain them through all conflict, are lost if we defend them by material means. There are other ways by which right can find its appropriate might.'

'If we could be assured of that we would all be fighters in the spirit!' cried Lavelle. 'But when did our nation win anything save when it stood armed and ready for the last sacrifice?'

'You will find,' answered the historian, 'that every great conflict has been followed by an era of materialism in which the ideals for which the conflict obstensibly was waged were submerged. The gain if any was material. The loss was spiritual. That was so inevitably because warfare implies a descent of the soul to the plane where it is waged, and on that plane it cannot act in fulness, or bring with it love, pity, or forgiveness, or any of its diviner elements. There is another reason why spiritual ideals may not be preserved by warfare, and that is because it is its nature to evoke hatred. Love and hate have a magical transforming power. They are the great soul changers. We grow through their exercise into the likeness of what we contemplate.[32] By intensity of hatred nations create in themselves the character they imagine in their enemies. Hence it comes that all passionate conflicts result in an interchange of characteristics. We might say with truth those who hate open a door by which their enemies enter and make their own the secret places of the heart.'

'That is a terrible thought,' said Lavelle. 'But is it more than the expression of an ethical exaltation beyond human nature? Is there not such a thing as a righteous anger which is proper to us and not ignoble, nor implicating us in such a tragic fate?'

'Can there be a beneficent union of what is good and evil in a single mood?'

'If warfare indeed brings on us such a lamentable destiny, by what means may right find its appropriate might? You seemed to affirm that the spiritual powers by themselves win victories for us. How may we be made certain of this, for no one will lay aside a powerful weapon until he is assured he may exert another equal or a greater power?'

The historian made answer, 'I came myself to such a certitude through experience, being led to brood upon the nature of the soul, when I was nearing completion of the history of our nation. Though everything was done better than I had thought possible I felt desolate in spirit and there came even an aversion to my work. The light which had hitherto inspired me seemed now to lead in a contrary direction. For as one whose eyes from gazing on vivid orange turn and rest on a vacancy finds it pervaded by a mist of blue, so my mind began to create in its emptiness the contrary of all I had loved and the lure of national ideals began to be superseded by imaginations of a world state. Where I might have been led by this reaction I do not know but that I met and afterwards became one of a company of men existing in many lands who were unknown to the world and were bent on the conquest of that vast life which is normally subconscious to us, so that they might have more than speculative knowledge and be nearer to what they truly were.'

'Why was a quest so important pursued in secrecy?' asked Lavelle.

'It was necessary lest there might be diverted to outward argument and controversy the energies which were all needed for the ascent to spirit,[33] for this quest requires an heroic enthusiasm, a courage rising again and again from defeat with indestructible hope. There was also a wisdom in it, for the mood must be solemn when any would enter the cathedral of the universe. All enmities must be laid aside, as in the East the worshippers lay their sandals outside the mosque. A serenity of feeling in which all diversities are harmonized has to be attained, so that out of many a new being which can act with power might be created. In that psychic unity the faculties of each one in the group gradually became the possession of all, a possibility which Culain has already apprehended; and the will of many in unison was powerful enough to transcend the bodily life so that in meditation together consciousness rose like a tower into heaven, and we were able to bring back some knowledge of the higher law.'

'Was there not peril in this meditation that the most powerful character might impose his imagination upon the rest?' asked Leroy. 'An Indian faquir can impose his mental fantasy upon a crowd so that they will see him swallowing a poisonous snake which exists only in his imagination and their vision. And this would be easier with groups such as you describe stilled to one intent and porous to each other's emanations.'

'Of this, too, we were aware,' said Brehon. 'For we were guided by ancient wisdom, an experience garnered through generations. It is true that the purification of nature, obligatory if we were to succeed, makes the psyche sensitive and translucent so that the feelings and imaginations of others affect it swiftly, but the will at the same time is quickened to more intense activity and made positive, so that to perceive or receive the emanations of others is not to be overcome by them. It is because I was in so close a psychic unity with others, and that in a brotherhood which existed in many lands, that I was made certain feeling and imagination radiate their influence to the boundaries of the world soul as stars shed their light through space. These influences pour on us and through us and illuminate or darken our lives. I have come to believe even the solitary or captive can by intensity of imagination and feeling affect myriads so that he can act through many men and speak through many voices. The deeper the being the more powerful are its radiations.[34] So far as the intellectual transcends the physical so does the spiritual transcend the intellectual. The avatars of the spirit, the Christs and Buddhas, do more by single gentleness than conquerors with armies do, and build more enduring kingdoms in the spirit of man. The devotees of the spirit, though few, give light to many. With them the deed is done when the thought is born, for if it is of the spirit it has more than the swiftness of light, and a deeper penetrative power, and it illuminates many hearts which have as yet no light of their own. If a kingdom is won by force it must be sustained by force, and, as Leroy has said, there is no real freedom. But if there is reliance on spiritual law, if we seek to be truly ourselves, we draw others naturally to seek for a like fulness of their own being.'

'Our civilizations have not been built up by the spiritual imagination acting alone but by manifold labours of mind and body,' said Rian. 'I can imagine a house, but who could live in the house of my dream unless the builders remake it in the substance of this world? If poets or music makers never went beyond the ecstasy of conception or brought down from heaven what they had seen or heard would not our life be the poorer? Would we have any civilization at all?'

'We do not lessen the power of the outer man by increasing the power of the spiritual man, for the spirit cannot be quickened without the strength of imagination and intellect being also increased.[35] Nor can the life of man be spiritual only, for he must oscillate between Heaven and Earth until he has reached his own centre and the immortal stills all in its own being. Until we can act from our own centre our ascents to Heaven involve reactions to outward life, but the soul returns to Earth, wrapping its memories of Heaven about it like a cloth, and shining as Moses going down from the Holy Mount. Its deeds then are of a lordlier character and reflect the magnificence of its imaginations. As men come higher to the immortal their civilizations will transcend ours as the Parthenon transcended the huts of those who herded their flocks in a more ancient Attica.'

XVII

'All distinctions of nationality seem to dissipate in a haze in this transcendentalism,' Lavelle protested. 'I mistrust the philosophy which universalizes overmuch. I admit a being which is the fountain of all being, but what emerges from that fountain is diversity of beauty in nature and humanity. You spoke of ancient Attica. We find there as in Egypt, China, India, and other lands, a character in the culture which does not appear elsewhere, and this, I think, arose because the more sensitive minds in every country came into contact with archetypal images of a nature peculiar to these regions of the earth. If for every man on earth there is a divinity in the heavens who is his ancestral self, should there not also be a varied and diviner nature overshadowing this earth we know and influencing it as the soul the body? The ancients spoke of a many-coloured earth[36] above this and temples wherein the gods do truly dwell, and may not these be the archetypes of our civilizations and the spiritual basis of nationalities? I must believe there are differences above as below. When we come to our own immortal it cannot be that we cease to have individual character. We cannot in the perfection of the spirit be only perfect images of each other. I believe also in the heaven of which earth is a shadow there are the divine originals[37] of the lands we know. Is not this what was meant by the saying, "In our Father's House are many mansions?" As I listen to you these diversities of beauty and culture which have enriched the world, which have, as I think, their root in a deeper being and should be defended as part of the divine polity, all seem to face before some gigantic and undefined ideal. Must national distinctions be lost, and if so to what world order are we tending?'

'I think,' said the old man, 'we are evolving through all our activities, through politics as through the arts and sciences to realization of our full human stature, and in that realization nothing that is rightly related to our humanity can be lost, no spiritual influence from earth or sky. If those influences you speak of are Heaven born the more humanity is transparent to spirit the more will life be penetrated by them. An oracle of the Oversoul states the law "Seek first the kingdom of Heaven and everything else will be added to you." How by this quest may we attain so rich a being? Because as the psyche evolves, and we become ourselves more fully, we awaken and attract all the powers and elements which are akin to our expanding consciousness. As we absorb so we radiate influences equal to our intensity of life. We have not yet come to the limit of our faculties. There are uncharted regions of psychic nature to which the perfected faculties give us access and which we may aspire to rule. The ear has not attained that infinitude of hearing in which sounds not only human but celestial are apprehended. The heart has not attained its infinity of feeling, nor the intellect its full power of penetration, nor has the will yet found its conscious root in the power which sustains the cosmos. With those who recognize this incompleteness there can be neither certainty nor finality in the relation of existing human groups to each other. But to you who have gone beyond the bodily life and have apprehended a spiritual nature I would point out a more excellent way than conflict. There is a justice, a law, which operates beneath all physical appearances. It is this which has brought us together to-night. It was spiritual affinity[38] not the power of empire which constrained us, though the law may use material agencies to carry out its decrees. The forces which shut us in whether they know it or not are the servants of that law which shapes outward circumstance in harmony with inward nature. Because life is so moulded for all of us there is no way of bringing about the perfecting of human relations other than by the transfiguration of the individual. Everything we do unaccompanied by an evolution of our consciousness to a higher being is but futile readjustment of surfaces. However we toil, alter, or build we can give nothing more than is in ourselves, and at the close of our ceaseless multiplication the total remains the same. I rely absolutely on this justice in the universe. I will not protest against anything which happens to me because that would be to protest against my kingship over my own destiny. I am moved here and there by what I am. If there is pain to me in these happenings I shall try to discover where there was misdirection of will which brought it about. Those who begin to live consciously in the spirit must be guided by an ethic based on the nature of the ancestral self or heavenly man. In that being, as Culain has said, all human life is reflected, so that none can be our enemies, and we can overcome only by the fierce and tender breath of love, if love be the heavenly name of that which yearns in us to be intimate with the innermost of all life. Once that spiritual awakening has begun for any the old life should be over, and they should no longer be concerned in the politics of time, and should leave the life of conflict and passion and fit themselves for the politics of eternity. Men cling because of old habit to formulae they have really outgrown and which have lost their lure. Below the old ideals vaster desires spring up, to win mastery over the elements, to chase the divinities. For a time they try to achieve the new ends by the old methods. But it is in vain, for nothing can be won save by the full devotion of the heart. If we do not enlarge the political ideals with the expanding spiritual consciousness, if we shut any out of our heart by making emotional or intellectual boundaries to human brotherhood, if any race or class are excluded, we pervert the spiritual energies whose natural flow is from each to all; and these energies, diverted from their natural goal, turn backwards and downward, and poison the very deeps of life, and they there generate spiritual pestilences, hates, frenzies, madnesses, and the sinister ecstasy making for destruction which is the divine power turned to infernal uses. Through ignorance of spiritual law idealists who take to warfare are perpetually defeated, for they do not realize the dark shadow which follows all conflict and which must follow this present conflict by the perversion of spiritual forces. These perverted energies endanger human life, not merely because they lead men to conflict with each other, but because they bring about a warfare of nature on humanity. We have supposed of the Universe it is a spiritual being, and the elements have intellectual guidance. The possibility of direct control of these nature forces through a growing comprehension of their relation to our own intellectual being has been referred to here. These powers await our sovereignty. There are legions of allies for us in air, in earth, in sea, ready to do our bidding when we come to our full stature and can command them with wisdom and power. But it is an error, I think, to suppose of them that they are not moved by us now, for there is perpetual communication between the elements in our being and their counterparts in nature. If we poison or infect them by our frenzies and passions, the distraught powers bring about cataclysms, earthquakes, and subsidences, and the evil humanity is shaken off the back of nature. The old poet who said, "There is not a breathing of the common wind that will forget thee" was wiser than he knew. We ray our influence not only on each other but on Nature, which more slowly, but inevitably, operates her own justice. Who can say there was no conscious intent in Nature when Atlantis sunk under water; who can say our mad humanity is not making inevitable a similar doom for this continent? I say that for those whose spiritual nature has awakened the old life should be over and they should be the fighters in the spirit and use immortal powers. Nor need there be fear lest by this re-direction of energy strength should be lost to any cause which has a basis in the spirit. In the ascent to Heaven, as Socrates said, we create a multitude of high and noble thoughts, our own nature expanding until at last we attain a science which is equal to a beauty so vast. Our science tells us that the impact of a heavenly body on the sun makes it to glow with a fiercer heat. Even so when the soul ascends to the spiritual sun[39] a more blinding radiance is emitted from that being. It is the benediction on Earth for yielding to Heaven the things which are Heaven's, and this benediction falls on the path by which the soul had mounted upwards, and it illuminates and strengthens what it touches, the power as it flows outward following the chain of thought and mood by which the soul had ascended. Indeed the soul is perpetually receiving this benediction, for, as I said, every imagination of man is the opening or the closing of a door to the divine world, and in whatever way he truly approaches it it meets him. From that being in which he lives and moves a light enters through every transparency, however momentary, of his nature, and it extends itself through all that is akin to it. That which enters us is the sap of the eternal sacred tree whose roots are in the heavens and whose branches grow downward to earth. Whatever way we approach it it answers us. It entered into Lavelle as a boy upon his mountain, and was with Culain in his dark streets, and with Heyt in his state laboratories and thought of a demiurgic power, and with Leroy in his passion for freedom. It endows one with power and bestows abundantly of life on another, and to all who make sacrifice it responds by a law which is so wonderful that if it was understood it would be the delight of the heart. I do not think of it as law. I call it rather Own-Being. The yearning of our innermost life is for that sweet and stern and infallible justice, which brings us to Heaven or Hell as our desires rise or fall in the scale of being. We are the children of Deity, and with us consciousness extends from the dim flicker in heart or brain up to the Heaven of Heavens. We live in many worlds, but the links are lost between the divided portions of our manifold being so that we forget in waking what we were in dream, or what majesty was ours in the regions beyond dream. While we are on this earth matter conditions energy and dominates life. In the mid region which we also inhabit energy or desire is the master and mind and matter its slaves. But in that heaven world in which man attains his full stature the soul is master and whenever it imagines or wills the energies and elements act in obedience to it. Those who would mould life in accord with divine nature must remember until their faculties are perfected they look at it through the stained glass of the personal and be watchful lest they limit in imagination that which is boundless. They must equal themselves to its vastness, for does not the Scripture say, "Be ye perfect even as the Father in Heaven is also perfect."[40] Those who seek for beauty will never master its magic unless they also have power, and those who seek for power will find that the mighty surrenders itself fully only to that which is most gentle; and we shall be repulsed perpetually until we have made perfect in ourselves those elements out of which both we and the universe are fashioned and which, made pure, will relate us to the vaster life of the cosmos.[41] Therefore we ought to regard none who differ from us as enemies but to contemplate them rather with yearning as those who possess some power or vision from which we are shut out but which we ought to share. If we seek for the fulness of being there can be no decay of what is beautiful in the world, for what is right always exercises its appropriate might. If we do not realize this it is because we do not know the sum total of our character and what uncomprehended elements in ourselves and others defeat what is noblest. But if we seek for the highest in ourselves and have this reliance on the law to justify and sustain us we shall see the Kingdom. Yes, we shall rule in the Kingdom.'

'It seems easy,' said Rian, 'to reshape the world simply by going on thinking and imagining and leaving to others the execution of what we devise. I do this in my own art, but the philosophy seems to have a kind of incompleteness when applied to the shaping of human destiny.'

'It is not easy,' answered the old man. 'To cross that red midregion[42] between heaven and earth is to undertake labours greater and more painful than those fabled of Hercules. In that red midregion the martyrdom of the passionate soul, its crucifixion in the spirit, takes place, until all that is gross is etherealized and it yields itself finally in absolute resignation to the ancestral being. It is not easy to stay the will against the desire of the world or to draw ourselves from the attraction of that magnet, as Leroy knows. But if we persist a time comes when the spiritual outweighs the bodily with us, and it will be so with all men, and finally they will, at first with pain, but in the end with rejoicing, journey in multitude to the Land of Promise. They will do so because man is spiritual at the root and cannot escape from himself for ever and the promise of the spirit to the spark wandering in the immensity of its own being was "I will not leave thee nor forsake thee!" '

XVIII

Leroy, a very sincere, but rarely a solemn being for long, grew restless towards the close of Brehon's commentary on the symposium, and broke a rather strained silence with one of his whimsies.

'I once had a vision of a funeral service in the other world before I was born, where I was committed to the grave of this body, and the angelic being who presided murmured something about his hopes for a joyful resurrection of their brother who was now buried in matter. But I felt there was little real confidence in his voice, and when he departed I heard a dialogue between a sceptical spirit who said he did not believe any came back from Earth to Heaven. He had met none. The other spirit, more credulous, thought there was good evidence that certain beings had risen out of the grave of the body, but the sceptic said if they had they were merely cases of premature burial. I have felt while I listened to you all I was prematurely buried myself and was still under that ancient domination of Heaven from which I hoped I had escaped.'

'Oh, you need not be afraid,' cried Rian. 'Your egomania is so concentrated it will persist when all the rest of us have gone back into the primeval silences, and you will be a solitary of the universe wandering about in quest for something to revolt against.'

'Well!' said Leroy, 'let us discover who are truly human. What do you think of all this?' He turned to Rudd, and that prisoner, long baffled in his efforts to understand things remote from his mentality, and at last irritated, broke out with much profanity that he never heard so much folly. One world was enough for him; one small country all he could think about. The empire found half a world too big to govern. It could only hold together by exterminating any who did not submit to it. If he had to comprehend three worlds before he could act in this he would go mad. He hated being bullied in the name of a law he had no share in making. He hated being instructed how to live in the name of science which was unintelligible, and most of all he hated being told in the name of God how to think. And after this, and much else, he walked indignantly to the other end of the room.

'I have much sympathy with Rudd,' said Rian. 'He expresses emotions we have all shared, and which, I fancy, had as much to do with bringing us here as these fine imaginations of the Oversoul. I cannot think of him as influenced by beauty or any of the other divinities. I think he belongs to your household, Leroy.'

'I accept him.'

'How did you come to share in this, Mara?' Rian asked another prisoner.

'Oh, because I wanted to be with Lavelle and you,' was the answer.

'I am afraid that is the mob instinct. It is a sub-species of Culain's mood. You lose your identity in that of others. What drew you to fight, Owen?'

'I wanted excitement, I am afraid. I never felt really alive until I was body and soul in our conspiracy.'

'It was the same mood which drew Leroy out of Paradise millenniums ago. What was your inspiration, Gavin?'

'I think the thought of death for our country was sweet to me.'

'Ah, your emotions must seem lovely to you before you are stirred by them. You comrade dimly with Lavelle. And you, Morane?'

'I was in a rage with life I think.'

'That rage with you I know rose out of pity. You were born under the same star as Culain. And you, Brugha?'

'I heard rebellion talked since I was a child. It was so with my family for generations. They were in every insurrection. It is a tradition with us.'

'That is ancestor worship. I could not place you in any of our categories unless I knew the mood of the first ancestor. He may have been another Leroy. The others are asleep and I am not going to waken them for the purpose of this symposium. It comes to an end. I wonder if I had heard all this a year ago would it have made any difference. It can make little difference now.'

A silence came over the room. Rian, who sat on the floor, watched Lavelle, who was in one of the windows. He saw after a while the dark head begin to nod, the lips to move and murmur. Being himself tired he wondered at the inexhaustible energy of mind which could so pursue beauty, for he knew by the movement of head and lips the poet had returned to his art. Lavelle began writing on a scrap of paper in the dim light, and when he had finished Rian came and sat beside him.

'Your imagination is a river running forever,' he said. 'What is it you write? I hope it is not a swan-song.'

'I was completing the last poem in a Book of Voyages wherein I, like the poets of our country before me, tell of journeyings to the Land of Immortal Youth.'

'We may soon be travellers there ourselves if all that legend relates of the other worlds be true. I myself only wanted to make this world lovely. I never tried to scale the heavens to look on another beauty. But I would like to hear the adventures of your voyager.'

'It is a dream about one who died in an old insurrection of our people hundreds of years ago. I had thought it finished but I was moved by what was said here to-night to add some interpretation to the dream.'

Lavelle's lips moved soundlessly for a little as if he was trying to find if memory ran easily, and then, in a voice low at first but which soon became rich and vibrant, he chanted the story he had imagined of Michael, a voyager to the Heaven World. Leroy, Rian, and the old historian alone listened, for the others had composed themselves to sleep, which they did soon, being weary, and Culain sat with his head bowed on his arms on the table, and none knew whether he was in a sleep or was meditating.

XIX

MICHAEL

A wind blew by from icy hills,
Shook with cold breath the daffodils,
And shivered as with silver mist
The lake's pale leaden amethyst.
It pinched the barely budded trees
And rent the twilight tapestries:
Left for one hallowed instant bare
A single star in lonely air
O'er stony lanes the bitter wind
Had swept of all their human kind.

Ere that the fisher folk were all
Snug under thatch and sheltering wall,
Breathing the cabin's air of gold,
Safe from blue storm and nipping cold.
And, clustered round the hearth within,
With fiery hands and burnished chin,
They sat and listened to old tales,
Or legends of gigantic gales.
Some told of phantom craft they knew
That sailed with a flame-coloured crew,
And came up strangely through the wind
Havens invisible to find
By those rare cities poets sung,
Cresting the Islands of the Young.

How do the heights above our head,
The depths below the water spread,
Waken the spirit in such wise
That to the deep the deep replies,
And in far spaces of the soul
The oceans stir, the heavens roll?

Michael must leave the morrow morn
The countryside where he was born;

And all day long had Michael clung
Unto the kin he lived among.
But at some talk of sea and sky
He heard an older mother cry.
The cabin's golden air grew dim:
The cabin's walls drew down on him:
The cabin's rafters hid from sight
The cloudy roof-tree of the night.
And Michael could not leave behind
His kinsmen of the wave and wind
Without farewell. The way he took
Ran like a twisted, shining brook,
Speckled with stones and ruts and rills,
'Mid a low valley of dark hills,
And trees so tempest-bowed that they
Seemed to seek double root in clay.

At last the dropping valley turned:
A sky of murky citron burned.
Above through flying purples seen
Lay pools of heavenly blue and green.
From the sea rim unto the caves
Rolled on a mammoth herd of waves.
While all about the rocky bay
Leaped up grey forests of wild spray,
Glooming above the ledges brown
Ere their pale drift came drenching down.

Things delicate and dewy clung
To Michael's cheeks. The salt air stung.
From crag to crag did Michael leap
Until he overhung the deep;
Saw in vast caves the waters roam,
The ceaseless ecstasy of foam,
Whirlpools of opal, lace of light
Strewn over quivering malachite,
Ice-tinted mounds of water rise
Glinting as with a million eyes,
Reel in and out of light and shade,
Show depths of ivory or jade,
New broidery every instant wear,
Spun by the magic weaver, Air.

Then Michael's gaze was turned from these
Unto the far, rejoicing seas,
Whose twilight legions onward rolled,
A turbulence of dusky gold,
A dim magnificence of froth,
A thunder tone which was not wrath,

The Interpreters

But such a speech as earth might cry
Unto far kinsmen in the sky.
The spray was tossed aloft in air:
A bird was flying here and there.
Foam, bird, and twilight to the boy
Seemed to be but a single joy.
He closed his eyes that he might be
Alone with all that ecstasy.

What was it unto Michael gave
This joy, the life of earth and wave?
Or did his candle shine so bright
But by its own and natural light?
Ah, who can answer for what powers
Are with us in the secret hours!
Though wind and wave cried out no less,
Entranced unto forgetfulness,
He heard no more the water's din;
A golden ocean rocked within.
A boat of bronze and crystal wrought
And steered by the enchanter, Thought,
Was flying with him fast and far
To isles that glimmered, each a star
Hung low upon the distant rim,
And then the vision rushed on him.

The palaces of light were there,
With towers that faded up in air,
With amethyst and silver spires.
And casements lit with precious fires,
And mythic forms with wings outspread,
And faces from which light was shed.
High upon gleaming pillars set,
On turret and on parapet,
The bells were chiming all around
And the sweet air was drunk with sound.

Too swift did Michael pass to see
Ildathach's mystic chivalry
Graved on the walls, its queens and kings
Girt round with eyes and stars and wings.
The magic boat with Michael drew
To some deep being that he knew,
Some mystery that to the wise
Is clouded o'er by Paradise.
Some will that would not let him stay
Hurried the boat away, away.
At last its fiery wings were still,
Folded beneath some heavenly hill.

But was that Michael light as air
Was travelling up the mighty stair?
Or had impetuous desire
Woven for him that form of fire,
Which with no less a light did shine
Than those with countenance divine,
Who thronged the gateway as he came,
Faces of rapture and of flame,
The glowing, deep, unwavering eyes
Of those eternity makes wise.
And lofty things to him were said
As to one risen from the dead.
What there beyond the gate befell
Michael could never after tell.

Imagination still would fail
Some height too infinite to scale,
Some being too profound to scan,
Some time too limitless to span.
Yet when he lifted up his eyes
That foam was grey against the skies,
That same wild bird was on the wing,
That twilight wave was glimmering.
And twilight wave and foam and bird
Had hardly in his vision stirred
Since he had closed his eyes to be
Of that majestic company.

And can a second then suffice
To hurry us to Paradise?
What seemed so endlessly sublime
Shrink to a particle of time?
Why was the call on Michael made?
What charge was on his spirit laid?
And could the way for him be sure
Made by excess of light obscure?
However fiery is the dream,
How faint in life the echoing gleam!
And faint was all that happed that day
As home he went his dreamy way.

And now has Michael, for his share
Of life, the city's dingy air,
By the black reek of chimneys smudged
O'er the dark warehouse where he drudged,
Where for dull life men pay in toll
Toil and the shining of the soul.

The Interpreters

Within his attic he would fret
Like a wild creature in a net,
And on the darkness he would make
The jewel of a little lake,
A bloom of fairy blue amid
The bronze and purple heather hid;
Make battlemented cliffs grow red
Where the last rose of day was shed,
Be later in rich darkness seen
Against a sky of glowing green.
Or he would climb where quiet fills
With dream the shepherd on the hills,
Where he could see as from high land
The golden sickle of the sand
Curving around the bay to where
The granite cliffs were worn by air,
And watch the wind and waves at play,
The heavenly gleam of falling spray,
The sunlit surges foam below
In wrinklings as of liquid snow.
And he could breathe the airs that blew
From worlds invisible he knew:
How far away now from the boy!
How unassailable their joy!

'Oh, Lavelle! Lavelle!' cried Rian, 'I know those hills and little lakes. Shall we ever see them again?'

So Michael would recall each place
As lovers a remembered face.
But, though the tender may not tire,
Memory is but a fading fire.
And Michael's might have sunken low,
Changed to grey ash its coloured glow,
Did not upon his hearing fall
The mountain speech of Donegal,
And that he swiftly turned to greet
The tongue whose accent was so sweet;
And found one of that eager kind,
The army of the Gaelic mind,
Still holding through the Iron Age
The spiritual heritage,
The history from the gods that ran
Through many a cycle down to man
And soon with them had Michael read
The story of the famous dead,

From him who with his single sword
Stayed a great army at the ford,
Down to the vagrant poets, those
Who gave their hearts to the Dark Rose;
And of the wanderers who set sail
And found a lordlier Innisfail,
And saw a sun that never set
And all their hearts' desires were met.

How may the past, if it be dead,
Its light within the living shed?
Or does the Ever-living hold
Earth's memories from the Age of Gold?
And are our dreams, ardours, and fires
But ancient unfulfilled desires?
And do they shine within our clay,
And do they urge us on their way?
As Michael read the Gaelic scroll
It seemed the story of the soul;
And those who wrought, lest there should fail
From earth the legend of the Gael,
Seemed warriors of Eternal Mind,
Still holding in a world grown blind,
From which belief and hope had gone,
The lovely magic of its dawn.

Thrice on the wheel of time recurred
The season of the risen Lord
Since Michael left his home behind
And faced the chilly Easter wind,
And saw the twilight waters gleam
And dreamed an unremembered dream.
Was it because the Easter time
With mystic nature was in chime
That memory was roused from sleep,
Or was deep calling unto deep?
The Lord in man had risen here,
From the dark sepulchre of fear,
Was wilful, laughing, undismayed,
Though on a fragile barricade
The bullet rang, the death star broke,
The street waved dizzily in smoke,
And there the fierce and lovely breath
Of flame in the grey mist was death.
Yet Michael felt within him rise
The rapture that is sacrifice.
What miracle was wrought on him,
So that each leaden-freighted limb
Seemed lit with fire, seemed light as air?

How came upon him dying there,
Amid the city's burning piles,
The vision of the mystic isles?
For underneath and through the smoke
A glint of golden waters broke:
And floated on that phantom tide,
With fiery wings expanded wide,
A bark of bronze and crystal wrought
And steered by the enchanter, Thought.
And noble faces glowed above,
Faces of ecstasy and love,
And eyes whose shining calm and pure
Was in eternity secure,
And lofty forms of burnished air
Stood on the deck by Michael there.
And spirit upon spirit gazed,
And one to Michael's lips upraised
A cup filled from that Holy Well
On which the Nuts of Wisdom fell.[43]
And as he drank there reeled away
Vision of earth and night and day,
And he was far away from these,
Afloat upon the heavenly seas.

'Here the voyage as I had written it ended,' said the poet. 'But I have added what follows in interpretation, for indeed I was moved by what was said in this room.'

'Are you at this hour forgetting your own ideals?' asked Rian.

'You shall judge,' answered Lavelle, continuing his narrative.

I do not know if such a band
Came from the Many-Coloured Land:
Or whether in our being we
Make such a magic phantasy
Of images which draw us hence
Unto our own magnificence.
Yet many a one a tryst has kept
With the immortal while he slept,
Woke unremembering, went his way.
Life seemed the same from day to day,
Till the predestined hour came,
A hidden will leaped up in flame,
And through its deed the risen soul
Strode on self-conquering to the goal.

This was the dream of one who died
For country, said his countryside.
We choose this cause or that, but still

The Everlasting works its will.
The slayer and the slain may be
Knit in a secret harmony.
What does the spirit urge us to?
Some sacrifice that may undo
The bonds that hold us to the clay,
And limit life to this cold day?
Some for a gentle dream will die:
Some for an empire's majesty:
Some for a loftier humankind,
Some to be free as cloud or wind,
Will leave their valley, climb their slope.
Whate'er the deed, whate'er the hope,
Through all the varied battle cries
A Shepherd with a single voice
Still draws us nigh the Gates of Gold
That lead unto the heavenly fold.
So it may be that Michael died
For some far other countryside
Than that grey island he had known.
Yet on his dream of it was thrown
Some light from that consuming Fire
Which is the end of all desire.
If men adore It as the power,
Empires and cities, tower on tower,
Are built in worship by the way,
High Babylon or Nineveh.
Seek It as love and there may be
A Golden Age and Arcady.[44]
All shadows are they of one thing
To which all life is journeying.

When he had made an end Rian said, 'Where, I wonder, in this universe of many dimensions shall we really go after death? Is there one heavenly house for us all, or will we live in ourselves as so many suppose, our genius playing a fantasy on our memories and desires? I remember one mystic telling me that we all had a genie like Aladdin, and it would build marvellous palaces for us and exalt our dreams into unimaginable light. Such solitary magnificence would please Leroy more than me. I am a sociable person, but I am now too drowsy for more speculation.' Leroy, as tireless in mind as Lavelle, would have made a commentary on all that had been said, but he saw Lavelle was sinking into reverie and was not inclined for further speech, so he made a pretence of imitating Rian who was trying to sleep in a chair. But no sleep during the night came to that restless soul.

XX

From the recess of the window Lavelle gazed into the night enveloping the monstrous fabric of the city. In an abeyance of will brought about by weariness he became oppressed by the melancholy which so often arises through contemplation of an external vastness in which humanity becomes dwarfed, and what seemed lofty in the heart shrivels to littleness by the measurement of the eye. Beyond the murky city shining seas were rolling by shadowy mountains, and over them heavens which lost themselves in their own depths, rumouring their own infinitudes, fainting and faltering in their speech, for light, though it be swiftest of all things, ere it has found a final resting-place or hamlet in the gloom, the worlds it spake of have long ceased to be. The stare of the night seemed pitiless and immutable, and he did not then remember that those heavens had always echoed his mood and were gay or solemn as he was exultant or mournful, reflecting as a glass from hour to hour the transformations in his own spirit. The poetic nature has all childhood's excess of emotion, and in an anguish such as the heart of childhood might hold he thought of the Golden Age passed away from the world and the terrrible and material powers ruling in the Iron Age. Through a night of time endless to his imagination he foresaw the martyrdom of those who like himself had nourished longing for the light and an earth made gay by a laughter which was worse than sobbing. Out of this meditation arose an immense pity for life; and because the sadness was spiritual and was not for himself, was indeed self-forgetful, it was marvellously rolled away and a deep serenity took its place. He felt the universe was sweet at heart, and that same majesty which had played with him as a boy among the hills was with him and he knew it would be with him to the end, and by it all dreams would be fulfilled. He murmured to himself the words of promise 'Long lost hearts burn in the oil of the lamp of the King.' Like a spell the utterance quickened a memory which had kept his life austere for many years, and a young beauty which had been made dust glowed before him as if it had never perished. She seemed to live in a luminous and blessed air, and was running to him along hills strangely like the hills his boyhood knew, and face and eyes were more ecstatic than life. 'Oh, Magic! Magic!' he whispered, calling her by the sweet name his fancy had bestowed on so vivid and lovely a girlhood. Then form and face faded, swallowed up in the Ever-living out of which they came, and her last look seemed to echo back the promise of the words, 'Long lost hearts burn in the oil of the lamp of the King.' And then his yearning brought him nigh to the fountain in which that and all other beauty had been born; and he knew that all that was cast up by it was lovely, and if rust or decay came over the spirit they were burned away as it fell back into the fountain where it received once more the primal blessings of youth, ecstasy, and beauty. In that hour innumerable images of life, hopes, and dreams hitherto uncomprehended, causes to which he had closed his heart, men from whom he had been remote in soul, all came nigh him with some revelation of their inmost being in which they reflected the ancient beauty. In each was some ray of Eternal Mind. The Eternal Mind going forth knew itself in them, and they returning knew themselves in it. The All-seeing and All-knowing had not withheld life from any, and while they were sustained by It and It had not condemned them, it was not for man to take life away. He remembered the words of the old man, 'We should cast none out of the heart.' And brooding on himself he saw how he had closed the doors to many by devotion to one form of beauty only, and he realized that what was cast out of the heart must force entry by pain, for life would be denied entry to none of its realms. All this was revealed to him when thought had ceased, and he was carried beyond himself, and his spirit seemed to be bathed by some shoreless ocean of sweet unterminable being. Never was he so remote from the vision of life, and never more intimate with being. Everything was understood. Everything was loved. Everything was forgiven. He knew after that exaltation he could never be the same again. Never could he be fierce or passionate. And his wisdom must be to retain this serenity, and he forbore to think of the conflict that had brought him there, and he stilled every earthly memory lest he might be cast out from the spirit. Through the night he sat with closed eyes made radiant within and sustained by that profundity of being men worship as the Father. At last his eyes opened. A dawn was beginning to lighten in the East. Gold began to mix with the blue, and the armada which had been floating invisibly in the high air was fired by light from a sun not yet over the horizon. He saw the old historian seated beside him. His eyes were fixed on Lavelle, and he whispered to the poet, 'You have come nigh to the Kingdom. You have seen the Kingdom.' Because of that recognition Lavelle felt the old man more the intimate of his spirit than even that beauty he had so long remembered and loved, but which had never shared with him the revelation of the Eternal.

As the dawn kindled, the tumult in the city, which had been stilled for a while, broke out again furiously. There were shouts and concussions and reverberations. The prisoners in the great room woke from uneasy slumbers. The conflict came closer to the great building in which they were confined and the rattle was deafening. Leroy, alert as ever, was first to understand what was taking place. 'Our comrades are winning in the city,' he cried. 'They are encircling the arsenal.'

He had hardly spoken when the door opened and an officer appeared, who said, 'We may have to evacuate this building and fight our way through the city. We cannot take prisoners with us. I have to tell you if we evacuate we shall blow up the arsenal.' The prisoners were silent for a moment, but Leroy, always generous, said, 'This prisoner,' pointing to Heyt, 'is not of us. He is here by error. He is for empire and is not worthy to die with us.' He told the officer who Heyt was, and the officer, startled by his name, sent for another who recognized the president of the Air Federation. Lavelle would have intervened on behalf of the old historian. But Brehon placed his hand gently on the arm of the poet and he knew it was forbidden. The Imperialist, moved by what he had heard and understanding these men were different from all he had imagined of them, hesitated for a moment as if he would have said or urged something. Then he shook his head as if he realized how impossible it now was to effect anything, and he left them without a word and went out to make the world in his own image.

AT THE DAWN OF THE KALIYUGA[1]

Where we sat on the hillside together that evening the winds were low and the air was misty with light. The huge sunbrowned slope on which we were sitting was sprinkled over with rare spokes of grass; it ran down into the vagueness underneath where dimly the village could be seen veiled by its tresses of lazy smoke. Beyond was a bluer shade and a deeper depth, out of which, mountain beyond mountain, the sacred heights of Himalay rose up through star-sprinkled zones of silver and sapphire air. How gay were our hearts! the silent joy of the earth quickened their beating. What fairy fancies alternating with sweetest laughter came from childish lips! in us the Golden Age whispered her last, and departed. Up came the white moon, her rays of dusty pearl slanting across the darkness from the old mountain to our feet. 'A bridge!' we all cried, 'Primaveeta, who long to be a sky-walker, here is a bridge for you!'

Primaveeta only smiled; he was always silent; he looked along the gay leagues of pulsating light that lead out to the radiant mystery. We went on laughing and talking; then Primaveeta broke his silence.

'Vyassa,' he said, 'I went out in thought, I went into the light, but it was not that light. I felt like a fay; I sparkled with azure and lilac; I went on, and my heart beat with longing for I knew not what, and out and outward I sped till desire stayed and I paused, and the light looked into me full of meaning. I felt like a spark, and the dancing of the sea of joy bore me up, up, up!'

'Primaveeta, who can understand you?' said his little sister Vina, 'you always talk of the things no one can see; Vyassa, sing for us.'

'Yes! yes! let Vyassa sing!' they all cried; and they shouted and shouted until I began:

NOTE: Kaliyuga. The fourth, the *black* or iron age, our present period, the duration of which is 432,000 years. It began 3,102 years B.C. at the moment of Krishna's death, and the first cycle of 5,000 years will end between the years 1897 and 1898.

At the Dawn of the Kaliyuga

'Shadowy petalled, like the lotus, loom the mountains with their snows:
Through the sapphire Soma rising, such a flood of glory throws
As when first in yellow splendour Brahma from the lotus rose.

'High above the darkening mounds where fade the fairy lights of day,
All the tiny planet folk are waving us from far away;
Thrilled by Brahma's breath they sparkle with the magic of the gay.

'Brahma, all alone in gladness, dreams the joys that throng in space,
Shepherds all the whirling splendours onward to their resting place,
Where at last in wondrous silence fade in One the starry race.'

'Vyassa is just like Primaveeta, he is full of dreams to-night,' said Vina. And indeed I was full of dreams; my laughter had all died away; a vague and indescribable unrest came over me; the universal air around seemed thrilled by the stirring of unknown powers. We sat silent awhile; then Primaveeta cried out: 'Oh, look, look, look, the Devas! the bright persons! they fill the air with their shining.'

We saw them pass by and we were saddened, for they were full of solemn majesty; overhead a chant came from celestial singers full of the agony of farewell and departure, and we knew from their song that the gods were about to leave the earth which would nevermore or for ages witness their coming. The earth and the air around it seemed to tingle with anguish. Shuddering we drew closer together on the hillside while the brightness of the Devas passed onward and away; and clear cold and bright as ever, the eternal constellations, which change or weep not, shone out, and we were alone with our sorrow. Too awed we were to speak, but we clung closer together and felt a comfort in each other; and so, crouched in silence; within me I heard as from far away a note of deeper anguish, like a horn blown out of the heart of the ancient Mother over a perished hero: in a dread moment I saw the death and the torment; he was her soul-point, the light she wished to shine among men. What would follow in the dark ages to come, rose up before me in shadowy, over-crowding pictures; like the surf of a giant ocean they fluctuated against the heavens, crested with dim, giantesque and warring figures. I saw stony warriors rushing on to battle; I heard their fierce hard laughter as they rode over the trampled foe; I saw smoke arise from a horrible burning, and thicker and blacker grew the vistas, with here and there a glow from some hero-heart that kept the true light shining within. I turned to Primaveeta who was crouched beside me: he saw with me vision for vision, but, beyond the thick black ages that shut me out from hope, he saw the resurrection of the True, and the homecoming of the gods. All this he told me later, but now our tears were shed together. Then Primaveeta rose up and said,

'Vyassa, where the lights were shining, where they fought for the True, there you and I must fight; for, from them spreads out the light of a new day that shall dawn behind the darkness.' I saw that he was no longer a dreamer; his face was firm with a great resolve. I could not understand him, but I determined to follow him, to fight for the things he fought for, to work with him, to live with him, to die with him; and so, thinking and trying to understand, my thoughts drifted back to that sadness of the mother which I had first felt. I saw how we share joy or grief with her, and, seized with the inspiration of her sorrow, I sang about her loved one:

> 'Does the earth grow grey with grief
>   For her hero darling fled?
> Though her vales let fall no leaf,
>   In our hearts her tears are shed.
>
> 'Still the stars laugh on above,
>   Not to them her grief is said;
> Mourning for her hero love
>   In our hearts her tears are shed.
>
> 'We her children mourn for him,
>   Mourn the elder hero dead;
> In the twilight grey and dim,
>   In our hearts the tears are shed.'

'Vyassa,' they said, 'you will break our hearts.' And we sat in silence and sorrow more complete till we heard weary voices calling up to us from the darkness below: 'Primaveeta! Vyassa! Chandra! Parvati! Vina! Vasudeva!' calling all our names. We went down to our homes in the valley; the breadth of glory had passed away from the world, and our hearts were full of the big grief that children hold.

Æ.

'GO OUT IN THOUGHT'[1]

Said a writer of the last century, 'If Christ be then mediator betwixt God and man, how shall ever man assume the Christ-like virtue, seeing that such function must always be too high for him? And if I say that mediation between man and man is of the same nature, I know not if I shall be understood.' Perhaps the mystic whom we have quoted is, in that sentence as in others, more fully understood to-day than in his own time.

In his instruction to those who desired to follow the path of life Buddha enjoined a special form of meditation. He said: 'With thine heart full of compassion go out in thought towards the east and the north and the west and the south; with love and pity go out towards all that lives.' Was that instruction merely aimed at promoting the spiritual growth of the man who thus meditated in solitude? The mystic has an ill-based philosophy if he thinks so, for none of us can grow in any other way than by taking up the work of mediation to which our first quotation refers. Let us look into it and see what we have to do. Let us see the worst of a situation before we try to mend it; and a full view will include the causes that led to it, as well as any factors now tending to maintain or alter it. When the survey is finished we shall know how to proceed.

We have been born into a civilization than which humanity can never have seen a worse, taking it all in all. The evil picture omits not a single discouraging element. To escape its horrors an increasing number year by year commit suicide; an increasing number become insane; year by year the average length of life decreases.

It is a civilization based wholly on selfishness. Growing up through the centuries, it is, in its political, social, and economic forms, the crystallized outer expression of an inner principle, *Every man for himself.* It is a universal fight for possessions, represented by money, and the weakest come off worst. Everything that we eat, wear, or use, has involved at least the underpayment, usually the sweating, of someone whose life is a long and despairing struggle for the pence that constitute his wage. The employer gets what he can from the overworking and underpayment of his employee, who in his turn must buy his necessaries at the lowest possible rate. These necessaries are produced under scarcely human conditions by the very lowest in the social scale, who, requiring to make every farthing do its utmost, *must* sweat others as they are sweated themselves. The whole picture is of a hideous conflict of man with man; part voluntary, mostly necessitated by the iron conditions of the age. And from it all comes up from a million lips the cry of pain that has long ceased to be a prayer. For the prayer awakened no response, brought no relief, and life remains unlit even by hope. And all the while the great nations half hang back and half press forwards, amassing mighty armaments, awaiting the inevitable crash.

So the prospect is the worst, the most painful, apparently the most hopeless that humanity has yet looked upon. Many rush in with their hearts on fire, proposing this and the other remedy. But they forget that whatever their remedy, and whatever its temporary success, it is temporary only. The cause of all the misery, *Every man for himself, every nation against the world,* remains untouched. Since selfishness as the one basis of action has at last created a hell through the centuries, outer alterations in the structure hardly mean even a momentary alleviation of the suffering, only a little shifting in the play of the scorching flames. Were the whole structure destroyed and all its elements flung into the melting-pot, it could but reëmerge. The same cause could but produce the same result.

Over this bleak and frozen scene the warm winds that herald the spring have begun to blow, and the icy hand of winter loosens its grasp. Of late years much has been said and thought of brotherhood, and in many countries. The same impulse has touched thousands of hearts, so that in full consciousness they have turned to each other and made little groups known by many names, but all pledged to the service of the moving power within them. And day by day the ripple widens out over hearts and minds so that men begin to say: Surely a new day has dawned. They talk much of brotherhood, some holding it but as a palliative to the evils; some as the very way of Nature herself as she weaves together the unit threads into a pattern, makes a multiple life from many single lives, who thereafter enter upon and share a new level of being and consciousness; some as the divine breath of the Oversoul, seeking to make of all humanity a sounding-board for its everlasting harmonies. The lonely feel no longer quite so lonely, they know not why; the fierce battle between man and man is not quite so fierce; the tension relaxes a little; small kindlinesses multiply; men grieve more for the sorrows of the others, they lead lives a little less centred; the veils between heart and heart thin away.

The winter-frozen earth remains long locked in ice, though the warm winds of the spring play above it, but its winter days have in truth departed. So among men the old forms and institutions stand and will stand for long yet, but the awful life has gone out of them. They will pass away slowly, and in their midst and out of their ruins will arise the temples of the new order. And all forms and institutions that shall come hereafter shall be the crystallization and outcome of the spirit of brotherhood, which they shall realize and conserve.

Do we come at last to an understanding of that mediation between man and man whereof our quotation spoke; between man and man, and between class and class? If a man speak his trouble to another, is it not lessened; and apart from words of reply, apart even from bodily presence, is it not continually lessened, because shared, by every sympathetic *thought* of that other? So the teaching of Buddha stands to-day, and with every thought we can lift a little of the burdens of those whom these eyes may never see, but whose pain the heart has felt.

THE HERO IN MAN[1]

I

There sometimes comes on us a mood of strange reverence for people and things which in less contemplative hours we hold to be unworthy; and in such moments we may set side by side the head of Christ and the head of an outcast, and there is an equal radiance around each, which makes of the darker face a shadow and is itself a shadow around the head of light. We feel a fundamental unity of purpose in their presence here, and would as willingly pay homage to the one who has fallen as to him who has become a master of life. I know that immemorial order decrees that the laurel and the crown be given only to the victor, but in those moments I speak of a profound intuition changes the decree and sets the aureole on both alike.

We feel such deep pity for the fallen that there must needs be a justice in it, for these diviner feelings are wise in themselves and do not vaguely arise. They are lights from the Father.[2] A justice lies in uttermost pity and forgiveness, even when we seem to ourselves to be most deeply wronged; or why is it that the awakening of resentment or hate brings such swift contrition?

We are ever self-condemned; and the dark thought which went forth in us brooding revenge, when suddenly smitten by the light, withdraws and hides within itself in awful penitence. In asking myself why it is that the meanest are safe from our condemnation when we sit on the true seat of judgment in the heart, it seemed to me that their shield was the sense we have of a nobility hidden in them under the cover of ignoble things; that their present darkness was the result of some too weighty heroic labour undertaken long ago by the human spirit; that it was the consecration of past purpose which played with such a tender light about their ruined lives, and it was more pathetic because this nobleness was all unknown to the fallen and the heroic cause of so much paon was forgotten in life's prison-house.

While feeling the service to us of the great ethical ideals which have been formulated by men, I think that the idea of justice intellectually conceived tends to beget a certain hardness of the heart. It is true that men have done wrong – hence their pain: but back of all this there is something infinitely soothing, a light which does not wound, which says no harsh thing, even although the darkest of spirits turns to it in its agony, for the darkest of human spirit has still around him this first glory which shines from a deeper being within, whose history may be told as the legend of the Hero in Man.

Among the many immortals with whom ancient myth peopled the spiritual sphere of humanity are some figures which draw to themselves a more profound tenderness than the rest. Not Aphrodite rising in beauty from the faery foam of the first seas, not Apollo with sweetest singing, laughter, and youth, not the wielder of the lightning, could exact the reverence accorded to the lonely Titan chained on the mountain, or to that bowed figure heavy with the burden of the sins of the world; for the brighter divinities had no part in the labour of man, no such intimate relation with the wherefore of his own existence so full of struggle. The more radiant figures are prophecies to him of his destiny, but the Titan and the Christ are a revelation of his more immediate state; their giant sorrows companion his own, and in contemplating them he awakens what is noblest in his own nature; or, in other words, in understanding their divine heroism he understands himself. For this in truth it seems to me to mean: all knowledge is a revelation of the self to the self, and our deepest comprehension of the seemingly apart divine is also our furthest inroad to self-knowledge; Prometheus, Christ, are in every heart; the story of one is the story of all; the Titan and the Crucified are humanity.

If, then, we consider them as representing the human spirit and disentangle from the myths their meaning, we shall find that whatever reverence is due to that heroic love which descended from heaven for the redeeming of a lower nature, must be paid to every human being. Christ is incarnate in all humanity. Prometheus is bound for ever within us. They are the same. They are a host, and the divine incarnation was not spoken of one, but of all those who descending into the lower world tried to change it into the divine image and to wrest out of chaos a kingdom for the empire of light. The angels saw below them in chaos a senseless rout blind with elemental passion for ever warring with discordant cries which broke in upon the world of divine beauty; and that the pain might depart, they grew rebellious in the Master's peace, and descending to earth the angelic lights were crucified in men; leaving so radiant worlds, such a light of beauty, for earth's grey twilight filled with tears, that through this elemental life might breathe the starry music brought from Him. If the 'Foreseer' be a true name for the Titan, it follows that in the host which he represents was a light which well foreknew all the dark paths of its journey; foreseeing the bitter struggle with a hostile nature, but foreseeing perhaps a gain, a distant glory o'er the hills of sorrow, and that chaos, divine and transformed, with only gentle breathing, lit up by the Christ-soul of the universe.[3] There is a transforming power in the thought itself: we can no longer condemn the fallen, they who laid aside their thrones of ancient power, their spirit ecstasy and beauty, on such a mission. Perhaps those who sank lowest did so to raise a greater burden, and of these most fallen it may in the hour of their resurrection be said, 'The last shall be first.'

So, placing side by side the head of the outcast with the head of Christ, it has this equal beauty – with as bright a glory it sped from the Father in ages past on its redeeming labour. Of his present darkness what shall we say? 'He is altogether dead'? Nay, rather with tenderness forbear, and think that the foreseeing spirit has taken its own dread path to mastery; that that which foresaw the sorrow foresaw also beyond it a greater joy and a mightier existence, when it would rise again in a new robe, woven out of the treasure hidden in the deep of its submergence, and shine at last like the stars of the morning triumphant among the Sons of God.

II

Our deepest life is when we are alone. We think most truly, love best, when isolated from the outer world in that mystic abyss we call soul. Nothing external can equal the fulness of these moments. We may sit in the blue twilight with a friend, or bend together by the hearth, half whispering, or in a silence populous with loving thoughts mutually understood; then we may feel happy and at peace, but it is only because we are lulled by a semblance to deeper intimacies. When we think of a friend, and the loved one draws nigh, we sometimes feel half-pained, for we touched something in our solitude which the living presence shut out; we seem more apart, and would fain wave them away and cry, 'Call me not forth from this; I am no more a spirit if I leave my throne.' But these moods, though lit up by intuitions of the true, are too partial, they belong too much to the twilight of the heart, they have too dreamy a temper to serve us well in life. We should wish rather for our thoughts a directness such as belongs to the messengers of the gods, swift, beautiful, flashing presences bent on purposes well understood.

What we need is that interior tenderness shall be elevated into seership, that what in most is only yearning or blind love shall see clearly its way and hope. To this end we have to observe more intently the nature of the interior life. We find, indeed, that it is not a solitude at all, but dense with multitudinous being: instead of being alone we are in the thronged highways of existence. For our guidance when entering here many words of warning have been uttered, laws have been outlined, and beings full of wonder, terror, and beauty described. Yet there is a spirit in us deeper than our intellectual being which I think of as the Hero in man, who feels the nobility of its place in the midst of all this, and who would fain equal the greatness of perception with deeds as great. The weariness and sense of futility which often falls upon the mystic after much thought is due to this, that he has not recognized that he must be worker as well as seer, that here he has duties demanding a more sustained endurance just as the inner life is so much vaster and more intense than the life he has left behind.

Now the duties which can be taken up by the soul are exactly those which it feels most inadequate to perform when acting as an embodied being. What shall be done to quiet the heart-cry of the world: how answer the dumb appeal for help we so often divine below eyes that laugh? It is the saddest of all sorrows to think that pity with no hands to heal, that love without a voice to speak, should helplessly heap their pain upon pain while earth shall endure. But there is a truth about sorrow which I think may make it seem not so hopeless. There are fewer barriers than we think: there is, in truth, an inner alliance between the soul who would fain give and the soul who is in need.[4] Nature has well provided that not one golden ray of all our thoughts is sped ineffective through the dark; not one drop of the magical elixirs love distils is wasted. Let us consider how this may be. There is a habit we nearly all have indulged in. We weave little stories in our minds, expending love and pity upon the imaginary beings we have created, and I have been led to think that many of these are not imaginary, that somewhere in the world beings are living just in that way, and we merely reform and live over again in our life the story of another life. Sometimes these faraway intimates assume so vivid a shape, they come so near with their appeal for sympathy that the pictures are unforgettable; and the more I ponder over them the more it seems to me that they often convey the actual need of some soul whose cry for comfort has gone out into the vast, perhaps to meet with an answer, perhaps to hear only silence. I will supply an instance. I see a child, a curious, delicate little thing, seated on the doorstep of a house. It is an alley in some great city, and there is a gloom of evening and vapour over the sky. I see the child is bending over the path; he is picking cinders and arranging them, and as I ponder, I become aware that he is laying down in gritty lines the walls of a house, the mansion of his dream. Here spread along the pavement are large rooms, these for his friends, and a tiny room in the centre, that is his own. So his thought plays. Just then I catch a glimpse of the corduroy trousers of a passing workman, and a heavy boot crushes through the cinders. I feel the pain in the child's heart as he shrinks back, his little lovelit house of dreams all rudely shattered. Ah, poor child, building the City Beautiful out of a few cinders, yet nigher, truer in intent than many a stately, gold-rich palace reared by princes, thou wert not forgotten by that mighty spirit who lives through the falling of empires, whose home has been in many a ruined heart. Surely it was to bring comfort to hearts like thine that that most noble of all meditations was ordained by the Buddha.[5] *'He lets his mind pervade one quarter of the world with thoughts of Love, and so the second, and so the third, and so the fourth. And thus the whole wide world, above, below, around, and everywhere, does he continue to pervade with heart of Love far-reaching, grown great and beyond measure.'*

That love, though the very fairy breath of life, should by itself and so imparted have a sustaining power some may question, not those who have felt the sunlight fall from distant friends who think of them; but, to make clearer how it seems to me to act, I say that love, Eros, is a being. It is more than a power of the soul, though it is that also; it has universal life of its own, and just as the dark heaving waters do not know what jewel lights they reflect with blinding radiance, so the soul, partially absorbing and feeling the ray of Eros within it, does not know that often a part of its nature nearer to the sun of love shines with a brilliant light to other eyes than its own. Many people move unconscious of their own charm, unknowing of the beauty and power they seem to others to impart. It is some past attainment of the soul, a jewel won in some old battle which it may have forgotten, but none the less this gleams on its tiara and the star-flame inspires others to hope and victory.

If it is true here that many exert a spiritual influence they are unconscious of, it is still truer of the spheres within. Once the soul has attained to any possession like love, or persistent will, or faith, or a power of thought, it comes into spiritual contact with others who are struggling for these very powers. The attainment of any of these means that the soul is able to absorb and radiate some of the diviner elements of being. The soul may or may not be aware of the position it is placed in or its new duties, but yet that Living Light, having found a way into the being of any one person, does not rest there, but sends its rays and extends its influence on and on to illumine the darkness of another nature. So it comes that there are ties which bind us to people other than those whom we meet in our everyday life. I think they are most real ties, most important to understand, for if we let our lamp go out, some far away who had reached out in the dark and felt a steady will, a persistent hope, a compassionate love, may reach out once again in an hour of need, and finding no support may give way and fold the hands in despair. Often we allow gloom to overcome us and so hinder the bright rays in their passage; but would we do it so often if we thought that perhaps a sadness which besets us, we do not know why, was caused by someone drawing nigh to us for comfort, whom our lethargy might make feel still more his helplessness, while our courage, our faith, might cause 'our light to shine in some other heart which as yet has no light of its own'?

III

The night was wet; and, as I was moving down the streets, my mind was also journeying on a way of its own, and the things which were bodily present before me were no less with me in my unseen travelling. Every now and then a transfer would take place, and some of the moving shadows in the street would begin walking about in the clear interior light. The children of the city, crouched in the doorways, or racing through the hurrying multitude and flashing lights, began their elfin play again in my heart; and that was because I had heard these tiny outcasts shouting with glee. I wondered if the glitter and shadow of such sordid things were thronged with magnificence and mystery for those who were unaware of a greater light and deeper shade which made up the romance and fascination of my own life. In imagination I narrowed myself to their ignorance, littleness and youth, and seemed for a moment to flit amid great uncomprehended beings and a dim wonderful city of palaces.

Then another transfer took place and I was pondering anew, for a face I had seen flickering through the warm wet mist haunted me; it entered into the realm of the interpreter, and I was made aware by the pale cheeks, and by the close-shut lips of pain, and by some inward knowledge, that there the Tree of Life[6] was beginning to grow, and I wondered why it is that it always springs up through a heart in ashes: I wondered also if that which springs up, which in itself is an immortal joy, has knowledge that its shoots are piercing through such anguish; or again, if it was the piercing of the shoots which caused the pain, and if every throb of the beautiful flame darting upward to blossom meant the perishing of some more earthly growth which had kept the heart in shadow.

Seeing too how many thoughts spring up from such a simple thing, I questioned whether that which started the impulse had any share in the outcome, and if these musings of mine in any way affected their subject. I then began thinking about those secret ties on which I have speculated before, and in the darkness my heart grew suddenly warm and glowing, for I had chanced upon one of those shining imaginations which are the wealth of those who travel upon the hidden ways. In describing that which comes to us all at once, there is a difficulty in choosing between what is first and what is last to say: but, interpreting as best I can, I seemed to behold the onward movement of a Light, one among many Lights,[7] all living throbbing, now dim with perturbations, and now again clear, and all subtly woven together, outwardly in some more shadowy shining, and inwardly in a greater fire, which, though it was invisible, I knew to be the Lamp of the World. This Light which I beheld I felt to be a human soul, and these perturbations which dimmed it were its struggles and passionate longing for something, and that was for a more brilliant shining of the light within itself. It was in love with its own beauty, enraptured by its own lucidity; and I saw that as these things were more beloved they grew paler, for this light is the love which the Mighty Mother[8] has in her heart for her children, and she means that it shall go through each one unto all, and whoever restrains it in himself is himself shut out; not that the great heart has ceased in its love for that soul, but that the soul has shut itself off from influx, for every imagination of man is the opening or the closing of a door to the divine world: now he is solitary, cut off, and, seemingly to himself, on the desert and distant verge of things: and then his thought throws open the swift portals; he hears the chant of the seraphs in his heart, and he is made luminous by the lighting of a sudden aureole. This soul which I watched seemed to have learned at last the secret love: for, in the anguish begotten by its loss, it followed the departing glory in penitence to the inmost shrine where it ceased altogether; and because it seemed utterly lost and hopeless of attainment and capriciously denied to the seeker, a profound pity arose in the soul for those who, like it were seeking, but still in hope, for they had not come to the vain end of their endeavours. I understood that such pity is the last of the precious essences which make up the elixir of immortality, and when it is poured into the cup it is ready for drinking. And so it was with this soul which grew brilliant with the passage of the eternal light through its new purity of self-oblivion and joyful in the comprehension of the mystery of the secret love, which, though it has been declared many times by the greatest of teachers among men, is yet never known truly unless the Mighty Mother has herself breathed it in the heart.

And now that the soul had divined this secret, the shadowy shining which was woven in bonds of union between it and its fellow-lights grew clearer; and a multitude of these strands were, so it seemed, strengthened and placed in its keeping: along these it was to send the message of the wisdom and the love which were the secret sweetness of its own being. Then a spiritual tragedy began, infinitely more pathetic than the old desolation, because it was brought about by the very nobility of the spirit. This soul, shedding its love like rays of glory, seemed itself the centre of a ring of wounding spears: it sent forth love and the arrowy response came hate-impelled: it whispered peace and was answered by the clash of rebellion: and to all this for defence it could only bare more openly its heart that a profounder love from the Mother Nature might pass through upon the rest. I knew this was what a teacher, who wrote long ago, meant when he said: 'Put on the whole armour of God,' which is love and endurance, for the truly divine children of the Flame are not armed otherwise: and of those protests, sent up in ignorance or rebellion against the whisper of the wisdom, I saw that some melted in the fierce and tender heat of the heart, and there came in their stead a golden response which made closer the ties, and drew these souls upward to an understanding and to share in the overshadowing nature. And this is part of the plan of the Great Alchemist whereby the red ruby of the heart is transmuted into the tenderer light of the opal; for the beholding of love made bare acts like the flame of the furnace: and the dissolving passions, through an anguish of remorse, the lightnings of pain, and through an adoring pity, are changed into the image they contemplate, and melt in the ecstasy of self-forgetful love, the spirit which lit the thorn-crowned brows, which perceived only in its last agony the retribution due to its tormentors, and cried out, 'Father, forgive them, for they know not what they do.'[9]

Now although the love of the few may alleviate the hurt due to the ignorance of the mass, it is not in the power of anyone to withstand forever this warfare; for by the perpetual wounding of the inner nature it is so wearied that the spirit must withdraw from a tabernacle grown too frail to support the increase of light within and the jarring of the demoniac nature without; and at length comes the call which means, for a while, release, and a deep rest in regions beyond the paradise of lesser souls. So, withdrawn into the Divine Darkness, vanished the Light of my dream. And now it seemed as if this wonderful weft of souls intertwining as one being must come to naught; and all those who through the gloom had nourished a longing for the light would stretch out hands in vain for guidance: but that I did not understand the love of the Mother, and that although few, there is no decaying of her heroic brood; for, as the seer of old caught at the mantle of him who went up in the fiery chariot, so another took up the burden and gathered the shining strands together: and to this sequence of spiritual guides there is no ending.[10]

Here I may say that the love of the Mother, which, acting through the burnished will of the hero, is wrought to highest uses, is in reality everywhere, and pervades with profoundest tenderness the homeliest circumstance of daily life; and there is not lacking, even among the humblest, an understanding of the spiritual tragedy which follows upon every effort of the divine nature bowing itself down in pity to our shadowy sphere; an understanding in which the nature of the love is gauged through the extent of the sacrifice and the pain which is overcome. I recall the instance of an old Irish peasant, who, as he lay in hospital wakeful from a grinding pain in his leg, forgot himself in making drawings, rude yet reverently done, of incidents in the life of the Galilean teacher. One of these which he showed me was a crucifixion, where, amidst much grotesque symbolism, were some tracings which indicated a purely beautiful intuition; the heart of this crucified figure, no less than the brow, was wreathed about with thorns and radiant with light: 'For that,' said he, 'was where he really suffered.' When I think of this old man, bringing forgetfulness of his own bodily pain through contemplation of the spiritual suffering of his Master, my memory of him shines with something of the transcendent light he himself perceived; for I feel that some suffering of his own, nobly undergone, had given him understanding, and he had laid his heart in love against the Heart of Many Sorrows, seeing it wounded by unnumbered spears yet burning with undying love.

Though much may be learned by observance of the superficial life and actions of a spiritual teacher, it is only in the deeper life of meditation and imagination that it can be truly realized; for the soul is a midnight blossom which opens its leaves in dream, and its perfect bloom is unfolded only where another sun shines in another heaven: there it feels what celestial dews descend on it, and what influences draw it up to its divine archetype:[11] here in the shadow of earth root intercoils with root and the finer distinctions of the blossom are not perceived. If we knew also who they really are, who sometimes in silence, and sometimes with the eyes of the world at gaze, take upon them the mantle of teacher,[12] an unutterable awe would prevail: for underneath a bodily presence not in any sense beautiful may burn the glory of some ancient divinity, some hero who has laid aside his sceptre in the enchanted land to rescue old-time comrades fallen into oblivion: or again, if we had the insight of the simple old peasant into the nature of this enduring love, out of the exquisite and poignant emotions kindled would arise the flame of a passionate love which would endure long aeons of anguish that it might shield, though but for a little, the kingly hearts who may not shield themselves.

But I too, who write, have launched the rebellious spear, or in lethargy have ofttimes gone down the great drift numbering myself among those who not being with must needs be against: therefore I make no appeal; they only may call who stand upon the lofty mountains; but I reveal the thought which arose like a star in my soul with such bright and pathetic meaning, leaving it to you who read to approve and apply it.

IV. THE GAELIC AWAKENING

THE LEGENDS OF ANCIENT EIRE[1]

A reverend and learned professor in Trinity College, Dublin, a cynic and a humorist, is reported once to have wondered 'why the old Irish, having a good religion of their own, did not stick to it?' Living in the 'Celtic twilight,' and striving to pierce backward into the dawn, reading romance, tradition and history, I have endeavoured to solve something of the mystery of the vast 'Celtic phantasmagoria,' I can but echo the professor. In these legends, prodigal of enchantment, where Gods, heroes and bright supernatural beings mingle, are at league or war together, I have found not misty but clear traces of that old wisdom-religion once universal. There are indeed no ancient Irish Scriptures I am aware of, but they were not needed. To those who read in the Book of Life, philosophy and scripture are but as blinds over the spiritual vision. But we to-day – lost children of the stars – but painfully and indirectly catch glimpses of the bright spheres once our habitations, where we freely came and went. So I will try to tell over again some of these old stories in the light of philosopy spoken later. What was this old wisdom-religion? It was the belief that life is one; that nature is not dead but living; the surface but a veil tremulous with light – lifting that veil hero and sage of old time went outwards into the vast and looked on the original. All that they beheld they once were, and it was again their heritage, for in essence they were one with it – children of Deity. The One gave birth to the many, imagining within itself the heaven of heavens, and the heavens, and spheres more shadowy and dim, growing distant from the light. Through these the Rays ran outward, falling down through many a starry dynasty to dwell in clay. Yet – once God or Angel – that past remains, and the Ray, returning on itself, may reässume its old vesture, entering as a God into the Ancestral Self.[2] Every real scripture and every ancient myth, to be understood truly, must be understood in this light. God, the angelic hierarchies, the powers divine and infernal, are but names for the mightier Adam[3] in whose image man was made and who is the forgotten Self in humanity.

Mystic symbolism is the same the world over, and applying it to the old Celtic romances, phantasy and faeryland are transformed into history and we are reading about the ancient Irish Adepts.

Ireland was known long ago as the Sacred Island. The Gods lived there; for the Tuatha De Dannans who settled in Eire after conquering the gigantic races of Firbolgs and Fomorians (Atlanteans) were called Gods, differing in this respect from the Gods of ancient Greece and India, that they were *men who had made themselves Gods* by magical or Druidical power. They were preëminently magi become immortal by strength of will and knowledge. Superhuman in power and beauty, they raised themselves above nature; they played with the elements; they moved with ease in the air. We read of one Angus Oge, the master magician of all, sailing invisibly 'on the wings of the cool east wind'; the palace of that Angus remains to this day at New Grange, wrought over with symbols of the Astral Fire and the great Serpentine Power. The De Dannans lived in the heart of mountains (crypts for initiation), and to-day the peasant sometimes sees the enchanted glow from the green hills he believes they still inhabit. Perhaps he believes not foolishly, for, once truly occult, a place is preserved from pollution until the cycle returns, bringing back with it the ancient Gods again.

The cycle of the Gods is followed in Irish tradition by the cycle of the heroes. The Gods still mingled with them and presumably taught them, for many of these heroes are Druids. Finn, the hero of a hundred legends, Cuchullin, Diarmud, Oisin and others are wielders of magical powers. One of the most beautiful of these stories tells of Oisin in Tir-na-noge. Oisin with his companions journeys along the water's edge. He is singled out by Niam, daughter of Mannanan, king of Tir-na-noge, the land of the Gods. She comes on a white horse across the seas, and mounting with her Oisin travels across the ocean; after warring with a giant Fomor he passes into Tir-na-noge, where for a hundred years he lives with Niam and has all that heart could wish for. But desire for Eire arises within him and returning, he falls off the magic steed, and becomes an old man weary with years. It is purely occult. Oisin, Niam, her white steed, Tir-na-noge, the waters they pass over, are but names which define a little our forgotten being. Within Oisin, the magician, kindles the Ray, the hidden Beauty. Let us call it by what name we will, so that we spare the terms of academic mysticism or psychology. It is the Golden Bird of the Upanishads; the Light that lighteth every man; it is that which the old Hermetists knew as the Fair or the Beautiful – for Niam means beauty; it is the Presence, and when it is upon a man every other tie breaks; he goes alone with It, he is a dying regret, an ever-increasing joy. And so with Oisin, whose weeping companions behold him no more. He mounts the white horse with Niam. It is the same as the white horse of the Apocalypse, whereon one sits called Faithful and True. It is the power on which the Spirit rides. Who is there, thinking, has felt freed for a moment from his prison-house, and looking forth has been blinded by the foam of great seas, or has felt his imagination grow kingly in contemplation – he has known its impelling power; the white horse is impatient of restraint.

As they pass over the waters 'they saw many wonderful things on their journey – islands and cities, lime-white mansions, bright greenans and lofty palaces.' It is the mirror of heaven and earth, the astral light, in whose glass a myriad illusions arise and fleet before the mystic adventurers. Haunt of a false beauty – or rather a veil hung dazzling before the true beauty, only the odour or incense of her breath is blown through these alluring forms. The transition from this to a subtler sphere is indicated. A hornless deer, chased by a white hound with red ears, and a maiden tossing a golden lure, vanishes for ever before a phantom lover. The poet whose imagination has renewed for us the legend has caught the true significance of these hurrying forms:

'The immortal desire of immortals we saw in their eyes and sighed.'

'Do not heed these forms!' cries Niam. Compare with this from another source: 'Flee from the Hall of Learning, it is dangerous in its perfidious beauty. . . . Beware, lest dazzled by illusive radiance thy Soul should linger and be caught in its deceptive light. . . . It shines from the jewel of the Great Ensnarer.'[4] There are centres in man corresponding to these appearances. They give vision and entrance into a red and dreadful world, where unappeasable desire smites the soul – a dangerous clairvoyance. But in the sphere beyond their power has to be conquered, and here Oisin wars with the giant Fomor. De Dannan and Fomorian passed from Eire wrestle still in the invisible world, say the legends. We, too – would-be mystics – are met on the threshold of diviner spheres by terrible forms embodying the sins of a living past when we misused our spiritual powers in old Atlantean days. These forms must be conquered and so Oisin battles with the Fomor and releases the power – a princess in the story. This fight with the demon must be fought by everyone who would enter the land of the Gods, whether in conscious occult adventure or half-consciously after death, when the strange alchemist Nature separates the subtile from the gross in the soul in this region which Oisin passes through. Tir-na-noge, the land of Niam, is that region the soul lives in when its grosser energies and desires have been subdued, dominated and brought under the control of light; where the Ray of Beauty kindles and illuminates every form which the imagination conceives, and where every form tends to its archetype. It is a real region which has been approached and described by the poets and sages who, at all times, have endeavoured to express something of the higher realities. It is not distant, but exists in earth as the soul within the body, and may be perceived through and along with the surface forms. In a sense it corresponds with the Tibetan Devachan,[5] and in this region Oisin lives for a hundred years, until desire to see Eire once more arises and he parts from Niam. For the details of his return, the drowsy land in which he slumbers; how he fell off the white horse and became an old man with the weariness of his hundreds of years upon him – I must refer the reader to the legends. He will read not alone of Oisin, but of many an old hero, who, hailed by the faery (divine) voice, went away to live in the heart of green hills (to be initiated) or to these strange worlds.

Dear children of Eire, not alone to the past but to to-day belong such destinies. For if we will we can enter the enchanted land. The Golden Age is all about us, and heroic forms and imperishable love. In that mystic light rolled round our hills and valleys hang deeds and memories which yet live and inspire. The Gods have not deserted us. Hearing our call they will return. A new cycle is dawning and the sweetness of the morning twilight is in the air. We can breathe it if we will but awaken from our slumber.

II

In the recently published *Story of Early Gaelic Literature,* attention is directed to the curious eastern and pantheistic character of some archaic verses. Critics are for ever trying to show how some one particular antique race was the first begetter of religion and mystic symbolism. Perplexed by the identity between the myths and traditions of different countries, they look, now here, now there, for the original. But it was not in any land but out of the Christ-Soul of the universe that true wisdom at all times was begotten. Some ignorant peasant, some Jacob Boehme,[6] is pure and aspires, and lo! the God stirs within him and he knows the things that were taught in elder days and by unknown people. Our own land, long ago, had its Initiates in whom the eye of the seer was open. This eye[7] concealed in the hollow of the brain, is the straight gate and the narrow way through which alone the mortal may pass and behold the immortal.

The Legends of Ancient Eire

It is now closed in most men. Materialism, sensuality and dogmatic belief have so taken the crown and sceptre from their souls that they enter the golden world no more knowingly – they are outcast of Eden. But the Tuatha De Dannans were more than seers or visionaries. They were magicians – God and man in one. Not alone their thought went out into the vast, but the Power went along with it. This mystic Power is called the Serpentine Fire.[8] It is spiritual, electric, creative. It develops spirally in the ascetic, mounting from centre to centre, from the navel to the heart;* from thence it rises to the head. He is then no more a man but a God; his vision embraces infinitude.

The action of this Power was symbolized in many ways, notably by the passage of the sun through the zodiacal signs† (centres in the psychic body). A stone serpent was found a little while ago in Ireland marked with twelve divisions. The archaic verses alluded to have the same meaning:

'I am the point of the lance of battle. [The spinal cord, the
  Sushumna nadi of Indian psychology.]
I am the God who creates in the head of man the fire of the thought.
Who is it throws light into the meeting on the mountain? [The meeting
  of the mortal and the immortal on Mount Meru, the pineal gland.]
Who announces the ages of the moon? [The activity of the inner
  astral man.]
Who teaches, the place where couches the sun?' [Spirit.]

The Serpentine Power is the couch of the sun, the casket of spirit. Hence the Druids or Magi who had mastered this power were called Serpents. Though St. Patrick is said to have driven the serpents out of Ireland, traces still remain of the serpent wisdom. Lest the interpretation given above should seem arbitrary I will trace further explicit references to the third eye. Diarmuid, the hero and darling of so many story-tellers, whose flight with Grania forms one of the most mystic episodes in Celtic romance, is described as having a spot in the centre of his forehead which fascinated whoever gazed. He is called the 'Son of the Monarch of Light.' He is the Initiate, the twice-born. This divine parentage has the sense in which the words were spoken, 'Marvel not that I said unto thee, ye must be born again.' In the same sense a Druid is described as 'full of his God.' From the mystic Father descends the Ray, the Child of Light. It is born in man as mind, not reasoning, earthly nor sensual, but as the heaven-aspiring, thinking mind. In itself it is of the nature of fire.

* 'He that believeth on me, out of his belly shall flow rivers of *living waters. This spake he of the Spirit.*' – *John*, vii, 38.
† 'The twelve signs of the zodiac are hidden in his body.' – *Secret Doctrine*, II. 619.

The man who knows it becomes filled with light, aye, he moves about in light within himself.

The following description of a giant, taken from the story of Diarmuid, refers to still another aspect of our occult nature.

'He has but *one eye only* in the fair middle of his black forehead. . . . He is, moreover, so skilled in magic that fire could not burn him, water could not drown him, and weapons could not wound him. . . . He is fated not to die until there be struck upon him three blows of the iron club he has. He sleeps in the top of that Quicken tree by night, and he remains at its foot by day to watch it. . . . The berries of the tree have the virtues of the trees of faeryland.'

The Quicken tree is the network of nerves in the magnetic astral body. Readers of the Upanishads will remember the description of the arteries, thin as a hair split a thousand times, which proceed from the heart, and in which the Ego rests during deep sleep. It has just the same significance in the legend. The meaning will be still better understood by a comparison of the youthful Finn in his encounter with a similar one-eyed Titan. There is a most interesting version of this in Curtin's *Irish Myths and Folk-Tales*. Too long to quote in its entirety, the story runs as follows. Finn meets a giant who carries a salmon in his hand. This Titan has 'but one eye as large as the sun in the heavens.' He gives the fish to Finn to cook. The moment the giant closed his eye he began to breathe heavily. 'Every time he drew breath he dragged Finn, the spit, the salmon, and all the goats to his mouth, and every time he drove a breath out of himself he threw them back to the places they were in before.' While Finn is cooking the salmon he burns it, and in trying to hide the blister he burns his thumb. To ease the pain he put his thumb between his teeth, and chewed it through to the bone and marrow. He then received the knowledge of all things. He was drawn up the next minute to the giant's eye, and plunged the hot spit (a bar of red-hot iron, says another account) into the eye of the giant. He passes the infuriate giant at the door of the cave something after the fashion of Ulysses, by driving the flocks out and himself escaping under the fleece of the largest goat or ram.

The meaning of this story, with all its quaint imagery, is not difficult. It is an allegory describing the loss of the third eye. The cave is the body. The fish is a phallic symbol, and the cooking of it refers to the fall of the early ethereal races into generation and eventually into gross sensuality. The synthetic action of the highest spiritual faculty, in which all the powers of man are present, is shown by the manner in which everything in the cave is dragged up to the giant's head. When Finn destroys the eye by plunging into it a bar of red-hot iron, it simply means that the currents started in the generative organs rose up through the spinal cord to the brain, and, acting upon the pineal gland, atrophied or petrified it. The principle of desire[9] is literally the spirit of the metal iron, and a clairvoyant could see these red fires mounting up by the way of the spinal canal to the brain and there smothering any higher feelings. The escape of Finn under the fleece of the ram means that, having destroyed the spiritual eye, he could only use the organ of psychic clairvoyance, which is symbolized here, as in the mysticism of other countries, by the ram.

This symbolism, so grotesque and unmeaning to-day, was once perfectly lucid and was justified in its application. A clairvoyant could see in the *aura* of man around every centre the glow, colour and form which gave rise to the antique symbol. One of the Gods is described as 'surrounded by a rainbow and fiery dews.' Cuchullin, whose hair, dark (blue?) close to the skin, red beyond, and ending in brilliant gold, makes Professor Rhys elaborate him into a solar myth, is an adept who has assimilated the substance of the three worlds, the physical, the psychic and the heavenworld; therefore his hair (aura) shows the three colours. He has the sevenfold vision also, indicated by the seven pupils in his eyes. Volumes of unutterably dreary research, full of a false learning, have been written about these legends. Some try to show that much of the imagery arose from observation of the heavenly bodies and the procession of the seasons. But who of the old bards would have described nature other than as she is? The morning notes of Celtic song breathe the freshness of spring and are full of joy in nature. They could communicate this much better than most of their critics could do. It is only the world within which could not be rendered otherwise than by myth and symbol. We do not need scholarship so much as a little imagination to interpret them. We shall understand the divine initiators of our race by believing in our own divinity. As we nourish the mystic fire, we shall find many things of the early world, which now seem grotesque and unlovely to our eyes, growing full of shadowy and magnificent suggestion. Things that were distant and strange, things abhorrent, the blazing dragons, winged serpents and oceans of fire which affrighted us, are seen as the portals through which the imagination enters a more beautiful, radiant world. The powers we dared not raise our eyes to – heroes, dread deities and awful kings – grow as brothers and gay children around the spirit in its resurrection and ascension. For there is no pathway in the universe which does not pass through man, and no life which is not brother to our life.

Æ

THE MOUNTAINS[1]

While we live within four walls we half insensibly lose something of our naturalness and comport ourselves as creatures of the civilization we belong to. But we never really feel at home there, though childhood may have wreathed round with tender memories old rooms and the quaint garden-places of happy unthinking hours. There is a house, a temple not built with hands; perhaps we thought it a mere cabin when we first formed it, and laid aside humbly many of our royal possessions as we entered, for the heavens and the heaven of heavens could not contain all of our glory. But now it seems vast enough, and we feel more at home there, and we find places which seem nearer of access to our first life. Such are the mountains. As I lie here on the monstrous mould of the hillside covered with such delicate fringes of tiny green leaves, I understand something of his longing who said: 'I lift up mine eyes to the hills, from whence cometh my aid.' Oh, but the air is sweet, is sweet. Earth-breath, what is it you whisper? As I listen, listen, I know it is no whisper but a chant from profoundest deeps, a voice hailing its great companions in the æther spaces, but whose innumerable tones in their infinite modulations speak clear to us also in our littleness. Our lips are stilled with awe; we dare not repeat what here we think. These mountains are sacred in our Celtic traditions. Haunt of the mysteries, here the Tuatha de Danaans once had their home. We sigh, thinking of the vanished glory, but look with hope for the fulfilment of the prophecy which the seer of another line left on record, that once more the Druid fires should blaze on these mountains. As the purple amplitude of night enfolds them, already the dark mounds seem to throw up their sheeny illuminations; great shadowy forms, the shepherds of our race, to throng and gather; the many-coloured winds to roll their aerial tides hither and thither. Eri, hearth and home of so many mystic races, Isle of Destiny, there shall yet return to thee the spiritual magic that thrilled thee long ago. As we descend and go back to a life, not the life we would will, not the life we will have, we think with sorrow of the pain, the passion, the partings, through which our race will once more return to nature, spirit and freedom.

> We turned back mad from the mystic mountains
>   All foamed with red and with faery gold;
> Up from the heart of the twilight's fountains
>   The fires enchanted were starward rolled.
>
> We turned back mad—we thought of the morrow,
>   The iron clang of the far-away town:
> We could not weep in our bitter sorrow
>   But joy as an arctic sun went down.

Æ.

ON AN IRISH HILL[1]

It has been my dream for many years that I might at some time dwell in a cabin on the hillside in this dear and living land of ours, and there I would lay my head in the lap of a serene nature, and be on friendly terms with the winds and mountains who hold enough of unexplored mystery and infinitude to engage me at present. I would not dwell too far from men, for above an enchanted valley, only a morning's walk from the city, is the mountain of my dream. Here, between heaven and earth and my brothers, there might come on me some foretaste of the destiny which the great powers are shaping for us in this isle, the mingling of God and nature and man in a being, one, yet infinite in number. Old tradition has it that there was in our mysterious past such a union, a sympathy between man and the elements so complete, that at every great deed of hero or king the three swelling waves of Fohla responded: the wave of Toth, the wave of Rury, and the long, slow, white, foaming wave of Cleena. O mysterious kinsmen, would that to-day some deed great enough could call forth the thunder of your response once again! But perhaps he is now rocked in his cradle who will hereafter rock you into joyous foam.

The mountain which I praise has not hitherto been considered one of the sacred places in Eire, no glittering tradition hangs about it as a lure; and indeed I would not have it considered as one in any special sense apart from its companions, but I take it here as a type of what any high place in nature may become for us if well loved; a haunt of deep peace, a spot where the Mother lays aside veil after veil, until at last the great Spirit seems in brooding gentleness to be in the boundless fields alone. I am not inspired by that brotherhood which does not overflow with love into the being of the elements, not hail in them the same spirit as that which calls us with so many pathetic and loving voices from the lives of men. So I build my dream cabin in hope of this wider intimacy:

On An Irish HIll

> A cabin on the mountain side hid in a grassy nook,
> Where door and windows open wide, where friendly stars
>   may look;
> The rabbit shy can patter in; the winds may enter free
> Who throng around the mountain throne in living ecstasy.
> And when the sun sets dimmed in eve and purple fills the air,
> I think the sacred Hazel Tree is dropping berries there
> From starry fruitage waved aloft where Connla's well o'er-
>   flows:
> For sure the immortal waters pour through every wind that
>   blows.
> I think when night towers up aloft and shakes the trembling dew,
> That every high and lonely thought that thrills my being
>   through
> Is but a shining berry dropped down through the purple air,
> And from the magic tree of life the fruit falls everywhere.[2]

The Sacred Hazel was the Celtic branch of the tree of life; its scarlet nuts gave wisdom and inspiration; and fed on this ethereal fruit, the ancient Gael grew to greatness. Though to-day none eat of the fruit or drink the purple flood welling from Connla's fountain,[3] I think that the fire which still kindles the Celtic races was flashed into their blood in that magical time, and is our heritage from the Druidic past. It is still here, the magic and mystery; it lingers in the heart of a people to whom their neighbours of another world are frequent visitors in the spirit and over-shadowers of reverie and imagination.

The earth here remembers her past, and to bring about its renewal she whispers with honeyed entreaty and lures with bewitching glamour. At this mountain I speak of it was that our greatest poet, the last and most beautiful voice of Eiré, first found freedom in song, so he tells me: and it was the pleading for a return to herself that this mysterious nature first fluted through his lips:

> Come away, O human child,
> To the woods and waters wild
> With a faery hand in hand:
> For the world's more full of weeping than you can understand.[4]

Away! yes, yes; to wander on and on under star-rich skies, ever getting deeper into the net, the love that will not let us rest, the peace above the desire of love. The village lights in heaven and earth, each with their own peculiar hint of home, draw us hither and thither, where it matters not, so the voice calls and the heart-light burns. Some it leads to the crowded ways; some it draws apart: and the Light knows, and not any other, the need and the way.

If you ask me what has the mountain to do with these inspirations, and whether the singer would not anywhere out of his own soul have made an equal song, I answer to the latter, I think not. In these lofty places the barriers between the sphere of light and the sphere of darkness are fragile, and the continual ecstasy of the high air communicates itself, and I have also heard from others many tales of things seen and heard here which show that the races of the Sidhe are often present. Some have seen below the mountain a blazing heart of light, others have heard the musical beating of a heart, or faery bells, or aerial clashings, and the heart-beings have also spoken; so it has gathered around itself its own traditions of spiritual romance and adventures of the soul.

Let no one call us dreamers when the mind is awake. If we grew forgetful and felt no more the bitter human struggle–yes. But if we bring to it the hope and courage of those who are assured of the nearby presence and encircling love of the great powers? I would bring to my mountain the weary spirits who are obscured in the fœtid city where life decays into rottenness; and call thither those who are in doubt, the pitiful and trembling hearts who are sceptic of any hope, and place them where the dusky vapours of their thought might dissolve in the inner light, and their doubts vanish on the mountain top where the earthbreath streams away to the vast, when the night glows like a seraph, and the spirit is beset by the evidence of a million suns to the grandeur of the nature wherein it lives and whose destiny must be its also.

After all, is not this longing but a search for ourselves, and where shall we find ourselves at last? Not in this land nor wrapped in these garments of an hour, but wearing the robes of space whither these voices out of the illimitable allure us, now with love, and anon with beauty or power. In our past the mighty ones came glittering across the foam of the mystic waters and brought their warriors away.

Perhaps, and this also is my hope, they may again return; Manannan,[5] on his ocean-sweeping boat, a living creature, diamond-winged, or Lu,[6] bright as the dawn, on his fiery steed, maned with tumultuous flame, or some hitherto unknown divinity may stand suddenly by me on the hill, and hold out the Silver Branch with white blossoms from the Land of Youth, and stay me ere I depart with the sung call as of old:

> Tarry thou yet, late lingerer in the twilight's glory;
> Gay are the hills with song: earth's faery children leave
> More dim abodes to roam the primrose-hearted eve,
> Opening their glimmering lips to breathe some wondrous story.

On An Irish Hill

Hush, not a whisper! Let your heart alone go dreaming.
Dream unto dream may pass: deep in the heart alone
Murmurs the Mighty One his solemn undertone.
Canst thou not see adown the silver cloudland streaming
Rivers of faery light, dewdrop on dewdrop falling,
Starfire of silver flames, lighting the dark beneath?
And what enraptured hosts burn on the dusky heath!
Come thou away with them for Heaven to Earth is calling.
These are Earth's voice–her answer–spirits thronging.
Come to the Land of Youth: the trees grown heavy there
Drop on the purple wave the starry fruit they bear.
Drink! the immortal waters quench the spirit's longing.
Art thou not now, bright one, all sorrow past, in elation,
Filled with wild joy, grown brother-hearted with the vast,
Whither thy spirit wending flits the dim stars past
Unto the Light of Lights in burning adoration.[7]

1896.

THE AWAKENING OF THE FIRES[1]

When twilight flutters the mountains over
The faery lights from the earth unfold,
And over the hills enchanted hover
The giant heroes and gods of old:
The bird of æther its flaming pinions
Waves over earth the whole night long:
The stars drop down in their blue dominions
To hymn together their choral song:
The child of earth in his heart grows burning
Mad for the night and the deep unknown;
His alien flame in a dream returning
Seats itself on the ancient throne.
When twilight over the mountains fluttered
And night with its starry millions came,
I too had dreams; the thoughts I have uttered
Come from my heart that was touched by the flame.[2]

I thought over the attempts made time after time to gain our freedom; how failure had followed failure until at last it seemed that we must write over hero and chieftain of our cause the memorial spoken of the warriors of old, 'They went forth to the battle but they always fell;' and it seemed to me that these efforts resulted in failure because the ideals put forward were not in the plan of nature for us; that it was not in our destiny that we should attempt a civilization like that of other lands. Though the cry of nationality rings for ever in our ears, the word here has embodied to most no other hope than this, that we should when free be able to enter with more energy upon pursuits already adopted by the people of other countries. Our leaders have erected no nobler standard than theirs, and we who, as a race, are the forlorn hope of idealism in Europe, sink day by day into apathy and forget what a past was ours and what a destiny awaits us if we will but rise responsive to it. Though so old in tradition this Ireland of to-day is a child among the nations of the world; and what a child, and with what a strain of genius in it! There

The Awakening of the Fires

is all the superstition, the timidity and lack of judgment, the unthought recklessness of childhood, but combined with what generosity and devotion, and what an unfathomable love for its heroes. Who can forget that memorable day when its last great chief was laid to rest? He was not the prophet of our spiritual future; he was not the hero of our highest ideals; but he was the only hero we knew. The very air was penetrated with the sobbing and passion of unutterable regret. Ah, Eri,[3] in other lands there is strength and mind and the massive culmination of ordered power, but in thee alone is there such love as the big heart of childhood can feel. It is this which maketh all thy exiles turn with longing thoughts to thee.

Before trying here to indicate a direction for the future, guessed from brooding on the far past and by touching on the secret springs in the heart of the present, it may make that future seem easier of access if I point out what we have escaped and also show that we have already a freedom which, though but half recognized, is yet our most precious heritage. We are not yet involved in a social knot which only red revolution can sever: our humanity, the ancient gift of nature to us, is still fresh in our veins: our force is not merely the reverberation of a past, an inevitable momentum started in the long ago, but is free for newer life to do what we will with in the coming time.

I know there are some who regret this, who associate national greatness with the whirr and buzz of many wheels, the smoke of factories and with large dividends; and others, again, who wish that our simple minds were illuminated by the culture and wisdom of our neighbours. But I raise the standard of idealism, to try everything by it, every custom, every thought before we make it our own, and every sentiment before it finds a place in our hearts. Are these conditions, social and mental, which some would have us strive for really so admirable as we are assured they are? Are they worth having at all? What of the heroic best of man; how does that show? His spirituality, beauty, and tenderness, are these fostered in the civilizations of to-day? I say if questions like these bearing upon that inner life wherein is the real greatness of nations cannot be answered satisfactorily, that it is our duty to maintain our struggle, to remain aloof, lest by accepting a delusive prosperity we shut ourselves from our primitive sources of power. For this spirit of the modern, with which we are so little in touch, is one which tends to lead man further and further from nature. She is no more to him the Great Mother so reverently named long ago, but merely an adjunct to his life, the distant supplier of his needs. What to the average dweller in cities are stars and skies and mountains? They pay no dividends to him, no wages. Why should he care about them indeed. And no longer concerning himself about nature what wonder is it that nature ebbs out of him. She has her revenge, for from whatever standpoint of idealism considered the average man shows but of pigmy stature. For him there is no before or after. In his material life he has forgotten or never heard of the heroic traditions of his race, their aspirations to godlike state. One wonders what will happen to him when death ushers him out from the great visible life to the loneliness amid the stars. To what hearth or home shall he flee who never raised the veil of nature while living, nor saw it waver tremulous with the hidden glory before his eyes? The Holy Breath from the past communes no more with him, and if he is oblivious of these things, though a thousand workmen call him master, within he is bankrupt, his effects sequestered, a poor shadow, an outcast from the Kingdom of Light.

We see too, that as age after age passes and teems only with the commonplace, that those who are the poets and teachers falter and lose faith: they utter no more of man the divine things the poets said of old. Perhaps the sheer respectability of the people they address deters them from making statements which in some respects might be considered libellous. But from whatever cause, from lack of heart or lack of faith, they have no real inspiration. The literature of Europe has had but little influence on the Celt in this isle. Its philosophies and revolutionary ideas have stayed their waves at his coast: they had no message of interpretation for him, no potent electric thought to light up the mystery of his nature. For the mystery of the Celt is the mystery of Amergin the Druid.[4] All nature speaks through him. He is her darling, the confidant of her secrets. Her mountains have been more to him than a feeling. She has revealed them to him as the home of her brighter children, her heroes become immortal. For him her streams ripple with magical life and the light of day was once filled with more aerial rainbow wonder. Though thousands of years have passed since this mysterious Druid land was at its noonday, and long centuries have rolled by since the weeping seeress saw the lights vanish from mountain and valley, still this alliance of the soul of man and the soul of nature more or less manifestly characterizes the people of this isle. The thought produced in and for complex civilizations is not pregnant enough with the vast for them, is not enough thrilled through by that impalpable breathing from another nature. We have had but little native literature here worth the name until of late years, and that not yet popularized, but during all these centuries the Celt has kept in his heart some affinity with the mighty beings ruling in the unseen, once so evident to the heroic races who

The Awakening of the Fires

preceded him. His legends and faery tales have connected his soul with the inner lives of air and water and earth, and they in turn have kept his heart sweet with hidden influence. It would make one feel sad to think that all that beautiful folklore is fading slowly from the memory that held it so long, were it not for the belief that the watchful powers who fostered its continuance relax their care because the night with beautiful dreams and deeds done only in fancy is passing: the day is coming with the beautiful real, with heroes and heroic deeds.

It may not be well to prophesy, but it is always permissible to speak of our hopes. If day but copies day may we not hope for Ireland, after its long cycle of night, such another glory as lightened it of old, which tradition paints in such mystic colours? What was the mysterious glamour of the Druid age? What meant the fires on the mountains, the rainbow glow of air, the magic life in water and earth, but that the Radiance of Deity was shining through our shadowy world, that it mingled with and was perceived along with the forms we know. There it threw up its fountains of life-giving fire, the faery fountains of story, and the children of earth breathing that rich life felt the flush of an immortal vigour within them; and so nourished sprang into being the Danaan races, men who make themselves gods by will and that magical breath. Rulers of earth and air and fire, their memory looms titanic in the cloud stories of our dawn, and as we think of that splendid strength of the past something leaps up in the heart to confirm it true for all the wonder of it.

This idea of man's expansion into divinity, which is in the highest teaching of every race, is one which shone like a star at the dawn of our Celtic history also. Hero after hero is called away by a voice ringing out of the land of eternal youth, which is but a name for the soul of earth, the enchantress and mother of all. There as guardians of the race they shed their influence on the isle; from them sprang all that was best and noblest in our past, and let no one think but that it was noble. Leaving aside that mystic sense of union with another world and looking only at the tales of battle, when we read of heroes whose knightly vows forbade the use of stratagem in war, and all but the equal strife with equals in opportunity; when we hear of the reverence for truth among the Fianna, 'We the Fianna of Erin never lied, falsehood was never attributed to us' – a reverence for truth carried so far that they could not believe their foemen even could speak falsely – I say that in these days when our public life is filled with slander and unworthy imputation, we might do worse than turn back to that ideal Paganism of the past, and learn some lessons of noble trust, and this truth that greatness of soul alone insures final victory to us who live and move and have our being in the life of God.

In hoping for such another day I do not of course mean the renewal of the ancient order, but rather look for the return of the same light which was manifest in the past. For so the eternal Beauty brings itself to the memory of man from time to time brooding over nations, as in the early Aryan heart, suffusing life and thought with the sun-sense of pervading Deity, or as in Greece where its myriad rays, each an intuition of loveliness, descended and dwelt not only in poet, sage and sculptor, but in the general being of the people. What has been called the Celtic renaissance in literature is one of the least of the signs. Of far more significance is the number of strange, dreamy children one meets, whose hearts are in the elsewhere, and young people who love to brood on the past I speak of which is all the world to them. The present has no voice to interpret their dreams and visions, the enraptured solitude by mountain or shore, or what they feel when they lie close pressed to the bosom of earth, mad with the longing for old joys, the fiery communion of spirit with spirit, which was once the privilege of man. These some voice, not proclaiming an arid political propaganda, may recall into the actual: some ideal of heroic life may bring them to the service of their kind, and none can serve the world better than those who from mighty dreams turn exultant to their realization: who bring to labour the love, the courage, the unfailing hope, which they only possess who have gone into the hidden nature and found it sweet at heart.

So this Isle, once called the Sacred Isle[5] and also the Isle of Destiny, may find a destiny worthy of fulfilment: not to be a petty peasant republic, nor a miniature duplicate in life and aims of great material empires, but that its children out of their faith, which has never failed, may realize this immemorial truth of man's inmost divinity, and in expressing it may ray their light over every land. Now, although a great literature and great thought may be part of our future, it ought not to be the essential part of our ideal. As in our past the bards gave way before the heroes, so in any national ideal worthy the name, all must give way in its hopes, wealth, literature, art, everything before manhood itself. If our humanity fails us or becomes degraded, of what value are the rest? What use would it be to you or to me if our ships sailed on every sea and our wealth rivalled the antique Ind, if we ourselves were unchanged, had no more kingly consciousness of life, nor that overtopping grandeur of soul indifferent whether it dwells in a palace or a cottage?

If this be not clear to the intuition, there is the experience of the world and the example of many nations. Let us take the highest, and consider what have a thousand years of empire brought to England.

Wealth without parallel, but at what expense! The lover of his kind must feel as if a knife were entering his heart when he looks at those black centres of boasted prosperity, at factory smoke and mine, the arid life and spiritual death. Do you call those miserable myriads a humanity? We look at those people in despair and pity. Where is the ancient image of divinity in man's face: where in man's heart the prompting of the divine? There is nothing but a ceaseless energy without; a night terrible as hell within. Is this the only way for us as a people? Is nature to be lost; beauty to be swallowed up? The crown and sceptre were taken from us in the past, our path has been strewn with sorrows, but the spirit shall not be taken until it becomes as clay, and man forgets that he was born in the divine, and hears no more the call of the great deep in his heart as he bows himself to the dust in his bitter labours. It maddens to think it should be for ever thus, with us and with them, and that man the immortal, man the divine, should sink deeper and deeper into night and ignorance, and know no more of himself than glimmers upon him in the wearied intervals of long routine.

Here we have this hope that nature appeals with her old glamour to many, and there is still the ancient love for the hero. In a land where so many well nigh hopeless causes have found faithful adherents, where there has been so much devotion and sacrifice, where poverty has made itself poorer still for the sake of leader and cause, may we not hope that when an appeal is made to the people to follow still higher ideals, that they will set aside the lower for the higher, that they will not relegate idealism to the poets only, but that it will dwell in the public as the private heart and make impossible any national undertaking inconsistent with the dignity and beauty of life? To me it seems that here the task of teacher and writer is above all to present images and ideals of divine manhood to the people whose real gods have always been their heroes. These titan figures, Cuculain, Finn, Oscar, Oisin, Caolte, all a mixed gentleness and fire, have commanded for generations that spontaneous love which is the only true worship paid by men. It is because of this profound and long-enduring love for the heroes, which must be considered as forecasting the future, that I declare the true ideal and destiny of the Celt in this island to be the begetting of a humanity whose desires and visions shall rise above earth illimitable into godlike nature, who shall renew for the world the hope, the beauty, the magic, the wonder which will draw the buried stars which are the souls of men to their native firmament of spiritual light and elemental power.

For the hero with us there is ample scope and need. There are the spectres of ignoble hopes, the lethal influences of a huge material civilization wafted to us from over seas, which must be laid. Oh, that a protest might be made ere it becomes more difficult, ere this wild, beautiful land of ours be viewed only as a lure to draw money from the cockney tourist, and the immemorial traditions around our sacred hills be of value only to advertise the last hotel. Yet to avert the perils arising from external causes is but a slight task compared with the overcoming of obstacles already existent within. There is one which must be removed at whatever cost, though the hero may well become the martyr in the attempt. It is a difficulty which has its strength from one of the very virtues of the people, their reverence for religion. This in itself is altogether well. But it is not well when the nature of that religion enables its priests to sway men from their natural choice of hero and cause by the threat of spiritual terrors. I say that where this takes place to any great extent, as it has with us, it is not a land a freeman can think of with pride. It is not a place where the lover of freedom can rest, but he must spend sleepless nights, must brood, must scheme, must wait to strike a blow. To the thought of freedom it must be said to our shame none of the nobler meaning attaches here. Freedom to speak what hopes and ideals we may have; to act openly for what cause we will; to allow that freedom to others – that liberty is denied. There are but too many places where to differ openly from the priest in politics is to provoke a brawl, where to speak as here with the fearlessness of print would be to endanger life. With what scorn one hears the aspiration for public freedom from lips that are closed with dread by their own hearthside! Let freedom arise where first it is possible in the hearts of men, in their thoughts, in speech between one and another, and then the gods may not deem us unworthy of the further sway of our national life. I would that some of the defiant spirit of the old warrior brood were here, not indeed to provoke strife between man and man, or race and race, but rather that we might be fearless in the spirit of one who said 'I do not war against flesh and blood, but against principalities and powers' – and against influences which fetter progress, against an iron materialism where the beauty of life perishes, let us revolt, let us war for ever.

But with all this I, like others who have narrowly watched the signs of awakening life, do not doubt but that these things will pass as greater potencies throng in and impel to action. Already the rush of the earth-breath begins to fill with elation our island race and uplift them with the sense of power; and through the power sometimes flashes the glory, the spiritual radiance which will be ours hereafter, if old prophecy can be trusted and our hearts prompt us true. Here and there some rapt dreamer more inward than the rest sees that Tir-na-noge was no fable, but is still around him with all its mystic beauty for ever. The green hills grow alive with the star-children fleeting, flashing on their twilight errands from gods to men. When the heart opens to receive them and the ties which bind us to unseen nature are felt our day will begin and the fires awaken, our isle will be the Sacred Island once again and our great ones the light-givers to humanity, not voicing new things, but only of the old, old truths one more affirmation; for what is all wisdom, wherever uttered, whether in time past or to-day, but the One Life, the One Breath, chanting its innumerable tones of thought and joy and love in the heart of man, one voice throughout myriad years whose message eterne is this – you are by your nature immortal, and you may be, if you will it, divine.

Æ.

PRIEST OR HERO?[1]

*'I think I could turn and live with animals, they are so placid and
   self-contained,
I stand and look at them long and long.
They do not sweat and whine about their condition,
They do not lie awake in the dark and weep for their sins, . . .*

*No one kneels to another, nor to one of his kind that lived thousands
   of years ago.'* – Walt Whitman.

I have prefixed some ideas about spiritual freedom addressed to the people of Ireland with these lines from the poet of another land, because national sentiment seems out of date here, the old heroism slumbers, alien thought and an exotic religion have supplanted our true ideals and our natural spirituality. I hoped that the scornful words of one who breathed a freer air might sting to shame those who have lost altogether the sentiment of human dignity, who have still some intuitions as to how far and how wisely a man may abase himself before another, whether that other claim divine authority or not. For this is the true problem which confronts us as a nation, and all else is insignificant beside. We have found out who are the real rulers here, who dictate politics and public action with no less authority than they speak upon religion and morals. It was only the other day that a priest, one of our rulers, declared that he would not permit a political meeting to be held in his diocese, and his fiat was received with a submission which showed how accurately the politician gauged the strength opposed to him. And this has not been the only occasion when this power has been exerted: we all know how many national movements have been interfered with or thwarted; we know the shameful revelations connected with the elections a few years back; we know how a great leader fell; and those who are idealists, God's warriors battling for freedom of thought, whose hope for the world is that the intuitions of the true and good divinely implanted in each man's breast shall supersede tradition and old authority, cannot but feel that their opinions, so

Priest or Hero?

much more dangerous to that authority than any political ideal, must, if advocated, bring them at last to clash with the priestly power. It is not a war with religion we would fain enter upon; but when those who claim that heaven and hell shut and open at their bidding for the spirit of man, use the influence which belief in that claim confers, as it has been here, to fetter free-will in action, it is time that the manhood of the nation awoke to sternly question that authority, to assert its immemorial right to freedom.

There lived of old in Eri a heroic race whom the bards sang as fearless. There was then no craven dread of the hereafter, for the land of the immortals glimmered about them in dream and vision, and already before the decaying of the form the spirit of the hero had crossed the threshold and clasped hands with the gods. No demon nature affrighted them: from them wielding the flaming sword of will the demons fled away as before Cuculain[2] vanished in terror shadowy embattled hosts. What, I wonder, would these antique heroes say coming back to a land which preserves indeed their memory but emulates their spirit no more? We know what the bards thought when heroic Ireland became only a tradition; when to darkened eyes the elf-lights ceased to gleam, luring no more to the rich radiant world within, the Druidic mysteries, and the secret of the ages. In the bardic tales their comrade Ossian voices to Patrick[3] their scorn of the new. Ah, from the light and joy of the faery region, from that great companionship with a race half divine, come back to find that but one divine man had walked the earth, and as for the rest it was at prayer and fasting they ought to be! And why? Because, as Patrick explained to Ossian, if they did not they would go to hell. And this is the very thing the Patricks ever since have been persuading the Irish people to believe, adding an alien grief unto their many sorrows, foisting upon them a vulgar interpretation of the noble idea of divine justice to cow them to submission with the threat of flame. Ossian, chafing and fuming under the priestly restriction, declared his preference for hell with the Finians to paradise with Patrick. His simple heroic mind found it impossible to believe that the pure, gentle, but indomitable spirits of his comrades could be anywhere quenched or quelled, but they must at last arise exultant even from torment. When Ossian rejects the bribe of paradise to share the darker world and the fate of his companions, there spake the true spirit of man; spark of illimitable deity; shrouded in form, yet radiating ceaselessly heroic thoughts, aspirations, deathless love; not to be daunted, rising again and again from sorrow with indestructible hope; emerging ever from defeat, its glooms smitten through and through with the light of visions vast and splendid as the heavens. Old bard, old bard, from Tir-na-noge where thou, perchance wrapt by that beauty which called thee from earth, singest immortal songs, would that one lightning of thy spirit could pierce the hearts now thronged with dread, might issue from lips which dare not speak.

I do not question but that the heroic age had its imperfections, or that it was not well that its too warlike ardour was tempered by the beautiful, pathetic and ennobling teaching of Christ. The seed of new doctrines bore indeed many lovely but exotic blossoms in the saintly times, and also many a noxious weed. For religion must always be an exotic which makes a far-off land sacred rather than the earth underfoot: where the Great Spirit whose home is the vast seems no more a moving glamour in the heavens, a dropping tenderness at twilight, a visionary light on the hills, a voice in man's heart; when the way of life is sought in scrolls or is heard from another's lips. The noxious weed, the unendurable bitter which mingled with the sweet and true in this exotic religion was the terrible power it put into the hands of men somewhat more learned in their ignorance of God than those whom they taught: the power to inflict a deadly wrong upon the soul, to coerce the will by terror from the course conscience had marked out as true and good. That power has been used unsparingly and at times with unspeakable cruelty whenever those who had it thought their influence was being assailed, for power is sweet and its use is not lightly laid aside.

As we read our island history there seems a ruddy emblazonry on every page, a hue shed from behind the visible, the soul dropping its red tears of fire over hopes for ever dissolving, noble ambitions for ever foiled. Always on the eve of success starts up some fatal figure weaponed with the Keys of the Hereafter, brandishing more especially the key of the place of torment, warning most particularly those who regard that that key shall not get rusty from want of turning if they disobey. It has been so from the beginning, from the time of the cursing of Tara, where the growing unity of the nation was split into fractions, down to the present time. I often doubt if the barbarities in eastern lands which we shudder at are in reality half so cruel, if they mean so much anguish as this threat of after-torture does to those who believe in the power of another to inflict it. It wounds the spirit to the heart: its consciousness of its own immortality becomes entwined with the terror of as long enduring pain. It is a lie which the all-compassionate Father-Spirit never breathed into the ears of his children, a lie which has been told here century after century with such insistence that half the nation has the manhood cowed out of it. The offence of the dead chief whose followers were recently assailed weighed light as a feather in the balance when compared with the sin of these men and their shameful misuse of religious authority in Meath a little while ago. The scenes which took place there, testified and sworn to by witnesses in the after trials, were only a copy of what generally took place. They will take place again if the necessity arises. That is a bitter fact.

A dim consciousness that their servitude is not to God's law but to man's ambition is creeping over the people here. That is a very hopeful sign. When a man first feels he is a slave he begins to grow grey inside, to get moody and irritable. The sore spot becomes more sensitive the more he broods. At last to touch it becomes dangerous. For from such pent-up musing and wrath have sprung rebellions, revolutions, the overthrow of dynasties and the fall of religions, aye, thrice as mighty as this. That thought of freedom lets loose the flood-gates of an illimitable fire into the soul; it emerges from its narrow prison-cell of thought and fear as the sky-reaching genie from the little copper vessel in the tale of Arabian enchantment; it lays hand on the powers of storm and commotion like a god. It would be politic not to press the despotism more; but it would be a pity perhaps if some further act did not take place, just to see a nation flinging aside the shackles of superstition; disdainful of threats, determined to seek its own good, resolutely to put aside all external tradition and rule; adhering to its own judgment, though priests falsely say the hosts of the everlasting are arrayed in battle against it, though they threaten the spirit with obscure torment for ever and ever: still to persist, still to defy, still to obey the orders of another captain, that Unknown Deity within whose trumpet-call sounds louder than all the cries of men. There is great comfort, my fellows, in flinging fear aside; an exultation and delight spring up welling from inexhaustible deeps, and a tranquil sweetness also ensues which shows that the powers ever watchful of human progress approve and applaud the act.

In all this I do not aim at individuals. It is not with them I would war but with a tyranny. They who enslave are as much or more to be pitied than those whom they enslave. They too are wronged by being placed and accepted in a position of false authority. They too enshrine a ray of the divine spirit, which to liberate and express is the purpose of life. Whatever movement ignores the needs of a single unit, or breeds hate against it rather than compassion, is so far imperfect. But if we give these men, as we must, the credit of sincerity, still opposition is none the less a duty. The spirit of man must work out its own destiny, learning truth out of error and pain. It cannot be moral by proxy. A virtuous course into which it is whipt by fear will avail it nothing, and in that dread hour when it comes before the Mighty who sent it forth, neither will the plea avail it that its conscience was in another's keeping.

The choice here lies between Priest and Hero as ideal, and I say that whatever is not heroic is not Irish, has not been nourished at the true fountain wherefrom our race and isle derive their mystic fame. There is a life behind the veil, another Eri which the bards knew, singing it as the Land of Immortal Youth. It is not hidden from us, though we have hidden ourselves from it, so that it has become only a fading memory in our hearts and a faery fable upon our lips. Yet there are still places in this isle, remote from the crowded cities where men and women eat and drink and wear out their lives and are lost in the lust for gold, where the shy peasant sees the enchanted lights in mountain and woody dell, and hears the faery bells pealing away, away, into that wondrous underland whither, as legends relate, the Danann gods withdrew. These things are not to be heard for the asking; but some, more reverent than the rest, more intuitive, who understand that the pure eyes of a peasant may see the things kings and princes, aye, and priests, have desired to see and have not seen; that for him may have been somewhat lifted the veil which hides from men the starry spheres where the Eternal Beauty abides in the shining – these have heard and have been filled with the hope that, if ever the mystic truths of life could be spoken here, there would be enough of the old Celtic fire remaining to bring back the magic into the isle. That direct relation, that vision, comes fully with spiritual freedom, when men no longer peer through another's eyes into the mysteries, when they will not endure that the light shall be darkened by transmission, but spirit speaks with spirit, drawing light from the boundless Light alone.

Leaving aside the question of interference with national movements, another charge, one of the weightiest which can be brought against the priestly influence in this island, is that it has hampered the expression of native genius in literature and thought. Now the country is alive with genius, flashing out everywhere, in the conversation even of the lowest: but we cannot point to imaginative work of any importance produced in Ireland which has owed its inspiration to the priestly teaching. The genius of the Gael could not find itself in their doctrines; though above all things mystical it could not pierce its way into the departments of super-nature where their theology pigeon-holes the souls of the damned and the blessed. It knew of the Eri behind the veil which I spoke of, the Tir-na-noge which as a lamp lights up our grassy plains, our haunted hills and valleys. The faery tales have ever lain nearer to the hearts of the people, and whatever there is of worth in song or story has woven into it the imagery handed down from the dim druidic ages. This is more especially true to-day, when our literature is beginning to manifest pre-eminent qualities of imagination, not the grey pieties of the cloister, but natural magic, beauty, and heroism. Our poets sing of Ossian wandering in the land of the immortals; or we read in vivid romance of the giant chivalry of the Ultonians, their untamable manhood, the exploits of Cuculain and the children of Rury, more admirable as types, more noble and inspiring than the hierarchy of little saints who came later on and cursed their memories.

The genius of the Gael is awakening after a night of troubled dreams. It returns instinctively to the beliefs of its former day and finds again the old inspiration. It seeks the gods on the mountains, still enfolded by their mantle of multitudinous traditions, or sees them flash by in the sunlit diamond airs. How strange, but how natural is all this! It seems as if Ossian's was a premature return. To-day he might find comrades come back from Tir-na-noge for the uplifting of their race. Perhaps to many a young spirit starting up among us Caolte might speak as to Mongan, saying: 'I was with thee, with Finn.' Hence, it may be, the delight with which we hear Standish O'Grady declaring that the bardic divinities still remain: 'Nor, after centuries of obscuration, is their power to quicken, purify, and exalt yet dead. Still they live and reign, and shall reign.' After long centuries – the voice of pagan Ireland! But that does not declare it: it is more: it is the voice of a spirit ever youthful, yet older than all the gods, who with its breath of sunrise-coloured flame jewels with richest lights the visions of earth's dreamy-hearted children. Once more out of the Heart of the Mystery is heard the call of 'Come away,' and after that no other voice has power to lure: there remain only the long heroic labours which end in companionship with the gods.

These voices do not stand for themselves alone. They are heralds before a host. No man has ever spoken with potent utterance who did not feel the secret urging of dumb, longing multitudes, whose aspirations and wishes converge on and pour themselves into a fearless heart. The thunder of the wave is deeper because the tide is rising. Those who are behind do not come only with song and tale, but with stern hearts bent on great issues, among which, not least, is the intellectual liberation of Ireland. That is an aim at which some of our rulers may well grow uneasy. Soon shall young men, fiery-hearted, children of Eri, a new race, roll out their thoughts on the hillsides, before your very doors, O priests, calling your flocks from your dark chapels and twilight sanctuaries to a temple not built with hands, sunlit, starlit, sweet with the odour and incense of earth, from your altars call them to the altars of the hills, soon to be lit up as of old, soon to be the blazing torches of God over the land. These heroes I see emerging. Have they not come forth in every land and race when there was need? Here, too, they will arise. Ah, my darlings, you will have to fight and suffer: you must endure loneliness, the coldness of friends, the alienation of love; warmed only by the bright interior hope of a future you must toil for but may never see, letting the deed be its own reward; laying in dark places the foundations of that high and holy Eri of prophecy, the isle of enchantment, burning with druidic splendours, bright with immortal presences, with the face of the everlasting Beauty looking in upon all its ways, divine with terrestrial mingling till God and the world are one.

There waits brooding in this isle a great destiny, and to accomplish it we must have freedom of thought. That is the greatest of our needs, for thought is the lightning-conductor between the heaven-world and earth. We want fearless advocates who will not be turned aside from their course by laughter or by threats. Why is it that the spirit of daring, imaginative enquiry is so dead here? An incubus of spiritual fear seems to beset men and women so that they think, if they turn from the beaten track seeking the true, they shall meet, not the divine with outstretched hands, but a demon: that the reward for their search will not be joy or power but enduring pain. How the old bard swept away such fears! 'If thy God were good,' said Ossian, 'he would call Finn into his dun.' Yes, the heroic heart is dear to the heroic heart. I would back the intuition of an honest soul for truth against piled-up centuries of theology. But this high spirit is stifled everywhere by a dull infallibility which is yet unsuccessful, on its own part, in awakening inspiration; and, in the absence of original thought, we pick over the bones of dead movements, we discuss the personalities of the past, but no one asks the secrets of life or of death. There are despotic hands in politics, in religion, in education, strangling any attempt at freedom. Of the one institution which might naturally be supposed to be the home of great ideas we can only say, reversing the famous eulogy on Oxford, it has never given itself to any national hero or cause, but always to the Philistine.

With the young men who throng the literary societies the intellectual future of Ireland rests. In them are our future leaders. Out of these as from a fountain will spring – what? Will we have another generation of Irishmen at the same level as to-day, with everything in a state of childhood, boyish patriotism, boyish ideals, boyish humour? Or will they assimilate the aged thought of the world and apply it to the needs of their own land? I remember reading somewhere a description by Turgenieff of his contemporaries as a young man: how they sat in garrets, drinking execrably bad coffee or tea. But what thoughts! They talked of God, of humanity, of Holy Russia; and out of such groups of young men, out of their discussions, emanated that vast unrest which has troubled Europe and will trouble it still more. Here no questions are asked and no answers are received. There is a pitiful, blind struggle for a nationality whose ideals are not definitely conceived. What is the ideal of Ireland as a nation? It drifts from mind to mind, a phantom thought lacking a spirit, but a spirit which will surely incarnate. Perhaps some of our old heroes may return. Already it seems as if one had been here; a sombre Titan earlier awakened than the rest who passed before us, and sounded the rallying note of our race before he staggered to his tragic close. Others of brighter thought will follow to awaken the fires which Brigid[4] in her vision saw gleaming beyond dark centuries of night, and confessed between hope and tears to Patrick. Meanwhile we must fight for intellectual freedom; we must strive to formulate to ourselves what it is we really wish for here, until at last the ideal becomes no more phantasmal but living; until our voices in aspiration are heard in every land, and the nations become aware of a new presence amid their councils, a last and most beautiful figure, as one after the cross of pain, after the shadowy terrors, with thorn-marks on the brow from a crown flung aside, but now radiant, ennobled after suffering, Eri, the love of so many dreamers, priestess of the mysteries, with the chant of beauty on her lips and the heart of nature beating in her heart.

Æ.

CHIVALRY[1]

I read in one of the Celtic stories, a tale rudely told but instinct with a magnificent spirit of chivalry, how Maeve, queen of the Olnemacta, stood upon the walls of her liss and saw below the Knights of the Red Branch[2] arrayed and ready for battle against her; and as her druid pointed out one famous hero after another – Concobar, most subtle of princes, Cuculain the champion, Conal, Laegaire, and the rest, how a glow of heroic admiration lit up her speech: 'Noble and regal is the description,' cried the queen. 'Noble and regal are they of whom it is said,' her druid also spoke. Not the fear of conquest, not death, could still the impartial love of beauty, wisdom, and courage shining even in a foe. Such was the tradition of Celtic chivalry. It has almost passed into the night, this great and fearless spirit. Whatever honeyed words are addressed by one nation to another have good material expectation, the making of some advantageous treaty, at the back of them. Let that hope be shattered, and where is the chivalry? And between public men the tone is equally ignoble: to praise an opponent, to grant him sincerity and patriotism, seems almost a betrayal of one's own party. But could we not hail like Maeve with equal joy whatever of beautiful or good shines in those who are opposed to us? How meagre then would appear the hostile array! The distinctions of party, the pride of nationality, have no place in those who see One alone living in all. With this ideal before us we declare ourselves free from all parties and to belong to one nation only. Our people are humanity and our foes are yet to be discovered. Whoever deny us we shall not deny. If they are witty at our expense they shall have made us to laugh also; and if they are cruel we will remember that we can only be hurt by departing from our own ideals. We shall hail whatever is beautiful in them as their contribution to a common cause. And indeed it seems to us that it is only through such tolerance and mutual recognition that the dream brooded upon with awe and hope by so many great thinkers in the past will ever become possible, that spiritual fusion of nations where a limitless spirit pervades a multiform life, and one eternal will inspires all with equal intent. Though this divine event be far off in the sunset of time, it is not too early to begin our efforts while the clash and roar of battle are about us. While we are in the turmoil, O spirit of ancient chivalry, return again to us. Return, return!

Pan.

IN THE SHADOW OF THE GODS[1]

When the children of Miled, as old tradition tells, overran Ireland, the Danann gods retired into the deeps of the sacred mountains, and there in inviolable secrecy they pursued their magical arts, being advised to this withdrawal by Manannán, wisest of the divine magi. Perhaps it may be that the younger race had vividly imprinted on their minds the glory of the departing Titans and it went in endless repetition from generation to generation, for these tales are still on the peasant's tongue, and the mystical reverie is still in his heart as he moves over the bogland or on the lonely mountains. It may be he communes with a memory, but I prefer to think these visitations of awe and beauty are the shadows of the still living gods engaged in their mysterious toil. They may not come forth, but they draw to them every dreamy heart; at the waving of their magic sceptres the peasant becomes oblivious of his sordid lot and is haunted by immemorial hopes and desires. In many a remote valley which the mountains ring about with a rampart of pearl can be found a world of thought so strange that many will scarce credit it. People are so possessed with belief that it even overmasters in them the sorrow of death; and there are cottages in Mayo where there is no weeping over the departed, for the dropping of tears or the sound of sobbing would draw the Phantom Hounds to chase the soul newly gone forth from the body; so, until it has passed safely into the other world, they weep not, or if they must it is in some distant spot. We hear of comings and goings between the faery world and this: I was pointed out the great-grandchild of a faery who had chosen a mortal lover, and still from the raths comes the old unweary merriment, the sound of music and dance alluring as when Etaine the queen and Connla of the Radiant Hair were called so many thousand years ago.

From frequent hearing of these tales I can still think of the Ireland of to-day as the Land of the Living Heart; and whenever I see a peasant standing alone, or a girl by the cabin door at evening, I question whether some transient, exultant moment may not have revealed to them the beautiful Angus passing like a star through the grey dusk, and ask in my heart with that tender familiarity which comes so rarely to the lips: 'What do you wonder at, asthore? What's away in yonder grey? Ah, dream-fed hearts, what old desire, what ancient beauty, forgotten in cities and palaces, paces before your cabin door?' I think myself into something of their mystic inheritance, and shape in song the stories which I hear. This, of a young farmer who was called away, was told me while passing through the desolate bogland at Erris, and I have tried to retell it, to give to others the feeling it gave to me:

> It's a lonely road through bogland to the lake at Carrowmore,
> And a sleeper there lies dreaming where the water laps the shore.
> Though the moth-wings of the twilight in their purple are unfurled,
> Yet his sleep is filled with music by the Masters of the World.
>
> There's a hand as white as silver that is fondling with his hair:
> There are glimmering feet of sunshine that are dancing by him there:
> And half open lips of faery that were dyed to richest red
> In revels where the Hazel Tree its holy clusters shed.
>
> 'Come away,' the red lips whisper, 'all the earth is weary now.
> 'Tis the twilight of the ages and it's time to quit the plough.
> Oh, the very sunlight's weary ere it lightens up the dew,
> And its gold is changed and faded ere its falling down to you.
>
> 'Though your colleen's heart be tender a tenderer heart is near,
> What's the starlight in her glances when the stars are shining here?
> Who would kiss the fading shadow when the flower face glows above?
> 'Tis the Beauty of all Beauty that is calling for your love!'
>
> Oh, the mountain-gates of dreamland are opened once again;
> And the sound of song and dancing falls upon the ears of men;
> And the Land of Youth lies gleaming far beyond our earthly strife,
> And the old enchantment lingers in the honey-heart of life.

Dream or real? Do not ask me too strictly. All things are dream save only the spirit which gazes on the phantasmagoria, and those dreams endure most which most fitly accord with its immortality. The tales told ere Patrick came to Ireland may yet outlast the memory of his teaching, for they still have an endless progeny of song and story, while the new creed is sterile for all its cathedral glories and the illuminations on its altars. The elder gods will conquer: their allies are air, river, cloud, hill, twilight, and dawn, which whisper of them but never of a Judæan divinity.[2] The truth is every country must have a religion of its own, and a universal *form* of religion is a chimera: though there is but one Breath it has many voices, and in this land it will cry for ever its wild and wondrous story of beauty and immortal joy, and call away its votaries to no pale paradise where humility is crowned, but to elemental sway and to conflict with the gods themselves. 'I would thy God were matched with my Oscar!' says Oisin in defiance to Patrick. They are matched. Belief in man's divinity and innate power exist still amid all the teaching of man's helplessness, which is one of the favourite themes of the Patricks. A man came to a priest in Galway a little while ago asking him to work spells on an ailing cow. The priest refused. 'But you should pray,' he said, 'and trust to the mercy of Almighty God.' The answer was delightful. 'It's a poor thing for a man with a large family to trust to the mercy of Almighty God!' He believed in a possible power in the human spirit: the other seemed a little hollow. Take off the veil of superficial habit, and in these poor peasants you will find, filling the recesses of their nature, thoughts of supramundane beings, not angelic but faery, the shadow of the gods.

The decay of the beautiful Gaelic speech is responsible for the loss of many a song and story and the death of many an old custom: but as they die out in one direction they awaken to new life in another. The genius of our modern writers has caught the last tales told in the cabins, and the dying fall of the songs: they have given them new meaning. They retell the old stories with a hitherto unknown splendour, and find in them a universal significance and fitting symbols for moods which never die. The battle fought in the tumultuous dawn-light of legend, between gods and demons at Moytura on the shores of the west, has been retold with profound spiritual significance by Larminie, and in his mystic drama it becomes the eternal battle between good and evil. Lu the Sun-god, whose sling brings victory to the Dananns, Balor of the Evil Eye, whose glance could turn armies to stone, are still with us. The battle is over in the heavens perchance, but it has yet to be fought out on earth, and the interest we feel in the antique story is that it is the fittest symbol for the conflict to-day:

> When in my shadowy hours I pierce the hidden heart of hopes and fears
> They change into immortal joys or end in immemorial tears:
> Moytura's battle still endures, and in this human heart of mine
> The golden sun-powers with the might of demon darkness intertwine.
>
> I think that every teardrop shed still flows from Balor's eye of doom,
> And gazing on his ageless grief my heart is filled with ageless gloom.
> I close my ever weary eyes and in my bitter spirit brood
> And am at one in vast despair with all the demon multitude.

> But in the lightning flash of hope I feel the Sun-god's fiery sling
> Has smote the horror in the heart where clouds of demon shades take wing.
> I lay my heavy grief aside and seize the flaming sword of will.
> I am of Dana's race divine and know I am immortal still.

I think it must be the near by presence of the immortals which in some interior way is the basis of the peasant's love for his country. In other lands people love their nation: here they love most the land itself. It is not that their lot is pleasant there, for these enchanted skies look down upon a poverty which abases the soul to witness. I never knew what power it had until returning from a brief visit beyond the water I saw in the early dawn the sacred hills shining in the holy light, and could have knelt down to hail them. What lies in thy heart, O Eiré, dearer than the heart of our beloved, nearer, sweeter, more alluring than all else, if it be not that there is somehow in thee a pathway to the original Heart of all from which we came, to which we must return? I read in some old tale that in Eiré was one of the four paradises of the ancient world, by which I understand that the visible world is the shadow of the invisible, and that here some rarer, purer atmosphere makes possible access into one of the intellectual sections which glitter in the Over-world. Geography is yet in its infancy. We have mapped out but one of the films which float around the true earth. It seems indeed so solid, this film; but there are hours when it fades from our gaze and becomes only a vanishing shadow, and the Rainbow Land of Plato, the Golden Isle of Apollo, the Hy Brasil of Celtic legend, with their splendours of mountainous light, flame and press upon the spirit.[3] Why cannot we put off into these glittering oceans whose foamlight tosses before the inner eye and seek for the Isles of the Immortals? We linger on the hither side of so great a glory, waiting, longing, until the magic vision passes, and then we dream that it is a dream. But though we delude ourselves thus, it is such exultations, such reveries as these we remember most, and count these hours happy, not those in which we have the pride of fancied truth to support us. There is a test of truth for the mystic which is not yet accepted by men: that vision, that thought, which fills him with profoundest life has most of truth. It is the spirit which is most unspeakable, and has therefore to be missed out in the telling, which gives that life. But what words, what song, could render the rapture, mystery, and light of those wild hours when earth fades and we are in a strange world, but with more certitude, more hope, than we feel with the most familiar faces and the most beloved heart beside us. Wild hours, come again! Wild hours, that bear us away!

The Descent of the Gods

Burning our hearts out with longing
    The daylight passed:
Millions and millions together,
    The stars at last!

Purple the woods where the dewdrops
    Pearly and grey,
Wash in the cool from our faces
    The flame of day.

Glory and shadow grow one in
    The forest dense:
Laughter and peace in the stillness
    Our spirits sense.

Hopes all unearthly are thronging
    In hearts of earth;
Tongues of the star-light are calling
    Our souls to birth.

And from the heavens their secrets
    Drop one by one,
Where time is for ever beginning
    And time is done.

There light eternal is over
    Chaos and night,
Singing with dawn-lips for ever,
    'Let there be light!'

And too for ever in twilight
    Time slips away,
Closing in darkness and rapture
    Its awful day.

                        Æ.

AN IRISH MYSTIC'S TESTIMONY[1]

Through the kindness of an Irish mystic, who is a seer, I am enabled to present here, in the form of a dialogue, very rare and very important evidence, which will serve to illustrate and to confirm what has just been said above about the mysticism of Ireland. To anthropologists this evidence may be of more than ordinary value when they know that it comes from one who is not only a cultured seer but who is also a man conspicuously successful in the practical life of a great city:

Visions. –

Q. – Are all visions which you have had of the same character?

A. – 'I have always made a distinction between pictures seen in the memory of nature and visions of actual beings now existing in the inner world. We can make the same distinction in our world: I may close my eyes and see you as a vivid picture in memory, or I may look at you with my physical eyes and see your actual image. In seeing these beings of which I speak, the physical eyes may be open or closed: mystical beings in their own world and nature are never seen with the physical eyes.'

Otherworlds. –

Q. – By the inner world do you mean the Celtic Otherworld?

A. – 'Yes; though there are many Otherworlds. The *Tir-na-nog*[2] of the ancient Irish, in which the races of the *Sidhe* exist, may be described as a radiant archetype of this world, though this definition does not at all express its psychic nature. In *Tir-na-nog* one sees nothing save harmony and beautiful forms. There are other worlds in which we can see horrible shapes.'

Classification of the 'Sidhe'. –

Q. – Do you in any way classify the *Sidhe* races to which you refer?

A. – 'The beings whom I call the *Sidhe,* I divide, as I have seen them, into two great classes: those which are shining, and those which are opalescent and seem lit up by a light within themselves. The shining beings appear to be lower in the hierarchies; the

opalescent beings are more rarely seen, and appear to hold the positions of great chiefs or princes among the tribes of Dana.'
Conditions of Seership.[3] –

Q. – Under what state or condition and where have you seen such beings?

A. – 'I have seen them most frequently after being away from a city or town for a few days. The whole west coast of Ireland from Donegal to Kerry seems charged with a magical power, and I find it easiest to see while I am there. I have always found it comparatively easy to see visions while at ancient monuments like New Grange and Dowth, because I think such places are naturally charged with psychical forces, and were for that reason made use of long ago as sacred places. I usually find it possible to throw myself into the mood of seeing; but sometimes visions have forced themselves upon me.'

The Shining Beings. –

Q. – Can you describe the shining beings?

A. – 'It is very difficult to give any intelligible description of them. The first time I saw them with great vividness I was lying on a hill-side alone in the west of Ireland, in County Sligo: I had been listening to music in the air, and to what seemed to be the sound of bells, and was trying to understand these aerial clashings in which wind seemed to break upon wind in an ever-changing musical silvery sound. Then the space before me grew luminous, and I began to see one beautiful being after another.'

The Opalescent Beings. –

Q. – Can you describe one of the opalescent beings?

A. – 'The first of these I saw I remember very clearly, and the manner of its appearance: there was at first a dazzle of light, and then I saw that this came from the heart of a tall figure with a body apparently shaped out of half-transparent or opalescent air, and throughout the body ran a radiant, electrical fire, to which the heart seemed the centre. Around the head of this being and through its waving luminous hair, which was blown all about the body like living strands of gold, there appeared flaming wing-like auras. From the being itself light seemed to stream outwards in every direction; and the effect left on me after the vision was one of extraordinary lightness, joyousness, or ecstasy.

'At about this same period of my life I saw many of these great beings, and I then thought that I had visions of Aengus, Manannan, Lug, and other famous kings or princes among the Tuatha De Danann; but since then I have seen so many beings of a similar character that I now no longer would attribute to any one of them personal identity with particular beings of legend; though I believe that they correspond in a general way to the Tuatha De Danann or ancient Irish gods.'

Stature of the 'Sidhe'. –

Q. – You speak of the opalescent beings as great beings; what stature do you assign to them, and to the shining beings?

A. – 'The opalescent beings seem to be about fourteen feet in stature, though I do not know why I attribute to them such definite height, since I had nothing to compare them with; but I have always considered them as much taller than our race. The shining beings seem to be about our own stature or just a little taller. Peasant and other Irish seers do not usually speak of the *Sidhe* as being little, but as being tall: an old schoolmaster in the West of Ireland described them to me from his own visions as tall beautiful people, and he used some Gaelic words, which I took as meaning that they were shining with every colour.'

The worlds of the 'Sidhe'. –

Q. – Do the two orders of *Sidhe* beings inhabit the same world?

A. – 'The shining beings belong to the mid-world; while the opalescent beings belong to the heaven-world. There are three great worlds which we can see while we are still in the body: the earth-world, mid-world, and heaven-world.'[4]

Nature of the 'Sidhe'. –

Q. – Do you consider the life and state of these *Sidhe* beings superior to the life and state of men?

A. – 'I could never decide. One can say that they themselves are certainly more beautiful than men are, and that their worlds seem more beautiful than our world.

'Among the shining orders there does not seem to be any individualized life: thus if one of them raises his hand all raise their hands, and if one drinks from a fire-fountain all do; they seem to move and to have their real existence in a being higher than themselves, to which they are a kind of body. Theirs is, I think, a collective life, so unindividualized and so calm that I might have more varied thoughts in five hours than they would have in five years; and yet one feels an extraordinary purity and exaltation about their life. Beauty of form with them has never been broken up by the passions which arise in the developed egotism of human beings. A hive of bees has been described as a single organism with disconnected cells; and some of these tribes of shining beings seem to be little more than one being manifesting itself in many beautiful forms. I speak this with reference to the shining beings only: I think that among the opalescent or *Sidhe* beings, in the heaven-world, there is an even closer spiritual unity, but also a greater individuality.'

Influence of the 'Sidhe' on Men. –

Q. – Do you consider any of these *Sidhe* beings inimical to humanity?

A. – 'Certain kinds of the shining beings, whom I call wood beings, have never affected me with any evil influences I could recognize. But the water beings, also of the shining tribes, I always dread, because I felt whenever I came into contact with them a great drowsiness of mind and, I often thought, an actual drawing away of vitality.'

Water Beings Described. –

Q. – Can you describe one of these water beings?

A. – 'In the world under the waters – under a lake in the West of Ireland in this case – I saw a blue and orange coloured king seated on a throne; and there seemed to be some fountain of mystical fire rising from under his throne, and he breathed this fire into himself as though it were his life. As I looked, I saw groups of pale beings, almost grey in colour, coming down one side of the throne by the fire-fountain. They placed their head and lips near the heart of the elemental king, and, then, as they touched him, they shot upwards, plumed and radiant, and passed on the other side, as though they had received a new life from this chief of their world.'

Wood Beings Described. –

Q. – Can you describe one of the wood beings?

A. – 'The wood beings I have seen most often are of a shining silvery colour with a tinge of blue or pale violet, and with dark purple-coloured hair.'

Reproduction and Immortality of the 'Sidhe'. –

Q. – Do you consider the races of the *Sidhe* able to reproduce their kind,[5] and are they immortal?

A. – 'The higher kinds seem capable of breathing forth beings out of themselves, but I do not understand how they do so. I have seen some of them who contain elemental beings within themselves, and these they could send out and receive back within themselves again.

'The immortality ascribed to them by the ancient Irish is only a relative immortality, their space of life being much greater than ours. In time, however, I believe that they grow old and then pass into new bodies just as men do, but whether by birth or by the growth of a new body I cannot say, since I have no certain knowledge about this.'

Sex among the 'Sidhe'. –

Q. – Does sexual differentiation seem to prevail among the Sidhe races?

A. – 'I have seen forms both male and female, and forms which did not suggest sex at all.'

'Sidhe' and Human Life. –

Q. – (1) Is it possible, as the ancient Irish thought, that certain of the higher *Sidhe* beings have entered or could enter our place of life by submitting to human birth? (2) On the other hand, do you consider it possible for men in trance or at death to enter the *Sidhe* world?

A. – (1) 'I cannot say.' (2) 'Yes; both in trance and after death. I think any one who thought much of the *Sidhe* during his life and who saw them frequently and brooded on them would likely go to their world after death.'

Social Organization of the 'Sidhe'. –

Q. – You refer to chieftain-like or prince-like beings, and to a king among water beings; is there therefore definite social organization among the various *Sidhe* orders and races, and if so, what is its nature?

A. – 'I cannot say about a definite social organization. I have seen beings who seemed to command others, and who were held in reverence. This implies an organization, but whether it is instinctive like that of a hive of bees, or consciously organized like human society, I cannot say.'

Lower 'Sidhe' as Nature Elementals. –

Q. – You speak of the water-being king as an elemental king; do you suggest thereby a resemblance between lower *Sidhe* orders and what mediaeval mystics called elementals?

A. – 'The lower orders of the *Sidhe* are, I think, the nature elementals of the mediaeval mystics.'[6]

Nourishment of the Higher 'Sidhe'. –

Q. – The water beings as you have described them seem to be nourished and kept alive by something akin to electrical fluids; do the higher orders of the *Sidhe* seem to be similarly nourished?

A. – 'They seemed to me to draw their life out of the Soul of the World.'

Collective Visions of 'Sidhe' Beings. –

Q. – Have you had visions of the various *Sidhe* beings in company with other persons?

A. – 'I have had such visions on several occasions.'

And this statement has been confirmed to me by three participants in such collective visions, who separately at different times have seen in company with our witness the same vision at the same moment. On another occasion, on the Greenlands at Rosses Point, County Sligo, the same *Sidhe* being was seen by our present witness and a friend with him, also possessing the faculty of seership, at a time when the two percipients were some little distance apart, and they hurried to each other to describe the being, not knowing that the explanation was mutually unnecessary. I have talked with both percipients so much, and know them so intimately that I am fully able to state that as percipients they fulfil all necessary pathological conditions required by psychologists in order to make their evidence acceptable.

FACE TO FACE WITH NATURE[1]

Review of *Among the Gnomes*, by Franz Hartmann

One rises from a perusal of this charming little book with a refreshing sense of having really learned something of the Gnomes, and with a greater sympathy, a wider understanding, of the world of 'inorganic' matter.

The scene of the story is laid in the mysterious Untersberg, or 'Mountain on the Lower World,' a snow-capped wing of the frontier mountains separating Austria from Germany. This cavernous monster is known by the inhabitants around to be the abode of certain kinds of elemental creatures, and to this eerie spot a party of scientists set out, their object being to prove that there is no sub-physical world. Having reached the Cave of the Dragon, they are suddenly overtaken by a storm, and one of their number, an Irishman named Patrick Mulligan, is knocked senseless and tumbles right out of his body into the realm of the Gnomes. Arrived there he meets the Princess Adalga, and all his subsequent adventures are made in her company.

One of the best chapters in the book is that devoted to a description of the various classes of Gnomes, as follows:

Pigmies, 'whose office it was to direct the currents of vital electricity in the earth to all places where the roots of the plants that grew upon the surface required it. This they did while they were in their disembodied state, when each of them was, so to say, like a magnetic current.'

Vulcani, 'who were principally occupied with mineral life, having in their charge the growth and transformation of metals. Their substance consisted of a certain force . . . which might be called an electro-magnetic fire. By an exercise of their will they were able to send a current of such vital electricity into a mineral vein and cause gold and silver, iron and copper, to grow.'

Cubitali. 'The substance of which they were formed was a kind of explosive force, which means that they could contract their fluidic bodies and expand them very rapidly, when the quick expansion caused a kind of explosion with a destructive effect . . . Their principal occupation was the blasting of air and the cutting of rocks.'

Acthnici, 'said to create heat and cause upheavings of the earth.'

Sagani. 'Their principal occupation was to contruct the astral modes of plants after a certain type for each species, which they did by the power of their imagination.'

'All the gnomes . . . in their ethereal shape could travel with the velocity of a thought . . . but in their corporeal state their locomotion was comparatively slow, and the atmospheric air, not being their own element, caused great obstacles to their locomotion.'

Throughout the whole book the author indulges in satire at the expense of materialism and the dogmatic tone of modern science. Many capital illustrations are to be found in the book.

G.R.

V. FOUNTAIN OF INSPIRATION

SONG AND ITS FOUNTAINS[1]

TO
VIOLET
AND
DIARMUID

[The text on this page was printed on the dust-jacket of the first edition of *Song and Its Fountains*. Although unsigned, it is almost certainly by A.E.]

The writer in this book continues the mystical meditation begun in his *Candle of Vision*. In the earlier volume he was intent on images which had form because it was easier to reason over things which had shape and body than about bodiless things. In the later book, having come to think that a poem is an intricately organised form of thought born in a sphere of being behind dream, he tries to track song back to its secret fountain in the psyche. He surmises a transcendental being or genie in the innermost which is wakeful while the body sleeps, and discusses the commerce between deep inner being and outer being. He speaks of poetry as oracles breathed from inner to outer being and tries to discover how much comes from the outer mind and how much from the genie within. To illustrate his thesis he takes a number of his own verses and tells the psychic circumstances connected with their making. He thinks there should be as much interest in the truth about the making of a thing as about the thing that is made.

In what follows I have tried to track song back to its secret fountains. As I have thought it unnatural to see together in galleries pictures unrelated to each other, or taken from the altars for which they were painted, so I have thought it unnatural for lyric to follow lyric in a volume without hint of the bodily or spiritual circumstance out of which they were born. I have here placed some songs in their natural psychic atmosphere. Those who cannot follow my reasoning may perhaps be amused or interested by the fantasy a poet built about his life and poetry.

A.E.

I

A child sits on the grass or strays in darkening woods, and its first going inward in dream may make inevitable a destiny.[2] When inner and outer first mingle[3] it is the bridal night of soul and body. A germ is dropped from which inevitably evolves the character and architecture of the psyche. It is seed[4] as truly as if it were dropped into earth or womb. Only what is born from it is a spirit thing, and it grows up and takes its abode in the body with its other inhabitants, earth-born or heaven-born. There may be many other minglings of heaven and earth in childhood which beget a brood which later become desires, thoughts or imaginations, but the earliest are the masters and they lie subtly behind other impulses of soul.

This I found many years ago when I began to practise a meditation the ancient sages spoke of. In this meditation we start from where we are and go backwards through the day,[5] and later, as we become quicker in the retracing of our way, through weeks, through years, what we now are passing into what we did or thought the moment before, and that into its antecedent;[6] and so we recall a linked medley of action, passion, imagination or thought. It is most difficult at first to retrace our way, to remember what we thought or did even an hour before. But if we persist the past surrenders to us and we can race back fleetly over days or months. The sages enjoined this meditation with the intent that we might, where we had been weak, conquer in imagination, kill the dragons which overcame us before and undo what evil we might have done.[7] I found, when I had made this desire for retrospect dominant in meditation, that an impulse had been communicated to everything in my nature to go back to origins. It became of myself as if one of those moving pictures we see in the theatres, where in a few moments a plant bursts into bud, leaf and blossom, had been reversed and I had seen the blossom dwindling into the bud. My moods began to hurry me back to their first fountains. To see our lives over again[8] is to have memories of two lives and intuitions of many others,[9] to discover powers we had not imagined in ourselves who were the real doers of our deeds, to have the sense that a being, the psyche, was seeking incarnation in the body. As a tribe of gay or dusky winged creatures we followed might lead us home to their nest, so a crowd of delicately coloured desires led me back to the moment in childhood when, about four or five years of age, beauty first dawned on me. I had strayed into a park, and I remembered how I lay flat on grass overcome by some enchantment flickering about a clump of daffodils. A little later I read a child's story, and in this what fascinated me was that the hero had a magic sword with a hilt of silver and a blade of blue steel. The word 'magic'[10] stirred me, though I knew not what it meant, as if there was some being within me which could foresee the time when the whole universe from wheeling stars to the least motion of life would appear to be wrought by, or depend on, the magic of some mighty mind. It lay in memory, that word, without meaning, until a dozen years later its transcendental significance emerged as a glittering dragon-fly might come out of a dull chrysalis. But the harmony of blue and silver at once bewitched me. I murmured to myself, 'blue and silver! blue and silver!' And then, the love of colour awakened, a few days later I saw primroses and laid the cool and gentle glow of these along with the blue and silver in my heart, and then lilac was added to my memory of colours to be treasured. And so, by harmony or contrast, one colour after another entered the imagination. They became mine or were denied, as they could or would not shine in company with those delicate originals of blue and silver. This love of colour seemed instinctive in the outer nature, and it was only in that retrospective meditation I could see that the harmonies which delighted me had been chosen by a deeper being and were symbolic of its nature and not of that unthinking child's.

I think it was because in the first contact of soul and body I could remember beauty was born, that later in life I accepted ideas, philosophies and causes for the beauty they suggested, and I have always shrunk from any activity in which I could not see that magic thing.

As my meditation revealed to me the birth here of the aesthetic sense, so it revealed to me when the sympathy for revolt was born. I was lying on my bed, a boy of fifteen or thereabouts. The faculty of dreaming while I was awake had then become active, though I hardly know whether what I have to tell was a dream of the waking self or revelation from some more ancient inner being. In my fantasy I was one of the Children of Light in some ancestral paradise, and it was rumoured to us there were Children of Darkness,[11] and the thought of them was fearful and abhorrent to us. But I in my imagination had wandered far outside the circle of light into a wilderness of space, and, far from that paradise, I became aware of a dark presence beside me, and I trembled because I knew it was one of the Children of Darkness. But this being whispered gently to me, 'We of the Darkness are more ancient than you of the Light,' and, at the saying of that, I forsook my allegiance to the Light, and my whole being yearned to lose itself in that Divine Darkness. This imagination of boyhood long forgotten I rediscovered years after in that retrospective meditation as the company of thoughts marched back with me along the road I had travelled. I knew in this lay the root of my many revolts against accepted faiths, and how later I could write a flaming rhetoric on behalf of those in my own country who were in revolt against its orthodoxies: exulting over the soul, resolutely putting aside all external tradition and rule, adhering to its own judgment, though priests falsely say the hosts of the Everlasting are arranged in battle against it, though they threaten the spirit with obscure torment for ever and ever: still to persist, still to defy, still to obey the orders of another captain, that unknown deity within whose trumpet-call sounds louder than all the cries of men.

I wrote so fiercely because the idea of revolt had incarnated in the hot body of youth and the gentleness of the whisper from the divine darkness was forgotten; and I did not then know that every passionate energy which goes forth evokes at once its contrary or balancing power, and that wisdom lies in the transmutation or reconcilement of opposites,[12] and, if we were gentle enough, the God would give us a star to lead. The spirit of revolt sank later to more mystical depths, but it was from that original fountain of dream that many poems came like that I wrote where the man cries to the angel:

> They are but the slaves of Light
> Who have never known the gloom,
> And between the dark and bright
> Willed in freedom their own doom . . .
>
> Pure one, from your pride refrain,
> Dark and lost amid the strife,
> I am myriad years of pain
> Nearer to the fount of life.
>
> When defiance fierce is thrown
> At the God to whom you bow,
> Rest the lips of the Unknown
> Tenderest upon my brow.

In that retrospect, too, I regained memory of the greatest of all wonders in my boyhood, when I lay on the hill of Kilmasheogue and Earth revealed itself to me as a living being, and rock and clay were made transparent so that I saw lovelier and lordlier beings than I had known before, and was made partner in memory of mighty things, happenings in ages long sunken behind time. Though the walls about the psyche have thickened with age and there are many heavinesses piled about it, I still know that the golden age[13] is all about us and that we can, if we will, dispel that opacity and have vision once more of the ancient Beauty.

There was another divine visitation in boyhood when I was living in the country and was told of a woman who was dying, how, a quarter of an hour or so before she went, she wept that she was unable to rise and nurse a sick neighbour; and there came on me a transfiguring anguish because of this self-forgetfulness of hers, and though the mood was too high for me to sustain, and I passed from it to many egoisms, yet this was the starting-point of whatever selflessness was in my life. Yet because the love of beauty was the first-born of the union between soul and body I could never be like Plotinus and place the good above the beautiful.[14]

One after another the desires and idealisms of later life were, in that retrospect, traced back to their fountains. There grew up the vivid sense of a being within me seeking a foothold in the body, trying through intuition and vision to create wisdom there, through poetry to impose its own music upon speech, through action trying to create an ideal society, and I was smitten with penitence because I had so often been opaque to these impulses and in league with satyr or faun in myself for so many of my days.

Yet this meditation, which discovers another being within us,[15] unites us to it in some fashion,[16] and in retrospect we seem to have lived two lives, a life of the outer and a life of the inner being. I do not know indeed, but I suspect of that inner being that it is not one but many; and I think we might find if our meditation was profound that the spokes of our egoity ran out to some celestial zodiac. And, as in dream the ego is dramatically sundered into This and That and Thou and I, so in the totality of our nature are all beings men have imagined, aeons, archangels, dominions and powers, the hosts of darkness and the hosts of light, and we may bring this multitudinous being to a unity and be inheritors of its myriad wisdom.

As I tracked the congregation of desires in myself back to their fountains in childhood I began to see too in those with whom I was intimate that each had some governing myth, that somewhere in their past, from the first bridal of soul and body, a germinal mood had been born which had grown to dominion over everything else in them. I can see to-day the central idea I surmised forty-five years ago in the young Yeats grown to full self-consciousness. I remember as a boy showing the poet some drawings I had made and wondering why he was interested most of all in a drawing of a man on a hill-top, a man amazed at his own shadow cast gigantically on a mountain mist, for this drawing had not seemed to me the best. But I soon found his imagination was dominated by his own myth of a duality in self, of being and shadow.[17] I think somewhere in his boyhood at the first contact of inner and outer he became aware of a duality in his being. In his earlier poetry one could pick out twenty lines showing how he was obsessed with this myth, how frequently and almost unconsciously the same idea recurs.

> Never with us where the wild fowl chases
> Its shadow along in the evening blaze.

or

> A parrot swaying on a tree
> Rages at its own image in the enamelled sea.

or

> Nought they heard for they were ever listening
> The dewdrops to the sound of their own dropping.

or

> The boy who chases lizards in the grass,
> The sage who deep in central nature delves,
> The preacher waiting the ill hour to pass,
> All these are souls who fly from their dread selves.

There are many such images in his early poetry. Then the mood ceased to haunt individual lines but became the subject of a long poem. I remember when we were walking along Leinster Road his telling me the first conception of *The Shadowy Waters*. His hero, a world-weary wanderer, was trying to escape from himself. He captures a galley in the waters. There is a beautiful woman among the captives. He thinks through love he may have this escape and casts a magical spell on Dectora, but he finds the love so created only echoes back to him the imaginations of his own heart of which he is already weary, and in the original form of the poem he unrolled the spell and went alone seeking for the world of the immortals. I think when the poet came himself to love, the thought of that lonely journey to the Everliving grew alien to his mood; and the poem was altered, losing, as I think, the noble imaginative logic of its first conception, for in the new ending the love won by the magic art becomes an immortal love. Concealed or unconcealed, this preoccupation of the poet with that dualism of being and shadow is in much that he has written, until at last it becomes self-conscious in the *Vision,* a gigantic philosophy of self and anti-self. I asked him could he remember at what moment in boyhood he was first conscious of this duality. But the poet is creative rather than introspective, and I do not think he had noticed how his final philosophy lay in germ in his earliest imaginations. There must have been many other contacts of inner and outer in his boyhood, for there are many coloured threads woven in the rich tapestry of his poetry.

I think if we were truly wise in our analysis we could discover those dominant moods, and we might almost re-create for ourselves how in some reverie in childhood by river or road, in wood or on hill, faery first nodded at him, or how, and awakening what desire, the Mystical Rose[18] opened first a burning blossom in his imagination.

I can surmise the character of the first illumination in Wordsworth, the most retrospective of poets, who knew also that in those illuminations a being was seeking incarnation in him, and in Shelley, Keats and other poets when they were first met by their souls.[19] I rarely see a child alone without wondering on what mysterious river consciousness is drifting. There is enchantment in those first adventures afloat on the canoe of dream, though the reverie may be like that doomful slumber Keats imagined.[20]

> A poor Indian's sleep
> While his boat hastens to the monstrous steep
> Of Montmorenci.

The child does not know the distant thunder of the deep he goes to, which brings not a flutter to his heart that dreams. We cannot waken the dreamer or point him out his fate. That is ordained by the past,[21] for the soul in its first kiss of the body renews an ancient love; and in this kiss, however gentle, are all the desires which brought it back to the world.

> Call not thy wanderer home as yet
> Though it be late.
> Now is his first assailing of
> The invisible gate.
> Be still through that light knocking. The hour
> Is thronged with fate.
>
> To that first tapping at the invisible door
> Fate answereth.
> What shining image or voice, what sigh
> Or honied breath,
> Comes forth, shall be the master of life
> Even to death.

Satyrs may follow after. Seraphs
On crystal wing
May blaze. But the delicate first comer
It shall be king.
They shall obey, even the mightiest,
That gentle thing.

All the strong powers of Dante were bowed
To a child's mild eyes,
That wrought within him that travail
From depths up to skies,
Inferno, Purgatorio
And Paradise.

Amid the soul's grave councillors
A petulant boy
Laughs under the laurels and purples, the elf
Who snatched at his joy,
Ordering Caesar's legions to bring him
The world for his toy.

In ancient shadows and twilights
When childhood had strayed,
The world's great sorrows were born
And its heroes were made.
In the lost boyhood of Judas
Christ was betrayed.

Let thy young wanderer dream on,
Call him not home.
A door opens, a breath, a voice
From the ancient room,
Speaks to him now. Be it dark or bright,
He is knit with his doom.

II

While I was yet a boy I began to run in and out of the house of dream, and as I went inward I grew older. An age of the spirit would fall upon me, and then I would come out of reverie and be the careless boy once more. Yet something of that ancientness of the psyche within clung to the boy, and began to part me from the thoughts of those about me. I at last realized with a kind of anguish that I was becoming a solitary, that a gulf had widened between myself and normal human life, between myself and home and love, the things in which most find a rich content. In the house of dream I entered there was neither home nor love, but beyond me in its labyrinths were intimations of primaeval being and profundities like the Pleroma.[22] That myth of the Children of Light and the Children of Darkness was only one of many such myths telling in symbol of dawn-distant antecedents of human life, of revolts in heaven and the descent of the spirit to earth. They were strange inhabitants of the soul of the boy, for, when I first was visited by such imaginations, there was nothing in the culture with which I was familiar which might give birth to them.[23]

Looking back on the past I have vivid sense of a being seeking incarnation here, beginning with those faint first intuitions of beauty, and those early dreamings which were its forerunners. It was no angelic thing, pure and new from a foundry of souls, which sought embodiment, but a being stained with the dust and conflict of a long travel through time, carrying with it unsated desires, base and august, and, as I divined of it, myriads of memories and a secret wisdom. It was not simple but infinitely complex,[24] as a being must be which has been in many worlds and all it had experienced has become part of it. If there was an original purity of being it had become corrupted, yet not altogether, for there was in it, I believe, some incorruptible spiritual atom,[25] carrying with it maybe some memory of its journeyings with deity. It had worshipped in many houses of prayer and kept the reverence it had paid, and had been in many a gay and many a ruined heart. Out of ancient happiness it could build intoxicating images of life, and out of ancient sorrows it could evoke a desolating wisdom that would crucify the infant joy ere it could run to its light.

It was such a being I surmised within me, trying to tune the body to be sensitive to its own impulses by a glamour cast upon desire, and also by vision, dream and the illuminations of intuition and conscience. They impelled often in such contrary directions these impulses, that I divined a dual nature in the psyche. It was a being in part avidly desirous of life, while another part was cold to this, but was endlessly seeking for the Spirit.[26] I am going to set down as clearly as I can a record of some of these inbreathings, so that it may be seen out of what argument with myself I came to think as I do of the psyche as a being pre-existent to the body and seeking incarnation in it. I have already in *The Candle of Vision* tried to illuminate that nature normally invisible to us. But I was there intent on images which had form, because it is easier to reason over things which have shape and body than about bodiless things. Intuition, feeling, thought are too swift in their coming and going, too elusive for a decisive argument over their nature. Though they may shake us by what they import, though what they in an instant hint at may be sacred to us, their coming and going are too swift for precise thought about themselves. In normal thought the fusion between inner and outer is so swift that it deceives the most attentive sense into the idea of unity, and we come to believe that there is no other creator of thought than the thinker who resides in the brain, who is with us from moment to moment, and we do not know what rays from how many quarters of the heavens are focussed on the burning point of consciousness.

I had brooded much, hoping to weave a net which would hold these glittering visitors long enough for argument over where they were born and the manner of their coming. Then I remembered that a poem is the most intricately organized form of thought, and in the coming into being of poetry there is the greatest intensity of consciousness. Here we can recall more of the circumstance of creation than we can about more transient intuitions and ideas, though what they had to tell us may have been more profound than the thought which took shape in a lyric and remained with us. I could remember enough of the circumstance in which a lyric was born to weave an argument over it as I could about the images we see in vision or dream. In dream there is a dramatic sundering of the psyche.[27] One part of us is seer and another is creator. The seer of dream is unconscious of creation. He looks on the forms which appear as he might look on a crowd drawn together by impulses not of his creation. He does not think all this when he dreams, but, when he wakens and remembers, he knows that the creator of dream had a magical power transcending anything which he could do in his waking state. It can project crowds of figures, set them in motion, make them to move with perfect naturalness, and wear the fitting expression for the deeds they do. Yet in the waking state of the dreamer, let him be given canvas, paints and brushes, and he might boggle as a child would over the drawing of a figure. The creator in dream is swift inconceivably. What seems a long dream to the seer of dream often takes place in an instant, and may be caused by sound or touch which wakens him. Transformations, too, take place in dream which suggest a genius to which psychic substance[28] is instantly malleable. If I tell a dream I had it may make this clearer.

In this dream I found myself in a room crowded with objects of art. Set apart on an easel was a picture. I looked at it and I wondered within myself how the artist painted so marvellous a sky. Then in my dream the painting, which was about two feet in length, was on the instant enlarged to about six feet, and every colour the artist had used was left isolated from every other brushful of paint with a space of white canvas between each. I looked closely and saw that the dusky luminous sky I had wondered at had been made so to glow by touches of a pale rose violet laid alongside touches of a pale bluish green, each colour keying up its delicate contrary. This dream I remembered, and I tried to make a replica of the picture the next day.

Is there not something beyond reason, something magical, in that swift analysis transfiguring the dream picture in response to a silent desire? You may say I, as an artist, must have known Monet and his school made scientific use of pure, broken and contrasted colour. But my dream was not thinking about a technical theory. The essential thing about it was that it was a vision. I was looking on a picture I could see clearly; and then came the astonishing enlargement of it, the analysis of colour, every brushful of paint isolated, with the untouched white of the canvas showing between touch and touch. The seer in dreams is apart from the creator. It is not unreasonable to surmise an intellectual creator able to work magically upon psychic substance. Sometimes, indeed, at the apex of dream I have almost surprised the creator of it peering in upon me as if it desired by these miracles to allure me to discovery of itself. In the exploration of dream we acquire some knowledge of the workings of that mysterious psyche. And at times in the making of poetry I have been able to discover the true creator of the poem withdrawn far within from the waking consciousness. The poem seemed like an oracle delivered to the waking self from some dweller or genie in the innermost.[29] I propose to tell what I could discover about that psyche from the oracles I received and the manner of their coming. I think there should be as much interest in the truth about the making of a thing as in the thing that is made. If I choose to speak about my own poetry it is not because I think it is so fine a thing that what I say about it should be of interest to others, but because in the making of poetry I discovered, as I did in the exploration and analysis of dream, something about the nature of that psyche which began incarnating in me in early boyhood. Though I think in all speech, even the lightest, there is, in final analysis, mystery as profound as there is in the lordly speech of the prophets,[30] I choose to speak about the making of poetry, because, by reason of the intensity of consciousness involved in its making, I could remember more of the circumstance than that about ordinary speech, and was more aware of the duality in my being, of the interactions between inner and outer, and of the same mystery in its making as there is in the creation of dream. For those who cannot follow with confidence my reasoning there may be some interest or amusement in studying the fantasies a poet built about his life and his poetry.

III

How is poetry born in us? There is, I think, some commerce between the outer and an inner being. Some character in aspiration determines the character of inspiration. In our meditation we are all consciously or unconsciously votaries of the Holy Breath.[31] Our meditation is sacrifice[32] and some one of its tongues of intellectual fire descends upon us. St. Paul says there are diversities of powers but they all spring from the same Breath. To one may come the discerning of spirits,[33] to another speaking with tongues, which I interpret to have, among others, these meanings, poetry, music, eloquence.[34] In my imagination of his wisdom the purified psyche is a focus or burning point through which that which is in itself infinite or boundless manifests as pure light through a prism does, becoming sevenfold; and these intellectual fires are for ever playing upon us, and we apprehend them as wisdom, thought, power, love, music or vision. By whatever way we ascend to that spirit it answers. I think poetry is one way in which it answers aspiration, and we receive, interpret or misinterpret the oracle as our being here is pure or clouded. To me it was only after long reverie that a song would come as a bird might fly to us out of the vast hollows of the air. I sometimes felt like that Merlin of legend who mused long by the margin of the great deep before a ninth wave bore the infant Arthur to his feet. There was always an element of the unexpected in the poetry itself, for it broke in upon and deflected the normal current of consciousness. I would be as surprised at the arising within me of words which in their combination seemed beautiful to me as I would have been if a water-lily had blossomed suddenly from the bottom of a tarn to make a shining on its dark surfaces. The words often would rush swiftly from hidden depths of consciousness and be fashioned by an art with which the working brain had but little to do.

Many poems were the residue or essence of waking dream. It is not true that we must fall asleep to dream. The dream consciousness may flood the waking,[35] and that waking consciousness may have little more to do with the moulding of the dream than the seer of dream in sleep has to do with the creation of the images by which he is surrounded. The waking dream may be likened to a living creature which invades us and obliterates all else in us until it has told its story. As a boy I was often overpowered by waking dreams; and their intensity was such that in them I would forget myself and the earth I walked on, and be in another nature, or thousands of years behind time. Some of these dreams were symbolic, and I surmise of others that they were memories of ancient life, or of experience which after death had gone into the heavenworld, and had there been thrice refined until little remained but essence that had become part of an immortal memory: and out of that enduring memory they were breathed into the mind of the boy to give age or wisdom to his thought, or to bring the being who lived to-day to some unity of purpose with the ancestral selves.

These waking dreams would fall upon me at any time, while I was at work, or in the streets, or in the country roads at night. Once I was walking down a passage in the great building where I was employed over forty years ago, a passage which led from one office to another; and in that dim lighted corridor my imagination of myself was suddenly changed, and I was a child and was looking upwards to a dawn of faintest yellow behind snowy peaks made blue and shadowy by that glow. The mound on which I stood was brown and bare as if it had been baked by the heat of fierce suns. The boy I had become was gazing in adoration at the high and holy light. He was celestially transparent, pure and virgin. He chanted a divine name, and a fire that was heaven-born leaped up from the heart, and for an instant the child was a delicate lyre whose strings quivered echoing the song of Brahma. Then all that faded and I was again in the offices at Pims; and I am afraid for the moment I was not doing their work, but was finding words which might hold that remote ancestral memory:

> Faint grew the yellow buds of light
> Far flickering beyond the snow,
> As, leaning o'er the shadowy white,
> Morn glimmered like a pale primrose.

Before that glamour had obliterated the corridor I was intent on the work I had to do, and this interruption of vision was like the sudden flowing into a cloudy river of crystal clear water from some tributary descending from high hills.

I must tell some other waking dreams before I can begin my speculation in regard to them. In such a waking vision I passed out of an ancient city built by the sea. It was steeped in the jewel glow and gloom of evening. There walked with me a woman whose face I could not see, for my head was downcast and I was rapt in my musing. It needed not that I should lift my eyes to see an image that was burning in my heart. I had gone from body to soul in my brooding, and the image was nigher to the inner eyes than it could ever be to the waking sight. We passed beyond the city gates, walking silently along the sands to a distant headland. The sea and sand swept by my downcast eyes in fantasmal flowings troubling not my thought. We came at last to the headland, climbed up a little way and sat down, and still no word was spoken. The love which was in my heart drew me inwards, and I was breaking through one ring of being after another seeking for that innermost centre where spirit could pass into spirit. But when the last gate was passed I was not in that spirit I adored, but trembled on the verge of some infinite being; and then consciousness was blinded and melted into unconsciousness, and I came at last out of that trance feeling an outcast on the distant and desert verge of things, though there was a cheek beside mine and I felt a wetness and I did not know whether it was the dew of night or weeping. Then the dream closed. I had learned to be still when such visitations came, not to alter, not to remould. It was as truly dream and uncreated by the waking consciousness as any of the images which visited me in sleep. The dream, which was burdened with such intensities of emotion, when it departed left behind a slight lyric which could not hold or hardly hint at the love which had passed from earth to heaven and had forgotten the love which gave it wings to rise.

> As from our dream we died away
> Far off I felt the outer things,
> Your wind-blown tresses round me play,
> Your bosom's gentle murmurings.
>
> And far away our faces met
> As on the verge of the vast spheres,
> And in the night our cheeks were wet,
> I could not say with dew or tears.
>
> O gate by which I entered in!
> O face and hair! O lips and eyes!
> Through you again the world I win,
> How far away from paradise!

Why was this dream projected into the waking consciousness? It was not drawn out by affinity with any earthly desire, for I had not then come to love in life. I do not think I could say of any of my earlier poems that I had learned in experience or suffering here what was transmuted into song. Indeed I would reverse the order and say rather that we first imagine, and that later the imagination attracts its affinities, and we live in the body what had first arisen in soul.[36] I had the sense that that far-travelled psyche was, in this and other waking dreams, breathing into the new body it inhabited some wisdom born out of its myriad embodiments. In this dream I was warned that love was a tale which already had been told, and I must not be allured by the romance of love, and that even from the noblest beauty the wonder would die swiftly. There came to me many oracles out of the psyche with this wisdom in their music.

> O beauty, as thy heart o'erflows
> In tender yielding unto me,
> A vast desire awakes and grows
> Unto forgetfulness of thee.

or

> Beauty, the face, the touch, the eyes,
> Prophets of thee, allure our sight
> From that unfathomed deep where lies
> Thine ancient loveliness and light.

As the sun in high air may be splintered into many stars upon moving waters, so the intensity of that dream was reflected in many a river of emotion. I look back with sadness upon a wisdom which too often was unregarded. But another wisdom was born from the conflict between cold spirit and flaming heart. I was not strong enough to go 'alone to the Alone,'[37] but, if I could not be the ascetic mystic, neither could I be content with the contrary and competing passions. They gave something to each other, for the tenderness which is in our passionate earthly affections began to invade the heavens, and the heavens seemed to the imagination to glow with the infinite of all that here was brief and exquisite. What was gross divested itself of its sensual commonness to take on a beauty stolen from the spirit. There is, I think, some necessity for the descents of the spiritual into the bodily to gather strength,[38] while the demoniac in us is for ever trying to make captive the spiritual beauty to sweeten its dark delights. I found, a melancholy wisdom, how many before myself had come to that perilous state where the evil in us has learned how to disguise itself in the apparel of light. It is vain to say the demon does not worship the beautiful. That worship is in almost all art and literature. It is in those strange heads drawn by Da Vinci where spirit and sense co-exist in an almost sinister companionship in the same face, where there are lips that allure and eyes that are scornful. It is in the lovely faces painted by Rossetti where lips and burning eyes betray a thirst which could not be allayed in any spiritual paradise, or in lyrics of Heine, half-fairy, half-sensual. The tragedy of that mood was sung by Keats in *La Belle Dame sans Merci*. Half-way between spirit and matter there is a state where good and evil wear one face.

'There came and looked him in the face
An angel beautiful and bright,
And that he knew it was a fiend
That miserable knight.'

They are the fortunate who know what dark passion may be hidden by the cheat of loveliness. Even when we think desire is left behind, on a sudden the desires we thought dead will rise from their grave in our meditation as if they were penitent, looking at us with angelic lips and eyes, and if we yield to their enchantment we may find they have become more terrible than when they were clothed in flesh. When desires die in the body they may reincarnate in the psyche,[39] and may in our heavenward travelling fright us with terror as incubi or succubi.[40]

IV

It may appear to many that I accept with a trust too easy and complete whatever revelation may be in those waking dreams. I have not passed the possibility that the psyche may be a story-teller with its own art of glorifying its memories. The ancient seers spoke of a state of soul[41] where, released from the heaviness of our life, and nearer to its own divine root, memories of this life were transfigured, or purified, until nothing remained but what had affinity with its own immortality.[42] And in telling these waking dreams, which affected life and thought so much, I have had in mind that possibility. But I was certain that they were not creations of the waking consciousness. I was sure of this, as I was sure that the seer in dream is not the creator, and I felt I must explore into their origin. I think there are many possible explanations. They may be regarded as memories of past life, or as memories transfigured in the psyche, or as symbolic dream, or as moments in the lives of other beings attracted and related to me by some mystical affinity in our natures. I think too we may attract images to ourselves out of the book of life, the memory of nature[43] where they live 'thinking the thought and performing the deed.' If I choose between these interpretations I do so for the most part by indications in myself which I find difficult to explain, though I will later try to make clear why I think some are ancestral memories, that is, connected in some way with the pre-existence of the psyche,[44] and why some are transient fusions of my own consciousness with the consciousness of others. I noticed about these waking dreams that sometimes they would seem to be related to each other. That is, a second or third waking dream would seem to come out of the same remote life. I had another lapse into that distant country where the young boy stepped out of a hut on the hillside to worship the dawn and chanted the ineffable name before it. In this the boy was on a hump of hill with other children. The hill sloped down into a vagueness below, where dimly a village could be seen veiled by its tresses of lazy smoke. And beyond this were the same mountains as the boy had seen at dawn. The children were in so lovely a mood of gaiety that the Golden Age might have been whispering its last in them ere it departed. To the boy the hollow of air was not empty but seemed filled with the bright ones, the devas,[45] and he longed to be a sky-walker with them. His life was half with them and only half with his laughing companions. Then the mood in the boy changed from gaiety to one of fathomless sorrow, for something within him told him that the light of the world had gone out, the Iron Age[46] had begun, and Earth was mourning in her deep heart. The last avatar[47] of the spirit was dead, and nevermore or for long ages would there be any coming again of that hero. The sorrow of the long dead boy was recreated in the living; and by the living a song was made echoing the anguish of earth.

> Does the Earth grow grey with grief
> For her hero darling fled?
> Though her vales let fall no leaf,
> In our hearts the tears are shed.
>
> Still the stars laugh on above;
> Not to them her grief is said.
> Mourning for her hero love,
> In our hearts the tears are shed.
>
> We, her children, mourn for him,
> Mourn the elder hero dead.
> In the twilight grey and dim,
> In our hearts the tears are shed.

The dream was unfolding itself swiftly as in the vision of the boy at dawn. But it grew blurred ere it closed, for the waking mind would not be still, and began to take part that it might weave a story out of the unfolding dream and so broke its continuity. But it opened in perfect harmony with the earlier dream as if it was another episode of mystical childhood five thousand years ago. I have noticed in other imaginations which came at different times a congruity with each other, as if characters and their setting were out of the same remote civilization. When the waking mind did not intervene, but was silently intent, the absorption at times would be as complete as if I had been in trance. Once I was moving in such a waking dream over a mountain road at night, absorbed by creatures of the imagination which held mystical converse with each other, and, when a man vaulted over a wall beside me, the thud of his feet on the path brought me back so violently[48] from what a distance in time that my heart began an abnormal thumping, and I had to lean half-fainting against the wall to recover from that rude awakening.

I am trying to unveil some of the secret sources of poetry, and in what manner outer is moulded by inner. And I must tell yet another tale of glamour cast on the waking consciousness before I begin any speculation on it. In this I was parted from my normal self and had become another person, a kinsman in mood but unlike in circumstance. I was with a companion looking over a valley, a lovely land of woods and waters. And trees and lake, earth and air, seemed in the evening glow to be in a trance of still delight, that joy of nature when the mighty Master is busy with His art and His creations feel the moulding touch of their creator. But I was shut out, exiled from intimacy with that myriad beauty, the life which breathed everywhere subtle and penetrating, which brought all but the gazer into unity with itself. I was shut out, for I had been traitor to earth and had forgotten it, having been long at other labours. Then a yearning had arisen in me to revisit the places of childhood, but the doors were closed to me. Earth denied me her blessing. I was no longer one of her children. Yet she had once, as I now knew, played in my heart, run in my limbs and laughed through my lips. The things I had laboured at in the city, which there seemed so mighty, here dwindled to the insignificance of dust beside the miracle of pure life I had lost, having fallen outside the circle of spirit. I realized this loss in an exquisite anguish in my heart, and then my companion broke silence, she who had played with me here in childhood and had returned with me, and I knew that her reverie was filled with as deep a regret as my own, for she said sadly, 'How innocent our childhood was!' Then the glamour of that tragic summer night was over and I was myself once more. You may say that that man I dreamed of was not in essence different from the dreamer. Yet while the glamour was on me I was that man, and knew from what labours and from what a life he had come to revisit this place, and they were not my labours nor my life. It was only for an instant in that poignancy of regret, knowing then what he had lost, that the circles of our being intersected. I had no feeling that this waking dream recreated for me anything I had already endured in an anterior life. The residue of that dream was a poem I called *A Summer Night*.

Her mist of primroses within her breast
Twilight hath folded up, and o'er the west,
Seeking remoter valleys, long hath gone,
Not yet hath come her sister of the dawn.
Silence and coolness now the earth enfold,
Jewels of glittering green, long mists of gold,
Hazes of nebulous silver veil the height,
And shake in tremors through the shadowy night.
Heard through the stillness, as in whispered words,
The wandering God-guided wings of birds
Ruffle the dark. The little lives that lie
Deep hid in grass join in a long-drawn sigh
More softly still;[49] and unheard through the blue
The falling of innumerable dew
Lifts with grey fingers all the leaves that lay
Burned in the heat of the consuming day.
The lawns and lakes lie in this night above,
Admitted to the majesty above.
Earth with the starry company hath part:
The waters hold all heaven within their heart
And glimmer o'er with wave-lips everywhere
Lifted to meet the angel lips of air.
The many homes of men shine near and far,
Peace-laden as the tender evening star.
The late home-coming folk anticipate
Their rest beyond the passing of the gate,
And tread with sleep-filled hearts on drowsy feet.
Oh, far away and wonderful and sweet
All this, all this. But far too many things
Obscuring, as a cloud of seraph wings
Blinding the seeker to the Lord behind,
I fall away in weariness of mind,
And think how far apart are I and you,
Beloved, from those spirit children who
Felt but one single Being long ago,
Whispering in gentleness and leaning low
Out of Its majesty as child to child.
I think upon it all with heart grown wild,
Hearing no voice, howe'er my spirit broods,
No whisper from those dense infinitudes,
This world of myriad things whose distance awes.
Ah me: how innocent our childhood was!

I had often at other times the sense that for an instant, an unforgettable moment, the circle of my being intersected with others, and that I had been admitted into the secrecy of other hearts.

These people were all strange to me, men, women or children, except at the point of intersection. It was not, I think, merely a transfer of images such as may take place in thought-transference. I have told in *The Candle of Vision* how my mind was once flooded with images. There was an old man in a little shop, a red-haired watchful girl, a cobbled street outside; I might have supposed all this was only what we call imagination but that I had an impulse to question my office companion about his people, and I found I had seen his father and sister. I had really been adventuring in the mind of another. There was there no identity of emotion. It was only the transfer of images from an active to a vacant mind. But I brooded much over the limitless possibilities of that momentary clairvoyance, and when I came to have waking dreams like that of the statesman mourning over a lost intimacy with spiritual nature, I felt a conviction that consciousness had melted into unity with another being through some transient affinity of mood. In thinking over such experiences, I have felt that not only are we fed out of an immortal memory but we have secret ties with the living.[50] I can only interpret these experiences by accepting what Kant wrote:

> I am much disposed to assert the existence of immaterial natures in the world and to place my own soul in the class of these beings. It will hereafter, I know not where or when, yet be proved that the human soul stands even in this life in indissoluble connection with all immaterial natures in the spirit world, that it reciprocally acts upon these and receives impressions from them.

The truth of that will never, I think, be proved by any dialectic, but by experience when we may meet in the body those we have first known in the secrecy of spirit and speak to each other about the moment when soul was nearer to soul than our own bodies are to us. I had but one constant mood of preoccupation with the spirit; and but rarely in my meditation did I brood upon other things, and because of this the points of intersection or mingling with other souls were only at moments of spiritual gain or defeat. I have often thought the great masters, the Shakespeares[51] and Balzacs,[52] endowed more generously with a rich humanity, may, without knowing it, have made their hearts a place where the secrets of many hearts could be told; and they wove into drama or fiction, thinking all the while that it was imagination or art of their own, characters they had never met in life, but which were real and which revealed more of themselves in that profundity of being than if they had met and spoken day by day where the truth of life hides itself under many disguises. When we sink within ourselves, when we seem most alone, in that solitude we may meet multitude. The psyche, when it has evolved a higher quality of that element which mirrors being, and by which it becomes self-conscious, may become not only aware of its own spirit but of that relation with other spirits which Kant divined.[53] Here we may find one of the secret sources of drama, poetry and wisdom. The psyche may, by the evolution of this sensitiveness, through love and sympathy, come to know that the whole of life can be reflected in the individual and our thoughts may become throngs of living souls.

V

The sages who spoke of that retrospective meditation[54] said also that by following it we could regain memory of past lives. The meditation does not bring us only to the fountains of beauty or desire or fear in this life. Wisdom, fear, desire have a remote ancestry, and if the meditation is intense enough it may recall what tragedy in the past gave birth to wisdom or fear in this life,[55] what vision of the heavens revealed a new star by which the mariner might guide the barque of the soul. When I was young, and these whisperings and breathings out of the past brought me to the belief that I was on a journey between two eternities,[56] I was not content with spiritual memories but desired to know what else there was to be known, what kind of being walked in ancient cities, what its labours were, its loves, tragedies and delights. But in this curiosity I was not sustained from within. When I sought for spiritual wisdom out of that ancestral memory I had the sense of being sustained, but not when I sought for the personal.[57] Once I was met by a terror frightening me from my meditation. In my brooding there had been born the sense that in some life before this there had been mighty happenings, aspirations, downfall and a tragic defeat. I began a concentration on that intuition. But there was some wisdom within me greater than my own which stayed me, for I had hardly begun my meditation than I was enveloped by that terror I spoke of, the fear that there would be revelation of things I could not endure; the resurrection of tragedies and crucifixions of the heart; of things I had done which were awful and unspeakable, the punishment for which was yet to fall. I knew not what I had done, whether my will had dared to storm the heavens, and had been hurled back and had itself been broken, and in its madness had reversed its heaven-assailing desires and the divine powers had been turned to infernal uses, and even love had been crucified in its despair. I seemed to be warned that if I persisted in this meditation I would arouse dragons that lay in slumber. I would be beset by powers I was too feeble now to master, and they would make wreck of the life which was slowly gathering itself from that defeat of the spirit. I was so overcome by this terror that I stayed the meditation, and a poem I had begun evoking that past was left uncompleted for thirty years. I could not continue it after two lines had come to my lips lest the very words might wind into their music the passion which once had made wreckage of the soul. It was only when I was old and desire had no power over me, that one day the poem completed itself. I do not think it was the poem I would have written if I had persisted in that tragic meditation. It had become wisdom rather than memory.

> Not by me these feet were led
> To the path beside the wave,
> Where the naiad lilies shed
> Moonfire o'er a lonely grave.
>
> Let the dragons of the past
> In their caverns sleeping lie.
> I am dream-betrayed, and cast
> Into that old agony.
>
> And an anguish of desire
> Burns as in the sunken years,
> And the soul sheds drops of fire
> All unquenchable by tears.
>
> I, who sought on high for calm,
> In the Ever-living find
> All I was in what I am,
> Fierce with gentle intertwined,
>
> Hearts that I had crucified,
> With my heart that tortured them –
> Penitence, unfallen pride,
> These my thorny diadem.
>
> Thou wouldst ease in heaven thy pain,
> O thou fiery, bleeding thing.
> All thy wounds will wake again
> At the heaving of a wing.
>
> All thy dead with thee shall rise,
> *Dies irae.* If the soul
> To the Ever-living flies
> There shall meet it at the goal

> Love that time had overlaid,
> Deaths that we again must die –
> Let the dragons we have made
> In their caverns sleeping lie!⁵⁸

This poem I call *Resurrection,* and it may explain why I speak of certain poems as oracles out of the psyche. They breathed out of some deep-remembered wisdom warning or guidance, for when the words swam up into consciousness there was more in them than the waking self had thought or known. I divined from it that before the psyche can be absorbed in spirit – the son in the bosom of the Father – there must be resurrection of the past, a resurrection of memory of all the evil we have done, and that agony must be endured.⁵⁹ After that may come the resurrection of what was lovely and beloved, of which I wrote elsewhere:

> I know when I come to my own immortal I will find there
> In a myriad instant all that the wandering soul found fair,
> Empires that never crumbled and thrones all glorious yet,
> And hearts ere they were broken and eyes ere they were wet.

It was from the early verses I wrote I had the clearest conviction of something in the deeps of being wiser than myself, with an age in thought and emotion which was not at all in the waking consciousness. I have told how when I was a boy I began to run in and out of the house of dream, and as I went inward an age of the spirit fell upon me, and then I would come out and be the careless boy once more with all youth in his emotions and acts. I must make plainer what I mean by this age of thought superimposed upon the outward nature. Sometimes, as I have said, the dream consciousness would flood the waking. At other times I would be drawn inward, and in that mid-world of the psyche there would arise not merely visions of things I held to be memories, but imaginations, tales and myths would arise which were purely symbolic. One of these early imaginations was a tale I wrote as *The Cave of Lilith.* It was born swiftly within me. There were three beings in the tale, an enchantress who symbolized that Maya⁶⁰ in which we look outside ourselves and gaze on the mirror of being rather than on being itself. There was a bad singer who symbolized the psyche caught in that Maya, and there was a Wise One who symbolized the Spirit. In my imagination Lilith the enchantress was exultant over the souls she kept in her cave, and she cried out to the Wise One:

'My illusions are sweeter to them than truth. I offer every soul its own

shadow. I pay them their own price. I have grown rich though the simple shepherds of old gave me birth. Men have made me.[61] The mortals have made me immortal. I rose up like a vapour from their first dreams, and every sigh since then and every laugh remains with me. I am made up of hopes and fears. The subtle princes lay out their plans of conquest in my cave, and there the hero dreams, and the lovers of all time write in flame their history. I am wise holding all experience to tempt, to blind, to terrify. None shall pass by me. The stars and the starry crown are not yours alone to offer, and every promise you make I make also. I offer the good and bad indifferently. The lover, the poet, the mystic, and all who would dream of the first fountain I delude with my mirage. I was the Beatrice who led Dante upward. The gloom was in me and the glory was mine also and he went not out of my cave. The stars and shining of heaven were illusions of the infinite I wove about him. A nutshell would have contained the film. I smote on the heart-chords the manifold music of being, God is sweeter in the human than the human in God. Therefore he rested in me. There is that fantastic fellow who slipped by me. Could your wisdom not retain him? He returned to me full of anguish. I wound my arms around him like a fair melancholy, and now his sadness is as sweet to him as hope before his fall. Listen to his song.'
A voice came from the depths chanting a sad knowledge:

> What of all the will to do?
> It has vanished long ago,
> For a dream-shaft pierced it through
> From the unknown archer's bow.
>
> What of all the soul to think?
> Someone offered it a cup,
> Filled with a diviner drink
> And the flame has burned it up.
>
> What of all the hope to climb?
> Only in the self we grope
> To the misty end of time.
> Truth has put an end to hope.
>
> What of all the heart to love?
> Sadder than for will or soul,
> No light lured it on above.
> Love has found itself the whole.

This fragment of a tale may make clear the mystery of such imaginations, how going inward I would be met by myth and dream, and they would unfold themselves with a swift concentration, though at the time I wrote this poem and imagined this myth the outward self, as Yeats recalls in his Memories, was stumbling and chaotic in speech, and, as I know, as confused and stumbling in mind, until I went into those mysterious depths of consciousness where I found the psyche waiting to initiate me into its own wisdom. There are many coloured tributaries of the river of life here which flow into it from uncharted regions of being. How can we explain the mystery of imagination, the power we discover in ourselves which leaps upon us, becoming master of ideas, images and words, taking control of these from the reasoning mind, giving to them symbolic meanings, until images, ideas and words, swept together, become an intellectual organism by some transcendental power superior to all reasoning? It is as mysterious as the growth of an organism in nature which draws from earth by some alchemy the essences it transmutes and makes subservient to itself. There was a greater age of thought in the imagination of *The Cave of Lilith* than there was in the outer mind,[62] a wisdom which had ransacked the treasure-house of thought, but had grown weary because thought of itself leads nowhere, but blows the perfume from every flower, and cuts the flower from every tree, and hews down every tree in the valley, and in the end goes to and fro gnawing itself in a last hunger.

I will try later to give reasons why I infer an interior creator of poetry and myth, a being with pre-natal wisdom, which exists in all of us trying to become self-conscious in the body. There are two wisdoms in us, the wisdom we are born with and the wisdom we acquire.[63] The outer mind grows but slowly to maturity, and even at its culmination it is never so wise as that other enriched by the garnered wisdom of countless lives. In the poetry of my boyhood there was, I think, some breathing of that inner wisdom. Its wisdom was not learned in any suffering here, and whatever anguish it may have been born out of lay far behind time.[64]

When I was about twenty-eight I began rapidly to adjust myself to the life about me, to lose the old confused timidity, and to talk with easy assurance to others. But while the outer mind became almost sage compared with the rambling immaturity of the young man, my most matured thought would seem young and immature whenever the psyche breathed its own wisdom. I had the gift of good health, the capacity to feel intense delight, and I never had any outward satiety such as follows a too avid thirst for pleasure. Yet, while the outer nature would be rapt in its imagination of love, there would break in upon its delight some oracle out of the psyche, a being to which our delight in beauty here was but a play which had lost meaning long ages ago.

We are desert leagues apart,
Time is misty ages now
Since the warmth of heart to heart
Chased the shadows from my brow.

Oh, I am so old, meseems
I am next of kin to Time,
The historian of her dreams
From the long-forgotten prime.

You have come a path of flowers.
What a way has mine to roam,
Many a fallen empire's towers,
Many a ruined heart my home.

No, there is no comfort, none.
All the dewy tender breath
Idly falls when life is done
On the starless brow of death.

Though the dream of love may tire,
In the ages long agone
There were ruby hearts on fire –
Ah, the daughters of the dawn!

Though I am so feeble now,
I remember when our pride
Could not to the Mighty bow.
We would sweep His stars aside.

Mix thy youth with thoughts like those –
It were but to wither thee,
But to graft the youthful rose
On the old and flowerless tree.

Age is no more near than youth
To the sceptre and the crown,
Vain the wisdom, vain the truth,
Do not lay thy rapture down.

I said I surmised a duality in the psyche, for the oracles it delivered in song often seemed to lead to opposing eternities. The wisdom before which love grew chill would be opposed by oracles speaking of an immortality of love. At one moment the psyche would seem to be redeemed from that passion; and then there would be an illumination of vision, and desire and imagination would be inflamed, and images would rush at me out of the deeps of life as creatures which had been long beloved, and which had been reborn to renew again their ecstasy. They carried with them in fantasy the setting of their lives, palaces and cities that had long crumbled into dust, and I was as ready to yield to love as if it had been born for the first time and had never known of its many cruelties and anguishes. This which follows was written close on the time when *The Grey Eros* was written.

The blue dusk ran between the streets. My love was winged within my mind.
It left day and yesterday and thrice a thousand years behind.
To-day was past and dead for me, for from to-day my feet had run
Through thrice a thousand years to walk the ways of ancient Babylon.
On temple top and palace roof the burnished gold flung back the rays
Of a red sunset that was dead and lost beyond a million days.
The tower of heaven turns darker blue, a starry sparkle now begins.
The mystery and magnificence, the myriad beauty and the sins
Come back to me. I walk beneath the shadowy multitude of towers.
Within the gloom the fountain jets its pallid mist in lily flowers.
The waters lull me and the scent of many gardens, and I hear
Familiar voices, and the voice I love is whispering in my ear.
Oh, real as in dream all this; and then a hand on mine is laid,
The wave of phantom time withdraws, and that young Babylonian maid,
One drop of beauty left behind from all the flowing of that tide,
Is looking with the self-same eyes, and here in Ireland by my side.
Oh, light our life in Babylon, but Babylon has taken wings,
While we are in the calm and proud procession of eternal things.

In that fierce illumination which gave birth to the poem I was surrounded by a wavering of phantom pictures. A dusky beauty all in rose and gold flowed to me. There were high buildings, strange cars or chariots, a great room with stone walls and an iron door, as if the whole of some gorgeous past wished to renew itself at that instant. Years after I read about some half-buried city in Bashan that the iron doors were still in the stone walls.

Here were voices out of the deep of being, an Eros that seemed to have run its race, and an Eros eager as if it ran to meet its first love. I have found this duality in everything in my life, and I can only surmise some wisdom, above the outworn heart and an eager heart, which understands that we cannot be wholly of this world or wholly of the heavenworld, and we cannot enter that Deity out of which came good and evil, light and darkness, spirit and matter, until our being is neither one or the other, but a fusion of opposites,[65] a unity akin to that Fulness where spirit, desire and substance are raised above themselves and exist in that mystic unity of all things which we call Deity.[66]

VI

I have spoken of certain poems as oracles out of the psyche, by which I imply they were conceived and fashioned by some high part of our dramatically sundered being and were breathed into the waking consciousness. I realize that what I have already written might have other interpretations, though I have never been able to explain the flooding of the waking consciousness with a dream story otherwise than by assuming it was a projection from a genie in some deep of our being. But at other times I found the relation between inner and outer not so debatable. I woke up one morning and some lines of verse tumbled out of the dream state into the waking.

> A wind blew by from icy hills,
> Shook with cold breath the daffodils,
> And shivered as with silver mist
> The lake's pale leaden amethyst.
>
> It pinched the barely budded trees,
> And rent the twilight tapestries,
> Left for one hallowed instant bare
> A single star in lonely air.

After these followed a line which seemed to have no relation to the preceding lines:

> The city with its burning piles.

I had an instinct that rather a long poem had been completed in dream, and that all I had to do was to let the poem drift into consciousness. Walking about the hills, in a few days the poem was completed. After about two hundred lines had been written down

> The city with its burning piles

fell into its proper place, and the plan of the poem *Michael* first became clear to myself. I noted that towards the close of the poem there were some verses suggesting that the real fountain of many acts lay in the kingdom of sleep.

> For many a one a tryst has kept
> With the immortal while he slept,
> Woke unremembering, went his way,
> Life seemed the same from day to day,
> Till the predestined hour came,
> A hidden will leapt up in flame,
> And through its deed the risen soul
> Strides on self-conquering to its goal.

Here at least was partial discovery in what region of our being was the foundry where poetry was fashioned. About eight or nine lines there could be no doubt. But at another time the revelation was complete. I was surprised by a sudden fiery rushing out of words from within me, and I took paper and pencil and wrote as rapidly as fingers could move the words which came to me; and I was aware from the first that all was complete, and the verses altogether seemed to float about the brain like a swarm of bees trying to enter a hive. It may be that they did not all find entry. I did not know what idea was in the poem until it was written down. It seemed to be a wild dialogue between the shadowy self and some immortal consciousness which was making vast and vague promises to the lower if it would but surrender itself to the guidance of that heavenly shepherd.

> 'Who art thou, O glory,
> In flame from the deep,
> Where stars chant their story,
> Why trouble my sleep?
> I hardly had rested,
> My dreams wither now,
> Why comest thou crested
> And gemmed on thy brow?'
> 'Up, shadow, and follow
> The way I will show.
> The blue-gleaming hollow
> To-night thou shalt know,
> And rise mid the vast to
> The fountain of days,
> From whence we had passed to
> The parting of ways.'

> 'I know thee, O glory,
> Thine eyes and thy brow,
> With white fire all hoary,

Come back to me now.
Together we wandered
In ages agone,
Our thoughts as we pondered
Were stars at the dawn.
My glory has dwindled;
My azure and gold;
Yet you keep enkindled
The sun-fire of old.
My footsteps are tied to
The heath and the stone,
My thoughts earth-allied-to.
Ah, leave me alone.
Go back, thou of gladness,
Nor wound me with pain,
Nor smite me with madness,
Nor come nigh again.'

'Why tremble and weep now,
Whom stars once obeyed?
Come forth to the deep now
And be not afraid.
The Dark One is calling,
I know, for his dreams
Around us are falling
In musical streams.
A diamond is burning
In deeps of the Lone,
Thy spirit returning
May claim for its throne.
In flame-fringed islands
Its sorrows shall cease,
Absorbed in the silence
And quenched in the peace.
Come lay thy poor head on
My heart where it glows
With love ruby red on
Thy heart for its woes.
My power I surrender,
To thee it is due,
Come forth, for the splendour
Is waiting for you!'

I do not think it a very good poem whatever dream may be in it. Nor do I wish to distinguish my verses from the poetry of others as being communicated in any abnormal way, as I believe all poetry is born beneath the dream consciousness. I have only been more curious than others about the forge in which poetry is fashioned, and when, as in that wild dialogue between Glory and Shadow, I know that the waking consciousness had nothing whatever to do with the making of it, and not until it was written down did I know the purport of what was written, I could only assume an internal creator. In almost everything I wrote, even though the words did not rush so swiftly from inner to outer, I had this element of surprise in the uprising of poetry when the superficial consciousness is made brilliant by a light or power flooding it from within.

Where, then, are the ideas in poetry given an organic form? Where are the images we see in symbolic dream set in motion? Whence come vision and high imagination? I think they come from a centre of consciousness behind the sphere of dream. Here I pass from experience to rely on intuition and the wisdom of others. It is to the seers who wrote the Upanishads[67] I turn for illumination. They speak of four states of the soul – waking, dreaming, deep sleep and spirit waking – the last a state in which the spirit is unsleeping in its ecstasy of infinite vision.[68] I quote in what follows from an interpretation of my own of those four phases of soul the seers spoke of.

> The Vedic seers had a more grandiose tale
> Of what lay in the secrecy of sleep,
> The soul gone into itself, its gates
> Barred upon earth, earth's magic stilled within
> The sleepy mind, the candles of dream all blown.
> when sleep is dreamless the gold-gleaming genius[69]
> Awakens laughing, immortal, so they say,
> Making music, chariot, dance and song,
> Cities and palaces and lamps in heaven,
> And meadows for the dancing feet, and lakes
> Gaudy with light, and flaring forest glades
> Where wind bewildered the mad sun-fire reels,
> And rainbow-tinted the lovely dryads whirl
> In carnival, a lustrous mirage for ever
> Glowing and changing at the heart's desire,
> As if the Arabian genii were its slaves.
> And after that glorying in beauty and power
> The genius becomes inexpressibly old,
> Returning into the Ancient of Days. It must
> As the diver under deep water must
> Rise to the air for life, so every night
> The soul must rise and go unto its Father,
> For a myriad instant breathing eternity.
> And then, returning by the way it came,
> It wakes here to renew its cyclic labours.

In that mysterious journeying from time to eternity, where the soul moves on to ever higher planes of its own being, there must be many transformations of the psyche. Something I think goes with it from this world to that other. 'The gods feed upon men.' Something comes back with it from Heaven to Earth. 'The gods nourish us.' There is, I believe, some commerce between this world and that other. As our aspiration is, so is our inspiration. The higher nature takes our fragmentary knowledge, thought, experience, and our aspiration, which is sacrifice, and it is transfigured, made whole and returned to us. What is earth-born is lifted up and perfected, shot through and through with the light of that higher world where the psyche nigh to its divine root imagines the perfection or truth in all things. Much must be lost of that transcendental lucidity and beauty of the heavenly consciousness when the psyche sinks through murky clouds of desire back to the body again.[70] But something returns. There are many I know who are not mystics who do yet before sleeping confide their questioning to a wisdom they divine is unsleeping while the body sleeps. The doctor is confirmed in his diagnosis. The scientist receives his flash of intuition about the laws of nature. The worshipper is endowed with inward peace, or the stirring of conscience tells him where he has erred and strayed. The poet feels the Magician of the Beautiful stirring in his imagination. It is, I think, in one of the higher transfigurations of the psyche beyond the mid-world of dream, in that phase where it is creator, that poetry is born. The seer of the Upanishads speaks of that state.[71]

> There are no chariots there nor streets for chariots. The soul makes himself chariots and streets for chariots. Nor are any delights there nor joys nor rejoicings. The soul makes for himself joys and rejoicings . . . For the soul of man is creator.

The words of the seer imply that there come up to that high world images of the earth-world, chariots, lotus ponds, joys and rejoicings; and, taking images and ideas, the god-lit psyche makes its magical play as a great poet transfiguring the things his eyes have seen and making of them a wonder-world of his own, of magic casements, perilous seas and forlorn fairylands. Here, too, the soul being immortal, would be memories of its journeyings from the beginning of time, of religions and civilizations which are all built about some divine idea, some hope of liberty, power or beauty breathed into men from the divinity which overshadows them. The soul returns by the way it came from those high spheres to the body to take up its labours in this world. What are its labours? It has to make conquest of this world, become master of the nature which envelops us, until the eternal is conscious in us, and we have made this world into a likeness or harmony with the Kingdom of Light. As our being here becomes transparent to the Light we receive more and more of the true. Intuitions begin to leap up in us every instant, and we receive, according to our capacity, vision, imagination, knowledge of past and future, illuminations about the nature of things, wisdom and poetry. The fountain of all these lies deep within us where the psyche in ceaseless ecstasy responds to the Will[72] that moves the universe and translates the wisdom of that being into the intellectual fires of the Paraclete, and its fiery tongues[73] give the divine signature to our thoughts.[74] The divine receives from the mortal and returns our sacrifice changed by some heavenly alchemy into substances which have the divine signature upon them. That high centre within us where the images of earth are so glorified and returned to us I call the Mount of Transfiguration,[75] and one of the earliest breathings out of the psyche which came to me spoke of this transfiguration.

> Those delicate wanderers,
> The wind, the star, the cloud,
> Ever before mine eyes
> As to an altar bowed,
> Light and dew-laden airs
> Offer in sacrifice.
>
> The offerings arise,
> Hazes of rainbow light,
> Pure crystal, blue and gold,
> Through dreamland take their flight,
> And mid the sacrifice
> God moveth as of old.
>
> In miracles of fire
> He symbols forth His days,
> In dreams of crystal light
> Reveals what pure pathways
> Lead to the soul's desire
> The silence of the height.

VII

Earth does not give us more 'sweet things out of our corruption' than the soul gives us for the dust of thought if it was gathered while we were travelling towards the Spirit. I know many will say if they knew all I had read or experienced before the poem was shaped they could find all the materials ready for fusion without calling on some high genie in consciousness to account for a lustre to me otherwise inexplicable. The effort to reassemble the ingredients of poetry pre-existing before the poem was made at immense length in *The Road to Xanadu,* but the logic of that analysis would almost lead to the assumption that when the palette is spread with colour it accounts for the masterpiece. In my own retrospective meditation I could discover often the elements later fused into poetry without this to me lessening the mystery. I remember reading about forty years ago a criticism of Hegel's philosophy of the Absolute becoming self-conscious in the unfolding of the universe. The writer's objection was that no change could take place in that which was already absolute and perfect, but that it might be said of the divine mind in its going forth through nature. I do not know why this logic remained in memory. A little later I found some Indian mystic correlating divine mind with primordial substance. In my own imagination I had thought of primordial substance as the mirror of that Mind and therefore the Ancient Beauty.[76] So were assembled in my mind before the birth of a poem the ideas implicit in it. But when the poem was born it was as much a surprise to me as if a flower had suddenly glowed before me in the hollow of air.

> Its edges foamed with amethyst and rose,
> Withers once more the old blue flower of day.
> There where the aether like a diamond glows
> Its petals fade away.
>
> A shadowy tumult stirs the dusky air:
> Sparkle the delicate dews, the distant snows;
> The great deep thrills, for through it everywhere
> The breath of Beauty blows.
>
> I saw how all the trembling ages past,
> Moulded to her by deep and deeper breath,
> Near to the hour when Beauty breathes her last
> And knows herself in death.

The verses came to me almost as swift as thought one evening while I was sitting on some rocks. There was no preconsciousness of the idea before I began to murmur line after line. I was unconscious of creation. It is true that antecedent to the poem there were certain ideas gathered months before, but not at all in memory when the poem came to me. The ideas were there as colours might lie on a palette, but the artist who blended them and who made the design was behind the consciousness which received the words. Whatever went to making an intricate harmony of colour and sound, the imagination of the ending of the long tale of time, of nature become so ethereal that it was the perfect mirror of deity, and the withdrawal of the universe into the Pleroma, all that was wrought in some secret laboratory within the psyche. I remember my own delighted surprise when a line came,

> Withers once more the old blue flower of day,

as if it had been read in the song of another poet. I can only assume that the philosophical antecedents in some way followed the psyche into that high state where, as the seers tell us, the gold-gleaming genius makes beauty, joys, rejoicings, dance and song, and it changed the dry-as-dust logic into colour and music and a rapture of prophecy.

I do not know in the ascension to the spiritual of our earth-born ideas as they reach the immortal whether they break out in a glory of words, a glory of images or a glory of thought, or whether these coexist in a glory of being. What comes back to us from that high sphere loses beauty in its descent, as Ishtar[77] in the Chaldean myth had crown and sceptre and the royalty of her robes taken from her when descending from heaven to earth. I know that there is loss, for once consciousness was kindled in me in the deep of sleep. I was in some profundity of being. There was neither sight nor sound, but all was a motion in deep being. Struggling desperately to remain there, I was being dragged down to the waking state, and then what was originally a motion in deep being broke into a dazzle of images which symbolized in some dramatic way the motion of life in that profundity. And still being drawn down there came a third state in which what was originally deep own-being, and after that images, was later translated into words. This experience I told to Yeats, who said he had an identical experience of the three states. But even what I remembered of this threefold change may itself have been but remembered symbolic dream. But I surmise that whatever faint relation to divine being there may be in our waking thought, as it ascends to the fourth state of spirit-illumination,[78] the germinal idea is perfected. From the segment the circle is completed, and its perfection is the mirroring in the psyche of the archetype of the idea in the divine mind. Here we only receive frail echoes in words which do not hold at all or only a faint trace of the pristine and magical beauty, as in a muddy street may shine faintly in its wetness the reflection of a star.

I discovered too that when the waking consciousness imagined it had found matter for fine poetry in something heard or read, and it tried to shape the idea into poetical form, it often received no aid from the genie within. The India sages[79] say the spirit is not taken by thought. It takes whom it wills. By this I understand that wisdom in such matters comes from within. The idea brings itself to birth. I once read a fragment quoted from the Vaishnava scriptures about the childhood of Krishna;[80] how he ran on all fours over the household, yet the sages spoke of him as the Ancient and Unborn; how he played with the milkmaids, yet he was called the Purest of the Pure and the most ascetic of sages allowed the claim. From this I turned away with the outer mind and I tried to imagine a poem of lovers in the Indian forest, where men and maidens went past the body and saw within each other god and goddess, Radha and Krishna.[81] But the poem would not write itself. Then the psyche some years after projected into the waking consciousness its own transfiguration of the fragment, completing the cycle of life from birth to death, in which there is always the mystery of fallen life and unfallen majesty together in the same being.

I paused beside the cabin door and saw the King of Kings at play,
Tumbled upon the grass I spied the little heavenly runaway
The mother laughed upon the child made gay by its ecstatic morn,
But yet the sages spake of It as of the Ancient and Unborn.
I heard the passion breathed amid the honeysuckle-scented glade,
And saw the King pass lightly from the beauty that He had betrayed.
I saw him change from love to love. But yet the pure allowed His claim
To be the purest of the pure, thrice holy, stainless, without blame.
I saw the open tavern-door flash on the dusk a ruddy glare,
And saw the King of Kings outcast reel brawling through the starlit air.
But yet He is the Prince of Peace whom the ancient wisdom tells,
And by their silence men adore the lovely silence where He dwells.
I saw the King of Kings again, a thing to shudder at and fear,
A form so darkened and so marred that childhood fled if it drew near.
And yet He is the Light of Lights whose blossoming is Paradise,
That Beauty of the King which dawns before the seer's enraptured eyes.
I saw the King of Kings again, a miser with a heart grown cold;
And yet He is the Prodigal, the Spendthrift of the Heavenly Gold,
The largesse of whose glory crowns the blazing brows of cherubim,
And sun and moon and starry fires are jewels scattered forth by Him.
I saw the King of Kings descend the narrow doorway to the dust
With all his fires of morning still, the beauty, bravery and lust,
And yet He is the life within the Ever-living Living Ones,
The Ancient with Eternal Youth, the cradle of the infant suns,
The fiery fountain of the stars, and He the golden urn where all
The glittering spray of planets in their myriad beauty fall.

I had always the sense of a will above my own, and if I turned from it I had no inspiration. My friend Yeats believes poetry to be fashioned more by the conscious mind, but how could he choose so perfectly among words if there was not a perfection of which he was unconscious which was within him to guide his choice? I did find as I grew older that I had a more conscious art in verse-making, as if the psyche had found a place in the waking mind and there was less of a dramatic sundering between the creative and the receiving consciousness. A poem like that from which I quoted my interpretation of the Upanishadic teaching about the phases of sleep seemed to me the outcome of the external mind grown to some maturity of its own, and able to act and think from its own centre,[82] whereas when I was young I had little but intuition. In my age, too, I think I shape poetry more out of my experience of life, as in the poem *Germinal* in the first chapter of this book. The things I did when I was younger have been brooded over, and something of the brooding has gone inward to the realm of the Interpreter and been returned with some wisdom of the Interpreter added to it. But though the later poems appear to be more the product of the conscious waking mind, I am not sure that I am not deceived about this, and they may be as much born in the deeps of being as the earlier verses which came like words whispered from another nature. I do not know whether I am still receiving oracles out of the psyche, or whether I am not like that sad singer lost in the Caves of Lilith, playing with symbols left in a temple from which the divinity had departed, where the ancient ritual is still sung but in the absence of the indwelling god.

VIII

I am a far exile from that great glory which inhabits the universe, and can but peer through some momentary dusky transparency in my nature to a greater light than the light of day. I know the royal road is by practice of the great virtues. But I cannot speak that language or urge those obligations, I who have been angry and sensual. I can only speak where I have been faithful. I have never ceased from the inward search, and might by that faithfulness have gone far if I had not a rabble of desires tugging me by the skirts to travel alluring roads in the world of illusion. I could peer only a little way, apprehending behind form the Creator, behind thought the Thinker, behind intuition the Seer, behind conscience the Love, and in fallen life some still unfallen majesty, and even in the basest desires could find signs of their spiritual ancestry.

> There was never sin of thine
> But within its heart did dwell
> A beauty that could whisper thee
> Of the high heaven from which it fell.

I tell what I have surmised or discovered, by reason perhaps of that uncorrupted spiritual atom in my nature. I know there must be error even in our highest approaches to the true if the whole nature has not been purified and made transparent. Emanations from our dark untransmuted desires must discolour our vision.[83] The deepest things in my life came to me in the form of poetry, and I brooded upon every circumstance in its uprising that I might discover its ancestral fountain. However slight may be the song contrasted with the great poetry of the world, it was as high above my normal mood as that great poetry is above mine. I could not but wonder at it, for at times there was some magic in its coming which seemed almost to dissolve the personality. A music would be born in the deeps of being which could not get completely incarnated in the words, but which swept them together until they were not at all like the stumbling, almost inarticulate, speech of the boy. I remember as if yesterday that day in my youth when a mystical music was born in me before ever thought came or the words that followed.

When the breath of twilight blows to flame the misty skies,
All its vaporous sapphire, violet glow and silver gleam,
With their magic flood me through the gateway of the eyes.
I am one with the twilight's dream.

When the trees and skies and fields are one in their dusky mood
Every heart of man is rapt within the mother's breast.
Full of peace and sleep and dream in the vasty quietude,
I am one with their hearts at rest.

From our immemorial joys of hearth and home and love,
Strayed away along the margin of the unknown tide,
All its reach of soundless calm can thrill me far above
Words or touch from the lips beside.

Aye, and deep and deep and deeper let me drink and draw
From the olden fountain more than light or peace or dream;
Such primaeval being as o'erfills the heart with awe
Growing one with its silent stream.

By the magic of that music which so rose within me the universe seemed to reel away from me, and to be remote and unsubstantial as the most distant nebulae, and for some minutes I was able to re-create within myself the musical movement of the power, and could stay the soul upon the high uplands. But it quickly vanished as a dream might go after our waking, and try as I might I could not recall it again. But for a moment I understood what power might be in sound or incantation. It made me understand a little those mystics who speak of travelling up a Jacob's Ladder of Sound to the Logos,[84] the fountain of all melody. I found later if meditation on the Spirit is prolonged and profound enough we enter on a state where our being is musical, not a music heard without but felt within as if the soul itself had become music,[85] or had drawn nigh to the ray of the Logos, the Master Singer, and was for that instant part of its multitudinous song. While *By the Margin of the Great Deep* was being conceived I felt that music in my being before the words were swept together, a state akin to that I experienced waking in dream when I followed in their descending order the phases from deep own-being through images or symbols to their last echo in words. I held these memories with others akin to them, hoping that at last I might understand the psyche and come to some mastery of the hidden powers. I do not think we shall ever come to truth otherwise than by such gropings in the cave of the soul, when with shut eyes we are in a dim illuminated darkness, and seek through transient transparencies to peer into the profundities of being. It is the most exciting of all adventures, the exploration of the psyche, even though the windows out of which we gaze are soon darkened for us by our own bodily emanations. Yet there are enchanted moments when we have vision, however distant, of the divinities who uphold the universe. It is true we are at an immense distance from their greatness, and see them as a shepherd boy far away among his hills might see the glittering of the army of a great king, and he is awed by the majesty and bows low at the vision of greatness, and dreams over it when the army is past and he turns to his humble task with his sheep. So remotely is it I have apprehended splendours overshadowing my insignificance. They stand over all of us. I think if we chose the least inspiring among those we know, one seeming not at all puissant or entitled to respect, and could know of the immortal powers which uphold the frailty of his being, his darkened life would seem to the imagination to move in a blaze of glory.[86]

There are many who would speak lightly of the serious mood in which I pondered over the songs which I think of as oracles out of the psyche. Yet they themselves may pay reverence to the voices of conscience or of intuition which also are oracles out of undiscovered depths in their own being, and intuition and conscience may utter themselves in song as well as in fugitive illuminations of mind, heart or will. My meditations were all intent on the discovery of the nature of soul and spirit. I write now in age, remembering indeed the circumstance about the writing of poetry, but there is some blurring of intensity and keenness of mind, and I cannot re-create the old intensity of emotion or thought.

No sooner does there come illumination than it is gone. I cannot stay it for an instant. Time inexorably hurries us from the god who dies away in hazes of memory, hurries us from exultation, exquisite ardours, emotions and anguish, and from the dead with whom we had willingly died so that we might go hand in hand with them into the darkness. I have deferred too long this work, for I can no more evoke the magic of moods that might have brought with me those who read, and I would not have been so frail a guide for them in the labyrinths of being. But as we near the end of our stay here, knowing we must soon start on other travelling, we begin thought on what we would take with us. In our last meditations we gather together in soul[87] what was most precious to pay for a habitation in the country in which we shall be newcomers. The seers who had known not only life but death said that what we think of last here is the starting-point of life in that other world, and that death is the beginning of a long meditation in which soul returns to spirit, the Son to the Father, as a prince who has led armies goes back to his king with the spoils of conquest. As we travel inward from time to the Ever-living we shall, if our thought be set on that and not on the desires of the body, regain what had passed from us here. As I get older my poetry seems to be less revelation out of the psyche than the summing up of whatever wisdom the outer mind had gathered. But almost the last poem which seemed to me to come out of the genie in the innermost with the old authenticity made promise that no precious thing would be lost, and when we went inward to our own immortal we would regain all that Time had taken away.

> Be not so desolate
> Because thy dreams have flown,
> And the hall of heart is empty
> And silent as stone,
> As age left by children
> Sad and alone.
>
> Those delicate children,
> Thy dreams, still endure.
> All pure and lovely things
> Wend to the Pure.
> Sigh not. Unto the fold
> Their way was sure.
>
> Thy gentlest dreams, thy frailest,
> Even those that were
> Born and lost in a heart-beat,
> Shall meet thee there.
> They are become immortal
> In shining air.
>
> The unattainable beauty,
> The thought of which was pain,
> That flickered in eyes and on lips
> And vanished again;
> That fugitive beauty
> Thou shalt attain.

Those lights innumerable
That led thee on and on,
The masque of time ended,
Shall glow into one.
They shall be with thee for ever,
Thy travel done.

IX

I think all true poetry was conceived on the Mount of Transfiguration and there is revelation in it and the mingling of heaven and earth. The Mount is a symbol for that peak of soul when, gone inward into itself, it draws nigh to its own divine root, and memory and imagination are shot through and through with the radiance of another nature. It is not alone poetry definitely mystical which is so conceived. The romantic imagination, equally with the mystical, released from the clog of our slower, more static nature, blossoms into its own ideal. There the imagination might move with the wizard airy glow of the *Ancient Mariner* or *Kubla Khan,* or have the stained glass richness of the *Eve of St. Agnes,* or the heart-choking sweetness of Shelley's music, or the phantom beauty of *Usheen* in Tirnanoge, or build itself a *Palace of Art* with exquisite enamellings on its cloud-built chambers. Whatever is germinal here finds there its perfection and culmination. Our inspiration will be as our aspiration. A seer in the Upanishads said of the seeker:

> Let him approach it saying, 'This is the Mighty.'
> He becomes mighty. Let him approach it saying,
> 'This is the Wise.' He becomes filled with wisdom.
> Let him approach it saying, 'This is the Maker of the
>   Song.' He becomes the Maker of the Song.

There are many who are not consciously mystical but who do yet before they sleep rest on and confide to some dweller in the innermost their problems, having found that what was obscure often became clear on their waking. Some healers I have known refer their doubts about a diagnosis to this wisdom which has never been to the schools. From this being comes the revealing flash to the scientist, the intuition about law or the movement of forces; and knowledge might rightly come from a ray of that Mind which is Shepherd over the vast horde of elements and powers, for the maker of the law needs no mechanism to discover the law. I do not know of any psychology which so spiritually excites me as this of the nightly return of the soul to the divine order, that we who through the day are absorbed in petty labours do go back to an unfallen nature, unto our own high magnificence, and are in council with the Cosmocratores.[88] Our Eden is not left behind time, but is all about us and within us, a paradise to be regained as we regain the innocence of wisdom. Many a time has this thought comforted me in fœtid slum and murky alley where the devil hath his many mansions. Passing through these I would remember the peaks reached in meditation, and the wisdom of the seers who taught that all these creatures slip away from their wretchedness, from that diabolical riot to the ancient beauty. For every one of these wretched were spoken the comforting words of the Ancestral Self, 'I will not leave thee or forsake thee,' and again of all these it was written, 'Their angels do always behold the face of the Father.'

By many a dream of God and man my thoughts in shining flocks were led,
But as I went through Patrick Street the hopes and prophecies were dead.
The hopes and prophecies were dead. They could not blossom where the feet
Walked amid rottenness nor where the brawling shouters stamped the street.
Where was the beauty that the Lord gave men when first they towered in pride?
But one came by me at whose word the bitter condemnation died.
His brows were crowned with thorns of light. His eyes were bright as one who sees
The starry palaces shine o'er the sparkle of the heavenly seas.
'Is it not beautiful?' He cried, 'Our Fairyland of Heart's Desire
Is mingled through the mire and mist, yet stainless keeps its lovely fire.
The pearly children with blown hair are dancing where the drunkards reel:
The cloud-frail daffodils shine out where filth is splashing from the heel.
O sweet and sweet and sweet to hear, the melodies in rivers run.
The rapture of their crowded notes is yet the myriad voice of One.
Those who are lost and fallen here to-night in sleep shall pass the gate,
Put on the purples of the King and know them masters of their fate.
Each wrinkled hag shall reassume the blooms and hues of Paradise,

Each brawler be enthroned in calm among the children of the Wise.
Yet in the council with the gods no one will falter to pursue.
His lofty purpose but come forth the cyclic labours to renew,
And take the burden of the world and dim his beauty in a shroud
And wrestle with the chaos till the Anarch to the light be bowed.
We cannot for forgetfulness forgo the reverence due to them
Who wear at times they do not guess the sceptre and the diadem.
As bright a crown as thus was theirs when first they from the Father sped.
Yet look with deeper eyes and still the ancient beauty is not dead.'
He mingled with the multitude. I saw their brows were crowned and bright,
A light about the shadowy heads, a shadow round the brows of light.

It is implied in this that we came to this world by our own will and for some purpose, and this thought has been with me since I was a boy, when I broke out in a fierce revolt at the idea that I was born into this world not by my own will and would be punished if I neglected to do what I had never undertaken to do. I remember the deep peace which came to me when I had the intuition that Christ, Prometheus, are in every heart,[89] that we all took upon ourselves the burden of the world like the Christ, and were foreseers as Prometheus was of the agony of the labour he undertook, until the chaos is subdued and wrought in some likeness to the image in the divine imagination.

It will be seen that I look on the poet as prophet. I think, indeed, that almost the only oracles which have been delivered to humanity for centuries have come through the poets,[90] though too often they have not kept faith with the invisible and have been guilty of the sin of simony. But at times they still receive the oracles, as did the sybils of old, because in the practice of their art they preserve the ancient tradition of inspiration and they wait for it with airy uplifted mind. They know, as Corot knew about painting, that you must go a little beyond yourself, and whatever revelation of beauty, of the spirit, has been in Europe for many centuries has come, not from the Churches, who hold they already have truth, but from the poets who are still the seekers, and who at times have that lordly utterance as if the God was speaking through His prophets.

Let no one assume that I claim for even their highest utterance that infallibility which those who do not desire to think ask from their teachers, but it is through the poets and musicians alone that we get the sense of a glory transmitted from another nature, and as we mingle our imagination with theirs we are exalted and have the heartache of infinite desire. Truth for us cannot be in statements of ultimates but in an uplifting of our being,[91] in which we are raised above ourselves and know that we are knocking at the door of the Household of Light. The poets and the great masters of music are those who have the expectation of inspiration. They wait upon the gods though they may not know when they turn inward in reverie what being it is upon whom they wait. They receive according to the quality of their desire. It may be with one but a momentary glow, an inner music imposed upon the words they use, a heartache in lovely distances, a tenderness dropping through the air, a love breathed upward through the dark clay, a beauty born out of suffering or a blinding revelation. But the oracle has in it some magic of a higher nature woven into music so that it can be remembered and may re-create the wonder out of which it was born. It is probable that the bad hexameters in which the Oracles of Apollo were delivered in the decadence of the mysteries continued the tradition of a time when the Earth-born waited on the Heaven-born in a rapt awe and the immortals uttered their oracles, a divine speech, through the purity of prophet or priest.[92] No Church to-day can convince me that it is inspired until the words arising from it even in anger break in a storm of beauty on the ear.

X

I have been exploring so far as I might into the psyche and the worlds it moves in, and its action upon waking consciousness. I had vivid memories of the projection of dream stories from inner to outer, of waking and finding words rushing out of dream into waking, of what seemed to me transient intersectings of the circle of my own being with the lives of others brought about by some spiritual affinity. I have told something of these. About a large part of the verse I wrote I have no such vivid memories, for the fusion between inner and outer was too swift, and I could not get evidence of the duality between creator and recipient which I surmised. If I had not these other memories I might have thought there was nothing in poetry more than an intensity of waking imagination. But in that retrospective meditation I found things which were curious, a guidance from within in regard to my intellectual interests. I had begun after I was thirty or thereabouts to evolve a quick superficial intelligence, interests in art, economics and politics and the ideas which excited my own generation. It was that quickness of mind which enabled me a little later to live as a critic of politics, economics and literature. I never found conscience or intuition staying my mind when I engaged in these necessary duties. But if I thought of using imagination apart from these obligations, to draw upon the psyche to aid me in works of imagination other than mystical poetry or mystical prose, I would find no inspiration. I could imagine easily original plots for stories or plays, but never received any impulse to write them. I had no glow of excitement at the thought of writing a great story or a great play. It was not my Dharma,[93] as the Indians would say. Everyone in their philosophy has some particular work to do, and to desert that and attempt the work of others, however estimable, is full of danger. Everything of which I had inner approval was related to the search for the spirit, and when I would bend my mind upon other things, try for instance to plan out a long tale, I would find myself led back to my own centre. Imagination would move as a bubble under water which is for ever seeking to rise to its native air. It may be delayed under rock or water-weed, but it slips ever upward until at last it comes to the surface. I remember I once planned out a tale about a novelist who had gone into the country to write a long story. There were two characters, a man and a woman, who had begun to live with a vivid actuality in his mind. He could see them moving about and he knew what was in their thoughts. It was their custom in the evening to walk along a ridge of rock which ran out into the sea. They would sit there and talk. The man had a rich vitality and many ambitions, but the whole life of the girl was rooted in that country of mountains, lakes and sea. There was love but some sundering of ideals between these twain. While the story-teller was putting his imagination into words he was visited by a friend who enquired about his work. He told him a little about the two characters he had imagined, and his friend cried out, 'But I know two people exactly like that,' and he went on talking about them. As he talked the story-teller suddenly realized that what he thought was pure imagination was really a vision of life, for his friend had told him things about the man and woman which he had already known and written down. He said nothing, but, when his friend had gone, he surrendered himself more and more to his imagination about the two. The artist in him demanded a rather tragic end of the spiritual conflict. Some months later the story-teller's friend visited him again, and the story-teller asked him about those two who were so like his imagined characters. The friend told him about a trouble which had risen between them, and the story-teller suddenly realized that his own powerful imagination had been moulding their actions toward a tragic end. And in my imaginary tale the story-teller in a panic went a long journey to break in upon the man and girl and tell them what havoc he had been making of their love, and it was he and not they themselves who had brought them to this tragic sundering of their lives.

When I had imagined so far I lost interest in the tale and the man. I began to think of that mystical girl, and could see her alone and without any unhappiness, not with that lover but with a thousand loves. And the moment I saw her so, the bubble of the spiritual imagination, which had been hindered on its way to light by that cloud of circumstance, slipped from beneath the last obstruction, and a poem which seemed to have been waiting for a mood in which it could incarnate began at once to sing itself in my mind.

> A myriad loves
> Her heart would confess
> That thought but one
> To be wantonness.
>
> And this was why
> She could not stay,
> From the gilded fireside
> Running away,
>
> To be on the hillside,
> Gay and alone,
> A twilight Sibyl
> With rock for her throne.
>
> There she was sweetheart
> To magical things,
> To cloudland, woodland,
> Mountains and springs.
>
> She yielded to them,
> But was not the less
> Pure, but the more,
> For that wantonness.
>
> For through these lovers
> Her spirit grew
> To be clear as crystal
> And cool as dew.
>
> Their bridal gift
> Was to make her be
> Initiate
> Of their company;

To know the lovely
Voices of these,
Of light, of earth,
Of wind and of trees,

Whose wisdom flowed
From a fullness, yea,
From bygone ages
And far away.

So thronged was her spirit
It seemed a pack
That carried the moon
And stars on her back.

When the spirit wakens
It will not have less
Than the whole of life
For its tenderness.

And that was why
She could not stay,
From the gilded fireside
Running away.

She laughed in herself
On her seat of stone.
'It would be wanton
To love but one.'

I could tell many tales of what at first seemed a wandering of the imagination, but from which I was finally led back to my destiny as mystical poet. I felt as if there was a shepherd within who brought back the flock of strayed desires and fancies to a fold which was their own. Even in my economic studies which led me to write *The National Being* I was brought to think less of circumstance than of the spirit behind national movements, and from that I was brought to the more completely mystical mood of *The Interpreters,* where the politic of the characters is traced back to motions in Anima Mundi.[94] However I might wander in imagination, misled by desires, fantasy or ambition, an uneasy undercurrent set in, and I was guided back to the path from which I had so often strayed. I came at last almost to believe that, like Ulysses in the Platonic myth,[95] I had chosen before birth a life in which I was primarily to be mystic, and I could not conflict with that primal will without finding many of the inhabitants of the soul deserting me. It is not merely in moral crises that interior guidance begins to manifest as conscience. There is not a moment in life, not the least action or thought, where the spiritual law if supplicated is not ready to declare itself.[96]

Do I build too much upon too slight foundations? But do we not all in life follow the faintest stars which flicker in the gloom of being? Do we not really trust these faint lights of intuition, because they are lights, more than reason, which is often too slow a councillor for us to resort to. They may seem to mislead us, those lights, but one never went out before another and brighter light had glowed to lead us out of that cave of the body[97] in which we are confined. Life and feeling are too swift runners for us to run alongside them unless we have as guide a pace-maker, intuition, which is swift as any.

XI

I had found the genie in the innermost sometimes overcoming me by an enchantment of dream flooding the waking consciousness, not merely when I was meditative, but when I was at other work or walking in the streets or on country roads. At other times I found the poem or the idea of a poem rushing directly on me out of sleep as if it were an outcast from light. Again I found the inspiration for poetry in what I believe was a momentary fusion of my own being with the souls of others brought into a psychic intimacy by some affinity of emotion or thought. I have now to tell how a symbolic vision or dream was projected into the waking consciousness while I was engaged in meditation. In this meditation, when I had closed my eyes, the psyche became like one of those crypts of the mysteries where, as the ancients relate, they saw images of gods and immortals in a clear, immovable and blessed light. But what I first saw was not a clear light, but the darkness of the cave, that cloudy gloom we peer into when we shut out the light of this world. Then the gloom began to become alive with moving forms. I was looking into an immense chamber in which huge misshapen beings, part monster animal, part giant man, moved restlessly. The only clear light in that darkness was a kind of fiery twilight glittering with stars, the gleaming from a golden throne at the far end of that chamber, a light, it seemed, caught from a last inflammation in the sky which came through a gigantic doorway facing the throne. On this throne sat one who seemed to be King, a being of a higher order than those misshapen creatures who prowled about the hall. There was a dim radiance about his head. He seemed sunken in melancholy, oblivious of the monsters sprawling before him. Beside the King, with a hand upon the throne, was a slender beautiful girl. Then my own understanding was quickened, for the genie in the innermost who projected these images before the inner eye had flooded the mind with understanding, and I knew at once this King was Nuada of the Silver Hand,[98] who was King of the Tuatha De Danann[99] when they were overcome by the dark Fomorian powers.[100] Some time before this I had been reading ancient Irish saga, and one scholar had found something which linked Nuada to a Norse divinity,[101] a god who sacrificed himself, and I had said to myself, 'Nuada may be the Prometheus of the ancient Irish.' My interpretation of the vision was that I had gone asleep and had carried this speculation into the psyche and up to that higher state of soul where the imagination 'goes forth' to use Blake's phrase, 'in its uncurbed glory.' And it had imagined in completeness a vast myth, and, when later I began my nightly meditation, I was met in the mid-world by these images projected from the Mount of Transfiguration. The dream-pictures had a swift movement and as swift an interpretation. I knew as I looked on these images that Nuada was the heroic heaven-descended will, and he had come with other divine companions to earth to conquer it and bring wisdom to its dark inhabitants. But the brightness of the immortals had been obscured by a sorcery breathing out of earth. These monstrous shapes were earth-born passions and desires which had enslaved the incarnate divinity. The divine powers had on earth been turned to infernal uses. Angus, the Celtic Eros, was singing love songs for the Fomorians. Diancecht, the god physician, had become healer of their loathsome diseases. Dana clothed their terrible desires with beauty. Ogma, the champion, taught them the arts of war. Only Nuada remembered the heroic thought which had brought himself and his companions from heaven to earth. Sometimes in this mythological vision there would be images. Then these would disappear and the mind would comprehend swiftly the meanings, leaping the void between one series of images and another. I knew that slender lovely woman was Armid, and she was asking Nuada to tell the story which he alone remembered, for the immortals had passed away from themselves and had forgotten all. Then the high King told her the story of the gods from the dawn of time when the divine world was fashioned, and how its dark image, the underworld, came into being, and how at last the peace of the divine world was shattered by the anguish in the underworld, for sorrow had grown to be more powerful than joy. Then Nuada had summoned the immortals to a great adventure of conquest and healing. All the immortals promised aid. They descended the ladder of the spheres and came at last to earth where they were at first welcomed, but were at last overcome by its sorcery, and now the immortals only held sway over its dark inhabitants when by their arts, out of the glory still within them, they made lovely to the Fomorians their own bestial desires.

After the first vision of the great palace of the King the images faded and there came the swift leaping of the mind in interpretation. Then the images broke in again on the trembling screen of the interior light, for Armid, frightened by the hoggish lust of one of the Fomorians, and shivering through all her body, fled from the hall through the great door, and raced blindly on and on until the cold waters stayed her, and she paused, holding her heart that fluttered like a bird at the long peril of the night in time. She grew still at last pacing to and fro by the sea. Then a light came from the west as if the sunken sun was re-arising. It grew greater coming swiftly across the waters, sending long lanes of fire before it. Out of that glory of light came a great flame-coloured warrior on a winged steed. It was Lug, the sun god, riding out of the Land of Promise. Then the images faded again, and for the first time my thought followed the ancient saga where Lug sent by the door-keeper a message to the High King that a champion had come to him out of the Land of Promise. Here the ancient story fitted itself into my dream. But when Lug entered the palace chamber the vision departed once more from the Saga, for the newcomer was invisible to all but the King. Lug stood beside Nuada and told him to command the Fomorians to be still. The hall became silent, for when the King willed the Fomorians must obey. Then Lug told the King that he, Nuada, the power that was will, alone was real, that Angus, Ogma, Dana, Diancecht and the rest were but phantom images of the immortals, the shadows of love, beauty or thought; and, by the power of Lug, the King was lifted above himself to his ancient divinity, and he saw all about him the true immortals, each speaking to him out of their own high ecstasy. They made promises to be truly with him at his labours until the great battle of Moytura to be fought at the end of time. The immortals then vanished and Nuada was left once more brooding in the great chamber, and the Fomorians there again began their restless prowling.

The vision seemed to me to be like one of those sacred mysteries enacted in crypt or sanctuary where those who had been purified could see in a mystic light the images of gods and immortals, that glass of which St. Paul, who uses often the language of the mystery cults, spoke saying, 'we see now in the glass darkly.'[102] I knew that such things could be, for once in my youth there came a visitor to our city who made clear my inner sight, and he showed me in that glass of æther images of magical things, of mystery celebrations and the unfolding of the wings of the psyche from the husk of the body, and of the return of the Son to the bosom of the Father,[103] all as if enacted by radiant figures in that mystic light.

Song and its Fountains

This projection of a myth about Nuada of the Silver Hand I understood to be an invitation to me to write what I saw or understood in a long narrative poem, and I was moved to write a thousand lines or more. But my talent was lyrical and ran only to brief intensities. I was deflected, too, by my labours in this world, where I was sent here and there to organise farmers, and I could not maintain any high exaltation or continuity of mood. The mystical narrative was dropped and I only printed one fragment of what I had written. This was the voice of Dana[104] speaking to Nuada revealing the true nature of the Mighty Mother, the goddess, not of earthly love, but of a divine tenderness and pity.

> I am the tender voice calling away,
> Whispering between the beatings of the heart,
> And inaccessible in dewy eyes
> I dwell, and all unkissed on lovely lips,
> Lingering between white breasts inviolate,
> And fleeting ever from the passionate touch,
> I shine afar till men may not divine
> Whether it is the stars or the beloved
> They follow with rapt spirit. And I weave
> My spells at evening, folding with dim caress,
> Aerial arms and twilight dropping hair,
> The lonely wanderer by wood or shore,
> Till, filled with some vast tenderness he yields,
> Feeling in dreams for the dear mother heart
> He knew ere he forsook the starry way,
> And clings there, pillowed far above the smoke
> And the dim murmur from the duns of men.
> I can enchant the trees and rocks, and fill
> The dumb brown lips of earth with mystery,
> Make them reveal or hide the God, myself
> Mother of all, but without hands to heal,
> Too vast and vague, they know me not, but yet
> I am the heartbreak over fallen things,
> The sudden gentleness that stays the blow,
> And I am in the kiss that foemen give
> Pausing in battle, and in the tears that fall
> Over the vanquished foe, and in the highest,
> Among the Danaan gods, I am the last
> Council of mercy in their hearts where they
> Mete justice from a thousand starry thrones.
> My heart shall be in thine when thine forgives.

I have condemned myself many times for my lack of persistence and of faith that the genie in the innermost would have given inspiration to complete a narrative which I thought needed too lordly a style for my talent. The symbolic interpretation of the ancient story was projected into my mind when I was intent on meditation. It was the vastest of any imaginations I had. I had the sense while it was present to consciousness that it was a symbolic message which I was to interpret and retell. But I failed in this as in so many other things, never having confidence in my own powers until I grew old and began to receive praise at a time when the powers were going inward from a body which was no longer tremulously sensitive and could not melt at an idea, and the psyche had almost lost its free gay movement in the upper airs.

There are many who have symbolic dreams, and if they brooded on them I am sure they would come to have faith in that dweller in the innermost. As they see images in the inner light they may come to understand how in the mysteries to those who were purified, the Wise Ones[105] could on that clear and blessed light bring images of their inner selves, of gods and immortals, before them, so that they might know something of their own yet unveiled magnificence and 'to feel that they are greater than they know.'

XII

The high noon of time is past. We are nearing to its twilight, but are like children who run about and play and do not hear the voices calling them homewards, though indeed they are weary and their play has not in it the young delight of their dawn. How may we start on this travel? The scriptures, which are the high Oracles of the Oversoul, have told us the way. But they speak a language so high that but few can understand its symbolism, for it is to most of us like a speech maintained in the court of a great king, an ancient aristocratic speech, while the rabble without think, chatter and barter with each other in a vulgar tongue from which courtesy, dignity and beauty are absent. I cannot speak that high language of the seers who wrote the scriptures of the world. I am as a child puzzled and enchanted by the wood into which he has strayed, who has the feeling that there is One who is playing hide-and-seek with it in the tangle, and the child peers through the leaves for a presence which always eludes it. I have never had the high vision of those who have gone into the deeps of being and who have returned rapture-blinded by the glory, and cried out in a divine intoxication to the Light of Lights:[106]

Spread thy rays and gather them. The Light which is thy fairest form – I am what He is.

I am a far exile from that great glory, and can but peer through a dusky transparency to a greater light than the light of day. That greater light shines behind and through the psyche. It is the light of spirit which transcends the psyche as the psyche in its own world transcends the terrestrial ego. The psyche has a dual nature,[107] for in part it is earth-bound, and in part it clings to the ancient spirit. I do not think many have brooded long enough in that distinction of soul and spirit which St. Paul made when writing to his friends at Corinth. He speaks of many unexplained things, of a third heaven, of soul and spirit, of psychic bodies and spiritual bodies, of a mysterious power which seems to be the fountain of all psychic powers, which enables one to discern spirits, and gives to another eloquence, speaking with tongues, poetry in fact, and to another magical or healing power. Some of these powers I tried to wake, but I will not here speak of them, for I am trying to supplicate the flame which gives wisdom rather than that which gives power. While I could comprehend a little about the nature of the psyche, I could not apprehend at all the spirit which transcends the soul, for, as the seers said of it, it is eternal, invisible and universal. Yet because it is universal we are haunted by it in every motion of mind. It is at the end of every way. It is present in sunlight. It nods at us from earth or air. As we pursue it it ever eludes us, but it becomes more and more present until all that we see or are swim in a divine æther. I understand out of what emotion the Greek poet Aratus cried:

Full of Zeus are the cities. Full of Zeus are the harbours. Full of Zeus are all the ways of men;

for at times the familiar city in which I spent my life became strange to me, and its buildings, its ways, its lights and its darkness seemed but a magical movement in being. I did not know myself, nor did the dark crowds who went on their errands, but all, unknown to themselves, were on some secret mission which, when the multitudinous meditation was ended, would bring them to some divine consummation in the Great Deep or Holy Sepulchre.[108] That which is thought cannot grasp the thinker. The psyche is an entity, but what can we affirm of the spirit? We cannot say it is more within the heart than it is in air, or sunlight, rock or sea, or that it is more in Heaven than Earth. It is within us and without us. When we love we are really seeking for it, and I think our most passionate kisses are given to that Lover who will not surrender to us. It cannot be constrained. But there are enchanted hours, when it seems to be nigh us, nigher to us than the most exquisite sweetness in our transitory lives. They tell in sacred story of those the spirit took to itself who had the infinite vision.[109] I never came nigh that infinitude, but because I sought for it I was often happy and content knowing it was all about me. If I had stirred it would have vanished. I never had other than a child's vision of the Father.

> I, with remembrance of our childhood only,
> Was stayed astonished at so vast a youth
> That bloomed suddenly through grey stones and air,
> Laughing, whirling, juggling its shining balls
> In their azure goblets, playing at hide-and-seek,
> An elf in the ivory delicate wild rose,
> Dilated in the zenith, sparkling afar,
> Here blurring the brown rough earth with beauty,
> Dancing to a grey beard as to a child.
> O thou Ancient with Youth, dost thou see in me
> The airy child who may so soon go forth?
> Art thou the companion who shalt take my hand
> In the dark valley? Wilt thou wear again
> The shapes that were thy lovely hiding places
> Where I found thee of old, secret in eyes,
> Inviolate on lips, and in the heart unconquerable?
> There was always for thee a door of escaping
> Through which I could not follow. Even now
> Tenderly frolic and intimate, if I would stay thee
> Thou art gone inward, and thy light as lost
> As the flying fishes, a pearly shadow that leaps
> From the dark blue to slide in the dark blue.
> As the high emperor I have never
> Worshipped thee, making my dreams majestical
> With thrones girt by the warriors of heaven,
> My secret was thy gentleness. I know
> No nurse had ever crooned a lullaby
> So softly as thou the music that guides the loud
> Tempest in its going forth. I know full well
> When thou dancest into the heart that it may be
> The rending of the heart. Yet the saints found
> Clinging unto thee that their anguish burned
> Upward to unimaginable delight,
> I had not passion to press so to thee,
> To know thee as the Mighty and the Wise.
> But that I followed with so light a love
> I was repaid, for every hour was filled
> With a new changing beauty that was still
> The ancient beauty. Here it glows on me
> Within thy many-coloured garden, twilight,
> A beauty that has never been before
> Save for one silvery bloom, the Evening Star.

For that enchantment one needs no projection from the dream consciousness. It does not arise in dream. The spirit is with us even in the day, and I could not trace back to any artificer in the psyche the poetry which apprehends the presence here of the spirit. In my retrospective meditation I noted that never in the dream consciousness had I any direct exalted sense of the presence of that spirit. In dream were beauty, imagination, desire or terror, but all things in that mid-world of dream existed by way of fantasy or symbolism whether the dream was projected into the waking state or was experienced in sleep. While the dream consciousness flooded me I was mystic rather than spiritual: that is, true being was hidden under a mask. Out of the dream consciousness came beauty, but never under the influence of dream did I seem near to the spirit as when the exalted waking soul brooded upon the world. I sometimes think the spirit is so with us here because the purpose of the highest is the conquest and transmutation of the lowest.[110] The ancient seers warned us against the heavenworld and that it seduced by its sweetness and stayed us on our way to true being[111] Does the Divine deny its light to those who would go back to the heavens before they have fulfilled their labours here? I remember the promise of the god to Thrice-Great Hermes, if he followed the straight way, was not beauty in a heavenworld but an illumination in this world.

It will everywhere meet thee and everywhere be seen of thee plain and easy, when thou dost not expect or look for it. It will meet thee waking, sleeping, sailing, travelling, by night, by day, when thou speakest or keepest silence. For there is nothing which is not the image of God.

It is, I sometimes think, in this world, not in another, that revelation will come and the purpose of incarnation be realized; and to come to our true wisdom we must think of Heaven and Hell as equally dragons in the path, both forms of the Maya which besets us and blinds the spiritual sight.

XIII

What transformations may take place in our nightly travelling from our house of clay to the heaven of heavens. The seers who had gone into the highest being said that the soul in the profoundest deep of sleep touches on infinity. I know nothing myself though I may surmise or imagine much. My farthest travelling inward was but a footstep. I would be overcome by a magic too mighty for me to hold back and would fall into the oblivion of slumber. But how many times when I meditated before sleeping did I not seem to myself to be sinking into light. How often when waking had I not the feeling that I had been cast forth and was rejected by heaven. Almost I looked for the waving of the flaming sword which nothing that is earthly can pass. I tried passionately from departing lights, fleeting visionary presences and intuition, to conjecture what wonders the soul may have known, with what beings it may have been in some high companionship. Even in this world at times I had been aware of lordly beings. Once when I was young I had evoked the divine powers, supplicating their help in some work I was doing. I said to them, 'I am trying to bring back your ancient reign,' and I was answered, as I think, for as I was speaking later that night I, who was normally stuttering and stammering, suddenly felt as if I was thrust aside in my own body, and it was entered by some being who filled me with light, and I heard a voice speak through me to those about me, a voice like the voice Yeats spoke of,

> the burning, live, unshaken voice
> Of those who it may be can never die,

and I could see the amazed faces of those accustomed to my stumbling talk. After its aid given that being departed from me, but left images and memories of its habitation in me, and all night long I was following up these flying traces and came at last to a vision of beings of flame in some place of wonder in Anima Mundi. At another time in my youth, when I was worn out, one of these beings leaned out of the air above me in my room, and from its hands came flaming emanations that poured on me and through me, and I was as one lifted from almost death to life, and felt for months after that a fiery invigoration of mind and body. I have no doubt there are beings as far transcending us in wisdom and power as we may transcend the amœba. In our journeyings inward to deep own-being there may be grandiose transfigurations of the psyche and we may at last be partakers in divine mysteries. When St. Paul spoke of being caught up to the third heaven I believe he was in the same high plane of being the Indian seers spoke of. The genius in deep sleep they say may take many forms for himself as he comes to the sphere of creation. This high state we all enter, when we waken remembering not at all what we were or did, though we may have been changed inconceivably. Only the initiates into the highest mysteries could remember, and for them it might be as with St. Paul that it was not lawful to speak of what was remembered. For the rest there might be nothing at all remembered but some symbolic dream, or a vague psychic unrest or longing, or a fiery exaltation in the midst of their forgetfulness. I sometimes think that the whole life of the soul, since it was first outbreathed by Deity, must be a struggle to find or re-create outside itself all that it first had within itself in the Pleroma. The soul fallen outside the divine circle begins to create in fantasy its lost infinitude. Something of the kind may take place in our microcosmic life when the soul wakens here. Its imaginations, philosophies, mysticism, its ardours and passions, may be symbols, echoes or images of its being in a higher state. To take an imagination which springs up in us, and to try to deduce from this what reality it mirrored, might seem almost as hopeless a task as for the non-mathematical mind to deduce what lies beneath formulae like the square root of minus one. Often I had an evidential emptiness about the reality behind my imaginations which might be mathematically symbolized by that formula, but yet something in me had flared out in a congregation of wild images which I contemplated with an intuition that what seemed so coherent within its own wildness must have some root in reality. A Christian philosopher, considering what he called the extravagant speculations of the Gnostics, did yet say nobly of them, 'We must remember that the mind of man is made in the image of God and therefore even in its wildest speculations it follows an image of truth.' It is only that noble attitude of his I have to uphold me when I begin to consider another poem of my own. I had wakened from sleep with a rare exaltation, but had not even a dream to hint by its symbolism at what lay beneath that exaltation. Yet something in my forgetfulness was trying to create phantasmal images in poetry of some almost inconceivable adventure of the psyche. I do not know whether the imagination which was born in the waking consciousness had any relation to the being from which it had passed, but what follows was the outcome of that high exaltation, of the reason for which I knew nothing, for there was nothing in this world but ashes of some starry fires or dust of some heaven-assailing will.

>   See, where the light streams over Connla's Fountain
>   Starward aspire.
>   The sacred sign upon the holy mountain
>   Shines in white fire.
>   Wavering and flaming yonder o'er the snows
>   The diamond light
>   Melts into silver, or to sapphire glows
>   Night beyond night.
>   And from the heaven of heavens descends on earth
>   A dew divine.
>   Come, let us mingle in the starry mirth
>   About the shrine.

O earth, enchantress, mother, to our home
In thee we press,
Thrilled by thy fiery breath and wrapt in some
Vast tenderness.
The homeward birds uncertain o'er their nest
Wheel in the dome,
Fraught with dim dreams of some enraptured rest,
Another home.
But gather ye to whose undarkened eyes
Night is as day.
Leap forth, immortals, birds of paradise,
In bright array.
Clothed as with shining tresses of the sun,
And by his name
Call from his haunt divine the ancient one,
Our Father Flame,
Aye, from the wonder light, heart of our star,
Come now, come now;
Sun-breathing spirit, ray thy lights afar.
Thy children bow,
Hush with more awe the heart. The bright-browed races
Are nothing worth
By those dread gods from out whose awful faces
The Earth looks forth
Infinite pity set in calm, whose vision cast
Adown the years
Beholds how beauty burns away at last
Their children's tears.
Now while our hearts the ancient quietness
Floods with its tide,
The things of air and fire and height no less
In it abide,
And, from their wandering over sea or shore,
They rise as one
Unto the vastness, and with us adore
The midnight sun,
And enter the innumerable All,
And shine like gold,
And starlike gleam in the immortals' hall,
The heavenly fold,
And drink the sun breaths from the Mother's lips
Awhile, and then
Fail from the light and drop in dark eclipse
To earth again,
Roaming along by heaven-hid promontory
Or valley dim,
Weaving a phantom image of the glory
They knew in Him.

> Out of the fullness flow the winds. Their song
> Is heard no more,
> Or hardly breathes a mystic sound along
> The dreamy shore.
> Blindly they move, unknowing, as in trance,
> Their wandering
> Is half with us, and half an inner dance
> Led by the King.

I had no memory of so high an adventure of the psyche, only a fire which seemed to have fallen out of heaven, and tried to recreate the intensity from which it had fallen, 'weaving a phantom image of the glory,' but it was so vivid that I was conquered by the fantasy and brooded on it as if it was revelation. The fantasy so created may not have had any more relation to truth than the relation Neander surmised lay in the vast mystical speculation of the Gnostics. A child as it grows up often carries a likeness to its parent, the germ out of which it came holding within itself somehow and unconsciously to itself an image of its begetter. In the same way the psyche, which in its own realm may have vision of infinite grandeurs, when it narrows itself to our clay may hold within itself some seed of its own high being, and in the house it builds for itself in the brain it may instinctively put forth symbolic images of its own primal magnificence.

It may be because of this the poets use at times a lordlier language than their contracted life here could justify. If not true to outward being, it may yet be true to inward or deep own-being. The fallen divinity for an instant forgets that it is fallen and speaks as to immortals.

There is as great a mystery about our least motion as there is about our whole being. We are affected by the whole cosmos. Emanations from most distant planets pour on us and through us. Everything is related to everything else. 'Thou canst not stir a stone without troubling of a star.' Let us still life to the utmost quietude, and what we feel in the stillness is pregnant as if there were multitudes in that intensity of loneliness. The universe seems involved in the simplest motion of mind. Just as the needle-point of a nerve in the eye is sensitive to light from the whole of the heavens spread above us, so at moments we feel that all knowledge is within us. But we have not yet evolved mind to be the perfect instrument to mirror universal mind as the eye mirrors infinitudes of light and darkness. But out of that centre in us through which all the threads of the universe are drawn there may come at times flashes of supernature; and by these flashes we live and hope and aspire, though nothing may remain when they go but some shadowy tale or vague exultant imagination like that poem about the mysteries I had written.

I feel what I have said about imagination to be very inadequate as portraiture. Even the simplest emotions need a more transcendental and complicated mathematic than the scientist devotes to the mysterious activity of the atom. How can words portray truly any emotion when the whole of life is involved in its parts, all the past, and, for all we know, the eternity we think of as the future?

> To bring this loveliness to be
> Even for an hour, the builder must
> Have wrought in the laboratory
> Of many a star for its sweet dust.
>
> Oh, to make possible that heart,
> And that gay breath so lightly sighed,
> What agony was in the art,
> How many gods were crucified!

Words can never be a perfect mirror for that complexity.[112] But we must needs use them if only to have guidance to that point within us where the whole universe focuses its light on one fiery centre.

XIV

'The One became many,' said the ancient seers. Everything therefore is divinely descended. Nothing came forth from that Majesty in which we may not discover some traces of its royal lineage. That is the excuse for the meditation on this book. Our lightest thoughts, our most fugitive ideas, do in obscure ways act and move by some magic like that which moves the universe. With this idea in mind I have taken thoughts and fancies which, compared with the imaginations of the great masters, are of slight value, and have tried to track them a little nearer to their fountains. In this I was following as I could the wisdom of Socrates, where in *The Banquet* he speaks of a meditation which leads us into the mid-world of desires, thoughts and imaginations. I was seeking the fountains of beauty and poetry, trying also to discover what I might of that Daimon or Genie who overshadows us and at times speaks through us. I did not attain 'a science equal to a beauty so vast': and I must often appear as one confused or bewildered in his thinking, or to be self-deceived. There is indeed a riotous fertility of fancy which at times chokes us and blinds us on our way to the True. When we would 'explore the river of the soul whence or in what order we have come so that we may ascend whence we came' we are bewildered by imaginations like those elf-girls, each lovelier than the other, who in an Eastern tale try to allure the seeker from the Waters of Immortality. It is difficult to weed the garden of the soul from the quick springing up of the blossoms of illusion, for we have not plucked up one when another enchants us. We, by some magic, do make spiritual the images of earth so that feet which may only be whiteness of clay seem airy feet that might run along the clouds, and light limbs seem fashioned out of some burnished and exquisite air, and dawn and night ravished of colours and stars to make a beauty that glows pleroma-like. So over the images we see a glamour is cast, and if we succumb to it and clasp the image there is nothing left but fading fire or crumbling form. Such a rabble of imaginations beset us that it is difficult to distinguish false from true, and we have little to guide us but intuition, which tells us to follow only those images which seem to have a lamp of spiritual meaning within them, which are not opaque but transparent, which do not stay us by their beauty, but suggest a lordlier beauty than their own. I think as we go inward images and ideas begin to glow as transparencies. They lead us beyond themselves and liberate us as Wordsworth does when he wrote:

> Thy friends are exultations, agonies,

which illuminates our darkness like the angel who released Peter from prison. So in what I have written I told only of those imaginations which seemed to have a lamp of spiritual meaning within them. My own Daimon, in one of the earliest inspirations I had, warned me – [113]

> Oh, be not led away
> Lured by the colour of the sun-rich day.
> The gay romance of song
> Unto the spirit life doth not belong.
> Though far-between the hours
> In which the Master of Angelic Powers
> Lightens the dusk within
> The holy of holies, be it thine to win
> Rare vistas of white light . . .

and I have always feared to yield to beauty which had not that lamp. Yet I have not written this book to my satisfaction, feeling throughout I have blundered and erred, and the lamp of intuition I held was often dim or went out altogether. I delayed too long, and things I would have spoken about have died away in remote distances of soul.

In my retrospective meditation I could recall form or circumstance, but could not arouse vivid feeling about them once more in myself. But I think the problems arising over imagination and poetry ought to be discussed, not merely by those psychologists who have themselves neither imagination nor poetry, and are without experience, but by those who have a higher imagination than mine and a keener analytic faculty, so that the element of magic and wonder about even the lightest motions of mind might be made manifest.

Even if we do not come to unity with the spirit there is a great gain from this meditation in which we try by a divine alchemy to transmute the gross into the subtle and pure, for very soon our whole being begins to circle around an invisible sun, and we are drawn more and more to it; and though it may be aeons before we come nigh it, yet we feel as Adam might have felt, the outcast from Paradise, after long penitence, if he had seen faintly flickering through the outer darkness of the world in which he laboured the shining of the lost Eden, and knew it was not altogether lost but was accessible after purification. To have this surety is no light thing. Though we fall and fail times without number, there are hours of resurrection when the fallen angels of the heart begin to wear again their ancient angel faces, and we are melted in an anguish of exquisite joy, knowing that the dead may rise. Or earth itself may become living and play with us, and we may know what lovely allies there are for us in wood, rock, mountain, hollow of air or along the silent shores.

> Now the quietude of earth
> Nestles deep my heart within,
> Friendships new and strange have birth
> Since I left the city's din.
>
> Here the tempest stays its guile,
> Like a big kind brother plays,
> Romps and pauses here awhile
> From its immemorial ways.
>
> Now the silver light of dawn,
> Slipping through the leaves that fleck
> My one window, hurries on,
> Throws its arms around my neck.

Darkness to my doorway hies,
Lays her chin upon the roof,
And her burning seraph eyes
Now no longer keep aloof.

And the ancient mystery
Holds its hands out day by day,
Takes a chair and croons with me
By my cabin built of clay.

THE END

JAGRATA, SVAPNA AND SUSHUPTI.[1]

While the philosophical concepts of ancient India, concerning religion and cosmogony, are to some extent familiar and appreciated in these countries, its psychology, intimately related with its religion and metaphysics, is comparatively unknown. In Europe the greatest intellects have been occupied by speculations upon the laws and aspects of physical nature, while the more spiritual Hindus were absorbed in investigations as to the nature of life itself; by continual aspiration, devotion, introspection and self-analysis, they had acquired vast knowledge of the states of consciousness possible for man to enter upon; they had laid bare the anatomy of the mind, and described the many states that lay between the normal waking condition of man, and that final state of spiritual freedom and unity with BRAHMA,[2] which it was the aim alike of religion and science to bring about. Most interesting among their ideas, was their analysis of the states of consciousness upon which we enter during sleep. Roughly speaking, they may be divided into two, which together with the waking state, make a trinity of states through which every person passes, whether he be aware of it or not. These states are known as: Jagrata, waking; Svapna, dreaming; and Sushupti, deep sleep. The English equivalents of these words give no idea of the states. Passing out of Jagrata, the Indians held that, beyond the chaotic borderland, we entered, in Svapna and Sushupti, upon real states of being. Sushupti, the highest, was accounted a spiritual state; here the soul touches vaster centres in the great life and has communion with celestial intelligences. The unification of these three states[3] into one is one of the results of Raj-Yoga;[4] in this state the chela keeps memory of what occurred while his consciousness was in the planes of Svapna and Sushupti. Entrance upon these states should not I think be understood as meaning that the mind has deserted its fleshly tabernacle in search of such experience.[5] Departure from the physical form is no more necessary for this than for clairvoyance, but a transfer of the consciousness in us from one plane to another is necessary.

Now as we generate Karma[6] in the dreaming and deep sleep

states which may either help or hinder the soul in its evolution,[7] it is a matter of importance that we should take steps to promote the unification of these states, so that the knowledge and wisdom of any one state may be used to perfect the others. Our thoughts and actions in the waking state react upon the dreaming and deep sleep, and our experiences in the latter influence us in the waking state by suggestion and other means. The reason we do not remember what occurs in Svapna and Sushupti is because the astral matter which normally surrounds the thinking principle is not subtle enough to register in its fullness the experience of any one upon the more spiritual planes of consciousness.[8] To increase the responsiveness of this subtle matter we have to practise concentration, and so heighten the vibrations, or in other words to evolve or perfect the astral principle. Modern science is rapidly coming to the conclusion that the differences perceived in objects around us, are not differences in substance, but differences of vibration in one substance. Take a copper wire; pass electrical currents through it, gradually increasing their intensity, and phenomena of sound, heat and light will be manifest, the prismatic colours appearing one after the other. Similarly by an increased intensity in the performance of every action, the consciousness is gradually transferred from the lower to the higher planes. In order to give a point, or to direct the evolving faculties into their proper channel, continual aspiration is necessary. Take some idea – the spiritual unity of all things, for example – something which can only be realized by our complete absorption in spiritual nature; let every action be performed in the light of this idea, let it be the subject of reverent thought. If this is persisted in, we will gradually begin to become conscious upon the higher planes, the force of concentration carrying the mind beyond the waking into Svapna and Sushupti. The period between retiring to rest and awakening, formerly a blank, will begin to be spotted with bright lights of consciousness, or, as we walk about during the day such knowledge will visit us. 'He who is perfected in devotion findeth spiritual knowledge springing up spontaneously in himself,'[9] says Krishna. Patanjali recommends dwelling on the knowledge that presents itself in dreams; if we think over any such experience, many things connected with it will be revealed, and so gradually the whole shadowy region will become familiar and attractive, and we will gain a knowledge of our own nature which will be invaluable and which cannot otherwise be acquired.

F.

CONCENTRATION[1]

Beyond waking, dreaming and deep sleep is Turya.[2] Here there is a complete change of condition; the knowledge formerly sought in the external world is now present *within* the consciousness; the ideations of universal mind are manifest in spiritual intuitions. The entrance to this state is through Jagrata, Svapna and Sushupti, and here that spiritual unity is realized, the longing for which draws the soul upwards through the shadowy worlds of dreaming and deep sleep. I have thought it necessary to supplement the brief statement made in the previous number by some farther remarks upon concentration, for the term applied without reference to the Turya state is liable to be misunderstood and a false impression might arise that the spiritual is something to be sought for outside ourselves. The waking, dreaming and deep sleep states correspond to objective worlds, while Turya is subjective, including in itself all ideals. If this is so, we can never seek for the true beyond ourselves;[3] the things we suppose we shall some time realize in spiritual consciousness must be present in it now, for to spirit all things are eternally present. Advance to this state is measured by the realization of moods; we are on the path when there surges up in the innermost recesses of our being the cry of the long imprisoned souls of men; we are then on our way to unity.

The Bhagavad-Gita[4] which is a treatise on Raj Yoga,[5] gives prominence to three aspects of concentration. Liberation[6] is attained by means of action, by devotion, by spiritual discernment: these aspects correspond respectively to three qualities in man and nature, known as Tamas, Rajas and Satva.[7] The Tamas is the gross, material or dark quality; Rajas is active and passional; the attributes of Satva are light, peace, happiness, wisdom. No one while in the body can escape from the action of the three qualities, for they are brought about by nature which is compounded of them. We have to recognize this, and to continue action, aspiration and thought, impersonally or with some universal motive, in the manner nature accomplishes these things. Not one of these methods can be laid aside or ignored, for the Spirit moveth within all, these are its works, and we have to learn to identify ourselves with the moving forces of nature.

Having always this idea of brotherhood or unity in mind, by action – which we may interpret as service in some humanitarian movement – we purify the Tamas.

By a pure motive, which is the Philosopher's Stone,[8] a potent force in the alchemy of nature, we change the gross into the subtle, we initiate that evolution which shall finally make the vesture of the soul of the rare, long-sought for, primoridal substance.[9] Devotion is the highest possibility for the Rajas: that quality which is ever attracted and seduced by the beautiful mayas of fame, wealth and power, should be directed to that which it really seeks for, the eternal universal life; the channels through which it must flow outwards are the souls of other men, it reaches the One Life through the many. Spiritual discernment should be the aim of the Satva, 'there is not anything, whether animate or inanimate which is without me,'[10] says Krishna, and we should seek for the traces of THAT in all things, looking upon it as the cause of the alchemical changes in the Tamas, as that which widens the outflowing love of the Rajas. By a continued persistence of this subtle analytic faculty, we begin gradually to perceive that those things which we formerly thought were causes, are in reality not causes at all; that there is but one cause for everything, 'The Atma by which this universe is pervaded. *By reason of its proximity alone the body, the organs, Manas and Buddhi apply themselves to their proper objects as if applied (by some one else).*' (The Crest Jewel of Wisdom). By uniting these three moods, action, devotion and spiritual discernment, into one mood, and keeping it continuously alight, we are accompanying the movements of spirit to some extent. This harmonious action of all the qualities of our nature, for universal purposes without personal motive, is in *synchronous vibration* with that higher state spoken of at the beginning of the paper; therefore we are at one with it. 'When the wise man perceiveth that the only agents of action are these qualities, and comprehends that which is superior to the qualities, he attains to my state. And when the embodied self surpasseth these three qualities of goodness, action and indifference – which are co-existent with the body, it is released from rebirth and death, old age and pain, and drinketh of the water of immortality.'[11]

COMFORT[1]

We are continually called upon to give comfort, and it is a problem to many what to say. For there are people who can see no outlet from their pain other than this, that they shall obtain that which they desire. The lover longs for the one who is absent or cold; the poor demand wealth; the tortured cry out for relief from suffering; and so on through all phases of human life we continually meet such people. We, perhaps free from such afflictions, have schooled ourselves into a heroic mood. These are not things to sorrow over, we think; therefore, we are in a dilemma. We cannot aid them, for their ideals often seem ignoble to us – their wish accomplished would only bring on the renewal of old pain, and bind them closer to the weary wheel. Yet we cannot be cold, we who would identify ourselves with all life, for the soul must 'lend its ear to every cry of pain, like as the lotus bares its heart to drink the morning sun.' In the many cases where the suffering is unavoidable, and cannot be otherwise received, what are we to do? Some, a little above the ignoble view that the only relief is in the satisfaction of desire, say reverently to those in pain: 'It is God's will,' and some accept it as such with dull resignation. But with some the iron has entered the soul – the words are empty. 'What have I to do with God, or He with me?' they demand in their hearts. They join in the immemorial appeal and fierce revolt which at all times the soul of man makes against any external restraint. We who are disciples of old wisdom may touch some chord in them which may awaken eternal endurance.

It is not, we say, a pain imposed upon us by any eternal power; but the path we tread is one which we ourselves very long ago determined. To the question, 'What have we to do with God?' we make answer that we are the children of Deity – bright sparks born in that Divine flame,[2] the spirit in its primal ecstasy reflected in itself the multitudinous powers that throng in space. It was nourished by Divine love, and all that great beauty thrilled through it and quickened it. But from this vision which the spirit had, it passed to climb to still greater heights – it was spiritual, it might attain divinity.

The change from the original transcendental state of vision to that other state of *being*, of all-pervading consciousness, could only be accomplished by what is known as the descent into matter where spirit identifies itself with every form of life, and assimilates their essences. This cyclic pilgrimage it undertook,[3] foreseeing pain, but 'preferring free will to passive slavery, intellectual, self-conscious pain, and even torture, "while myriad time shall flow," to inane, imbecile, instinctual beatitude,' foreseeing pain, but knowing that out of it all would come a nobler state of life, a divinity capable of rule, a power to assist in the general evolution of nature. It is true in the experience of many that going deep within themselves, an elemental consciousness whispers comfort; it says all will be well with us; it is our primal will which so orders. And so we justify the pain and hearts that break; and that old appeal and fierce revolt we make dies out in the inner light which shines from 'the Goal, the Comforter, the Lord, the Witness, the resting-place, the Asylum, the Friend.' We can then once more go forth with the old, heroic, Titan will for mastery, seeking not to escape, but rather to meet, endure, and assimilate sorrow and joy alike; for so we can permeate all life – life which is in its essence one. This is the true centre on which all endurance must rest; this is the comfort the soul may take to itself; and beyond and after this we may say we struggle in a chaos indeed, but in a chaos whose very disorder is the result of law. That law is justice that cannot err. Out of confidence in this justice may spring up immortal hopes; our motives, our faith shall save us. We may dare more, give ourselves away more completely, for is not the root of this law declared to be beauty, harmony, compassion. We may trust that our acts shall have full fruition, and remain careless of the manner, nor seek for such results. We may look upon it if we will as the sweetest of the sweetest, the tenderest of the tenderest; and this is true, though still it is master of the fiery pain. Above all it is the law of our own being; it is at one with our ancestral self. In all this lies, I think, such consolation as we may take and offer for pain. Those who comprehend, in their resignation, shall become one with themselves: and out of this resignation shall arise will to go forth and fulfil our lofty destiny.

REVIEW[1]

The Treasure of the Humble. By Maurice Maeterlinck. [London: George Allen.]

I confess that Maeterlinck as dramatist does not attract me. He is always an artist, but an artist concerned too much with the morbid and gruesome to have any very pleasurable hold on the mind. The works which we return to are those which radiate sunlight. These twilight emotions and pathetic privacies, which are so frequently the subject of M. Maeterlinck's art, leave an after-sensation of sickliness, and to get rid of the unpleasant memory we carefully put the books out of sight. In *The Treasure of the Humble* the author reverts more to himself, and his faculty of delicate perception which, when concerned with tragic action, seems to be led by its own sensitiveness into a region of overwrought emotions where the heart is perpetually strained, here is more beautifully revealed in divining the laws and principles of the invisible spiritual spheres which environ us. The tremulous sensitiveness which enables M. Maeterlinck to sense so many hidden influences, to be in a way a revealer of the unseen, is, I think, also the cause of his main drawbacks as a teacher. 'No sooner do we speak than something warns us that the divine gates are closing,' he says in the essay on 'Silence.' That surely is the extreme statement of the visionary whose joy is mainly in perception. Others no less mystic have spoken, feeling the doors were open behind them and that celestial powers went forth charioted on the voice. Silence is no nearer than sound to that which moves through all. M. Maeterlinck is a little too much enamoured of the charms of the negative; he signs too much for us to withdraw. Yet, having made Silence his theme, what he says is lit up by true intuitions; the noiseless revelations taking place in the soul have hardly in modern literature a more subtle recorder. ' "We do not know each other yet," ' some one writes to him, ' "we have not yet dared to be silent together." ' He comments as follows:

'And it was true: already did we love each other so deeply that we shrank from the superhuman ordeal. And each time that silence fell upon us – the angel of the supreme truth, the messenger that brings to the heart the tidings of the unknown – each time did we feel that our souls were craving mercy on their knees, were begging for a few hours more of innocent falsehood, a few hours of ignorance, a few hours of childhood. . . .'

Again he says, and with what profound truth:

'It is an entire destiny that will be governed by the *quality* of this first silence which is descending upon two souls. They blend: we know not where, for the reservoirs of silence lie far above the reservoirs of thought, and the strange resultant brew is either sinisterly bitter or profoundly sweet. Two souls, admirable both and of equal power, may yet give birth to a hostile silence, and wage pitiless war against each other in the darkness: while it may be that the soul of a convict shall go forth and commune in divine silence with the soul of a virgin.'

These essays, variously titled, have all for their theme the midworld between soul and spirit, a region of strange perceptions, which, as M. Maeterlinck points out, is becoming more irradiated year by year for men. What he has to say is told with unfailing charm and dignity. Even if we do not agree with him in his attitude, and that is but seldom, we feel that he is always dealing with realities. It is a book of beautiful starlight perceptions – most beautiful. It is a curious thing that M. Maeterlinck seems to have gone far into the mystic worlds without any vivid sense of the preëminence of human consciousness over all it surveys, a sense which most mystics attain. The spirit has never spoken to him as to Blake:

> 'If thou humblest thyself thou humblest me:
> Thou also dwellest in eternity.'

There are no lightning flashes, no sudden lustres from the light beyond the darkness, but all is calm, serene and noble, a nature still and perceptive of the tide of light rounding the dark shoulder of the world.

AN EASTERN CANDLE OF VISION[1]

I live in Ireland, and have no personal knowledge of the psychic revival you refer to as existing in your own country, and any answers I could make to your questions, based as they would be on hearsay, would be without value. Personal intimacy with movements is necessary before one can criticize or make suggestions with regard to them. I have had no experience of what is called Spiritualism, though I have read a number of works by spiritualists, but I have not been sufficiently interested in the results recorded to make investigations on my own account. The spirit of man while it is in the body, manifesting through the poets, artists, musicians and mystics, seems to me to have access to a deeper life than entities out of the body speaking through mediums. Platitudes, whether uttered by the living or the dead, are equally uninteresting to me, and I have not yet, in the literature of Spiritualism, come upon thoughts which were worth remembering, or if there were wise things said, they had already been said better in literature deriving its inspiration from other sources. I do not deny the sincerity of mediums or that psychic manifestations take place, but, admitting that the phenomena are genuine, they are so stupid in most cases that I see no reason why I should study them with more seriousness than I should study the utterances of a drunken man. Like the utterances of the drunken man, they may be of interest to psychologists and those who study the workings of the subconscious mind, but spiritual wisdom must, I believe, be attained otherwise, and the way has been pointed out by many mystics. I think, for example, that in the Yoga Sutras[2] of Patanjali a more scientific method of attaining certainty about spiritual things is outlined than can be found in any of the publications of Psychical Research Societies or spiritualists which I have read. The question of immortality is not one to be decided by abstract argument, but by evidence, and I believe many who have followed the instruction given by the Indian sage have acquired psychic and spiritual vision, and have been able to see directly into spheres of being invisible to others and to see the dead, and had not to rely on the utterances of mediums, coloured by their own personality, the character of the subconscious mind, or influenced telepathically by the presence of others, and who were probably as inaccurate in their interpretation of the thought of the disembodied as they would be in their interpretation of the thought of the living. For myself, I desire to hear with my own ears and to use my own spiritual vision, and to discuss what I hear and see with those who can also hear and see, as we do in regard to things of this world, and I do not want to listen to utterances by mediums or to trust to second-hand evidence. I doubt whether the spiritual life of humanity can be deepened by psychic phenomena, though they have the general interest and importance all things relating to our complex being have. Whenever through any medium come utterances of the high quality and beauty we find in the Upanishads, Bhagavad-Gita, Gospels, Tao or Hermetic books, I will feel a passionate interest in the medium and the source of the inspiration. While the utterances are, as at present, subhuman in the average of intellect displayed, I cannot see how the highest interests of the nation can be served by them.

THE CITY WITHOUT WALLS[1]

INTRODUCTION

For many years I had the idea of compiling an Anthology from the sacred and half-sacred literatures of the world, so that those who read might be released from the confining notion of truth in one Scripture only, and come to know to what harmony of vision came the seers who, in India, China, Palestine, Egypt, Greece or Arabia, turned their thoughts to the Oversoul. I had gathered here and there from my reading the wisdom of those seers upon creation, life, death, conduct, immortality and the heaven-world. But, when I read *The City Without Walls,* I knew there was no need to continue this labour for the compiler of this Anthology had, in a mood akin to my own, ransacked the Scriptures, Christian, Buddhist, Brahmin, Chinese, Egyptian for their profundities and exaltations, and also a wide range of secular literature where it becomes half-sacred because the intensity of the soul has burned away for a time its dross, and there is a transparency through which there comes some transcience of the Everlasting Light. In a long life Mrs. Osgood has gathered together these precious fires, now burning as the soul came nigh to heaven, or again as it looked on the loveliness of earth, or in love or in sorrow found some star of leading which if followed might lead the soul to the mystic Jerusalem. I do not know of any better book to dispel, without controversy, the arrogance of ignorance . . . of those who speak about the heathen and the pagan of whose lives they know nothing, and whose wisdom they have never read . . . a custom which is very common in many countries, among people who read little. . . . How great a vision is born from the reading of this book, a vision of innumerable ladders reaching up to the heavens, and of innumerable descents of the spirit. The Communion of Saints is enlarged for us and St. Francis walks hand in hand with Akhnaton, and St. Teresa is one in her ecstasy with Kabir, and hundreds . . . are here found speaking so harmoniously together that we divine their wisdom comes from one fountain. This is the special virtue of the Anthology that it liberates and enlarges the soul, and shows a shining host of friends where before it had thought there was only a malign darkness.

The reader will find much heavenly and much lovely human wisdom within the pages of this book. It is not to be read through at one sitting, but is to be taken up and closed again when one has found a starry thought which we can walk away with and make our own, and then the pages can be opened once more. Good thinking and wisdom come from taking one thought at a time as the Japanese bring out one picture and let its beauty be before their eyes for days ere another picture is brought out and displayed. There is material in the Anthology for a rich spiritual culture. I hope it will be bought by many so that it may lie easily to the hand for the wisdom in it is of the kind that can easily be carried in the memory, and there is no other wisdom that can be of any service to us.

A.E.

VI. THE MYTHIC IMAGINATION

THE MASK OF APOLLO[1]

A tradition rises within me of quiet, unrumoured years, ages before the demigods and heroes toiled at the making of Greece, long ages before the building of the temples and sparkling palaces of her day of glory. The land was pastoral, and over all the woods hung a stillness as of dawn and of unawakened beauty deep breathing in rest. Here and there little villages sent up their smoke and a dreamy people moved about. They grew up, toiled a little at their fields, followed their sheep and goats, wedded, and grey age overtook them, but they never ceased to be children. They worshipped the gods in little wooden temples, with ancient rites forgotten in later years.

Near one of these shrines lived a priest – an old man – who was held in reverence by all for his simple and kindly nature. To him, sitting one summer evening before his hut, came a stranger whom he invited to share his meal. The stranger seated himself and began to tell the priest many wonderful things – stories of the magic of the sun and of the bright beings who move at the gateways of the day. The old man grew drowsy in the warm sunlight and fell asleep. Then the stranger, who was Apollo, arose, and in the guise of the priest entered the little temple, and the people came in unto him one after the other.

First came Agathon, the husbandman, who said: 'Father, as I bend over the fields or fasten up the vines I sometimes remember that you said the gods can be worshipped by doing these things as by sacrifice. How is it, father, that the pouring of cold water over roots or training up the vines can nourish Zeus? How can the sacrifice appear before his throne when it is not carried up in the fire and vapour?'

To him Apollo, in the guise of the old man, replied: 'Agathon, the father omnipotent does not live only in the æther. He runs invisibly within the sun and stars, and as they whirl round and round they break out into streams and woods and flowers, and the clouds are shaken away from them as the leaves from off the roses. Great, strange, and bright, he busies himself within, and at the end of time his light shall shine through, and men shall see it moving in a world of flame. Think then, as you bend over your fields, of what you nourish and what rises up within them. Know that every flower as it droops in the quiet of the woodland feels within and far away the approach of an unutterable life and is glad. They reflect that life as the little pools the light of the stars. Agathon, Agathon, Zeus is no greater in the æther than he is in the leaf of grass, and the hymns of men are no sweeter to him than a little water poured over one of his flowers.'

Agathon, the husbandman, went away, and he bent tenderly in dreams over his fruits and his vines, and he loved them more than before; and he grew wise as he watched them and was happy working for the gods.

Then spake Damon, the shepherd: 'Father, while the flocks are browsing dreams rise up within me. They make the heart sick with longing. The forests vanish, and I hear no more the lambs' bleat or the rustling of the fleeces. Voices from a thousand depths call me; they whisper, they beseech me. Shadows more lovely than earth's children utter music, not for me though I faint while I listen. Father, why do I hear the things others hear not – voices calling to unknown hunters of wide fields, or to herdsmen, shepherds of the starry flocks?'

Apollo answered the shepherd: 'Damon, a song stole from the silence while the gods were not yet, and a thousand ages passed ere they came, called forth by the music; and a thousand ages they listened, and then joined in the song. Then began the worlds to glimmer shadowy about them, and bright beings to bow before them. These, their children, began in their turn to sing the song that calls forth and awakens life. He is master of all things who has learned their music. Damon, heed not the shadows, but the voices. The voices have a message to thee from beyond the gods. Learn their song and sing it over again to the people until their hearts, too, grow sick with longing, and they can hear the song within themselves. Oh, my son, I see far off how the nations shall join in it as in a chorus, and, hearing it, the rushing planets shall cease from their speed and be steadfast. Men shall hold starry sway.'

The face of the god shone through the face of the old man, and it was so full of secretness that, filled with awe, Damon, the herdsman, passed from the presence, and a strange fire was kindled in his heart. The songs that he sang thereafter caused childhood and peace to pass from the dwellers in the woods.

Then the two lovers, Dion and Neæra, came in and stood before Apollo, and Dion spake: 'Father, you who are so wise can tell us what love is, so that we shall never miss it. Old Tithonus nods his grey head at us as we pass. He says only with the changeless gods has love endurance, and for men the loving time is short, and its sweetness is soon over.'

Neæra added: 'But it is not true, father, for his drowsy eyes light when he remembers the old days, when he was happy and proud in love as we are.'

Apollo answered: 'My children, I will tell you the legend how love came into the world, and how it may endure. On high Olympus the gods held council at the making of man, and each had brought a gift, and each gave to man something of their own nature. Aphrodite, the loveliest and sweetest, paused, and was about to add a new grace to his person; but Eros cried: "Let them not be so lovely without; let them be lovelier within. Put your own soul in, O mother." The mighty mother smiled, and so it was. And now, whenever love is like hers, which asks not return, but shines on all because it must, within that love Aphrodite dwells, and it becomes immortal by her presence.'

Then Dion and Neæra went out, and as they walked home through the forest, purple and vaporous in the evening light, they drew closer together. Dion, looking into the eyes of Neæra, saw there a new gleam, violet, magical, shining – there was the presence of Aphrodite; there was her shrine.

After came in unto Apollo the two grandchildren of old Tithonus, and they cried: 'See the flowers we have brought you! We gathered them for you in the valley where they grow best!' Apollo said: 'What wisdom shall we give to children that they may remember? Our most beautiful for them!' And as he stood and looked at them the mask of age and secretness vanished. He appeared radiant in light. They laughed in joy at his beauty. Bending down he kissed each upon the forehead, then faded away into the light which is his home.

As the sun sank down amid the blue hills, the old priest awoke with a sigh, and cried out: 'Oh, that we could talk wisely as we do in our dreams!'

1893.

THE STORY OF A STAR[1]

The emotions that haunted me in that little cathedral town would be most difficult to describe. After the hurry, rattle, and fever of the city, the rare weeks spent here were infinitely peaceful. They were full of a quaint sense of childhood, with sometimes a deeper chord touched – the giant and spiritual things childhood has dreams of. The little room I slept in had opposite its window the great grey cathedral wall; it was only in the evening that the sunlight crept round it and appeared in the room strained through the faded green blind. It must have been this silvery quietness of colour which in some subtle way affected me with the feeling of a continual Sabbath; and this was strengthened by the bells chiming hour after hour. The pathos, penitence, and hope expressed by the flying notes coloured the intervals with faint and delicate memories. They haunted my dreams, and I heard with unutterable longing the dreamy chimes pealing from some dim and vast cathedral of the cosmic memory, until the peace they tolled became almost a nightmare, and I longed for utter oblivion or forgetfulness of their reverberations.

More remarkable were the strange lapses into other worlds and times. Almost as frequent as the changing of the bells were the changes from state to state. I realized what is meant by the Indian philosophy of Maya.[2] Truly my days were full of Mayas, and my work-a-day city life was no more real to me than one of those bright, brief glimpses of things long past. I talk of the past, and yet these moments taught me how false our ideas of time are. In the Ever-living yesterday, to-day, and to-morrow are words of no meaning. I know I fell into what we call the past, and the things I counted as dead for ever were the things I had yet to endure. Out of the old age of earth I stepped into its childhood, and received once more the primal blessing of youth, ecstasy, and beauty. But these things are too vast and vague to speak of, the words we use to-day cannot tell their story. Nearer to our time is the legend that follows.

I was, I thought, one of the Magi of old Persia,[3] inheritor of its unforgotten lore, and using some of its powers. I tried to pierce through the great veil of nature, and feel the life that quickened it within. I tried to comprehend the birth and growth of planets, and to do this I rose spiritually, and passed beyond the earth's confines into that seeming void which is the matrix where they germinate. On one of these journeys I was struck by the phantasm, so it seemed, of a planet I had not observed before. I could not then observe closer, and coming again on another occasion it had disappeared. After the lapse of many months I saw it once more, brilliant with fiery beauty. Its motion was slow, revolving around some invisible centre. I pondered over it, and seemed to know that the invisible centre was its primordial spiritual state, from which it emerged a little while and into which it then withdrew. Short was its day; its shining faded into a glimmer, and then into darkness in a few months. I learned its time and cycles; I made preparations and determined to await its coming.

The Birth of a Planet

At first silence and then an inner music, and then the sounds of song throughout the vastness of its orbit grew as many in number as there were stars at gaze. Avenues and vistas of sound! They reeled to and fro. They poured from a universal stillness quick with unheard things. They rushed forth and broke into a myriad voices gay with childhood. From age and the eternal they rushed forth into youth. They filled the void with revelling and exultation. In rebellion they then returned and entered the dreadful Fountain. Again they came forth, and the sounds faded into whispers; they rejoiced once again, and again died into silence.

And now all around glowed a vast twilight; it filled the cradle of the planet with colourless fire. I felt a rippling motion which impelled me away from the centre to the circumference. At that centre a still flame began to lighten; a new change took place, and space began to curdle, a milky and nebulous substance rocked to and fro. At every motion the pulsation of its rhythm carried it farther and farther away from the centre; it grew darker, and a great purple shadow covered it so that I could see it no longer. I was now on the outer verge, where the twilight still continued to encircle the planet with zones of clear transparent light.

As night after night I rose up to visit it they grew many-coloured and brighter. I saw the imagination of nature visibly at work. I wandered through shadowy immaterial forests, a titanic vegetation built up of light and colour; I saw it growing denser, hung with festoons and trailers of fire, and spotted with the light of myriad flowers such as earth never knew. Coincident with the appearance of these things I felt within myself, as if in harmonious movement, a sense of joyousness, an increase of self-consciousness: I felt full of gladness, youth, and the mystery of the new. I felt that greater powers were about to appear, those who had thrown outwards this world and erected it as a palace in space.

I could not tell half the wonder of this strange race. I could not myself comprehend more than a little of the mystery of their being. They recognized my presence there, and communicated with me in such a way that I can only describe it by saying that they seemed to enter into my soul, breathing a fiery life; yet I knew that the highest I could reach to was but the outer verge of their spiritual nature, and to tell you but a little I have many times to translate it; for in the first unity with their thought I touched on an almost universal sphere of life, I peered into the ancient heart that beats throughout time; and this knowledge became changed in me, first into a vast and nebulous symbology, and so down through many degrees of human thought into words which hold not at all the pristine and magical beauty.

I stood before one of this race, and I thought, 'What is the meaning and end of life here?' Within me I felt the answering ecstasy that illuminated with vistas of dawn and rest. It seemed to say:

'Our spring and our summer are an unfolding into light and form, and our autumn and winter are a fading into the infinite soul.'

I questioned in my heart, 'To what end is this life poured forth and withdrawn?'

He came nearer and touched me; once more I felt the thrill of being that changed itself into vision.

'The end is creation, and creation is joy. The One awakens out of quiescence as we come forth, and knows itself in us; as we return we enter it in gladness, knowing ourselves. After long cycles the world you live in will become like ours; it will be poured forth and withdrawn; a mystic breath, a mirror to glass your being.'

He disappeared, while I wondered what cyclic changes would transmute our ball of mud into the subtle substance of thought.

In that world I dared not stay during its period of withdrawal; having entered a little into its life, I became subject to its laws; the Powers on its return would have dissolved my being utterly. I felt with a wild terror its clutch upon me, and I withdrew from the departing glory, from the greatness that was my destiny – but not yet.

From such dreams I would be aroused, perhaps, by a gentle knock at my door, and my little cousin Margaret's quaint face would peep in with a 'Cousin Robert, are you not coming down to supper?'

Of these visions in the light of after thought I would speak a little.

All this was but symbol, requiring to be thrice sublimed in interpretation ere its true meaning can be grasped. I do not know whether worlds are heralded by such glad songs, or whether any have such a fleeting existence, for the mind that reflects truth is deluded with strange phantasies of time and place in which seconds are rolled out into centuries and long cycles are reflected in an instant of time. There is within us a little space through which all the threads of the universe are drawn; and, surrounding that incomprehensible centre,[4] the mind of man sometimes catches glimpses of things which are true only in those glimpses; when we record them the true has vanished, and a shadowy story – such as this – alone remains. Yet, perhaps, the time is not altogether wasted in considering legends like these, for they reveal, though but in phantasy and symbol, a greatness we are heirs to, a destiny which is ours though it be yet far away.

1894

A DOOMED CITY[1]

Lights flew about me; images sparkled in the imperishable Akasa. Oh. such ancient, ancient places and peoples! Such forms of primitive grandeur and antique simplicity! I was thrilled through with strangeness, and anon quickened with a familiar sense as when one returns to the scenes of childhood and the places of long ago. Then the visions faded away, and I became folded up in blackness; out of the stillness came forth again the light of the elder day; the blackness grew thick with stars; I saw burning skies fading into dawn; over distant hills danced up the star of day; it brought others with it to pale soon in the grey light; from the roof of a high building I watched it shadowed by a multitude of magical spires and turrets which rose up darkly from a great city erected on the plain. I looked down through the gloom into the square below; already there was a stir; I could see black forms moving about; they plied at ponderous engines. I could hear cries of wrath from these giants; then a stony despair came over me, for I knew the Golden Age had passed away, and the earth was crowded with these pitiless and inhuman races, the masters of all magical arts. Proud, exultant, tireless heroes of old *Atlantis*,[2] this was your day of glory! What sin of all your sins did I witness? I watched from above, without comprehending it, the stir and rage; then suddenly impelled, I raised my eyes once more to the holy light. There I saw a new wonder borne high on the luminous air. His starry front proclaimed him straight one of the Children of the Wise – one of divine race. The brilliant moon-coloured lord – a vast phantom – floated erect with outstretched arms over the city; his shadowy hair drifted about him like a grey mist seen against the dawn. He glanced hither and thither beneath, and his hands swayed rhythmically as if he were weaving some enchantment; the rainbow fires danced about him; they flew here and there; I watched those radiant messengers; where they fell below, the toilers stopped suddenly as if stricken by light, looking vaguely about and above, seeing nothing; I knew then that the Lord was unknown to them. One after another I saw the toilers so touched steal away from labour, and far beyond I could see the road over the hills darkened here and there with moving forms passing hurriedly from the city. I looked up again; the Wise One was nigh the parapet I leaned on; I trembled being so near. I had but to stretch out my hands to touch greatness. I looked at the wonderful eyes; they were lightless as if the power were turned within; but they flashed anon, the fire in them seeming suddenly to run out from sphere deep-hidden in sphere; they were upon me.

I looked up. 'Lord, why or whither should I fly as all these do?'

His thought answered me: 'Your eyes are not yet sealed. See for thyself.'

Forthwith the eye of old memory opened, and the earth in its fairy-first beginning returned to me. I wandered – a luminous shadow; without eyes I saw the glory of life; without ears I heard its marvellous song; without nostrils I knew its sweet odours. I, the seer, lived in and shared the imagination of the Mighty. I knew the old earth once more, clear, transparent, shining, whose glory was self-begotten, flung up from its own heart, kindling the air with the reflection of its multitudinous fires. The fires ran in and out of the heart, in tides of crimson and torrents of gold, through veins of lilac, azure, and deepest blue. A million creatures ran free with indescribably flashing movement within them – the lustrous populace of the elements. Then the vision of the earth moved onwards and darkened, and the fiery heart was shadowed slowly from the eye of man who fell from dream and vision into deed and thought;[3] for his deeds he needed power, and for his thoughts messengers; he took the creatures of the elements; they became his servants to do his will, and his will was darkness; he moulded them into shapes of passion and hatred. As he sank deeper he knew them no longer from himself, though what he willed was accomplished by them. As he moved from place to place they followed in hordes, and the fiery tides – their habitation – rolled along with them beneath the earth. When cities were builded these terrible armies were thronged thick around, within, and under; in air, in fire, in earth, and in the hidden waters. Then I saw below me where the fires were gathering, surging, pressing, ready to leap forth and devour; there passed upwards from them, continually, strange beings, shadowy creatures of the underworld called forth by the will of the giants who meditated the destruction of another city; they entered into these giants who sent them forth again. Full of terror I cried out –

'The fires will follow! Oh, look, look, how ruddy and red they glow! They live, and they send forth living creatures!'

I looked up, but the Wise One had gone away, I knew not where. Then I arose hurriedly, went downward and out of the city. I fled, without stopping, across the mountain-path, until I left far behind the city and the doomed giants.

Æ.

THE MYSTIC NIGHTS' ENTERTAINMENT[1]

We went forth gay in the twilight's cover;
The dragon Day with his ruddy crest
Blazed on the shadowy hills hung over
The still grey fields in their dewy rest.

We went forth gay, for all ancient stories
Were told again in our hearts as we trod;
Above were the mountain's dawn-white glories;
We climbed to it as the throne of God.

We pitched our tents in a sheltered nook on the mountain side. We were great with glee during the day, forecasting happy holidays remote from the crowded city. But now as we sat round the camp fire at dusk silence fell upon us. What were we to do in the long evenings? I could see Willie's jolly face on the other side of the fire trying to smother a yawn as he refilled his pipe. Bryan was watching the stars dropping into their places one by one. I turned to Robert and directed the general attention to him as a proper object for scorn. He had drawn a pamphlet on some scientific subject from his breast-pocket and was trying to read it by the flickering light.

'Did you come up to the mountains for this,' I asked, 'to increase your knowledge of the Eocene age? Put it by, or – we will send it up as a burnt offering to the stars.'

'Well,' he said, looking rather ashamed, 'one must do something, you know. Willie has his pipe, Bryan is holding some mysterious intercourse with the planets, and you have the fire to take care of. What is one to do?'

This went to the root of the matter. I pondered over it awhile, until an idea struck me.

'There is Bryan. Let him tell us a story. He was flung into life with a bundle of old legends. He knows all mystery and enchantment since the days of the Rishees, and has imagined more behind them. He has tales of a thousand incarnations hidden away in secretness. He believes that everything that happened lives still in the memory of Nature, and that he can call up out of the cycles of the past heroic figures and forgotten history, simply by his will, as a magician draws the elemental hordes together.'

'Have a dragon and a princess in it,' said Willie, settling himself into an attitude of listening.

'Or authentic information about the Eocene man,' suggested Robert.

'I could not tell a story that way,' said Bryan simply. 'I could never invent a story, though all the characters, heroes and princes, were to come and sit beside me so that I could describe them as they really were. My stories come like living creatures into my mind; and I can only tell them as they tell themselves to me. Today, as I lay in the sunlight with closed eyes, I saw a haze of golden light, then twilight trees appeared and moving figures and voices speaking; it shaped itself into what is hardly a story, but only an evening in some legendary existence.'

We waited while Bryan tried to recall his misty figures. We were already in sympathy with his phantasmal world, for the valleys below us were dim-coloured and quiet, and we heard but rarely and far away the noises of the village; the creatures of the mountain moved about in secretness, seeking their own peculiar joys in stillness amid dews and darkness. After a little Bryan began

THE GARDENS OF TWILIGHT.[2]

I saw in my vision one of the heroes of the antique world. He rode for many, many days, yet saw no kindly human face. After long wanderings and toils he came to the Gardens of Twilight, the rich and rare gardens of the primeval world, known by rumour to the ancient Greeks as the Hesperides. He looked around with wonder; the place was all a misty dazzle with light, a level light as of evening that flowed everywhere about; the air was rich with the scent of many blossoms; from each flower rose an odour that hovered about it as a delicate vapour. While he gazed, one of the spirits of the garden came nigh him in the guise of a beautiful human child.

'How came you here?'

'I wandered for many years,' he said, 'I fought with the dragons that lie coiled in citron scales on the highways; I warred against oppression; I made justice to prevail, and now that peace is on the land I might have rested with peace in mine own heart, but I could not yet. So I left behind the happy hearths and homes of men and rode onward, a secret fire burning ceaselessly within me; I know not in what strange home it will be still. But what gardens are these?'

'They are the Gardens of Twilight,' answered the child.

'How beautiful then must be the Gardens of Day! How like a faint fine dust of amethyst and gold the mist arises from the enchanted odorous flowers! Surely some spirit things must dwell within the air that breaks so perpetually into hues of pearl and shell!'

'They are the servants of Zeus,' the child said. 'They live within these wandering airs; they go forth into the world and make mystery in the hearts of men.'

'Was it one such guided me thither?'

'I do not know; but this I know, whether led by the wandering spirits or guided by their own hearts, none can remain here safely and look upon the flowers save those who understand their mystery or those who can create an equal beauty. For all others deadly is the scent of the blossoms; stricken with madness, they are whirled away into the outer world in fever, passion and unending hunger and torment.'

'I do not care if I pass from them,' said the wanderer. 'It is not here my heart could be still and its desire cease, but in the first Fountain.'

They passed on and went deeper into the Gardens of Twilight, which were ever-changing, opalescent, ever-blushing with new and momentary beauty, ever-vanishing before the steady gaze to reveal beneath more silent worlds of mystic being. Like vapour, now gorgeous and now delicate, they wavered, or as the giant weeds are shadowy around the diver in the Indian wave sun-drenched through all its deeps of green. Sometimes a path would unfold, with a million shining flowers of blue, twinkling like stars in the Milky Way, beneath their feet, and would wind away delicately into the faery distances.

'Let us rest,' said the child, leaning against a tree. She began swaying a hand to and fro among the flowers; as her fingers touched the bell-like blooms of burning amethyst they became stained with the rich colour; she seemed to lose herself in dreams as one who toils not for delight, living ever amid rich joys. He wondered if she was as unreal as the gardens, and remembering her words, they seemed familiar as if they were but echoes of the unuttered thoughts that welled up as he moved about. While he watched the flitting phantasmagoria with a sense expectant of music which never came, there arose before him images of peace, vanishing faster than passion, and forms of steadfast purity came nigh, attired, priestess-like, in white and gold; they laid their heads against his breast; as he looked down, their eyes, eager and flamelike, grew passionate and full of desire. He stretched out his hand to pluck blossoms and twine wreaths for their beautiful heads.

'Do not! Do not!' cried the child. 'See how every blossom has its guardian!'

There were serpents coiling about the roots of every flower, or amid the leaves, waiting with undulating head and forked tongue to strike the uncautious hand. He shook off the drowsy influence of the scents and o'er-burdened air; the forms vanished. He remembered the child's words: 'None can remain in safety save those who understand the mystery, or those who can create an equal beauty.' He began to ponder over the meaning of the gardens.

'While we sit here, late lingerers in the glory of the twilight, I will tell you a story which my fancy brings me,' he said. 'I thought one came here long ago and built himself a mighty world in a dream of many hundred years.'

'He had lived with kings and counsellors; he had wrought in magical arts, and the great and wise of the earth were his fellows. When a time came for him to depart he turned away sadly from the towers of men. He passed, without knowing it, through the strange defiles which lead to these gardens; but the light did not break upon him in iridescent waves foamy with flowers and sparkling with vanishing forms; the light was hidden in the bosom of the twilight; it was all-pervading but invisible; the essence of the light bathed his soul; the light was living; the light was exhaustless; by it everything was born; touched by it everything went forth in ecstasy, blind, seeking for realization.

'The magician brought with him the seeds of human desire and wisdom and aspiration. The light broke into his moody forgetfulness and kindled long-forgotten fires. He awoke from his darkness and saw before him in happiest vistas the island city of his longing. Around him were the men and women he knew; acting on his secret wishes the multitudes hailed him as king, they bowed before him as wise, they worshipped him as all-powerful. It was not strange to him, and rapt in royal imaginations for countless years he held sway over the island city. He dreamed of it as a poet, and there was no more beautiful city than this city of his dream. There were palaces that shot up, pinnacle upon pinnacle, amid the jewel-light of the stars; there were courts and porticoes full of mysterious glory and gloom, magnificence and darkness; there were fountains that jetted their pearly mists into the light; around them with summer in their hearts lay the island inhabitants, each one an angel for beauty. As the dream of the magician deepened in rapture, the city wavered and changed more continually; its towers pierced more daringly into the way of the stars; for the darkness below he summoned birds of fire from the aerial deeps; they circled the palaces with flaming wings; they stained the air with richest dyes and rained forth emerald and blue and gold on the streets and sculptured walls and the inhabitants in their strange joys.

'His dream changed; he went forth no more but shut himself up in his palace with his wisest princes, and as he took counsel with them, the phantasmal and brilliant towers without faded and fell away as a butterfly droops its wings. For countless years he lived in the intoxication of thought; around him were sages who propounded wisest laws, and poets who sang of love, humanity and destiny. As his dream deepened still more in its rapture, they sang of mightier themes; there was continual music and light; there was no limit of glory or dominion which the human soul might not aspire to; his warriors stepped from star to star in dreams of conquest, and would have stayed the seraph princes of the wind and wave and fire, to make more radiant the retinue of this magician of the Beautiful.

'Again his desire changed. He sought to hold no further sway over these wide realms beyond him; he shut himself up in an inner chamber in lonely meditation, and as he entered into a deeper being the sages and poets, who were with him at his royal feasts, vanished and were no more. He, the wise mind, pondered within himself, finding joy in the continual inward birth of thought following thought, as in lonely seas wave rolls upon wave. From all things he had known or experienced he drew forth their essence and hidden meaning, and he found that he had been no less a king in his old unconsciousness than he now was, and that at all times nature had been obeisant and whatever had happened had still been by his own will. Through the light, thin fretted by the fire of his aspiration, he sometimes seemed to see the Shining Law in all things and the movement throughout the thought-swept fields of heaven of the universal imagination. He saw that this, too, had been a minister to him. He drew nigh to himself – divinity. The last rapture of his soul was this radiant self-conception. Save for this vesture[3] the light of illusion fell from him. He was now in a circle of whitest fire, that girdled and looked in upon the movements of worlds within its breast. He tried to expand and enter this flaming circle; myriads of beings on its verges watched him with pity; I felt their thought thrilling within me.

' "He will never attain it!"

' "Ah, the Beautiful Bird, his plumage is stained!"

' "His glory will drag him down!"

' "Only in invisible whiteness can he pass!"

' "How he floats upwards, the Beautiful Bird!"

'These voices of universal compassion did not reach him, rapt in aspiration and imperious will. For an instant – an eternity – the infinitudes thrilled him, those infinitudes which in that instant he knew he could never enter but as one with all on the days of the great return. All that longed, all that aspired and dared, all but the immortal were in that moment destroyed, and hurled downwards from the highest heaven of life, the pilgrim spark began once more as a child to live over again the round of human days.'

'The spirit of the place o'ermastered you,' said the child. 'Here many come and dream; and their dream of joy ended, out of each dreaming sphere comes forth again in pain the infant spirit of man.'

'But beyond this illusive light and these ever-changing vistas – what lies? I am weary of their vanishing glories. I would not wish to mount up through dreams to behold the true and fall away powerlessly, but would rather return to earth, though in pain, still eager to take up and renew the cyclic labours.'

'I belong to the gardens,' said the child, 'I do not know what lies beyond. But there are many paths leading far away.'

Before them where they stood branched out paths of rich flowers. Here a region of pinks lured on to vistas of delicate glory; there ideal violet hues led to a more solemn beauty; here the eyes were dazzled by avenues of rich, radiant, and sunny green; another in beautiful golden colours seemed to invite to the land of the sun, and yet another winded away through soft and shadowy blues to remote spiritual distances. There was one, a path of white flowers ending in light no eye could pierce.

'I will choose this – the path of white flowers,' he said, waving farewell to the child. I watched the antique hero in my vision as he passed into the light; he seemed to shine, to grow larger; as he vanished from my eyes he was transfigured, entering as a god the region of gods.

NIGHT ON THE MOUNTAINS

'Did you really dream all that?' said Willie. 'How jolly it must be! It is like stepping from sphere to sphere. Before the night of one day you are in the morning of another. I suppose you have some theory about it all – as wonderful as your gardens?'

'Yes!' said our sceptic, 'I had an uneasy consciousness it was not all pure story. I felt an allegory hiding its leanness somewhere beneath the glow and colour.'

'What I want to know is how these things enter the imagination at all!'

'With what a dreadfully scientific spirit you dissect a fantasy! Perhaps you might understand if you recall what sometimes happens before sleep. At first you see pictures of things, landscapes, people you know; after a time people and places unknown before begin to mingle with them in an ever-widening circle of visions; the light on which these things are pictured is universal, though everyone has around himself his own special sphere of light; this is the mirror of himself – his memory; but as we go deeper into ourselves in introspection we see beyond our special sphere into the great or universal light, the memorial tablet of nature; there lie hidden the secrets of the past; and so, as Felix said a little while ago, we can call up and renew the life of legend and tradition. This is the Astral Light of the mystics. Its deeper and more living aspect seems to inflame the principle of desire in us. All the sweet, seductive, bewitching temptations of sense are inspired by it. After death the soul passing into this living light goes on thinking, thinking, goes on aspiring, aspiring, creating unconsciously around itself its own circumstance in which all sweetest desires are self-fulfilled. When this dream-power is exhausted the soul returns again to earth. With some this return is due to the thirst for existence; with some to a perception of the real needs of soul.'

'Do you really believe all that?'

'Oh yes! But that is only a general statement.'

'I wonder at your capacity for believing in these invisible spheres. As for me I cannot go beyond the world I live in. When I think of these things some dreadful necessity seems heaped upon me to continue here – or, as you might put it, an angel with a flaming sword keeps everywhere the avenues to the Tree of Life.'[4]

'Oh!' said Willie, 'it seems to me a most reasonable theory. After all, what else could the soul do after death but think itself out? It has no body to move about in. I am going to dream over it now. Good-night!'

He turned into the tent and Robert followed him. 'Well, I cannot rest yet,' said Bryan, 'I am going up for a little to the top of the hill. Come, Felix, these drowsy fellows are going to hide themselves from the face of night.' We went up, and leaning on a boulder of rock looked out together. Away upon the dream-built margin of space a thousand tremors fled and chased each other all along the shadowy night. The human traditions, memories of pain, struggle, hope and desire floated away and melted in the quietude until at last only the elemental consciousness remained at gaze. I felt chilled by the vacancies. I wondered what this void was to Bryan. I wished to see with his eyes. His arm was around my shoulder. How I loved him – my nearest – my brother! The fierce and tender flame, comrade to his spirit, glowed in my heart. I felt a commingling of natures, something moved before my eyes. 'Look, Bryan!' I whispered, 'this is faery!' A slight upright figure, a child, stood a little apart shedding a delicate radiance upon the dusky air. Curiously innocent, primeval, she moved, withdrawn in a world only half-perceived of gorgeous blossoms and mystic shadows. Through her hair of feathery brown drifting about her the gleam of dust of gold and of rich colour seemed to come from her dress. She raised her finger-tips from the flowers and dashed the bright dew aside. I felt something vaguely familiar about the gesture. Then Bryan said, 'It is one of the Children of Twilight.' It was a revelation of his mind. I had entered into the forms of his imagination.

'This is wonderful, Bryan! If I can thus share in the thought of one, there can be no limit to the extension of this faculty. It seems at the moment as if I could hope to finally enter the mind of humanity and gaze upon soul, not substance.'

'It would be a great but terrible power. As often as not we imagine ourselves into demons. Space is thronged with these dragon-like forms, chimaeras of the fearful mind. Every thought is an entity.[5] Some time or other I think we will have to slay this brood we have brought forth.'

But as we turned backwards I had no dread or thought of this future contest. I felt only gay hopes, saw only ever-widening vistas. The dreams of the Golden Age, of far-off happy times grew full of meaning. I peopled all the future with their splendour. The air was thronged with bright supernatural beings, they moved in air, in light; and they and we and all together were sustained and thrilled by the breath of the Unknown God.

As we drew nigh to the tent, the light of the fire still flickering revealed Robert's face within. He was sleeping. The warmth of the sun had not yet charmed away the signs of study and anxious thought.

'Do you know the old tradition that in the deepest sleep[6] of the body the soul goes into itself? I believe he now knows the truth he feared to face. A little while ago he was here; he was in doubt; now he is gone unto all ancient things. He was in prison; now the Bird of Paradise has wings. We cannot call him by any name, for we do not know what he is. We might indeed cry aloud to his glory, as of old the Indian sage cried to a sleeper, "Thou great one, clad in white raiment; Soma: King!" But who thinking what he is would call back the Titan to this strange and pitiful dream of life? Let us breathe softly to do him reverence. It is now the Hour of the King,

> 'Who would think this quiet breather
>   From the world had taken flight?
> Yet within the form we see there
>   Wakes the Golden King to-night.
>
> 'Out upon the face of faces
>   He looked forth before his sleep;
> Now he knows the starry races
>   Haunters of the ancient deep;

> 'On the Bird of Diamond Glory
>   Floats in mystic floods of song;
> As he lists, Time's triple story
>   Seems but as a day is long.
>
> 'When he wakes – the dreamy-hearted –
>   He will know not whence he came,
> And the light from which he parted
>   Be the seraph's sword of flame;
>
> 'And behind it hosts supernal
>   Guarding the lost Paradise,
> And the Tree of Life eternal
>   From the weeping human eyes.'

'You are an enchanter, Bryan. As you speak I half imagine the darkness sparkles with images, with heroes and ancient kings who pass, and jewelled seraphs who move in flame. I feel mad. The distance rushes at me. The night and stars are living, and – speak unknown things! You have made me so restless I will never sleep.'

I lay down. The burden of the wonder and mystery of existence was upon me. Through the opening of the tent the warm night air flowed in; the stars seemed to come near – nearer – full of kindly intent – with familiar whispering; until at last I sank back into the great deep of sleep with a mysterious radiance of dream showering all about me.

Night the Second

> The skies were dim and vast and deep
>   Above the vales of rest;
> They seemed to rock the stars asleep
>   Beyond the mountain's crest.
>
> Oh, vale and stars and rocks and trees,
>   He gives to you his rest,
> But holds afar from you the peace
>   Whose home is in His breast!

The massy night, brilliant with golden lights enfolded us. All things were at rest. After a long day's ramble among the hills, we sat down again before our fire. I felt, perhaps we all felt, a mystic unquiet rebelling against the slumbrous mood of nature rolled round her hills and valleys.

'You must explain to us, Bryan, why it is we can never attain a real quiet, even here where all things seem at peace.'

'We are aliens here, and so do not know ourselves. We are always dreaming of some other life. These dreams, if we could only rightly interpret them, would be the doors through which we might pass into a real knowledge of ourselves.'

'I don't think I would get much wisdom out of my dreams,' said Willie. 'I had a dream last night; a lot of little goblin fellows dancing a jig on the plains of twilight. Perhaps you could tell us a real dream?'

'I remember one dream of the kind I mean, which I will tell you. It left a deep impression upon me. I will call it a dream of

THE NORTHERN LIGHTS

I awoke from sleep with a cry. I was hurled up from the great deep and rejected of the darkness. But out of the clouds and dreams I built up a symbol of the going forth of the spirit – a symbol, not a memory – for if I could remember, I could return again at will and be free of the unknown land. But in slumber I was free. I sped forth like an arrow. I followed a secret hope, breasting the currents of life flowing all about me. I tracked these streams winding in secretness far away. I said, 'I am going to myself. I will bathe in the Fountain of Life;' and so on and on I sped northwards, with dark waters flowing beneath me and stars companioning my flight. Then a radiance illumined the heavens, the icy peaks and caves, and I saw the Northern Lights. Out of the diamond breast of the air I looked forth. Below the dim world shone all with pale and wintry green; the icy crests flickered with a light reflected from the shadowy auras streaming over the horizon. Then these auras broke out in fire, and the plains of ice were illumined. The light flashed through the goblin caves, and lit up their frosty hearts and the fantastic minarets drooping above them. Light above in solemn array went forth and conquered the night. Light below with a myriad flashing spears pursued the gloom. Its dazzling lances shivered in the heart of the ice; they sped along the ghostly hollows; the hues of the orient seemed to laugh through winter; the peaks blossomed with sparry and crystalline flowers, lilac and white and blue; they faded away, pearl, opal and pink in shimmering evanescence; then gleams of rose and amethyst travelled slowly from spar to spar, lightened and departed; there was silence before my eyes; the world once more was all a pale and wintry green. I thought of them no more, but of the mighty and unseen tides going by me with billowy motion. 'Oh, Fountain I seek, thy waters are all about me, but where shall I find a path to Thee?' Something answered my cry, 'Look in thy heart!' and, obeying the voice, the seer in me looked forth no more through the eyes of the shadowy form, but sank deep within itself. I knew then the nature of these mystic streams; they were life, joy, love, ardour, light. From these came the breath of life which the heart drew in with every beat, and from thence it was flashed up in illumination through the cloudy hollows of the brain. They poured forth unceasingly; they were life in everyone; they were joy in everyone; they stirred an incommunicable love which was fulfilled only in yielding to and adoration of the vast. But the Fountain I could not draw nigh unto; I was borne backwards from its unimaginable centre, then an arm seized me, and I was stayed. I could see no one, but I grew quiet, full of deep quiet, out of which memory breathes only shadowiest symbols, images of power and Holy Sages, their grand faces turned to the world, as if in the benediction of universal love, pity, sympathy, and peace, ordained by Buddha; the faces of the Fathers, ancient with eternal youth, looking forth as in the imagination of the mystic Blake, the Morning Stars looked forth and sang together. A sound as of an 'OM' unceasing welled up and made an aureole of peace around them. I would have joined in the song, but could not attain to them. I knew if I had a deeper love I could have entered with them into unending labours amid peace; but I could only stand and gaze; in my heart a longing that was worship, in my thought a wonder that was praise. 'Who are these?' I murmured. The Voice answered, 'They are the servants of the Nameless One.[7] They do his bidding among men. They awaken the old heroic fire of sacrifice in forgetful hearts.' Then the forms of elder life appeared in my vision. I saw the old earth, a fairy shadow ere it yet had hardened, peopled with ethereal races unknowing of themselves or their destinies and lulled with inward dreams; above and far away I saw how many glittering hosts, their struggle ended, moved onward to the Sabbath of Eternity. Out of these hosts, one dropped as a star from their heart, and overshadowed the olden earth with its love. Wherever it rested I saw each man awakening from his dream turned away with the thought of sacrifice in his heart, a fire that might be forgotten, but could never die. This was the continual secret whisper of the Fathers in the inmost being of humanity. 'Why do they not listen?' I marvelled. Then I heard another cry from the lower pole, the pit; a voice of old despair and protest, the appeal of passion seeking its own fulfilment. Alternate with the dawn of Light was the breath of the expanding Dark where powers of evil were gathered together. 'It is the strife between light and darkness which are the world's eternal ways,' said the Voice, 'but the light shall overcome and the fire in the heart be rekindled; men shall regain their old angelic being, and though the dark powers may war upon them, the angels with their love shall slay them. Be thou ready for the battle, and see thou use only love in the fight.' Then I was hurried backward with swift speed, and awoke. All I knew was but a symbol, but I had the peace of the mystic Fathers in my heart, and the jewelled glory of the Northern Lights all dazzling about my eyes.'

'Well, after a dream like that,' said Willie, 'the only thing one can do is to try and dream another like it.'

THE ENCHANTMENT OF CUCHULLAIN[1]

By Æ. and Aretas.

While our vision, backward cast,
Ranged the everliving past,
Through a haze of misty things –
Luminous with quiverings
Musical as starry chimes –
Rose a hero of old times,
In whose breast the magic powers
Slumbering from primeval hours,
Woke at the enchantment wild
Of Aed Abrait's lovely child;
Still for all her Druid learning
With the wild-bird heart, whose yearning
Blinded at his strength and beauty,
Clung to love and laughed at duty.
Warrior chief, and mystic maid,
Though your stumbling footsteps strayed,
This at least in part atones –
Jewels were your stumbling-stones!

I

The Birds of Angus

The birds were a winging rapture in the twilight. White wings, grey wings, brown wings, fluttered around and over the pine trees that crowned the grassy dun. The highest wings flashed with a golden light. At the sound of voices they vanished.

'How then shall we go to the plains of Murthemney? We ought not to be known. Shall we go invisibly, or in other forms? We must also fly as swiftly as the birds go.'

'Fly! yes, yes, we shall – fly as the birds. But we shall choose fairer forms than these. I know where the Birds of Angus flock. Come, Liban, come!'

The crypt beneath the dun was flooded with light, silvery and golden, a light which came not from the sun nor from the moon; a light not born from any parent luminary, and which knew nothing opaque. More free than the birds of the air were the shadowy forms of the two daughters of Aed Abrait, as they gazed out from that rock-built dun upon a place their mortal feet had never trod. Yet timidly Liban looked at her more adventurous sister. Fand floated to the centre of the cavern, erect and radiant. Her eyes followed the wavy tremulous motion of the light as it rolled by. They seemed to pierce through earth and rock, and search out the secret hollows of the star, to know the vastness, and to dominate and compel the motion of the light. Her sister watched her half curiously and half in admiration and wonder. As the floating form grew more intense the arms swayed about and the lips murmured. A sheen as of many jewels played beneath the pearly mist which enrobed her; over her head rose the crest of the Dragon; she seemed to become one with the shining, to draw it backwards into herself. Then from far away came a wondrous melody, a sound as of ancient chiming of the stars. The sidereal rivers flowed by with more dazzling light, and the Birds of Angus were about them.

'Look, Liban, look!' cried the Enchantress. 'These of old were the chariots of the children of men. On these the baby offspring of the Gods raced through the nights of diamond and sapphire. We are not less than they though a hundred ages set us apart. We will go forth royally as they did. Let us choose forms from among these. If the Hound should see us he will know we have power.'

With arms around each other they watched the starry flocks hurtling about them. The birds wheeled around, fled away, and again returned. There were winged serpents; might which would put to flight the degenerate eagle; plumage before which the birds of paradise would show dull as clay. These wings dipt in the dawn flashed ceaselessly. Ah, what plumage of white fire rayed out with pinions of opalescent glory! What feathered sprays of burning amethyst! What crests of scarlet and gold, of citron and wavy green! They floated by in countless multitudes; they swayed in starry clusters dripping with light, singing a melody caught from the spheres of the Gods, the song which of old called forth the earth from its slumber. The sound was entrancing. Oh, fiery birds who float in the purple rivers of the Twilight, ye who rest in the great caverns of the world, whoever listens to your song shall grow faint with longing, for he shall hear the great, deep call in his heart and his spirit shall yearn to go afar; whatever eyes see you shall grow suddenly blinded with tears for a glory that has passed away from the world, for an empire we no longer range.

'They bring back the air of the ancient days. Ah! now I have the heart of the child once again. Time has not known me. Let us away with them. We will sweep over Eri and lead the starry flocks as the queen birds.'

'If we only dared. But think, Fand, we shall have every wizard eye spying upon us, and every boy who can use his freedom will follow and thwart us. Not these forms, but others let us take. Ah, look at those who come in grey and white and brown! Send home the radiant ones. We will adventure with these.'

'Be it so. Back to your fountains, O purple rivers! King-Bird, Queen-Bird, to your home in the hollows lead your flock!' So she spoke, but her words were shining and her waving arms compelled the feathered monarchs with radiations of outstretched flame. To the others: 'Rest here awhile, sweet singers. We shall not detain you captive for long.' So she spoke, but her hands that caressed laid to sleep the restless pulsation of the wings and lulled the ecstatic song.

Night, which to the eye of the magian shows more clearly all that the bright day conceals, overspread with a wizard twilight the vast hollow of the heavens. Numberless airy rivulets, each with its own peculiar shining, ran hither and thither like the iridescent currents streaming over a bubble. Out of the still duskier, more darkly glowing and phantasmal depths stared the great eyes of space, rimmed about with rainbow-dyes. As night moved on to dawn two birds shot forth from the dun, linked together by a cord of golden fire. They fled southwards and eastwards. As they went they sang a song which tingled the pulses of the air. In the dark fields the aureoles around the flowers grew momentarily brighter. Over the mountain homes of the Tuatha de Danaans rose up shadowy forms who watched, listened, and pondered awhile. The strayed wanderers amid the woods heard the enraptured notes and forgot their sorrows and life itself in a hurricane of divine remembrance. Where the late feast was breaking up the melody suddenly floated in and enwreathed the pillared halls, and revellers became silent where they stood, the mighty warriors in their hands bowed low their faces. Still on and on swept the strange birds flying southwards and eastwards.

> Still in many a peasant cot
> Lives the story unforgot
> While the faded parchments old
> Still their rhyming tale unfold.
> There is yet another book
> Where thine eager eyes may look.
> There within its shining pages

Lives the long romance of ages,
Liban, Fand, their glowing dreams,
Angus' birds, the magic streams
Flooding all the twilight crypt,
Runes and spells in starry script;
Secrets never whispered here
In the light are chanted clear.
Read in it the tales of Eri
If the written word be weary.

Never is there day so gleaming
But the dusk o'ertakes it;
Never night so dark and dreaming
But the dawn awakes it:
And the soul has nights and days
In its own eternal ways.

II

Cuchullain's Dream

The air was cool with the coming of winter; but with the outer cold came the inner warmth of the sun, full of subtle vitality and strength. And the Ultonians had assembled to light the yearly fire in honour of the Sun-God, at the seven-days' feast of Samhain. There the warriors of Ulster rested by the sacred fire, gazing with closed eyes upon the changing colours of the sun-breath, catching glimpses of visions, or anon performing feats of magic when they felt the power stirring within their breasts. They sang the songs of old times, of the lands of the West, where their forefathers lived ere the earth-fires slew those lands, and the sea-waves buried them, leaving only Eri, the isle where dwelt men so holy that the earth-fires dared not to assail it, and the ocean stood at bay. Lightly the warriors juggled with their great weapons of glittering bronze; and each told of his deeds in battle and in the chase; but woe to him who boasted or spoke falsely, magnifying his prowess, for then would his sword angrily turn of itself in its scabbard, convicting him of untruth.

Cuchullain, youngest but mightiest of all the warriors, sat moodily apart, his beardless chin resting in the palms of his hands, his eyes staring fixedly at the mirror-like surface of the lake upon whose sloping bank he rested. Laeg, his charioteer, lying at full length upon the greensward near by, watched him intently, a gloomy shadow darkening his usually cheerful face.

'It's a woman's trick, that,' he muttered to himself, 'staring into the water when trying to see the country of the Sidhe, and unworthy of a warrior. And to think of him doing it, who used to have the clearest sight, and had more power for wonder-working than anyone else in the lands of the West! Besides, he isn't seeing anything now, for all the help of the water. When last I went to the dun some women of the Sidhe told me they had looked up Cuchullain and found he was getting too dim-eyed to see anything clearly now, even in his sleep. It's true enough, but to hear it said even by women!'

And the discontented charioteer glanced back contemptuously at a group of women a short distance away, who were following with their eyes a flock of wild birds circling over the plain.

'I suppose they want those birds,' he continued, conversing familiarly with himself. 'It's the way of women to want everything they see, especially if it's something hard to catch, like those wild birds.'

But Laeg's cynicism was not so deep as to keep his glance from lingering upon the bevy of graceful maidens and stately matrons. Their soft laughter reached his ear through the still evening air; and watching their animated gestures he idly speculated upon the plan he felt sure they were arranging.

'Yes; they want the birds. They wish to fasten the wings to their shoulders, to make themselves look like the women of the Sidhe. They know Cuchullain is the only man who can get the birds for them, but even Emer, his wife, is afraid to ask him. Of course they will coax that patient Ethné to do it. If she succeeds, she'll get no thanks; and if she fails she'll have all the blame, and go off by herself to cry over the harsh words spoken by Cuchullain in his bad temper. That's the way of Ethné, poor girl.'

He was right in his conjecture, for presently Ethné left the group and hesitatingly approached the giant warrior, who was still gazing vacantly at the glassy surface of the water. She touched him timidly on the shoulder. Slowly he raised his head, and still half dazed by his long staring, listened while she made her request. He rose to his feet sleepily, throwing out his brawny arms and expanding his chest as he cast a keen glance at the birds slowly circling near the ground.

'Those birds are not fit to eat,' he said, turning to her with a good-natured smile.

'But we want the wings to put on our shoulders. It would be so good of you to get them for us,' said Ethné in persuasive tones.

'If it's flying you wish to try,' he said, with a laugh, 'you'll need better wings than those. However, you shall have them if I can get within throwing distance of them.'

He glanced around for Laeg. That far-seeing individual was already yoking the horses to the chariot. A moment later, Cuchullain and the charioteer were dashing across the plain behind the galloping steeds. As they neared the birds, Cuchullain sent missiles at them from his sling with such incredible rapidity and certainty of aim that not one of the flock escaped. Each of the women was given two of the birds; but when Ethné, who had modestly held back when the others hurried forward to meet the returning chariot, came to receive her share, not one remained.

'As usual,' said Laeg stolidly, 'if anyone fails to get her portion of anything, it's sure to be Ethné.'

'Too true,' said Cuchullain, a look of compassion softening his stern features. He strode over to Ethné, and placing his hand gently on her head said: 'Don't take your disappointment to heart, little woman; when any more birds come to the plains of Murthemney, I promise to get for you the most beautiful of them all.'

'There's a fine brace of them now, flying towards us,' explained Laeg, pointing across the lake. 'And I think I hear them singing. Queer birds, those; for I see a cord as of red gold between them.'

Nearer and nearer swept the strange beings of the air, and as their weird melody reached the many Ultonians at the Samhain fire, the stalwart warriors, slender maidens, the youthful and the time-worn, all felt the spell and became as statues, silent, motionless, entranced. Alone the three at the chariot felt not the binding influence of the spell. Cuchullain quietly fitted a smooth pebble into his sling. Ethné looked appealingly at Laeg, in whose sagacity she greatly trusted. A faint twinkle of the eye was the only sign that betrayed the thought of the charioteer as he tried to return her glance with a look of quiet unconcern. She hastened after Cuchullain, who had taken his stand behind a great rock on the lake shore which concealed him from the approaching birds.

'Do not try to take them,' she entreated; 'there is some strange power about them which your eyes do not see; I feel it, and my heart is filled with dread.'

The young warrior made no reply, but whirling his sling above his head sent the missile with terrific force at the two swan-like voyagers of the air. It went far astray, and splashed harmlessly into the lake, throwing up a fountain of spray. Cuchullain's face grew dark. Never before in war or the chase had he missed so easy a mark. Angrily he caught a javelin from his belt and hurled it at the birds, which had swerved from their course and were now flying swiftly away. It was a mighty cast, even for the strong arm of the mightiest warrior of Eri; and the javelin, glittering in the sun, was well on the downward curve of its long flight, its force spent, when its point touched the wing of the nearest bird. A sphere of golden flame seemed to glitter about them as they turned downward and disappeared beneath the deep waters of the lake.

Cuchullain threw himself upon the ground, leaning his broad shoulders against the rock.

'Leave me,' he said in sullen tones to Ethné; 'my senses are dull with sleep from long watching at the Samhain fire. For the first time since I slew the hound of Culain my right arm has failed me. My eyes are clouded, and strange music murmurs in my heart.'

His eyes closed, his heavy breathing was broken by sighs, and anguish distorted his features. Ethné watched him awhile, and then stole quietly back to where the warriors were, and said to them:

'Cuchullain lies slumbering by yonder rock, and he moans in his sleep as if the people of the Sidhe were reproaching his soul for some misdeed. I fear those birds that had the power behind them. Should we not waken him?'

But while they held council, and some were about to go and awaken him, Fergus mac Roy, foster-father of Cuchullain, arose, and all drew back in awe, for they saw the light of the Sun-God shining from his eyes, and his voice had the Druid ring as he said in stern tones of command:

'Touch him not, for he sees a vision; the people of the Sidhe are with him; and from the far distant past, even from the days of the sunken lands of the West, I see the hand of Fate reach out and grasp the warrior of Eri, to place him on a throne where he shall rule the souls of men.'

To Cuchullain it did not seem that he slept; for though his eyelids fell, his sight still rested on the calm surface of the lake, the shining sand on the shore, and the great brown rock against which he reclined. But whence came the two maidens who were walking toward him along the glistening sand? He gazed at them in speechless wonder; surely only in dreamland could so fair a vision be seen. In dreamland, yes; for a dim memory awoke in his breast that he had seen them before in the world of slumber. One wore a mantle of soft green, and her flaxen hair, strangely white but with a glint of gold, fell about her shoulders so thickly it seemed like a silken hood out of which looked a white face with gleaming violet eyes. The other maiden had dark brown eyes, very large, very luminous; her cheeks were rosy, with just a hint of bronzing by the sunshine, a dimple in her chin added to the effect of her pouting red lips; her dark brown hair was unbound and falling loosely over her deep crimson mantle, which reached from her waist in five heavy folds. The recumbent warrior felt a weird spell upon him. Powerless to move or speak, he saw the two maidens advance and stand beside him, the sunlight gleaming upon their bare arms and bosoms. They smiled upon him and uplifted their arms, and then from their fingers

The Enchantment of Cuchullain

there rained down upon him blinding lightnings, filaments of flame that stung like whipcords, a hail of rainbow sparks that benumbed him, darting flames that pierced him like javelins; and as he gazed upward through that storm of fire, writhing in his agony, he saw still their white arms waving to and fro, weaving a network of lightnings about him, their faces smiling upon him, serene and kindly; and in the eyes of her with the crimson mantle he read a tenderness all too human. Eyes that shone with tenderness; white arms that wove a rainbow-mesh of torturing fires about him; his anguish ever increasing, until he saw the arms stop waving, held for an instant aloft, and then swept downward with a torrent of flame and a mighty crash of sound like the spears of ten thousand warriors meeting in battle, and then – he was alone, staring with wide-open eyes at the blue, cloud-mirroring surface of the lake and the white sand gleaming on the shore.

'Trouble me not with questions,' said Cuchullain to the warriors gathered about him. 'My limbs are benumbed and refuse to obey me. Bear me to my sick-bed at Tete Brece.'

'Shall we not take you to Dun Imrish, or to Dun Delca, where you may be with Emer?' said they.

'No,' he replied, a shudder convulsing his strong frame; 'bear me to Tete Brece.'

And when they had done so, he dwelt there for a year, and on his face was always the look of a slumberer who is dreaming; not once did he smile, nor did he speak one word during that year.

> When the soul has many lives
>   Fettered by forgetfulness,
> Hands that burst its long-worn gyves
>   Cruel seem and pitiless.
>
> Yet they come all tenderly,
>   Loved companions of the past;
> And the sword that sets us free
>   Turns our pain to peace at last.
>
> What shadows turn his eyes away
>   Who fain would scale the heavenly heights;
> There shines the beauty of a day,
>   And there the ancient Light of Lights.
>
> And while be broods on visions dim
>   And grows forgetful of his fate,
> The chariot of the Sun for him
>   And all the tribal stars await.

III

The Slumber of Cuchullain, and the Message of Angus

Within the door at Tete Brece, under the shadow of the thatch, the couch of Cuchullain was placed, so that if he willed he could gaze over the rich green fields to the distant rim of blue hills. Yet rarely opened he his eyes or gazed with outward understanding during that weary year. Often the watchers round his bed, looking on the white rigid face, wondered if he were indeed living. But they dared not awaken him, for the seers had found that his slumber was filled with mystic life, and that it was not lawful to call him forth. Was the gloom of the great warrior because he was but the shadow of his former self, or was that pale form indeed empty? So pondered Fergus, Conail, Lugard and Ethné, faithful companions. But he in himself was wrapped in a mist of visions appearing fast and vanishing faster. The fiery hands that smote him had done their work well, and his darkness had become bright with remembrance. The majesty of elder years swept by him with reproachful glance, and the hero cowered before the greatness of his own past. Born out of the womb of the earth long ago in the fulness of power – what shadow had dimmed his beauty? He tracked and retraced countless steps. Once more he held sceptred sway over races long since in oblivion. He passed beyond the common way until the powers of the vast knew and obeyed him. As he looked back there was one always with him. Lu, the Sun-God, who in the bright days of childhood had appeared to him as his little feet ran from home in search for adventures. Remote and dim, nigh and radiant, he was always there. In solemn initiations in crypts beneath the giant hills he rose up, gemmed and starred with living fires, and grew one with the God, and away, away with him he passed into the lands of the immortals, or waged wars more than human, when from the buried lands of the past first came the heroes eastward to Eri and found the terrible Fomorian enchanters dwelling in the sacred isle. In dream Cuchullain saw the earth-scorning warriors rise up and wage their battles in the bright æther, and the great Sun-Chieftain, shining like gold, lead his glittering hosts. In mountainous multitudes the giantesque phantoms reeled to and fro, their mighty forms wreathed in streams of flame, while the stars paled and shuddered as they fought.

There was yet another face, another form, often beside him; whispering, luring, calling him away to he knew not what wild freedom. It was the phantom form of the child of Aed Abrait, with dark flowing tresses, mystic eyes, her face breathing the sweetness of the sun, with all the old nobility of earth, but elate and apart, as one who had been in the crystal spheres of the unseen and bathed in its immortalizing rivers and drunk the starry dews.

'Come, Cu. Come, O hero.' she whispered. 'There are fiery fountains of life which will renew thee. We will go where the Sidhe dwell, where the golden life-breath flows up from the mountains in a dazzling radiance to the ever-shining regions of azure and pearl under the stars. Glad is everything that lives in that place. Come, Cu, come away.' And she passed from beside him with face half turned, calling, beckoning, till in his madness he forgot the bright Sun-God and the warriors of Eri awaiting his guidance.

It was again the feast of Samhain. About twilight in the evening a shadow darkened the door. A man in a blue mantle stood outside; he did not enter but looked around him a little while and then sat down, laughing softly to himself. Fergus, Conail and Lugard rose simultaneously, glad of the pretence of warning off the intruder as a relief from their monotonous watch.

'Do you not know,' said Conail sternly, 'that one lies ill here who must not be disturbed?'

The stranger arose.

'I will tell you a tale,' he said. 'As I was strolling through the trees I saw a radiance shining around the dun, and I saw one floating in that light like a mighty pillar of fire, or bronze ruddy and golden: a child of the Sun he seemed; the living fires curled about him and rayed from his head. He looked to the north and to the west, to the south and to the east, and over all Eri he shot his fiery breaths rainbow-coloured, and the dark grew light before him where he gazed. Indeed if he who lies here were well he would be mightiest among your warriors. But I think that now he clasps hands with the heroes of the Sidhe as well, and with Druid power protects the Ultonians. I feel happy to be beside him.'

'It is Lu Lamfada guarding the hero. Now his destiny will draw nigh to him again,' thought Cu's companions, and they welcomed the stranger.

'I see why he lies here so still,' he continued, his voice strange like one who is inspired while he speaks. 'The Sidhe looked out from their mountains. They saw a hero asleep. They saw a God forgetful. They stirred him to shame by the hands of women. They showed him the past. They said to Fand and Liban, "Awake him. Bring him to us. Let him come on the night of Samhain." They showed the chosen one from afar, in a vision while hid in their mountains. The Tuatha de Danaans, the immortals, wish for Cuchullain to aid them. The daughters of Aed Abrait are their messengers. If Fand and

Liban were here they would restore the hero.'

'Who are you?' asked Laeg, who had joined them.

'I am Angus, son of Aed Abrait.' While he spoke his form quivered like a smoke, twinkling in misty indistinctness in the blue twilight, and then vanished before their eyes.

'I wonder now,' muttered Laeg to himself, 'if he was sent by the Sidhe, or by Liban and Fand only. When one has to deal with women everything is uncertain. Fand trusts more in her beauty to arouse him than in her message. I have seen her shadow twenty times cooing about him. It is all an excuse for love-making with her. It is just like a woman. Anything, however, would be better for him than to lie in bed.' He went off to join the others. Cuchullain was sitting up and was telling the story of what happened last Samhain.

'What should I do?' he asked.

'Go to the wise King,' said Laeg, and so they all advised, for ever since the day when he was crowned, and the Druids had touched him with fire, a light of wisdom shone about Concobar the King

'I think you should go to the rock where the women of the Sidhe appeared to you,' said Concobar when appealed to.

So Laeg made ready the chariot and drove to the tarn. Night came ere they reached it, but the moon showed full and brilliant. Laeg waited a little way apart, while Cuchullain sat himself in the black shadow of the rock. As the warrior gazed into the dark, star-speckled surface of the waters, a brightness and a mist gathered over them, and there, standing with her robe of green down-dropping to her feet and trailing on the wave, her pale flaxen hair blown around her head, was Liban. She smiled strangely as before, looking through him with her subtle eyes.

'I am one of the Sidhe,' she said, and her voice sounded like a murmur of the water. 'You also, O warrior, though forgetful, are one of us. We did not indeed come to injure you, but to awaken remembrance. For now the wild clouds of demons gather from the neighbouring isles and we wish your aid. Your strength will come back to you exultant as of old. Come with me, warrior. You will have great companions. Labraid, who wields the rapid fires as you the sword, and Fand, who has laid aside her Druid wisdom longing for you.'

'Whither must I go with you, strange woman?' asked Cuchullain.

'To Mag-Mell.'

'I will send Laeg with you,' said Cuchullain. 'I do not care to go to an unknown place while I have my duties here.' He then went to Laeg, asking him to go with Liban.

'He is longing to go,' thought Laeg, 'but he mistrusts his power to get away. He has forgotten all he knew and did not wish to appear nothing before a woman. However, it can do no harm if I go and see what they do.'

>Oh, marvel not if in our tale
>   The gleaming figures come and go,
>More mystic splendours shine and pale
>   Than in an age outworn we know.
>
>Their ignorance to us were wise:
>   Their sins our virtue would outshine:
>A glory passed before their eyes:
>   We hardly dream of the divine.
>
>In mystic worlds may come romance,
>   With all the lures of love and glamour;
>And woesome tragedy will chance
>   To him whom fairy forms enamour.
>
>There slain illusions live anew
>   To stay the soul with coy caresses;
>But he who only loves the True
>   Slays them again, and onward presses.
>
>For golden chains are yet but chains,
>   Enchanted dreams are yet but dreaming;
>And ere the soul its freedom gains
>   It bursts all bonds, destroys all seeming.

IV

THE MAIDENS OF THE SIDHE

'Yes, I'll go with the maid in the green mantle,' muttered Laeg to himself; 'but I'll don the crimson mantle of five folds which it is my right to wear in the land of the Sidhe, even though my earthly occupation is only the driving of a war-chariot.'

He began chanting softly; a golden gleam as of sunshine swept circling about him; then as the chant ceased a look of wild exultation came to his face, and he threw up his arms, so that for an instant he had the aspect he wore when guiding the great war-chariot of Cuchullain into the thick of the battle. His swaying form fell softly upon the greensward, and above it floated a luminous figure clad in a crimson mantle, but whose face and bare arms were of the colour of burnished bronze. So impassive and commanding was his face that even Liban faltered a little as she stole to his side. Cuchullain watched the two figures as they floated slowly over the dark expanse of the lake, till they suddenly disappeared, seemingly into its quiet surface. Then with his face buried in his hands he sat motionless, absorbed in deep thought, while he waited until the return of Laeg.

The recumbent form of Liban rose from the couch where it had lain entranced. Before her stood the phantom figure of Laeg. All in the house save herself were asleep, but with the conscious sleep of the Sidhe, and their shades spoke welcome to Laeg, each saying to him in liquid tones such as come never from lips of clay:

'Welcome to you, Laeg; welcome because of her who brings you, of him who sent you, and of yourself.'

He saw about him only women of the Sidhe, and knew that he was in one of the schools established by the wise men of Eri for maidens who would devote their lives to holiness and Druid learning; maidens who should know no earthly love but fix their eyes ever on the light of the Sun-God. But not seeing Fand among them, he turned with an impatient gesture to Liban. She read his gesture aright, and said:

'My sister dwells apart; she has more knowledge, and presides over all of us.'

Leaving the room, she walked down a corridor, noiselessly save for the rustle of her long robe of green, which she drew closely about her, for the night was chill. An unaccustomed awe rested upon her, and to Laeg she whispered:

'The evil enchanters have power to-night, so that your life would be in danger if you had not the protection of a maiden of the Sun.'

But a smile wreathed for an instant the bronze-hued face of the shadowy charioteer, as he murmured in tones of kindness near to pity, softening his rude words:

'Till now nor Cuchullain nor I have ever felt the need of a woman's protection, and I would much rather he were here now than I.'

Drawing aside a heavy curtain, Liban entered her sister's room. They saw Fand seated at a little table. A scroll lay on it open before her, but her eyes were not fixed on it. With hands clasped under her chin she gazed into the vacancies with eyes of far-away reflection and longing. There was something pathetic in the intensity and wistfulness of the lonely figure. She turned and rose to meet them, a smile of rare tenderness lighting up her face as she saw Liban. The dim glow of a single lamp but half revealed the youthful figure, the pale, beautiful face, out of which the sun-colours had faded. Her hair of raven hue was gathered in massy coils over her head and fastened there by a spiral torque of gleaming gold. Her mantle, entirely black, which fell to her feet, made her features seem more strangely young, more startlingly in contrast with the monastic severity of the room. It was draped round with some dark unfigured hangings. A couch with a coverlet of furs, a single chair of carved oak, the little table, and a bronze censer from which a faint aromatic odour escaping filled the air and stole on the sense, completed the furniture of the room, which might rather have been the cell of some aged Druid than the chamber of one of the young maidens of Eri, who were not overgiven to ascetic habits. She welcomed Laeg with the same terms of triple welcome as did the mystic children of the Sun who had first gathered round him. Her brilliant eyes seemed to read deep the soul of the charioteer.

Then Liban came softly up to her, saying:

'Oh, Fand, my soul is sad this night. The dark powers are gathering their strength to assail us, and we shall need to be pure and strong. Yet you have said that you feel no longer the Presence with you; that Mannanan, the Self of the Sun, shines not in your heart!'

Fand placed her hand upon her sister's flaxen head, saying with a voice of mingled joy and pathos:

'Peace, child; you, of us all, have least to fear, for though I, alas! am forsaken, yet He who is your Father and Yourself is even now here with you.'

Liban fell on her knees, with her hands clasped and her eyes uplifted in a rapture of adoration, for above her floated one whom she well knew. Yet unheeding her and stern of glance, with his right arm outstretched, from which leaped long tongues of flame, swordlike, into space, Labraid towered above gazing upon foes unseen by them. Slowly the arm fell and the stern look departed from the face. Ancient with the youth of the Gods, it was such a face and form the toilers in the shadowy world, mindful of their starry dynasties, sought to carve in images of upright and immovable calm amid the sphinxes of the Nile or the sculptured Gods of Chaldæa. So upright and immovable in such sculptured repose appeared Labraid, his body like a bright ruby flame, sunlit from its golden heart. Beneath his brows his eyes looked full of secrecy. The air pulsing and heaving about him drove Laeg backward from the centre of the room. He appeared but a child before this potent spirit. Liban broke out into a wild chant of welcome:

> 'Oh, see now how burning,
>   How radiant in might,
> From battle returning
>   The Dragon of Light!
> Where wert thou, unsleeping
>   Exile from the throne,
> In watch o'er the weeping,
>   The sad and the lone.

>The sun-fires of Eri
> Burned low on the steep;
>The watchers were weary
> Or sunken in sleep;
>And dread were the legions
> Of demons who rose
>From the uttermost regions
> Of ice and of snows;
>And on the red wind borne,
> Unspeakable things
>From wizard's dark mind borne
> On shadowy wings.
>The darkness was lighted
> With whirlwinds of flame;
>The demons affrighted
> Fled back whence they came.
>For thou wert unto them
> The vision that slays;
>Thy fires quivered through them
> In arrowy rays.
>Oh, light amethystine,
> Thy shadow inspire,
>And fill with the pristine
> Vigor of fire.
>Though thought like a fountain
> Pours dream upon dream,
>Unscaled is the mountain
> Where thou still dost gleam,
>And shinest afar like
> The dawning of day.
>Immortal and starlike
> In rainbow array.'

But he, the shining one, answered, and his voice had that melody which only those know whom the Sun-breath has wafted into worlds divine:

'Vaunt not, poor mortal one, nor claim knowledge when the Gods know not. He who is greatest among all the sons of evil now waits for the hour to strike when he may assail us and have with him all the hosts of the foes of light. What may be the issue of the combat cannot be foreseen by us. Yet mortals, unwise, ever claim to know when even the Gods confess ignorance; for pride blinds all mortals, and arrogance is born of their feebleness.'

Unabashed she cried out:

'Then rejoice, for we have awakened Cu, the warrior-magician of old times, and his messenger is here.'

Then he answered gently, pityingly:

'We need the help of each strong soul, and you have done well to arouse that slumbering giant. If through his added strength we conquer, then will he be the saviour of Eri; beloved by the Gods, he will cease to be a wild warrior on earth, and become a leader of mortals, aiding them on the way to the immortals. Wisely have you awakened him, and yet – '

He smiled, and such was the pity in his smiling glance that Liban bowed her head in humiliation. When she raised it he was gone, and Laeg also had vanished. She arose, and with a half-sob threw herself into the arms of her sister. So they stood, silent, with tearless eyes; for they were too divine for tears, although, alas! too human.

Slowly the chariot rolled on its homeward way, for Laeg, seeing the weakness and weariness of Cuchullain, held the great steeds in check; their arched necks and snorting breath resenting the restraint, while the impatient stamping of their hoofs struck fire from the pebbly road.

'Well,' said Cuchullain moodily, 'tell me what happened after you went away with that woman of the Sidhe.'

Briefly and without comment of his own Laeg stated what he had seen. Then long Cuchullain pondered; neither spoke, and the silence was broken only by the stamping of the steeds and the rumble of the chariot wheels. Dark clouds drifted athwart the moon, and the darkness gave more freedom of speech, for Cuchullain said in measured, expressionless tones:

'And what do you think of all this?'

'What do I think?' burst forth Laeg with sudden fire; 'I think you had better be leaving those women of the Sidhe alone, and they you. That Fand would lose her soul for love, and the spell they've cast over you is evil, or it wouldn't make a warrior like you as helpless as a toddling babe.'

In letting loose his pent-up wrath Laeg had unconsciously loosened as well the reined-in steeds, who sprang forward impetuously, and the jolting of the car was all that Cuchullain could bear in his enfeebled state. Recovering himself, the charioteer drew them in check again, inwardly upbraiding himself for his carelessness.

Sorrowful and broken was the voice of the warrior as he said:

'On the morrow, Laeg, you shall bear a message to Emer. Tell her the Sidhe have thrown a spell of helplessness upon me while deceiving me with false visions of my aiding them in their war with the evil enchanters. Ask Emer to come to me, for her presence may help to rouse me from this spell that benumbs my body and clouds my mind.'

Then Laeg sought to console him, saying:

'No, no; the Sidhe wrong no one. Their message to you was true; but their messengers were women, and you were a warrior. That is why the mischance came, for it is ever the way with a woman to become foolish over a warrior, and then there is always a muddle. And when Emer comes – ,' he checked his indiscreet utterance by pretending to have a difficulty in restraining the horses, and then added confusedly: 'Besides, I'd rather be in your plight than in Fand's.'

'Has Emer come?' asked Cuchullain, drawing himself up on his couch and resting on his elbow.

'Yes,' said Laeg dejectedly; 'I have brought her. She has been talking to me most of the journey. Now she'll be after talking to you, but you needn't mind; it isn't her usual way, and she isn't as unreasonable as might be expected. She puts most of the blame of your illness on me, though perhaps that is because it was me she was talking to. Insists that as I can go to the Plain of Fire where the Sidhe live I ought to be able to find a way of curing you. She has expressed that idea to me many times, with a fluency and wealth of illustration that would make a bard envious. Here she comes now. I'll just slip out and see if the horses are being properly cared for.'

He had not overstated the case, for the sweet face of Emer was clouded with wrath as she approached the sick-bed of her husband. Bitterly she reproached him for what she claimed was only a feigned illness, and expressed her conviction that no theory would account for his conduct save that, faithless to her his wife, he had fallen in love. But Cuchullain made no answer, for not only was he invincible in battle, but also wise in the matter of holding his tongue when a woman warred against him with words.

'You are looking stronger,' said Laeg, when next he saw him alone.

'Yes,' he returned, 'the speech of Emer has roused me a little from my torpor. I have been thinking that possibly we were wrong in disregarding the message brought by the women of the Sidhe. They surely have power to break this spell, and doubtless would have done so had you not fled from them so inconsiderately.'

'I was thinking the same when Emer was coming here with me,' observed Laeg. 'Her speech roused me a little too.'

Cuchullain was silent awhile and then said reflectively:

'Do you think we could find Liban again?'

'There would be no difficulty about that,' Laeg replied drily.

'Then,' said Cuchullain with sudden energy, 'let us go once more to the rock of the visions.'

Our souls give battle when the host
    Of lurid lives that lurk in Air,
And Ocean's regions nethermost,
    Come forth from every loathsome lair:

For then are cloudland battles fought
    With spears of lightning, swords of flame,
No quarter given, none besought,
    Till to the darkness whence they came

The Sons of Night are hurled again.
    Yet while the reddened skies resound
The wizard souls of evil men
    Within the demon ranks are found.

While pure and strong the heroes go
    To join the strife, and reck no odds,
For they who face the wizard foe
    Clasp hands heroic with the Gods.

What is the love of shadowy lips
    That know not what they seek or press,
From whom the lure for ever slips
    And fails their phantom tenderness?

The mystery and light of eyes
    That near to mine grow dim and cold;
They move afar in ancient skies
    Mid flame and mystic darkness rolled.

Oh, hero, as the heart o'erflows
    In tender yielding unto me,
A vast desire awakes and grows
    Unto forgetfulness of thee.

V

THE MANTLE OF MANNANAN

Again Liban stood before them, and her eyes were full of reproach.

'You doubt the truth of my message,' she said. 'Come, then, to the Plain of Fire, and you shall see the one who sent me.'

'I doubt you not,' said Cuchullain quietly; 'but it is not fitting that I should go when the message is brought by a woman, for such is the warning I have had in vision from Lu Lamfada. Laeg shall go with you, and if he brings back the same message, then I shall do the bidding of the Sidhe, and wage war against the evil enchanters, even as when a lad I vanquished the brood of wizards at Dur-mic-Nectan.'

'Where did Liban take you this time, Laeg? Have you brought back a message from the Sidhe?'

'I have seen the Chief,' said Laeg, whose doubts had vanished and whose whole manner had changed. 'Cuchullain, you must go. You remember how we went together to Brusna by the Boyne, and what wonders they showed us in the sacred crypt. Yet this is a place more marvellous – thrice. Well indeed did Liban call it the Plain of Fire, for a breath of fire is in the air for leagues and leagues around. On the lake where the Sidhe dwell the fishers row by and see nothing, or, mayhap, a flicker of phantasmal trees around the dun. These trees are rooted in a buried star beneath the earth; when its heart pulsates they shine like gold, aye, and are fruited with ruby lights. Indeed this Labraid is one of the Gods. I saw him come through the flaming rivers of the underworld. He was filled with the radiance. I am not given to dread the Sidhe, but there was that in him which compelled awe; for oh, he came from the homes that were anciently ours – ours who are fallen, and whose garments once bright are stained by the lees of time. He greeted me kindly. He knew me by my crimson mantle with five folds. He asked for you; indeed they all wish to have you there.'

'Did he say aught further?'

'No, he spoke but little; but as I returned by Mag Luada I had a vision. I saw you standing under the sacred Tree of Victory. There were two mighty ones, one on each side of you, but they seemed no greater than you.'

'Was Fand there?' asked Cuchullain.

'Yes,' said Laeg reluctantly; 'I saw her and spoke to her, although I did not wish to. I feared for myself. Ethné and Emer are beautiful women, but this woman is not like them. She is half divine. The holiest of Druids might lose his reason over her.'

'Let us go thither,' said Cuchullain.

The night was clear, breathless, pure as a diamond. The giant lights far above floated quietly in the streams of space. Below slept the lake mirroring the shadowy blue of the mountains. The great mounds, the homes of the Sidhe, were empty; but over them floated a watchful company, grave, majestic, silent, waiting. In stately procession their rich, gleaming figures moved to and fro in groups of twos and threes, emblazoning the dusky air with warm colours. A little apart, beyond the headland at the island's edge, two more commanding than the rest communed together. The wavering water reflected headlong their shining figures in its dark depths; above them the ancient blue of the night rose as a crown. These two were Labraid and the warrior of Murthemney restored to all his Druid power. Terrible indeed in its beauty, its power, its calm, was this fiery phantasmal form beside the king of the Sidhe.

'We came to Eri many, many ages ago,' said Labraid; 'from a land the people of to-day hold no memory of. Mighty for good and for evil were the dwellers in that land, but its hour struck and the waters of the ocean entomb it. In this island, which the mighty Gods of Fire kept apart and sacred, we made our home. But after long years a day came when the wise ones must needs depart from this also. They went eastward. A few only remained to keep alive the tradition of what was, the hope of what will be again. For in this island, it is foretold, in future ages will arise a light which will renew the children of time. But now the world's great darkness has come. See what exhalations arise! What demons would make Eri their home!'

Away at the eastern verge a thick darkness was gathering; a pitchy blackness out of which a blood-red aerial river rolled and shot its tides through the arteries of the night. It came nigher. It was dense with living creatures, larvae, horrible shapes with waving tendrils, white withered things restless and famished, hoglike faces, monstrosities. As it rolled along there was a shadowy dropping over hamlet and village and field.

'Can they not be stayed? Can they not be stayed?' rang the cry of Fand.

The stern look on Cuchullain's face deepened.

'Is it these pitiful spectres we must wage war against? Labraid, it is enough. I will go – alone. Nay, my brother, one is enough for victory.'

Already he was oblivious of the Sidhe, the voices of Fand and Laeg calling him. A light like a wonder-mist broke dazzling about him. Through a mist of fire, an excess of light, they saw a transcendent form of intensest gold treading the air. Over the head of the god a lightning thread like a serpent undulated and darted. It shed a thousand dazzling rays; it chanted in a myriad tones as it went forward. Wider grew the radiant sphere and more triumphant the chant as he sped onward and encountered the overflow of hell. Afar off the watchers saw and heard the tumult, cries of horrible conflict, agonies of writhing and burning demons scorched and annihilated, reeling away before the onset of light. On and still on he sped, now darkened and again blazing like the sun.

'Look! Look!' cried Laeg, breathless with exultation as the dazzling phantom towered and waved its arms on the horizon.

'They lied who said he was powerless,' said Fand, no less exultant.

'Cu, my darling,' murmured the charioteer; 'I know now why I loved you, what burned within you.'

'Shall we not go and welcome him when he returns?' said Liban.

'I should not advise it,' Laeg answered. 'Is it to meet that fury of fire when he sinks back blind and oblivious? He would slay his dearest friend. I am going away from here as fast as I can.'

Through the dark forests at dawn the smoke began to curl up from dun and hamlet, and all unconscious of the war waged over their destinies, children awoke to laugh and men and women went forth to breathe the sweet air of morning.

Cuchullain started from a dream of more ancient battles, of wars in heaven. Through the darkness of the room he saw the shadowy forms of the two daughters of Aed Abrait; not as before, the mystic maidens armed with Druid power, but women, melting, tender, caressing. Violet eyes shining with gratitude, darker eyes burning with love, looked into his. Misty tresses fell over him.

'I know not how the battle went,' he sighed. 'I remember the fire awoke . . . Lu was with me. . . . I fell back in a blinding mist of flame and forgot everything.'

'Doubt it not. Victory went with thee, warrior,' said Liban. 'We saw thee: it was wonderful. How the seven splendours flashed and the fiery stars roved around you and scattered the demons!'

'Oh, do not let your powers sink in sleep again,' broke forth Fand. 'What are the triumphs of earthly battles to victories like these? What is rule over a thousand warriors to kingship over the skyey hosts? Of what power are spear and arrow beside the radiant sling of Lu? Do the war-songs of the Ultonians inspire thee ever like the terrible chant of fire? After freedom can you dwell in these gloomy duns? What are the princeliest of them beside the fiery halls of Tir-na-noge and the flame-built cities of the Gods? As for me, I would dwell where the great ones of ancient days have gone, and worship at the shrine of the silent and unutterable Awe.'

'I would go indeed,' said Cuchullain; 'but still – but still –; it is hard to leave the green plains of Murthemney, and the Ultonians who have fought by my side, and Laeg, and – '

'Laeg can come with us. Nor need Conchobar, or Fergus or Conail be forgotten. Far better can you aid them with Druid power than with the right arm a blow may make powerless in battle. Go with Laeg to Iban-Cind-Trachta. Beside the yew-tree there is a dun. There you can live hidden from all. It is a place kept sacred by the might of the Sidhe. I will join you there.'

A month passed. In a chamber of the Dun of the Yew-tree, Fand, Cuchullain and Laeg were at night. The two latter sat by an oaken table and tried by divination to peer into the future. Fand, withdrawn in the dark shadow of a recess, lay on a couch and looked on. Many thoughts went passing through her mind. Now the old passion of love would rise in her heart to be quenched by a weary feeling of futility, and then a half-contempt would curl her lips as she saw the eagerness of her associates. Other memories surged up. 'Oh, Mannanan, Father-Self, if thou hadst not left me and my heart had not turned away! It was not a dream when I met thee and we entered the Ocean of Fire together. Our beauty encompassed the world. Radiant as Lu thy brother of the Sun we were. Far away as the dawn seems the time. How beautiful, too, was that other whose image in the hero enslaves my heart. Oh, that he would but know himself, and learn that on this path the greatest is the only risk worth taking! And now he holds back the charioteer also and does him wrong.' Just then something caused her to look up. She cried out, 'Laeg, Laeg, do you see anything?'

'What is it?' said Laeg. Then he also looked and started. 'Gods!' he murmured, 'Emer! I would rather face a tempest of Fomorian enchanters.'

'Do you not see?' repeated Fand scornfully. 'It is Emer the daughter of Forgall. Has she also become one of the Sidhe that she journeys thus?'

'She comes in dream,' said Laeg.

'Why do you intrude upon our seclusion here? You know my anger is no slight thing,' broke out Cuchullain, in ready wrath hiding his confusion. The shadow of Emer turned, throwing back the long, fair hair from her face the better to see him. There was no dread on it, but only outraged womanly dignity. She spake and her voice seemed to flow from a passionate heart far away brooding in sorrowful loneliness.

'Why do I come? Hast thou not degraded me before all the maidens of Eri by forsaking me for a woman of the Sidhe without a cause? You ask why I come when every one of the Ultonians looks at me in questioning doubt and wonder! But I see you have found a more beautiful partner.'

'We came hither, Laeg and I, to learn the lore of the Sidhe. Why should you not leave me here for a time, Emer? This maiden is of wondrous magical power: she is a princess in her own land, and is as pure and chaste to this hour as you.'

'I see indeed she is more beautiful than I am. That is why you are drawn away. Her face has not grown familiar. Everything that is new or strange you follow. The passing cheeks are ruddier than the pale face which has shared your troubles. What you know is weariness, and you leave it to learn what you do not know. The Ultonians falter while you are absent from duty in battle and council, and I, whom you brought with sweet words when half a child from my home, am left alone. Oh, Cuchullain, beloved, I was once dear to thee, and if to-day or to-morrow were our first meeting I should be so again.'

A torrent of self-reproach and returning love overwhelmed him. 'I swear to you,' he said brokenly, through fast-flowing tears, 'you are immortally dear to me, Emer.'

'Then you leave me,' burst forth Fand, rising to her full height, her dark, bright eyes filled with a sudden fire, an image of mystic indignation and shame.

'If indeed,' said Emer softly, 'joy and love and beauty are more among the Sidhe than where we dwell in Eri, then it were better for thee to remain.'

'No, he shall not now,' said Fand passionately. 'It is I whom he shall leave. I long foresaw this moment, but ran against fate like a child. Go, warrior, Cu; tear this love out of thy heart as I out of mine. Go, Laeg, I will not forget thee. Thou alone hast thought about these things truly. But now – I cannot speak.' She flung herself upon the couch in the dark shadow and hid her face away from them.

The pale phantom wavered and faded away, going to one who awoke from sleep with a happiness she could not understand. Cuchullain and Laeg passed out silently into the night. At the door of the dun a voice they knew not spake:

'So warrior, you return. It is well. Not yet for thee is the brotherhood of the Sidhe, and thy destiny and Fand's lie far apart. Thine is not so great but it will be greater, in ages yet to come, in other lands, among other peoples, when the battle fury in thee shall have turned to wisdom and anger to compassion. Nations that lie hidden in the womb of time shall hail thee as friend, deliverer and saviour. Go and forget what has passed. This also thou shalt forget. It will not linger in thy mind; but in thy heart shall remain the memory and it will urge thee to nobler deeds. Farewell, warrior, saviour that is to be!'

As the two went along the moonlit shore mighty forms followed, and there was a waving of awful hands over them to blot out memory.

In the room where Fand lay with mad beating heart tearing itself in remorse, there was one watching with divine pity. Mannanan, the Golden Glory, the Self of the Sun. 'Weep not, O shadow; thy days of passion and pain are over,' breathed the Pity in her breast. 'Rise up, O Ray, from thy sepulchre of forgetfulness. Spirit, come forth to thy ancient and immemorial home.' She rose up and stood erect. As the Mantle of Mannanan enfolded her, no human words could tell the love, the exultation, the pathos, the wild passion of surrender, the

The Enchantment of Cuchullain

music of divine and human life interblending. Faintly we echo – like this spake the Shadow and like this the Glory.

The Shadow

Who art thou, O Glory,
   In flame from the deep,
Where stars chant their story,
   Why trouble my sleep?

I hardly had rested,
   My dreams wither now:
Why comest thou crested
   And gemmed on thy brow?

The Glory

Up, Shadow, and follow
   The way I will show;
The blue gleaming hollow
   To-night we will know,

And rise mid the vast to
   The fountain of days;
From whence we had passed to
   The parting of ways.

The Shadow

I know thee, O Glory:
   Thine eyes and thy brow
With white fire all hoary
   Come back to me now.

Together we wandered
   In ages agone;
Our thoughts as we pondered
   Were stars at the dawn.

My glory has dwindled,
   My azure and gold:
Yet you keep enkindled
   The Sun-fire of old.

My footsteps are tied to
   The heath and the stone;
My thoughts earth-allied-to –
   Ah! leave me alone.

Go back, thou of gladness,
   Nor wound me with pain,
Nor smite me with madness,
   Nor come nigh again.

The Glory

Why tremble and weep now,
   Whom stars once obeyed?
Come forth to the deep now
   And be not afraid.

The Dark One is calling,
   I know, for his dreams
Around me are falling
   In musical streams.

A diamond is burning
   In depths of the Lone
Thy spirit returning
   May claim for its throne.

In flame-fringed islands
   Its sorrow shall cease,
Absorbed in the silence
   And quenched in the peace.

Come lay thy poor head on
   My breast where it glows
With love ruby-red on
   Thy heart for its woes.

My power I surrender:
   To thee it is due:
Come forth, for the splendour
   Is waiting for you.

THE CHILDHOOD OF APOLLO[1]

It was long ago, so long that only the spirit of earth remembers truly. The old shepherd Admetus sat before the door of his hut waiting for his grandson to return. He watched with drowsy eyes the eve gather, and the woods and mountains grow dark over the isles – the isles of ancient Greece. It was Greece before its day of beauty, and day was never lovelier. The cloudy blossoms of smoke, curling upward from the valley, sparkled a while high up in the sunlit air, a vague memorial of the world of men below. From that, too, the colour vanished, and those other lights began to shine which to some are the only lights of day. The skies drooped close upon the mountains and the silver seas like a vast face brooding with intentness. There was enchantment, mystery, and a living motion in its depths, the presence of all-pervading Zeus enfolding his starry children with the dark radiance of æther.

'Ah!' murmured the old man, looking upward, 'once it was living; once it spoke to me. It speaks not now; but it speaks to others I know – to the child who looks and longs and trembles in the dewy night. Why does he linger now? He is beyond his hour. Ah, there now are his footsteps!'

A boy came up the valley driving the grey flocks which tumbled before him in the darkness. He lifted his young face for the shepherd to kiss. It was alight with ecstasy. Admetus looked at him with wonder. A golden and silvery light rayed all about the child, so that his delicate ethereal beauty seemed set in a star which followed his dancing footsteps.

'How bright your eyes!' the old man said, faltering with sudden awe. 'Why do your limbs shine with moonfire light?'

'Oh, father,' said the boy Apollo, 'I am glad, for everything is living to-night. The evening is all a voice and many voices. While the flocks were browsing night gathered about me. I saw within it and it was everywhere living. The wind with dim-blown tresses, odour, incense, and secret falling dew, mingled in one warm breath. They whispered to me and called me "Child of the Stars," "Dew Heart," and "Soul of Light." Oh, father, as I came up the valley the voices followed me with song. Everything murmured love. Even the daffodils, nodding in the olive gloom, grew golden at my feet, and a flower within my heart knew of the still sweet secret of the flowers. Listen, listen!'

There were voices in the night, voices as of star-rays descending.

>Now the roof-tree of the midnight spreading
>   Buds in citron, green, and blue:
>From afar its mystic odours shedding,
>   Child, on you.

Then other sweet speakers from beneath the earth, and from the distant waters and air, followed in benediction, and a last voice like a murmur from universal nature:

>Now the buried stars beneath the mountains
>   And the vales their life renew,
>Jetting rainbow blooms from tiny fountains,
>   Child, for you.
>
>As within our quiet waters passing
>   Sun and moon and stars we view,
>So the loveliness of life is glassing,
>   Child, in you.
>
>In the diamond air the sun-star glowing
>   Up its feathered radiance threw;
>All the jewel glory there was flowing,
>   Child, for you.
>
>And the fire divine in all things burning
>   Yearns for home and rest anew,
>From its wanderings far again returning,
>   Child, to you.

'Oh, voices, voices,' cried the child, 'what you say I know not, but I give back love for love. Father, what is it they tell me? They embosom me in light, and I am far away even though I hold your hand.'

'The gods are about us. Heaven mingles with the earth,' said Admetus, trembling. 'Let us go to Diotima.[2] She has grown wise brooding for many a year where the great caves lead to the underworld. She sees the bright ones as they pass by, though she sits with shut eyes, her drowsy lips murmuring as nature's self.'

That night the island seemed no more earth set in sea, but a music encircled by the silence. The trees, long rooted in antique slumber, were throbbing with rich life; through glimmering bark and drooping leaf a light fell on the old man and boy as they passed, and vague figures nodded at them. These were the hamadryad souls of the wood. They were bathed in tender colours and shimmering lights draping them from root to leaf. A murmur came from the heart of every one; a low enchantment breathing joy and peace. It grew and swelled until at last it seemed as if through a myriad pipes that Pan the earth spirit was fluting his magical creative song.

They found the cave of Diotima covered by vines and tangled trailers at the end of the island where the dark-green woodland rose up from the waters. Admetus passed, for he dreaded this mystic prophetess; but a voice from within called them:

'Come, child of light: come in, old shepherd, I know why you seek me!'

They entered, Admetus trembling with more fear than before. A fire was blazing in a recess of the cavern, and by it sat a majestic figure robed in purple. She was bent forward, her hand supporting her face, her burning eyes turned on the intruders.

'Come hither, child,' she said, taking the boy by the hands and gazing into his face. 'So this pale form is to be the home of the god. The gods choose wisely. They take no wild warrior, no mighty hero to be their messenger, but crown this gentle head. Tell me, have you ever seen a light from the sun falling on you in your slumber? No, but look now. Look upward.'

As she spoke she waved her hands over him, and the cavern with its dusky roof seemed to melt away, and beyond the heavens the heaven of heavens lay dark in pure tranquillity, in a quiet which was the very hush of being. In an instant it vanished, and over the zenith broke a wonderful light.

'See now,' cried Diotima, 'the Ancient Beauty! Look how its petals expand, and what comes forth from its heart!' A vast and glowing breath, mutable and opalescent, spread itself between heaven and earth, and out of it slowly descended a radiant form like a god's. It drew nigh, radiating lights, pure, beautiful, and star-like. It stood for a moment by the child and placed its hand on his head, and then it was gone. The old shepherd fell upon his face in awe, while the boy stood breathless and entranced.

'Go now,' said the sibyl, 'I can teach thee naught. Nature herself will adore you, and sing through you her loveliest song. But, ah, the light you hail in joy you shall impart in tears. So from age to age the eternal Beauty bows itself down amid sorrows, that the children of men may not forget it, that their anguish may be transformed, smitten through by its fire.'

THE FOUNTAINS OF YOUTH[1]

I heard that a strange woman, dwelling on the western coast, who had the repute of healing by faery power, said a little before she died. 'There's a cure for all things in the well at Ballykeele': and I know not why at first, but her words lingered with me and repeated themselves again and again, and by degrees to keep fellowship with the thought they enshrined came more antique memories, all I had heard or dreamed of the Fountains of Youth; for I could not doubt, having heard these fountains spoken of by people like herself, that her idea had a druid ancestry. Perhaps she had bent over the pool until its darkness grew wan and bright and troubled with the movements of a world within and the agitations of a tempestuous joy; or she had heard, as many still hear, the wild call to 'Come away,' from entreating lips and flame-encircled faces, or was touched by the star-tipped fingers, and her heart from the faery world came never back again to dwell as before at ease in this isle of grey mists and misty sunlight. These things are not fable only, for Ireland is still a land of the gods, and in out of the way places we often happen on wonderlands of romance and mystic beauty. I have spoken to people who have half parted from their love for the world in a longing for the pagan paradise of Tir-na-nóg,[2] and many who are outwardly obeisant to another religion are altogether pagan in their hearts, and Meave[3] the Queen of the Western Host is more to them than Mary Queen of Heaven. I was told of this Meave that lately she was seen in vision by a peasant, who made a poem on her, calling her 'The Beauty of all Beauty': and the man who told me this of his friend had himself seen the jetted fountains of fire-mist winding up in spiral whirls to the sky, and he too had heard of the Fountains of Youth.

The natural longing in every heart that its youth shall not perish makes one ponder and sigh over this magical past when youth, ecstasy, and beauty welled from a bountiful nature at the sung appeal of her druid children holding hand in hand around the sacred cairn. Our hearts remember:

The Fountains of Youth

A wind blows by us fleeting
   Along the reedy strand:
And sudden our hearts are beating
   Again in the druid-land.

All silver-pale, enchanted,
   The air-world lies on the hills,
And the fields of light are planted
   With the dawn-frail daffodils.

The yellow leaves are blowing
   The hour when the wind-god weaves,
And hides the stars and their glowing
   In a mist of daffodil leaves.

We stand in glimmering whiteness,
   Each face like the day-star fair,
And rayed about in its brightness
   With a dawn of daffodil air.

And through each white robe gleaming,
   And under each snow-white breast,
Is a golden dream-light streaming
   Like eve through an opal west.

One hand to the heart, another
   We raise to the dawn on high;
For the sun in the heart is brother
   To the sun-heart of the sky.

A light comes rising and falling,
   As ringed in the druid choir
We sing to the sun-god, calling
   By his name of yellow fire.

The touch of the dew-wet grasses,
   The breath of the dawn-cool wind,
With the dawn of the god-light passes
   And the world is left behind.

We drink of a fountain giving
   The joy of the gods, and then –
The Land of the Ever-living
   Has passed from us again.

Passed far beyond all saying,
   For memory only weaves
On a silver dawn outraying
   A cloud of daffodil leaves.

And not indirectly through remembrance only, but when touched from within by the living beauty, the soul, the ancient druid in man, renews its league with the elements; and sometimes as the twilight vanishes and night lays on the earth her tender brow, the woods, the mountains, the clouds that tinted like seraphim float in the vast, and the murmur of water, wind and trees, melt from the gaze and depart from the outward ear and become internal reveries and contemplations of the spirit, and are no more separate but are part of us. Yet these vanishings from us and movements in worlds not realized, leave us only more thirsty to drink of a deeper nature where all things are dissolved in ecstasy, and heaven and earth are lost in God. So we turn seeking for the traces of that earlier wisdom which guided man into the Land of Immortal Youth, and assuaged his thirst at a more brimming flood at the Feast of Age, the banquet which Manannán the Danann king instituted in the haunt of the Fire-god, and whoever partook knew thereafter neither weariness, decay, nor death.

These mysteries, all that they led to, all that they promised for the spirit of man, are opening to-day for us in clear light, their fabulous distance lessens, and we hail these kingly ideals with as intense a trust and with more joy, perhaps, than they did who were born in those purple hours, because we are emerging from centuries indescribably meagre and squalid in their thought, and every new revelation has for us the sweetness of sunlight to one after the tears and sorrow of a prison-house. The well at Ballykeele is, perhaps, a humble starting point for the contemplation of such mighty mysteries; but here where the enchanted world lies so close it is never safe to say what narrow path may not lead through a visionary door into Moy Argatnel, the Silver Cloudland of Manannán, where

'Feet of white bronze
Glitter through beautiful ages.'

The Danann king with a quaint particularity tells Bran in the poem from which these lines are quoted, that

'There is a wood of beautiful fruit
Under the prow of thy little skiff.'

What to Bran was a space of pale light was to the eye of the god a land of pure glory, Ildathach[4] the Many-coloured Land, rolling with rivers of golden light and dropping with dews of silver flame. In another poem the Brugh by the Boyne, outwardly a little hillock, is thus described:

'Look, and you will see it is the palace of a god.'

The Fountains of Youth

Perhaps the mystic warriors of the Red Branch saw supernatural pillars blazoned like the sunset, and entered through great doors and walked in lofty halls with sunset-tinted beings speaking a more beautiful wisdom than earth's. And they there may have seen those famous gods[5] who had withdrawn generations before from visible Eiré: Manannán the dark blue king, Lu Lamfáda with the sunrise on his brow and his sling, a wreath of rainbow flame, coiled around him, the Goddess Dana in ruby brilliance, Nuada silver-handed, the Dagda with floating locks of light shaking from him radiance and song, Angus Oge, around whose head the ever-winging birds made music, and others in whose company these antique heroes must have felt the deep joy of old companionship renewed, for were not the Danann hosts men of more primeval cycles become divine and movers in a divine world. In the Brugh too was a fountain, to what uses applied the mystical imagination working on other legends may make clearer.

The Well of Connla,[6] the parent fountain of many streams visible and invisible, was the most sacred well known in ancient Ireland. It lay itself below deep waters at the source of the Shannon, and these waters which hid it were also mystical, for they lay between earth and the Land of the Gods. Here, when stricken suddenly by an internal fire, the sacred hazels of wisdom and inspiration unfolded at once their leaves and blossoms and their scarlet fruit, which falling upon the waters dyed them of a royal purple; the nuts were then devoured by Fintann the Salmon of Knowledge, and the wisest of the druids partook also. This was perhaps the greatest of the mysteries known to the ancient Gael, and in the bright phantasmagoria conjured up there is a wild beauty which belongs to all their tales. The suddenly arising forests of golden fire, trees whose roots drew honey sweetness from the dreams of a remote divinity, the scarlet nuts tossing on the purple flood, the bright immortals glancing hither and thither, are pictures left of some mystery we may not now uncover, though to-morrow may reveal it, for the dawn-lights are glittering everywhere in Ireland. Perhaps the strange woman who spoke of the well at Ballykeele, and others like her, may know more about these fountains than the legend-seekers who so learnedly annotate their tales. They may have drunken in dreams of the waters at Connla's well, for many go to the Tir-na-nóg in sleep, and some are said to have remained there, and only a vacant form is left behind without the light in the eyes which marks the presence of a soul. I make no pretence of knowledge concerning the things which underlie their simple speech, but to me there seems to be for ever escaping from legend and folk-tale, from word and custom, some breath of a world of beauty I sigh for but am not nigh to as these are. I think if that strange woman could have found a voice for what was in her heart she would have completed her vague oracle somewhat as I have done:

> There's a cure for all things in the well at Ballykeele,
> Where the scarlet cressets o'erhang from the rowan trees;
> There's a joy-breath blowing from the Land of Youth I feel,
>   And earth with its heart at ease.
>
> Many and many a sun-bright maiden saw the enchanted land
> With star-faces glimmer up from the druid wave:
> Many and many a pain of love was soothed by a faery hand
>   Or lost in the love it gave.
>
> When the quiet with a ring of pearl shall wed the earth
> And the scarlet berries burn dark by the stars in the pool,
> Oh, it's lost and deep I'll be in the joy-breath and the mirth,
>   My heart in the star-heart cool.
>
> Æ.

A DREAM OF ANGUS OGE[1]

The day had been wet and wild, and the woods looked dim and drenched from the window where Con sat. All the day long his ever restless feet were running to the door in a vain hope of sunshine. His sister Norah to quiet him had told him over and over again the tales which delighted him; the delight of hearing which was second only to the delight of living them over himself, when as Cuculain he kept the ford which led to Ulla, his sole hero heart matching the hosts of Meave; or as Fergus he wielded the sword of light the druids made and gave to the champion, which in its sweep shore away the crests of the mountains; or as Brian, the ill-fated child of Turenn, he went with his brothers in the ocean-sweeping boat further than ever Columbus travelled, winning one by one in dire conflict with kings and enchanters the treasures which would appease the implacable heart of Lu. He had just died in a corner of the room from his many wounds when Norah came in declaring that all these famous heroes must go to bed. He protested in vain, but indeed he was sleepy, and before he had been carried half way to the room the little soft face drooped with half-closed eyes, while he drowsily rubbed his nose upon her shoulder in an effort to keep awake. For a while she flitted about him looking, with her dark shadowy hair flickering in the dim, silver light like one of the beautiful heroines of Gaelic romance, or one of the twilight race of the Sidhe. Before going she sat by his bed and sang to him some verses of a song, set to an old Celtic air whose low intonations were full of a half soundless mystery:

> 'Over the hill-tops the gay lights are peeping:
> Down in the vale where the dim fleeces stray
> Ceases the smoke from the hamlet upcreeping:
> Come, thou, my shepherd, and lead me away.

'Who's the shepherd?' said the boy, suddenly sitting up.
'Hush, alannah: I will tell you another time.' She continued still more softly:

> 'Lord of the Wand, draw forth from the darkness
>   Warp of the silver, and woof of the gold:
> Leave the poor shade there bereft in its starkness:
>   Wrapped in the Fleece we will enter the Fold.
>
> 'There from the many-orbed heart where the Mother
>   Breathes forth the love on her darlings who roam,
> We will send dreams to their land of another
>   Land of the Shining, their birthplace and home.'

He would have asked a hundred questions, but she bent over him, enveloping him with a sudden nightfall of hair to give him his goodnight kiss, and departed. Immediately the boy sat up again, all his sleepiness gone. The pure, gay, delicate spirit of childhood was darting at ideas dimly perceived in the delicious moonlight of romance which silvered his brain, where many airy and beautiful figures were moving: the Fianna with floating locks chasing the flying deer, shapes more solemn, vast, and misty, guarding the avenues to unspeakable secrets; but he steadily pursued his idea.

'I guess he's one of the people who take you away to faeryland. Wonder if he'd come to me? Think it's easy going away;' with an intuitive perception of the frailty of the link binding childhood to earth in its dreams. (As a man Con will strive with what passionate intensity to regain that free gay motion in the upper airs.) 'Think I'll try if he'll come;' and he sang, with as near an approach as he could make to the glimmering cadences of his sister's voice:

> 'Come, thou, my shepherd, and lead me away:'

He then lay back quite still and waited. He could not say whether hours or minutes had passed, or whether he had slept or not, until he was aware of a tall golden-bearded man standing by his bed. Wonderfully light was this figure, as if the sunlight ran through his limbs: a spiritual beauty was on the face, and those strange eyes of bronze and gold with their subtle intense gaze made Con aware for the first time of the difference between inner and outer in himself.

'Come, Con, come away!' the child seemed to hear uttered silently.

'You're the Shepherd,' said Con, 'I'll go.' Then suddenly: 'I won't come back and be old when they're all dead?' a vivid remembrance of Ossian's fate flashing upon him.

A most beautiful laughter, which again to Con seemed half soundless, came in reply. His fears vanished: the golden-bearded man stretched a hand over him for a moment and he found himself out in the night, now clear and starlit. Together they moved on as if

A Dream of Angus Oge

borne by the wind, past many woods and silver gleaming lakes, and mountains which shone like a range of opals below the purple skies. The Shepherd stood still for a moment by one of these hills, and there flew out riverlike a melody mingled with a tinkling as of innumerable elfin hammers, and there was a sound of many gay voices where an unseen people were holding festival, or enraptured hosts who were let loose for the awakening, the new day which was to dawn, for the delighted child felt that faeryland was come over again with its heroes and battles.

'Our brothers rejoice,' said the Shepherd to Con.

'Who are they?' asked the boy.

'They are the thoughts of our Father.'

'May we go in?' Con asked, for he was fascinated by the melody, mystery and flashing lights.

'Not now. We are going to my home where I lived in the days past when there came to me many kings and queens of ancient Eiré, many heroes and beautiful women, who longed for the druid wisdom we taught.'

'And did you fight like Finn, and carry spears as tall as trees, and chase the deer through the woods, and have feasting and singing?'

'No, we, the Dananns, did none of those things; but those who were weary of battle, and to whom feast and song brought no pleasure, came to us and passed hence to a more wonderful land, a more immortal land than this.'

As he spoke he paused before a great mound grown over with trees, and around it silver clear in the moonlight were immense stones piled, the remains of an original circle, and there was a dark, low, narrow entrance leading within. He took Con by the hand, and in an instant they were standing in a lofty, cross-shaped cave built roughly of huge stones.

'This was my palace. In days past many a one plucked here the purple flower of magic and the fruit of the tree of life.'

'It is very dark,' said the child disconsolately. He had expected something different.

'Nay, but look: you will see it is the palace of a god.' And even as he spoke a light began to glow and to pervade the cave, and to obliterate the stone walls and the antique hieroglyphs engraven thereon, and to melt the earthen floor into itself like a fiery sun suddenly uprisen within the world, and there was everywhere a wandering ecstasy of sound: light and sound were one; light had a voice, and the music hung glittering in the air.

'Look, how the sun is dawning for us, ever dawning; in the earth, in our hearts, with ever youthful and triumphant voices. Your sun is but a smoky shadow, ours the ruddy and eternal glow; yours is far away, ours is heart and hearth and home; yours is a light without, ours a fire within in rock, in river, in plain, everywhere living, everywhere dawning; whence also it cometh that the mountains emit their wondrous rays.'

As he spoke he seemed to breathe the brilliance of that mystical sunlight and to dilate and tower, so that the child looked up to a giant pillar of light having in his heart a sun of ruddy gold which shed its blinding rays about him, and over his head there was a waving of fiery plumage, and on his face an ecstasy of beauty and immortal youth.

'I am Angus,' Con heard; 'men call me the Young.[2] I am the sunlight in the heart, the moonlight in the mind; I am the light at the end of every dream, the voice for ever calling to come away; I am desire beyond joy or tears. Come with me, come with me: I will make you immortal; for my palace opens into the Gardens of the Sun, and there are the fire-fountains that quench the heart's desire in rapture.' And in the child's dream he was in a palace high as the stars, with dazzling pillars jewelled like the dawn and all fashioned out of a living and trembling opal. And upon their thrones sat the Danann gods with their sceptres and diadems of rainbow light, and upon their faces infinite wisdom and imperishing youth. In the turmoil and growing chaos of his dream he heard a voice crying out, 'You remember, Con, Con, Conaire Mor, you remember!' and in an instant he was torn from himself and had grown vaster and was with the Immortals, seated upon their thrones, they looking upon him as a brother, and he was flying away with them into the heart of the gold when he awoke, the spirit of childhood dazzled with the vision which is too lofty for princes.

Æ.

RELIGION AND LOVE[1]

I have often wondered whether there is not something wrong in our religious systems in that the same ritual, the same doctrines, the same aspirations are held to be sufficient both for men and women. The tendency everywhere is to obliterate distinctions, and if a woman be herself she is looked upon unkindly. She rarely understands our metaphysics, and she gazes on the expounder of the mystery of the Logos with enigmatic eyes which reveal the enchantment of another divinity. The ancients were wiser than we in this, for they had Aphrodite and Hera and many another form of the Mighty Mother[2] who bestowed on women their peculiar graces and powers. Surely no girl in ancient Greece ever sent up to all-pervading Zeus a prayer that her natural longings might be fulfilled; but we may be sure that to Aphrodite came many such prayers. The deities we worship to-day are too austere for women to approach with their peculiar desires, and indeed in Ireland the largest number of our peole do not see any necessity for love-making at all, or what connection spiritual powers have with the affections. A girl, without repining, will follow her four-legged dowry to the house of a man she may never have spoken twenty words to before her marriage. We praise our women for their virtue, but the general acceptance of the marriage as arranged shows so unemotional, so undesirable a temperament, that it is not to be wondered at. One wonders was there temptation.

What the loss to the race may be it is impossible to say, but it is true that beautiful civilizations are built up by the desire of man to give his beloved all her desires. Where there is no beloved, but only a housekeeper, there are no beautiful fancies to create the beautiful arts, no spiritual protest against the mean dwelling, no hunger to build the world anew for her sake. Aphrodite is outcast, and with her many of the other immortals have also departed. The home life in Ireland is probably more squalid than with any other people equally prosperous in Europe. The children begotten without love fill more and more the teeming asylums. We are without art; literature is despised; we have few of those industries which spring up in other countries in response to the desire of woman to make gracious influences pervade the home of her partner, a desire to which man readily yields, and toils to satisfy if he loves truly. The desire for beauty has come almost to be regarded as dangerous, if not sinful; and the woman who is still the natural child of the Great Mother and priestess of the mysteries, if she betray the desire to exercise her divinely-given powers, if there be enchantment in her eyes and her laugh, and if she bewilder too many men, is in our latest code of morals distinctly an evil influence. The spirit, melted and tortured with love, which does not achieve its earthly desire, is held to have wasted its strength, and the judgment which declares the life to be wrecked is equally severe on that which caused this wild conflagration in the heart. But the end of life is not comfort but divine being. We do not regard the life which closed in the martyr's fire as ended ignobly. The spiritual philosophy which separates human emotions and ideas, and declares some to be secular and others spiritual, is to blame. There is no meditation which if prolonged will not bring us to the same world where religion would carry us, and, if a flower in the wall will lead us to all knowledge, so the understanding of the peculiar nature of one-half of humanity will bring us far on our journey to the sacred deep. I believe it was this wise understanding which in the ancient world declared the embodied spirit in man to be influenced more by the Divine Mind[3] and in woman by the Mighty Mother, by which nature in its spiritual aspect was understood. In this philosophy, Boundless Being, when manifested, revealed itself in two forms of life, spirit and substance; and the endless evolution of its divided rays had as its root impulse the desire to return to that boundless being. By many ways blindly or half consciously the individual life strives to regain its old fullness. The spirit seeks union with nature to pass from the life of vision into pure being; and nature, conscious that its grosser forms are impermanent, iş for ever dissolving and leading its votary to a more distant shrine. 'Nature is timid like a woman,' declares an Indian scripture. 'She reveals herself shyly and withdraws again.' All this metaphysic will not appear out of place if we regard woman as influenced beyond herself and her conscious life for spiritual ends. I do not enter a defence of the loveless coquette, but the woman who has a natural delight in awakening love in men is priestess of a divinity than which there is none mightier among the rulers of the heavens. Through her eyes, her laugh, in all her motions, there is expressed more than she is conscious of herself. The Mighty Mother through the woman is kindling a symbol of herself in the spirit, and through that symbol she breathes her secret life into the heart, so that it is fed from within and is drawn to herself. We remember that with Dante, the image of a woman became at last the purified vesture of his spirit through which the mysteries were revealed.[4] We are for ever making our souls with effort and pain, and shaping them into images which reveal or are voiceless according to their degree; and the man whose spirit has been obsessed by a beauty so long brooded upon that he has almost become that which he contemplated, owes much to the woman who may never be his; and if he or the world understood aright, he has no cause of complaint. It is the essentially irreligious spirit of Ireland which has come to regard love as an unnecessary emotion and the mingling of the sexes as dangerous. For it is a curious thing that while we commonly regard ourselves as the most religious people in Europe, the reverse is probably true. The country which has never produced spiritual thinkers or religious teachers of whom men have heard if we except Berkeley and perhaps the remote Johannes Scotus Erigena, cannot pride itself on its spiritual achievement; and it might seem even more paradoxical, but I think it would be almost equally true to say that the first spiritual note in our literature was struck when a poet[5] generally regarded as pagan wrote it as the aim of his art to reveal –

> In all poor foolish things that live a day
> Eternal beauty wandering on her way.

The heavens do not declare the glory of God any more than do shining eyes, nor the firmament show His handiwork more than the woven wind of hair, for these were wrought with no lesser love than set the young stars swimming in seas of joyous and primeval air. If we drink in the beauty of the night or the mountains, it is deemed to be praise of the Maker, but if we show an equal adoration of the beauty of man or woman, it is dangerous, it is almost wicked. Of course it is dangerous; and without danger there is no passage to eternal things. There is the valley of the shadow beside the pathway of light, and it always will be there, and the heavens will never be entered by those who shrink from it. Spirituality is the power of apprehending formless spiritual essences,[6] of seeing the eternal in the transitory, and in the things which are seen the unseen things of which they are the shadow. I call Mr. Yeats' poetry spiritual when it declares, as in the lines I quoted, that there is no beauty so trivial that it is not the shadow of Eternal Beauty. A country is religious where it is common belief that all things are instinct with divinity, and where the love between man and woman is seen as a symbol, the highest we have, of the union of spirit and nature, and their final blending in the boundless being. For this reason the lightest desires even, the lightest graces of women have a philosophical value for what suggestions they bring us of the divinity behind them.

As men and women feel themselves more and more to be sharers of universal aims, they will contemplate in each other and in themselves that aspect of the boundless being under whose influence they are cast, and will appeal to it for understanding and power. Time, which is for ever bringing back the old and renewing it, may yet bring back to us some counterpart of Aphrodite or Hera as they were understood by the most profound thinkers of the ancient world; and woman may again have her temples and her mysteries, and renew again her radiant life at its fountain, and feel that in seeking for beauty she is growing more into her own ancestral being, and that in its shining forth she is giving to man, as he may give to her, something of that completeness of spirit of which it is written, 'neither is the man without the woman nor the woman without the man in the Highest.'

It may seem strange that what is so clear should require statement, but it is only with a kind of despair the man or woman of religious mind can contemplate the materialism of our thought about life. It is not our natural heritage from the past, for the bardic poetry shows that a heaven lay about us in the mystical childhood of our race, and a supernatural original was often divined for the great hero or beautiful woman. All this perception has withered away, for religion has become observance of rule and adherence to doctrine. The first steps to the goal have been made sufficient in themselves; but religion is useless unless it has a transforming power, unless it is able 'to turn fishermen into divines,' and make the blind see and the deaf hear. They are no true teachers who cannot rise beyond the world of sense and darkness and awaken the links within us from earth to heaven, who cannot see within the heart what are its needs, and who have not the power to open the poor blind eyes and touch the ears that have heard no sound of the heavenly harmonies. Our clergymen do their best to deliver us from what they think is evil, but do not lead us into the Kingdom. They forget that the faculties cannot be spiritualized by restraint but in use, and that the greatest evil of all is not to be able to see the divine everywhere, in life and love no less than in the solemn architecture of the spheres. In the free play of the beautiful and natural human relations lie the greatest possibilities of spiritual development, for heaven is not prayer nor praise but the fullness of life, which is only divined through the richness and variety of life on earth. There is a certain infinitude in the emotions of love, tenderness, pity, joy, and all that is begotten in love, and this limitless character of the emotions has never received the philosophical consideration which is due to it, for even laughter may be considered solemnly, and gaiety and joy in us are the shadowy echoes of that joy spoken of the radiant Morning Stars, and there is not an emotion in man or woman which has not, however perverted and muddied in its coming, in some way flowed from the first fountain. We are no more divided from supernature than we are from our own bodies, and where the life of man or woman is naturally most intense it most naturally overflows and mingles with the subtler and more lovely world within. If religion has no word to say upon this it is incomplete, and we wander in the narrow circle of prayers and praise, wondering all the while what is it we are praising God for, because we feel so melancholy and lifeless. Dante had a place in his Inferno for the joyless souls,[7] and if his conception be true the population of that circle will be largely modern Irish. A reaction against this conventual restraint is setting in, and the needs of life will perhaps in the future no longer be violated as they are to-day; and since it is the pent-up flood of the joy which ought to be in life which is causing this reaction, and since there is a divine root in it, it is difficult to say where it might not carry us; I hope into some renewal of ancient conceptions of the fundamental purpose of womanhood and its relations to Divine Nature, and that from the temples where woman may be instructed she will come forth, with strength in her to resist all pleading until the lover worship in her a divine womanhood, and that through their love the divided portions of the immortal nature may come together and be one as before the beginning of worlds.

1904.

VII. THE DESCENT OF THE GODS

There is no imagination of mine about Avatars in this book. No more than an artist could paint the sun at noon could I imagine so great beings. But as a painter may suggest the light on hill or wood, so in this fantasy I tried to imagine the spiritual excitement created by two people who pass dimly through the narrative, spoken of by others but not speaking themselves. I have, I fear, delayed too long the writing of this, for as I grow old the moon of fantasy begins to set confusedly with me. *The Avatars* has not the spiritual gaiety I desired for it. The friends with whom I once spoke of such things are dead or gone far from me. If they were with me, out of dream, vision and intuition shared between us, I might have made the narrative to glow. As it is, I have only been able to light my way with my own flickering lantern.

A.E.

THE AVATARS[1]

TO
W.B. YEATS

I

In the winter twilight a young man was flying from civilization. His way lay between many snow-covered hills. Why was he flying from city to mountain? On the morning of that wintry day his city had appeared to him to be an evil wrought by sorcerers, who, at the close of their labours, had summoned fog, gloom and cold, a grey consistory, to intervene between the heart and heaven. He had watched from his window dejected figures looming and vanishing in the fog, their world a blur of grey mist above, a blur of murky brown underfoot. He had thought for an instant a picture might be made of these sad shadows darkling and fading in the cloudy air, but shrank from the idea of giving permanence to what was not in itself desirable life. A wind had swept the fog from the street, but the thinning mist revealed only the dull darkness of the houses opposite, in bleak unlikeness to the City the artist imagination would build on earth.

'It must be sorcery keeps the world as it is,' he had thought. And fancy had created a vivid grotesque, a council of wizards riding high on the steely air, monstrous shapes with eyes opaque as stone, like to that fabled Balor of the Evil Eye,[2] but petrifying hearts, not bodies, with a glance. If not like these in body, like these in soul must have been the creators of that dark industrial architecture which made a gloom in the air. He thought of the minds darkened in those mills, face and form losing comeliness, the mechanical eliminating use of the joyous creative faculty. He had himself been manacled to the mechanical world when a boy. He recalled his agony at the dimming of imaginative life in dull labours; an agony which one day grew unendurable, and impelled him there and then to escape, prepared to let body starve rather than soul. The exaltation of revolt carried him far from the city, a vagabond truly, but happy, restored to the everlasting companions, air and light, who flung their arms about him. He had journeyed on and on over an earth rich with lakes and woods, with noons misty with light, and mountains that in the evening seemed to ascend in flame. They were all calling him to be of their brotherhood. It was then he first felt their beauty was transparent. Some being, remote yet intimate, peered at him from the deeps of air. The apparitions of light, cloud, mountain and wood underwent a transfiguration into life, a vaster remoter self or oversoul to his own being. So, spell-stricken, he had passed from wonder to wonder, until at last the western sea stayed his travelling. There he met Michael Conaire, who became to him an elder brother; and, by his help, Paul came to be the artist which was nature's intent for him. The thought of that old friend had come to him in his despondency as light draws the lost traveller in some midnight valley. With an impetuous obedience to impulse in which he never failed, he had hastened to pack up the materials of his art. In his hurrying mind the air was shining, the foam was leaping, the snow was pure on mountain and field, the fire was on the hearth and the whimsical elder was beside it, all that would meet him at the end of his journey. So he started on his second flight from civilization. An hour after the dull city and its melancholy slaves were behind him. He wondered if time would ever come when they would revolt as he had done, return to nature and let that mother restore their lost likeness in soul and body to the ancestral beauty. Only a god, he thought, could arouse them from their stupor. As he drew nigh at twilight to that western land he loved, half in a dream he watched from the silently running car the fields white without a gleam; the hills a chilly violet against a sky of lemon light; the cottages on the hillside; tall smoke rising up through stillest air; here and there a glint of gold from door or window. It was all so pure and cold and lovely that he closed his eyes to lay it reverently in the chamber of beautiful memories. Then his mood of half dream became wholly dream, and passed into trance, and vision came strangely to him with power and the sense of purpose.[3]

In that illumination of vision he was brought to a cottage on some mountainside. He knew not where. He saw, by a light in himself which made the dusk lucid, the snow pale as pearl lying on rock and ridge and roof with a blue lustre taken from a sky with just awakening stars. One window only was aglow piercing the whitewashed walls, and about that homestead a delicate nimbus was spread as if rayed from a lovely life hidden within. Above the cottage rose two watchers, crested with many-coloured lights, gigantic forms that seemed shaped from some burnished and exquisite fire. They held swords of wavering flame as if guardians of some precious thing. There was gentleness amid the awe the vision created: and it was all marvellously clear, clearer than anything imagination had ever beheld and beyond his own imagination beautiful.

Paul opened his eyes and, starting up, he looked wildly about him, but he could see nothing but the dark ridged mountains rising on either side of the valley road. The only lights were the stars and the far lights of homes on the hillside, and he knew not where to search for that cottage of wonder. He sank back, closing his eyes that he might see again, but the vision had vanished, and memory could not recreate it in its first magical lustre. He groaned in himself that he should have started up and had lost maybe some further revelation. The car ran on along the snowy road, the driver, unconscious of the mad imaginations of his silent passenger, hurrying him from the valley of vision. At last there came a twist in the road, and then the shadowy shining of a lake below battlements of rock, and beyond that dim sea, and beyond that still dimmer mountains. Paul recalled his thoughts from their wild careering as the car turned into an avenue. In a moment he was before an open door; there was a hall ruddy with light and a figure with arms uplifted in welcome.

II

'Dear Paul, I felt at midday you were coming. You sent your thought flying before you. I have been looking along the road for an hour or more.' Behind Conaire was his wife, kind as himself, the silent and affectionate listener to interminable rhapsody and speculation from the talkative philosopher. Conaire was radiant in the anticipation of a less silent hearer. He foresaw colloquies stretching beyond midnight with the artist he had fostered. That night truly he was stirred as Paul hesitatingly told of the vision in the dark valley. Conaire sat up quivering with excitement.

'There is a prologue in heaven to that,' he began impressively. 'I know now why I met you seven years ago. I know why you revolted against the mechanical. I know why you and I are what we are. I know why Lavelle fashioned poetry out of legend and coloured it with fairy. I know why Brehon turned to a language which had become almost a tradition, and why the enthusiasts of a rural civilization began their labours. They were all fore-runners. Now there will be spiritual adventures, knights-errant, dragons to be slain, black magic and divine enchantments. I would not now exchange this my age for any other; not to sit at the Banquet and hear the wisdom of Socrates: not to be in Babylon with the great king: not to see Solomon bewitch the Queen of Sheba!'

'Incurable romantic! Tell me about the prologue in heaven,' said Paul, amused and pleased as all are when thought of theirs is taken by another, and the psychic juggler tosses it in the air, and it breaks out into many shining forms with faces looking in every direction. It was to warm himself at this glow of fancy he had fled from the city. 'I came here to have my gloom lit up by the torch of your mind. Begin in heaven, dear friend, and you can descend by way of the half-gods to the hearth where I sit. Make the journey as long as you like. I am excited about that aureoled cottage with its watchers. I never dreamed earth had such fiery gigantic citizens. My being leaped up in light when I saw them. Do you think it more than imagination?'

'It is not imagination. It is seership.[4] Listen, Paul. When I was young the whole world was at war, as you know. You could not remember the agony but you know the black night which settled on men's souls after it. I thought the Iron Age was to be with us for ever, that beauty was to be but a memory, that earth deserted by the gods was to spin desolate in space. You know what infinite sorrow the heart can feel when we are young. In the midnight of my despair I too had a vision. My sleep broke into a dazzle of light, and I was raised above myself to be with the immortals. They glimmered starlike about me, each in the image by which they were fabled. They were gazing silently at a ruddy divinity who was waving his hand from the heaven world at the troubled earth. It was Ares, proud, for he had drawn men in millions to act in his greatest drama. The gentler deities held counsel together. The memory of that tragedy must be obliterated. The curtain of blackness which would fall when it was over must be lifted on a new drama to be enacted, a drama like one of the beautiful plays of antiquity in which gods took part as hero or heroine. Such was the play of Helen which made men realize that beauty was a divinity. Such was the play of Radha and Krishna which taught lovers how to evoke god and goddess in each other.[5] Only a deity could undo what a deity had done. So now there must be born on earth divine shepherds to lead men back to ancient happiness and beauty. The immortals, gazing on earth, communed as to where the incarnation would take place. In the Old World the hearts of men were so heavy that they could not be uplifted even by a god. In the New World the hearts of men were so fierce that not even the power of the immortals could save their avatar if he did not worship the idols men had there set up. There was India always ready to prostrate itself before a divinity. But India had many avatars, and if a new avatar came it would still be prostrate and gentle and would not rise up in pride. Then one pointed to a land where lived a perfectly impossible people with whom anything was possible. And when he had pointed it out, all the immortals turned their eyes and looked on me and I awoke.'

'Your imagination leaps by the tipsiest stepping-stones from darkness to light with seven-leagued boots,' said Paul, contrary

The Avatars

from old custom, yet all the while willing to be convinced life's darkness could be transmuted into precious fires. 'But if you took any two dreams by any two other people and made them stepping-stones for your seven-leagued imagination, into what incredible regions in space and time would you not be carried?'

'There are not two stepping-stones only. But by treading on these I can see the stepping-stones behind me and others ahead,' Conaire answered, delighted at an opposition which was a signal to summon up whole legions of theory. 'My vision doubtless appears to you more personal fantasy than an image of truth. But truth may be revealed in symbol. When we fall asleep after a day of anxiety our desires often dramatize themselves in dream which is a true symbol of our waking state. The circumstance of the dream may be incredible. What it symbolizes is a truth. In the secrecy of sleep, in that state we call dreamless, we wake to a life of divine reality.[6] When we emerge from that state its realities may dramatize themselves in symbolic dreams, and these realities must drape themselves in whatever shapes they can find. The circumstance of the dream may be incredible and yet the idea symbolized may be worthy philosophic scrutiny. I know,' continued Conaire with a deprecating movement of hands and features, 'my mind is encrusted with fantasies. I built them up as a defence against the grey folk who were ever assailing me with the wish that I become as colourless as themselves. For that habit of mind the penalty is, I receive truth only through a mist of fantasy. But I have come to believe my dream, however fantastic, mirrored some reality in divine consciousness brooding on the future, devising religions, philosophies, arts, sciences and civilizations, and breathing forth the moods by which acceptance is made possible. I think your vision was of some reality while mine was symbolic.[7] You must not think of gods or avatars as fountains only of theological piety. In the ancient world any around whom nations pivoted to new destinies were regarded as avatars.[8] So the goddess was surmised in Helen, the god in Alexander or Cuchulain. You must not allow your mind to be dominated by traditions of the avatars of theology. Plato says if there be any gods they certainly do not philosophize, and I am equally certain they are not like even the saintliest of archbishops. They are, I fancy, more like poets who live their own lordly imaginations. It is not an incredible speculation that one of these divine poets has taken a body in this world, and is now as child or man in that aureoled cottage on the mountainside. Are not the greater poets half gods, and why should we shrink from belief in one who is fully conscious of his divinity?'

'I would undertake labours like those of Hercules to learn the truth about my dream,' cried Paul. 'But what have the gods been doing since the Council in Heaven? Tell me about the forerunners. You have a segment of the divine circle, and I expect an imagination like yours to complete the full orb for me.'

'It is not so easy as that,' returned the philosopher. 'An ancient scripture says, "The Wise Ones guard well the home of Nature's order. They assume excellent forms in secret." Whatever happens I am sure will be surprising however we speculate. Ares is the only deity who repeats himself. The warrior mind in heaven as on earth is devoid of imagination. Was there ever clearer evidence of flagging invention than in the Russian revolution following the French? The *dramatis personae* were the same in both dramas. A half-witted king, a haughty queen, angry philosophers, magicians, charlatans, ferocious dictators, *jacquerie* and peasant wars. But it is a fascinating subject for speculation how, after thought in Heaven on the affairs of Earth, the Divine Will might be transmuted into earthly activities. The ancients spoke of Fountains welling out of Hecate, by which symbols they expressed their belief that from the heart of divine nature there was a ceaseless flow of spiritual energy on all that live. In many lands there are legends of these sidereal Fountains – in our own country also. It was by breathing the exhalations from mystic nature the Sibyls were inspired to prophecy. This indicated the belief of the ancients that ideas born in the Heaven world descended to the Earth dwellers by these ethereal streams. We can imagine one of these Fountains[9] feeding with spiritual vitality the people among whom the incarnation is to take place, first coloured by the presence of the god; and the spiritually sensitive, awakened to a new consciousness by the current laving heart and mind, stirred to give it expression and so becoming forerunners of the Avatar. These naturally would seek symbols and affinities in myth, legend and tradition of ages when this commerce between Heaven and Earth was understood. What is spoken of as the mystic paganism of our poets is not merely a protest against mechanical life, but is the desire of the soul to live amid its spiritual affinities. The very names they use, the names of ancient gods and heroes, have a power of evocation. Those who, allured by the magic of rhythm, murmur these names, whether they know it or not, are weaving spells and incantations. The powers evoked flow to them out of the Ever Living. The earth is changed for them; and all this prepares the way for the Avatar; for, if there were no forerunners, there would be none who could understand his voice. The forerunners arouse ideas latent in the character of the people. The Avatar wakens these to full consciousness and indicates their final goal. The purpose of an Avatar is to reveal the spiritual character of a race to itself.'

'Can you say of us that we do not know our own spiritual character?' asked Paul.

'Do you know when you listen to orchestra what next shall follow on the music sounding on the air, whether flute or violin shall most intoxicate the sense? But whatever instrument dominates, if the work be by a great master, we feel the sequence was inevitable even if unforeseen. The master knows the quality of the instrument and its full tones. We do not know until the master has played on the instrument what music it can make. We do not know ourselves but we are known. The spiritual cultures we associate with Greece, Egypt, India, Persia, China or Judea were all in the divine consciousness before they were in the human. I can imagine, before the awakening of Greece, before a poet had sung to a lyre or a statue was carved, the Lords of the world, who know what is within, perceiving the latent instinct for beauty, and that some divine messenger incarnated to be its Avatar. It may have been that being, fabled long after as Apollo, by whom was awakened that consciousness which culminated in epic, drama, statue, temple; and which realized its divine origin in a philosophy which declared that Deity was Beauty in its very essence. Can we say of our own people what one mood is dominant, as we can say in ancient Greece there was the passion for beauty, or in ancient India there was the longing for spiritual truth?'

'But,' said Paul, 'you came out of that high conclave with the thought we were an impossible people. Why, if that be so, should everything be possible?'

'The marriage of Heaven and Earth has not taken place here as among the races I have mentioned,' returned the philosopher placidly. 'Where it has taken place men can live by reason. We have not that rational life. We live by intuition or instinct. At times our life is golden. At other times we are like demons from Eblis.'

'I am in a mood to believe anything tonight,' said Paul. He moved about the room restless as the orange-glow dancing and dwindling on the wall, an echo in light of the ruddy hearth. Then he went to the window and looked out on a mountainous earth, all blue, fairy and still in its mask of snow. It seemed more imagination than reality. The sky leaning over the lofty crags was like a face all majesty of expression yet without features. The sense of it being living overcame him. It seemed to draw nearer and nearer, to be at the window, intense with spirit being. The window for an instant was a portal into eternity. He came back to Conaire. 'I do not understand myself. I know nothing about life. This morning I felt as if iron bars were to close about us for ever and I hurried here like the condemned escaping from a dungeon. Tonight I feel as if I had but to lift my hands and call "Be ye lifted up, ye everlasting doors," and that apparition of earth and sky would be rolled up as a curtain. But,' he said dejectedly, 'they would not be lifted up. We are only children tilting at unassailable walls.'

'It is in the awakening of an eye the dead shall be raised,' said Conaire. 'Was it with those eyes you saw the fiery watchers on the hillside? I think you are a natural seer, but you have been content as an artist with the images you created for yourself. An Eastern sage said we could climb into Heaven by brooding on knowledge which came in dream. If you brood on your vision it may start you on some marvellous travelling. Remember the Persian poet:

> a single Alif were the clue,
> Could we but find it, to the Treasure House
> And peradventure to the Master too.'

III

A mood at once gay and solemn is born in the soul when it first discovers a path to light out of the dark cavern of the body, and is made aware of wide realms to travel in with a higher order of beings as companions. Such a mood overwhelmed Paul when he laid his head on a pillow and closed his eyes to sleep. He found, not the accustomed shade into which consciousness fades, but a jewel lustre as if whatever being had imparted to him its own vision, by that momentary commerce with him had made everything radiant, leaving behind it shining memories of its own nature and its travel from Heaven to Earth.

In that mood of mingled awe and exaltation Paul pursued the trail of glittering images. He seemed to himself to be borne up on a river of luminous and living air, and to be carried in vision into the heart of a great mountain. When he had passed within there was no hill, but a dazzle of light cast up from some interior fountain. He was aware of lofty beings there, kinsmen of those fiery watchers who kept guard on the mountain ridges. He did not feel anything was strange, for he seemed to have some ancient knowledge of it all. There was a spirit in him, too, deeper than conscious thought, which knew of a vaster life beyond all vision. He would have drawn nigher those lordly ones, but there was some constraint on him which he could not break, and at last there came relaxing of the will and he slept. It may have been that spirit within him desired to part from the waking self before it passed through the gateway of light to high adventures of its own. However it may have been, when Paul awoke he felt inexpressibly young and happy as if he had been reborn and baptized with some glorious fire. His limbs were light to move, and his fancies like a gay multitude of fish, flying to and fro, sunlit in water. He dressed and went out, climbing the snow-covered ridge that rose behind the house, so that his eyes might drink in all his heart loved. The world without, like his world within, was all radiance in the dawn. The sea was a waste of quivering light. The lake was frozen silver. In the mountainous lands the heights were glittering with gold, and the hollows blue, lustrous and ethereal as the abyss of air overhead. Here and there was a starry sparkling as of diamonds and opals scattered in the light. Here and there were patches of dark grey or purple or green rock, vestiges of the rugged country he knew before, but now veiled by the purity and frailty of snow. He breathed with delight the clear, cold, life-giving air. Every atom in his being was fiery. Never did he feel charged with so intense a vitality. He interpreted the universe by his own being and had the sense of life throughout dense infinitudes. He lifted up his hands crying out as one spirit to another, as if he knew in those wide spaces there was that which could hear him and could answer to his call. Then he heard a shout and saw a ruddy little figure, Conaire's only child, flying to him over the snow. She flung herself on the young artist whom she loved. Paul lifted the girl in his arms and, talking gaily to her, went back to the house.

IV

What was told of that mystic Babylon of the Apocalypse, the haunt of every unclean spirit, might have been spoken of the cities of the Iron Age dominated by the dark mechanic genius. They were haunted by yet more evil divinities and knew it not. The stars were not darkened over them. The sun shone on their streets. The clouds were snowy and spiritual as of old. All the tapestry of the heavenly house hung and flamed overhead, but there was midnight about them in Anima Mundi.[10] In vain was the wealth created bartered for beauty. It could not purchase a light by which the soul could see it, and because of that psychic night, what was lovely to the eyes could not make gay the soul. As there are houses haunted by the shades of those who in them have done evil, so were the cities haunted by evil memories. The shades grew thicker about them through centuries as the ocean of life bathing them became more impregnated by the emanations of men leprous with sensuality, blind with fear or smouldering with hate. The larvae of the dead hung about the living with unsatiated passion, and a base desire was never solitary, for it summoned up legions of evil affinities to urge it to its consummation.[11] As the lights of the soul became extinguished, its darkened halls and corridors were thronged by sinister inhabitants breathing animalism and corruption. They held revelry within and hence came frenzies, obsessions and unappeasable desires. The body, possessed by the shades, was made meet for its inhabitants. The character of the goat, the hog and the rat began to appear in men's faces and to efface the divine signature. In the Babylons of the ancient earth there was beauty and magnificence even of sin. Beauty was born in their courts and byways because mechanical devices had not yet been set to do the work of man. The imagination was still artificer, and the slave might hold commerce with heaven and be a creator at his labours. But, as the demon of the mechanical began to dominate the cities of the Iron Age, it brought life itself into subservience to it. The looms of the soul became silent and rich webs of fantasy no longer poured from them. The potter no more shaped his vessel with delight, moulding about it the dancing figures which were in his heart. No song sounded over labour, for the machine chanted its iron dronings by day and by night, and the sorcery made men to forget the soul had once been as illuminated as nature. The heart was ever heavy, and few were those who could hold back the gloom by creating their own light. The imagination could no more conceive of lordly life, and multitudes fell blindly into a mould devised that society might have the precision of the machine. The artificers of this vast degradation wrought on the unillumined nature so that, if any had the dream of freedom, they were made to seem the enemies of all by which men lived. By identity of character souls become welded together in the psychic world, and tend there to become entities, beings made out of multitudes, the dominant passion as soul moving all to act together as a single being.[12] To the divine vision these cities of the Iron Age appeared as monstrous beasts, the dragon devourers of virgin life. Unable themselves to give birth to vital beings, they became insatiable vampires drawing youth out of nature to themselves to replace the life which became so rapidly burnt out, so decadent and decrepit, that none could trace ancestry beyond a grandsire who had been born in the cities. As the cities exercising this magnetic power grew more thronged the country became more desolate and deserted. The Earth itself for leagues about them suffered a blight so that there was less magic in woodland or glade. These seemed empty of their elemental populace, dryad and hamadryad, the gentle silvery presences blowing their horns, or making with childlike voices melodies with no passion or pain in them; or else the power to see and hear there had been lost and a world of ethereal beauty had drifted beyond human cognisance. It was in one of the blackest of these cities Paul had heard a voice like that which cried in the mythic Babylon, 'Come out of her, my people,' and had fled away from it to hear the voice of the Earth Spirit, to listen to its multitudinous meditation, and to be inspired to become one of its instruments so that the spirit might not pass forgotten from the minds of men.

V

As a cloud fades leaving bare the fields of heaven, so the cloud of snow crumbled from rock, hill and hollow. Summer came, and Paul, still under the enchantment, lingered in the western land. Such moods of majesty and sweetness arose in him that he felt omnipresence was working the same miracles in his soul that it wrought out of earth, turning dark clay into the brilliance of leaf and flower. Nothing that lived close to the earth could altogether escape the wizardry. There was a spirit in the wild people who lived among the hills which was not in the people of the cities. They belonged, however remotely, to some mystic empire. The dullest peasant might break silence with a phrase in which the mountains seemed to speak rather than a man. Even in their orgies there was a leaven of imagination, and a spiritual light glowed, however fitfully, amid the bestial as a star might glow in the darkness of a tarn. Daily Paul was discovering the affinity between these people, himself and that mystic nature. In a late twilight he sat on a rock above a mountain road. From that twilight nigh the earth the night rose up from one blue heaven to another, and he stayed gazing through the night until his soul became one with the stillness, prolonging his reverie until it seemed to become part of the reverie of Earth itself or to take colour from its imaginations. An incoherent babbling broke the silence. It came from a man staggering along the road below. That drunken babble outraged the solemn ceremonial whereby the Lights nightly unveil the infinite which is the symbol of God, and the Ivory Gate seemed to close at the sound. Then there was again silence, and Paul, peering through the dusk, saw the drunkard had fallen in the middle of the road. He clambered down from his seat on the rocks; and, as he bent to lift the fallen man out of danger from any cart which might pass in the darkness, he heard a half-inarticulate crooning and caught the words of an old song full of gentleness and beauty: 'She passed the sally garden on little snow-white feet,' and Paul knew that, through the fever and blind disorder of the reeling senses, the soul of that man was following images which were quiet and lovely, and it too belonged to the mystic empire.

Paul had brooded on that rocky ridge night after night, for he was painting the mountain which rose beyond the wooded valley and the long lake, and he carried memory of shadowy form and dim illumination to the hours of light when he could work. One morning he brought his picture to the rocky seat to compare the forms revealed by day with his memory of them shrouded in the summer night. As he brooded on the picture he felt a quickening of imagination. He closed his eyes and he saw again the huge mountain in the dim night, but now a light glowed above the high plateau and wavering flames streamed up into the air. His fingers began to quiver as if what he had imagined had run from head to hand, and he took the brushes and began to paint that mystic light above the high land. He was inspired by something beyond himself. The hand moved almost without guidance from the mind. Yet when he had ended, the psychic illumination on the mountain did not appear alien to earth but a portion of natural beauty.

'What is that light on the hill?' asked an eager and imperative voice. Paul turned. He had never seen a more beautiful boy than this who stood before him. The sunlight through the yellow curls made them glow like an aura of fire. The eyes, strange, innocent and intense, were like pools of blue light in the shadowed face. Paul's own eyes remained fixed on the boy and he could not move them, so stricken was he with that beauty. The child of a peasant, he thought. What a wonder. He might be tending sheep, but no sheep were visible.

'I do not know,' he answered at last, for the boy's eyes dazzled him, and his mind was confused as the mind is oft-times by the eyes of women. 'I imagined it there. It might be a palace of the Sidhe who were the old gods of our people. You may have heard of them.'

'Old people speak of them,' said the boy. 'I have not seen them though they call me a changeling.'

'Why do they call you that?' asked Paul.

'I will not do the things they wish me to do. I will not be made to learn like the others. I will not be shut out of the air. I run away.'

'Do you not want to know what others know?' asked Paul.

'I know what they think,' answered the boy. 'They have no light in their minds unless I blow into them. Then I can make them think what I will.'

'What do you make them do?' asked Paul, amused at the young dictator whose years might number twelve or fourteen. He thought the boy might indeed move people to do anything by his beauty.

'I imagine them wearing gay colours and they begin to wear them. I imagine them dancing in curves like the clouds and they begin to dance,' said the boy.

Paul, who was now in imagination devising a picture of the lad as a shepherd on the hills, and who wished to know where he could find him again, asked, 'What is your name?'

'Aodh,' answered the boy.

'I have not seen you before. Where do you live?'

The boy waved a hand to a ridge made faint and blue by many miles of air and heat and light.

'There!' he said. 'It was to see the sea I came here.'

'So far!' said Paul. 'How tired you must be!'

The boy laughed, and before Paul could find words to delay him he ran up the hill as lightly as another might run down. Paul saw the golden curls in a last flashing against the blue sky as the light figure leaped over the ridge of rock. I am sure to meet him again, he thought; but many years were to pass before he again saw Aodh.

VI

The boy went on lightly leaping from rock to rock, choosing always the high ridges for his path. He had delight in his airy leapings like to that the soul feels when it wakes in dream and is buoyed on air and exults, because the vast dragging of earth no more ties its feet to heath or stone, and it can, though wingless, wander at its will like a bird. In fancy this tireless child thought of leaping from crest to crest of the long blue waves of hills. Why could he not do it? He imagined the run and the mad gathering of power for the leap, and in the very act of imagining he had left the body behind. What had happened? The air in which he floated was vibrant with timeless melody, a sound as beautiful and universal as the light. Where was he? Earth was vanishing, swallowed up in a brightness fiery as the sun, and mountains, crags and vales were fading from vision as if consumed by the ecstasy of the fire. A moment more and he would have passed from the illusion of boyhood. He was reaching up to some immeasurable power which was himself when consciousness faded. When it awoke again he heard voices speaking above him.

'It is time to awaken him. The seer cannot be held to the eyes. The being cannot be tied to the body.'

He looked up. He saw a figure thrice the height of mortals, a body gleaming as if made of golden and silver airs. It was winged with flame above the brows. The eyes which looked on him were still as if they had gazed only on eternities, and the boy cried and knew not why he uttered the words.

'I know you, Shepherd of the Starry Flocks. What soul do you now draw from the abyss?'

There were others, a high companionship, but he saw only for an instant a light of calm and lordly faces, and the next instant he was standing on the mountain grass, his limbs still bent for the leap he had imagined. He shook his ruddy curls in perplexity as he looked about him. The air was still and empty of sound or light, save the light from the far fire in the sky, and it seemed a grey twilight to the light which had vanished. 'The sun is dark to-day,' he said to himself. He felt a chill which was spiritual such as one might feel who is solitary on a lost planet. He flung himself on the heather and, with face buried in his arms shutting out the world, he began to think about himself. He lay there for hours, and when he rose to journey homewards the setting sun was reddening the battlement of the rocks and the valleys were brimming up with purple shadow. He walked on and on over the ridges and at last came to a cottage in the mountainside. As he entered he flung off the sadness which had beset him and spoke sweetly to the elders he called grandfather and grandmother. He ate the porridge and milk the old woman gave to him, and talked about the sea and the artist who was painting the mountain, but did not speak of the shining figure he had called the Shepherd of the Starry Flocks. He knew, though he was loved, that they looked doubtfully at times upon this child of their child, and that they wondered often if he was indeed a changeling as the people of the hills said of him. He knew this, for he could see their thoughts as he could feel their love. He went out after that and ran about the fields with other children, racing and shouting with them until voices from distant cottages began to call them home, and he too went back to the cottage where he lived, and, climbing a ladder, went into a little room where his bed lay close to a window looking across the valley and lake. Beyond that was the same great mountain which he had watched with the artist in the morning. He took up a fiddle which lay on a box and he began in the dark to play a melody of his own imagining. In the room below the old man, drowsing by a turf fire, heard the music and it awakened long-sleeping emotions. His heart was melted as when he was young, and he sat with wet eyes listening until the music ceased and there came a creaking which showed the boy had climbed into his bed.

It may have been an hour or hours may have passed. Aodh sat up in his bed. He looked through the open window. He saw the great mountain beyond the dark valley and the lake, but now it was crested with a glowing light like that he had seen in Paul's imagination. The boy's eyes were starry in the dark. The light beckoned him to it. He must go. In a moment he was out in the night and was hastening down the valley. He felt tireless and full of power as if he had not already roamed for many miles. The rocks glimmered greyly in the summer night. He leaped them more lightly than he had leaped them in the dawn. Then he left the rocky fields behind and entered the black woods silvered here and there by flakes of moonfire. His feet moved as surely through the mazes of the blackness as through the light, and at last he came to the reed-fringed margin of the lake. He thought he saw silvery forms looking at him from the water but heeded them not. He strode along swiftly by the lake to its eastern shore, where he turned and entered anew the blackness of the woods which covered the mountain to its knees. The boy climbed upwards. He felt the huge mountain to be living. It poured its strength into him. There was a vibration in the air like that melody of the aether which had sounded on his ear, but now it grew until the mountain seemed mad with song. As he climbed from the last trees he saw far above him the light brightening on the highest plateau, and he ran up the steep side in his eagerness lest it might fade before he came. There were voices mingling with the music, voices ethereal and divinely gentle, yet with all the power of that great tone out of which they rose. As he overcame the last steep rock and stood on the turf of the plateau his eyes were dazzled, for there rose into the blue night a mighty and many-coloured palace, its pillars, walls and towers all luminous opal enwrought with precious fires and carven over with mythic forms. From the great gate came a blinding light, but the boy unterrified passed through it; and he was in the lofty hall and, through a light intense but clear, he saw many immortals shining as that figure he had beheld in dream, but beyond his dream in majesty, each on their thrones, with calm faces turned to him. As the child strode into the hall, the immortals from their thrones descending stood with bowed heads, for the child who was there was one of themselves, one who had left the Imperishable Light, laying aside sceptre and diadem and had narrowed himself to that body that he might waken the souls in the abyss of earth.[13] At that moment Aodh was divested of the childhood into which he had imagined himself, and he towered up to a consciousness unimaginable and not to be fully remembered by his mortality, for it enveloped Earth and Heaven. He was struggling, when he awakened at dawn in his room, to recapture a lost magnificence of power. Had he been singing a song which went in every direction and into thousands of hearts? Had he blown shining images into myriads of darkened souls? Had he taken these from eternity to scatter the fiery seed through humanity? Or was the fiery seed already sown and did he but blow it to a vivid flame? The child mind was bewildered, and it was long before Aodh came to a surety about himself, for even the immortals when they put on mortality are but a little part of themselves, a spark in the immensity of their own fiery being.[14]

VII

Men are never nearer to the gods or more partakers of their ecstasy than when they are creators. Paul, incessantly creative, was the happiest of men. Seated in a glade of the forest he could see the branches, green-burdened and wind-swayed, make fire and darkness to reel to and fro on the russet floor. He watched the flying of tattered flame and purple shadow; and the mad dance of colour evoked whirling figures which rushed out of the house of the soul to mix with the reeling light. He could see swirling draperies, flushed faces, loosened and rippling hair, the glint of a white arm, a gleaming neck, the dance of lovely feet, all sun-flecked, dazzling and bewildering as the anarchy of flame and darkness in which they rioted. His heart was singing as his brush moved swiftly. If we were many-armed as an Indian god, he thought, one might keep pace with imagination. But the phantasmal figures went on dancing, being gay of themselves with a life of their own, and they would not be stayed in any one movement however beautiful. He pretended unhappiness, but all the while was delighted at his own swift mastery in evolving rhythm from chaos. So swiftly did his brush move that he surprised his hand shaping form ere an image had become present to consciousness. And suddenly he knew that the daimon, which had let loose the whirling figures, had also liberated energies which played on the strings of the body, directing hand and mind; and, if the mind wavered for a moment, the guidance of the hand was sure. For an instant he rose above himself and became one with that creative genius which is behind all conscious motion of the mind. He felt in that instant his being was rooted in some paradise of fiery and beautiful forms, ready to rush out through any open door to populate earth with their ecstatic life. Where did it all come from? Had there been a dance like that in some forest of antiquity with only the Eternal Mind to remember its beauty, and was it from that treasure-house the flock of images escaped? He went on painting, intoxicated with the beauty he saw and the beauty he imagined. The forest depths before him were a dazzle of green and sparry scintillations. Branches were suddenly burnished with vivid colour as suddenly vanishing. Patches of orange flame awoke, blazed on the russet floor, then darkened to purple. There was incessant birth and death of light. Through it all went the dance of lovely shapes. Then into the figures of imagination a living figure raced, a girl running down the glade, the sunlight on her blue dress flecking it with a glow rich as the bloom on a peacock's tail. It was Conaire's child. She slipped behind him to look at the picture.

'Oh, Paul, how lovely! I want to dance! I want to dance!' and she went whirling about, face, flickering hair and dress fretted with light like the figures of his dream. At last she flung herself down on the moss beside him.

'Why isn't Aoife here to dance with me? She is like a daffodil in the sun – all burning.'

'Who is this wonderful Aoife?'

'Aoife! The mountain, the lake and the woods as far as you can see are hers. I call her the Princess, because though she is only my age everybody has to be her servant.'

'Must an old woman of twelve even be her slave?'

'Oh, Paul, I can't help it. I think she gets inside me, and can run in and out of me as if I was a cave. She sets me on fire.'

'She keeps you to do her mischief for her as another young person keeps me!'

'No. It is not like that,' said the child mysteriously. 'She is like someone in the fairy tales. I never told anybody but you. I hear music inside the rocks when she is with me. Sometimes there are people like twinkling mists who come out of the mountain to look at her. And tall silvery people grow from the trees, gleaming people with long purple hair. I was frightened when I saw them, but Aoife laughed and clapped her hands, and they all faded back into the trees.'

'You and your Aoife are living in fairyland now, sweetheart. And to think they are sending you both out of fairyland to Europe where never a dryad has been seen for thousands of years! Why are they doing it?'

'Father and mother think I ought to learn languages where they are spoken.'

'Oh, Olive dear, don't let them take all the fairy out of your mind. If you do, the hills, when you come back, will be only rocks empty of music, and the bark door of the trees will be shut so that not a dryad can slip through to play with you.'

'It is cruel of you even to think that. Why should I grow out of seeing things any more than you?'

She sat looking at him reproachfully, the child's lovely face a pure oval, the eyes a rich grey with a spark of silver like a little star dancing in each, the fair hair falling in curves and clusters; and all of such beauty that Paul, gazing on her, lapsed into one of those mystical moods which what was beautiful more and more evoked in him. And she was no longer Conaire's child, but a fragile exquisite imagination of the Master of all arts who dreamed and devised it within and without, and held it together, face, eyes, innumerable hair, heart beating adorably, breathing body, grace of limb, through every motion, speaking through it to him, evolving it until it became the perfect mirror of the immortal thought in the immortal mind and could be a dwelling-place for the gentleness in that majesty. He murmured in his heart over this little citizen of the mystic empire, 'Oh, if you should ever become an exile!' And a wild protest burned in him because the great Artist seemed to set out his masterpieces carelessly and without defence, so that miracles of beauty might be marred, and the lamp set within them be dimmed. And then something within him cried, 'No! no! The Master never fails in His art. Through life, and through death to life again, He follows His works, and He will not cease until He has fashioned in immortal substance what was but evanescent air.' He shook off his sadness and said gaily:

'No! You will never be out of hail of fairyland! Never! Yet it is tragic this going away to-morrow. But I'll steal you all for myself now, and we will row on the lake, and come to our own enchanted island, and light a fire there, and signal to the stars when they come out, and I'll have a whole afternoon of my dearest to remember when she is away.'

He had been folding easel, gathering up brushes, paints and canvas; and with the child moving happily beside him he walked down the glade, and crossed a rushy field to a wooded promontory running out into the lake. His own cottage was there, built a little way from the trees. He cried to his elderly house-keeper: 'Margaret. I want tea and a kettle full of water and a boat-load of cakes, for we are going to be wrecked on a desert island, and the earth will have to race a million miles from where it is before we get back.'

He rowed out leisurely into the haze of sunny mist which lay on the lake, half rowing, half drifting, to a wooded island from which great branches stretched far out, sheltering lustrous shallows and inlets. It was a place in which he often sought solitude, and the mood of the Earth became life for him as he rested there, and the vision of the Earth was speech and no other speech was needed.[15] They lay on the mosses, sometimes watching through half-closed eyes the roof of sunlit leaves quivering as if millions of emerald, blue and yellow birds were fluttering above them, sometimes watching the diamond dance of lights on the water. The lake, as the long afternoon ended, was burnished with gold and that melted into every iridescence. Paul with a half-sigh woke out of his dream, and then there was a bustle for fallen branches. The fire was lit, the kettle was boiled, the feast was spread. He invented many fantasies for their common delight. The isle became movable as the carpet of the magicians of Arabia, and he brought it to Eastern seas, or planted it as an oasis beside the ruins of great cities, and they had imaginary adventures with dusky races, and both agreed that when they died the island must go with them to Paradise. At last, looking through the leaves, Paul saw the Evening Star sparkling above the cliffs, and he said sadly, 'Our day is over.' They went to the boat and he rowed it back silently to the shore. The child stood looking at him when they landed. He saw her eyes were wet. She took his hand, pressed it to her wet cheek, and then ran away as if she could not bear a longer parting. He followed the little figure with his eyes until it was swallowed up in the darkening twilight. Over the hills the stars were moving in the paths appointed them, and it seemed that she, no less than the other stars, was guided on her way by the Great Shepherd.

VIII

'How great a hollow in life can be made by the absence of a very small person,' said Conaire unhappily. He had come to Paul's cottage a month or two later. He moved restlessly about the room. 'The flame of a candle is a minute thing. But when it goes out, what a great darkness there is!'

'Why did you let Olive go so far away?' asked Paul.

'Truly I do not know. I think some magic constrained me. There is a young girl a little older than Olive who will be a great lady, for hers are the forests, lakes and mountains all about us. When she first saw Olive some years ago she took possession of her as a young queen might, and Olive seems to belong to her more truly than to me or her mother. She is a beautiful quivering fire, this young Aoife. When I wanted Olive to remain here she blazed at me. I felt as if an indignant goddess was shrivelling me with lightning, and I was like some old half-wit who had halted a procession of princes. They have gone to a very rare and distinguished school. I could not myself afford this for Olive. But the guardians of that young Aoife – who ought rather to be called her slaves, for they are obedient to her whims as the genii to Aladdin and his lamp – when told she would not move unless Olive went with her, in their lordly way insisted that payment was their duty as they existed only for the happiness of their young despot. Do you know, Paul, if your vision of the warriors of heaven had been about a great house and not a cottage, I might have thought the Avatar to come was a goddess and that this wonder child was she. Well, while Olive is away I must try to find other lights to illuminate my darkness. Let us talk of that child we imagined as Avatar. The thought of him is often in my mind.'

'He is often in my mind,' said Paul. 'Come, I will show you something'; and he left the cottage and walked through the woods until he came to a glade where was his studio, a building of wood all white with white pillars about it like a Greek temple. Conaire followed him within. The artist took two pictures and a drawing in coloured chalks and set them side by side on a ledge. The first was that cottage aureoled with light with its divine guardians holding their swords of wavering flame. The second was that dark mountain he had painted with its dragon crest of fire. The third was a pastel of the head of the boy who had been with him on the hill. It was a face full of light, a blue sky behind the head making the gold of his hair like curling flames.

'These three,' he said, 'have come, I hardly know why, to be connected together in my mind.' He told Conaire about the boy who spoke to him for so few moments and passed lightly leaping up the hill. Conaire's eyes lit with excitement.

'Did you never think to trace the boy?'

'I did indeed, for his image had begun more and more to glow in my imagination. But when I thought of seeking him out in that countryside to which he was going I felt as if a constraining will was laid upon mine, and I was not to unveil the mystery of that boy. In his own time he will reveal himself, and he is not to be revealed by another. Oh, I have thought about him, and,' he said hesitantly, as if he was half ashamed to be so impressed by the transient vision of a peasant boy, 'I had a dream in which he came to a palace of the gods, and they stood bowed before him. I do not know why it is, but the image of that boy darkens everything else in my imagination.'

'And that dark flame-fringed mountain?' asked his friend. 'What are your thoughts about that?'

'I do not know what I think. I hardly felt it was my own fingers guided the brushes, and it has haunted me ever since – that mountain. I look at it as some ancient might have looked at Mount Olympus or the fabulous Meru.[16] I imagine a gate to the secret of the world in its heart. I find myself thinking of what may be hidden in it before I sleep, and when I waken sometimes I have the sense that I have been there with shining companions.'

Then the elder began to conjure up out of memory or fantastic imagination a mysterious wisdom about the earth and its sacred places.

'To the ancients,' he said, 'Earth was a living being. We who walk upon it know no more of the magnificence within it than a gnat lighting on the head of Dante might know of the furnace of passion and imagination beneath. Not only was Earth a living being having soul and spirit as well as body, but it was a household wherein were god folk as well as the whole tribe of elemental or fairy lives. The soul of Earth is our lost Eden.[17] This was the Ildathach[18] or Many-coloured Land of our ancestors, and of which Socrates too spoke, saying Earth was not at all what the geographers supposed it to be, and there was a divine earth superior to this with temples where the gods do truly dwell. Our souls put on coats of skin. That is, they were lost in our bodies here, and at last we fell together outside the divine circle and came to live on surfaces, not even dreaming that within the earth is a spirit which towers up within itself from clay and rock to the infinite glory. Only the poets and mystics have still some vision of the lost Eden. The gods are still in the divine household, and the radiance over the palaces of light appears at times to seers like yourself as dragon-crests of flame or rivers of light running out to the stars. It is time for us to be travelling inward, and, if there be an Avatar to come, he may show us the way once more as did the Avatars of the past. How do I know all this? The Earth Spirit has been talking to me ever since I came here, telling me the meanings of all I have read and many things which never were written, and it confirmed that dream I told you about, that there would come a day when the immortals once more would walk among us and be visible heroes to us.'

Paul looked affectionately at his old friend to whom the universe was such a romance, and he would have asked a question which, he knew, would have started Conaire on a monologue of an hour, when there was a sound of footsteps behind him. He turned and saw a slight figure with a beautiful elfish face, who walked as if his body was charged with energy. It was another friend, Felim Carew, the poet, who began at once with a tempest of friendly denunciation.

'I have found you out at last – you who denounced the money kings for their monstrous greed. But their sin was innocence compared with yours. They only kept money for themselves, a thing which is not worth keeping. I do not grudge it to them any more than I grudge straws and feathers to a madman. But you discovered here a world of unfallen beauty, beauty for which we starved, and you kept the beauty to yourself. I am going to write an epic like Dante and put you in the lowest hell, face to face with Satan's masterpiece of ugliness. It will be a punishment for your silent greed in keeping to yourself the loveliest country on earth. Is it any wonder you paint pictures which people fall over each other to possess when you have not even to exercise imagination? You have only to pick up the loveliness which lies all about you while we have to sweat blood to make a thing of beauty. Oh, but that is wonderful!' His quick eyes had been roaming about while he talked, and he had seen the aureoled cottage with its divine watchers. 'You must tell me about that! It is you have become the poet. But I have broken in between you and your friend!'

'No,' said Conaire. 'You only continue what we were speaking of, the mystery and magnificence of this mountainous nature. Earth, I see, has accepted you, for she inspires you to continue our conversation.' He looked with great friendliness on the new-comer. Each had heard the artist speak of the other and they at once slipped into what seemed an old intimacy.

'I walked my way up here. I knew I had come into a country which was still in the divine keeping. I was on a hillside last evening and I watched girls and children lighting a fire. And I swear to you, Paul, there was some master of their souls and bodies who lived within them all and made every motion rhythmical and beautiful, as if a greater than Phidias had invented the harmony of their movements with each other, with clouds, blown boughs and the quivering waters of a stream. For three marvellous moments the invisible artist made masterpiece after masterpiece, and then, as if he had run to other souls to make another wonder, the rhythm was broken, and the children parted as leaves might fall from a withering blossom. Your eyes should have seen it. How could I put that visible magic into poetry! But you are not going to keep this enchanted land to yourself. I'll make it famous. No, I won't. You are right to be reticent. The earth will call to it all whom it thinks worthy. I am going to write better poetry than anyone, for I will wrestle with earth and will not let it go until it blesses me.'

'Shall we initiate him into the mysteries?' the artist asked Conaire.

'Let him brood on the pictures, and if he is to be initiated it will appear from his interpretation.'

The poet looked at the three pictures, and, after a silence of some moments, he turned to the others.

'A divine child! A manger, heavenly guarded! A holy mountain!'

'He is accepted,' said Conaire, and the three talked late into the night.

IX

The poet, who had neither dream nor vision to build on, was strangely the most earnest in faith that the darkness of earth was to be invaded from the heavens, and yet he would not have any search made for the Avatar.

'He will reveal himself in his own time. Though as yet he may be only a boy he may be doing his work. He may be like that Cuchulain of the Irish hero tales of whom it was said, "This man protects Ireland more when he sleeps than when he wakes!" Do we know what happens when we sleep and pass beyond dream? We do not know what we do. We do not know what an avatar may do when his body is still.[19] He may narrow himself here into the being of a child. But is he narrowed in that other world beyond dream – the world of spirit waking? Your visions and imaginations and the imaginations of others may be fiery arrows shot by a being all light. I may be here because I am called. I think I am. I was for a year in that New World of marvellous cities. Nothing that the most fantastic imagination dreamed of Babylon or Nineveh comes near the reality of these gigantic heaven-assailing cities. You stand in the heart of one and look up from the gloom of the street, and a thousand feet or more above you the sunlight blazes on great towers and terraces. There may be a dazzle of flame where burnished plates of metal, silvery or bronze, catch fire from the sun and burn like giant candles. There are tall towers all a glitter of glass. And, oh, the wonder at night! There are lights faint as stars on the topmost storeys, and the stars themselves seem but the continuation of a fabulous architecture reaching up to infinity. These cities are the last trap set for the spirit of man to draw him from nature and from himself. The people who live in them are kind, but, oh, so unhappy. They fly from one sensation to another and the way from body to soul is lost. If they close their eyes they are in a darkness which frightens them. They cannot bear to be still or alone. They are thirsty for beauty but cannot create it within themselves. When they meet a soul, truly living, natural and prodigal in itself, they are filled with wonder. They try to express their reverence by filling up every moment for it with the sensations which have atrophied their own imaginations. Ninety per cent of their people live in these unimaginable cities which they began lifting to the clouds three hundred years ago when the race was in its childhood. They created out of an abundant physical energy a prodigious mechanism which goes on swelling out of its own inherent vitality, building and organizing, until the mechanism has overwhelmed life. They cannot help themselves, poor people. They were born into the mechanistic maze and do not know the way out. There was never anything in the world so pitiful as their souls. They are rich inconceivably without, but paupers within, supplicating alms from any stray genius. They have become alien to nature, the ancient Mother. In its silences and lonelinesses they might meet the outcast majesty of spirit; and to the poor soul that outcast majesty would be a thing of terror. They would not recognize it as themselves. How could they be saved? If I was dictator I would take them in hundreds of thousands, and chain each one as a solitary to a stone in the desert or to a rock in the hills, give them a blanket or two and a little food. I would chain them to the rock as Prometheus was chained, and let the infinite heavens, sun, moon, stars and wind, be tormentors in their solitude until they had made friends with sky, sun, stars, moon, wind and earth, and they found in the anger of the gods there was a love; until the silences became friendly and the hollows of air no longer a void, and the stones were sweet to the touch. I cast all my thoughts about this on the air to a hundred million listeners and then flew over here to know what you were doing. It is enchanted, this western land of yours, not for its mountains, not for lake, river and heath, but because it seems alive. And, Paul, there are the strangest folk here, drawn, as I think I was and you were, by that mystic nature. I walked day after day and felt the mountains were swallowing me up. It is not the poet you knew who is here, but the Earth Spirit who sits and prattles by your hearth. Make the most of it while it is with me for it may leave me, though I will never leave it, but will pursue it and cry to it as Jacob to the angel, "I will not let you go until you bless me." '[20]

Paul and Conaire sat listening, pleased by the fantasy of the poet, and, as Paul looked at the elfish figure, it seemed to his imagination to be enveloped in a dark blue shining air, transparent as the blue of night, and there seemed innumerable sparks flashing like gold in that dark purity of blueness.

'Even the ruins of humanity here,' the poet went on, 'have some wild poetry in them. I was walking on a mountain road the day before yesterday and an old man came along, the remains of a magnificent human being, with a ruined beauty on his face. The old man was hugging his body to himself with his arms, shaking and swaying in his grief. And his sorrow was so great that he must speak it, even if it was only to another vagabond like himself. He stayed me and said, "Over those hills I wandered forty years ago. Nobody but myself knows what happened under the thorn tree forty years ago. The fret is on me! The fret is on me! God speaks out of His darkness, 'I have and I have not. I possess the heavens. I do not possess the world.' Abroad if you meet a countryman he will give you the bit and the sup. But if you come back to your own country after forty years it is not the potato and bit of salt you get, but only 'Who's that ould fellow?' The fret is on me! The fret is on me!" Was the old man drawn back at the end of his days to remember a young beauty? "Nobody knows but myself what happened under the thorn tree forty years ago!" Will that remembered beauty be the candle which will light him into Paradise? Oh, they are strange these mountain folk! What wisdom is born in their silences! I found a boy tending sheep a hundred miles from this, and he was staring at the sky and I asked him what he thought, and he said: "I am thinking we once lived in the Sun." But he had no words to tell of the great glory he had imagined. I found an old woman listening to a music coming out of the hills. She was muttering to herself, "They are singing there. They are dancing there tonight," and I tell you, Paul, I heard a faint tinkling coming out of a ridge of rock as of innumerable elf creatures playing on I know not what magical instruments. Besides these folk whose minds have been shaped for centures by the earth they lived on, there are many refugees from cities as you are. The masters of the world who organized production and found that wheat could be grown here and fruit there, and cattle fattened most economically in other places, left out of their calculations these mountainy places where there could be no cheap mass production. But, neglecting these, they made it possible for rebels against the mechanical to live there, people who can, by the produce of two or three acres, feed themselves and escape slavery. There are odd groups of workers in arts and crafts, little colonies of earth lovers. There is a dark, fierce, fantastical man you must know. His name is Gregor. There is a sculptor and his wife I met. There are obscure mystics scattered about everywhere. I never met such adorable wild people. They all seem to have woven into them some tapestry of nature and their being is shot through and through with threads of light. They are the nucleus of an army in conflict with the vast mechanism of the world.[21] They are mobilizing the great silences, mountains, lakes, sun and wind; things that have no hands to smite, making ready for the last battle between light and darkness. They will make themselves invincible by these gentle eternal things, and, by God, they will win even if the battle should last ten thousand years. This country of stones the masters of the world neglected. It is there the temple of the future will be built.'

Paul and Conaire had the delight men have who listen to praise of their best-beloved. Then the poet began again:

'I am not going to leave this country. I will tramp about it until I find the place where earth is most friendly to me and will sing to me most. I am going to be lazy,' he said with a whimsical smile, 'and let the Earth Spirit make my songs for me as it makes your pictures for you. I saw lovely things of yours in the galleries. But,' his restless eyes had been looking about the studio, 'you keep the masterpieces for yourself.'

'Yes,' said Paul, 'all of a certain character I keep. I do not like parting from them. They seem to belong to each other and throw a reflected light from picture to picture.'

'Yes, I see that. It is a new realm of nature you are revealing. They connect with each other as we do. We are like planets drawn to circle about an invisible sun. The only thing of interest about us now is what reflected lights may shine on us from whatever divinity is to be the new lamp of the world.'

X

It was Midsummer Eve. A fairy stillness was in the air. The only glow came from that girdle of green fire which all night long lay about the earth in midsummer nights. Paul and the poet sat on a hillock looking over tide-deserted sands to a long black ridge lying like some monstrous animal half on earth and half crouched in water. There were apparitions like silver stars that glowed and went out and glowed again and ran along the blackness of the ridge.

'See, the lights of fairy!' whispered Paul. 'They hold festival to-night. It is Midsummer Eve. Do you see? Below there on the sands! Those tall flame-coloured people who move in some mystic ritual!'

'How lovely! How wonderful! Their dance seems to be god-guided. Are they those who never fall out of Eden? They move all with the innocence of unfallen life. Are we to go back to their world?'

'No. These are only the slaves of light. That life lies far behind us. We, I think, shall go back to a brighter light than that which opened up the story of the cycles.'

'Something is going to happen, Paul. What is it? Is a new religion to be born? What magic will it exercise over us? I hope it will be the magic of the Gay. Are they not terrible in their sadness these religions of the Iron Age? The Light is never hailed with joy. "The Light shineth in the darkness and the darkness comprehendeth it not."[22] "He came to His own and His own received Him not." The mystery is told in tears as if we must understand sorrow better than joy. The real betrayal of Jesus was not by Judas but by the other apostles who would not speak of the laughter of Jesus, He who went to feastings and merriments, gay at heart as all must be who know their immortality. I pine for something gay and beautiful. I swear to you, Paul, I want to wear cap and bells before the Throne, to clash cymbals and dance, not abase myself before the Lord with my nose in the dust and my hinder parts pointed to the heavens like crawling saints in the religious pictures.'

They both broke into laughter. The spell of the fairy stillness was broken. They rose and went their ways, the poet to Conaire whose guest he was.

Paul went his own way, but after his lively companion had departed, the spell of Midsummer Night – the most enchanted night in the year, when the barriers between this world and that other are fragile – fell on him again. There was a wild restlessness in body and soul. Imaginations crowded on him. His feet, unconsciously to himself, began to move swiftly, driven by an energy born in the psyche. He drew nigh his cottage but turned away again and strode across the dark miles of sand. He walked like one pursued not by terrifying but by noble furies who pelted him with celestial fire. He was overwhelmed. His body was unable to bear the hurricane of power; and at last, below that long black ridge of rock, half fainting, he sat down on a stone and buried his head upon his knees. As he sat there he became more still. The horizon of soul seemed to widen, to spread far beyond the body to a distant light. Whether it rushed at him or whether he was borne to it he could not afterwards say. But in imagination he was buoyed up on some shining aether which welled, a dazzling fountain, from the heart of earth. Where the fountain broke out of Anima Mundi in the blinding centre he saw the likeness of a being white as the sunfire.[23] What was that being? A celestial singer? A heavenly poet? A magician of the beautiful? From it poured dazzling images and forms of ethereal loveliness. It was that being that had blown on him with fiery breath. From it came that hurricane of imaginations. The light illuminated earth and its children from within. It searched out every heart. It came with a burning message to those who seemed to wear the colour of truth. Paul remembered ancient legends of his country of a Fountain which flowed invisibly bathing the soul. He was wondering what god had unsealed the fountain, and then the fierce illumination faded. But, before it departed, eyes that seemed to have looked only on eternity looked into his own, and he was awed as if omniscience was pondering upon him. With its fading came the face of a child, and then he was back in himself and was seated on his stone alone in the night looking over the desert miles of sand. He sat there long and long, and at last went homewards, filled with a spiritual exaltation. He knew the tongues of fire with which he had been baptized would be wisdom in him, and the will of the power would be seen in the work of his hands.

XI

The day following that midsummer night was heavenly still and clear. A pure and silver glory pervaded the blue air. The clouds on far horizons bowed low like young awed cherubim. The waters in the lake hardly stirred, parting their lips as if to sing but were silent, breathing only joy deep in each other. Everything, light, water, air, cloud and rocky earth, seemed to belong to an unfallen nature. Paul himself, the last night's tumult of vision and imagination stilled, felt ethereally light within. He might have been one of the earth's unfallen children ere Eden was clouded from our eyes. He sat as in a trance gazing on a nature that seemed living from earth to utmost distances of sky. It was gazing at him, that living nature, as he was gazing into it. The magical fingers of air and light made music in his being, playing as on a lute strung by Heaven. How had man lost that vision of infinite life? What had they thought precious enough to turn them from the endless wonders created by the mighty artist who at his feet made the melody of the flowers, each a miracle of art, wild rose, orchid, honeysuckle, fern. If they had been dilated to the immensity of space they would still have been flawless. There were depths within these marvellous depths, worlds within worlds, and heavens beyond the heaven of heavens, each with its divine populace.[24] The majesty which held constellations and galaxies, suns, stars and moons inflexibly in their paths, could yet throw itself into infinite, minute and delicate forms of loveliness with no less joy, and he knew that the tiny grass might whisper its love to an omnipotence that was tender towards it. What he had felt was but an infinitesimal part of that glory. There was no end to it.

There was a rustle of feet in the grass behind him. He turned and saw Carew, who came and sat down beside him and lay there in a long silence. Some magic had stilled for a while the restless flame of his mind, and it was only after an hour had passed that he began to speak, dreamily.

'I think the Golden Age has returned. Everything one imagined seems possible. This day is the forgiveness of sins, and when the God forgives there is no withholding of love. Everything is as it was on the first day. We are made virginal and receive once more the primal blessings of ecstasy and beauty. If one of the gods leaned out of that hollow air now and said, "Felim, come with me," I would take his hand and climb up the airy way to his home, and think it only natural that we should be friends, his greatness and my littleness. I would sing him my songs and he would make wonders for me by his art. Paul, there must be some way of getting out of the body. While I was lying here I asked myself why were we prisoners. Why are we so tied to grass and stones – tied to ourselves still more? I am like a thief pent in solitary confinement in a cell. I am packed round with thick clay and bound to the bone. Outside I can see what treasures there are, what galleys laden with stars sail to unknown beaches. How rich the Kingdom must be when the King can scatter his jewels so prodigally on moths and butterflies! If I could get out of my cell, the psyche would have wings for far flights. What a universe there would be to loot if we were out of our cells! If the Lord hears me talking He will know what to expect if I break prison.' He laughed. 'Oh, I am so happy to-day I could clap my hands and dance. But no, I must not. I feel tender to everything living. See, I lift my feet from the ground lest I hurt my fellow-prisoners, grass and flowers. O little pimpernel, who stare up at me so gallantly, do not fear me. I am no ogre. I am only a little looser on my legs than you are. You too, little ruddy star, will get free. It may be aeons away, but assuredly you will get free, and you will mount so high that you will glow on air, a burning blossom, looking down on earth below, and its people will fold their palms and adore you. Everything, little pimpernel, is hurrying godwards, and you will get there, changing from flower to star on the way. You believe that, Paul?'

'Yes, I believe everything you say.'

'And why not? The atom is always trembling into the infinite in our imagination, and it is right, for the atoms are the creation of the infinite and they bear signs of that majestic ancestry. The final gift of the infinite to its children will be itself. I am prodigal of intuitions to-day. Is there not something different in earth as if it had wakened from long sleep, its soul had come back to its body. And now it has wakened, its body is flushed with magical life. That is not the water of yesterday, nor the air, nor the earth. Some heavenly wine is mixed with the water, and in the air we breathe there is a mingling of the Holy Breath.[25] Earth is living under our feet. It was in a world like this ages ago all the mythologies and fairy tales were born. And they were all true, true to something in our own being. Once more there can be natural spirituality.[26] I went out early this morning and I was reborn. Why do we ever sleep at the hour of miracles? I made then this song, or it made itself for me:

'O, dark holy magic,
To steal out at dawn,
To dip face and feet in grasses
The dew trembles on,
Ere its might of spirit healing
Be broken by the dawn.

'O, to reel drunken
On the heady dew;
To know again the virgin wonder
That boyhood knew;
While words run to music, giving voices
To the voiceless dew.

'They will make, those dawn-wandering
Lights and airs,
The bowed worshipping spirit
To shine like theirs.
They will give to thy lips an aeolian
Music like theirs.

'That natural spirituality is growing around us in the folk we meet. Conaire has natural spirituality. So have you. It is in many others and you must meet them, Paul. You are becoming a hermit with only mountains and stones for companions. They are good company. But I want you to give up this afternoon and night to me and come for a tramp. You shall choose your own way. Spiritual gravitation[27] will bring us to our kinsmen, or if it brings us only to other hills, then these are our kinsmen also. There are adorable people living about among these mountains whom you would love. It is as easy to walk in and out of their minds as if you had known them for a million years. I feel so certain you must meet some of these spiritual kinsmen that I will not show you the way. They may not be better company than the stones of the field with which you are in league. But they know you are there and they will talk to you and are as transparent as crystal. I called them by their Christian names when I met them first. It is delightful to speak by their intimate names to friends without knowing what other names they have.'

XII

'I will take, then, the hill road southward,' said Paul. 'It is easier to walk on the high ridges than on the level road.'

'Yes, I found that. It must have been on a hill-top that Antaeus wrestled with Hercules. It is on the hills the Earth Spirit puts fire into one's feet every time we touch her. Is it that earth breath you painted in serrations of flame about the sacred mountain?'

'That was a vision. I only know after a while when I lie on the hillside with closed eyes that the dusk disappears under my eyelids. I see waves of brilliant colour. Never is imagination so vivid. The barrier between worlds is fragile there and one can peer from this world to that as through a transparency.'

All roads are easy to the traveller with whom imagination is a companion. The leagues dwindle to furlongs and the mountains to mounds. After a time they paused at the highest point of the ridge. The artist lay back on the heather, while his friend wandered about. Paul looked up into blue deeps of air. Like those seers before whose gaze, concentrated on a crystal, visionary forms appear, he had found his magic mirrors for vision in deep pools of water and the vaster ocean of air. Gazing into the first mirror of water he had passed through it into lustrous worlds which lay within the being of earth; and often looking into that other mirror of cloudless blue he had seen its depths stained with brilliant colour: palaces glowing with amethyst, gold and every hue of the rainbow, and there moved the cloud-brilliant populace of sky. One mirage of remote beauty after another had enchanted his eyes fixed on that mirror. Gradually he lost himself in those depths. He heard faintly the footsteps of his friend who moved about, and at last, half in a dream, he heard the voice of the poet. He looked round. Carew with shut eyes was standing beside him, his hands groping as if to touch some invisible thing. The poet's voice came to him wholly out of his dream.

'I feel blown by an invisible wind inward. Though I am steady on my legs I tell you I am dream-tipsy. I have been tossed between moon and sun and stars and visions of water, wind, hills and forests. They come to me as ancient intimates. I had known them millions of years ago. They were once within me. We parted from ourselves, I know not how or why. We have played hide-and-seek with each other through the aeons. And now they come near. The spirit in them is as near to me as the beatings of my own heart. Now we meet again it is like the meeting of lovers who had parted but yesterday. The immortals never forget their loves through all inbreathings and outbreathings of the universe. Come with me, Paul. There is endless wonderful travelling here. There are divine transfigurations that await us. We will be changed inconceivably as we go on. I am changed within myself. My feet here are tied to stone and grass. But I, where am I? Am I treading the meadows of the sun? What are these burning blossoms that glow by their own light? Who are those about me who look as if they were consumed from within by love for some ineffable beauty? There is ecstasy under their closed eyelids. Their feet are god-guided as if they were dancers at the bridal of Love and Death.'

As his companion spoke Paul almost came to community of vision with the poet. He saw lovely forms which seemed to emit light, and half saw the rapture of faces lit by the last ecstasy of surrender to a divinity which drew them into itself. The poet became silent, as if in his mystic travelling he had come to a being for whose remote wonder no words in human speech had any affinity. At last he came back to earth, his eyes blinking like one who has come out of a blazing room into the darkness of night.

'Where am I? How dark it is! How remote is everything! I am outcast from heaven. I was melting into divinity, and there came some flicker of earth into my soul, and I am here again. I am only a vagrant poet, and how little and tremulous is my song!'

'You see, as the poets ages ago saw into Ildathach, the many-coloured land. It was so Bran saw through this world the blossoms burning in some heavenly forest. I could follow you but a little. You went away from me. Another time we must try to see together.'

They walked on silently, Paul leading the way into a country which was unknown to him. Earth had grown multicoloured. Through hazes of light the ridges glowed with pale gold. The hollows of the valleys were pools of blue and purple shade. At last they dropped to lower levels. Paul saw a house which even at a distance created a sense of beauty and fitness as if it was as natural an outcrop of earth as rocks or trees.

'It was an artist built that: I wonder who?'

'That was designed by Mark, the sculptor I spoke to you about. Mary his wife told me he sat for days looking at that recess within the hills until the image of the house arose before him. He says that is the form the stones there would have dreamed themselves into if they had dreams.'

The door to it was open, and there was nobody in sight. The poet entered as if sure of welcome. He turned into a great room. There were many figures in clay. He pointed to some of these.

'Those are Mark's, and these,' pointing to a multitude of little figures, 'are done by the young folk about here. Mark teaches them to play with clay, while Mary inspires them to sing and dance and even to make songs for themselves. The making of figures is a delightful play to them. They never had thought of praise or profit. See how good this is in intention!'

He held up a little group of two girls leaning against a rock.

'Has it not a natural grace? Look at those weeders! What rhythm in their bent bodies! And that dancer! Does she not seem as if she was foam tossed up from some invisible fountain?'

The artist was delighted with the play of the children. But his eyes were more drawn by the sculptor's own imaginations. He stood long before one figure whose whiteness rose out of stone as if it was earth-born. An uncouth animal shape was heaving its haunches out of clay with its forefeet straining against the earth for complete emancipation. And itself seemed to be changing; for, as in the centaur the human rises out of the animal, so from that monstrous earth-born creature rose a lovely winged figure with face cast upward as if it was beating its way into air. As the monster had struggled out of earth and rock so out of the brute the psyche was winging its way into the heavenly aether.

'That is genius,' he thought. Then he saw a relief. There were two airy figures flying wingless as if by their own volition. One was pointing exultantly earthwards where a skull lay. Over the relief was carven the words, 'That was once thy dwelling-place.' There was another mystical figure, Minerva rising from the head of a Jove with the vast blind face of an earth god. In all this mystic sculptor's work was the sense of transfiguration and escape. Paul would have lingered but Felim drew him outside. 'Mark and Mary must be near by. Ah, there is Mary!'

A graceful dark-eyed girl a little way from the house sat between tree-roots leaning back against the trunk and looking over a valley now growing to a rich gloom.

'Mary, this is Paul.'

The girl greeted the new-comer as if he was a pleasant thought of her own which had just come into her mind.

'You must not think it was I who brought him here.' The poet insisted upon the philosophy of their coming. 'It was the law of spiritual gravitation.'

'It is a good law, Felim,' said the girl.

'I was going to ask for Mark, but it seemed to show mistrust in the law.'

'Here he comes,' the girl smiled. 'See the law guiding his feet!'

The sculptor greeted Paul with the same air of natural acquiescence in intimacy that his wife had. The poet assumed control over the gathering. His quickened imagination started him on a speculation over what they were doing.

'We have been in the studio. I see something there you do not see. You are rooted here as Paul is in his own place. It is I who have been the roamer over hundreds of miles of country. There are tribes of folk who are our spiritual kinsmen inspired to do just such things.

There are potters and painters and poets of sorts like myself, drifted out of the suffocation of the cities. What I see is an identity of character and inspiration in all they and you are doing. It is the birth of a new culture.[28] They are all tipsy with dream as indeed I am myself. It was so all the great cultures of the past began, not in great cities. They died in the cities. But they were born in remote country places, in mountain valleys and on hills, with whisperings and breathings out of a mysterious nature. There was a music made by some Master-Singer and all who were bathed by the music had to dance to the tune. That unity of mind you see in ancient civilizations is beginning here. Do not the arts in the Egypt of antiquity seem to us in retrospect to be the creation of one mighty mind, the moulder of generations. The least workman who decorated a mummy-case had something in him guiding his fingers, something that was akin to the solemn temple-builders and the carver of sphinx and statue. Is there not the same harmony with all its variety in the Grecian mind? So it was with Chinese, Chaldeans, Hindus and Mayas. I think the invisible player now is pulling out a new stop on his organ, and the music with a new note is quickening many spirits.'

'I like to hear Felim talking,' said the girl. 'He is like a gilded herald running before a great king blowing a trumpet. But you are hungry men. After supper I want to hear all about the celestial musician.'

'He is always telling me things I know already,' said Mark, 'though I did not know them until he had spoken. He makes me feel as if I was dark and blind with unrealized profundities.'

'He is a disturber of slumber,' said Mary. 'I know I shall go to bed to-night with a thousand torches blazing under my eyelids. But I will forgive if he comes now and will talk after. He will turn our daily bread into the substance of fairy.'

XIII

They sat later in the warm and friendly night. Beyond the valley a vast moon rose redly over dark hills.

'What a night! Heaven and Earth seem one being.' Carew spoke dreamily.

'The universe is an everyday companion, Felim,' the girl spoke. 'But it is too silently wise. You are a rarer visitor and the gods gifted you with flowing speech. You were to talk to us about the Master-Singer and the new music to which we are to move.'

'If you brood on what Mark is already doing and on what you yourself are doing, you have your answer. What is in the minds of the children who flock to you? What about those two delightful young people who tell you their dreams?'

'Ah, you remember Rory and Aileen! They are wonderful. I met them to-day, oh so proud and dignified. They spoke to me as if they were ancients of the earth, far older than I was. They had been reading a coloured history of Egypt, and discovered they had lived before, for old Egyptian men came living out of the book. There were temples and sphinxes hovering about them. A tall Eyptian rose out of Rory, while Aileen was changed to a dusky girl with black braided hair, and the boy and girl bowed to each other solemnly and said "We meet again." The rest of their day was a longing for that ancient home of theirs. They told me with wounded dignity, "We'd go there if they'd let us. They never think when they call us children and send us to bed that we are old like that inside." '

'How enchanting! What a romance their lives must be!'

'They go on marvellous adventures in their imagination. Their imagination is so vivid I think they do not know whether they lived them or only imagined them. They become all kinds of great people. Once they were air chiefs, not of boats like those which fly over our heads, but boats which blew themselves along. And in one of these boats they went back through a thousand ages and came to themselves as they were in old De Danann times. Once they dreamed themselves into the heart of a mountain, and they told me when they were there there was no mountain at all but a blaze of light like the sun within the world.'

'It is out of such children the new world will be born,' said Felim. 'Are they not dancing to a new music, linking heaven and earth in their hearts?'[29] Out of these adventures and memories will come what age in the thought, what skill in the deed, what gaiety in the heart.'

'I think myself,' said the girl, 'their dreaming began when the Fairy Fiddler first came here.'

'Who is the Fairy Fiddler?'

'A peasant boy. A strange and most beautiful child. They call him a changeling and think he is not right in his head. He has never been to school. But he plays marvellously on his fiddle. I think he must be like the poet of the Kalevala:[30]

> Winds and waters my instructor.

After I heard him I lay down and cried and cried, for he made me feel the happiness and heartache of infinite desire. I first saw him on a rock by the roadside, his long gold hair blown back by the wind. He was playing to some children and it was the loveliest sight, the boy-player, the whirling of colour, the rippling of hair and the twinkling of feet. When I would have spoken to him he was gone, and the children scattered, their dance broken like a flower that had tumbled into pieces. The boy roams by himself over the country. I believe he must be a changeling as they say, for when I close my eyes and think about him I seem to see fairy lights dancing about his head.'

Felim's hand pressed Paul's in the dark.

'That must be your boy,' he whispered.

'Do you not sometimes find,' the girl went on, 'that those you meet often create ideal images of themselves on the heart, and seem to be changing into light?'

'Why should they not when for every man on earth there is a Seraph in his beauty in the divine world! What we really love in others is not what they seem to the outer but to the inner vision. I believe,' said the poet, catching fire from his own thought, 'that the psyche[31] holds in itself the most wonderful and indescribable forms in which it robes itself in its travelling through the spheres. I am sure, Mary, behind that mask of girlhood there is a nymph, a dryad, an oread, a goddess and I know not what other creatures. Perhaps there is an angel. There certainly is a pixie.'

'There is, Felim,' said the girl, laughing. 'She is here now listening to a kinsman's voice.'

'You think I am not serious! Come and look at Paul's pictures. He is a seer and he is painting the earth visible and invisible, all the shapes the soul takes in its travel from earth to sky.'

'Yes, if we may, we would be happy, Mark and I.'

'You will see how much kinship there is between his art and Paul's. They are players on different instruments but in the same new orchestration of life.'

'I wish the music you imagine would draw our friend Gregor into its harmony. He haunts those who have faith yet he derides them. Yet there must be some deep fountain of faith in him, if, as you say, it is spiritual gravitation brings us together. I think that he is striding up the road. He must have sent a thought of himself before him.'

'You must meet him, Paul,' said Felim. 'There is a kind of lofty, dark, exasperated nobility about him. He will attack us, but it will be out of a profundity of feeling which measures everything by its own depths. Is that Gregor?' he called out as a tall dark figure passed beneath them on the mountain road. 'Come up. Here is Paul Heron I want you to meet.'

The man he called climbed up to the grassy mound, lifted a hand vaguely in greeting to them all, then laid himself down beside them, silent at first as if he continued a reverie that had absorbed him before he was called. The poet, who had elements of subtle impishness in him, wished to rouse that dark exasperation of protest he had spoken of as characteristic. He dangled a provocative fancy before the new-comer.

'I always thought the Golden Age never really departed from earth. Driven out of cities and palaces it still lingers in remote valleys like this. I am now certain of this, because it has even cast its spell on Gregor.'

'On a night like this you could almost impose your fancy on me. God knows I wish I could think with you people whom I love more than any in the world. I would be much happier. But it is all self-begotten fantasy this idealism of yours. It is like the flickering of light over immovable stone; or at highest, but mirrored majesties, the reflections many times reverberated of profundities in the universe, and no more real than reflections are. Truth must be a state of being, and must include in unity or identity of consciousness the vast masonry of this earth, the deeps of space, the stars that move so resistlessly, as well as flowers and grass and you and I.[32] I love listening to you, but I keep touching the granite with my fingers to keep my sense of the profundity and strength of things.'

'Is not imagination our best way to apprehend truth? Is not what you have just said an imagination no less than Felim's fantasy?'

'Whatever reality is on us must be in the will. It is only when we will we find something real in ourselves, when we find we can stay ourselves against the stream of things, against our thoughts which bewilder us, even against love. Our imaginations are unreal and come and go. Desires too have their flow and ebb. All are phantasmal. The will[33] only is the self-moving. When it is keen and burnished like a star it may become kin with or slip into unity with the will that sustains all things. The ancients knew this. A seer in the Upanishads spoke of the hierarchy of human faculties, and, above poetry in speech, above thought, above imagination, mind, wisdom or understanding, he placed strength, and said, "One strong man can make a thousand men of understanding tremble."[34] It is, he said, by strength the earth stands, the sky stands, the mountains stand and the divinities rule. So I try to nourish the will and send what fiery arrows may be in my quiver against that world order which keeps the will in abeyance.'

'But are not the faculties a high companionship of equals in essentials rather than a hierarchy?' asked the artist, who himself gave first place to the creative imagination.

'It is possible we may rise to a state where the faculties in their perfection will be blended into a unity. But here only the exercise of the will makes us aware of a reality in ourselves. I am not able to sustain that unrelaxing intensity of will that I spoke of. I am susceptible to influences from people like yourselves. Nature too has her own magic and can melt me as indeed I was melted last night. You who are the naturally spiritual could not, I think, have known of the exquisite anguish of joy at an awakening of the spirit I felt, I who had lived for forty years in cities, and had never realized in the haste and brilliance of life without, that within, under closed eyelids, there was a midnight of black unalterable air. I did not suspect that inner darkness until my first coming to this country many years ago. I lay on the hillside and found a brilliance of colour under the sheltered sight and wondered at it. When I went back to the city it had gone. But I became filled with a passion to have this sweetness of light within me and so I returned here. It seems a frail beginning for what later brought about an avalanche in my life. It was first an aesthetic, but it was changed later into a spiritual impulse. How great a price we must pay to be made luminous within! Every desire, every thought, is either the opening or the closing of a door to that light. A passionate desire and there is an instant thickening of the walls.[35] To bring about a resurrection I had to give up my place in the world, my ambition, my power, my mistresses, the riot of the senses, and at last I settled here, seeking for allies in the silences of the hills, in water, grass, stones, the sweet immortal things. But even here I can only sustain the soul from slipping back by a never-ceasing will. I realized that only when I willed was I real to myself, and that all else was fugitive and phantasmal. That is why I dare not surrender to the luxury of dream. I do not dare to travel your road. Yet indeed last night I was melted as I had never been melted before, and I was made partner in some marvellous sweetness in the universe. I had all your faith for an hour, and believed like a child that all the fairy tales might be true, and I might yet come to the Land of Promise – oh, I was just such another sweet fool as yourselves, and had a bitter time exorcising this frailty.'

'But that was a great happiness, Michael,' the girl said softly.

'Yes, but I do not know whether it was not the ancient sensuousness transfigured taking on a more exquisite form. If I had surrenderd myself to it I might have been dream-betrayed into my old passions once more. There's many a lovely Paradise in Hell, you know. If we rest in them, the old dragons of lust rise again out of a sweet cheating of the senses. There can be for me only the way of the will. Now you know, dear people, why I am at war with the world, and why, though I love you and your ideas, I dare not admit them, for they might not be to me what they are to you, and the famished devil in me might take hold of them to deliver my soul once more into safe keeping of the body.'

There was a journey of many miles before Paul and Felim could come to home and bed. They rose with regret. There were promises of further meetings as they said good-night to the others.

On their way homeward the poet said, 'Did not spiritual gravitation bring you to your own kin? There are many like these you can meet in further travelling. And you will meet them.' He said of Gregor: 'Though he is at war with the civilisation where he was once a great figure, his enemies truly are not without but within the house of the soul. Because of that intimate conflict he is becoming a much greater writer. All his fiery arrows are sped from a bow bent in the passion of that intimate conflict. He makes his nobilities, as we all do, out of the struggle with what is base in us. I hope his battle will not be over too soon for him, for there is no one writes with such power. When he has expelled the demons in his soul he may become a saint. But, in that regained innocence of being, a great captain in the battle between darkness and light may be lost.'

XIV

A gusty energy was in the air. Paul, stayed by rain at his door, looked up at the cyclopean world of cloud piled fabulously in precipices of lustrous pearl, cataracts of light, pools of blue fringed by glades of dazzling whiteness, miracles wrought by the wizard air, dissolving as swiftly as they were created, shedding from roots of cloud shadowy driftings of rain. A huge arch of seven quivering fires straddled across the valley. Beneath it, over wrinkled hollow and hill, waves of vivid green and gold rippled, chased incessantly by purple shadows. A hawk soared up as if it sought home in that cloudland. Brooding on the dissolving wonder Paul remembered Gregor's belief that all without us, whatever is seen on earth or in the heavens, even the noblest images, were but Maya.[36] A despondency fell upon him. He went indoors. Here all about him was the work of seven years, since on that midsummer eve a new purpose had been given to his art. Were he and his friends like that hawk he had imagined, allured by a cloudland of images unsubstantial as those dissolving mists? A vast hope had been born among them, its father a dream, its mother a vision. It had been fed by intuition and imaginations. But might it not all be Maya? No embodiment of that hope had appeared in the world. He moved about among the paintings he had retained in the belief that, gathered together, in them finally might be seen the spirit of a new cycle. As he looked on them something of his despondency passed. Nature at least was living. The earth to him had been a mighty mother, majestically garrulous of the multitudes in her household, speaking to him in images which had come to him as he sat amid rocks on the mountain. Here were beings which were but coils of dazzling fire with faces of an ancient wisdom; dragon-crested divinities; beings like those spoken of in old mythologies; centaurs winged with flame, also the gentler beings who peered silently from the waters with blooms of delicate flame about their heads, or who rose, a glimmering brightness out of the rocks or emerged from the trees; sibyls breathing the mystical exhalations from earth while priests listened to the god-intoxicated utterance. Here, too, were images of a primaeval humanity which had drifted before him, and cities whose beauty was only in the eternal memory. Earth had spoken to him, not in words, but in that many-coloured speech of varied forms, and he had recorded it so far as his mastery over his art had enabled him. He moved from picture to picture, his despondency not altogether dispelled. The companionship between divinity and the human soul is unequal. While the divinity speaks to us we are exalted, but when the oracles are voiceless there is a sadness such as the unilluminated never know,[37] for the spirit takes whom it wills, and it cannot be constrained even when to ourselves we are most solitary and need it most.

'I have been too much alone,' he thought, and he understood why it was men and women sought each other, blotting out by one beloved face the majesty whose forms and faces are legion. Then he roused himself, and taking a canvas he began to work steadily on it. At last came a moment of relaxed attention and he had the sense he was no longer alone. There was a faint stir behind him. He turned. Leaning by the open door was a slender girl in a soft blue dress, her fair hair falling in clusters about the pure oval of her face. He rose, and as he moved to his visitor he saw a little silvery spark in the rich grey of the eyes, affectionate, doubtful, mocking, questioning. Then in an instant he remembered when he last saw that face.

'Olive! what ages since I saw you!'

They stood looking at each other with the questioning gaze of those who had been darlings of each other's hearts, and who wonder what years of separation have made of each other.

'I do not realize you as the little girl whose hair I used to ruffle.'

'Are you not ashamed, you an artist, to remember that you did such a thing?' said that mocking affectionate voice. 'It is as wicked, is it not – a sin against beauty – to disturb a tress as to burn the Alexandrine Library?' And at the saying of this he knew she had grown up and had run away from him and become another person, and he would have to know her all over again. There came to his mind the words of an Indian folk-song:

> She has become a woman, Her eyes have caught the dancing of her feet.

She came into the great room and walked about lightly from picture to picture.

'Oh!' she cried, almost becoming the eager child again. She began to look at him with the old affection.

'You are just the same: you have painted the people who used to look out of the trees. But these I do not know.' She pointed to some of the more majestic figures. 'These are great people. You will tell me about them.'

He began to speak hesitantly about what he was doing, for she did not know the long background of meditation out of which the images came. But she was intuitive and eager, and soon she had by a passionate inquisition extracted the wonder tale by which he and his friends were inspired.

'Oh, it is wonderful! And how, thinking all this, could you look so dejected as you were when I came in first. I watched you. You looked as if the universe had no light for you. Yet it is really lit up by a blaze of fairy torches.'

'I think I have been too much alone lately. I have seen but little of my friends for some time. I have no ever-burning lamp within me, and my friends must feed the lamp with the oil of their ideas.'

'You have been living too much among shadows and apparitions, Paul. No, not living. It cannot be life when you are always looking at images, however noble. To have vision is not to live. I must bring Aoife here. If you see her all the world will turn to gold.'

'The friend you called the Princess?'[38]

'Yes, but she is more than a princess, more than a queen. She is like Helen of Troy, or one of the great heroines from the old epics. She sets fire to all about her.'

'How have you come to love the thought of Helen and Troy burned?' he bantered her. 'Is your ideal woman one who wrecks a civilization?'

'It is we who make civilisations and we have the right to break them,' the girl laughed. 'Do you not realize that it is we who, with youth, with beauty, inspire all the hurried steps men take to the age of gold? I would like to overthrow the hateful civilisation we live in to-day. I could imagine Aoife leading against it armies she had made mad.' She laughed at her own fantasy. 'I see I must teach you world history as I see it. You only know what men have done. Civilization began in some primaeval forest when a woman first plucked a flower and put it in her hair, and appeared like a spirit to her savage lover. Men would have been content with cave dwellings if women had not insisted on palaces, the counterpart in marble of a queen's beauty. The world will be reborn when some great beauty appears, a being so wonderful that men will feel life must be built anew around her. There should be a golden turbulence of rapture when a divine beauty passes by. But you are one of those people who are only fully awake when you are half asleep. That is, you go inside yourself and light candles there. But you must not go inward out of sight, Paul.' She laid her hand on his arm and shook him with the lovely familiar petulance of her childhood.

Paul, delighted to have again the old intimacy, made himself humble with promises to be her slave as of old, but she would not have this.

'No, you must not. I love to twist people round my little finger. But if they go round I cannot endure them.'

As he talked with the girl he felt some curiosity about that friend she called the Princess, for he divined she was talking a gallant language that was not learned in any school but had come from contact with some other who had brought her out of childhood into an incandescent girlhood.

'You are to come with me. Father and Mother have come back also. And I am never going away again. And you are to tell me everything about your wonderful boy. I am to became an initiate of the guild, am I not?'

XV

Some little time after the return of Conaire's daughter, Felim broke in upon Paul one afternoon.

'Paul, you must stand up and gird yourself, for Conaire's prophecy is to be fulfilled. There are dragons and black enchantments to be overcome. I was with Gregor last evening, "The great beast is aroused," he said. "The hunt will soon begin." But it is the dragon who is to hunt us. There may now be only the lifting of an eyelid or the twitching of a tail, but the beast is gathering itself for a leap.'

'What are you talking about?' asked Paul, lifting dream-cloudy eyes from his canvas.

'I say the lords of that monstrous mechanism, the State, have found the unrest in the world has its roots here. It is we, the spiritual anarchists, pagan poets and vagabond idealists, who have injected our own wildness into the social order. The slaves of the machine are becoming restless. No, it is not a passion for a new sharing out of wealth. The machine is efficient. Nobody is hungry now though the spirit may be starved. Everyone now is clothed in body though there may not be a rag of coloured fire about the psyche. No one is insecure, no one is homeless, unless they close their eyes to be bleak and homeless in the inner dark. It is the beginning of a spiritual renaissance. The State has nothing more to promise humanity, and when that is realized allegiance falls away. The spirit of man has lost itself in many illusions, and last of all it lost itself in the most pitiful illusion of any, the illusion of economic security and bodily comfort. These now fail to satisfy it, and there is nothing for it but spiritual adventures. Subconsciously it begins to remember ancient majesties, for in the midst of plenty without it is hollow and empty within.'[39]

'How are we the disturbers of the peace? I am glad to hear it. But I feel innocent for myself of any part in so good a work.'

'Do you not know there are a score of fierce idealists in these regions spitting out their scorn on the comfortable world – Gregor the most powerful, whose books are read everywhere, and whose analysis cuts to the bone? Now there are warnings uttered about anarchists who would wreck the first perfectly organized society the world has known. The air quivers with anathemas from State and Church. They stir up passion which they can direct if need be. They can let loose on the idealists the wild beasts who kill in the name of the State. They can let loose a horde of wild fanatics who will rend us in the name of God.'

'Your dragon is a very wild and glittering beast. But it does not terrify me. I wish you would speculate rather how those empty souls are to be made full. I ask about this, for before you came I was pondering over a man who left me an hour ago. I had thought of him as a magnificent unimaginative animal, but I think he suddenly conceived greatly about himself and I am responsible. I saw him first breaking stones lazily by the roadside. I never saw such a shapely creature. His body had the superb anatomies of the Adam of Michelangelo. Apollo in exile might have worn such a guise in dread of some more terrible divinity. As I imagined him so I painted him. He sat for me without showing the least interest in what I was making. Here is the picture. I call it "A God in Exile." '

The painting was of a man in rough patched trousers, a shirt open at breast and throat, while the sleeves were rolled up, showing those divine contours of throat, chest and arms of which Paul has spoken. The man was breaking stones, a humble task, but all about him, seen against the blue air, the fantasy of the artist had painted white, gold and rose-coloured flames swirling about the figure as if they blazed from a fire form only half hidden beneath the human disguise.

'What a magnificent creature!'

'When I had finished I drew him to see what I had made of him. He stood for a while looking silently, and then he drew himself up; said haughtily, "What am I doing here!" and stalked out as if he was going to storm the heavens. Yet he might as conceivably in that new dilation of his being become the pursuer of nymphs as some of the ancient divinities were. When the gods cannot find the way back to their skies they too often descend in their thoughts to the fairer among the daughters of men.'

'Ought I to be sorry for the nymph his eye singled out?' asked the poet. 'He might be a wonderful lover. But I feel what you imply that our idealists have made the lives men live empty, but do not help those they have disillusioned to make a fulness.'

'I find little imagination about life itself. I read books prophetic about the future. But the writers conceive only of more perfect mechanisms, not of a lordlier humanity. One will imagine airships of more electrical swiftness, or a force which might dissolve the bones of the world, or a boat which might sink under water to the harbours of sunken Atlantis. They imagine nothing about ourselves. Yet what could be more exciting than such speculations? Whether, for instance, in ten thousand years we may not all be able to send our thoughts as we will to distant friends and to have a like intimacy for ourselves: whether the psyche might not become so sensitive to the forces which pour on and through us that it might be able to reflect the multitudinous life of humanity in itself as the eye reflects a heaven of clouds and stars. Again, it is worth while brooding over whether we might not be able to extend consciousness into nature and interpret to ourselves the life on rock, water, earth or tree. It is conceivable also that there is an element of infinity at the root of every sense.[40] It is manifest in the sense of sight which reaches out beyond sun and moon into the galaxies of stars and suns in the Milky Way. Might we not develop hearing to embrace the things beyond the seas and stars? Have not you and I heard voices of our friends speaking to us in intensity while they were yet many miles away? Have not you and I heard a musical vibration in the air and melodies from unseen players? It was not the physical ear heard but the power of hearing within. In the course of aeons that power might come to as wide a range as the power of sight and the myriad voices of nature be all intelligible to us. Our prophets do not speculate on human destiny, whether that other world which shines invisibly about us might not gradually become as native to us as this: whether we might not find the wings of the psyche unfolding and a spiritual body be born from the womb of this mortal body. We have in us in germ such powers as I spoke of. Their development is not incredible. Dilated to their perfection they would make all I have imagined possible for us.'

'Yes, I know, you old wizard, when you talk about your pictures I can see them glowing in some aether about you. I look round but do not see an enchanter's wand. Yet you practise enchantments on myself and others.'

The forms of imagination with Paul had begun to glow as vividly as life. When talking about what he had seen he would sometimes conjure up the image and had been able to make it shine in the poet's mind. This was the casting of enchantments of which Felim had affectionately accused him. They were very close to each other these two, and thought was hardly born in one before it appeared in the mind of the other. Something of a like intimacy had grown up between these two and their other friends. Ideas flowed from mind to mind.[41] Even without speech they became sharers of each other's wisdom. Paul and Felim began a speculation, whether this was the natural consequence of some identity of mood, or whether they were all bathed by some river of life whose ripples broke on the shores of the soul. Then the door was momentarily darkened and Conaire's daughter came in. She ran to Paul, taking his two hands and wringing them, her face pale and bright like a distraught angel, her lovely eyes agonised by some tragic happening.

'Oh, Paul, she has gone! Aoife has gone! I do not know where. She went away three days ago with some man, a stranger. She has not returned. She has sent no message. Oh, Paul, what can be done? What could have happened? You cannot feel it. You have never known her. To me she was like an angel of the Sun. I was only a little moon to her fire. Oh, if she should not come back! What can I do? What can we do?

XVI

Very gently Paul spoke to the distressed girl:
'Tell me how this happened.'
'I had been with Aoife all day. She walked back with me the road over the hill. As we came near the top where the cromlech is, I thought I saw a light on the road, but there was no light. As we came to the cromlech I saw a tall figure of a man against the blue-green sky. He stood there until we were beside him. Then Aoife stopped. They looked at each other. He said to her:
'It is time for the play to begin. The chorus know their parts.'

'I am ready,' said Aoife.

'She turned then to me, kissed me and said "Good-night, my child." She seemed to me to have grown indescribably remote and great. I felt like a child who had been dismissed to its bed. I could say or do nothing. I watched them take the path down the valley, and oh, Paul, as they went there seemed a blue and golden light enveloping both, and they did not seem human to me but to be like some marvellous spirits journeying the earth. It is now three days since they went, and she has not returned. She has not even sent a message. What does it all mean? Who could the stranger be?'

'How did he appear to you?'

'I thought at first he was a peasant. He was dressed like one very simply. His head was bare and a great mane of yellow golden hair rose up from his forehead and fell to his shoulders. It was like a lion's mane. His face I thought very noble, and his eyes, when he turned them on me for an instant, had a light in them which seemed to come from something further and deeper than the sky. As he turned away with Aoife I saw what seemed like a violin-case slung over his shoulders.'

'It is the child of your vision, the boy on the mountain. Mary's Fairy Fiddler now grown up,' said Felim, who had listened intently. 'Dream and vision are to be justified. The play is to begin. It must be a great play to be heralded by miracles in so many souls. We are the chorus, we and others we do not know, who have been prepared for many years to play our parts. Do not be distressed,' he said to the girl. 'They are immortals. They do not err and lose their way in life as we do. You should be exalted rather, being a character in so great a tale, a tale which may be told for ages about these two. What did you want your princess to become? To settle down as the beloved of someone of her own rank, to bear him children, have a brief summer of beauty and be forgotten. For what she does now I think she will never be forgotten. These twain may be a pivot round which the imagination of the world will wheel to new spiritual destinies.'

'Yes,' said the girl. 'I feel she must take her own way. There is something great, unheard of before, in Aoife. She might have been a queen, but she laughed at an infatuated young prince who thought his rank made him an equal. If she reverses the tale of Cophetua's queen I will not be saddened. She would know it was a King of men in disguise. I only become wild knowing nothing.'

'She does not stoop choosing such a companion, who is, I am sure, great beyond our dreaming of him. Already there are many whose imaginations, they know not why, follow him as planets circle around the sun. Do not be deceived by the guise in which he appears.[42] The wise ones assume excellent forms in secret. Did an

Avatar ever sit on a throne? Have they not always gone about the world as vagrants? How could they make us believe in the riches of their world if they did not despise the riches of this?'

'You truly believe, then,' she asked of Paul, 'that this is the strange boy of whom you spoke to me?'

'I am certain as Felim of this.'

'Oh, I am already lighter of heart. I feel it must be so and this is that unimagined thing I always felt must be her destiny. I have no heart sadness now, only an excitement of spirit. But I am too excited to talk. I must be alone with all you have said. You remember, Paul, the stone on which I used to sit when I was a little girl and tried to puzzle things out for myself, and I would not have even you with me until everything was clear. I am going there again. I am sure the hills will not let me think falsely. They will not tell me a lie.'

She went from them. Perhaps because they, like her, had gone on some inner quest, they did not speak to each other about what she had told them. Felim, watching the girl flitting through the wood, began to speak of her.

'She has a spirit flashing like quicksilver. I am glad you initiated her into our mystery, for she herself must be one of the chorus. I remember her a small girl. You were away then. She had come back from her school on holiday. She brought me into the wood where you painted those dancing figures, and made me tell her every secret of the universe that I knew. To please her was a poet's whole-time work without holiday. I had begun to think of other things. She saw my lapse and stamped at me indignantly like a young queen. I was delighted with that imperiousness which brought me to her feet. It was about her I wrote those verses I call "Distraction." Do you remember?

'I lapse from her sweet play. Although
My heart had hardly beat
For a dream instant, the wild child
Stamps with imperious feet.

'Wind-quickened shook the forest boughs,
Green glitterings died and came.
O'er her young stormy beauty broke
Ripples of shade and flame.

'I wake, my lovely child, I wake.
I fly thy slave to be,
Forgive, O voices from the deep,
Yet come again to me.

'I think she has the genius for living and she may find her way into the heart of our mystery more than any of us. We turn what we imagine into poetry and art. She will live what she imagines. You and I would not dare to follow those two on their wanderings. But that girl will not rest until she has found them. She will be like a shadow following their footsteps until her heart, not her head, finds what it sought for.'

XVII

The spiritual are swift transmitters of thought.[43] Among those mystical communities, which had sought refuge from a civilization they hated amid the mountainy regions, rumours of a spiritual excitement created by two divinely beautiful visitors began to spread, as in India knowledge of distant happenings spreads from city to city. The rumours began weeks after the vanishing of Aoife. They came first from the far south. To those who heard the rumours it seemed as if, after dark aeons that had lain like frost on the heart, the ice was melting and the spring of a new golden age was stealing upon the earth. The strangers had come to those communities who were creating through the arts a culture in harmony with their spiritual intuitions. By the presence of these two the days had been coloured with a rich wonder. Something, rumour at first did not say what, had been added to drama, dance and song. Then came stories of men and women raised above themselves in some transfiguration so that they saw each other in some shining way in moonlit dances in forest glades, in dances which had been taught them by the mystic visitors, for as they swayed in the dance their feet came to be lighter, to have the gay movement of dream. As the dancers looked at each other, they saw bodies no longer lit by the moonlight but which seemed to glow from within and to be radiant with starry colours and plumes of delicate flame. In their enchantment they were god and goddess to each other. It seemed natural in that moment of exaltation. Surprise came only when the music died out and dance and dream had ended, and the strangers had gone away from them, leaving the dancers to sorrow and wonder over the dying glory in themselves. From another came a tale of a music played amid the rocks which melted those who heard it in its ecstasy, so that their own being became a music, and nature itself a divine tone in which earth and heaven were dissolved. Others told of lovely genii seen in the air who seemed to wait on the two strangers, and who made a shining drama of their words so that the meanings were exalted. And as the days passed, Paul, Felim and Olive could follow the route of the mystic revellers which brought them nearer and nearer to those who waited their coming in a passion of longing. Through those days Conaire's daughter had been still. The distress she felt at first at the vanishing of her friend had gone. It may be she was moved by the belief of her friends that we have only to be ourselves and what is our own must come to us and we cannot lose what is our own. But one morning that restraint was gone. A fairy excitement invaded her. She took the road over the mountains southward. Her body seemed to herself light as air. She felt as one might who knows her feet are god-guided, and though she did not know what would be her way, she went happily on her blind and rapt wandering.

On the evening after she came into the room where Paul was with Felim and said:

'I have seen them.'

They remained silent but turned intent eyes on her. They knew without asking who those were she spoke of, and waited for her speech.

'When I woke yesterday morning I felt like a boat whose anchor had been lifted and the wind was blowing it out of harbour. Yet I did not know where to go or what I was to do. I waited for some understanding and then I felt as if Aoife had taken me by the hand. I walked away over the mountain road. I knew I was called to her, that I was going to meet her. I was not tired by the long road, nor was I uncertain, and that fairy exaltation never left me until at evening I saw about twenty-five or thirty people in a glade and above the glade the hill rose steeply. Aoife was there. I sat down beside her. She patted my hand but said nothing. They were all listening to a half-musical play composed by a young man I heard spoken of as Rory. He and his sister were both actors in the play. I thought it beautiful. In it the soul was led by music to the fairy world. There were songs by invisible singers hidden behind rocks or trees on the hills. Song and music became more ethereal as they came from the heights. But the real wonder came when the voices had died upon the hills, for there then sounded a melody played on a violin, a music not born out of any human emotion, but the melody of aether itself, a tapestry of sound wavering between earth and heaven. I felt if that magical curtain lifted I would be in Paradise. When it died inaudible by the ear it was still audible by the spirit. I saw the boy and girl as in a trance holding each other's hands while they listened to a finale more marvellous than anything they had imagined. When that music ended, the man you spoke of as Aodh came down the slope to Aoife. Some went away at once as if they could not endure human speech after so much beauty and must be alone to caress the memory. But Aodh and Aoife moved on together; and, as in trance where one is moved from beyond oneself, I followed with six or seven others. The young musician and his sister, Mark and Mary were among them. But for what seemed like a spell laid upon us I think we would have been too awed to follow. We came to a mossy hollow on the hillside just above the road. It overlooked a valley which was growing vast and vague and blue in the twilight. We sat down on moss or stones. I felt as we do in dreams where consciousness stirs and we know our waking selves are in the dream world and we see wonders unrolled before us in the wizardry of dream. I was in some way beyond dream. I heard Aoife speaking about the young man's musical fantasy, and how it was right to make beautiful images because we became what we imagine. The realists who think they are closer to truth are no less depicting a world created by imagination though it is begotten by dark desires. The universe itself was nothing but Imagination ceaselessly creative.[44] The Imagination and Will which uphold it are in us also, so that we can make our own world and transfigure it out of the glory still within us. We were not what we seemed but children of the heavens. The body even is a palace all marvellous within. It has secret radiant gateways opening inward to light. It has wings which could be unfolded. All the precious fires of Elohim[45] are co-mingled in us. She said there were many who came in the past from that heaven world of light, divine poets, who made known the paths between earth and heaven. This they did less by speech than by opening the blind eyes, and showing images of gods and immortals in a clear, immovable and blessed light. As I listened, my eyes, which had been fixed on Aoife, passed for a moment to the blue twilight air which was over the valley. It seemed to me there was a secret shining in it like that blessed light she spoke of, and I saw in it radiant forms in harmony with her words. When she spoke of the body as lit with precious fires, a figure upon that mystic screen, which had been shadowy, began to glow, and it became transparent, a dazzling opalescence, and there were lights in it like sunfire for brilliancy. It was so glorious that I remembered the prophet who said of the soul that it had been on the holy mountain of God and walked amid the stones of fire where every precious stone was its covering. Then that radiant psyche itself became transfigured and was changed to a dark divine majesty, and as I looked I heard her speaking of the return of the Son to the Father. She told tales of those divine poets, Apollo, Krishna, Lugh, and as she spoke there were majestic images in that shining aether as if they were all still living in the eternal memory. I cannot now speak of all I saw there. I must brood over it lest it fades from me like a dream when we wake. But there were figures on that aether like some you, Paul, had painted, and I knew that you had looked into that shining glass. Through it all Aodh sat silently, but I thought he was the magician who made these living pictures to glow in the twilight air. When Aoife ended she and Aodh went away from us. I went home with Mary and stayed with her that night. What I tell you is but a little part of mysteries which are too great for my understanding. I feel very young, a child who has strayed into the company of immortals and heard them talking in their own speech and it was too high for me.'

She looked at them silently for a moment and then left them, going to Conaire's house.

XVIII

'That young girl has been burdened with great mysteries,' said the poet. 'You were right to question nothing, to ask no more. These are things which are lost through speaking of them.[46] It would be wrong to break her mood of wonder. In solitude, in that mood, she may recall and make those marvels all her own. When she has made them secure in memory she will tell us about them and I am sure she will understand. I do not believe vision is vouchsafed to any without its interpretation. I think she told us what she did lest it might fade away or some cloud come between her waking mind and the light which was born in her. I think that you and I understand that imparting of mystical vision. Before Aodh and Aoife went on their wanderings, images like those Olive spoke of shone before you in reverie. I am less of a seer than you are. Yet I have long had the feeling that there was some shepherd of my spiritual life. It is difficult to give reasons for this conviction. Nor do you want them. You have the same certitude. But you are an artist and can give permanence to your vision, and those who have vision can say "Yes, I have seen just such forms." But moods are bodiless things, and however we speak of them we cannot compare them with the moods of others, so that we may be made certain of the identity of moods and that they come from the same source. A few days ago that Spirit which made its promise to man, "I will not leave thee or forsake thee," renewed to me that ancient promise, and I seemed in my solitude to be with that which endures from everlasting to everlasting. What can we bring back from these visitations? We are dark and blind with a glory of being. But the words that fly up to the brain in our intoxication are too feeble a net to catch Leviathan. What have we to give to others? Only a few half-mad words! What had I to give to others but this with no precise revelation in it, nothing to make a philosophy out of.

'The pool glowed to a magic cauldron
O'er which I bent alone.
The sun burnt fiercely on the waters;
The setting sun;
A madness of fire. Around it
A dark glory of stone.

'O mystic fire!
Stillness of earth and air!
That burning silence I
For an instant share.
In the crystal of quiet I gaze
And the god is there.

'Within that loneliness
What multitude!
In the silence what ancient promise
Again renewed!
Then the wonder goes from the stones,
The lake and the shadowy wood.

'The mood in that is any man's heritage. A lonely herdsman in Tartary, a hunter on Peruvian hills, might meet the All-pervading. It is not by brooding on such illuminations we will discover the guidance of the spiritual Shepherd we imagine.'

'Why not?' asked Paul.

'I think we must look for it in a quality of thought, a character or tendency in many people such as historians find in their summing up of past cultures, who know that beauty was the mask the ancient Greeks sought to lift to discover deity, who find a common mind in the Egyptians, the Hindus, the Chaldeans or the Chinese. If there is a new outbreathing from the Earth Spirit, as we imagine, it may be we are too intimate with it for understanding. It is the spiritual air we breathe and it cannot now be objective to us. A little longer waiting and what is hidden may rush out and act through many men and speak through many voices. I talk quietly with you, but all the while the psyche in me is dancing the gayest dance. I am as blind and mad and happy as I was when I was a boy and rolled naked in the wet grasses or drew the living air into myself or hugged the earth, having found they were all living. No child ever laid its head against its mother's breast with more tender an intimacy. To-day I feel just as blind and mad and happy. Our dream is coming true. All the things which seemed remote and fabulous, tales of a golden age, of gods mingling with men, things sunken from belief on remote horizons of time, now seem to rise to us, to be true once more. I shall never be able to transfigure myself into a grandeur to meet them as people do when kings and princes come to their city. I could only be like that acrobat who did all his tricks in tumbling before the shrine of the Virgin as his best worshipping of the goddess. I have, alas, no skill as an acrobat. Come with me, Paul, and we will be forerunners. I will chant my poems and you will carry your pictures of the gods and I will cry "These come after us! These come after us! Look out for the immortals." '

'It is easy for you who carry your songs in your head. I could not carry my pictures. I must be a pavement artist. Give me a smooth pavement and I will colour it with fairy.'

That inward awe and excitement of spirit they felt translated itself into a light-hearted fantasy of thought and speech. How should they greet the divine strangers if they met them on the highway knowing that these were immortals in human guise? Should they prostrate themselves before the divinities?

'No! no!' said Felim. 'We would do none of these things. What are the gods but elder brothers to us.[47] We are of the same lineage. I will pay reverence to those who transcend me, but I will not abase myself. I do not think the immortals wish any of their kin, however lowly, to degrade themselves into being flatterers of their majesty as the church-goers do, hoping to propitiate a vain deity. How could the gods delight in seeing us abase ourselves before them as worms or miserable sinners? We should be natural with the immortals as the children in a great house are natural with their elders. Anyhow we will think more truly when, like Olive, we each enter our own solitude. I leave you to yours,' and went away.

But Paul was not to be left long to his solitude, for Michael Gregor came to him and began to speak to him about a plot he had discovered to tie together the loose ends of society, bringing all the refugees and vagrants from civilization under the mechanism of the State.

'Our freedom is dangerous to it.'

XIX

'I declare to Heaven, which does not mind in the least, that there must be a devil in one if one is to understand the diabolism of the State. The State is the devil, or rather a multitude of devils. Its name is legion. It has been questing all about this region to find the fountain of unrest in society. At first men went about alone. But yesterday I found some dark and surly brutes together, exotic to this country, and I guess by that old devil not yet dead in me, that they intend some devilry. There is a festival in the village to-night. I am guessing they will be there and for some bad purpose. I am going to watch them.'

He walked restlessly about the room, casting a glance every now and then at the paintings.

'I am not an initiate of your guild, though you, Felim, Conaire and our other friends are more to me than any others. I have still something of that ancient devil in me which makes me an alien. But you fit in somewhere with all I hold in spirit to be true and good. Even these majestical images which you have painted and which my reason declares to be self-begotten fantasies, born out of a poetical nature – like that, and like nothing else in heaven or earth – now when I look at them, somehow beyond reason, catch at my spirit and seem in some unplumbed deep of me to symbolize a reality. I say to myself, after all, why should not the universe, through all its infinitudes, hold such beings even if my outer mind can't find a glimmer of substance in the imaginations? I am lately feeling more of a difference between inner and outer. I am with you against the world. I would fight for you in the hope that your dreams might after all be true. I might after death wake amid heavenly things and be hailed there as a martyr who had died for a beauty he had never seen. You who are naturally spiritual can adventure into fantasy. I, most of whose life was spent chasing illusions, can find peace only in imagining a deep of being beyond sight or sound.[48] My heart holds to something that may be cold to you, too vast or too vague to warm the heart. I am not a poet like Felim, who can put into words the secret things in his soul. But I found in a poem of his a mood which comes close to that which is my comfort:

> 'The skies were dim and vast and deep
> Above the vale of rest.
> They seemed to rock the stars to sleep
> Beyond the mountain's crest.
>
> 'I sought for graves I had mourned, but found
> The roads were blind. The grave,
> Even of love, heart-lost, was drowned
> Under time's brimming wave.
>
> 'Huddled beneath the wheeling sky
> Strange was my comfort there:
> That stars and stones and love and I
> Drew to one sepulchre.'

'The mood in that is a current that sets to the great deep. You are as near to it as any of us,' said Paul.

'I have lately allowed myself to dream a little. I found the old devil in me was not so clever as he was, and did not seize upon the beauty to hide himself in it. I feel a little high and beyond myself to-night. Maybe it is because I can drink the cup of dream and find no poison in the cup, not a heartache in it. What is it in me? Is it a long winter changing to spring? I am elated as I have not been since I was an innocent boy. Or is it the magic of earth? But I must go. I have to track my devils.'

'I will come with you,' said Paul. He was unusually stirred about his friend, and wondered what had brought about the change, the exaltation of mind he felt about Gregor. For a while there was silence, except for the sound of their feet on the hard road.

'The men of science tell us that almost the instant a footfall sounds here the vibration ripples about the Pleiades. Would it be right if we interpreted their esoteric mathematic to mean that our least motions send a quiver through omnipresence?[49] I mistrust any speculation which cannot be stated in the natural speech of man. When thought hides itself in monstrous equations, or in pedantic dialectic, I am sure it is misshapen thought. I am sure it must be useless for man. Yet, if what we do runs through infinitude, we in turn must be penetrated by terrors and grandeurs pouring on us and through us out of the vastness. All wisdom must be uttered to us. You and I carry the universe in our packs. But blind and deaf to it all, I am hunting some low brutes who I suspect are sent here on some devilish mission.'

'You may be wiser than you know. That intuition of yours about devils in your neighbourhood may be the one thing out of all your subconscious omniscience that you most need to know.'

A man and girl hurrying, passed them on the way. Paul heard the girl's voice in a strange eagerness saying to the man, 'I hear the two will be there,' and on the hearing of this a sudden excitement fell upon him also.

'We will follow these,' he said. 'I think they must be going to that festival you spoke of.'

Paul was wondering whether those long sequences of vision, dream and intuition were coming to a consummation. To his dilated consciousness the night seemed dense with majestic beings intent on all that was happening. The road turned and widened and he saw a crowd, a dark blur of forms thrown into a silhouette by a lantern held low by someone beyond. He heard the sound of a voice which thrilled him while he was yet too remote to hear its meanings. He hurried to be closer, and above that dark blurring of heads he saw, illuminated by the low-swung light, two faces which remained with him for ever. They overtopped the crowd. There was a godlike head, a mane of golden hair rising above the brow and falling to the shoulder. What ancientness there was in its youth! And beside it the face of a woman. Paul thought of all the goddesses men had imagined in stone or colour for its peer and could not find it. He saw with the greatest lucidity the contours of face, the light of the eyes. It was only afterwards he knew that he could not have seen what he remembered with such distinctness by that flickering lantern light, and there must have been spirit perception added to bodily vision. Aoife was speaking and he began to hear what was said, something about a return to ever-living nature, how men would leave their dark cities, their dead religions, their grey churches and twilight sanctuaries, turning to the altars of the hills, soon to be lit up as of old. 'Ah, my darlings, you must fight and you must suffer. You must endure loneliness, the coldness of friends, the alienation of love, warmed only by the interior hope of a future you must toil for but may never see, laying down in dark places the foundations of that holy earth of prophecy, with the face of the everlasting beauty glowing through all its ways, divine with terrestrial mingling till God and the world be one.' Then someone gave a signal. There was a rush of dark figures towards Aodh and Aoife, and to Paul's imagination an unearthly blackness seemed to envelop those hurrying figures and made them seem ministers of some divinity of evil.

'Oh, the devils,' he heard Gregor speaking, as he rushed forward. Paul followed. He saw the head of Aodh with its glittering golden mane rise more lionlike. A light seemed to ray from him. Then Paul was thrust on one side. A surly voice growled, 'Keep out of this. Don't interfere.' Unheeding he hurried after Gregor. A bludgeon fell on him and he knew no more of what happened until he came at last to an agonising consciousness. He was in his own room. There was a fierce aching in his head. He saw Conaire's daughter beside him. Her eyes were on him. They held so much anguish that he thought of angels in torture. When she saw his eyes open she knelt down by the couch on which he lay and took both hands.

'Oh, Paul, you at least are living.' Then he heard that Gregor was dead, the first martyr for a faith he did not hold. Aodh and Aoife had vanished. His mind was still so cloudy and confused that he could hardly follow her tale of what happened. The lantern was extinguished. There was a rush of those dark brutal strangers, and then a flight after the deed was done. When the crowd, so rudely broken up, drew itself together there was no trace at all of that lordly twain about whom had gathered so much wonder and mystery. There was a long search, but, living or dead, they had vanished. The girl, faltering in her tale, broke down: 'Oh, Paul, what has become of Aoife?' She wept kneeling beside him, and he, shaken and dazed and not yet understanding fully, could only stretch out a trembling hand to caress feebly the lovely, bowed and weeping head.

XX

A year had passed since Aodh and Aoife had gone from earthly knowledge of them. Conaire, his daughter and Carew were with Paul. They sat close to the open door of the great room crowded with his paintings. Through waving branches the descending sun shot flickering fingers of fire through the door, which touched those who sat there and the mystic figures on the walls so that they glowed momentarily with an almost super-physical light.

'It is little more than a year,' said Conaire, 'since that which began in our world as a dream and a vision fulfilled itself and departed. Already the story is becoming one of the great legends of the world like the story of Radha and Krishna or the tale of Helen. It is a fairy tale made real, a reversal of the tale of Cophetua. A beautiful woman who might, if she wished, have been a queen, and a peasant mystic, a child of earth, began a companionship. For a few months they came into the lives of others and created a spiritual wonder as they passed. Already pilgrims from many countries walk these mountainy roads, following what has been called the Route of the Mystic Revellers, and if they meet any who had seen Aodh or Aoife they look on such people with awe as people who with bodily eyes had looked upon immortals. Now a great temple is to be built at the place where the two disappeared, and in this are to be placed whatever in the arts, music, poetry or philosophy seems to have been born out of that spiritual wonder, or out of prescience of the coming of Aodh and Aoife, the paintings of Paul, the sculpture of Mark and his pupils. Every story of Aodh and Aoife, whatever was known of them is being reverently collected. A very rich culture has been born about us, a culture in which we find our own inmost intuitions reflected, a culture so harmonious in its parts that it seems almost the product of one mind. These strangers also who come here from whatever distant continents seem to me intimates of the soul, as much so as if they had lived with us for years and had sat by the hearth with us and shared our dreams. A moment after our meeting we can talk to them in that secret language of the heart we use with those who have been comrades in the spirit a long time together. It would almost appear that the needles of spiritual being pointed to this region and the travellers were guided to it.'

'It is not only these later pilgrims who were so guided,' said Felim. 'Were not we ourselves brought together by spiritual gravitation? You were born here. But what was it brought Paul or Mark or Gregor, or indeed most of these who are our spiritual kinsmen? I know I myself came on what seemed the whim of an instant, and I found in a few days more who could understand my language than I had known before in my lifetime. How did it happen? Were we called inwardly? Or is there some law in the being in which we live and move which draws affinities together, just as in ourselves if any mention Paris or Rome or San Francisco, all that we have known of these cities, all our memories of them, awake silently, come together and swim up in consciousness. Was the incarnation of a divine being so powerful a magnet that it drew secretly to itself those who had begotten in themselves a fire akin to that great fire. Or did the avatar choose its own, having an inward vision of the colours with which the soul shines so that he knew in whom there was a spark which could be blown into flame? How did Jesus or Buddha choose those who became disciples? John knew the prophet of the spirit because he was himself a seer, and he saw an aureole like wings around the head of the Avatar and knew what golden lamps were lit behind the brows. I can imagine a wider vision which could discern multitudes, and know to what order of being they belong by the light or the darkness about them. I am not going to rebel against being called. But I would like to believe that in some deep of my being I saw the Avatar and came to him by my own will. I dislike the idea of being only the slave of light.'

'I have never understood what is meant by those who talk of natural or spiritual law,' said Conaire. 'For whatever takes place seems to me to be but movement within divine being, and what people speak of as laws are but intuitions about the mode of that being. There is something in me which leads me to speculate beyond the doctrine of affinities, which yet is true; or beyond your idea that certain people are called, as I think they are, for I share in your intuition against all being ordered and that we are but the slaves of light. I think that at the root of our being we will what we do; that we choose our lives as in that myth in the Republic Plato imagines Ulysses choosing a quietness into which he would be reborn.[50] Prometheus, as many suppose, is not one being, but symbolizes a host of beings[51] who are ourselves, and that we, like the Titan, come to earth with a fire born in the heavens, and that like him we foresaw all that would happen. The Gnostics said of Christ that He was in all humanity, and the myth of His taking on Himself the burden of the sins of the world would, if this interpretation is true, have the same meaning as the Promethean myth. There are many such intimations by the seers and prophets that what we endure was brought about by our primal will and was foreseen. I have always been in revolt against any imagination of life which makes us the puppets of law or destiny or of beings outside ourselves. It was out of a like mood was born the indignation which made the Persian poet cry out:[52]

> 'What! from his helpless creatures be repaid
> Pure gold for what he lent us dross allayed!
> Sue for a debt we never did contract
> And cannot answer. O the sorry trade!

Whether the law seems benign to us or the divinity favourable to our desires, to have no part in our destiny is unpleasing to me. I feel that in some secrecy of our being we are the choosers, that we willed what we have done. Even if the outer being finds itself outcast, in prison, hopeless or suffering, the inner spirit knew what wisdom or power it would have through undergoing just such things. The moment of willing our fate may be at the first outbreathing of the universe. Or, before we are reborn, we may, as Plato suggests, choose the circumstance of our lives. Or it may be, as the Indian seers hold, we go back every night, when we are beyond dream, to a state of spirit-waking, where for an instant we are truly ourselves and have communion with the gods. There again we may will what is to be done, though when we waken we may not remember at all what majesties we have known; and from this state the soul receives impulses which are surprising to itself but which it yet obeys. My intuition is with the Indian seers and I think we have always freedom of choice.[53] If this philosophy is true, we are co-workers with divinities, what we endure we have willed; and if we find ourselves miserable or helpless here, we are not condemned to that pain by a deity outside ourselves. It is rather like the agony one suffers who has gone heroically into a fiery pit to rescue others, and there is a spiritual gain from it.'

'That is a noble and consoling doctrine,' said Paul. 'It implies in regard to the Avatar that we had enlisted under the banner of one who was greater than ourselves. If we were called, it was because we had already chosen. But what was it was devised? Is there any wisdom of past seers about the labours of Avatars. Were those who so excited our imagination to be called by that name? If so, what was their peculiar message. All those who spoke out of the divine world revealed some wisdom never before apprehended. What spiritual inheritance is made ours by the coming of Aodh and Aoife?'

XXI

'In India the seers spoke of the Manus,[54] who were the spiritual guides of humanity, as thinking out in their high regions the religions of the future. I am not a seer, but I had long ago, as you may remember, a dream which in its fantasy embodied the same idea. If we can imagine such beings having a vision of life from within, brooding over a race, or over humanity, then those moods which were most widely diffused among people might be the moods whose exaltation or transfiguration into heavenly counterparts it would be the art of Avatar to bring about. How are we to discover such a mood in ourselves? Fletcher makes the most heroic character in his play say of Deity:

> His hidden meaning dwells in our endeavours.

It is by intimate confession among ourselves how the universe has been changed to us, what secret lovely desires we have in our hearts, that we may discover a common intent, and come to believe that impulses springing up deeply within us were messages from gods. It may be that we shall never know what will be plain to those who come after us. Every wave of time has its own glitter. How few really enter intimately into the consciousness of those who come after them. I am the elder here, and even my dearest' – Conaire looked affectionately at his daughter – 'has a thousand moods which I can only adore without understanding. She has been baptized with radiant fires while I have only known the lustration of water. She acts by impulses from within while I only philosophize. I am all eagerness to leap from my wave of time here. But even if I could be as young as the youngest, I am certain that the Avatars plan not for their own day here, but for long centuries.[55] What in them is a divine intensity or fulness may be unrolled in time into an infinity of moods and ideas evolving new beauties like a flower in its growth, and this through many generations. In Plato perhaps came a full flowering of the conception of beauty in its very essence as Deity, and the seed of that idea may have been cast into his race a thousand years before. We surmise behind many statements a long ancestry of speculation. In one of the Vedic hymns the poet speculates whether the most high seer that lives in highest heaven can be self-conscious: "Perhaps he knows, perhaps even he knows not."[56] Was that born as a sudden intuition or did the doubt arise out of long and subtle speculations upon the nature of Deity. It is possible too that what is a long history for us may, to a being rooted in a timeless world, be but an instant in which he acts consciously, not in that moment only but through ages which are hereafter to us but now to him, and the meanings of all be known only in the history of a culture which has come to its culmination.'

While Conaire was speaking three people had entered the room silently and had seated themselves, Mark, Cluborn, one of the pilgrims from the New World who with the romantic generosity of his race had made possible the building of that temple of which the philosopher had spoken, a man who had made himself loved by a shining simplicity and friendliness. The third was the boy Rory Lavelle, whose uncle, also a poet, had perished in a revolt against the world state many years before.

'Is this a symposium on Aodh and Aoife?' asked Mark. 'May we listen?'

'Yes, and take part if you will. I was going to say that around every Avatar in the past a civilization had arisen, and in that civilization was the reflection of his spirit, and how difficult it was to discover by brooding over a few years meanings which were unrolled through long centuries. I am doubtful myself whether the creation of a civilization was in the will of Aodh or Aoife.'

'Why,' asked Felim impetuously, 'must we assume that to create a civilization was in the plan? Why inspire those who hate civilization and have fled from it? Might not the purpose be rather to bring us into communion with a living nature. What has civilization brought us but the triumph of the great heresy of separateness between ourselves and nature? Has there been any civilization which did not defend itself within walls of clay or stone from the Earth Spirit as from an enemy? I see your reproachful eyes,' he said to Conaire. 'I have wronged you. Brick, stone, mortar, cement or steel are not necessary ingredients in your civilization. If three people are together under the skies and the soul is conscious between them, that is civilization. Let us think what has been born among us here. Is it not that nature has become living to our imaginations, is itself an imagination of the lordliest kind which envelops us and cherishes us who turn to it as to an elder brother? Has not earth been tender towards us? Are not sunlight, twilight, colour, form, element, melted into meanings so that they seem but voices out of that ever-living nature? Does not the very air we breathe seem at times to be the Holy Breath? Are we not for ever passing into what we contemplate? Have not solid earth, stone and hill become transparent at times to us? As we become purified we have vision of a hitherto unknown virgin beauty and are awed and hallowed by the vision. Are we not made happy and blessed by a love breathed through the dark clay? There grows up a magic between men and women when they love. Has not such a magic grown between us and nature, and the heart chokes with love as it does when it is nigh the fulfilment of desire? Do we not go out at times from ourselves, our being expanded, so that we seem to mix with the life in nature as if we permeated it and had come together in the infinite yearning of centre and circumference for each other? In that co-mingling of natures the gates of the heart are unbarred for there is nought to defend. Our darkness becomes brimming with stars. Everything becomes holy. Even the dust becomes precious as light.' He turned to Paul. 'Is not this what your seership revealed? A nature living from depths to heights. What was it happened to you and to us after that secret baptism of the spirit was received? Is it not because of that baptism you cannot paint a valley but it seems as living as the quickness behind the brows? It is this sense of the universe as spiritual being which has become common between us, that a vast tenderness enfolds us, is about us and within us. It was that intimacy the Avatar came to quicken, he who had no roof over his head but the sky, to whom earth itself was hearth and home; and who knows what blazing pavements these rocky roads may not have been to his vision! There was that intimacy between man and nature at the beginning of the world. In the Golden Age we were not separate but one. Then we were half divine. What has been happening to us is that we have been lapsing back into that intimacy. Unawares almost we have strayed into the heavenly household and feel we are of divine kin. Outside that we are but men and women, and oh, how unhappy and how little are our joys.'

'Yes, we have all come to that faith,' said Paul, 'though the ecstasy does not leap upon us all so swiftly in contemplation. But I would say that this vision of an exhaustless ever-living nature is in all the ancient religions, is indeed what makes any religion possible, and what we were seeking for has a particular character or message. When Socrates has the vision of Deity as Beauty in its very essence; when the exalted seers of the Upanishads cry out, "This is the real, this is the true"; or when another seer cries out that God is love, they utter words which guide the soul for generations after them. Yet they were all speaking about the same profundity of being as Felim. What we are looking for is not a new heaven but a new ladder by which we may climb from earth to the ancient skies.'

XXII

'A new upward-leading path! But how shall we find that when so little has been told, though so much has been imagined. We have to ask ourselves what do we know certainly about Aodh. That he creates by imagination what he desires. Even as a child he said of those about him, "I imagine them wearing gay colours and they begin to wear them. I imagine them dancing in curves like the water and they begin to dance." What attribute do we give to gods? That they are creative. In what way? Krishna says of himself, "I am born through my own maya, the mystic power of self-ideation."[57] If Aodh be a divinity come to earth, he lived here as he lived in the heavens, creating what he desired.[58] There he may have been one of the high rulers of the spheres. Here instinctively as a child he began to use the same power, but as a child might use it. Soon he would be finding his way inward to light. He would reawaken to his own divinity. He would use greater powers. What was he doing while Aoife told those tales of gods and avatars? Was he not creating images of them on the spiritual air? Do any of us know all he did? If he had that greatness we imagine of him, we could hardly with our highest consciousness touch more than the lower fringes of a being towering into infinity. Certainly he was quickening imagination in us. Once I was walking along the sands at night, and I suddenly felt as if I was pelted with fire. I was so beaten by the fiery storm that I was nigh to fainting because of its almost unendurable intensity. For years afterwards that seed of fire cast into my soul was blossoming into imaginations, indeed into all I have done. Every imagination in itself was a spur to further imagination. It was, I believe, to kindle a creative imagination that Aodh was born into our sphere. What has happened to life? It has been frozen in monstrous mechanisms. The creative genius which is the soul of man, his very self, has become atrophied. What has united us all here? Were we not all rebels against those mechanisms? What is it but a delight in the creative arts links us with those who are our spiritual kinsmen? What is important in this is the mood of creation itself rather than what is created. It is in the ecstasy of creation that we are made aware of divine deeps in our own being. When that ever-living nature glowed before Felim, was it the vision which gave life? Did it not rather give impulse to creation, to transmute bodiless spirit into beauty, into melody? You felt master of your power when the wild beautiful words flew upward to be molten together into images, emotion and thought. You were writing poetry while Mark was modelling his imaginations. Was there not some magical change taking place inwardly, something more wonderful than the poem or the statue? It was the soul becoming itself in creation, using its god-descended power. We have in potency all the powers of the ancestral self. It is by their use we re-enter the heavens. What is the universe but ceaseless creation by the congregation of divine powers. We have through long ages imagined ourselves into what we are.[59] We have now to imagine ourselves back into light. The most mystic of all Scriptures says: "On that path to whatever place one would travel, that place one's own self becomes." '[60]

'Do we imagine ourselves what we wish to be?'

'Yes. Here in this world where time beats slowly, it is long ere we so change ourselves. But in that mid-world as we know from dream the creative power acts in an instant. We are not yet masters of the dream consciousness. When we create there we project in an instant images, scenes and incidents. But we have not yet learned consciously to use the power of imagination in that world upon ourselves, equalling ourselves to the gods. What did Aodh do to those he moved among? I think he brought a wisdom of imagination, a wisdom changing as we rise from one plane of being to another. Here it may begin with the imagination acting outward, creating music, picture, architecture, sculpture, poetry. It may be seen in the beauty of arts and crafts. As we ascend within ourselves, the imagination begins to act inwards, and as it acts our being becomes incandescent.'

'How would that inward imagination act?'

'How, but as Thrice Great Hermes was counselled by the god: "Increase thyself to an immeasurable greatness higher than all height, lower than all depth"; "Equal thyself to God."[61] That becomes possible for us because there is in us a centre through which all the threads of the universe are drawn, or a spirit in which the ideations of the divine mind are mirrored; and our imagination in its fiery brooding at last identifies itself with that and in that fusion the mortal reassumes its immortality.'

'Yes, but this majestic wisdom was also told by Avatars in the past. Are we not looking for some hitherto unheard-of wisdom?'

Conaire turned to Mark but he was one who spoke little, and he said only:

'I think if Aodh was an Avatar he was an Avatar of freedom. Whether as boy or man he passed by, he seemed to be free like those who have no fears about the morrow, or what he might eat or what he might wear. He had the air of one to whom earth was a gigantic genie who could be trusted to bring what he needed, as that genie did who was slave of the lamp. He looked as if he knew the rocks could put out hands to offer him bread, or the sky would drop down to bring him raiment. He had the air of a king who knows he has many allies and could call them from the silence of the hills. He was like that other Avatar –

> When but a child he ran away.

When he passed by me, even as a boy, I felt, that is, my soul within felt, as if it wanted to take off the clothes of the body and become a sky-walker, going where it willed, no longer earth-bound. I think that freedom is what the soul most needs, for here it is slave to such baubles of comfort or praise or profit. It may be Aodh who made me so free that the body seems but a dream wrapt round me, and when I wake in the morning I wonder how I came into so strange a thing. You know I have never had but one idea in what I modelled or carved but the liberation of the spirit. I have an intuition that once the spirit in us was pure and free we would find the universe rushing to us, as a friend might with outstretched hands, ready to pour all its treasures into us. Aodh walked as if he knew the proud earth was bowed before him. But I really cannot tell what I feel.' And then, as if abashed at his own unaccustomed talkativeness, the sculptor relapsed awkwardly into silence.

'That is an interpretation that I love,' said Conaire. 'But the Avatars of old were before Aodh in this. We are finding that the spirit can act through many men and speak with many voices. But there are others who have yet to speak who believe that an immortal walked the same earth as they did, and that they saw him with their own eyes.'

He had hardly spoken when Rory, the young musician, began to speak with an eagerness broken at times by the shyness of his youth. They all looked on him with kindness, for a spirit that was ancient with youth seemed to be stammering through the lips of boyhood.[62]

XXIII

'I think he came to make life a music; to unseal the music in nature. The universe we see is only a lovely dust raised by the vibration of that music. Aodh we knew as the Fairy Fiddler when he was a boy. He carried that violin with him to the end. Has not every Avatar his symbol, caduceus, lyre or cross! I think Aodh will carry that violin as long as he is in the memory of earth. When he played to us as children he did not only make the feet to dance but the heart. Every bit of us ran to some music. I lay awake at night trying to recapture a music that seemed to lead from that sound to the fountain of all melody. My soul was lifted up and itself became a music, that which lies behind the beating of the heart and the flowing of the blood. We dreamed a great deal, my sister Aileen and I. We sometimes dreamed the same dream and sometimes we went on ways of our own. The dreams I loved most seemed to bring me to some shoreless sea of melody like the voices of unnumbered seas in which stars danced and sang. Once I remembered in dream being laid down eastward, while a voice whispered in my ear, "Listen to the music, lose yourself in the music," and under my closed eyelids I looked into my heart, which glowed to a great orb of light, and out of the light came that music, the heart music the Indians call it, and I lost myself in the sound. I could not remember when I woke how far I had climbed up the musical stair of being. But I knew that music, song, was at the root of life. All this dreaming began when the Fairy Fiddler began to pass by us on his wanderings. I tried to make music myself, but there was a magic in Aodh's playing which made it seem a gate in the silence opening to a melody that was innumerable. After I heard him first I began to hear music among the hills, a melody in the aether. I came to think that we were to be changed in our nature; that, along with the infinity of light our eyes can see, there would gradually come the revelation of the universe as sound or music.[63] I think when first we began to see there was only a blindness of light. Then after that we began to distinguish what was near and what was far and the glory of many colours. And so we will first hear that great tone, and after we will know the distant voices of sun, moon and stars, and the carol the flowers make as they grow, and we will not be confused by these innumerable voices of things any more than we are by the innumerable colours and forms which all keep their place in the universe of light. So these voices far and near will keep their places in an infinite harmony, and – and –' The eager boy broke down, confused by the multitude of ideas which thronged for utterance, and for which he had no words. But the voice carried some of the music of which he spoke, and as he drew back, timid after his boldness, Mark, who was his special friend, laid his hand on the hand of the boy in the assurance of another's love for his imagination, and Conaire said:

'In what has just been said there is indeed the sense of something hitherto unheard of. If there ever was on earth before an Avatar revealing the music in the nature of things, the music he awoke has long trembled into silence. Though Apollo is depicted with his lyre, we do not know what songs he may have sung. Though there were those in the past who spoke about the music of the spheres, there was never a world religion with this as its root idea.' He would have gone on, but Olive, who had listened intent on all that had been spoken, stood up and began to speak with an eagerness no less impetuous than that of the young musician.

'You all speak as if there was but one in this wonder of our lives. You forget with Aodh there was Aoife. I listened to everything that was said, and it was beautiful and wonderful those visions of a living nature, or of the imagination climbing into heaven, or the freedom of the soul, or of the music that lies within life. But one Avatar might have revealed such things. Whatever mystery had to be revealed two had to come. In this Aoife was with Aodh. He said to her when they met: "It is time for the play to begin." She said: "I am ready," speaking of something preconceived and now to be fulfilled. What was the play to reveal? You have given answers according to your nature. You are all beautiful inhuman creatures' – she stamped her foot at them. 'You go on some rapt wandering of your own. You have no companions climbing with you into your heavens. There must be an ethic in every revelation of the spirit. What are we to do with each other from day to day? That must be our best wisdom. I am not wise of myself. I never had to fight with dark powers. I have been sheltered by affection. When I was a little girl Paul told me fairy stories, and Felim talked to me about a fairy universe, and I was with Aoife who showed me fairy itself and told me these fairy lands were only pleasure grounds where the soul died in dream. I know but little about Aodh though I think he must be some great one. I was close to Aoife all my life almost, yet she was as much a mystery to me as Aodh to you, and as great a wonder to all who met her. She glowed with an inner light as if her body was but a shade to a golden fire, or as if summer itself had taken form. Through her the ice of many hearts was broken up so that they knew the sweetness of life once more. This is as great a wonder as the opening of visionary eyes. Men are for ever roaming with adventurous minds. We brood with hungry hearts over life. You seek for the new, we try to transmute the old.[64] You exult if you discover a new star, a new starry country. We are happy if a cold heart melts into sympathy. Aoife passed like a gay transfiguring fire through life. She was beset even as a girl by those who desired that beauty to be beside them always. She slipped by them. She could with a word, a laugh, crumble whole lofty Himalayas of pretence, breaking up the moulds of mind in which so many imprison themselves. But she did not drive the soul naked out of the house of its self-imaginings but gave to each a star by which they might be guided. She spoke to others as if they were immortals, as if she saw seraph kings glowing through the dusky rags and tatters of the body. She told me I was to love only the immortal in people, to let none be comrade of my heart but those who had found the immortal in myself. I came to change from my childish delight in the fairy things, who thronged about her when we played long ago in the woods, to a feeling of awe. She grew up within swiftly and beyond me where I could not follow her. She was a being of a different order. Even if my eyes were shut beside her, the light from her made me to glow inwardly. Once I slept in the same room and had a dream which was, I think, more than a dream. There rose out of her sleeping body a glorious creature like the sun for brightness. I did not know where it went or what it did. But I said calmly, as one who knew, to another who was with me in my dream, "She is one of the Dawn Maidens," and after that her body to me was only a lovely disguise. I tried to interpret her ways and the swift unreasonable things she did as action by a spirit who saw what I could not see. She was a divine comrade who overlooked none and who heaped precious things on others. I think there must have been this divine companionship between Aodh and Aoife, the companionship of those who know themselves from earth to heaven, and it was such a divine companionship they wished to create. Did they not in the dances they taught, whether by music or motion or by some magic, make men and women so rapt and exalted in their imaginings that they became god and goddess to each other and knew that they must cling to that in each other for evermore? It was so heaven-making a companionship they came to inspire. It is wonderful to think of such a thing, to go on for ever under sun-rich, under star-rich skies, ever falling deeper into the enchantment of the universe, and to know there is no end to it, no end to the lovely things we discover in each other.' The girl looked with luminous, questioning eyes at those about her, at Paul her oldest friend, to see if they, if he, understood with what purpose Aodh and Aoife scattered largesse on the soul in their passing. She saw only love-tender eyes, and as if she was satisfied she sank back into her chair.

'Everyone among us has had the gift from heaven that he or she desired,' said Conaire; 'and you,' he turned to Cluborn, 'who have come from the New World, who made yourself friend of us all as if you had lived always among us, what meaning has all this to you?'

'The meanings are too great for me. I am like a scribe taking down the words of some infinitely wise person, words which he does not now understand, but on which he may brood hereafter. I was left with wealth, and as I was nothing of myself there seemed to be little I could do but to gather the harvest of past beauty, and I came to the Old World. Someone told me new and lovely things were being fashioned by artists and craftsmen in this region. I began my search. I found myself stirred with the discovery of a new art, a new mood in art. I walked from place to place, and one day I sat down by the roadside. Just before me the road rose to its crest, and then ran downward to a valley I could not see. Beyond the crest of the road there was nothing but a blue sky and far hills misty in light. I heard voices from unseen people coming up from below. I was suddenly quickened by a vibrant music in the voices. Then there rose over the ridge, walking swiftly – the memory will be with me for ever – a woman who moved like the Winged Victory, white garments, sunlit, wind-blown, flowing over shapely limbs, and a man more lordly than I had ever known man to be, with bare head, golden hair rising lion-like over the brows and blown behind him, and eyes fuller of light than the sky. They swept swiftly by me like flames, god and goddess, and the whole universe seemed to my imagination to be with them in their going. I heard a voice as of one who had passed beyond sorrow, who was speaking out of an eternity or fulness of joy: "Every beating of the wing of time is blessed. For every instant there is a God-born joy." They went on. I was overpowered by their coming, too blinded by that revelation to rise and go after. I found myself crying out words I had read in some Buddhist tract: "A fragrance blows from the leaders of the world by which all creatures are intoxicated."[65] Later I rose to follow a beauty greater than I had sought for or imagined possible. I came after a time to know those I had seen were Aodh and Aoife, and that this truly was the beauty I had come to seek. Yet when I knew this they had passed beyond any knowing of ours. That is why I have gone to every place they have been, and have written down all that was told to me that nothing might be lost. It may be some other brooding on all may come to a more profound wisdom than any of us and give the true story of Aodh and Aoife to the world.'

XXIV

'I wonder,' said Felim, 'what was implied in those shining sentences: "Every beating of the wing of time is blessed. For every instant there is a God-born joy"? Is it that for everyone of us there is a God-imagined path from which we have erred and strayed, and if we follow that path we are happy always and are beautiful to others? I have watched people for enchanted moments when every movement was rhythmical and they were in a more lovely harmony with nature and each other than the riders on the Parthenon. Only yesterday I saw a girl racing over the sands, and girl, sands, tumbling waters, light, cloud and shadow seemed not separate but one thing, as if some purity of the girl's being made it possible for the master of every art to draw her into a harmony with his other imaginations. I tried to put into words that God-guided enchantment:

> 'Thou slender of limb; thou lightness;
> Wild grace that flies
> Over the shining sands
> Under cloud-brilliant skies,
> What beauty flies within thee,
> Sped from what skies?
>
> 'Thee for an instant
> The God possesses,
> Is joy in thy fleet limbs,
> Gay feet and flying tresses.
> His lovely thought of thee, the Artist
> Delights in and caresses.
>
> 'Thou shalt remember hereafter
> Through sorrowful years,
> That wonder of all thy moments
> And pine for through tears,
> This moment that shall be for thee
> A fountain of tears.

'I might have been happier in my prophecy,' he said. 'I only thought then of her falling out of the divine procession and the sorrow of it.'

'Here is one,' said Conaire, 'who came last into our company, and from far away, and yet his fleeting vision of Aodh and Aoife in their secret joy may have in it as great a revelation as long brooding has brought to any of us. What was it you felt? That their being seemed to rise out of a shoreless sea of joy. I do not know whether there are such beings in the universe, but we are for ever brooding on such an eternal joy, we are for ever seeking a way to it in our hearts. To feel this was true about any is a great magic.'

'There are many who felt this enchantment,' said Cluborn. 'I found a house Aodh and Aoife had entered for an hour. The man who told me the tale said they filled the room with such a magic of light and loveliness that he had made a shrine of the room. He would let none enter it. He himself meditates long before he opens the door of the room, and he stands there silently trying to re-create in his heart the magic of the beauty he had known.'

'That is coming nigh idolatry,' said Felim. 'We shall next hear of prayers to the two, or of girls supplicating Aoife for happiness in love.'

'The story has gone into the world,' Conaire said. 'It cannot be recalled. It will take a thousand forms in the soul, and it will be well if there is nothing more sinister than a girl praying for herself and her lover. The story of Aodh and Aoife has started some who were naturally spiritual upon more heavenly travelling. But what will it bring to others? There never yet was a fire which did not cast dark shadows of itself. I wonder what dark counterpart of itself the story will create in some obscene souls.'

They then began to speak of other things. Mark brought out the plans of the temple he had made for the American. They were unrolled on the table and praised for their beauty. Here Cluborn desired to bring together everything born out of the quickening of the spirit in that region. Here were to be placed the art of Paul, Mark and many others, the works of poets, dramatists and imaginative craftsmen. They were talking about the divine innocence of some paintings done in a little colony of mystics, when Paul, near to the open door, heard footsteps. He moved to the doorway and saw there a man he knew a little and liked not at all. He was one of the famous story-tellers of his time. When he saw the artist, he spoke to him in the soft caressing voice of those who are accustomed to speak to women more than to men.

'No. I will not come in. I was passing and heard you lived here. This is but to call and say farewell. We have seen you but little for some years. You are a hater of cities, I hear. Your paintings I have seen, of course. Very distinguished. But rather remote, that stellar illumination in all of them. You know I am a creature of this world. I only came to this country looking for local colour, a romantic background for a tale which I think will be my masterpiece. You living here must, of course, be familiar with the story of the two who disappeared. A beautiful woman who might, I believe, have been a queen, met a peasant poet or musician. You understand the attraction opposite grades of society have for each other. The romance of it! They went rambling together in a country of lakes and hills. Of course she became his mistress. But none here believe it. They get angry at the thought. They will have it the companionship was platonic. But you and I understand life. We know that platonic affection is the most enchanting approach to bodily love. People imagine wonderful things about each other. They seem to be groping for the heavens and suddenly find themselves in each other's arms.[66] Religion, philosophy, poetry, music, all the arts indeed, beget lovely phantoms who lead us delicately to a simple act. We feel while possessing the beloved that fairy or goddess has come to us from their skies. Life has given me a tale better than any I ever imagined. Oh, I will make it beautiful, the tale of these two, Aodh and Aoife. What names for romance! What a setting for love, these mountains! these woods! How much more poetical than the hotel! I will send you this greatest of my love stories when it is printed. I know you will like it better than anything I have yet written. Well, after hail, it is now farewell.'

He made a gesture of departure. The subtly insinuating,

self-caressing voice ceased. The pale face turned away. Paul had listened without a word while his visitor was speaking. Then he turned within. The young musician's face was white, his eyes dark with anger. The girl was shuddering as if at some apparition of incredible and uncomprehended evil. Felim was exhausting all the demoniac resources of speech.

'That thing has worms slinking through its veins, not blood. It would pollute earth to bury him in it. He ought to be dropped off the planet with demons clawing him all the way to the bottomless pit. May nightmares squat on his chest, nightmares with sticky tongues passing him down their throats to blazing furnaces. How could you be still while he oozed out that leprosy of imagination? A word and we would have been at him like hounds.'

'Do not speak of him. Do not think of him!' the girl cried passionately. 'We grow like what we hate.'

'Oh, but – ' the poet protested, and then: 'Yes, you are right. In my rage at him I became a devil, and I had been climbing into heaven a moment before. How can I grow wings again!'

'No, do not let us forget him,' said Conaire. 'His interpretation of the story of Aodh and Aoife has a wisdom for us. Has any beauty been in the world which was not pursued by beasts? How rarely does any beauty enter the soul where there are not red goblins snatching at it, to make out of it more beautiful shapes for their own evil, turning the divine to infernal uses, sweetening some dark delight.'[67]

'I remember,' said Felim, 'Gregor telling us he dared not because of his past allow himself the luxury of dream, lest when he came back from his heaven he might find devils waiting for him in the pit. He had to cling to the austere opposite of all he had been.'

'But on that night of his death he told me,' said Paul, 'that he found he could permit himself to dream. The old devils in him were too feeble and famished to stir. Dear Michael, I wonder if he could share in our symposium how he would interpret the tale.'

'What we might now speculate about is, in what way the story will be refashioned by the imagination of the world. Not only the lecherous but many of finer nature will weave about it their own fantasy. Let us remember the austere profundities uttered by great Avatars and what was built on them. How the story of Jesus was smothered with monstrous growths. Some with a sadistic emotion brooded upon the torture of the God until the pain itself became a thing to be adored. There grew up a luxury of anguished emotion. Pain, if it comes naturally to us here, if it is endured with resignation, brings its own nobility. But to seek it for its own sake, that is devilish. The brooding on agonies, martyrdoms and crucifixions leads the soul into sinister by-ways. Out of that brooding upon the tortured God was born the mentality which made the dark ages hideous with religious persecutions, with the rack, the stake and the martyr's fire. The way out of that had to be by the drawn sword. The fantasies of great poets, too, like Dante and Milton, deflect us in another way from the true, for they send the imagination outward, whereas the aim of all high religion is to throw the imagination inward to being. Once the tale of Aodh and Aoife has entered the imagination of the world, the myth may grow prodigiously. The least incident recorded may excite artist or poet or story-teller; and, finally, what is born out of the tale may have as little relation to the original as Dante's *Inferno* has to the Sermon on the Mount. We cannot stay this growth, though we can foresee it. The Chinese sage Lâo-tze said, "To see things in germ, this I call intelligence."[68] It was to divine the outcome of all this we began our symposium. You cannot be confident that what glows with so pure a light in your minds will not multiply images and shadows of itself in others until it has lost all spiritual significance. We can understand why ancient Greek and Egyptian made mysteries of their most spiritual truths. These were communicated only after there had been purifications and vows that they would never be revealed. They knew that to spread wide the noblest ideas would be to degrade them, as Homer, a great secular genius, degraded the gods. Plato, who had the reverence of an initiate for the truth, would have exiled him from his ideal republic.[69] To give sacred mysteries to the mob is like a man casting the most beautiful of his children into the streets to be degraded by prostitution.

XXV

'If the light casts so dark a shadow,' asked Paul, 'what does a descent from Heaven give to us?'

'When the soul enters a higher heaven in its own nature it must have insight into lower deeps. We descend into these, not to surrender to them, not to be overcome, but to bring about a harmony or fusion of opposites. I think only by this fusion of opposites does the soul itself become strong.[70] We cannot go from earth leaving behind us untransmuted the elements and forces the soul had gathered about itself, the dross and slime of its life.'

'I sigh at the long, long labour,' said Felim. 'But I will try to think of that transmutation as making a heart friend out of an enemy.'

'Let us return,' said Conaire, 'to the interpretations of Aodh and

Aoife which have been made. If they were Avatars – they certainly moved among us with mysterious power – they differ from all Avatars of whom we have knowledge in this, that they left behind them no body of doctrine. No one has discovered sayings of Aodh or Aoife which, put together, might form a scripture. Whatever has been told about them, all that is wonderful, has come from vision or intuition of the onlooker. To interpret we have to go inward, to see things unseen by the bodily eyes, to hear things unheard by the sensual ear. The Avatars who went before had disciples to whom they spoke about creation, the architecture of the heavens. They left a wisdom about life and death, what to do and what not to do. Multitudes pondered over it all, and out of that pondering came theologies, philosophies, ethic, psychology, literature, arts, and last a civilization. The immaterial soul finally cast substantial shadows of itself in brick and mortar. Men were thus impelled to continue their labours in the world. But what are we to think of Avatars who come to us and do nothing in the manner of their fore-runners? We surmise a divinity within them. Whoever came nigh them had a quickening of soul. It became incandescent as torches set ablaze by the touch of fire. Why were these two so great, and yet so secret and silent? This secrecy and silence must have profound meanings. It was said of the Popol Vuh[71] that its wisdom was hidden from him who sees with his eyes, who hears with his ears. They were like that. Because of this I ask myself was it in their plan to create a civilization at all? They guarded their mystery. They played like two divine children, careless of our questioning, and only intuition can discover the meaning of that play which enchanted us. Was it in the plan we should be allured to build a new civilization out of a new culture. I think not. Why? Because I believe we are past the high noon of time and are drawing to its twilight. It is time for men to leave their labours here. Earth is crowded with the ruins of the cities they have built. They have come to age in soul. Even when the body is young and desirous, if we meditate on what we do we grow listless. We have lived through too many empires. Is there any mood of the heart told even by the great masters in literature which is not stale to us? Even from human love the enchantment has gone. If we are not pursuing the chase, if in stillness we turn inward, we find only a grey Eros without desire dwelling in the heart. Has there not been this earth-weariness among us all? Have we not come out of the world and found our happiness only pondering by the margin of the Great Deep? It was to people with this age of the soul that the avatars came, but as they passed by us, they made us feel we yet might bathe in some fountain and come to an immortality of youth? They left no wisdom for moralist or philosopher to dilate into systems which as they grew could only enslave us. They gave us no ethic, no commandment, to do or forbear. Such things are not natural. They do violence to the soul, begetting exaltations followed by despairs. No one can state a moral law which is sufficient for the infinite complexities of life. But as we grow nigher to deep own-being, our passions drop away from us. We act with tenderness to all for we enter the great unity of all-life. What we do is in natural accord with that divine nature which takes possession of us. The consequences of our acts, then, are like a fragrance blown over the world. It is time for us to go homeward, to climb the terraces of being by which we descended to this world. Do any of us feel inspired to labour at another civilization. Those who came to us gave us nothing but the certainty that they were divinities and a longing to be like them, to be with them whither they are gone. Nothing about them can be proven outwardly. It was only the visionaries who knew them, who were dazzled, seeing through the mask of the body some flashing of the plumes of the bird of paradise. I doubt if they were killed. I think they went inward and homeward. Gregor was the only martyr. Whatever they were, their secret remains inviolate from those who see with their eyes and hear only with their ears. Maybe to those who open those secret radiant gateways to light of which Aoife spoke, the mystery will be revealed. But it will be found there, not here.'

'Was I wrong in my thought to build a temple of the arts inspired by them?' the American asked.

'I do not think so. All that will be gathered there, the painting, the sculpture and whatever else, will not draw men out of themselves, but will light the candle of vision within the psyche.'

'What are we to do, then? How are we to climb those terraces of being you speak of when the avatars have told us nothing?'

'Are you certain about this? They did not speak in words, but did they not speak in other ways? Did they not create light within us? Did we not feel them in our very spirits? Can we say that they have departed and left not a gift behind until we use the candle of vision and explore the upper chambers of the soul? We might discover all the ways to these were lit. The links binding us to earth have been loosened, while the links binding us to each other have been made stronger. We tend to overflow into each other. What one knows all of us soon know. To one there came the vision of nature as a vast ocean of being bathing heart and mind. With another the universe is revealed as a music. A third feels the free gay movement of the upper airs, and the girders of the soul which bind it to earth are slackened. Another is moved to be co-worker with that imagination which everywhere is making, sustaining and re-creating the world.

Another feels that being as a profound tenderness enveloping all that lives. All have been raised above themselves and all have in some way imparted their vision to the rest. Is not this true? Do we not surmise swiftly the desire or thought in the heart of another even when the friend is distant? Do we not come to each other without outer asking? Did any send messages to bring us here? Did not our friend think of us and we came? To climb into heaven might be difficult for one alone. But when there are seven or eight we will and aspire with the strength of all. At last, like adventurers who have found a marvellous country beyond the seas and who settle there, we may make firm our place in that other world and be able to know each other there in whatever way the psyche appears to the psyche. I think, too, we will find others there inspired like us to such heavenly climbing. At last the bonds of matter will, I think, wear thin so that our life shall be more there than here. We may be able at last to live there completely, finding in it an ark of refuge from this world which our men of science tell us is growing old like the moon. Do you not like the idea of leaving the world by our own strength? I have always thought it an indignity that we should be thrust out of the body by the falling in of its rafters, or the crumbling of its walls of clay, being outcast against our will. There must be a lordly way out of the body by one of those secret radiant gateways into light. If we do not find this way, I think we must return again and again to the body until we have mastered the secret of death and can take that lordly way out by our own will.'

While the elder had been speaking, Paul had sunken into one of those visionary moods which had become habitual with him. In that visionary mood he saw in the centre of the circle in which they sat a light flashing like a diamond. From that light, as waves might ripple from a flung stone, its glow dilated until it enveloped them all. For an instant there was that light only, and then in another instant a figure was there glowing as if it had been a shape cast in fire. He knew that figure, though transfigured, the lion-like mane of golden hair, or was it flame, which rose above the brows, and the eyes that looked out of eternity. Swiftly it swept a hand round the circle, and Paul saw where the hand moved a light ran from heart to heart linking them as by a chain of fire. In another instant the royal phantom had vanished and the glow had gone inward. There was a silence in the room, a silence which was not physical, a silence of intent and listening souls. No one asked of another whether they had seen anything or of what they had been aware. They were raised above themselves, needing that silence for understanding. A voice would have drawn them outward. There were no voices. Each needed that quiet for himself, for the chain of fire that linked heart to heart had made them all for the moment one mood, one being.

XXVI

After a time the old man began again. His voice seemed to come from far away.

'It is strange that I who am old should yet feel in myself strength and understanding for so great an adventure. The world has become changed for me, as if I had raced back from age to childhood and its heart-charmed country. When I was a boy earth, all nature indeed, seemed tender to me, a presence which melted about me as a nurse who loves her children, plays with them, answering all their demands. To my fantasy the streams then babbled with laughter fed from lovely and hidden springs. Even the gay stars from their towers nodded at me, clapping their elfin hands above my play. When I grew up and became a man, the earth had become solid and nature opaque. Now in my age nature has become transparent once more – melted toward me in some more infinitely majestic way. I feel made young again so that I can undertake that great journey. We have all moved in soul into some new region where we will find each other in some new guise and we will not need to speak each other's names as we do here, but come to profounder intimacies. Perhaps spirit may flow into spirit, and this not with ourselves alone but with many others, so we shall grow into a myriad wisdom.'

'If we are going inward,' cried Felim, 'How shall we know each other there? I do not know myself when I dream. How shall I know you? Rory I might know if I heard a music, and Paul I shall know for he has long been able to make me see his imaginations. How could I know Olive unless she came to me as a silver glow with innumerable stars in it? Or Cluborn unless by a friendliness to all creatures? Maybe we shall be raised above ourselves, transfigured into some divine counterpart of ourselves! And what does going inward mean? I have had my glimpses of a world of light. But is that going inward? Is it not rather going outward to another more lovely Maya? Going inward must mean a miraculous change if not vision but being is dilated. We must feel stirring within life some motions of the great deep.'[72]

'Is there not some place in that sphere next to us where we could keep tryst?' Olive spoke impetuously. 'Where do you go, Paul, when you shut your eyes and run away from us? You can make Felim see what you see. And I have seen what you imagine often without your telling. You could give to us a place not here but there where we might meet. What does it matter if it be but an imagination if we can find our way there in soul!'

'I will try,' said Paul. He sat with shut eyes. His face was set with intensity of will. He was evoking in himself memory of a vision. His head turned slightly to one after another, as one who makes a lit candle to touch with its flame a circle of unlit candles. There began to glow in each the vision of a vast hall with high marvellous pillars, a hall lit with a delicate golden air.

'Oh, I know that place!' cried the girl.

'I know it,' said Felim.

'And I, and I,' came from one after another.

'I was outcast once from its light when I woke,' said the poet. 'I had seen wonderful things there I knew, but I could not bring them back. What a place to keep tryst in! Is it one of those temples Socrates spoke of in that divine world which is all around us, temples wherein the gods do truly dwell? What are we to do? When do we keep tryst there? If I cannot go with my waking consciousness, I will be there surely in soul while I sleep.

'The night after to-morrow is Midsummer Eve. The barriers between earth and heaven are fragile. Let us try to be with each other there. We can meet after and tell what we remember. Once we have surety that we can meet in soul we shall have taken the first step in the great journey.'

They were all gay at the thought of so great adventure. They felt a fresh spiritual intimacy. They were conscious that they were knit to each other as the climbers of high mountains are. If one slipped, the others would hold him fast.

'We must go now. We have many miles to walk,' said Mark.

Felim and the young musician went with him. They made gestures of farewell silently, as those do who know that departure is not farewell and that space is but a myth to soul.

Paul, Olive, Conaire and Cluborn watched for a while the figures fading in the summer night. Conaire and his New World visitor turned to Conaire's home. Paul and the girl walked slowly after them. The night was luminous. They could see from the hill road the earth, wrinkled with hill and hollow, lying like a vast sleeping creature. The lakes in the hollows glowed like dim moonstones. Paul and his companion did not speak. They who were closer to each other than any in the world beside were yet free, and could take lonely journeys in soul sure that they would not lose the way back to each other. They stood for a while at the crest of the hill road. It was there the Avatars had met and gone on their radiant journey together. In that pause of quietness Paul became aware that the years had changed him, that he had come to be within that life which as a boy he had seen nodding at him through the transparency of air or earth. For many years he had peered through that veil, but he himself, except for moments which were so transient that he was hardly aware of them until they were gone, had been outside the heavenly circle. Now something was living and breathing in him, interpenetrating consciousness, a life which was an extension of the life that breathed through those dense infinitudes. He could not now conceive of himself apart from that great unity. He knew he was, however humbly, one of the heavenly household. In that new exaltation the lights above, the earth below, were but motions of a life that was endless. He almost felt the will that impelled the earth on which he stood on its eternal round. Through earth itself as through a dusky veil the lustre of its vitality glowed. It shimmered with ethereal colour. Space about him was dense with innumerable life. He felt an inexpressible yearning to be molten into that, into all life. He thought of that great adventure he and his friends were beginning, and what transfigurations in life and nature it would mean. What climbing of endless terraces of being! He knew out of what anguish of body and soul, through what dark martyrdoms, come the resurrection and the life, but he thought of these in peace. At last he came back to earth and to his companion. She was still brooding as he had been, her face lifted up to the skies, intent on the same depths. She was unconscious of the one by her side, and at that moment he loved her more in forgetting than in remembering him.

THE END

THE ASCENDING CYCLE[1]

The teaching of the Secret Doctrine[2] divides the period during which human evolution proceeds upon this globe into seven periods. During the first three-and-a-half of these, the ethereal humanity who appeared in the First Race gradually become material in form, and the psychic spirituality of the inner man is transformed into intellectuality. During the remaining three-and-a-half periods, there is a gradual dematerialization of form; the inner man by slow degrees rises from mere brain intellection to a more perfected spiritual consciousness. We are told that there are correspondences between the early and later periods of evolution; the old conditions are repeated, but upon higher planes; we re-achieve the old spirituality with added wisdom and intellectual power. Looked at in this way we shall find that the Seventh Race corresponds to the First; the Sixth to the Second; and the Fifth Race (which is ours) corresponds with the Third. 'We are now approaching a time,' says the Secret Doctrine, 'when the pendulum of evolution will direct its swing decidedly upward, bringing humanity back on a parallel line with the primitive Third Root Race in spirituality.' That is, there will be existing on the earth, about the close of Fifth Race, conditions in some way corresponding with those prevailing when the Third Race men began their evolution. Though this period may be yet distant hundreds of thousands of years, still it is of interest to forecast that future as far as may be, for the future is concealed in the present, and is the outcome of forces working to-day. We may find out from this enquiry the true nature of movements like the Theosophical Society.

One of the most interesting passages in the Secret Doctrine is that which describes the early Third Race. 'It was not a Race, this progeny. It was at first a wondrous Being, called the "Initiator",[3] and after him a group of semi-divine and semi-human beings.' Without at all attempting to explain the real nature of this mysterious Being or Race, we may assume that one of the things hinted at is the consciousness of united being possessed by these ancient Adepts. Walking abroad over the earth as instructors of a

The Ascending Cycle

less progressed humanity, their wisdom and power had a common root. They taught truth from a heart-perception of life, ever fresh and eternal, everywhere pervading nature and welling up in themselves. This heart-perception is the consciousness of unity of inner being.[4] The pendulum of evolution which in its upward swing will bring humanity backwards on a parallel line with the primitve Third Root Race, should bring back something corresponding to this primeval hierarchy of divine sages. We should see at the end of the Kaliyuga[5] a new brotherhood formed from those who have risen out of material life and aims, who have conquered self, who have been purified by suffering, who have acquired strength and wisdom, and who have wakened up to the old magical perception of their unity in true Being. 'At the end of the Kali, our present age, Vishnu, or the "Everlasting King," will appear as Kalki, and establish righteousness upon earth. The minds of those who live at that time shall be awakened and become pellucid as crystal.' – (*Secret Doctrine* II, 483)

Passing beyond the turning point of evolution, where the delusion of separateness[6] is complete, and moving on to that future awaiting us in infinite distances, when the Great Breath shall cease its outward motion and we shall merge into the One – on this uphill journey in groups and clusters men will first draw closer together, entering in spirit their own parent rays,[7] before being united in the source of all light and life. Such a brotherhood of men and women we may expect will arise, conscious in unity, thinking from one mind and acting from one soul.[8] All such great achievements of the race are heralded long before by signs which those who study the lives of men may know. There is a gestation in the darkness of the womb before the living being appears. Ideals first exist in thought, and from thought they are outrealized into objective existence. The Theosophical Society was started to form the nucleus of a universal brotherhood of humanity,[9] and its trend is towards this ideal. May we not justifiably suppose that we are witnessing to-day in this movement the birth of a new race corresponding to the divine Initiators of the Third,[10] a race which shall in its inner life be truly a 'Wondrous Being.'[11] I think we will perform our truest service to the Society by regarding it in this way as an actual entity whose baby years and mystical childhood we should foster. There are many people who know that it is possible by certain methods to participate in the soul-life of a co-worker, and if it is possible to do this even momentarily with one comrade, it is possible so to participate in the vaster life of great movements. There will come a time to all who have devoted themselves to this ideal, as H.P. Blavatsky and some others have done, when they will enter into the inner life of this great Being,[12] and share the hopes, the aspirations, the heroism, and the failures which must be brought about when so many men and women are working together. To achieve this we should continually keep in mind this sense of unity; striving also to rise in meditation until we sense in the vastness the beating of these innumerable hearts glowing with heroic purpose: we should try to humanize our mysticism; 'We can only reach the Universal Mind through the minds of humanity,' and we can penetrate into their minds by continual concentration, endeavouring to realize their thoughts and feelings, until we carry always about with us in imagination, as Walt Whitman, 'those delicious burdens, men and women.'

G.W.R.

SHADOW AND SUBSTANCE[1]

Many are the voices that entreat and warn those who would live the life of the Magi.[2] It is well they should speak. They are voices of the wise. But after having listened and pondered, oh, that someone would arise and shout into our souls how much more fatal it is to refrain. For we miss to hear the fairy tale of time, the æonian chant radiant with light and colour which the spirit prolongs. The warnings are not for those who stay at home, but for those who adventure abroad. They constitute an invitation to enter the mysteries. We study and think these things were well in the happy prime and will be again in the years to come. But not yesterday only or to-morrow – to-day, to-day burns in the heart the fire which made mighty the heroes of old. And in what future will be born the powers which are not quick in the present?[3] It will never be a matter of greater ease to enter the path, though we may well have the stimulus of greater despair.[4] For this and that there are times and seasons, but for the highest it is always the hour. The eternal beauty does not pale because its shadow trails over slime and corruption. It is always present beneath the faded mould whereon our lives are spent. Still the old mysterious glimmer from mountain and cave allures, and the golden gleams divide and descend on us from the haunts of the Gods.

The dark age is our darkness and not the darkness of life. It is not well for us who in the beginning came forth with the wonder-light about us, that it should have turned in us to darkness, the song of life be dumb. We close our eyes from the many-coloured mirage of day, and are alone soundless and sightless in the unillumined cell of the brain. But there are thoughts that shine, impulses born of fire. Still there are moments when the prison world reels away a distant shadow, and the inner chamber of clay fills full with fiery visions. We choose from the traditions of the past some symbol of our greatness, and seem again the Titans or Morning Stars[5] of the prime. In this self-conception lies the secret of life, the way of escape and return. We have imagined ourselves into forgetfulness, into darkness, into feebleness. From this strange and pitiful dream of life, oh, that we may awaken and know ourselves once again.

But the student too often turns to books, to the words sent back to him, forgetful that the best of scriptures do no more than stand as symbols. We hear too much of study, as if the wisdom of life and ethics could be learned like a ritual, and of their application to this and that ephemeral pursuit. But from the Golden One, the child of the divine, comes a voice to its shadow. It is stranger to our world, aloof from our ambitions, with a destiny not here to be fulfilled. It says: 'You are of dust while I am robed in opalescent airs. You dwell in houses of clay, I in a temple not made by hands. I will not go with thee, but thou must come with me.'[6] And not alone is the form of the divine aloof but the spirit behind the form. It is called the Goal truly, but it has no ending. It is the Comforter, but it waves away our joys and hopes like the angel with the flaming sword. Though it is the Resting-place, it stirs to all heroic strife, to outgoing, to conquest. It is the Friend indeed, but it will not yield to our desires.[7] Is it this strange, unfathomable self we think to know, and awaken to, by what is written, or by study of it as so many planes of consciousness. But in vain we store the upper chambers of the mind with such quaint furniture of thought. No archangel makes his abode therein. They abide only in the shining. How different from academic psychology of the past, with its dry enumeration of faculties, reason, cognition and so forth, is the burning thing we know. We revolted from that, but we must take care lest we teach in another way a catalogue of things equally unliving to us. The plain truth is, that after having learned what is taught about the hierarchies and various spheres, many of us are still in this world exactly where we were before. If we speak our laboriously-acquired information we are listened to in amazement. It sounds so learned, so intellectual, there must needs be applause. But by-and-bye someone comes with quiet voice, who without pretence speaks of the 'soul' and uses familiar words, and the listeners drink deep, and pay the applause of silence and long remembrance and sustained after-endeavour. Our failure lies in this, we would use the powers of soul and we have not yet become the soul. None but the wise one himself could bend the bow of Ulysses. We cannot communicate more of the true than we ourselves *know*.[8] It is better to have a little knowledge and know that little than to have only hearsay of myriads of Gods. So I say, lay down your books for a while and try the magic of thought. 'What a man thinks, that he is; that is the old secret.' I utter, I know, but a partial voice of the soul with many needs. But I say, forget for a while that you are student, forget your name and time. Think of yourself within as the Titan, the Demi-god,[9] the flaming hero with the form of beauty, the heart of love. And of those divine spheres forget the nomenclature; think rather of them as the places of a great childhood you now return to, these homes no longer ours. In some moment of more complete imagination the thought-born may go forth and look on the olden Beauty. So it was in the mysteries long ago and may well be to-day. The poor dead shadow was laid to sleep in forgotten darkness, as the fiery power, mounting from heart to head,[10] went forth in radiance. Not then did it rest, nor ought we. The dim worlds dropped behind it, the lights of earth disappeared as it neared the heights of the Immortals. There was One seated on a throne, One dark and bright with ethereal glory. It arose in greeting. The radiant figure laid its head against the breast which grew suddenly golden, and father and son vanished in that which has no place nor name.

Æ.

THE RENEWAL OF YOUTH[1]

I

> I am a part of all that I have met;
> Yet all experience is an arch wherethro'
> Gleams that untravell'd world . . .
>   . . . Come, my friends,
> 'Tis not too late to seek a newer world.
>
> *Ulysses.*

Humanity is no longer the child it was at the beginning of the world. The spirit which, prompted by some divine intent, flung itself long ago into a vague, nebulous, drifting nature, though it has endured through many periods of youth, maturity, and age, has yet had its own transformations. Its gay, wonderful childhood gave way, as cycle after cycle coiled itself into slumber, to more definite purposes, and now it is old and burdened with experiences. It is not an age that quenches its fire, but it will not renew again the activities which gave it wisdom. And so it comes that men pause with a feeling which they translate into weariness of life before the accustomed joys and purposes of their race. They wonder at the spell which induced their fathers to plot and execute deeds which seem to them to have no more meaning than a whirl of dust. But their fathers had this weariness also and concealed it from each other in fear, for it meant the laying aside of the sceptre, the toppling over of empires, the chilling of the household warmth, and all for a voice whose inner significance revealed itself but to one or two among myriads.

The spirit has hardly emerged from the childhood with which nature clothes it afresh at every new birth, when the disparity between the garment and the wearer becomes manifest: the little tissue of joys and dreams woven about it is found inadequate for shelter: it trembles exposed to the winds blowing out of the unknown. We linger at twilight with some companion, still glad, contented, and in tune with the nature which fills the orchards with blossom and sprays the hedges with dewy blooms. The laughing lips give utterance to wishes – ours until that moment. Then the spirit, without warning, suddenly falls into immeasurable age: a sphinx-like face looks at us: our lips answer, but far from the region of elemental being we inhabit, they syllable in shadowy sound, out of old usage, the response, speaking of a love and a hope which we know have vanished from us for evermore. So hour by hour the scourge of the infinite drives us out of every nook and corner of life we find pleasant. And this always takes place when all is fashioned to our liking: then into our dream strides the wielder of the lightning: we get glimpses of a world beyond us thronged with mighty, exultant beings: our own deeds become infinitesimal to us: the colours of our imagination, once so shining, grow pale as the living lights of God glow upon them. We find a little honey in the heart which we make sweeter for some one, and then another lover, whose forms are legion, sighs to us out of its multitudinous being: we know that the old love is gone. There is a sweetness in song or in the cunning re-imaging of the beauty we see; but the Magician of the Beautiful[2] whispers to us of his art, how we were with him when he laid the foundations of the world, and the song is unfinished, the fingers grow listless. As we receive these intimations of age our very sins become negative: we are still pleased if a voice praises us, but we grow lethargic in enterprises where the spur to activity is fame or the acclamation of men. At some point in the past we may have struggled mightily for the sweet incense which men offer to a towering personality; but the infinite is for ever within man: we sighed for other worlds and found that to be saluted as victor by men did not mean acceptance by the gods.

But the placing of an invisible finger upon our lips when we would speak, the heart-throb of warning where we would love, that we grow contemptuous of the prizes of life, does not mean that the spirit has ceased from its labours, that the high-built beauty of the spheres is to topple mistily into chaos, as a mighty temple in the desert sinks into the sand, watched only by a few barbarians too feeble to renew its ancient pomp and the ritual of its once shining congregations. Before we, who were the bright children of the dawn, may return as the twilight race into the silence, our purpose must be achieved, we have to assume mastery over that nature which now overwhelms us, driving into the Fire-fold the flocks of stars and wandering fires. Does it seem very vast and far away? Do you sigh at the long, long time? Or does it appear hopeless to you who perhaps return with trembling feet evening after evening from a little labour? But it is behind all these things that the renewal takes place, when love and grief are dead; when they loosen their hold on the spirit and it sinks back into itself, looking out on the pitiful plight of those who, like it, are the weary inheritors of so great destinies:

then a tenderness which is the most profound quality of its being springs up like the outraying of the dawn, and if in that mood it would plan or execute it knows no weariness, for it is nourished from the First Fountain.[3] As for these feeble children on the once glorious spirits of the dawn, only a vast hope can arouse them from so vast a despair, for the fire will not invigorate them for the repetition of petty deeds but only for the eternal enterprise, [the purpose of the immemorial battle waged through all the ages,] the war in heaven,[4] that conflict between Titan and Zeus which is part of the never-ending struggle of the human spirit to assert its supremacy over nature. We, who lie, crushed by this mountain nature piled above us, must arise again, unite to storm the heavens and sit on the seats of the mighty.

[As the Titan in man ponders on this old, old purpose wherefore all its experience was garnered, the lightnings will once more begin to play through him and animate his will. So like the archangel ruined let us arise from despair and weariness with inflexible resolution, pealing once more the old heroic shout to our fallen comrades, until those great powers who enfold us feel the stirring and renewal, and the murmur runs along the spheres, 'The buried Titan moves once again to tear the throng from Him.']

II

We speak out of too petty a spirit to each other; the true poems, said Whitman:

Bring none to his or to her terminus or to be content and full,
Whom they take they take into space to behold the birth of stars, to learn one of the meanings,
To launch off with absolute faith, to sweep through the ceaseless rings and never be quiet again.

Here is inspiration – the voice of the soul. [And we, who professed to bring such wisdom, what have we to say? Have we uttered with equal confidence such hopes, or with such daring and amplitude of illustration? Let us confess we have not. There are one or two exceptions which will occur to everyone. Now, as we adventure afresh, let us see what it is has brought despondency and failure in our work upon us in the past. I think it is because we have been saying things we have never realized; we have been repeating without imagination the words of those few leaders. We have lowered their heroic tone because we thought we were speaking to a fallen people who could not respond to our highest. But it was not the way, it was not the way. It is not with the dust we have brotherhood, but with the ancient spirit it clouds over. To this spirit we must speak heart to heart as we know how. I would not willingly recognize aught in anyone but the divine.] Every word which really inspires is spoken as if the Golden Age had never passed. The great teachers ignore the personal identity and speak to the eternal pilgrim.[5] [Do we not treasure most their words which remind us of our divine origin? So we must in our turn speak.] Too often the form or surface far removed from beauty makes us falter, and we speak to that form and the soul is not stirred. But an equal temper arouses it. To whoever hails in it the lover, the hero, the magician, it will respond, but not to him who accosts it in the name and style of its outer self.[6] How often do we not long to break through the veils which divide us from some one, but custom, convention, or a fear of being misunderstood prevent us, and so the moment passes whose heat might have burned through every barrier. Out with it – out with it, the hidden heart, the love that is voiceless, the secret tender germ of an infinite forgiveness. That speaks to the heart. That pierces through many a vesture of the Soul. Our companion struggles in some labyrinth of passion. We help him, we think, with ethic and moralities. Ah, very well they are; well to know and to keep, but wherefore? For their own sake? No, but that the King may arise in his beauty. We write that in letters, in books, but to the face of the fallen who brings back remembrance? Who calls him by his secret name? Let a man but feel for what high cause is his battle, for what is his cyclic labour, and a warrior who is invincible fights for him and he draws upon divine powers. Our attitude to man and to nature, expressed or not, has something of the effect of ritual, of evocation. As our aspiration so is our inspiration. We believe in life universal, in a brotherhood which links the elements to man, and makes the glow-worm feel far off something of the rapture of the seraph hosts. Then we go out into the living world, and what influences pour through us! We are 'at league with the stones of the field'. The winds of the world blow radiantly upon us as in the early time. We feel wrapt about with love, with an infinite tenderness that caresses us. Alone in our rooms as we ponder, what sudden abysses of light open within us! The Gods are so much nearer than we dreamed. We rise up intoxicated with the thought, and reel out seeking an equal companionship under the great night and the stars.

Let us get near to realities. We read too much.[7] We think of that which is 'the goal, the Comforter, the Lord, the Witness, the resting-place, the asylum, and the Friend.'[8] Is it by any of these dear and familiar names? The soul of the modern mystic is becoming a mere hoarding-place for uncomely theories. He creates an uncouth symbolism, and blinds his soul within with names drawn from the Kabala[9] or ancient Sanskrit, and makes alien to himself the intimate powers of his spirit, things which in truth are more his than the beatings of his heart. Could we not speak of them in our own tongue, and the language of to-day will be as sacred as any of the past. From the Golden One, the child of the divine, comes a voice to its shadow. It is stranger to our world, aloof from our ambitions, with a destiny not here to be fulfilled. It says: 'You are of dust while I am robed in opalescent airs. You dwell in houses of clay, I in a temple not made by hands. I will not go with thee, but thou must come with me.' And not alone is the form of the divine aloof but the spirit behind the form. It is called the Goal truly, but it has no ending. It is the Comforter, but it waves away our joys and hopes like the angel with the flaming sword. Though it is the Resting-place, it stirs to all heroic strife, to outgoing, to conquest. It is the Friend indeed, but it will not yield to our desires. Is it this strange, unfathomable self we think to know, and awaken to, by what is written, or by study of it as so many planes of consciousness? But in vain we store the upper chambers of the mind with such quaint furniture of thought. No archangel makes his abode therein. They abide only in the shining. No wonder that the Gods[10] do not incarnate. We cannot say we do pay reverence to these awful powers. We repulse the living truth by our doubts and reasonings. We would compel the Gods to fall in with our petty philosophy rather than trust in the heavenly guidance. Ah, to think of it, those dread deities, the divine Fires,[11] to be so enslaved! We have not comprehended the meaning of the voice which cried, 'Prepare ye the way of the Lord,' or this, 'Lift up your heads, O ye gates. Be ye lifted up, ye everlasting doors, and the King of Glory shall come in.'"[12] Nothing that we read is useful unless it calls up living things in the soul. To read a mystic book truly is to invoke the powers. If they do not rise up plumed and radiant, the apparitions of spiritual things, then is our labour barren. We only encumber the mind with useless symbols. They knew better ways long ago. 'Master of the Green-waving Planisphere, . . Lord of the Azure Expanse, . . . it is thus we invoke,' cried the magicians of old.

And us, let us invoke them with joy, let us call upon them with love, the Light we hail, or the Divine Darkness[13] we worship with silent breath. That silence cries aloud to the Gods. Then they will approach us. Then we may learn that speech of many colours, for they will not speak in our mortal tongue; they will not answer to the names of men. Their names are rainbow glories. Yet these are mysteries, and they cannot be reasoned out or argued over. We cannot speak truly of them from report, or description, or from what another has written. A relation to the thing in itself alone is our warrant, and this means we must set aside our intellectual self-sufficiency and await guidance. It will surely come to those who wait in trust, a glow, a heat in the heart announcing the awakening of the Fire.[14] And, as it blows with its mystic breath into the brain,[15] there is a hurtling of visions, a brilliance of lights, a sound as of great waters vibrant and musical in their flowing, and murmurs from a single yet multitudinous being. In such a mood, when the far becomes near, the strange familiar, and the infinite possible, he wrote from whose words we get the inspiration:

To launch off with absolute faith, to sweep through the ceaseless rings and never be quiet again.

Such a faith and such an unrest be ours: faith which is mistrust of the visible; unrest which is full of a hidden surety and reliance. We, when we fall into pleasant places, rest and dream our strength away. Before every enterprise and adventure of the soul we calculate in fear our power to do. But remember, 'Oh, disciple, in thy work for thy brother thou hast many allies; in the winds, in the air, in all the voices of the silent shore.' These are the far-wandered powers of our own nature, and they turn again home at our need. We came out of the Great Mother-Life[16] for the purposes of soul. Are her darlings forgotten where they darkly wander and strive? Never. Are not the lives of all her heroes proof? Though they seem to stand alone the eternal Mother keeps watch on them, and voices far away and unknown to them before arise in passionate defence, and hearts beat warm to help them. Aye, if we could look within we would see vast nature stirred on their behalf, and institutions shaken, until the truth they fight for triumphs, and they pass, and a wake of glory ever widening behind them trails down the ocean of the years.

Thus the warrior within us works,[17] or, if we choose to phrase it so, it is the action of the spiritual will.[18] Shall we not, then, trust in it and face the unknown, defiant and fearless of its dangers. Though we seem to go alone to the high, the lonely, the pure, we need not despair. Let no one bring to this task the mood of the martyr or of one who thinks he sacrifices something. Yet let all who will come. Let them enter the path, 'Yes, and hope,' facing all things in life and death with a mood at once gay and reverent, as beseems those who are immortal – who are children to-day, but whose hands to-morrow may grasp the sceptre, sitting down with the Gods as equals and companions. 'What a man thinks, that he is: that is the old secret.' In this self-conception lies the secret of life, the way of escape and return. We have imagined ourselves into littleness, darkness, and feebleness. We must imagine ourselves into greatness. 'If thou wilt not equal thyself to God thou canst not understand God. The like is only intelligible by the like.' In some moment of more complete imagination the thought-born may go forth and look on the ancient Beauty. So it was in the mysteries long ago, and may well be to-day. The poor dead shadow was laid to sleep, forgotten in its darkness, as the fiery power[19] mounting from heart to head, went forth in radiance. Not then did it rest, nor ought we. The dim worlds dropped behind it, the lights of earth disappeared as it neared the heights of the immortals. There was One seated on a throne, One dark and bright with ethereal glory. It arose in greeting. The radiant figure laid its head against the breast which grew suddenly golden, and Father and Son vanished in that which has no place or name.

III

> Who are exiles? as for me
> Where beneath the diamond dome
> Lies the light on hills or tree
> There my palace is and home.

We are outcasts from Deity, therefore we defame the place of our exile. But who is there may set apart his destiny from the earth which bore him? I am one of those who would bring back the old reverence for the Mother, the magic, the love. I think, metaphysician, you have gone astray. You would seek within yourself for the fountain of life. Yes, there is the true, the only light. But do not dream it will lead you farther away from the earth, but rather deeper into its heart. By it you are nourished with those living waters you would drink. You are yet in the womb and unborn, and the Mother breathes for you the diviner airs. Dart out your farthest ray of thought to the original, and yet you have not found a new path of your own. Your ray is still enclosed in the parent ray, and only on the sidereal streams are you borne to the freedom of the deep, to the sacred stars whose distance maddens, and to the Lonely Light of Lights.[20]

Let us, therefore, accept the conditions and address ourselves with wonder, with awe, with love, as we well may, to that being in whom we move. I abate no jot of those vaster hopes, yet I would pursue that ardent aspiration, content as to here and to-day. I do not believe in a nature red with tooth and claw. If indeed she appears so terrible to any it is because they themselves have armed her. Again, behind the anger of the Gods there is a love. Are the rocks barren? Lay your brow against them and learn what memories they keep. Is the brown earth unbeautiful? Yet lie on the breast of the Mother and you shall be aureoled with the dews of faery. The earth is the entrance to the Halls of Twilight.[21] What emanations are those that make radiant the dark woods of pine! Round every leaf and tree and over all the mountains wave the fiery tresses of that hidden sun which is the soul of the earth and parent of your soul. But we think of these things no longer. Like the prodigal[22] we have wandered far from our home, but no more return. We idly pass or wait as strangers in the halls our spirit built.

> Sad or fain no more to live?
> I have pressed the lips of pain:
> With the kisses lovers give
> Ransomed ancient powers again.

I would raise this shrinking soul to a more universal acceptance. What! does it aspire to the All, and yet deny by its revolt and inner protest the justice of Law? From sorrow we shall take no less and no more than from our joys. For if the one reveals to the soul the mode by which the power overflows and fills it here, the other indicates to it the unalterable will which checks excess and leads it on to true proportion and its own ancestral ideal. Yet men seem for ever to fly from their destiny of inevitable beauty; because of delay the power invites and lures no longer but goes out into the highways with a hand of iron. We look back cheerfully enough upon those old trials out of which we have passed; but we have gleaned only an aftermath of wisdom, and missed the full harvest if the will has not risen royally at the moment in unison with the will of the Immortal, even though it comes rolled round with terror and suffering and strikes at the heart of clay.

Through all these things, in doubt, despair, poverty, sick, feeble, or baffled, we have yet to learn reliance. *'I will not leave thee or forsake thee'* are the words of the most ancient spirit to the spark wandering in the immensity of its own being.[23] This high courage brings with it a vision. It sees the true intent in all circumstance out of which its own emerges to meet it. Before it the blackness melts into forms of beauty, and back of all illusions is seen the old enchanter tenderly smiling, the dark, hidden Father[24] enveloping his children.

All things have their compensations. For what is absent here there is always, if we seek, a nobler presence about us.

> Captive, see what stars give light
> In the hidden heart of clay:
> At their radiance dark and bright
> Fades the dreamy King of Day.

We complain of conditions, but this very imperfection it is which urges us to arise and seek for the Isles of the Immortals.[25] What we lack recalls the fullness. The soul has seen a brighter day than this and a sun[26] which never sets. Hence the retrospect: 'Thou hast been in Eden the garden of God; every precious stone was thy covering, the sardius, topaz, and the diamond, the beryl, the onyx, the jasper, the sapphire, emerald. . . . Thou wast upon the holy mountain of God; thou hast walked up and down in the midst of the stones of fire.'[27] We would point out these radiant avenues of return; but sometimes we feel in our hearts that we sound but cockney voices, as guides amid the ancient temples, the cyclopean crypts sanctified by the mysteries. To be intelligible we replace the opalescent shining by the terms of the scientist, and we prate of occult physiology in the same breath with the Most High.[28] Yet when the soul has the vision divine it knows not it has a body. Let it remember, and the breath of glory kindles it no more; it is once again a captive. After all it does not make the mysteries clearer to speak in physical terms and do violence to our intuitions. If we ever use these centres,[29] as fires we shall see them, or they shall well up within us as fountains of potent sound. We may satisfy people's minds with a sense correspondence, and their souls may yet hold aloof. We shall only inspire by the magic of a superior beauty. Yet this too has its dangers. 'Thou hast corrupted thy wisdom by reason of thy brightness,' continues the seer.[30] If we follow too much the elusive beauty of form we will miss the spirit. The last secrets are for those who translate vision into being. Does the glory fade away before you? Say truly in your heart, 'I care not. I will wear the robes I am endowed with to-day.' You are already become beautiful, being beyond desire and free.

> Night and day no more eclipse
> Friendly eyes that on us shine,
> Speech from old familiar lips,
> Playmates of a youth divine.

To childhood once again.[31] We must regain the lost state. But it is to the giant and spiritual childhood of the young immortals we must return, when into their clear and translucent souls first fell the rays of the father-beings. The men of old were intimates of wind and wave and playmates of many a brightness long since forgotten. The rapture of the fire was their rest; their outgoing was still consciously through universal being. By darkened images we may figure something vaguely akin, as when in rare moments under the stars the big dreamy heart of childhood is pervaded with quiet and brimmed full with love. Dear children of the world, so tired to-day – so weary seeking after the light. Would you recover strength and immortal vigour? Not one star alone, your star, shall shed its happy light upon you, but the All you must adore. Something intimate, secret, unspeakable, akin to thee, will emerge silently, insensibly, and ally itself with thee as thou gatherest thyself from the four quarters of the earth. We shall go back to the world of the dawn, but to a brighter light[32] than that which opened up this wondrous story of the cycles. The forms of elder years will reappear in our vision, the father-beings once again. So we shall grow at home amid these grandeurs, and with that All-Presence about us may cry in our hearts, 'At last is our meeting, Immortal. O starry one, now is our rest!'

> Come away, oh, come away;
> We will quench the heart's desire
> Past the gateways of the day
> In the rapture of the fire.

1896

SELF-RELIANCE[1]

Perhaps it is now while we are in a state of transition, when old leaders have gone out of sight and the new ones have not yet taken their place in the van, that we ought to consider what we are in ourselves. Some questions we ought to ask ourselves about this movement: where its foundations were laid? what the links are? where is the fountain of force? what are the doors? You answer the first and you say 'America,' or you say 'India'. But if that old doctrine of emanations be true it was not on earth but in the heavenworld where our minds immortal are linked together. There it was born and well born, and grew downwards into earth, and all our hopes and efforts and achievements here but vaguely reflect what was true and perfect in intent above, a compact of many hearts to save the generations wandering to their doom. Wiser, stronger, mightier than we were those who shielded us in the first years; who went about among us renewing memory, whispering in our hearts the message of the meaning of life, recalling the immemorial endeavour of the spirit for freedom, knowledge, mastery. But it is our movement and not the movement of the Masters only. It is our own work we are carrying on; our own primal will we are trying to give effect to. Well may the kingly sages depart from bodies which were torment and pain to them. They took them on for our sakes, and we may wave them a grateful farewell below and think of the spheres invisible as so much richer by their presence, more to be longed for, more to be attained. I think indeed they are nearer heart and mind there than here. What is real in us can lose no brotherhood with such as they through death. Still flash the lights from soul to soul in ceaseless radiance, in endless begetting of energy, thought and will, in endless return of joy and love and hope. I would rather hear one word of theirs in my heart than a thousand in my ears. I would rather think of my guide and captain as embodied in the flame than in the clay. Although we may gaze on the grave, kindly face living no more, there can be no cessation of the magic influence, the breath of fire, which flowed aforetime from the soul to us. We feel in our profoundest hearts that he whom they call dead is living, is alive for evermore.

He has earned his rest, a deep rest, if indeed such as he cease from labour. As for us, we may go our ways assured that the links are unbroken. What did you think the links were? That you knew some one who knew the Masters?[2] Such a presence and such a Companion would indeed be an aid, a link. But I think wherever there is belief in our transcendent being, in justice, our spiritual unity and destiny, wherever there is brotherhood, there are unseen ties, links, shining cords, influx from and unbroken communication with the divine. So much we have in our own natures, not enough to perfect us in the mysteries, but always enough to light our path, to show us our next step, to give us strength for duty. We should not always look outside for aid, remembering that some time we must be able to stand alone. Let us not deny our own deeper being, our obscured glory. That we accepted these truths, even as intuitions which we were unable intellectually to justify, is proof that there is that within us which has been initiate in the past, which lives in and knows well what in the shadowy world is but a hope. There is part of ourselves whose progress we do not comprehend. There are deeds done in unremembered dream, and a deeper meditation in the further unrecorded silences of slumber. Downward from sphere to sphere the Immortal works its way into the flesh, and the soul has adventures in dream whose resultant wisdom is not lost because memory is lacking here. Yet enough has been said to give us the hint, the clue to trace backwards the streams of force to their fount. We wake in some dawn and there is morning also in our hearts, a love, a fiery vigour, a magnetic sweetness in the blood. Could we track to its source this invigorating power, we might perhaps find that as we fell asleep some olden memory had awakened in the soul, or the Master had called it forth, or it was transformed by the wizard power of Self and went forth to seek the Holy Place. Whether we have here a guide, or whether we have not, one thing is certain, that behind and within the 'Father worketh hitherto'. A warrior fights for us. Our thoughts tip the arrows of his quiver. He wings them with flame and impels them with the Holy Breath. They will not fail if we think clear. What matters it if in the mist we do not see where they strike. Still they are of avail. After a time the mists will arise and show a clear field; the shining powers will salute us as victors.

I have no doubt about our future; no doubt but that we will have a guide and an unbroken succession of guides. But I think their task would be easier, our way be less clouded with dejection and doubt, if we placed our trust in no hierarchy of beings, however august, but in the Law of which they are ministers.[3] Their power, though mighty, ebbs and flows with contracting and expanding nature. They, like us, are but children in the dense infinitudes. Something like this, I think, the Wise Ones would wish each one of us to speak: 'O Brotherhood of Light, though I long to be with you, though it sustains me to think you are behind me, though your aid made sure my path, still, if the Law does not permit you to act for me to-day, I trust in the One whose love a fiery breath never ceases; I fall back on it with exultation; I rely upon it joyfully.' Was it not to point to that greater life that the elder brothers sent forth their messengers, to tell us that it is on this we ought to rely, to point us to grander thrones than they are seated on? It is well to be prepared to face any chance with equal mind; to meet the darkness with gay and defiant thought as to salute the Light with reverence and love and joy. But I have it in my heart that we are not deserted. As the cycles wend their upward way the heroic figures of the dawn reappear. Some have passed before us; others in the same spirit and power will follow: for the new day a rearisen sun and morning stars to herald it. When it comes let it find us, not drowsy after our night in time, but awake, prepared and ready to go forth from the house of sleep, to stretch hands to the light, to live and labour in joy, having the Gods for our guides and friends.

Æ.

IRELAND BEHIND THE VEIL[1]

In the ages which lie far back of our recorded history many battles between gods and demons took place as told by the Celtic Homers. The hosts of light, a divine race known as the Tuatha de Danaan, made war upon the Fomors for possession of Eire. At the last great battle of Moytura came victory for the gods. One of our later singers, Larminie,[2] who has retold the story, has it that the demoniac nature was never really subdued. The bright Danaan and the dark Fomor no longer war in mystic worlds, but twine more subtly together in the human generations who came after, and now the battle is renewed in the souls of men. Indeed it seems that the fierce Fomor spirit is more rampant, makes itself more evident to the eyes of men, than the gentle, peaceful race who inherit the spirit bequeathed by the gods. It is our misfortune that the Fomorian Celt, who makes most noise, represents us before the world. He looms up variously as a drunken Paddy, a rowdy politician, a moonlighter, or a rackrenting landlord. There is a tradition current about the last which confirms my theory. It is that when the rebel angels were cast out of Paradise the good god put some of them into waste places, and some became landlords. So I am moving here on safe ground.

But, however it may be, of that other Eire behind the veil the world knows little. It is guessed only by some among ourselves. We may say one-half of Ireland is unsuspected by the other half: it is so shy of revealing itself. The tourist will never unmask it: nor will the folklorist who goes about his work in the scientific spirit of a member of the Royal Dublin Society. It is on his own telling that, bent on discovery, he panted his way up certain hills until he met a native. Our folklorist surveyed him through spectacles and went at once to business.

'Are there any myths connected with these hills, any ancient traditions, my good man?'

'Sor!'

'I mean are there any folk-tales current?'

'No, sor, I never heard tell of any.'

Our folklorist went his way down the mountain-side convinced that legend and faery were things of the past. Yet these very mountains have been to some what Mount Meru was to the Indian ascetic. They have seen the bright race of the Sidhe at midnight glow like a sunrise on the dark brow in rainbow-coloured hosts. They have heard the earthly silences broken by heart-capturing music. Where these mountains are and who it was that saw is of no moment. If I named the hills they would be desecrated by the curious bent equally on picnic and faeries. If I named the visionaries some people would be sure to get up a committee to investigate. It is the dark age. To the curious I would say that faery-land is the soul of earth and it lies as much about you in America as here, and friendship with your bright kinsmen in the unseen there is the surest way to friendship with them here when you pay us a visit. That the faery traditions have by no means passed away I am aware.

I was driving from the ancient city of Drogheda to New Grange, once the most famous magical and holy place in Ireland. My car-man after a little became communicative. He told me that many people still left little bowls of milk for the good people: a friend of his had seen them in their red jackets playing hurley: a woman near by had heard the faery chimes ringing clear over the deserted Druidic mound at Dowth. Then he grew apprehensive that he was telling too much and sounded me as to my own beliefs. My faeries were different from his. I believed in the bright immortals; he in the little elemental creatures who drape themselves with the pictures of the past, and misbehave in their heroic guise. But I sunk my differences and most positively affirmed my faith, adding a few tales to his own. 'Sor,' he said at last, in an awestruck tone, 'is it thrue they can take you away among themselves?' Still thinking of my bright immortals I expressed my downright conviction that such was the case. May the belief flourish! An old sergeant of the constabulary told me many tales. He had seen a water-spirit invoked: 'Man,' he said, 'it do put one in a sweat to see them.' He knew the spell but would not tell it. I might 'do some one a hurt with it.' A strain of the magical runs in the blood of the Celt and its manifestation is almost always picturesque and poetical. He has an eye to effect. Down in Kerry, a friend tells me, there lived a faery doctor whom he knew. This man was much pestered, as bigger magicians have been, by people who wanted to see something. One in particular was most persistent and the doctor gave way. He brought his neophyte into a lonely place where there was a faery rath. It was night: a wind colder than earthly began blowing: the magician suddenly flung his arms round his trembling companion, who had a vision of indescribable creatures fleeting past. Ever after, he had the second sight.

Stories like these could be endlessly multiplied. What it is these peasant seers really perceive we cannot say. They have only a simple language and a few words for all. A child wanders over the hillside while the silver blushes fade from the soft blue cheek of evening. The night drops with dew about him. The awe of the nameless also descends. And, as he stands entranced, the children of twilight begin to move softly beside him, wearing the masks of ancient queens with sweeping draperies of purple, gold and green: or stately warriors appear: or white-robed druids at their mystic rites. He relates, after, that the good people were about. But perhaps, child as he is, his eyes have looked upon some mighty mystery's re-enactment, some unveiling of the secrets of life and of death. It is a land full of enchantment.

That much of what is gathered by the folklorists misrepresents the actual vision, seems probable. The band of singers and writers in modern Ireland who directly relate their own dreams grow more mystic day by day. Another nature whispers busily in their brains. It has held its breath too long and now the faery soul of things exhales everywhere. I find a rhymer in *United Ireland* inspired because of the new light in his country:–

> 'Once more the thrilling song, *the magic art*,
> Fill with delight.'

The week before I was carried into wonderland by another poet who describes a Sunset City, a flame-built dun of the gods high over Slieve Cullen. He was perhaps unaware of the ancient tradition which declares that below this mountain Creidené, the Smith of the Tuatha de Danaan, worked. What was his toil? Another of these Smiths, Culain, the foster-father of the hero Cuculain, had his forge in the recesses of Slieve Fuad. A third had his smithy at Loch Len, now Killarney, where he worked 'surrounded by a rainbow and fiery dews.' Were not these Smiths the same as the mighty Kabiri, most mysterious of deities, fire-gods from whose bright furnaces shot the glow, the sparks which enkindled nations. In ancient Eire their homes lay below the roots of the mountains. Will they, awakening from their cyclic reverie, renew their labours as of old? Last year, to one who, lying on the mound at Ros-na-ree, dreamed in the sunlight, there came an awakening presence, a figure of opalescent radiance who bent over crying, 'Can you not see me? Can you not hear me? I come from the Land of Immortal Youth!' This world of Tir-na-nogue, the heaven of the ancient Celt, lay all about them. It lies about us still. Ah, dear land, where the divine ever glimmers brotherly upon us, where the heavens droop nearer in tenderness, and the stones of the field seem more at league with us; what bountiful gifts of wisdom, beauty, and peace dost thou not hold for the world in thy teeming, expanding bosom, O, Eire! There is no death in the silence of thy immovable hills, for in their starhearts abide in composed calm the guardians of the paths through which men must go seeking for the immortal waters. Yes, they live, these hills.

A little while ago a quite ordinary man, a careless, drinking, unthinking sort of fellow, strayed upon one of them in holiday time and awoke out of a lazy dream on the hillside crying that the 'mountain was alive!' The unseen archers had pierced his heart with one of their fiery arrows. I record his testimony with delight and add thereto a vagrant tribute:-

> A friendly mountain I know:
> As I lie on the green slope there,
> It sets my heart in a glow
> And closes the door on care.
>
> A thought I try to frame:
> I was with you long ago:
> My soul from your heart-light came:
> Mountain, is that not so?
>
> Take me again, dear hills:
> Open the door to me
> Where the magic murmur fills
> The halls I do not see,
>
> Thy halls and caverns deep,
> Where sometimes I may dare
> Down the twilight stairs of sleep
> To meet the kingly there.
>
> Sometimes with flaming wings
> I rise unto a throne,
> And watch how the great star swings
> Along the saphhire zone.
>
> It has wings of its own for flight;
> Diamond its pinions strong,
> Glories of opal and white,
> I watch the whole night long.
>
> Until I needs must lay
> My royal robes aside,
> And toil in a world of gray,
> Gray shadows by my side,

And when I ponder it o'er
Gray memories only bide:
But their fading lips tell more
Than all the world beside.

There is no country in the world whose ancient religion was more inseparably connected with the holy places, mountains, and rivers of the land than Ireland, unless perhaps it be America. We may say it was shaped by the gods. They have left their traces in the streams and lakes which sprung forth at their command. A deity presided over each: their magical tides were fraught with healing powers for they were mixed with elemental fire at their secret sources. We read of strange transformations taking place, of demigods who become rivers or are identified with mountains. After the battle of Gabra, where the Finian chivalry were overthrown, Caolte, one of the most mystic and supernatural of the warriors stormed the hill of Assaroe and dwelt therein expelling a horde of elemental beings. He appears in after years and was supposed to have become one of the divine race of the Tuatha. He came to Mongan, a prince of Ulster three centuries later, and hailed him as an old companion: 'You were with me – with Finn.' Do not these strange transformations hint at some vast and grandiose beliefs about the destiny of the human soul? It may become a guardian of men, of a divine being, enthroning itself at one of those places where from the star-soul of earth the light breaks through into our shadowy sphere. Whenever I grow ambitious I think of Caolte at Assaroe, and long for a mountain of my own with plenty of fire to scatter about.

It may be because the land is so full of memorials of an extraordinary past, or it may be that behind the veil these things still endure, but every thing seems possible here. I would feel no surprise if I saw the fiery eyes of the cyclopes wandering over the mountains. There is always a sense expectant of some unveiling about to take place, a feeling, as one wanders at evening down the lanes scented by the honeysuckle, that beings are looking in upon us out of the true home of man. While we pace on, isolated in our sad and proud musings, they seem to be saying of us 'Soon they will awaken. Soon they will come again to us'; and we pause and look around smitten through by some ancient sweetness, some memory of a life-dawn pure before passion and sin began. The feeling is no less prophetic than reminiscent, and this may account for the unquenchable hope in the future of Ireland which has survived centuries of turbulence, oppression and pain, and which exists in the general heart.

In sleep and dream, in the internal life, a light from that future is thrown upon the spirit which is cheered by it, though unable to phrase to itself the meaning of its own gladness. Perhaps these visions, to which the Celt is so liable, refer as much to the future as to the bygone, and mysteries even more beautiful than the past are yet to be unfolded. I think it is so. There are some to whom a sudden sun-luster from Tir-na-nogue revealed a hill on the western shore overlooking the Atlantic. There was a temple with many stately figures: below at the sea's edge jetted twin fountains of the golden fire of life, and far off over a glassy calm of water rose the holy city, the Hy-Brazil, in the white sunlight of an inner day.

ON THE MARCH[1]

The civilized races are extending their influences in every direction. A little while ago the French thought well to take Madagascar. There is a general rush for what is left of Africa. The frontier war in India is doubtless prompted by the best motives, and it is the purest humanity on our part to burn the villages and leave thousands of women and children homeless. Our troops are thanked for the admirable way in which it is done, and the only complaint seems to be that of the editor of the morning paper who sits like a divinity in distant contemplation, that there are not enough details to make his columns of really absorbing interest. A tiny voice here and there makes its protest in pity, but the millions read on complacently. Are our human hearts turned to stone that we take these things so easily? They are done far away. But to the eyes divine these distant tribesmen are our brothers as much as those we meet day by day; and our own life is wounded in every blow that is struck at them, and our own spirit, the spirit of humanity, is hunted and homeless in them, and their misery so far from our eyes creeps in at our hearts where we know it not, but we walk weighted with a gloom which will not lift until we learn that all life is one, and far and near are lost in the living recognition.

* * * * *

It is policy; it is cruel; but it is necessary, we hear indeed confessed. Our first necessity then is to be cruel. It is a utopian belief, doubtless, that I hold, but I do not think there was a single war of all our petty wars but could have been avoided by simple kindness on our part. If we did not so contemptuously refer to them as 'niggers', and think of them as barbarians. They have not our material force, our inventions in use, our telegraphs, or our tall silk hats – so they are barbarians. I am a heretic in regard to these matters. I ask with Mitchell, who was told of the laying of the Atlantic cable: 'Will a lie told at one end come out truth at the other?' The spiritual question is the only really important one. What does it matter: the silk hat, if it only covers a brain scheming for gold; or our mighty cities if they are not beautiful; or our intertwisted social scheme if our hold on each other comes simply from sheer desperation and not from love? The womb of beauty is sterile for us and will not produce for all our gold; and our artists seek their loveliest effects of colour and form in painting the temples and cities of the barbarians, and find the most perfect models in their superb manhood; and our writers collect from their folklore more spiritual tales, more lofty imaginings, than are to be found in the brains of litterateurs nourished on Herbert Spencer and Huxley.

* * * * *

It is policy. Fearful word! When the actions of our statesmen are clearly against any kindly human ideal, when they are altogether inexplicable in men who use the name of Christ as their teacher, when they cannot be defended on any ideal ground whatever – this word 'policy' is heard, and people silently slur over the sin. The fact is that to men and women who have any ideals, our parliaments, our senates, and our governing bodies, are the last places where they expect to hear uttered the secret wishes of their hearts or any echo of their hopes. There is something deadly in the atmosphere of these places. Keen, shrewd, cynical, doubtless well-meaning, our public men may be; but the Oversoul has never made use of their lips as a trumpet, and none have guided the people to lofty aspirations as did the king-initiates in earth's day of glory. Their every step is based on statistics and not on inviolable right. How they would laugh and stare, these legislators of ours, if one stood up in their assembly and based his claim of justice for a people, not on material grounds, but because it was shameful that the immortal spirit of man, pregnant with divinity, should be hampered and confined. Yes, they might laugh, but such things will be said yet again and again:

> 'Slowly comes a hungry people as a lion drawing nigher,
> Glares at one who nods and winks behind a slowly dying fire.'

Out of the degradation and sorrow of life, in every human heart awakens at last like a lion the untamable spirit, making its universal claims even to the very stars. These voices, these ideals, must be heard finally in our senates and parliaments, and be triumphant at last, and avatars descending from the invisible shall reign. What we will must finally be. Let us nourish ourselves with and proclaim such hopes, for only a vast hope can arouse men from so vast a despair.

On The March

* * * * *

Avatars,[2] kingly souls once on earth, and now again returning with the wisdom of a greater day, and the world-spirit urgent within their wills. I seem to see in this confused transition period a plan whereto all is tending; a true social state with divine dynasties and solar heroes at its head, like those who ruled Egypt in its mystic beginning. Already spirits with such imperial instincts begin to appear amongst us, laying a deeper foundation for the spiritual revolution. Who was that mysterious woman[3] who flaunted her belief in gods and the dim giantesque cosmogonies of the past in the face of materialistic science, and illustrated her beliefs too with such prodigal power? Who was that quiet man[4] who began to familiarize America with the magical beliefs of the ancient world? Forerunners of others, or perhaps of themselves! Anyhow, since they spoke to us, we have become expectant; at every voice sounding a little deeper than ordinary we stare, trying to pierce the disguise of the king; and we guess tremendous destinies in the yet dreamy tender faces of children – empire, or that thorny crown men place on the brows of those who rule when life is done.

* * * * *

We are not deluded when we so question appearances. Every man is a god in disguise. Some few appear more immediately radiant than others, but the final emergence is sure. Even in the present darkness we can scarce restrain exultant voices when we think of the dawning, the dawning within, where on the mountain-tops of meditation golden figures begin to leap and call, and the final trumpet is eternally sounding for our resurrection. The future races will be allied with their kinsmen in spiritual spheres, for so the world traditions have it that men and gods were united in the past; what was will be again; our hearts confirm it, that is enough; we care not for the old weary reasoning based on the senses; the mystic proof of an idea is the light it sheds, for every true thought is electric and descends like a shower of stars into the black night of the mind.

* * * * *

Finally there is work to be done. To resume again our timelong labour:

> 'Each to the other outstretching a hand,
> We wove a vasty circle
> And within it we gathered the world.'

So a Celtic poet sings the building of earth by the gods. We, too, whose obscure divinity is betrayed to ourselves by the vastness of our dreams, must (our task still in its inception) each to the other outstretch a hand, and still hold out even to hands that will not close on the grasp; for we cannot forego the reverence and love due to men because they are forgetful or overwhelmed by the chaos they live in. Whether the star of life shines behind faces rich with dusky colour, or through paler races; whether it is dimmed in luxury or in poverty; whether in nations far or near, it is still a ray of the Light of Lights, and our being is inadequate if we do not blend heart with heart and flame with flame. Do not think because you are alone that you can accomplish nothing, for every thought and aspiration to the divine is something gained in the eternal struggle, a wandering fire captured and transmuted for the building in pure light of the temple of the eternal beauty.

G.W.R.

TRANSFORMATIONS[1]

It was said by one who is accounted a spiritual king among men that the shining world was only for those who could return to youth again. But what miracle could give to age and weariness the faery heart of childhood if youth be not an eternal thing, a spirit which flashes indeed with lightness and laughter through lips that are young, but is none the less present under the disguise of age – more, I think, to be loved, more evidently to be known as an immortal when it laughs behind wisdom and a mortality whose transience is clear. It was not childhood[2] the king meant, but that which we feel to be for ever young within us, and childhood is no nearer than age to that. We know, we know what it means when the world which had been still for a while, suddenly on some morning trembles and flings aside its mask of chill indifference: the winds flow on us with ethereal tenderness: the mountains make nothing of their size, but nod and call to us beyond the city's roofs and spires: we cannot pluck a flower, it is all too living, its life is too much a part of our joy, and all life appears but a game of hide and seek we play with ourselves. We concealed ourselves of old in the great as well as the little things: we smile up at the blue sky and the suddenly softening majesty of eternal things shows that we have pierced another disguise. I have always loved those stories where children move without fear, familiarly, in enchanted castles amid dread beings, wizards and dragons, who seem somehow forced to companionship with them by the spell of youth, for it is one of the three master spells in life – the names of the others are beauty and love.

If I phrase lightly or fancifully the terms of this new intimacy, it is because I cannot find words endearing enough in academic philosophy. I cannot speak in scientific language. Who would describe the descent of a god as a psychical researcher the apparition of an ordinary respectable citizen, or say when thrilled by intensest compassion, 'My consciousness is on such-and-such a plane of being'? What meets us in these flashes is the Spirit looking out of its universal home. I believe the poet to be nearer the truth than the scientist. His observation is subjective: and in a living universe everything said of nature is false which does not convey its opulent vitality even in barren wilds and the seeming vacuity of space. This gay spirit of youth in man makes him a poet, for its vision is of the life behind the veil. It sees the hills as stars and sees truly, and infinite elfin forms in the woodland, and every sorrow throbs with a hidden heart of joy; and, ah, what tender revelations about men and women! They must needs be pathetic, but they are inspired with such hope:

> This mood hath known all beauty, for it sees
> O'erwhelmed majesties
> In these pale forms, and kingly crowns of gold
> On brows no longer bold,
> And through the shadowy terrors of their hell
> The love for which they fell,
> And how desire which cast them in the deep
> Called God too from his sleep.
> O pity, only seer, who looking through
> A heart melted like dew,
> Sees the long-perished in the present thus
> All-seeing eye in us,
> Whatever time thy golden eyelids ope
> They travel to a hope,
> Not only backward from these low degrees
> To starry dynasties,
> But looking far where now the silence owns
> And rules from empty thrones,
> Thou seest the enchanted halls of heaven burn
> When we in might return.
> Thy tender kiss hath memory we are kings
> For all our wanderings:
> Thy shining eyes already see the after
> In hidden light and laughter.

It is years ago since I first heard of the Divine Eye,[3] and I marvelled what the fire-gaze might hold within it – suns, stars, and all the fiery populace of space in one manifold vision flashing suddenly upon the spirit. I think now we might look with the Divine Eye in every hour. Is not love another name for the spirit, and whoever with pure love beholds anything sees in that glance as the spirit sees. There are, I know, other mighty things which the first morning glances of love cannot perceive, but it is none the less the Eye of the Lord which looks through its eyes, and that soul travels most swiftly to infinite vision who is most readily compassionate. With it these transformations happen daily, placing crowns upon uncrowned brows, and in hitherto ignored beings it beholds the kingly spirit moulding with infinite patience and tenderness the heavy unwilling clay. It knows lastly, then, that nothing exists without the support of the Mighty, and it cannot choose but be at league with its fellows. To have this knowledge in the heart, however simply it phrases its wisdom to itself, is better than to have all the story of human thought and its philosophies in the brain. The mind overweighted with a cumbrous metaphysic grows cold and chill and grey, but listening to the voice in the heart we feel lifted on light wings. O Golden Bird, I am only thy shadow and dwell in a shadowy world. Give me thy star-touching pinions. Give me thy wider vision,

> 'That I may see beneath the common things of day
> Eternal Beauty wandering on her way.'

Æ.

THE CHRIST[1]
The Mythic Christ

An animated discussion is proceeding in the religious world over a book just translated from the German of Dr. Arthur Drews, entitled 'The Christ Myth.' In Germany it is more than a discussion, it is a controversy raging round the old distinctions of ecclesiasticism, and as such it has a fascination for the typical Teutonic mind, which is apt to be influenced by the ideals of commerce and of the physical sciences. Such minds place more importance on personalities than on principles, for they do not see that consciousness is the reality and the physical man of seventy years' duration in time has *per se* no elements of inspiration or greatness. Those who have experienced a bit of the other world within themselves, feel constantly the inadequacy of the physical environment for the expression of their real life, and to them no historical event nor person is of value except as such events or persons have helped humanity to realize its destiny. And the careful analysis of the actual conditions of the life of any person who has become the centre of a religion shows how much like the life of other human mortals must be the activity and environment of any *person*. The greatness that appeals lies not in the person, and only the intimate disciples ever perceive the Teacher. The Saviour in a religion emerges when the person has become obscured by time, and the world seeking salvation has built up an Ideal Man from the composite of ideals, expressed in the sayings of the historical sage. The Saviour never exists as a man. He arises from the imagination of our aspiring race. He is made by man's need.[2] He is constructed by the thoughts of blind humanity, who sense an inner realer world not perceived by the physical senses, but who yet do not know the futility of the search in the eternal world for the talismanic Word.[3]

And they who make such an Idol would never perceive the Ideal were the actual historical person to meet them or even to live with them;[4] they would be looking for that which is physically impossible; they would require signs and wonders[5] and expect a combination of qualities and perfections and god-like attributes which, in the nature of things, are not capable of complete expression in one *physical* personality.

So what is interesting to us in this erudite philosophical investigation of the basis of the Christian religion, is not the disproving of the historical Jesus which has been often attempted before, but the proving of the antiquity of the Christ Idea and its essential value to the race. The author says, 'We are indeed faced with the strange fact that all the essential part of the Gospels, everything which is of importance for religious faith, such as especially the passion, death and resurrection of Jesus is demonstrably invented and mythical; but such parts as can at best be historical because of their supposed "uninventable" nature are of no importance for the character of the Gospel representation.'

This leads us to ask why 'the passion, death and resurrection of Jesus,' though demonstrably invented and mythical, is the essential part of the gospels? Does it not suggest an inner mystical meaning of the physically disproved events? The real mystics in Christendom know this – know that 'the true and only Saviour of every man or woman is the self-knowledge of Divine Truth.'

The Coming Christ

The times and seasons[6] of this physical earth find their counterpart in every moment of life, in every phase of human activity. Life is always ebbing or flowing, and we are only stating a fact of cosmic activity when we say that spirituality is more vital in human consciousness at one time in the history of races than at another.

Looking over the religious and philosophical world just now we see many evidences of quickened interest in the deep things of the spirit, many signs which indisputably mean that men are once again, as so often in the past, seeking the Christ, the spiritual haven of storm-driven humanity. Man as a race has gone out exploring for a period. He has examined his nature as mirrored in the earth and the physical world. But now the leaders of men in the sciences are asserting the impossibility of further explaining the meaning of our physical and psychic environment, and the Infinite Spirit of humanity is returning upon itself and crying 'Let Thy Light shine!' 'The Christ, the Christ!' and on all levels of consciousness this cry for the revelation of the Christ is being heard. Where shall we find him? Will he come as a man? Will he live a personal life and teach a new religion and morality? Are we to look to the East for a sign? Yes, in the East may be seen His Star. But think you, who know the satiation and limitation of our physical experiences, that we can confine the Christ to a locality in space, or to one human form?

Are we not weary of the periodic attempts to found religions and build temples that but imperfectly express the wonderful Temple not made by hands? Let us glorify man and no longer try to dwarf him before some external presentation which at its best can be but a faint reflection of 'The Light that never was on Sea or Land.' Not on the waves of space may be seen the Master, *except as a symbol*; and those who have glimpsed the Reality, who have sat at the feet of the Teacher, must watch and pray lest they enter into temptation.

Always, as the currents increase in voltage, there is stirring in all the members, and consequent confusion due to pressure. We become bewildered. We cry, 'What does it mean? Is the Christ within or without?'[7]

The purpose of the revitalization of the spiritual forces in humanity, the purpose of the 'Coming of Christ' will not be consummated if these inner fires are not protected. If there are no disciples whose consciousness is purified for His reception, there will be no manger, no place for him, and he will not be able to come near to men. He cannot contact humanity if there is no spiritual body for His use.[8] The currents will not be able to pass into the outer world and animate the aspirations of those who long for a Saviour, if there is no focus supplied by devoted and responsive souls. And the power of any organization for religious purposes depends on the strength of this inner body, this 'esoteric section' of true believers.

Such a period as this is a test of our Faith in the Kingdom of Heaven. For many anti-Christs, many pseudo-Christs will appear in our vision before we discover the true Celestial Inhabitant of our own inner kingdom, and learn that He is a citizen of Heaven, not of earth.

Y.O.

APPENDIX A:

THE THEOSOPHICAL MOVEMENT

LODGES OF MAGIC[1]

Nothing that has yet appeared in your magazine has been so much in concord with my own humble views as your Editorial in the October Number on 'Lodges of Magic'.

I am not a *proclaimed* Theosophist. I do not belong to the Society. For some reasons I am sorry; for many reasons I am glad. And one of the most cogent of the latter is the almost certain degeneracy of any Society or Sect formed by mortal hands. I mean no disrespect to the founders of the T. S. They were animated by the purest motives; inspired by the noblest resolves.

But, being human, they cannot control the admission of members. They cannot read the heart, nor know the mind. And, consequently, the T. S. is not representative of Theosophy, but only of itself – a gathering of many earnest seekers after truth, many powerful intellects, many saints, and many sinners and lovers of curiosity.

If I have learned aright the lesson you have endeavoured to teach, it is this. That development must be harmonious, and must be unconscious.

The danger which attends the *desire to know* is that the knowledge to be gained too often becomes the goal of our endeavours, instead of being the means whereby to become perfect. And by 'perfect' I mean Union with the Absolute.

A young man, whose intellect is of the keenest, and with great power of assimilating and applying knowledge, is devoured by a desire to attain a lofty ideal. He feels there may be something beyond the facts of material science, beyond the anthropomorphic religions of the day.

Drifting into that mysterious current which is now flowing through the Century, he becomes attracted by Theosophy. For awhile he studies it with avidity, strives to live 'the life', to permeate himself with its teaching.

His intellect is satisfied for the time.

But, alas! he commits the fatal fault of forgetting that he has a soul. He does not, indeed, forget that *he* is immortal, but he neglects to feed his soul on spiritual things.

His science becomes wider, he grasps the idea of universality – and generally becomes a rank pessimist.

But, through the above-mentioned fault, Mystic Union with the Higher Self becomes more and more phantasmal. He recognises its necessity, but postpones the ordeal.

'First let me prove the lower realms of Nature,' he cries, and plunges into the phenomena of spiritualism, table rapping, and the evocation of spooks. He declares that Knowledge is Power, and carries his assertion to no further issue. He is remonstrated with. He replies that it is necessary to test all experience, and construes that axiom into a law that Karma is to be moulded and shaped by the conscious Ego. Carried to a logical conclusion, his rendering of the axiom would lead him into the lowest depths of vice to the hurt of his higher nature. He would seek in this transient incarnation to gratify every lust, passion and ideal of his personality. Whereas, surely the true meaning of the *Law* is that the Ego *must* of necessity taste of every experience in its progression up the Scale; *must* pass through every grade, ascend every step of the ladder.

It does not mean that when we know the good we must follow evil, nor that our higher must sometimes be actively degraded to the level of our lower self.

And so, step by step, it seems to me our neophyte wanders towards the broad path that leadeth to destruction. Confident that he is able to use the little knowledge he has gained, assured of his own powers, and disdainful of the terrors that lie in lurk for him, he goes on his way. His weapon is Self-Confidence and his armour Ignorance.

There is no turning back when once the path is trod, and the only hope is in his being vanquished in the *first* trial. Should he conquer his earliest foe, he will only meet a direr fate.

Now, is this Theosophy? If so, I will have none of it. I own I should like to see phenomena, to 'call spirits from the vasty deep' with success.* But I do not flatter myself that this longing is of a pure nature. If I did not sometimes wish to take a short cut to knowledge, I should not be a man *as we know him*. But I believe this desire after manifestation to be of the earth, earthy. With faith we can do all things, yet we should not desire *to do* all things, but simply to have the faith.

I recognise the essentiality of establishing the scientific basis of

---

* It is not in the Theosophical Society that our correspondent can ever hope to evoke spooks or see any *physical* phenomena. – [ED.]

Theosophy, of studying it from all sides. I do not wish to be merely a metaphysical mystic. I am sadly afraid, however, that most of us followers of Theosophy are but just out of our swaddling clothes. We must have our toys and picture books.

My ideal is to worship the One God in spirit and in truth. Is that the aim of the T.S.? ...*

I have expressed myself to you, not with any wish to see my feeble endeavour in print, nor from any presumptuous thought that I have written anything new or authoritative. Much less have I written in any carping or judging spirit. I have no right or desire to criticise people better than myself, but I feel it on me to ask for an assurance that the T.S. as a whole is doing the work it is meant to do – not merely expanding the Intellect of the World, but also drawing the Soul of Humanity towards its Higher Self.

A.E.

P.S.–Is not the 'Esoteric Section' of the T.S. likely to run counter to the views of your Editorial on Lodges of Magic? Who is to ensure that the Esoteric Members are not only willing to, but *will* 'abide by its rules'?

6th November, 1888 A.E.

NOTE

Our correspondent's question is a natural one – coming from a European. No, it does not run counter, because it *is not* a lodge of *magic*, but of *training*. For however often the true nature of the occult training has been stated and explained, few Western students seem to realize how searching and inexorable are the tests which a candidate must pass before *power* is entrusted to his hands. Esoteric philosophy, the occult hygiene of mind and body, the unlearning of false beliefs and the acquisition of true habits of thought, are more than sufficient for a student during his period of probation, and those who rashly pledge themselves in the expectation of acquiring forthwith 'magic powers' will meet only with disappointment and certain failure. – [Ed.]

LODGES OF MAGIC.

MADAM,–

I have only two remarks on your notes to my letter published in the December Number of LUCIFER. – (1.) I do not 'hope' to see spooks by the help of the Theosophical Society. My baser part

---

* 'There is no Religion higher than Truth' is the motto of our Society. – [ED.]

sometimes desires manifestation, but I recognize such desire to be impure. I earnestly trust no Member of the Society will ever indulge in the evocation of phenomena, whether for curiosity, or for the gratification of the intellect.

(2.) I asked if the worship of the One God in spirit and in truth was the aim of the Society. You reply with the motto of the Society. But your real answer appears to be in the opening article of the Magazine on Denunciation.

I candidly think the formation of the Society was a mistake. Not a mistake in motive, but a mistake in generalship. The speed of the slowest ship marks the rate of progress of a fleet. The weak ones of the Society mark its position in the world. But if the Society has only helped *one* brother to right living, then it has done much to justify its existence, and I have naught to say.

My real reason in again addressing you is to call your attention to a Novel written by A. de Grasse Stevens. At page 141 is a reference to yourself as a Russian spy who was ejected from India by Lord Dufferin.

I have never before seen this curious slander in print, and, although you may consider it beneath contempt, I think it a pity to allow it altogether to escape notice.

The reprehensible conduct of the Publishers in allowing an Author to libel a living person, and that person a woman, is such that I do not care to express my opinion on paper more fully than in this letter.

I am, your most *faithful* servant,

A. E.

REPLY.

The Theosophical Society has 'helped' many and many of its 'brothers' to 'right living' – and this is its proudest boast.

I thank our Correspondent for his kind remarks about me. With regard to publishers in general, their 'reprehensible conduct' may perhaps find an excuse in the great law of the 'struggle for life'; this species having always been known to feed and thrive on the carrion of murdered reputations. As to the authoress of this would-be politico-social novel, a rather *green* than young American, it is said, her exceptional claim to distinction from other trans-Atlantic writers of her sex, would seem to be an intimate acquaintance with the lobby and the back stairs of politics.

Apart from the half-dozen living people whose reputations she slaughters on a single page, what this political Amazon invents is that:–

Appendix A: The Theosophical Movement

'.... Mme. Blavatsky, for many years carried on a secret correspondence with Monsieur Zinovief (?!), chief of the Asiatic Department,' and that 'but *for Lord Dufferin's clear-sightedness* Madame might still be carrying on her patriotic work' – presumably in India.

LIES from the first word to the last. I never knew a 'Monsieur Zinovief,' nor corresponded with one at any time. I *defy* any government in the world to produce the slightest evidence, *even inferential*, that I have ever been a spy, or corresponded *secretly* with any Russian authority. As to Lord Dufferin he reached India only after I left it. As I have answered fully the infamous libel in the *Pall Mall Gazette* of January 3, I hope the public will leave this fresh lie to share the fate of the many that preceded it – in the waste-paper basket of literature.

H. P. BLAVATSKY.

A WORD UPON THE OBJECTS OF THE THEOSOPHICAL SOCIETY[2]

1st:- To form the nucleus of a Universal Brotherhood of Humanity, without distinction of race, creed, sex, caste or colour.
2nd:- To promote the study of Aryan and other Eastern literatures, religions, philosophies and sciences, and demonstrate the importance of that study.
3rd:- To investigate unexplained laws of nature and the psychic powers latent in man.

Started a little under a quarter of a century ago, in an age grown cold with unbelief and deadened by inexplicable dogmas, the Theosophical Society has found adherents numerous enough to make it widely known, and enthusiastic enough to give it momentum and make it a living force. The proclamation of its triple objects – brotherhood, wisdom and power, acted like a trumpet call, and many came forth to join it, emerging from other conflicts; and out of silence and retirement came many who had grown hopeless but who had still the old feeling at heart.

For the first object no explanation is necessary; but a word or two of comment upon the second and third may help to show how they do not weaken, by turning into other channels, the intellectual energies and will, which might serve to carry out the first. In these old philosophies of the East we find the stimulus to brotherly action which might not be needed in an ideal state, but which is a help to the many, who, born into the world with a coldness of heart as their heritage, still wish to do their duty. Now our duty alters according to our conception of nature, and in the East there has been put forward, by men whom we believe to be the wise and great of the earth, a noble philosophy, a science of life itself, and this, not as a hypothesis, but as truth which is certain, truth which has been verified by eyes which see deeper than ours, and proclaimed by the voices of those who have become the truth they speak of; for as Krishna teaches Arjuna in the Dnyanishvari, 'on this Path to whatever place one would go that place one's self becomes!' The last word of this wisdom is unity. Underneath all phenomena and surviving all changes, a great principle endures for ever. At the great white dawn of existence, from this principle stream spirit and primordial matter; as they flow away further from their divine source, they become broken up, the one life into countless lives, matter into countless forms, which enshrines these lives; spirit involves itself into matter and matter evolves, acted upon by this informing fire.

These lives wander on through many a cycle's ebb and flow, in separation and sorrow, with sometimes the joy of a momentary meeting. Only by the recognition of that unity, which spiritually is theirs, can they obtain freedom.

It is true in the experience of the race that devotion of any life to universal ends brings to that life a strange subtle richness and strength; by our mood we fasten ourselves into the Eternal; hence these historic utterances, declarations of permanence and a spiritual state of consciousness, which have been the foundation of all great religious movements. Christ says, 'I and my Father are one.' 'Before Abraham was I am.' Paul says, 'In him we live and move and have our being.'

In the sacred books of India it is the claim of many sages that they have recognised 'the ancient constant and eternal which perishes not though the body be slain,' and there are not wanting to-day men who speak of a similar expansion of their consciousness, out of the gross and material, into more tender, wise and beautiful states of thought and being. Tennyson, in a famous letter published some time ago, mentioned that he had at different times experienced such a mood; the idea of death was laughable; it was not thought, but a state, 'the clearest of the clearest, the surest of the surest.' It would be easy to go on multiplying instances.

Now in a nature where unity underlies all differences, where soul is bound to soul more than star to star; where if one falters or falls the order of all the rest is changed; the duty of any man who perceives this unity is clear, the call for brotherly action is imperative, selfishness cannot any longer wear the mask of wisdom, for isolation is folly and shuts us out from the eternal verities.

The third object of the Society defined as 'the study of the psychic powers latent in man' is pursued only by a portion of the members, those who wish to understand more clearly the working of certain laws of nature and who wish to give themselves up more completely to that life in which they live and move and have their being; and the outward expression of the occult life is also brotherhood.

G.W.Russell, F.T.S.

TO THE FELLOWS OF THE THEOSOPHICAL SOCIETY[3]

March 26th, 1894.

Dear Brothers, – The time is now approaching when your delegates must again consider what is best to be done in this matter which has so long divided us. Statements have been made, and denials of these statements, and we have had time to reflect on the futility of both. I think there is scarcely one whose opinion has been changed. Those who accuse have remained in their first attitude, and those who said 'not guilty' say so still. Now all this is because each man fashions in his own way a soul behind every body or circumstance. It is impossible to acquire the certainty of right action when we judge from material evidence alone. Behind all we say or show lurk the infinite possibilities of occult nature; and I say that, unless our differences can be settled by an appeal to first principles, then our union as members in this Society was premature and a mistake, for we have had no real bond of union. But, before considering the principles which we all avow, I would like to emphasize and illustrate the impossibility for those who live only in this side of nature to have any real assurance that they are in the right as to what is beyond. I will take but two instances, though it would be possible to go through every detail of the evidence brought forward. A point which was strongly urged by Mrs. Besant, which was, indeed, the main feature in her statement and her chief ground of complaint, was that Mr. Judge wrote with his own hand, but in the handwriting of the Master, a message which he gave to her as Master's. It may be so. I cannot say. But, if written by his hand, is there any necessity to assume guilt? Who can say what was behind the hand that wrote, the will of the Adept or the will of Mr. Judge? Only the trained occultist who sees on other planes could say with certainty. I notice that not one of the accusers is in that position, for, so far as I am aware, no one has said, 'I know,' though many believe him guilty. To illustrate still further this uncertainty: it has been urged against the statement that he was forewarned of the private nature and the future hostile action of individuals, that he did yet at the same time show the most ample trust in them by letters offering aid in special furtherance of their projects. He may have done so. I cannot say. But if it is so, must we necessarily make the implication that the insight was at fault and the guidance did not exist? I can imagine in such a case that one could see hostility and foresee future defection as possible but yet not abate love or act otherwise than with the confidence of those who are blind beyond the hour. I am afraid there are but few would do it, for there are so few who have imagined it. But a great heart might so act for its own sake or the sake of others. It is always possible for one to rise above 'his stars'. Some word of love or trust might awaken the soul, whose attribute is freewill, to rise above the stream of tendency, and for this or for its own sake a great heart would abate nothing of its human kindness. It is a height which might be reached, and while I can so imagine it I shall not lessen the boundaries of my belief. For why should we choose to think the evil thing rather than the good? We – some of us at least – should have grown wiser, for we have had one such lesson before. I call to mind a letter of H.P.B.'s, which some could and did cry over. It was written with all the shame and pain of a noble heart forced to confess its own generosity, and to explain to pigs (myself one) who could not fathom the absoluteness of such a love, why it was that, with all her powers of insight, she seemed so often to be betrayed. She said in effect: I was bound to the ethics of those Masters of whom I am pupil and witness; and she illustrated by an aphorism that superb reliance upon the laws of life with which the occultist relinquishes worldly wisdom and expediency. It said that they who, from fear of danger to themselves, turn away from rather than feed and warm a hungry serpent, depart from the Law of Compassion. It said in effect what has been again reiterated, 'that our only justice is compassion'. If she had taught us nothing more she would still have earned our undying gratitude. Every act of the true Teacher is an application to human life of divine ideals. It is a hint at angelic laws. The very darkness of those great souls sheds a light on us, for their hearts are torn by a grief and love we do not comprehend. Their tears reveal a world-wide compassion. Their pain has a deep significance; for perhaps our sad souls, which look no more on the eternal Beauty, can easier read the mystery told in tears and understand sorrow better than joy. Be this as it may, it is still a terrible thing to crucify the Christ-Soul when it appears; even though through its torture come the revelation of transcendent laws and burning love – the nature of the Lions of the Flaming Heart.

And so, as there lies behind every act the possibility of a dual interpretation, we will never be enabled to judge of the right or wrong from appearances. The Great Ones, who with eyes of serene

Appendix A: The Theosophical Movement

regard look beyond the turmoil of the moment, wave aside such petty considerations. They await the verdict of the Law, which is most swift and irresistible in spiritual things. But we – who are not all agreed and have not this vision – are we then to be at strife for ever? Is there not some ground whereon we can at least *agree* to differ without anger? I think there is such a ground. Let us examine it.

At the initiation of this Society there were two great principles laid down by the founders, and adhesion to these was the essential condition of fellowship. By one of these it was declared that the utmost toleration should be shown for the beliefs of others. The second laid it down as a necessity that all who entered should have, or profess, a real desire for the welfare of the race. On these two great principles – the principles of Freedom and Brotherhood – we are avowedly agreed. Let us consider them with reference to the present crisis. Let us determine that, come what may, they shall not be broken. And first as to Freedom, the desire for which lies at the root of our self-conscious individual being – thought which for ever inspires; at this sacred watchword nations have risen up maddened and exultant, and the clang of martial arms has been heard, and the stony kings of the past been encountered in battle. I think we will have for ever to wage this battle. With other arms maybe; perhaps with the tender yet terrible breath of love we shall overthrow our foes, as to-day we strive with mind and tongue and pen for this old cause. Now one of the aspects which comes up most before us is the clamour against the psychic element in our nature. The demand for its repression has passed from the stage of moral disapproval to actual threats that the Society shall be purified completely. 'We shall have no physical phenomena.' I confess that at first to me all this was extremely laughable. I saw a vision of the ideal F.T.S. with all his chakras locked and labelled, 'No physical phenomena permitted.' But it is not a matter for laughter only. It is much graver. It means this: that a man shall not dare to use the powers which are his heritage as a being of divine descent; that he shall not dare to live his own life and do the deeds he would unless he explains how all is done, and tears open his heart and soul and reveals the things he holds most sacred for the satisfaction of the curious, the sceptic, the materialist. If he refuses his silence will be taken as evidence of guilt. It means also – if this clamour is successful – that we shall create a precedent, that we shall drive back into the darkness those who have broken the silence of ages, and essayed to teach a sense-soddened people that they are divine – that they are GODS, if they but will it so. And those who come forth as Teachers – shall we say to them. 'Do not use your powers to help us. Do not touch our souls within. Speak to us in the comon way. Teach us with manuals. Inspire us with lectures.' I tell you he is no real Teacher who cannot rise beyond the world of sense and darkness, and awaken the links within us from plane to plane; who cannot see within the heart what are its needs, and who has not the power to open the poor blind eyes and to touch the ears which have heard no sound of the heavenly harmonies. I say, he must be a MAGICIAN; he must know and exert power over the psychic world which you condemn because you yourselves are condemned by it, and shut out from it, and do not know your own souls at all. Shall we, then, ask our leaders, those who have loved and toiled and suffered for us, to explain point by point their action, to make all square. If we think to do this, we have tried too soon to enter the Path. We can never comprehend the actions of great natures by our reason; but they come that we may exercise our intuitions with regard to them. 'The wind bloweth where it listeth, and thou hearest the sound thereof, but canst not tell whence it cometh and whither it goeth; so is every one that is born of the Spirit.'

But you have the right to speak and express your doubts. That has never been denied. I would make in this matter the largest allowances for good intentions, and this without any mental reservation. Perhaps Mrs Besant was justified in bringing forward her suspicions and frankly stating them. It is better, much better, to be openly suspicious than to hide a secret fear of wrong. But it seems to me that with this statement her duty *ended*. Yet she has gone far beyond this. For – although by far the largest Section of the Society is united in its trust of Mr. Judge, thinking as one mind and loving as one heart, and although there are Branches and many scattered members elsewhere who share this confidence – she still pushes her attack, uses her influence, her eloquence, her weight; and when the members of the Indian Section clamour for the expulsion and disgrace of one whom their brothers love, I say IT IS A VIOLATION OF THE PRINCIPLE OF FREEDOM IN OUR RANKS, and I call upon all true men and women to rise up and protest against it.

Now think how greatly necessary it is that the soul should have freedom. I do not mean merely the freedom of life and of limb. This is less important. I mean the freedom of the soul, that it may choose its own heroes and ideals; may live its own life unfettered save by the rights of others – which are still its own rights. If we leave the body free to act as it will, and yet go away in our souls full of bitterness or scorn, we allow no real freedom, for we do still enchain our brother by our will. We confine him within the narrow boundary of our own expansion. We burn his soul inwardly by our hatred at its course. What even if it goes astray? It is taught by pain; it is purified

Appendix A: The Theosophical Movement 663

by suffering; it learns the truth in the only way truth can be learned – by living into it. And this is better than that it should rise up in mad revolt, and cry out against the world it was born in, and wreck itself in rage because debarred of that freedom for which it left its starry home.

And now as to Brotherhood. A brotherhood of men and women; vision ideal, the hope of generations of noble minds; it comes forth at last and we are at once put to the test. Are we to break the heart for the heart's own sake? Are we to refuse to now apply our talisman of love for some further good to be attained? Are we to deny our own share in another's life, no matter how dark? This is really what all the talk about purifying the Society comes to. Oh, aristocrats in virtue! dowered with all the Paramitas! a hemisphere is not far enough apart from vice but it still will soil your souls? Can you not rest satisfied with your mental isolation? Must you proclaim to the world the gulf between yourselves and such iniquity? I would not willingly debar myself from brotherhood with Satan, for what we call evil is half of the life of the embodied Self – the Deity. It is on this universal nature of the soul that all true brotherhood rests. For this of old the Christ-Spirit moved among publicans and sinners and lost no trace of its spotless purity. Perhaps it manifests with added wisdom in those who say we will have no more to do with one who is almost proved to be 'fraud, a liar, and a forgerer'. Let the purification be more complete. Separate all round. There are worse than he who has at least built up a hundred Lodges. I confess to greater sins than he is charged with; to years smothered with sensuality, lurid with anger, wrinkled with meanness, dark with fear. Why should I try to pose as among the elect? I will engage to find a hundred others in the Society who will state along with me that what he is charged with is nothing to what they have done. But we yet gravitate towards the spiritual, we comprehend dimly that greater life and the change it necessitates. Because I find in myself those things I would arise and fly from I make this protest, knowing what the needs of the soul are when it is quivering with pain at its own evil fate. Oh, to be so assailed and tortured! Or to be promised a condescending pardon: 'Confess all. Justify our suspicions. Vindicate our action. Then all will be forgiven and forgotten.' Amongst those who profess nothing it might pass. But in a Society which stands before the world as bringing a sweeter, kindlier, more tender, human creed – ah, God! it makes one feel sick to think of it!

And now I hope those great hearts will pardon us who have discussed their merits in time past and to-day. I hold it no less unethical to praise than to blame. For to raise questions of merit or demerit is to create vortices around the soul which may suck it into the gulf of personality. I call all to witness that it is not we who defend who have initiated this controversy, but those who attack. But a few words more. I have spoken of the psychic plane, and defended the right to openly use powers or teach in whatsoever way most reaches the heart. I have no particular affection for the psychic above all other planes. It is true H. P. B. warned us against its attractions; but she warned us against many other things also. She did not wish to debar us from any field of nature, but wrote over every portal we would enter, 'Be ye wise.' And one thing is clear ; we shall never acquire power in any other way than by its use. Millenniums of metaphysical meditation or study of *The Secret Doctrine* will never bring us to that state where the mystic Power will spring on us and recreate us Gods. Do not protest too much against phenomena, fraught with danger as they are. The issue is now before you. Will we as a community follow the absolute ideal good hitherto attained only by individuals, or must worldly expediency outweigh every higher consideration. This is the issue, and I for one think it is better than the Society should perish than that the right should not be done.

GEO. W. RUSSELL, F.T.S.

3. Upper Ely Place, Dublin.

ON THE SPUR OF THE MOMENT[4]

I am minded to put down some intuitions about brotherhood and trust in persons. A witty friend writes, 'Now that I have made up my mind, I intend looking at the evidence.' A position like that is not so absurd as at first it seems. It is folly only to those who regard reason alone and deny the value of a deep-seated intuition. The intuitive trust which so many members of the T.S. have in William Q. Judge, to my mind shows that he is a real teacher. In their deepest being they know him as such, and what is knowledge there becomes the intuition of waking hours. When a clamour of many voices arises making accusations, pointing to time, place and circumstance; to things which we cannot personally investigate, it is only the spirit within us can speak and decide. Others with more knowledge may give answering circumstances of time, place and act; but, with or without these, I back up my intuition with the reason – where the light breaks through, there the soul is pure. Says a brother truly:

'The list of his works is endless, monumental; it shows us an untiring soul, an immense and indomitable will, a total ignoring of himself for the benefit of his fellow-members. This is not the

Appendix A: The Theosophical Movement

conduct of the charlatan, nor of the self-seeker. It is that of one of those brave and long-tried souls who have fought their way down through the vistas of time so that they might have strength to battle now for those who may be weaker.'

Others may have been more eloquent and learned, but who has been so wise? Others may have written more beautifully, but who with such intimations of the Secret Spirit breathing within? Others have explained intellectually tattvas, principles and what not, but who like him has touched the heart of a hidden nobility? Has he not done it over and over again, as here?

'Do what you find to do. Desire ardently to do it, and even when you shall not have succeeded in carrying out anything but some small duties, some words of warning, your strong desire will strike like Vulcan upon some other hearts in the world, and suddenly you will find that done which you had longed to be the doer of. Then rejoice that another has been so fortunate as to make such a meritorious Karma.'

Or he speaks as a hero:

'To fail would be nothing, but to stop working for Humanity and Brotherhood would be awful.'

Or as one who loves and justifies it to the end:

'We are not Karma, we are not the law, and it is a species of that hypocrisy so deeply condemned by it for us to condemn any man. That the law lets a man live is proof that he is not yet judged by that higher power.'

To know of these laws is to be them to some extent. 'What a man thinks, that he is, that is the old secret.' The temple of Spirit is inviolate. It is not grasped by speech or by action. 'Whom the Spirit chooses, by him it is gained. The Self chooses his body as its own.' When the personal tumult is silenced, then arises the meditation of the Wise within. Whoever speaks out of that life has earned the right to be there. No cunning can simulate its accents. No hypocrisy can voice its wisdom. Whose mind gives out light – it is the haunt of the Gods. Does this seem too slight a guarantee for sincerity, for trust reposed? I know of none weightier. Look back in memory; consider how you have gained the truths you hold most sacred. Out of the martyrdom of opposing passions, out of the last anguish came forth the light. It was no cheap accomplishment. If some one meets us and speaks knowing of that law, we say inwardly, 'I know you have suffered, brother!' But here is one with a larger wisdom than ours. Here is one whose words to-day have the same clear ring. 'The world knows him not.' His own disciples hardly know him: he has fallen like Lucifer. But I would take such teaching as he gives from Lucifer himself and say, 'His old divinity remains with him still.'

'After all you may be mistaken,' someone says. 'The feet of no one are set infallibly on the path.' It may be so. Let us take that alternative. Can we reject him or any other as comrades while they offer? Never. Were we not taught to show to those on whom came the reaction from fierce effort, not cold faces, but the face of friendship, waiting for the wave of sure return? If this was a right attitude for us in our lesser groups, it is then right for the whole body to adopt. The Theosophical Society as a whole should not have less than the generous spirit of its units. It must exercise the same brotherly spirit alike to those of good or evil fame. Alike on the just and the unjust shines the Light of It, the Father-Spirit. Deep down in our hearts have we not all longed, longed, for that divine love which rejects none? You who think he has erred, it is yours to give it now. There is an occult law that all things return to their source, their cycles accomplished. The forces we expend in love and anger come back again to us thrilled with the thought which accepted or rejected them. I tell you, if worse things were true of him than what are said, if we did our duty simply, giving back in gratitude and fearfulness the help we had received from him, his own past would overcome the darkness of the moment, would strengthen and bear him on to the light.

'But,' some push it further; 'it is not of ourselves, but of this Society and its good name, we think. How can it accomplish its high mission in the world if we seem to ignore in our ranks the presence of the insincere person or fraud?'

I wish, my brothers, we could get rid of these old fears. Show, form, appearance and seeming, what force have they? A faulty face matters nothing. The deep inner attitude alone has power. The world's opinion implicates none of us with the Law. Our action may precipitate Karma, may inconvenience us for an hour; but the end of life is not comfort but celestial being; it is not in the good voice of the world to-day we can have any hope: its evil voice may seem to break us for a little; but love, faith and gratitude shall write our history in flame on the shadowy aura of the world, and the Watchers shall record it. We can lose nothing; the Society can lose nothing. Our only right is in the action, and half the sweetness of life consists in loving much.

While I wrote, I thought I felt for a moment the true spirit of this pioneer body we belong to. Like a diver too long under seas, emerging I inhaled the purer air and saw the yellow sunlight. To think of it! what freedom! what freshness! to sail away from old report and fear and custom, the daring of the adventurer in our hearts, having reliance only upon the laws of life to justify and sustain us.

Æ.

Appendix A: The Theosophical Movement

To the Editor of LUCIFER[5]

3. UPPER ELY PLACE, DUBLIN.
February 16th, 1895.

I observe that Mrs. Besant in LUCIFER, February issue, refers to the letter from a Master published in vol. ix, p.5. She seems to imply that the ethical principle on which the defence of Mr. Judge was based is contradicted by the teaching of the Master. I read the letter and thought of Blake's lines:-

> Thy heaven doors are my hell-gates.
> Both read the same book day and night,
> But you read black where I read white.'

Here are the Master's words. To my mind the meaning is clear, unmistakably clear:-
'The majority of the public Areopagus is generally composed of self-appointed judges, who have never made a permanent deity of any idol save their own personalities – their lower selves; for those who try in their walk in life to follow their *inner light* will never be found judging, far less condemning, those weaker than themselves.'

Here, too, is a clearly-defined principle:-

'*As an association* it has not only the right but the duty to uncloak vice and do its best to redress wrongs, whether through the voice of its chosen lecturers, or the printed words of its journals and publications – making its accusations, however, as impersonal as possible. But its Fellows, or members, have *individually* no such right. Its followers have, first of all, to set the example of a firmly outlined and as firmly applied morality, before they obtain the right to point out, even in a spirit of kindness, the absence of a like ethic unity and singleness of purpose in other associations or individuals. *No Theosophist should blame a brother, whether within or outside of the Association; neither may he throw a slur upon another's actions or denounce him, lest he himself lose the right to be considered a Theosophist.*'

These are grand words, and *they are not qualified*. May I also quote some words which Mrs. Besant once uttered in a more generous spirit than that which prompted her to call upon Mr. Judge for an explanation and defence. In LUCIFER, vol. v, p. 52, she is reported thus:-

'It is one of the rules of Theosophy that you must not use your power merely to defend yourself. (Laughter.) Permit me to say there is nothing laughable in that. You may not have the courage to do it, you may not have the heroism, but there is nothing greater than those who can stand attack, and remain silent under it. (Loud applause.)'

These words rang in my heart when I read them first. They need no comment of mine to show their application to-day. It is well in the midst of adventure and battle to recall forgotten wisdom and ideals which gave us early inspiration. I hope that it is not too much to ask that these words be again reprinted. Perhaps at the third call some may be aroused to question themselves, for the great principles of freedom and brotherhood are now before them, to choose or to reject. – Fraternally,

GEO. W. RUSSELL.

A BASIS FOR BROTHERHOOD[6]

Many have wondered how the study of ancient religions, philosophies and sciences, and the knowledge of the psychic powers latent in man, could in any way help forward that universal brotherhood, to work for which is the foremost aim of the Theosophical Society. In an ideal state, the love of a man for his comrade would be natural, and without motive; love would be part of life. But we have so far departed from the elemental attributes of being, that I do not slander men when I say that it is much easier to be indifferent than interested; our hates are more passionate than our loves. For one born into an age with universal coldness of heart as his heritage, but one thing remains, and that is to do his duty.

Now our conception of duty must depend upon our knowledge, and he to whom this last wish remains, must study the development of society, and the nature of the units of which it is composed. I do not think that there can be found any real basis for altruism in the speculations of modern science.

It coldly shows the necessity of coöperation in order that the Self may exist, but there is nothing in such a knowledge to give birth to that divine heroism which flings self-interest aside, when the interests of others are concerned. I do not mean to say that among materialists heroism does not exist; we all know it does, but it is in spite of their creed, and because man in his essence is good, not evil. One feels a strange reverence arise for that which has worked unceasingly for others, with no chilling of tenderness because no reward, or fruition of life, seemed possible in the hereafter. How many of those whose names are foremost now in philanthropic effort because their creed promises them much, would work as Charles Bradlaugh did, and as others have done, if they too had no

Appendix A: The Theosophical Movement 669

belief in a future state? I had better not think it out. Returning to those whose opinions are founded upon the theories of modern science alone, I say, if love does not already exist, there is nothing in their creed which would make altruism a duty – that which ought from the nature of things to be done. We must look elsewhere for a conception of a nobler scheme of things. Having satisfied ourselves that little light can be thrown upon our spiritual life by a study of force and matter alone, we should make sure that we have reasons for our belief in spirit, and that it is not a mere will-o-the-wisp we are following.

The examination of a few of the simpler experiments in hypnotism, if well considered will, I think, be sufficient for this purpose. They show clearly that within the mind there are agencies at work which the physicist cannot explain; factors in the evolution of man undreamt of by the Darwinian; for it is clear that in the scheme of development conceived of by Darwin, where the life evolved departs suddenly from the normal line, there is no provision made for intellectual sanity or clearness of vision. Hypnotic experiments show, on the contrary, that people who in the normal condition are ignorant or dull, show great powers of imagination; the faculty of vision becomes something almost miraculous in its acuteness, and there is a similar increase of intensity in the other faculties. This is beyond question, and is quite sufficient as evidence without investigating any of the rarer phenomena, such as clairvoyant vision, diagnosis of disease, or the appearance of the 'double'. The development of these powers not being due to conscious effort on the part of the individual who displays them, they must belong to a different stream of evolution. To put it shortly, while matter has been evolving upwards, ever tending towards rarer and finer forms and essences, capable of interpreting spirit; spirit has been involving itself into matter, following a line of development of its own, and it is from a knowledge of these forces, so potent for good or for evil, that our conceptions of duty must arise, and the brotherhood of humanity be built up in the ages to follow ours.

The methods of investigation employed in Europe, admirable for their accuracy in dealing with physical things, have been most barren of result touching the problems of life and mind. We meet everywhere confessions of inability to determine their character; they fall within the region of the 'unknowable'. Confessedly, then, as the bridge between mind and matter is impassable to the scientist, we must adopt other than material instruments and means in our search; and here the study of ancient literatures, sciences and religions helps us. The ern scientific investigator has, in his search, gone further and further away from the primeval fountain of life, and sits bewildered amid deserts of barren matter of his own creation, while those to whom matter has been but a passing illusion, have laid hold of the eternal.

I do not propose to make any analysis of the different religious systems. In their essence they are identical, though they differ somewhat from each other in the application of their ideal to life and conduct. They all postulate one universal, eternal life, from which all things proceed. This life periodically manifests, and as it outbreathes a great drama begins, in which Gods and men take part; worlds are generated, sphere within sphere,

> And beauty, wisdom, love and youth,
> By its enchantment gathered grow
> In age-long wandering to the Truth,
> Through many a cycle's ebb and flow.

From this it would follow that all life in its essence is one, and we should therefore expect to find that, the more spiritual self-consciousness was aroused, the more this unity would be felt, and from a deeper life there would come a wider vision.

It would seem that there is a law in these things; that every man must *become* for himself that life before he *knows* its meaning. But this at least he can know: that the way is clear. With the multitude of things observed by men of science, there is not one fact which contradicts this unity of life, and the intimate connection between mind and mind. In the *Journal of the Psychical Research Society,* January, 1884; we find that Society claims 'to have proved the reality of thought transference; of the transmission of thoughts, feelings, and images from one mind to another by no recognized channel of sense.' It has been no hasty conclusion; hundreds of the most carefully conducted experiments have proved that this psychic connection between mind and mind is no mere theory, but a fact in nature. Thoughts, feelings and images are communicable, not alone by speech and gesture, but also by the inherent energy of silent will. These do not pass in a miraculous way without bridge or medium of communication. A substance which we may call ether is diffused through space; it receives and registers these images generated in the mind, and its currents are capable of being controlled and directed by the will. This is the memory of nature, the 'book of life' of the Apocalypse. It is a vast storehouse in which are garnered up all the thoughts and feelings of men; not an action is unnoticed. All that is noble, all that is base; the god-like visions of the poet; love and consuming hatred; strange fantasies; the brooding of despair;

all that men desire, are caught and pictured in this universal ether which surges around and breaks in upon the consciousness of men.

W. Q. J.[7]

O hero of the iron age,
Upon thy grave we will not weep,
Nor yet consume away in rage
For thee and thy untimely sleep.
Our hearts a burning silence keep.

O martyr, in these iron days
One fate was sure for soul like thine:
Well you foreknew but went your ways.
The crucifixion is the sign,
The meed of all the kingly line.

We may not mourn – though such a night
Has fallen on our earthly spheres
Bereft of love and truth and light
As never since the dawn of years:-
For tears give birth alone to tears.

One wreath upon thy grave we lay
(The silence of our bitter thought,
Words that would scorch their hearts of clay),
And turn to learn what thou has taught,
To shape our lives as thine was wrought.

It is with no feeling of sadness that I think of this withdrawal. He would not have wished for that. But with a faltering hand I try to express one of many incommunicable thoughts about the hero who has departed. Long before I met him, before even written words of his had been read, his name like an incantation stirred and summoned forth some secret spiritual impulse in my heart. It was no surface tie which bound us to him. No one ever tried less than he to gain from men that adherence which comes from impressive manner. I hardly thought what he was while he spoke; but on departing I found my heart, wiser than my brain, had given itself away to him; an inner exaltation lasting for months witnessed his power. It was in that memorable convention in London two years ago that I first glimpsed his real greatness. As he sat there quietly, one among many, not speaking a word, I was overcome by a sense of spiritual dilation, of unconquerable will about him, and that one figure with the grey head became all the room to me. Shall I not say the truth I think? Here was a hero out of the remote, antique, giant ages come among us, wearing but on the surface the vesture of our little day. We, too, came out of that past, but in forgetfulness; he with memory and power soon regained. To him and to one other we **owe an** unspeakable gratitude for faith and hope and knowledge **born again.** We may say now, using words of his early years: 'Even **in hell** I lift up my eyes to those who are beyond me and do not deny them.' Ah, hero, we know you would have stayed with us if it were possible; but fires have been kindled that shall not soon fade, fires that shall be bright when you again return. I feel no sadness, knowing there are no farewells in the True: to whosoever has touched on that real being there is comradeship with all the great and wise of time. That he will again return we need not doubt. His ideals were those which are attained only by the Saviours and Deliverers of nations. When or where he may appear I know not, but I foresee the coming when our need invokes him. Light of the future æons, I hail, I hail to thee!

Æ.

STAND AND SERVE[8]

Let us respect and follow the true. Let us practise the sterling virtue of keeping company with our truest state of consciusness; that state that was discovered to us for a brief space, by the Fire in the Heart, when we threw in our lot with the Theosophical Movement. At that time we were determined to *stand* and *serve*. By the magic of the living Love let us retain that heroic determination.

The sorrow of battle is in complete victory. Not ours yet that passing sorrow, but the joy of the fight. Sound, then, the bugle-note of effort ever renewed. Voice the Leaders' call to follow. Heed the simple regulations of the army.

We will be unselfish; unselfish enough to be loyal. – G.R.

WORD AND THEORY[9]
TO THE EDITOR OF THE ETHICAL ECHO.

I have read with interest the discussion between C. W. and Mr Dick. C.W. declares that the attractive force in spiritual or religious theory does not differ in kind but only in degree from the attractive force in great literature. But surely to think so is to 'lose the sense of subtle distinctions' he lays so much stress upon. He instances the Divine Comedy as great literature, and though this to a great extent deals with religious theory, and so makes the distinction more

Appendix A: The Theosophical Movement 673

difficult of realisation, still we may accept it. Now there the really attractive force lies where it deals with the things men have already achieved, it touches the chords already touched, we are gratified by the expansion of emotions we already possess, and by the dilation of thought; the attractive force is almost purely mental.

But in spiritual or religious theory it is quite different; it is a thing *sui generis*, for it seeks, that is when it is true religion, to reveal the path to pure being, and to hint in such a way at the nature of consciousness, that we are drawn away more and more from interest in its manifestation as mind or emotion, to penetrate into that pure being which is the basis of all.

The theory of Re-incarnation, then, which implies an eternal spiritual being with a power of entering or permeating with part of itself a material form, in order to acquire experience, will have an interest for the spiritual mind quite distinct from the interest awakened by literature; its power is over the whole nature, not over the mind or emotions merely, for the mystic will seek to adjust his life to the needs of the Immortal within him, and by means of action, devotion, sacrifice, and deference to the eternal purpose, endeavour to draw out the latent unrealised being, and so unite the divine and human consciousness. Surely C. W. will admit the difference of the attractive force where acquired faculties are gratified, and in the case where these are subdued or readjusted in the hope of a yet unrealised being.

C. W. wishes to know what value Re-incarnation has as fact other than its value as theory. As theory, it leads to the adjustment of the nature to exalted ideals; as a realised truth it is the uncommunicable consciousness of eternal being; and here C.W. becomes as dogmatic in assertion as the Theosophist he condemns, and with less reason: he says this 'cannot be verified as facts are verified.' How does he know it is unverifiable? because when realised it is uncommunicable; because it is a theory each man must prove for himself. It seems to me that the facts of life and consciousness are the only facts we can verify, and all else is theory. How are the truths about human nature verified? Is it not by participation in that nature? Will thought alone do it? It will not. No ordinary man can, by thinking, understand the force of that mystic passion for the ideal which exalts some men into martyrs and heroes, for he must become in order to know; he will have to endure all sacrifice and action like them ere he in turn can understand the martyr's fire. It is because experience in life is more necessary than thought for the comprehending of these things, that Mr. Dick spoke of years of effort and experiment, and C. W. wishes to know what bearing this has upon the question at issue. Now there is a method of proving Re-incarnation; but it is not by mere thinking, nor by a critical analysis of consciousness: thought, and a knowledge of science and psychology may lead to the point where the theory appears the most reasonable or logical of theories; but it cannot lead beyond that point, nor grasp a truth greater than itself. Those who wish to prove it will have to make, during their lifetime, the complete sacrifice of the personal nature for the needs of soul. The way is always open.

With regard to the various theories about Heaven which C. W. thinks are mutually destructive; I think that it is quite possible that all may be true for the individuals holding them. Does he forget the famous line –

'Heaven's but the vision of fulfilled desire?'

C. W. must regard heaven as a material region, in which case his objection would be valid; but if it is looked upon as a subjective state of consciousness, then there is nothing improbable in the supposition that the mind when released from the restraint and clog of matter, goes on thinking, and aspiring, and realises for itself the ideals conceived on earth. It is quite conceivable that this is one of the states of *post-mortem* consciousness; and I think it is possible, by methods which it is out of place to indicate here, to come into contact with these dreaming souls, and so verify the truth of the Eastern Devachan. In conclusion, I think that the methods of literary criticism which C. W. applies to life and religion are quite inadequate for the purpose; the mind can only judge the things it is mindful of, and the final test of truth in these things is to have lived through them.

GEO. W. RUSSELL, F.T.S.

'WORD AND THEORY'
TO THE EDITOR OF THE ETHICAL ECHO

May I, in as brief a manner as possible, indicate in what lies the difference between C. W.'s views and my own, and this will show clearly how futile discussion carried on in this manner is. The books which hold the record of religious theory can be regarded in two ways; either as having poetic or literary value, or as being statements of fact. There are in the sacred books of the East many descriptions of Swargam or Devachan; they are very beautiful in the mere expression, and the states described can be related to states of consciousness experienced by the yet living man. We have all had, in

Appendix A: The Theosophical Movement

more or less brief moments, ecstasy and imaginary fulfilment of all desire, and so it is quite possible to read these accounts of Devachan as in some way descriptive of things we feel during life. This certainty is part of their attractive force; but (and this is the religious aspect) Devachan is said to be a real state of *post-mortem* consciousness, and the description is of fact in so far as words can convey any images of these things. Herein lies the whole difference between C. W. and the Theosophist. Now I should like to know what reason C. W. has for denying this aspect. What has he to say to the assertion of long experience? Many Theosophists speaking to-day, and in long past days, declare that they have had knowledge spiritually of these states. Why should C. W. brand them as fools? He says of the Theosophist who regards these things as facts, 'of the absurdity of his statement there would be no doubt at all.' I think when we consider how so many eminent thinkers hold in doubt and put forward in hesitation widely differing opinions on these matters, that C. W.'s attitude is quite unjustified. This habit of branding as 'absurd' opinions not shared by the writer is one of those freaks on which Matthew Arnold once lavished a good deal of delicate sarcasm. Practical students of occultism, who have explored into these mysteries, are very much in accord in their statements, and until C. W. adopts similar methods of investigation, his opinion on the reality of Kama Loka or Devachan has just the same value as any opinion uttered without thought or knowledge. C.W. raises so many other points that it is quite impossible to go into them in detail. He has found it necessary to occupy six columns in replying to an argument compressed into one. If I were to reply similarly expanding I would need two whole numbers of the ETHICAL ECHO to set forth my case, and the things C. W. would have to say in reply are such that I suppose a whole volume would not contain them. But it seems to me there is no advantage to be derived from discussing the nature of 'pure being' when C. W. is quite unprepared to admit even the immortality of the soul as preliminary to arriving at a mutual understanding. For, even supposing I had made it clear that the views I put forward were metaphysically correct, C. W. would probably retreat to this other position and ask me why do I believe in a soul at all. With regard to the quotation from Omar, this was used in illustration of my meaning, not as an argument. But as C. W. has been much concerned over the perversion of Omar's 'very much here-and-now philosophy,' to make it dovetail with Eastern theories, I will append further extracts from Omar, who, though not affiliated with any Sufi order, was saturated with Sufi philosophy. Omar thus declares the identity of his own spiritual essence with the Eternal:

> 'My body's life and strength proceed from Thee!
> My soul within and spirit of Thee!
> My being is of Thee, and Thou art mine,
> And I am Thine, since I am lost in Thee!'

Here is his doctrine concerning the after life:

> 'When this fair soul its mansion doth vacate
> Each element assumes its principal state.'

This is identical with the Theosophical theory, earth to earth, the shadow to the world of shadows, the soul to its fiery dreams in Devachan the place of souls, the spirit to spiritual spheres. C. W. has been quite misled as to Omar's philosophy; the allusions to the wine cup his matter-of-fact consciousness takes as evidence of Omar's living very much here-and-now in thought. When the Sufis speak of wine they mean spiritual life, the tavern is the cell of the ascetic, where he becomes intoxicated with divine things. Listen to Omar himself:

> 'The more I drink of *Being's wine*,
> More sane I grow, and sober than before!'

What I described as an 'eternal spiritual being with a power of entering or permeating matter with part of itself' Omar, as a poet, writes of thus:

> 'The eternal Saki from the bowl has poured
> Millions of bubbles like us, and will pour.'

And these bubbles, which are the transitory souls of men, before they expire utterly, cast upon the darkness their gold or crimson in visions of fulfilled desire or fiery torment; the Saki, the spirit, enduring eternally, entering new forms and departing again through the luminous doorways of heaven or hell. But it is useless to argue upon these things, it is useless to dilate upon the mystery of life to anyone when the dead words are like a barrier across his vision forever, and his intuition does not leap forth beyond them and their forms to grasp at truth.

GEO W. RUSSELL.

[This correspondence must now cease. – ED.]

APPENDIX B: THE RETURN

The text of 'The Return' exists in a number of holograph drafts, until recently in the possession of Monk Gibbon and now part of the collection acquired by the Library of Queen's University, Kingston, Ontario, and a typescript version, with holograph corrections, in the possession of the Harry Ransom Humanities Research Center, Austin, Texas.

We give below the text of the final draft version, then that of the typescript. In both texts, spelling mistakes have been silently corrected. A note by Monk Gibbon follows.

General Editors

THE RETURN

1

The time had now come when Christopher must return to the ancestral fountain of his life, as in the parable the Prodigal returned to the home of the mystic Father, but time had not yet come for him to pronounce the tragic self judgement 'I have sinned before Heaven and against thee and am no more worthy to be called thy son'. Not now could he have any wisdom about himself, he who lay there with a drugged consciousness in an alcove of the hall in the house he had made his home.

The day was dying. A herd of shadows, that through daytime hid amid the rafters, now began to drop from vault to stone pavement obliterating all but the round window high up where thin dragons in scarlet and gold still glowed because of some twilight inflammation in the heavens making a fiery eye for the dusk within. That fiery eye had for hours been growing to a blaze of incoherent light and then receding to stellar distances, swaying in some uncontrollable rhythm caused by the drug rioting in Christopher's blood. These hours had seemed centuries to him. What life he had beyond them was lost. To remember would have been to exercise the will, and the will for him had sunken beyond remote horizons of life.

At last he was able to close his eyes. But the entry into himself was not to be master there. For, as in dream the unity of being may be sundered into many beings, and the seer of dream gazes at creatures born out of himself who act with a life of their own, so about his drugged consciousness gathered beings to whom Christopher had been creator; imaginations, terrors and desires in the shapes in which he had fashioned them and into which he had breathed his own life.

The man lying there, now so feeble, had once been filled with power, but he had parted with it to his own creations, until at last there remained to him only that fluttering shock of consciousness which now in a kind of terror apprehended its own children passed from its sway and become mightier than itself.

Christopher had been one of the most famous if the least read, storytellers of his time, for there were few who could induce the sinister ecstasy which quickened those dark romances. In these by some perversion of his spirit, earth, the nature so kindly to most, was conceived of as a monstrous being at enmity with the heavenly light in man. That monstrous being was in his imagination one of the host which anciently had warred against heaven. It still continued the old revolt enveloping with its sorcery whatever on earth held allegiance to the light.

Yet Christopher departing in so blind a darkness from earth had a radiant dawn there, a youth transparent to spirit, when every thought broke into stars, and the powers of nature, now so dreadful to him, were but the vesture of angelic hierarchies and a divinity enfolding all. In that spiritual youth he had written the mystical romance of the Knight-Errant whose high will it was to redeem earth and bring it under the Empire of Light. It was easy then for Christopher to create a heroic counterpart of himself who could endure all things, and fight with dragons at the gateways of the underworld to rescue a princess made in the image of his Agnes who was then in a lovely and shining girlhood. Even in that early tale his readers had noticed with what horror he had surrounded the beast, the emanation of evil issuing from the Pit.

But his Agnes was long dead, and with her going the balance

Appendix B: The Return

between light and darkness in Christopher was upset. It was then that he came to conceive of the nature about him as in itself evil, everywhere threatening the spirit, dooming it to dark crucifixions and martyrdoms. As he grew older these imaginations became more sinister and had more and more horror and terror in them. There were tales of demoniac and elemental beings, earth's own natural children, the hosts of water, air, and fire, and the ministers of its will. There were tales of beings who once were, but now were no longer human, liliths, incubi, succubi, wizards, tormentors and inquisitors who to their warfare with the spirit brought all the hatred of these in whose own being the divine powers had been darkened and turned to infernal uses. In all these tales somewhere, seen faintly as in starlight was an image of Agnes, her beauty bowed to sorrow, and the anguish of her martyrdoms, as if it was the crucifixion of the spirit itself, became almost unendurable to the few who followed the tales and read them fearfully, for in these tales was all the anguish of Christopher's own soul.

He had come to seek in drugs a magic to bring forgetfulness, but these only brought him to a more fearful intimacy with the horrors whose sorcery he had divined. There had been trances where time had seemed to stand still while his soul was pressed close to the very soul of that darkness that he might know its most terrible secrets, and in that fearful intimacy the soul of Christopher had seemed so lost in its imaginations that it had itself become like that it contemplated and had share in the exultation of evil over good. So stair after stair the soul of Christopher descended into the pit, and as he descended his powers were taken from him as were Ishtar's in the Chaldean myth when she passed from heaven, until now there was but that fluttering speck of consciousness, soon to go out in this world, around which fluttered the beings he had created which had now taken possession of the house of the soul.

About their creator they gathered. As in old time a King might will to move from one to another of his dominions, and the whisper goes about 'He is going! He is going!' and his dignitaries, his queens, the captains of his legions make ready for his departure, and his chariots, his elephants, his camels, his horses with their riders are marshalled, so about Christopher gathered the creations of his imagination, dark or radiant. Though they were now more powerful than Christopher, yet were they linked to him by chains which could not be broken, and they must be with him and haunt him until he had brought about their transfiguration and they had reassumed their original shining in his soul.

They waited there for Christopher could not pass without them. Though they might not now enter every world he might enter, they would wait for his return. They could draw him out of any Paradise. No Paradise could be his immortally until they too were with him in that beauty they had before their fall.

The man who waited on Christopher came into the hall with a lamp which he placed on a table by Christopher's couch. He looked wth pity on his master, at the pallid face, over which fell the black hair tinged with grey. He asked a question, but Christopher made only a faint gesture of dismissal. The man went out softly. Christopher again sank into himself, and his reverie gradually faded into unconsciousness, and in that unconsciousness the soul of Christopher, a galleon freighted with all these wild imaginings, passed into the shining aether. He was captain of that wild crew, a captain they now heeded not. After a time the shining aether began to permeate and lave those images, and to bring them to life and light again and they spread about in phantom space, and when Christopher awoke he was living only in memory or phantasy but he knew it not. He seemed to himself to have but wakened out of sleep, and he was lying on the couch in that ancient building in a land of mountains, woods, lakes and desolate plains. He was master of his world. It would change at his desire but now he did not know it.

THE RETURN

The day was dying. In the gray hall the shadows, a phantasmal herd began to gather, prowling from niche to niche, dropping from vault to pavement, darkening all save the round window high up where twin dragons, writhing in scarlet and gold, still glowed from some twilight inflammation in the heavens and made a fiery eye for the dusk within. That fiery eye had for hours been growing to a glare of incoherent light and receding to stellar remoteness, swaying in some uncontrollable rhythm caused by the drug rioting in Michael Heron's veins. At one instant there was nothing before consciousness but that fiery entanglement of colour, and in the next it had reeled back to incalculable horizons pursued by the gloom. This madness of vision was evoked by drugs, and the sinister ecstasies and terrors which accompanied it were wrought by Michael's genius into tales which were the nightmares of art. From that ancient house, built in a land of forests, mountains and lakes, romance after romance had gone forth charged with an increasing spiritual terror. To him imagination everything in nature, its elements and arcane powers, were united in a cosmic conspiracy to assail beauty; and the vision of it martyred, or bowed to sorrow, made the reading of his tales an unendurable straining of the heart. Yet in his youth Michael had written the romance of spiritual courage. But the romance of Saint George was written while Agnes was still living in a youth where ecstasy and beauty seemed unquenchable; and inspired by that golden girlhood he could imagine himself into Saint George and go forth against the Dragon of Darkness and conquer it. He had imagined a spiritual chivalry not to be dismayed by any horror; but hardly had he done so when darkness swallowed up the light of his own soul, for Agnes had died, and since that agony the crucifixion of beauty had become a torturing obsession, the theme of tragic romances filled with a despairing mysticism. Because of that law which changes the soul into the image it contemplates, where it hates no less than where it adores, the soul of Michael Heron had become haunted with images of evil, and after these came imagination of their nature and consciousness, and at last it seemed to his readers that he had almost allied himself with the dark powers he had conceived of as plotting the martyrdom of the spirit. He had found a drug whose use inflamed imagination, and seemed to admit him into the secret consciousness of demons, until he felt, with the exultation of genius at complete mastery, he could make evil as intelligible as others could make the good. He had in the tale of The Liliths followed lust into its own sinister Eden. In another book he told of The Sorcerers who practised the magic of hate. In The Fate of the Gods was narrated the tragedy of those divine children who first came to Earth to redeem it and win it for the Empire of Light. Now, in a last madness of imagination, he was dreaming of the End of Time and the final defeat of Heaven, and the extinction of the Promethean fire by the gods of this World so that Earth might regain its ancient elemental consciousness untroubled by the spirit. All these had been imagined in the glooms of that grey chamber which was haunted by a wizard populace of chimeras, gnarled goblins, giants, monstrous and shaggy primitives, demons with eyes cold as stone, incubi and succubi, Liliths, lovely but lustrous with corruption, glowing elementals, red larvae of the passions, and amid these there was always a figure, blue eyed with shining hair, Agnes, the martyr whose lovely ardour all that wizard populace conspired to extinguish. These imaginations had been made living and each was endowed with some power from the protean being of its creator. That evening Michael lay on a couch facing the gloom where the fiery eye was expanding and receding. Behind him a window opened into the darkness of forests where last mighty elms overshadowed the house and rustled against its walls. In that recess the pale beautiful features, the dark bright eyes, the grey hair overhanging the forehead could hardly be seen. A man came in noiselessly bearing a lamp with the flame turned low. He placed the lamp on a table by the couch. He gazed with pity on the drugged figure as he asked whether there was more he could do, but there came only a flickering hand in dismissal without speech. The man wet out noiselessly not seeing the terror in Michael's eyes. In the dim light the face of the lamp bearer had assumed a sinister character, and in Michael's drug-dilated consciousness the man had towered up and become inhuman and his eyes like those of a bird of prey. The drug chained him to the couch, and in his madness he felt there could be no bodily escape, for soon a consistory of inhuman powers would be gathered about him. He closed his eyes seeking a place of refuge in the forest of imagination, but he had hardly entered its shades when he fell into the darkness of complete unconsciousness. In that sleep the soul of Michael Heron passed into the shining aether, a galleon freighted with a cargo of wild dream and passions; and that magical aether after a time began to permeate memory, dream and imagination with its light and to make all living. When Michael awoke he was in the shining aether but knew it not. The forms of life were present to consciousness as before. He seemed to be lying on his couch, and he was listening with a cold shrivelling of his flesh to the footfall of some inhuman creatures in the corridor. He knew those who were coming, and opening the casement he dropped on the grass without and ran on frantic feet through the thick midnight of the forest.

Appendix B: The Return

NOTE

MONK GIBBON

In his last letter to his son, Diarmuid, who was in America, AE, from his sick bed in Bournemouth suggested that Padraic Colum should write his life and that I should arrange and edit his multitudinous contributions to *The Irish Statesman*, presenting the material much as Eckermann presented the thought of Goethe, a project which I had long entertained but which Yeats discouraged when shown a rough sample.

AE had given me a brief list of the various pseudonyms beyond which he had had to shelter in each week's issue of the paper. When *The Living Torch* appeared, it received great praise from various sources. I had had no difficulty in discovering nuggets of gold in the leading articles, book reviews, etc. which came from his pen, a compendium of the reflections of a very great man; on writers, human nature, destiny and the contemporary political scene, all of it described by a sage who saw time as a not unduly important element in eternity.

In addition I asked Macmillans to supply me with any unpublished documents found amongst AE's papers at the time of his death, but these were brief and casual and I was unable to make use of any of them. The most interesting item consisted of six closely-related manuscript versions of what the author had evidently intended should be the opening pages of another prose book. I am afraid I gave them rather cursory attention. They were pinned together and entitled 'The Return', and the various revises differed very little from one another. A hurried first reading left me with the impression that they were intended to be the reminiscences of a drug-addict, a verdict that seems close to nonsense when I return to the text now after a lapse of forty-eight years. Viewed more closely there is no addict involved, only AE himself, plumbing the depths of the human spirit when it sinks into an area of distortion and despair. He was fond of quoting the Hindu contention that every rise in human apprehension entails the willingness to accept a corresponding descent. And he seems to be hinting at some such balance of destiny now. We are being asked to accept the horror of the pit because we have aspired to reach the heights.

The story starts on a note of melodrama; its style suggests almost the thriller of the mid-'thirties. Was AE making one last effort to reach a wider public? I reject the notion, although he is more successful in the medium – if one can call it that – than one would have expected. But, very soon, it becomes evident that he is launched once more on the old quest, the pursuit of an esoteric solution to the mystery of human consciouness, which had fascinated both him and the poet Yeats from their schooldays onwards. Indeed he outlines his own mental past in the paragraph which begins with a reminder of a 'youth transparent to spirit, when every thought broke into stars, and the powers of nature, now so dreadful to him, were but the vesture of angelic hierarchies and a divinity enfolding all'.

It is almost possible that 'The Return' is not a characteristic 'afterthought', but a last minute attempt to recast the message, latent in some much earlier unfinished manuscript – and to express this thought in a more modern idiom but with a noticeable measure of his earlier and more decorative language. I myself am out of sympathy with the whole 'bag of tricks' with which Yeats and his fellow initiates played in the very secret society with its separate Latin mottoes for each individual member. And I am almost equally critical of the Upper Ely Place group in whose mystical company AE laboured until – as he told me himself – his health forced him to abandon a path which he hoped would lead him into the promised land.

I am speculating most wildly, the faithful will say. But if any academic sleuth, or any person with predominantly theosophic bias, cares to produce a telling interpretation of 'The Return' I shall read it with great care and a modicum of sympathy. I myself am tied to earth. AE, which I published *The Seals* a year before his death, wrote to me to congratulate me on having used my earthly eyes so well here. 'You are lucky to have found yourself so young. Some of us never find ourselves at all.' He went on to refer to 'the rootless flowers of fantasy' which would have tempted him with their irrelevancy in his own youth. That phrase is highly significant. It suggests a repudiation almost of his Hindu convictions in favour of the Greek clarity of his later style. The one cardinal creed to which he clung till the end of his life was the doctrine of reincarnation. On his deathbed, he could say to a friend of the approaching change in his own spiritual status:- 'You know, it is going to be exciting!'

It was of course nonsense to write to me that I had found myself. Do any of us find ourselves? Of the various giants I have been fortunate enough to meet in my long life I would say that AE was unquestionably the greatest. Why? Because he mixed greatness and goodness in equal parts. His repeated attempts to find a more satisfactory wording for 'The Return' are, I believe, an indication that he was a tired man when he attempted this, and displeased by his own persevering efforts.

NOTES AND COMMENTARY

ABBREVIATIONS USED

Asc.	Ascent of Mount Carmel
B.U.	Bṛhadāraṇyaka Upaniṣad
Ch.U.	Chāndogya Upaniṣad
C.O.V.	The Candle of Vision
D.N.	The Dark Night of the Soul
Gita	Bhagavad Gītā
Gita Notes	Notes on the Bhagavad Gītā
Glo.	Theosophical Glossary
I.U.	Isis Unveiled
Kath.U.	Kaṭha Upaniṣad
Key	The Key to Theosophy
K.U.	Kena Upaniṣad
L.O.P.	Light on the Path
Mai.U.	Maitri Upaniṣad
Man.U.	Māṇḍukya Upaniṣad
Mun.U.	Muṇḍaka Upaniṣad
Ocean	The Ocean of Theosophy
S.D.	The Secret Doctrine
Selections	Selections from the Upanishads and the Tao Te King
S.F.	Song and Its Fountains
Sv.U.	Śvetāśvatara Upanisad
Tai.U.	Taittirīya Upaniṣad
T.M.	The Theosophical Movement
Tr.	Transactions of the Blavatsky Lodge
Voice	The Voice of the Silence
W.Q.J. Letters	Letters That Have Helped Me

[Quotations from the Upaniṣads are in Robert Hume's translation, unless otherwise indicated.]

THE CANDLE OF VISION

1. First published by Macmillan and Co., 1918.
2. 'Occultism teaches that no form can be given to anything, either by nature or by man, whose ideal type does not already exist on the subjective plane. More than this; that no such form or shape can possibly enter man's consciousness, or evolve in his imagination, which does not exist in prototype, at least as an approximation.' (*S.D.* I, p. 282 fn.)
3. The 'Great Mother' is a name often given to the primordial undifferentiated divine substance before it is differentiated into particular forms. (See *Tr.*, p. 140.)
4. The *Ṛg Veda* Hymn of Creation states: 'Desire first arose in It (the Unknowable Absolute).' Desire as the principle of differentiation is the source of all individualization. (See *B.U.* [*Selections*, p. 25].)
5. The metaphor of the spider and his thread recurs in the Upaniṣads. (*B.U.*, 2.1.10, also *Mai.U.*, 6.22.)
6. 'I created this universe by the mystic power of my illusion.' (*Gītā*, ch. IV, vs. 6; *Sv.U.*, 4.10.) Indian scriptures use similar terms, and *Īśvara* is said to produce the universe by magical powers. (*Māyā* means both illusion and creative magical power.)
7. 'In my Father's house are many mansions.' (*John* XIV.2.)
8. 'Heaven lies about us in our infancy.' (See Wordsworth: 'Ode: of Intimations of Immortality'.)
9. The symbol of a universal life-principle, common to many mystical and religious traditions, known as *alaya* in Tibetan Buddhism and *akaśa* or *mulaprakṛti* in Hindu systems.
10. 'It may be conceived that the ego in man is a monad that has gathered to itself innumerable experiences through aeons of time, slowly unfolding its latent potencies through plane after plane of matter. It is hence called the "*eternal pilgrim*".' (W.Q. Judge, 'The Synthesis of Occult Science', *The Path*, February 1892.)
11. In *B.U.* cosmic creation is likened to weaving 3.8.3–7 (cf. *Mun.U.*, 2.2.5).
12. A mystic term explained in *The Secret Doctrine* (I, pp. 93–4). The Voice which emerges from everlasting Silence is that aggregate of divine mind-beings who come forth at the dawn of manifestation to assist the work of cosmic evolution. As a body they constitute the ceaseless activity of noetic intelligence in matter.
13. The reference is to Elijah ascending to heaven in a chariot. (II *Kings* II. 11.)
14. We exile ourselves from our spiritual home by separative thoughts. Hence the Buddhists spoke of 'the great dire heresy of Separateness' (*Voice*, p. 9), and *Light on the Path* urges us to 'Kill out all sense of separateness.' (*L.O.P.*, p. 2.)
15. The Buddhist prefaces all teachings with the phrase, 'Thus have I heard', rather than proclaiming, 'Behold I know.' (*Voice*, pp. 29–30.)
16. This passage reflects A.E.'s deep fidelity to Eastern thought, especially to the teaching of the sage Patañjali. It was axiomatic in his philosophy of Yoga that 'realization is attained by dwelling upon the thing to be realized'.

689

17. A mythical or symbolic term which has a distinct significance in the teachings of Pythagoras and Plato. Theosophy teaches a similar doctrine of *yugas* or ages which are of definite duration and characterize the state of human consciousness on the globe during a specific evolutionary period. The death of Lord Krishna inaugurated the Kali Yuga or Iron Age for the majority of human beings on this planet though the mystic chronology of ages cannot be reckoned by clock time. Each age or *yuga* is a state of consciousness which is omnipresent yet modifiable by the relative degree of expression in any given period. It is possible for a variety of individuals to be living within different epicycles of influence whether Gold, Silver or Bronze, while being contemporaneous in the Iron Age. (See *Ocean*, p. 125, for chronology of *yugas*.)
18. Cf. Francis Thompson, 'In No Strange Land': "Tis ye, 'tis your estrangèd faces/That miss the many-splendoured thing.'
19. W.Q. Judge, writing to a spiritual aspirant, mentions this experience on the mystic path – 'It is a great advance that you hear the bells, which few hear, and evidence that you are where you can hear them; that is a great deal indeed. Do not look for the voice of the bells, but regard the *ideas* which thereupon come into the head, and apply to them the touchstone of your own Soul . . .' (*W.Q.J. Letters*, p. 9.) *The Voice of the Silence* speaks of different mystic sounds. (p. 11).
20. According to the Brahmins, the Iron Age began 5,085 years ago at the passing of Krishna and will extend altogether for 432,000 years. Hindu calculations of historical periods are not deterministic but merely indicative of a vast sweep of activity during a given epoch. Individual aspiration can recover the vibration of the Golden Age. *The Candle of Vision* seems to bear testimony to this possibility. (Cf. 'Conversations on Occultism', *The Path*, April 1894.)
21. As thoughts are regarded as energies, each thought has a magnetic link with others similar to it and attracts or is attracted to them.
22. 'Behind will stands desire', proclaimed the ancient Hermetic axiom. True prayer is an invocation of the Higher Self by an act of will grounded in the desire for the Good (as Plato would call it). (See *Key*, p. 68; also 'Conversations on Occultism', *The Path*, April 1894.)
23. This probably refers to W.B. Yeats, who drew much inspiration in his early years from A.E.'s eloquent renderings of mystical philosophy in verse and prose. There is the suggestion here of an alchemic attraction between them similar to the laws of affinity in the atomic world.
24. Buddha said to his disciples as he lay dying, 'Be ye lamps unto yourselves. Rely on yourselves.' (E.A. Burtt, *The Teachings of the Compassionate Buddha*, p. 49.)
25. 'MAGIC is spiritual WISDOM; nature, the material ally, pupil and servant of the magician.' (*I.U.* II, p. 590.)
26. W.Q. Judge wrote, 'So then, with the absolute knowledge that all your limitations are due to Karma, past or in this life, and with a firm reliance ever upon Karma as the only judge, which will be good or bad as you make it, yourself, you can stand anything that may happen and feel serene . . .' (*W.Q.J. Letters*, pp. 18–19.)
27. *The Voice of the Silence* says of such a man — 'Yea, he is mighty. The living power made free in him, that power which is HIMSELF, can raise the tabernacle of illusion high above the Gods, above great Brahm and Indra.' (*Voice*, p. 71.)
28. 'Those who believe in *Karma* have to believe in *destiny*, which, from birth to death, every man is weaving thread by thread around himself, as a spider does his cobweb; and this destiny is guided either by the heavenly voice of the invisible *prototype* outside of us, or by our more intimate *astral*, or inner man, who is but too often the evil genius of the embodied entity called man. Both

Notes and Commentary to pages 91–92 691

these lead on the outward man, but one of them must prevail; and from the very beginning of the invisible affray the stern and implacable *law of compensation* steps in and takes its course, faithfully following the fluctuations. When the last strand is woven, and man is seemingly enwrapped in the net-work of his own doing, then he finds himself completely under the empire of this *self-made* destiny . . .' (*S.D.* I, p. 639.)

29. 'As Krishna says in *Dnyaneshvari:* "When this Path is beheld . . . whether one sets out to the bloom of the east, or to the chambers of the west, *without moving*, O holder of the bow, *is the travelling in this road*. In this path, to whatever place one would go, *that place one's own self* becomes." "Thou art the Path", is said to the Adept Guru, and by the latter to the disciple, after initiation. "I am the way and the Path", says another MASTER.' (*Voice*, p. 14 fn.) The *Bṛadāraṇyaka Upaniṣad* refers to 'the small old path'.

30. 'The pivotal doctrine of the esoteric philosophy admits no privileges or special gifts in man, save those won by his own Ego through personal effort and merit throughout a long series of metempsychoses and reincarnations.' (*S.D.* I, p. 17.)

31. 'Genius is the very nature of spiritual entity itself of our Ego.' ('Genius', *Lucifer*, November 1889.)

32. '. . . *the hidden meaning of Apollo's HEPTACHORD – the lyre of the radiant god, in each of the seven strings of which dwelleth the Spirit, Soul and Astral body of the Kosmos* . . .' (*S.D.* I, p. 167.)

33. This is very similar to the practice of *dhāraṇā* or concentration, the first step in meditation taught by Patañjali in the *Yoga Sutras*. (Cf. bk. III, sutras 1–12.) *Dhāraṇā* is the fixing of the mind upon some point or idea initiating a smooth, uninterrupted flow of consciousness towards and through the object to be realized. If successfully mastered, the mind pierces the phenomenal veil surrounding the object and attains to noetic awareness of its true nature.

34. The procedure is well described in Sangharakshita's *A Survey of Buddhism* (p. 164).

35. It is the common experience of countless mystics that when they begin to walk the mystic path and aspire towards the higher life, the lower selfish nature begins to rebel against the new discipline. Sensing the withdrawal of attention away from itself, the ego begins to be filled with a foreboding of its own inevitable diminution and ultimate death. Summoning all its powerful illusions and cunning devices to its aid it declares war on the new endeavour and on its own higher nature. This 'civil war within the breast' has been symbolized in many a myth and allegorical tale. W.Q. Judge speaks about this in his exposition of the allegorical interpretation of the *Bhagavad Gītā*. (*Gita Notes*, pp. 34–5.) The same theme is elaborated upon in other mystical texts. (See, for example, *The Cloud of Unknowing*, ch. 69; also chs. 46, 64, 67; and St. John of the Cross, *D.N.*, bk. I, chs. 1–7; bk. II, ch. 23, no. 4, p. 183.)

36. This is what the Indian mystics call *tapas* (from the root *tap* meaning 'to heat'), the self-imposed discipline which kindles an inward fire whose heat burns away the impurities of the ego to allow the divine nature to shine forth. The alchemists clearly used a similar metaphor, and the language of St. John of the Cross (*D.N.*, bk. II, ch. 6, no. 6) displays a striking parallel. (Cf. also *Through the Gates of Gold*, pp. 25–30; *W.Q.J. Letters*, p. 15.)

37. *The Voice of the Silence* speaks of 'the fierce strife between the living and the dead' (p. 43). (The living spirit and the empty shadow of the ego.)

38. 'Attracted by the beauty or other seductive quality, for him, of this study, he enters upon the prosecution of it, and soon discovers that he arouses two sets of forces. One of them consists of all his friends and relations who do not view life

as he does, who are wedded to the "established order", and think him a fool for devoting any attention to anything else, while the general mass of his acquaintances and those whom he meets in the world, instinctively array themselves against one who is thus starting upon a crusade that begins with his own follies and faults, but must end in a condemnation of theirs, if only by the force of example. The other opponents are far more difficult to meet, because they have their camp and base of action upon the Astral and other hidden planes; they are all his lower tendencies and faculties, that up to this time have been in the sole service of material life. By the mere force of moral gravity, they fly to the other side, where they assist his living friends and relatives in their struggle against him.' (*Gita Notes*, pp. 18–19.)

39. '*Will* is a pure, colourless force which is moved into action by *desire*.' (*Gita Notes*, p. 36.)
40. After speaking of the supreme *Brahman*, the Upaniṣads and Śaṅkara made the great affirmation, 'TAT TVAM ASI' – 'That Thou Art' – pointing to the ultmate identity between our being and the Absolute Reality.
41. Here follows a visionary explanation of the *dhyāna* state which is the second stage of the whole meditation cycle called by Patañjali *saṁyama*.
42. The Buddhist text, *Dhammapada*, characterizes man as the sum-total of all his previous thoughts in all his previous lives. (Cf. ch. I, v. 1.)
43. 'The Path that leadeth on, is lighted by one fire – the fire of daring, burning in the heart.' (*Voice*, p. 59; see also *D.N.*, bk. I, ch. 8; bk. II, chs. 5, 20, 21, 'Love is like fire', says St. John, 'which ever rises', and *The Cloud of Unknowing*, chs. 68, 69, ch. 4, especially last paragraph, i.e., p. 58, and ch. 5.)
44. 'Yet stand alone and isolated, because nothing that is embodied, nothing that is conscious of separation, nothing that is out of the eternal, can aid you.' *(L.O.P.*, p. 3.) (See also *D.N.*, bk. II, ch. 6, especially sections 2 and 3: 'It (the soul) feels, too . . . friends.')
45. A.E. invokes the alchemical tradition to explain the psychological transformations that occur in the spiritual life. Alchemy was concerned with the transmutation of elements in three distinct realms: the terrestrial, the human and the cosmic. The true alchemist is concerned only with the latter two, giving all his efforts to the transmutation of the baser elements of the personal will into the refined gold of divine universal wisdom. (Cf. *Glo.*, 'Alchemy'; *D.N.*, bk. II, ch. 6, section 6, 'The soul is purified in this furnace like gold in a crucible.')
46. Śaṅkara in *The Crest Jewel of Discrimination* describes the 'sheaths' or 'vestures' of the soul, and St. John in *Dark Night of the Soul* speaks of the 'garments' or 'vestments' of the soul. (*D.N.*, bk. II, ch. 21.) Also *Gita Notes*, p. 26 – '. . . the soul, in order to at last reach the objective plane where its experience is gained, places upon itself, one after the other, various sheaths, each having its peculiar property and function.' The soul is thus shifting its locus of consciousness from one level (or sheath) to another, and thus, in a sense 'creating' a new vesture.
47. H.P. Blavatsky points to this central truth in *The Key to Theosophy* (p. 68) – 'Let no Theosophist, if he would hold to divine, not human truth, say that this "God in secret" listens to, or is distinct from, either finite man or the infinite essence – for all are one. Nor, as just remarked, that a prayer is a petition. It is a mystery rather; an occult process by which finite and conditioned thoughts and desires, unable to be assimilated by the absolute spirit which is unconditioned, are translated into spiritual wills and the will; such process being called "spiritual transmutation".'
48. If one is persistent in maintaining an undeviating line of life-meditation on the

highest Self, one's perceptions will be transformed so that they are consonant with an enlarged sense of being. The truest test of spirituality has always been the awakening of unbounded compassion.
49. Spiritual knowledge is the inalienable birthright of every human soul. In a universe governed at all levels by law and justice, this absolute spiritual equality implies that any individual who is willing and able to fulfil the impersonal condition of the spiritual life may enter into the luminous realm of pure vision. (Cf. *S.D.* I, p. 17.)
50. The man who comes out of the darkness of the cave of ignorance into the bright sunlight of eternal truth (in Plato's Allegory of the Cave) may at first find the daylight dazzling to his unaccustomed eyes, and Plotinus remarks, 'Like anyone just awakened, the soul cannot look at bright objects' (*Enneads* I, 6, 9, [O'Brien p. 42]). Both St. John of the Cross in *D.N.*, bk. II, ch. 5, and *The Cloud of Unknowing*, ch. 68, p. 135 ('. . . it is overwhelming spiritual light that blinds the soul that is experiencing it, rather than actual darkness or the absence of physical light'), describe this universal mystic experience. To Arjuna, granted the mystical vision of the Universal Divine Form of Krishna, it seems as if 'The glory and amazing splendour of this mighty Being may be likened to the radiance shed by a thousand suns rising together into the heavens.' (*Gītā*, ch. XI, p. 79; also see *S.D.* I, p. 255.)
51. This is the First Logos of whom it is said, '. . . the universal Deity is darkness, and from this Darkness issues the Logos . . .' (*Tr.*, p. 116.)
52. Cf. a striking section in the *Enneads* of Plotinus entitled 'The Descent of the Soul', wherein Plotinus lyrically describes the passage of the soul from high contemplative states to waking life. Such descriptions of rises and falls in consciousness are common in mystical literature. However, there is also the teaching that a point can be reached (called *titikṣa* in Mahayana Buddhism) in the life of the soul where an *unbroken* perception of divine consciousness is achieved. The spiritual adept then voluntarily ascends or descends the stairway of being at will in order to aid others.
53. '. . . the day-star (the sun) is only the reflection and material shadow of the Central Sun of truth, which illuminates the intellectual (invisible) world of Spirit and which itself is but a gleam borrowed from the ABSOLUTE.' (Quoted from Eliphas Lévi, *S.D.* I, p. 255.)
54. *Theosophical Glossary*, p. 255.
55. The image of a love, yearning to draw near to the beautiful object of his love, is one frequently employed by mystics – whether it be Plato in *Phaedrus*, the Sufi mystics, or St. Teresa of Avila.
56. The etymological origin of the word 'mystic' is the Greek term *mystes*, which signifies both a sealing of the lips as well as a closing of the eyes.
57. This is Virāj, the Deity manifested in the universe, in Indian thought.
58. Cf. Plato, *Phaedo*, 108C and thereafter, for a moving account of the earth as experienced by the wise and the innocent.
59. The Sanskrit word *deva* comes from the root *div*, 'to shine', and thus *deva* literally means 'the shining one'.
60. These are the ensouling spirits of the elements called elementals in modern Theosophy. Every tradition employed different names for them but, generally speaking, they are the invisible forces that operate behind the veil of manifest nature. They are esemplastic in so far as they are susceptible to the impress of human thought and can be directed by the will of powerful beings for both good and evil. On the terrestrial plane they are the invisible substrate of all natural forms. (See H.P. Blavatsky's article, 'Elementals', *Lucifer*, August 1893.)

61. '... as a fact insisted upon by generations of Seers, none of these Beings, high or low, have either individuality or personality as separate Entities...' (*S.D.* I, p. 275.)
62. The Highest Realization symbolized in the Indian apophatic tradition by Darkness – '... in the beginning, when the Infinitude was without form, and Chaos, or the outer Space, was still void, Darkness (i.e., *Kalahansa Parabrahm*) alone *was*. Then, at the first radiation of Dawn, the "Spirit of God" (after the First and Second Logos were radiated, the Third Logos, or Narayan) began to move on the face of the Great Waters of the "Deep".' (*Tr.*, p. 119.)
63. 'Alas, alas, that all men should possess Alaya, be one with the Great Soul, and that possessing it, Alaya should so little avail them! Behold how like the moon, reflected in the tranquil waves, Alaya is reflected by the small and by the great, is mirrored in the tiniest atoms, yet fails to reach the heart of all.' (*Voice*, pp. 26–7.)
64. Highly reminiscent of other accounts of visionary experiences by poets and mystics, especially Shelley; cf. *Prometheus Unbound*, Act II, Sc. V, and *Voice*, pp. 10–12, for similar reflections on the nature of mystical experience.
65. W.Q. Judge specifically mentions the sound of bells as being heard by the spiritual novice as his inner senses begin to awaken. (*W.Q.J. Letters*, p. 9.)
66. Suggestive of initiation ceremonies as recounted in the sacred texts of ancient Egypt. The transforming process of the initiatory rite is archetypal, transcending particular historical designations. The notion of a holy tribe of Divine King-Initiates is a central feature of Kabbalistic, Egyptian and Pythagorean thought. (See *S.D.* II, pp. 558–9.)
67. The rational or philosophical side of the mystical life is stressed here. A.E. sees this as an absolute necessity if one is to avoid the excesses of subjective experience and test the truth of one's insights against objective standards of philosophical reasoning. Plato called this method the 'giving an account' of one's notions and concepts according to first principles. (Cf. *Theaetetus*, 202B.)
68. W.Q. Judge remarks, '... that astral light exists in all places and interpenetrates everything, and is not simply in the free air alone. Further should he know that to be able to see as he sees in the light is not *all* of the seeing thus. That is, there are many sorts of such sight, *e.g.*, he may see now certain airy shapes and yet not see many others which at the same time are as really present there as those he now sees. So it would seem that there are "layers" or differences of states in the astral light. Another way to state it is that elementals are constantly moving in the astral light – that is, everywhere. They, so to say, show pictures to him who looks, and the pictures they show will depend in great part upon the seer's thoughts, motives and development.' (*W.Q.J. Letters*, p. 79.) *The Secret Doctrine* explains at great length that the earlier races of mankind in ages long past, in the civilization called Atlantis, were indeed of gigantic stature, so that legends and stories about giants are not fictitious but have a firm foundation in fact. (See section on 'Are Giants a Fiction?', *S.D.* II, p. 277.)
69. Reference is made here to the interpretation of memory and imagination found in the empiricist tradition from Hobbes to Mill. A.E. pleads for the Platonic interpretation, pointing to the divine source of man's higher faculties and powers.
70. This is the mystical Third Eye of intuition, the wisdom eye, the eye of Śiva. 'With the pure Heavenly Eye surpassing that of man, he sees beings as they pass away from one form of existence and take shape in another.' (*Sammānaphala Suttanta* [E.A. Burtt, *The Teachings of the Compassionate Buddha*, p. 106].)

Notes and Commentary to pages 103–107

71. As the microcosmic focus of a macrocosmic order, man is a unified aggregate of evolutionary forces and is allied to every atom in space.
72. El Dorado means literally 'the gilded city', a utopian term for the heavenly city, the New Jerusalem.
73. In order to know oneself one must come to know all of nature. One must study all grades of being as radiations of the Central Sun from the most universal to the most particular.
74. Reference to Plato's Allegory of the Cave in *The Republic*, bk. VII.
75. Reference is made here to latent faculties and powers in the human constitution known as *śaktis*. These perfections are attained as one ascends to a more divine order of reality. There are six major *śaktis* which have their reflections on earth as imagination, will, clairvoyance, etc. Such powers are latent in every man and can be aroused by ardent desire and intense discipline. (See *S.D.* I, pp. 292–3.)
76. In Eastern teachings this is referred to as the ākāśic record of spiritual evolution on the earth, an indelible account of universal patterns of Logoic activity on this globe. As a man passes beyond personal history and taps this universal storehouse of memory, he may gain glimpses of his true heritage and destiny.
77. A reference to awakening the inner eye. (See note 70.)
78. 'With the ancients the divine luminiferous substance which pervades the whole universe, the "garment" of the Supreme Deity, Zeus, or Jupiter.' (Cf. *Glo.*, 'Æther'.)
79. St. Paul, *Acts* XVII. 28. Also see Plotinus – 'It is because of the One that we breathe and have our being.' (*Enneads* VI, 9, 9 [O'Brien, p. 85].)
80. The human mind is constantly throwing off thought-energies which condense into palpable images in the medium of the astral light. Clairvoyants and sensitives may perceive such images as their senses function on the astral plane. All thinking beings participate in this great ocean of energies and images, and it is by virtue of this common medium that we communicate with and influence those around us in myriad unknown ways.
81. '. . . he who rightly inspects sacred matters ought to be both intelligent and strong, one of these without the other being imperfect. And for the same reason the symbol of the great Sphynx was established; the beast signifying strength, and the man wisdom.' (*Gita Notes*, p. 41.)
82. Shakespeare under Nirmāṇakāyic influences. (W.Q. Judge, *Echoes from the Orient*, p. 6.)
83. A.E. recognized that the meditative life bestows a certain degree of power upon the individual. He warns that unless we are willing continually to examine our motive, we may be easily misled or unconsciously do harm to others.
84. Buddhist meditation also enjoins us to pervade the whole world with love. (Cf. *Sutta-Nipāta*, quoted in *The Teachings of the Compassionate Buddha*, p. 46; see also Sangharakshita.) W.Q. Judge, whom A.E. intensely admired, expressed a similar idea. He recommended the gradual expansion of consciousness in concentric circles, including more and more within each circle of thought until one is attuned to the noumenal cosmos in Brahmā. *The Voice of the Silence* enjoins us similarly 'to feel thyself ALL-THOUGHT, and yet exile all thoughts from out thy Soul'. (*Voice*, p. 66.)
85. 'Realization comes from dwelling on the thing to be realized.' (W.Q. Judge expressing Patañjali's thought.)
86. *Transactions,* pp. 100, 108, 109, and 138. (See also Browning's poem, 'Paracelsus'.)
87. See *The Secret Doctrine* on atoms and monads (*S.D.* I, pp. 610–634).
88. See *The Secret Doctrine* passages on monads in 'Gods, Monads and Atoms' (*S.D.* I, pp. 610–634).

89. '... the (to us) invisible tablets of the Astral Light, "the great picture-gallery of eternity" – a faithful record of every act, and even thought, of man, of all that was, is, or ever will be, in the phenomenal Universe.' (*S.D.* I, p. 104.)
90. This is the power of psychometry and related powers, all aspects of what *The Secret Doctrine* calls *jñānaśakti*. 'The following are *some* of its manifestations *when placed under the influence or control of material conditions*. (a) The power of the mind in interpreting our sensations. (b) Its power in recalling past ideas (memory) and raising future expectation. (c) Its power as exhibited in what are called by modern psychologists "the laws of association", which enables it to form *persisting* connections between various groups of sensations and possibilities of sensations, and thus generate the notion or idea of an external object. (d) Its power in connecting our ideas together by the mysterious link of memory, and thus generating the notion of self or individuality; *some* of its manifestations when liberated *from the bonds of matter* are – (a) Clairvoyance, (b) Psychometry.' (*S.D.* I, p. 292.)
91. The astral light is a subtle essence that surrounds our globe and is visible to the clairvoyant.
92. According to Plato all interior images are phenomenal reflections of more noumenal essences residing in the causal planes of cosmos.
93. A sacerdotal caste which flourished in Britain and Gaul. The three chief commandments of their religion were: obedience to divine laws, concern for the welfare of mankind, and suffering with fortitude all the evils of life. (See *Glo.*, 'Druids'.)
94. Each human being is a lodestone which attracts elements in the objective world according to its nature. The powers of thought and volition can alter the quality and intensity of the magnetic relationship between the individual and his environment. C.G. Jung's concept of synchronicity is suggestive of this ancient law.
95. See *Yoga Aphorisms*, bk. I, p. 2. Cf. also, '... thy Soul as limpid as a mountain lake' (*Voice,* p. 32). Mahatma K.H. says on the importance of the calm, reflecting mind – 'It is upon the serene and placid surface of the unruffled mind that the visions gathered from the invisible find a representation in the visible world.' (Quoted in *T.M.*, Vol. II, p. 18.)
96. 'The "Power" and the "World-Mother" are names given to *kuṇḍalinī* – one of the mystic "Yogi Powers".' It is *Buddhi* considered as an active instead of a passive principle (which it is generally, when regarded only as the vehicle, or casket of the Supreme Spirit ATMA). It is an electro-spiritual force, a creative power which when aroused into action can as easily kill as it can create.' (*Voice,* p. 10 fn. 2.)
97. 'Then from the heart that Power shall rise into the sixth, the middle region, the place between thine eyes ...' (*Voice,* p. 10.)
98. This symbol is pictorially represented as two serpents intertwined around a rod. It is the wand of Mercury or Hermes. Metaphysically, it represents the fall of primordial spirit into gross terrestrial matter. Physiologically it represents the restoration of the equilibrium lost between Life as a unity, and the currents of Life performing various functions in the human body. (Cf. *Glo.,* 'Caduceus'.) This symbol is also linked in Theosophy to the spiral path of *kuṇḍalinī* (see note 96 above).
99. 'Fohat, then, is the personified electric vital power, the transcendental binding Unity of all Cosmic Energies, on the unseen as on the manifested planes, the action of which resembles – on an immense scale – that of a living Force created by WILL, in those phenomena where the seemingly subjective acts on the seemingly objective and propels it to action. Fohat is not only the living Symbol

and Container of that Force, but is looked upon by the Occultists as an Entity – the forces he acts upon being cosmic, human and terrestrial, and exercising their influence on all those planes respectively. On the earthly plane his influence is felt in the magnetic and active force generated by the strong desire of the magnetizer.' (*S.D.* I, p. 111.)

100. The adept is the master of all cosmic forces and can direct that energy at will. The medium, by contrast, is a slave to externalities and a passive instrument of pernicious forces in the astral light. (See H.P. Blavatsky's article 'Adeptship and Mediumship' in her *Collected Works.*)

101. *The Voice of the Silence* warns us of the 'perfidious beauty' of the Hall of Learning – '. . . stop not the fragrance of its stupefying blossoms to inhale' (p. 7.). 'The astral region, the psychic world of supersensuous perceptions and of deceptive sights – the world of mediums. It is the great "Astral Serpent" of Eliphas Lévi. No blossom plucked in those regions has ever yet been brought down on earth without its serpent coiled round the stem. It is the world of the Great Illusion.' (*Voice*, p. 7 fn. 1.)

102. 'The WISE ONES tarry not in pleasure-grounds of senses. The WISE ONES heed not the sweet-tongued voices of illusion.' '. . . seek not for thy Guru in those mayavic regions.' (*Voice*, p. 7.)

103. ' "The one Universal Light, which to Man is *Darkness*, is ever existent", says the Chaldean "Book of Numbers". From it proceeds periodically the ENERGY, which is reflected in the "Deep" or Chaos, the store-house of future worlds, and, once awakened, stirs up and fructifies the latent Forces, which are the ever present eternal potentialities in it.' (*S.D.* I, p. 337.)

104. The visionary is sensitive to sounds and images impressed in the medium of the astral light. If he is a high visionary he may be able to pass beyond the dregs of the lower astral and visit with the mind's eye the courts of king-initiates of the past or initiatory academies that flourished in ancient times. However, this is inferior to a true act of imagination in which one draws forth from divine mind, known as *ākāśa* or the *Mysterium Magnum,* the thought-forms which will benefit mankind as a whole. This is known in Hindu thought as *Kriyāśakti*, one of the great powers that crown the arduous efforts of the yogi. In the Pythagorean tradition it is the secret of the Tetraktys wherein man rises to the level of the gods. 'KRIYASAKTI. The mysterious power of thought which enables it to produce external, perceptible, phenomenal results by its own inherent energy. The ancients held that *any idea will manifest itself externally if one's attention is deeply concentrated upon it.* Similarly *an intense volition will be followed by the desired result.*' (*S.D.* I, p. 293.)

105. 'Plastic potency of thought . . .' (See *S.D.*; also cf. Coleridge on Imagination in *Biographia Litteraria* and Coleridge's 'Aeolian Harp', lines 44–48.)

106. 'But how are we to reach such an elevated status? By enlightened application of our precepts to practice. By use of our higher reason, spiritual intuition and moral sense, and by following the dictates of what we call "the still small voice" of our conscience, which is that of our EGO, and which speaks louder in us than the earthquakes and the thunders of Jehovah, wherein "the Lord is not".' (*Key*, p. 240.)

107. 'I established this whole universe with a single portion of myself, and remain separate.' (*Gītā*, ch. X.42, p. 76.) Theosophy teaches that we are constantly creating 'worlds' through our thoughts, feelings, attitudes and words. But as we do not 'remain separate' from them, as we get caught up in them and identify with them, we get involved in *māyā* and fail to see the shadow spheres for what they are – a mere mimicry of reality. The 'monkey' may well refer to what Hindu philosophers call the restless 'monkey mind'.

108. 'There are no chariots there, nor steeds for chariots, nor roadways. The Spirit of man makes himself chariots, steeds for chariots and roadways. Nor are any delights there, nor joys and rejoicings. The Spirit of man makes for himself delights and joys and rejoicings. There are no lotus ponds there, nor lakes and rivers. The Spirit of man makes for himself lotus ponds, lakes and rivers. For the Spirit of Man is Creator.' (*B.U.*, 4.3.10 [*Selections*, p. 12].)

109. The Upaniṣads speak, roughly, of four levels of consciousness or four selves – the bodily self, the phenomenal (empirical self), the transcendental self and the highest or absolute Self. This is given in the parable of the True Self in *Chāndogya Upaniṣad*, 8.3-12. (See also *Māṇḍukya Upaniṣad*, which gives a profound and mystical account of the four states of consciousness all in the space of its twelve brief verses. The commentaries on this Upaniṣad by Gauḍapāda and Śaṅkara provide us with perceptive insights through their analysis of the four states.)

110. The *Bhagavad Gītā* speaks of 'the spirit in the body' – the *dehin*. The Upanisads and the *Gītā* declare this to be the true Self of every individual.

111. St. John and other mystics say that the understanding has to be purged and purified and worldly reason has to be given up. This is what leads to the second night – the dark night of the soul – in St. John: '. . . likewise it must be blinded and darkened according to the part which has respect to God and to spiritual things, which is the rational and higher part . . .' (*Ascent*, bk. I, ch. 4.) Zen masters also urge a similar 'abasement' and abandonment of reason – hence the typical zen *koan* or apparently absurd story. Reason's net is too feeble to 'catch' this higher realm of consciousness.

112. 'The Universe was evolved out of its ideal plan, upheld through Eternity in the unconsciousness of that which the Vedantins call Parabrahm. This is practically identical with the conclusions of the highest Western Philosophy – "the innate, eternal, and self-existing Ideas" of Plato, now reflected by Von Hartmann. The "unknowable" of Herbert Spencer bears only a faint resemblance to that transcendental *Reality* believed in by Occultists, often appearing merely a personification of a "*force* behind phenomena" – an infinite and eternal *Energy* from which all things proceed. . . . Everything that *is*, *was* and *will be*, eternally IS, even the countless forms, which are finite and perishable only in their objective, not in their *ideal* Form. They existed as Ideas, in the Eternity, and, when they pass away, will exist as reflections.' (*S.D.* I, pp. 281–2.)

113. 'Occultism teaches that no form can be given to anything, either by nature or by man, whose ideal type does not already exist on the subjective plane. More than this; that no such form or shape can possibly enter man's consciousness, or evolve in his imagination, which does not exist in prototype, at least as an approximation.' (*S.D.* I, p. 282 fn.) 'Therefore *our* human forms have existed in the Eternity as astral or ethereal prototypes.' (*S.D.* I, p. 282.) By 'space' A.E. here means the formless *ākāśa*.

114. The Hindus believe that at the end of a vast period of manifestation (*mahāmanvantara*) the universe will dissolve back into the primordial chaos, into 'nothingness', until the time comes for the dawn of a new manifestation. (See *S.D.* I, p. 41.)

115. The English equivalent of the Kabbalistic term Adam Kadmon, meaning archetypal man, Humanity before the fall into matter or sin. Kabbalists refer to it as the ten Sephiroth on the plane of human perception. (Cf. *Glo.*, 'Adam Kadmon'.)

116. A Greek term used to designate extremely long periods of time and the activity of celestial beings in such epochs. It was adapted by the Gnostics to refer to various emanations of beings from the Deity. (See *Glo.*, 'Aeon'; cf. *S.D.* I, pp. 349–52.)

Notes and Commentary to pages 116–118

117. 'The whole of antiquity was imbued with that philosophy which teaches the involution of spirit into matter, the progressive, downward cyclic descent, or active, self-conscious evolution. The Alexandrian Gnostics have sufficiently divulged the secret of initiations, and their records are full of "the sliding down of Æons" in their double qualification of Angelic Beings and Periods: the one the natural evolution of the other. On the other hand, Oriental traditions on both sides of the "black water" – the oceans that separate the two *Easts* – are as full of allegories about the downfall of Pleroma, of that of the gods and Devas. One and all, they allegorized and explained the FALL as *the desire to learn and acquire knowledge* – to KNOW.' (*S.D.* I, pp. 416–7.)

118. Philosophers who spoke of the gnosis or spiritual knowledge (the *gupta vidyā* of the Hindus) which could only be attained by initiation into the Mysteries. They flourished in the first three centuries of the Christian era. Among them the best known were Valentinus, Basilides, Marcion and Simon Magus. (See *Glo.*, 'Gnosis', and 'Gnostics'.)

119. While no personal details of past lives survive in our memories, the soul may, in moments of high aspiration and untroubled reflection, reach back into reminiscences or soul memories of past lives. These may touch us as vivid flashes of perceptive insight or merely as suffused and dimly apprehended intimations of immortality. This is the process Plato is describing when he says (in *Phaedo, Meno,* and elsewhere) that all true knowledge is recollection. (See H.P.B.'s theosophical distinction between memory and reminiscence in *Key*, pp. 124–5.)

119a. Johann August Wilhelm Neander, *General Church History*, 1826–52.

120. This is, of course, a central concept in theosophical as in Platonic thought. The soul has eternally and innately within it, as part of its essential nature, true knowledge or wisdom, although its descent into the phenomenal world of becoming may temporarily obscure this knowledge. The spiritual path is a ceaseless striving to recover this forgotten gnosis.

121. Cf. letter from John Keats to George and Thomas Keats, January 5, 1818.

122. Cf. Emerson's essay entitled 'The Poet': 'For poetry was all written before time was, and whenever we are so finely organized we can penetrate into that region where the air is music.'

123. This sacred beverage of the Hindus corresponds to the Greek ambrosia or nectar quaffed by the gods of Olympus. Only initiated priests can taste the real soma, and they were allowed to drink it only after undergoing a period of discipline and meditation. Mystically it is in many respects the same as the Eucharistic Supper to the Christians. The soma is a plant and also an angel which connects the personal man with his divine nature, allowing him to mount to the highest Self and merge with the Christos within. (See *Glo.*, 'Soma'.)

124. The dream state or *svapnāvastha* is closely allied with the universal medium of the astral light and experiences therein conditioned by the constitution of the medium. As the astral light is sevenfold in nature, so too are the categories of dreaming. According to H.P. Blavatsky (in *Tr.*, p. 79) they may be roughly divided into the following classes:

'1. Prophetic dreams – connected directly with the Higher Self.
2. Allegorical – glimpses of reality distorted by the brain.
3. Mesmeric dreams – sent by adepts, good and bad.
4. Retrospective dreams – events in previous lives.
5. Warning dreams – for others who cannot be impressed themselves.
6. Confused dreams – the causes of which are discussed above in *Tr.*, p. 177.
7. Fanciful or chaotic dreams – owing to some external cause.

In deep sleep (*suṣuptāvastha*) the human soul withdraws entirely from the realm of objective experience beyond the highest dreaming state. It is here in a true subjective 'paradise' that it is refreshed for its return through the astral corridor to the waking state of *jāgratāvastha*. The true ego or spiritual intelligence is the experiencer on all these planes of being and during a normal twenty-four hour cycle it has encountered beings and images on many different planes of invisible nature.'

125. Of the Self that is awake while the body sleeps, it is said, 'Leaving the bodily world through the door of dream, the sleepless Spirit views the sleeping powers.' (*B.U.*, 4.3.11 [*Selections*, p. 13].) 'The Spirit sees not; yet seeing not, he sees. For the energy that dwelt in sight cannot cease, because it is everlasting. But there is no other besides the Spirit, or separate from him, for him to see.' (*B.U.*, 4.3.23 [*Ibid.*, p. 16].)

126. The dream state or *svapna* is usually a chaotic one since it is produced by a disordered throwing up, on the psychic plane, of images or experiences in the waking state. It is a plane still tied to the consciousness of the personal, egotistic mind, which is incapable of a higher continuity or a true harmonious order. It is the realm of psychic fantasy.

127. The *triloka* of Hindu thought. The ancient Vedic seers posited three worlds – *bhūrloka* (earth), *antarikṣaloka* (intermediate world) and *dyurloka* (divine or celestial sphere). These correspond to the three *avasthas* (state of consciousness) of the Upaniṣads (especially the *Māṇḍukya*) – *jāgrat* (waking), *svapna* (dreaming) and *suṣupti* (dreamless sleep). Beyond these lies the ineffable *turīya* state corresponding to the indescribable *Ātman*.

128. It is said of Sages that the common light of day is night to them and our night their true day. The type of light perceived by the senses is the most illusory aspect of existence, being the dimmest reflection of the noumenal light of the Spiritual Sun. The night of the senses signals the awakening of higher intuition normally eclipsed by the fever of sensation during the day.

129. 'I saw eternity the other night,/Like a great ring of pure and endless light,/All calm, as it was bright.' (Henry Vaughan, 'The World'.)

130. *The Secret Doctrine* treaches: 'The fundamental identity of all Souls with the Universal Over-Soul, the latter being itself an aspect of the Unknown Root; and the obligatory pilgrimage for every Soul – a spark of the former – through the Cycle of Incarnation (or "Necessity") in accordance with Cyclic and Karmic law, during the whole term.' (*S.D.* I, p. 17.) A parallel use of the same image is to be found in the depiction of the relation between the eternal flame of the individual divine Self and its personalities, the innumerable sparks that it shoots forth into the world of time. 'It is the Root that never dies, the Three-Tongued Flame of the four wicks', says a stanza in the mystical *Book of Dzyan*, and *The Secret Doctrine* explains – 'The "Three-tongued flame" that never dies is the immortal spiritual triad – the Atma-Buddhi and Manas – the fruition of the latter assimilated by the first two after every terrestrial life.' It goes on to add, 'Just as milliards of bright sparks dance on the waters of an ocean above which one and the same moon is shining, so our evanescent personalities – the illusive envelopes of the immortal MONAD-EGO – twinkle and dance on the waves of Maya.' (*S.D.* I, p. 237.)

131. Boatman ferrying souls of the dead across the river Styx. (Michael Grant and John Hazel, *Gods and Mortals in Classical Mythology*, p. 113.)

132. St. Paul, II *Corinthians* III.18.

133. Plotinus speaks of the 'estrangement' of the soul when it withdraws from the whole, and the idea of the incarnated soul as an exile from its divine home is to be commonly found in mystical literature.

134. A Phoenician term for the deities that presided over the Mysteries in Thebes,

Macedonia, Phrygia, Samothrace, etc. They were held by those peoples in the highest veneration and their real number has never been revealed, their occult meaning being very sacred. (See *Glo.*, 'Cabeiri'.)
135. According to H.P. Blavatsky's *The Secret Doctrine*, Hecate was an aspect of the moon or lunar side of cosmic creation (cf. *S.D.* I, p. 387). It is connected mysteriously with soma, the Sanskrit name for the moon and by derivation with the soma juice mentioned earlier.
136. Reference to Hindu mystical doctrine of *cakras* or centres of force and energy within the human being, which may be aroused or activated by meditation. The *cakras* are centres of the *kuṇḍalinī* force referred to earlier.
137. The term 'psychic' has several distinct meanings, yet it is most commonly associated with actions that occur on the astral plane. Higher psychic experiences can be sudden illuminations or mystical visions, whereas lower psychic experiences emanate from the irrational soul of man and partake of the most chaotic and potentially destructive portion of the astral light. Psychic action must always be contrasted with noetic action which springs from the spiritual soul and higher faculties in man. (See 'Psychic and Noetic Action', *Lucifer*, October 1890.)
138. '... none of us, and especially those who have heard of the Path or of Occultism or of the Masters, can say with confidence that he is not already one who has passed through some initiations with knowledge of them. We may be already initiated into some higher degree than our present attainments would suggest, and are undergoing a new trial unknown to ourselves.' (*Gita Notes*, p. 53.)
139. 'There must therefore be something eternally persisting, which is the witness and perceiver of every passing change, itself unchangeable.' (*Gita Notes*, p. 23.) 'The Spirit of man has two dwelling-places: both this world, and the other. The borderland between them is the third, the land of dreams. While he lingers in the borderland, the Spirit of man beholds both his dwellings.' (*B.U.*, 4.3.9 [*Selections*, p. 11].)
140. 'A clairvoyant can only see the sights properly belonging to the planes his development reaches to or has opened. And the elementals in those planes show to the clairvoyant only such pictures as belong to their plane. Other parts of the idea or thing pictured may be retained in planes not yet open to the seer.' ('Conversations on Occultism', *The Path*, June 1888.)
141. 'As a great fish swims along one bank of the river, and then along the other bank, first the eastern bank, and then the western, so the Spirit of man moves through both worlds, the waking world and the dream world.' (*B.U.*, 4.3.18 [*Selections*, p. 15].)
142. Intense and one-pointed aspiration lights up the whole being of man. '... when thine eye is single thy whole body also is full of light.' (*Luke*, XI,:34.) Also, *B.U.*, 4.4.2 (*Selections*, p. 23) says that 'the point of the heart grows luminous, and when it has grown luminous, it lights the soul upon its way'.
142a. *Ezekiel* XXVIII, 13–14.
143. A term used by disciples of spiritual teachers in the East to indicate the highest Self. It is the equivalent of *Ādi-Buddha* with Buddhist occultists, *Ātman* with the Brahmans and Christos with the ancient Gnostics.
144. 'When the Spirit of man enters into rest, drawing his material from this all-containing world, felling the wood himself and himself building the dwelling, the Spirit of man enters into dream, through his own shining, through his own light. Thus does the Spirit of man become his own light.' (*B.U.*, 4.3.9 [*Selections*, p. 12].)
145. Śaṅkara was the founder of the philosophical system called Advaita Vedānta which asserted that all existence is an illusory superimposition on the One

Reality called *Brahman*, which is identical with *Ātman*, the true Self. The supposed duality of perceiver and perceived is the result of the superimposition of a limited notion of self upon the One Reality. A comprehensive introduction to his teachings can be found in his *Crest Jewel of Discrimination*.
146. Suggestive of the Gnostic god Abraxas, who was the unfathomable fusion of good and evil. Man carries simultaneously within himself beings of light and darkness, the spiritual intelligence and the evil genius. That is why a total purification of one's nature is an essential prerequisite to the attainment of higher wisdom or power. Higher *manas* is that portion of the mind which gravitates towards universal good, and the lower *manas* is that portion which desires personal good or self-gratification.
147. 'Occultism is the general, all-inclusive term, the differentiating terms are White or Black; the same forces are used by both, and similar laws, for there are no special laws in this universe for any special set of workers in Nature's secrets. But the path of the untruthful and the wicked, while seemingly easy at first, is hard at last, for the black workers are the friends of no one, they are each against the other as soon as interest demands, and that may be anytime. It is said that final annihilation of the personal soul awaits those who deal in the destructive side of Nature's hall of experience.' ('Conversations on Occultism', *The Path*, October 1894.)
148. '... this destiny is guided either by the heavenly voice of the invisible *prototype* outside of us, or by our more intimate *astral*, or inner man, who is but too often the evil genius of the embodied entity called man. Both these lead on the outward man, but one of them must prevail.' (*S.D.* I, p. 639.)
149. Luke XI. 9.
150. Archaeus is the ' "Father-Ether", – the manifested basis and source of the innumerable phenomena of life.' (*S.D.* I, pp. 51–2.)
151. St. Teresa speaks of 'the inner castle' of the soul, and its 'mansions'. (See St. Teresa, *The Interior Castle*.)
152. '... not only is the Ego, or thinking man, Proteus, a multiform, ever-changing entity, but he is also, so to speak, capable of separating himself on the mind or dream plane into two or more entities' (*Tr.*, p. 74). Man, says Theosophy, is a unity in a diversity, and his lower, personal, transitory nature is formed of myriads of 'elementals' – points of life or energy, Leibnizian monads – all subservient to and dependent upon the divine and immortal spirit which is the true self of man. W.Q. Judge says about elementals – 'They are centres of force or energy which are acted on by us while thinking and in other bodily motions. We also act on them and give them form by a species of thought which we have no register of.' '... all atoms continually arriving at and departing from the "human system" are constantly assuming the impression conveyed by the acts and thoughts of that person, and therefore, if he sets up a strong current of thought, he attracts elementals in greater numbers, and they all take on one prevailing tendency or colour, so that all new arrivals find a homogeneous colour or image which they instantly assume. On the other hand, a man who has many diversities of thought and meditation is not homogeneous, but, so to say, parti-coloured, and so the elementals may lodge in that part which is different from the rest and go away in like condition.' ('Conversations on Occultism', *The Path*, May 1888.)
153. '... he is like Ain-Soph talking to Ain Soph, holding a dialogue with himself and speaking through, about, and to himself', says the *Transactions* (p. 74). An ancient Kabbalistic term meaning the boundless or limitless. It is the One, the highest abstraction, ineffable and inconceivable life, the Parabrahman of the Hindus. Deity is no-thing; it is nameless and therefore called Ain Soph

Notes and Commentary to pages 125–130

meaning No-thing. (See *Glo.*, 'En Soph'.)
154. These are the *vimānas* or sky-chariots of the Atlanteans. (See *S.D.* II, pp. 426-7.)
155. The fabled continent and civilization that was submerged in the Atlantic and Pacific Oceans prior to the emergence of civilizations in Asia and Europe. (cf. *S.D.* II, p. 314 fn.)
156. 'The world's great age begins anew, the golden years return.' (Shelley, 'Hellas' and also Virgil, *Eclogue* IV. l.3, 'The Golden Age returns'. ll. 1060-1.)
157. A.E. was clearly seeing visions of the civilization of the Atlanteans, imprinted on the astral light.
158. '. . . during the long night of rest called Pralaya, when all the existences are dissolved, the "UNIVERSAL MIND" remains as a permanent possibility of mental action, or as that abstract absolute thought, of which mind is the concrete relative manifestation.' (*S.D.* I, p. 38.) 'In strict truth, Universal Mind, being only another name for the Absolute, *out of time and space*, this Cosmic Ideation, or Mind, is not an evolution at all (least of all a "creation"), but simply one of the aspects of the former, which knows no change, which ever was, which is, and will be.' (*Tr.*, p. 22.)
159. There are planes of consciousness – 'globes', 'planets', as they are sometimes metaphysically called – which 'interpenetrate' the earth or mundane plane of consciousness we usually inhabit. A shift of consciousness, whether voluntary or involuntary, puts us in tune with these other planes or 'planets', and we may then see things from a wholly different perspective – 'as if from a different planet'. '*Our Globe, as taught from the first, is at the bottom of the arc of descent, where the matter of our perceptions exhibits itself in its grossest form. . . . Hence it only stands to reason that the globes which overshadow our Earth must be on different and superior planes. In short, as Globes, they are in* CO-ADUNITION *but not* IN CONSUBSTANTIALITY WITH OUR EARTH *and thus pertain to quite another state of consciousness.*' (*S.D.* I, p. 166.)
160. ' 'Tis by that sense alone which lies concealed within the hollow of thy brain . . .' (*Voice*, p. 18.) 'When the ascetic has completely mastered all the influences which the body has upon the inner man, and has laid aside all concern in regard to it, and in no respect is affected by it, the consequence is a removal of all obscurations of the intellect.' (Patañjali, *Yoga Aphorisms*, bk. III, no. 44, p. 55.)
161. The Sanskrit term *avatāra* refers to the incarnation of a god or divine being into the world. Hindu mythology speaks of many such divine incarnations at critical moments in the long history of humanity. A.E. does not, however, always use the term in its strict, traditional sense. The definition in the *Theosophical Glossary* is 'Divine incarnation. The descent of a god or some exalted Being, who has progressed beyond the necessity of Rebirths, into the body of a simple mortal. Krishna was an avatar of Vishnu. The Dalai Lama is regarded as an avatar of Avalokiteswara, and the Teschu Lama as one of Tsong-Kha-pa, or Amitabha.' (*Glo.*, 'Avatāra'.)
162. A.E. is saying that images of the past cannot be reflected in some universal medium in a flat, static two-dimensional way as in a mirror. But the astral light or 'ether' spoken of in Theosophy records the thoughts and energies as well as the events of the past, and thus all aspects or dimensions of events long gone by exist in this 'universal memory' as karmic seeds from which the present is being created and from which the future will be born.
163. 'Every person has about him a fluid, or plane, or sphere, of energy, whichever you please to call it, in which are constantly found elementals that partake of his nature. That is, they are tinted with his colour and impressed by his character.'

('Conversations on Occultism', *The Path*, September 1888.)
'As it (the elemental world) is automatic and like a photographic plate, all atoms continually arriving at and departing from the "human system" are constantly assuming the impression conveyed by the acts and thoughts of that person.' ('Conversations on Occultism', *The Path*, May 1888.)

164. 'In this realm (of the soul) the slightest thought becomes a voice or a picture. All thoughts make pictures. Every person has his private thoughts and desires.' ('Conversations on Occultism', *The Path*, January 1895.)

165. With the ancients, this is the luminous substance that pervades the whole of space, the lining or garment of the creative deity. It is the third of seven cosmic principles, standing above the astral light and below the *ākāśic* empyrean. The earth itself is but the most extreme solidification of aethereal substance. (See *Glo.*, 'Aether'.)

166. 'Then there is that which I referred to in a preceding conversation about the effect of our acts and thoughts upon, not only the portion of the astral light belonging to each of us with its elementals, but upon the whole astral world.' ('Conversations on Occultism', *The Path*, September 1888.) In his story, *The Skin of the Earth*, W.Q. Judge deals vividly with this theme of thought-impressions on the astral light.

167. 'Thus *reality* in the manifested world is composed of a *unity of units*, so to say, immaterial (from our stand-point) and infinite. This Leibnitz calls "Monads", Eastern philosophy *"Jivas"* – and Occultism gives it, with the Kabalists and all the Christians, a variety of names. They are with us, as with Leibnitz – "the expression of the universe", and every physical point is but the phenomenal expression of the noumenal, metaphysical point.' (*S.D.* I, pp. 629–30.)

168. '... these monads are representative Beings. Every monad reflects every other. Every monad is a living mirror of the Universe within its own sphere. And mark this, for upon it depends the power possessed by these monads, and upon this depends the work they can do for us; in mirroring the world, the monads are not mere passive reflective agents, but *spontaneously self-active*.' (*S.D.* I, p. 631.) 'Thus the Egg, on whatever plane you speak of, means the ever-existing undifferentiated matter which strictly is not matter at all but, as we call it, the Atoms. Matter is destructible in form while the Atoms are absolutely indestructible, being the quintessence of Substances. And here, I mean by "atoms" the primordial divine Units, not the "atoms" of modern Science.' (*Tr.*, p. 85.) Jesus' parable likening the kingdom of heaven to a mustard seed also points to the mighty power of the minute, the invisible, the unimportant, to produce the whole world of spiritual reality. (*Matthew* 13:31–2.)

169. In the *Chāndogya Upaniṣad* (6.12) the boy Svetaketu is taught that from the minute, almost invisible, divided seed of the fig a mighty banyan tree springs forth. Just so, 'that which is the finest essence – this whole world has that as its soul. That is Reality. That is Ātman. That art thou, Śvetaketu.'

170. 'There are but two ways of explaining the mystery of heredity; either the substance of the germinal cell is endowed with the faculty of crossing the whole cycle of transformations that lead to the construction of a separate organism and then to the reproduction of identical germinal cells; or, *those germinal cells do not have their genesis at all in the body of the individual, but proceed directly from the ancestral germinal cell passed from father to son through long generations.*' (*S.D.* I, p. 223 fn.)

171. The phrase is taken directly from Keats's 'Hyperion'.

172. 'Occultism regards every atom as an "independent entity" and every cell as a "conscious unit". It explains that no sooner do such atoms group to form cells,

than the latter become endowed with consciousness, each of its own kind, and with *free will to act within* the limits of law.' '. . . memory has no seat, no special organ of its own in the human brain, but that it has *seats* in every organ of the body.' ('Psychic and Noetic Action', *Lucifer*, October 1890.) 'This is the essence of Occult teaching – even in the Tantra works. Indeed, every organ in our body *has its own memory*. For if it is endowed with a consciousness "of its own kind", every cell must of necessity have also a memory of its own kind, as likewise its own *psychic* and *noetic* action.' (*Ibid.*)

173. Hindu three worlds. (See also note 127 above.)
174. Plato says that 'virtue is knowledge', that no gap can exist between theory and practice. The *Bhagavad Gītā* warns us that it would be foolish to think of *sāṁkhya* and *yoga* as separate doctrines, i.e., to imagine that theoretical understanding and practical discipline (*theoria* and *praxis*) can ultimately be separated. In the same vein, Spinoza declared that to attain to a certain plane of reality was identical with embodying a level of knowledge as well as a degree of virtue or energy.
175. Jesus – 'the kingdom of God is within you.' (*Luke* XVIII.21.)
176. See 'The Speech of the Gods', note 3.
177. The Vedas constitute the most sacred literature of Hindu mystical religion. The term *veda* is derived from the Sanskrit verb root *vid*, 'know', and the Vedas constitute the divine wisdom, eternal Truth, the *Sanātana Dharma*, recorded by the sages of the Golden Age in ancient India in magnificent hymns and poems of great power and imagination. There is, it is believed, the eternal, unrevealed, infinite and eternal Veda, of which the *saṁhitās* (recorded recursions) are but a manifested expression. The seers of ancient India *heard* and *saw* the divine Veda in moments of mystic revelation, and Vedic literature is thus regarded as *śruti*, 'revealed' literature – a revelation, however, quite different from the Christian sense of revelation in time by a personal God.
178. The idea of spiritual rebirth, a birth out of death, is common to all mystical traditions. Jesus says, 'He that findeth his life shall lose it: and he that loseth his life for my sake shall find it.' (*Matthew* X:39, 16:25; *Luke* IX:24.) Speaking again of this mystical rebirth he warns Nicodemus, 'Verily, verily, I say unto thee, Except a man be born again, he cannot see the kingdom of God.' *The Voice of the Silence*, in similar vein, advises the aspirant to the spiritual life, 'Give up thy life, if thou would'st live.' (p. 6.) The advice given by mystics of all ages and diverse traditions is that unless the individual goes through a process of 'dying to the world' he cannot attain the spiritual life. St. John of the Cross remarks – '. . . any soul that will ascend this mount in order to make of itself an altar whereon it may offer to God the sacrifice of pure love and praise and pure reverence, must, before ascending to the summit of the mount, have done these three things aforementioned perfectly. First, it must cast away all strange gods – namely, all strange affections and attachments; secondly, it must purify itself of the remnants which the desires aforementioned have left in the soul, by means of the dark night of sense whereof we are speaking, habitually denying them and repenting itself of them; and thirdly, in order to reach the summit of this high mount, it must have changed its garments, which, through its observance of the first two things, God will change for it, from old to new, by giving it a new understanding of God in God, the old human understanding being cast aside; and a new love of God in God, the will being now stripped of all its old desires and human pleasures, and the soul being brought into a new state of knowledge and profound delight, all other old images and forms of knowledge having been cast away, and all that belongs to the old man, which is the aptitude of the natural self, quelled . . .' (*Ascent*, bk. I, ch. 5); and 'a soul to attain to the state

of perfection, it has ordinarily first to pass through two principal kinds of night, which spiritual persons call purgations or purifications of the soul' (*Ibid.*, ch. 1); and indeed his profoundly perceptive description of two 'nights' is nothing but the record of the soul's descent into the valley of the shadow of death (dying to the world) in order to be raised into the sunlight of the Spirit. The author of *The Cloud of Unknowing* speaks movingly of the soul's experience of the two clouds – of forgetting and unknowing. 'We are apt to think that we are very far from God because of this cloud of unknowing between us and him, but surely it would be more correct to say that we are much farther from him if there is no cloud of forgetting between us and the whole created world. Whenever I say "the whole created world" I always mean not only the individual creatures therein, but everything connected with them. There is no exception whatever, whether you think of them as physical or spiritual beings, or of their states or actions, or of their goodness or badness. In a word, everything must be hidden under this 'cloud of forgetting'. (ch. 5.) For Eckhart, this 'dying' is a giving up of all sense knowledge, imagination, memory, understanding so that one may enter into 'the central silence' of the soul, 'where no creature dwells' and where one may find 'the barren God-head'. Every ancient religious tradition offers us myths about the descent into the realms of darkness and 'death' as a necessary precursor to birth in the world of the spirit – for example, Jesus' descent into Hell before the resurrection, Naciketas' sojourn in the Hall of Death in the *Kaṭha Upaniṣad* and Dionysus' descent into the underworld or Osiris' death and rebirth.

179. The subtle, mystical elements are here meant – spiritual essences – *tattvas*.
180. A reference to the New Testament story of the woman who touched Jesus' garment and was healed. Despite the thronging crowds, Jesus knew he had been touched for he felt that 'virtue had gone out of him.' (cf. *Mark* V, 24–35 an *Luke* VIII, 42–48.)
181. The ineffability of the incommunicable experience has been remarked on by all mystics and by commentators on mysticism such as William James. It is an experience as impossible to communicate to one who has not had it as is the taste of a fruit to one who has never eaten it. Socrates, in *Phaedrus*, says that to describe the soul as she really is is a task only the gods can undertake. The soul is not to be described to men who have not experienced its reality in their own hearts, but it may be dimly apprehended through myth and metaphor.
182. *Vāc*, 'Divine Speech', is the Word of which the whole universe is a manifestation.
183. 'Universal or Absolute Mind always *is* during Pralaya as well as Manvantara; it is immutable. The Ah-hi are the highest Dhyanis, the Logoi as just said, those who begin the downward evolution, or emanation. During Pralaya there are no Ah-hi, because they come into being only with the first *radiation* of the Universal Mind, which, *per se*, cannot be differentiated, and the radiation from which is the first *dawn* of Manvantara.' (*Tr.*, p. 20.)
184. 'Devanagari'. The name of the Sanskrit script or alphabet. Means 'the language of the gods' (lit., 'divine city writing'). (See Monier-Williams, *English-Sanskrit Dictionary*, p. 439ii.)
185. 'Sound is the characteristic of Akasa (Ether): it generates air, the property of which is Touch; which (by friction) becomes productive of Colour and Light (*Vishnu Purana*).' (*S.D.* I, p. 205.) Vach, the goddess of Speech (or Sound) is 'a form of Aditi – the principle higher than *Ether* – in Akasa, the synthesis of all the forces in Nature; thus Vach and Kwan-Yin are both the magic potency of Occult sound in Nature and Ether – which "Voice" calls forth Sien-Tchan, the illusive form of the Universe out of Chaos and the Seven Elements.' (*S.D.* I, p.

137.) It is said, in mystical philosophy, that the effects of *Fohat* or Cosmic Electricity 'include, among other things, Sound, Light, Colour, etc., etc.' (*S.D.* I, p. 554.)
186. Symbols are often called 'the language of the soul'. What cannot be expressed in words may be conveyed to the inner eye of the perceptive individual in a flash of intuition through the use of symbols. Ancient spiritual truths were often written down in glyphs and symbols of a universal nature. 'The religious and esoteric history of every nation was embedded in symbols; it was never expressed in so many words.' (*S.D.* I, p. 307.)
187. 'Psyche' is the word for butterfly in Greek and thus metaphorically for the human soul newly awakened from its chrysalis of blind matter.
188. In Indian mysticism, sounds and colours have direct correspondences (vowels are more important than consonants). Similar ideas concerning colour-sound correspondences are also found in Western mystics such as Jacob Boehme.
189. This is a reference to the Third Eye and the light in the centre of the forehead in Hindu and Buddhist mysticism.
190. 'Before the voice can speak in the presence of the Masters, it must have lost the power to wound.' (*L.O.P.*, p. 70.)
191. In Indian philosophy and mysticism true speech (*Vāc*) is directly connected with seeing into the heart of things. This 'seeing' is a flash of intuition. In Sanskrit ('the perfect language') every sound and name originally corresponded to the nature of the thing or activity.
192. Especially held to be true of Sanskrit letters. (See note 191 above.)
193. In Sanskrit the alphabet is arranged according to the mystically (and phonetically) correct order of sounds, i.e., vowels, gutturals, palatals, linguals, dentals, labials, etc.
194. It is said that the universe emerged from silence as the Word, which dispersed itself throughout space in the form of vibration. A common feature of all life is that it is vibratory, a result of the initial manifesting impulse of *Vāc* or *the Word*. Thus, audible sound is the external expression of inaudible forces which precede them. The utterance of various sounds awakens these energies to life as they are in sympathetic harmony with them. Speech and language have a truly spiritual basis as the offspring of *Vāc* and provide the means for creative action or true magic in the world.
195. *Genesis*, II, 20.
196. (See *C.O.V.*, note 115.) The 'Heavenly man' is Adam Kadmon in the Kabbalah (cf. *S.D.* II, p. 37), or primordial Puruṣa from whom issues forth the whole manifested universe. '*Every form on earth, and every speck (atom) in Space strives in its efforts towards self-formation to follow the model placed for it in the "HEAVENLY MAN".*' (*S.D.* I, p. 183.)
197. In the Vedic hymns Agni, the god of fire, the mediator and transmuter, is one of the most frequently invoked deities. Also invoked very often is the Sun ('the fire in the sky') in his different aspects – hidden and mystical, manifest, in the morning, in mid-heaven, in the evening. In the Vedas over forty names are used for the sun, each with a different mystical meaning and each invoking a distinct invisible force.
198. When, O Lord of the Word, the Wise established
Name-giving, the first principle of language,
Their inmost excellence, pristine and pure,
Hidden deep within, was brought to light through love.
(Hymn to Vāc)
199. The best example of this is Sanskrit, which is composed of fifty-two discrete sounds which represent the primary forces of invisible nature.

200. '*The spoken word has a potency unknown to, unsuspected and disbelieved in*, by the modern "sages". Because sound and rhythm are closely related to the four Elements of the Ancients; and because such or another vibration in the air is sure to awaken corresponding powers, union with which produces good or bad results, as the case may be.' (*S.D.* I, p. 307.)
201. The Oversoul is sometimes referred to as the *Anima Mundi*.
202. 'Now it has elsewhere been said: "This, namely, *a*, *u*, and *m* (= om), is the sound-form of this (*Ātman*, Soul)," (*Mai.U.*, 6.5). The Upaniṣad then proceeds to give the 'forms' or expressions of the Om at different levels of reality in the macrocosm and in man.
203. . . . the great Circle, or O, itself a symbol for the universe . . .' (*S.D.* I, p. 359.) The evolution of the entire universe from the One Absolute Reality may be represented by the circle with increasing differentiating points and lines within it. The circle seems to be a universal symbol of the ultimate reality and of eternity, containing, as it does, the potentiality of an infinity of meanings. 'The first and only form of the *prima materia* our brain-consciousness can cognise, is a circle. Train your thought first of all to a thorough acquaintance with a limited circle, and expand it gradually. You will soon come to a point when without its ceasing to be a circle in thought, it yet becomes infinite and limitless even to the inner perceptions. It is this circle which we call Brahmā, the germ, atom or *anu*: a latent atom embracing infinitude and boundless Eternity during Pralaya, an active one during the life-cycles; but one which has neither circumference nor plane, only limitless expansion. Therefore the Circle is the first geometrical figure and symbol in the subjective world, and it becomes a Triangle in the objective.' (*Tr.*, pp. 126–7.)
204. 'Electricity, light, heat, etc., have been aptly termed the "Ghost or Shadow of Matter in Motion", i.e., supersensuous states of matter whose effects only we are able to cognise.' (*S.D.* I, p. 146.)
205. 'In the "beginning", that which is called in mystic phraseology "Cosmic *Desire*" evolves into absolute Light. Now light without any shadow would be absolute light – in other words, absolute darkness – as physical science seeks to prove. That shadow appears under the form of primordial matter, allegorized – if one likes – in the shape of the Spirit of Creative Fire or Heat. If, rejecting the poetical form and allegory, science chooses to see in this the primordial Fire-Mist, it is welcome to do so. Whether one way or the other, whether Fohat or the famous FORCE of Science, nameless, and as difficult of definition as our Fohat himself, that Something "caused the Universe to move with circular motion", as Plato has it; or, as the Occult teaching expresses it: "*The Central Sun causes Fohat to collect primordial dust in the form of balls, to impel them to move in converging lines and finally to approach each other and aggregate.*" ' (*S.D.* I, p. 201.)
206. A.E.'s symbol is a variation of the ancient sacred symbol of the *svastika*. 'Few world-symbols are more pregnant with real occult meaning than the Swastica. It is symbolized by the figure 6; for, like that figure, it points in its concrete imagery, as the ideograph of the number does, to the Zenith and the Nadir, to North, South, West, and East; one finds the unit everywhere, and that unit reflected in all and every unit. It is the emblem of the activity of Fohat, of the continual revolution of the "wheels", and of the Four Elements, the "Sacred Four", in their mystical, and not alone in their cosmical meaning; further, its four arms, bent at right angles, are intimately related, as shown elsewhere, to the Pythagorean and Hermetic scales. One initiated into the mysteries of the meaning of the Swastica, say the Commentaries, "can trace on it, with mathematical precision, the evolution of Kosmos and the whole period of

Sandhyā". Also "the relation of the Seen to the Unseen", and "the first procreation of man and species". (*S.D.* II, p. 587.)
207. 'The centripetal and the centrifugal forces, which are male and female, positive and negative, physical and spiritual, the two being the one *Primordial* Force.' (*S.D.* I, p. 282 fn.) 'In Kosmos, the equilibrium must be preserved. The operations of the two contraries produce harmony, like the centripetal and centrifugal forces, which are necessary to each other − mutually interdependent . . .' (*S.D.* I, p. 416.) The entire universe is produced through these opposing movements and everything is sustained through the balance or equilibrium maintained between the two forces. The Chinese mystics (particularly the Taoists) explained the whole of the universe as an interplay between the *yin* and the *yang*, opposed to and yet eternally flowing into each other, and both contained, as the *yin-yang* diagram shows, within the other great circle. In the life of the mystic, it is the delicate balance to be preserved between the expansive outward flowing, all-embracing flow of *buddhi* (intuition) and the concentrating, focussing, one-pointed effort of *manas*. 'The active Power, the "Perpetual motion of the great Breath" only awakens Kosmos at the dawn of every new Period, setting it into motion by means of the two contrary Forces, and thus causing it to become objective on the plane of Illusion. In other words, that dual motion transfers Kosmos from the plane of the Eternal Ideal into that of finite manifestation, or from the *Noumenal* to the *phenomenal* plane.' (*S.D.* I, p. 282.)
208. Dualism is a characteristic of the world of manifestation. 'Light and darkness are the world's eternal ways.' (*Gītā*, ch. VIII, p. 62.)
209. '*Sloka* (1). THE LAST VIBRATION OF THE SEVENTH ETERNITY THRILLS THROUGH INFINITUDE. THE MOTHER SWELLS, EXPANDING FROM WITHIN WITHOUT LIKE THE BUD OF THE LOTUS . . . It is only when "the mother swells" that differentiation sets in, for when the first Logos radiates through primordial and undifferentiated matter there is as yet no action in Chaos.' (*Tr.*, p. 93.)
210. 'The Web is the ever-existent primordial substance − pure spirit to our conception − the material from which objective universe or universes are evolved. When the breath of fire or Father is upon it, it expands; that is to say, as subjective material it is limitless, eternal, indestructible. When the breath of the Mother touches it, that is, when the time of manifestation arrives and it has to come into objectivity of form, it contracts, for there is no such thing as an objective material form which is limitless.' (*Tr.*, pp. 127−8.)
211. In the *Bṛhadāraṇyaka Upaniṣad* we find the original, eternal *Ātman* or *Puruṣa*, wrapped in solitary contemplation, moving outward with the mental utterance 'I am', initiating the production of all creatures. (*B.U.*, 1.4.1.)
212. Varuṇa, in Indian mythology, was the god of the deep blue sky as well as of the ocean.
213. *M* is the last sound uttered by the closing of the mouth, hence, the last letter of AUM. It signifies the end, death, *pralaya*, etc. W.Q. Judge, writing about the occult and mystical significance of the OM, points out that, 'If these two sounds, (a and u) so compounded into one, were to proceed indefinitely, there would be of course no destruction of them. But it is not possible to continue the utterance further than the breath, and whether the lips are compressed, or the tongue pressed against the roof of the mouth, or the organs behind that used, there will be in the finishing of the utterance the closure or *M* sound, which among the Aryans had the meaning of *stoppage*. In this last letter there is found the destruction of the whole word or letter. To reproduce it a slight experiment will show that by no possibility can it be begun with *M*, but that *AU* invariably

commences even the utterance of *M* itself. Without fear of successful contradiction, it can be asserted that all speech begins with *AU*, and the ending, or destruction of speech, is in *M*.' ('AUM!', *The Path*, April 1886.)

214. 'Dreamless sleep is one of the seven states of consciousness known in Oriental esotericism. In each of these states a different portion of the mind comes into action; or as a Vedantin would express it, the individual is conscious in a different plane of his being.' (*S.D.* I, p. 47; also see previous note on dreams, note 124.)

215. The whole period of manifestation of the universe, cycle within cycle, follows the principle of the downward arc of involution and the upward arc of evolution. From the first flutter of differentiation, spirit involves itself in greater and greater individuation and through the differentiation of an ever-increasing multiplicity of forms. When the greatest possible differentiation of forms in the cycle has taken place and the lowest point of matter reached, the upward swing begins. Using the diversity of forms, spirit or consciousness begins to evolve *out* of them through the self-conscious affirmation of the unity of spirit that lies behind the multiplicity. Thus the consciousness is drawn away from the many and journeys back towards the One – spirit evolving out of matter.

216. Intuition is a distinct faculty which can be consciously aroused by the higher mind. It is the power of perceiving the formless essences of things.

217. 'That which in thee shall live forever, that which in thee *knows*, for it is knowledge, is not of fleeting life: it is the Man that was, that is, and will be, for whom the hour shall never strike.' (*Voice*, p. 34, also fn.) 'There must therefore be something eternally persisting, which is the witness and perceiver of every passing change, itself unchangeable. All objects, and all states of what western philosophers call Mind, are modifications, for in order to be seen or known by us, there must be some change, either partial or total, from a precedent state. The perceiver of these changes is the inner man – Arjuna-Krishna.' (*Gita Notes*, p. 23.)

218. Each individual contains within himself all the powers of the universe but we have only developed a tiny portion of these. Vast resources therefore lie hidden within us. ' . . . in man are the same powers and forces which are to be found anywhere in Nature. He is held by the Masters of Wisdom to be the highest product of the whole system of evolution, and mirrors in himself every power, however wonderful or terrible, of Nature; by the very fact of being such a mirror he is man.' (*Ocean*, p. 136.)

219. Cf. 'Ten Propositions of Oriental Psychology' by H.P. Blavatsky in *Isis Unveiled* (vol. II, pp. 587–90), Proposition eight, which states: 'Races of men differ in spiritual gifts as in color, stature or any other external quality . . .' As individuals possess different gifts and propensities, so do races and nations.

220. 'It was the "Golden Age" in those days of old, the age when the "gods walked the earth, and mixed freely with the mortals".' (*S.D.* II, p. 273.)

221. 'FROM THE FIRST-BORN (*primitive, or the first man*) THE THREAD BETWEEN THE SILENT WATCHER AND HIS SHADOW BECOMES MORE STRONG AND RADIANT WITH EVERY CHANGE (*re-incarnation*) . . . (*a*) This sentence: "The thread between the *silent watcher* and his *shadow* (man) becomes stronger" – with every re-incarnation – is another psychological mystery . . . the "Watcher" and his "Shadows" – the latter numbering as many as there are re-incarnations for the monad – are one. The Watcher, or the divine prototype, is at the upper rung of the ladder of being; the shadow, at the lower.' (*S.D.* I, pp. 264–5.)

222. The word for 'death' in many Indo-European languages has some such root. The Sanskrit root is the verb *mr* – to 'die'.

223. *Ma* = to measure. The word *māyā*, meaning 'illusion', comes from this root. (See Monier-Williams.)

Notes and Commentary to pages 143–146

224. Sanskrit root *man*, 'to think'.
225. Cf. Jacob Boehme, *The Signature of All Things*. Boehme, like Paracelsus and the Fire Philosophers of the Middle Ages, developed the doctrine of signatures, whereby one can evoke the spiritual essence behind a phenomenal object by 'reading' its root structure and form. This was especially important in the preparation of alchemical formulae from appropriate materials of the mineral, plant and animal kingdoms.
226. True intuition or *buddhi* is the seat of spiritual discrimination. Intellect devoid of intuition is analysis without insight, or what is referred to as 'head learning' as opposed to 'heart wisdom'. (For a complete classification of human principles see *Ocean*, p. 32 *et al.*)
227. In the Sanskrit alphabet the consonants are grouped in five articulatory classes and proceed in a natural order from the throat to the lips, i.e., gutturals, palatals, linguals, dentals and labials. (See note 193.)
228. 'All the thoughts and emotions, all the learning and knowledge, revealed and acquired, of the early races, found their pictorial expression in allegory and parable. Why? Because *the spoken word has a potency unknown to, unsuspected and disbelieved in*, by the modern "sages". Because sound and rhythm are closely related to the four Elements of the Ancients; and because such or another vibration in the air is sure to awaken corresponding powers, union with which produces good or bad results, as the case may be. No student was ever allowed to recite historical, religious, or any real events in so many unmistakable words, lest the powers connected with the event should be once more attracted. Such events were narrated only during the Initiation, and every student had to record them in corresponding symbols, drawn out of his own mind and examined later by his master, before they were finally accepted.' (*S.D.* I, p. 307.)
229. *Bhagavad Gītā*, ch. X.33, p. 75.
230. See earlier note on correspondences between colours and sounds, note 188.
231. See *Bṛhadāraṇyaka Upaniṣad*, 1.4.7; 3.9.10–18; 5.5.2–4; *Chāndogya Upaniṣad*, 3.13.1–6; 5.18.1–2; and *Aitareya Upaniṣad*, 1.4.
232. 'To see ... heaven in a wild flower'. (Blake, 'Auguries of Innocence'.) Saint-Martin says, '... I heard flowers that sounded.' (Underhill, *Mysticism*, p.7.)
233. *Genesis* II.5.
234. See note 6.
235. 'To see the world in a grain of sand' (Blake, 'Auguries of Innocence'.) As the Upaniṣads repeatedly affirm, the *Ātman* (soul) is identical with *Brahman*, and may be equally described as 'smaller than the smallest' and 'greater than the greatest'. '... this Soul of mine within the heart is greater than the earth, greater than the atmosphere, greater than the sky, greater than these worlds.' (*Ch.U.*, 3.14.3.)
236. A reference to the incident of the stealing of cows by the infant Hermes. At the end of the episode, Apollo appoints him protector of herdsmen, and he is sometimes known by the title *Nomios*, 'the pasturer'. (Grant and Hazel, p. 230.)
237. Cf. 'The kingdom of heaven is taken with violence.' (*Matthew* XI.12.)
238. *Matthew* V.48.
239. The phrase is originally found in *Daniel* VII.9. However, it also means the primeval spirit of wisdom in all religions; Brahma in the East and the Holy Ghost in Christianity; that which manifests through Adam Kadmon or the Universal Man, as the Kabbalists say, to become incarnate Humanity. Also regarded as the essence of cosmic force or electricity.

240. 'The human Will is all powerful and the Imagination is a most useful faculty with a dynamic force.' (*Ocean*, p. 139.)
241. 'Rāja-yoga' – the royal discipline; the 'kingly knowledge'. (Cf. *Gītā*, ch. IX.2, p. 64.) These are all phrases used for the high road of spiritual discipline.
242. It is said that Buddha once remarked that while 'miracles' could be worked by understanding the laws of invisible nature, the highest magic consists in the change brought about in the human heart.
243. Fire is the universal symbol in all mystical philosophies of the spirit and to have mastery of the Fire is to have become an initiated, perfected hierophant to whom the fire of the Holy Spirit is a continuous living reality. 'Deity is an arcane, living (or moving) FIRE, and the eternal witnesses to this unseen Presence are Light, Heat, Moisture.' (*S.D.* I, p. 2.) 'Fire and Flame destroy the body of an Arhat, their essence makes him immortal.' (*Bodhi-mur, Book II.*) 'The knowledge of the absolute Spirit, like the effugence of the sun, or like heat in fire, is naught else than the absolute Essence itself,' says Sankaracharya.' (*S.D.* I, p. 6.) 'Sankaracharya the greatest of the Esoteric masters of India, says that *fire* means a deity which presides over Time (kala).' (*S.D.* I, p. 86.)
244. The seven or forty-nine fires are, in Indian mysticism, references to the spiritual powers that lie hidden in man at different levels of his being corresponding to the living Divine Fire that pulsates through the planes of the universe. The individual's progress along the spiritual path may be depicted as a gradual awakening of these latent fires. '*To man, it gives all that it bestows on all the rest of the manifested units in nature; but develops, furthermore, the reflection of all its* FORTY-NINE FIRES *in him. Each of his seven principles is an heir in full to, and a partaker of, the seven principles of the "great Mother".'* (*S.D.* I, p. 291.) 'Every *fire* has a distinct function and meaning in the worlds of the physical and the spiritual. It has, moreover, in its *essential* nature a corresponding relation to one of the human psychic faculties, besides its well determined chemical and physical potencies when coming in contact with the *terrestrially* differentiated matter.' (*S.D.* I, p. 521.)
245. 'The Archaeus is of a magnetic nature, and *attracts or repels* other sympathetic or antipathetic forces belonging to the same plane. . . . The vital force is not enclosed in man, but radiates (within) and around him like a luminous sphere (aura) . . .' (Dr. F. Hartmann, *Life of Paracelsus*, quoted in *S.D.* I, pp. 538–9.) The arousal of the inward fires spoken of above creates a kind of luminous glow around the individual capable of being actually seen by the eye of a pure clairvoyant. It is this glow which has been traditionally represented, in both Eastern and Western iconography, by the halo around the head.
246. This is the fiery power of *kuṇḍalinī*. 'The "Power" and the "World-Mother" are names given to *kuṇḍalinī* – one of the mystic "Yogi powers". It is *Buddhi* considered as an active instead of a passive principle (which it is generally, when regarded only as the vehicle, or casket of the Supreme Spirit ATMA). It is an electro-spiritual force, a creative power which when aroused into action can as easily kill as it can create.' (*Voice*, p. 10 fn.) '*Kundalini*, the "Serpent Power", or mystic fire. *Kundalini* is called the "Serpentine" or the *annular* power on account of its spiral-like working or progress in the body of the ascetic developing the power in himself. It is an electric fiery occult or *Fohatic* power, the great pristine force which underlies all organic and inorganic matter.' (*Voice*, p. 13 fn.)
247. *The Voice of the Silence*, speaking of the ladder of the seven mystic sounds, says, 'The second comes as the sound of a silver cymbal of the Dhyanis, awakening the twinkling stars.' (*Voice*, p. 11.)
248. The Third Eye, see note 189.

249. Divine or white magic stresses the importance of purity of motive. If this is lacking, if the motive for investigating and arousing the powers latent in one's being is a personal and selfish one, then one is involved in the most dangerous of endeavours, one is lighting a match, as it were, in a dark magazine room full of gunpowder. Only the strictest adherence to a high level of virtue and pure altruism can guide us through this dangerous area, this path as fine as a razor's edge.

250. 'Verily I say unto you, All sins shall be forgiven unto the sons of men, and blasphemies wherewith soever they shall blaspheme; But he that shall blaspheme against the Holy Ghost hath never forgiveness, but is in danger of eternal damnation . . .' (*Mark* III, 28–29.) This sin against the Holy Ghost is related to the loss (or atrophy) of the Third Eye of wisdom, the divine eye or 'eye of Siva'. 'THE "THIRD EYE" IS INDISSOLUBLY CONNECTED WITH KARMA . . . The "eye of Siva" did not become entirely atrophied before the close of the Fourth Race. When spirituality and all the divine powers and attributes of the deva-man of the Third had been made the hand-maidens of the newly-awakened physiological and psychic passions of the physical man, instead of the reverse, the eye lost its powers. But such was the law of Evolution, and it was, in strict accuracy, no FALL. The sin was not in using those newly-developed powers, but in *misusing* them; in making of the tabernacle, designed to contain a god, the fane of every *spiritual* iniquity.' (*S.D.* II, p. 302.) The Breath is often the symbol of the highest spirit or deity in Indian thought. 'The One breathed, breathless', and the *Taittirīya Upaniṣad* says, 'For truly, breath is the life of beings; Therefore it is called the Life-of-all.' (2.3) In the *Chāndogya Upaniṣad* we find, 'Om! Verily, he who knows the chiefest and best, becomes the chiefest and best. Breath, verily, is the chiefest and best.' (*B.U.*, 6.1.1; *Ch.U.*, 5.1.1.)

251. Paul, I *Corinthians* XII. 7–10, 28.

252. 'Then from the heart that Power shall rise into the sixth, the middle region, the place between thine eyes, when it becomes the breath of the ONE-SOUL . . .' (*Voice*, p. 10); '. . . by that sense alone which lies concealed within the hollow of thy brain . . .' (*Ibid.*, p. 18); ' . . . as a lamp sheltered from the wind flickereth not' (*Gıta*, ch. VI.19, p. 47).

253. The creative fire of self-conscious mind, the use of which alone can enable man to return to his spiritual home.

254. 'What is the *real* object of modern education? Is it to cultivate and develop the mind in the right direction; to teach the disinherited and hapless people to carry with fortitude the burden of life (allotted them by Karma); to strengthen their will; to inculcate in them the love of one's neighbour and the feeling of mutual interdependence and brotherhood; and thus to train and form the character for practical life? Not a bit of it. And yet, these are undeniably the objects of all true education. No one denies it; all your educationalists admit it, and talk very big indeed on the subject. But what is the practical result of their action? Every young man and boy, nay, every one of the younger generation of schoolmasters will answer: "The object of modern education is to pass examinations", a system not to develop right emulation, but to generate and breed jealousy, envy, hatred almost, in young people for one another, and thus train them for a life of ferocious selfishness and struggle for honours and emoluments instead of kindly feeling.' (*Key*, pp. 265-6.)

255. Like many another mystic, A.E. cherished the doctrine of man's divine ancestry, of man as a fallen god, self-exiled from his heavenly home, a pure soul in essence, wearing the muddy and bedraggled garments of this earth, a prince in pauper's clothing. He is inherently capable of rising once again to loftier realms to reclaim his spiritual heritage. But, as A.E. points out, some of the

children of the Divine King, forgetful of their proud ancestry, believe themselves to be worms doomed to suffer from the eternal burden of original sin; others, no less ignorant, caught in the narrow dogma of materialistic theories of evolution, see themselves, alas, as the poor descendants of some primitive animal ancestors.

256. 'When he goes to sleep, these worlds are his. Then he becomes a great king, as it were. Then he becomes a great Brahman, as it were. He enters the high and the low, as it were. As a great king, taking with him his people, moves around in his own country as he pleases, even so here this one, taking with him his senses, moves around in his own body (*śarīra*) as he pleases . . . Verily, as a youth or a great king or a great Brahman might rest when he has reached the summit of bliss, so this one now rests.' (*B.U.*, 2.1.18–19.)

257. Parable of the Prodigal Son, *Luke* XV.11–32. There is also the story by Hans Christian Andersen about the prince who posed as a swineherd.

258. The Homeric epic of the wanderings and adventures of Ulysses has sometimes been interpreted as the obstacle-strewn journey of the soul through the travails of earth-life back to its own divine country.

259. '*Manas*, or the Thinker is the reincarnating being, the immortal who carries the results and values of all the different lives lived on earth or elsewhere.' (*Ocean*, p. 54.)

260. A phrase used by Jesus (*Luke* XVI. 8), and again by Paul (I *Thessalonians* V.5).

261. 'Elementals: Spirits of the Elements. The creatures evolved in the four Kingdoms or Elements – earth, air, fire, and water. They are called by the Kabbalists, Gnomes (of the earth), Sylphs (of the air), Salamanders (of the fire), and Undines (of the water). Except a few of the higher kinds, and their rulers, they are rather forces of nature than ethereal men and women. These forces, as the servile agents of the Occultist, may produce various effects; but if employed by "Elementaries" – in which case they enslave the mediums – they will deceive the credulous. All the lower invisible beings generated on the 5th, 6th, and 7th *planes* of our terrestrial atmosphere, are called Elementals: Peris, Devs, Djins, Sylvans, Satyrs, Fauns, Elves, Dwarfs, Trolls, Kobolds, Brownies, Nixies, Goblins, Pinkies, Banshees, Moss People, White Ladies, Spooks, Fairies, etc., etc., etc.' (*Glo.*, 'Elementals'.)

262. The astral man is akin to the *kāma rūpa* yet normally recoils from kamalokic shells.

263. Theosophy speaks of the sevenfold constitution of the human being, each principle distinct on its own plane and yet merging into that above and that below it. The Vedantins speak of the five *kośas* – sheaths or coverings of the true Self or *Ātman*.

264. It is recognized in Eastern thought that one may meet one's guru in sleep – in tranquil realms of the deepest sleep undisturbed by the chaos and turmoil of confused personal dreams.

265. Modern psychology does not take account of the highest aspects of man.

266. This is the *triloka* of the Hindus – *bhūrloka*, *antarikṣaloka* and *svargaloka* or *devaloka*.

267. 'There are no chariots there, no spans, no roads. But he projects from himself chariots, spans, roads. There are no blisses there, no pleasure, no delights. But he projects from himself blisses, pleasures, delights. There are no tanks there, no lotus-pools, no streams, but he projects from himself tanks, lotus-pools, streams. For he is a creator.' (*B.U.*, 4.3.10.)

268. According to the chronology of evolutionary cycles recorded in *The Secret Doctrine*, our race has come to a point where it is beginning to prepare the way for the coming sixth sub-race (ours being the fifth) which, it is said, will

demonstrate powers and faculties beyond anything we commonly witness in human beings today. Such a spiritual impulse will be felt by the intuitive long before it becomes manifest in the race. (Cf. *S.D.* II, pp. 445–6.)

269. In line with the teachings of the Buddha and Plato, both of whom exhorted men to think deeply for themselves and not expect to receive from others vicarious confirmation of the profoundest spiritual truth, H.P. Blavatsky wrote in her preface to *The Key to Theosophy*, 'To the mentally lazy or obtuse, Theosophy must remain a riddle; for in the world mental as in the world spiritual each man must progress by his own efforts. The writer cannot do the reader's thinking for him.' (p. xi.)

269a. This chapter was originally published in two instalments under the title 'The Children of Lir' in the *United Irishman* for 8 and 15 March 1902. The first instalment began with the paragraphs included now in square brackets; they were omitted when it was published in *The Candle of Vision*.

270. The story of manifestation recounted here is in accord with the cosmogonies of all ancient religions. Although terms and concepts change according to age and place, the vision behind them is the golden thread which binds together all human beings as inheritors of a common divine ancestry. Compare what A.E. says with the description of the boundless and eternal One in the *Ṛg Veda* Hymn of Creation –

>Nor Aught nor Nought existed; yon bright sky
>Was not, nor heaven's broad roof outstretched above.
>What covered all? what sheltered? what concealed?
>Was it the water's fathomless abyss?
>There was not death – yet there was nought immortal,
>There was no confine betwixt day and night;
>The only One breathed breathless by itself,
>Other than It there nothing since has been.
>Darkness there was, and all at first was veiled
>In gloom profound – an ocean without light . . .
>
>(*S.D.* I, p. 26)

271. 'The Tao that can be named is not the eternal Tao', says the *Tao Te Ching* at the very beginning. The Upaniṣads remind us that nothing in the end can be affirmed about the absolute *Brahman-ātman* save *neti-neti* ('not this, not that'). 'There the eye goes not; Speech goes not, nor the mind.' (*K.U.*, 3.) 'Wherefrom words turn back, together with the mind, not having attained.' (*Tai. U.*, 2.4.9.) It 'exceeds by measure of five fingers all that can be said about it', for it is beyond conceptions, beyond all categories and distinctions of human thought.

272. *Brahman* cannot be described, nothing may be affirmed of it, but it may be experienced in the depths of human consciousness.

273. 'Breath, verily, is the chiefest and best.' (*Ch. U.*, 5.1.1.) 'Now when the Breath was about to go off – as a fine horse might tear out the pegs of his foot-tethers all together, thus did it tear out the other Breaths all together. They all came to it and said: "Sir! Remain. You are the most superior of us. Do not go off".' (*Ibid.*, vs. 12.) 'Verily, they do not call them "Speeches", nor "Eyes" nor "Ears", nor "Minds". They call them "Breaths" (*prāṇa*), for the vital breath is all these.' (*Ibid.*, vs. 15)

274.
>Who knows the secret? who proclaimed it here?
>Whence, whence this manifold creation sprang?
>The Gods themselves came later into being.
>
>(*Ṛg Veda*, Hymn of Creations, *S.D.* I, p. 26)

275. The silence that precedes sound, the silence from which even the sacred Om emerges and into which it recedes (the Om without metres and measures, as the sage *Guaḍapāda* calls it) is the primeval silence higher than even the most sacred of sounds.
276. The symbol of the great World-Tree is common to a number of ancient mythologies. *The Secret Doctrine* describes the Indian symbol – 'Thus, the Asvattha, tree of Life and Being, whose destruction alone leads to immortality, is said in the Bhagavad Gītā to grow with its roots above and its branches below (ch. xv). The roots represent the Supreme Being, or First Cause, the LOGOS; but one has to go beyond those roots to *unite oneself with Krishna* . . . Its boughs are Hiranyagharba (Brahmā or Brahman in his highest manifestations, say Sridhara and Madhusudana), the highest Dhyan Chohans or Devas. The Vedas are its leaves. He only who goes *beyond* the roots shall never return, i.e., shall reincarnate no more during this "age" of Brahmā.' (*S.D.* I, p. 406.) In Nordic mythology, similarly, is to be found the all-important Yggdrasil tree, an equivalent symbol.
277. The whole manifested universe, according to ancient wisdom, springs from seven rays of the One Logos or seven streams or pathways issuing forth from the primordial fountain of life. '*The Seven Beings in the Sun are the Seven Holy Ones, Self-born from the inherent power in the matrix of Mother substance. It is they who send the Seven Principal Forces, called rays* . . .' (An occult commentary quoted in *S.D.* I, p. 290.)
278. The Absolute *Brahman* transcends the duality of spirit and matter (substance), according to the most ancient teachings of the mystics, reiterated by Theosophy.
279. The Night of Brahmā, as the Hindus call it, when there is no manifested universe.
280. A.E. believed that the creative God of the first book of *Genesis* is *not* the highest divine principle, but rather the First Logos.
281. Seven Dhyan Chohans or seven Dhyani Buddhas. (See note 277 above.)
282. *Ṛg Veda* Hymn of Creation:
   The Most High Seer that is in highest heaven,
   He knows it – or perchance even He knows not.
                                                             (*S.D.* I, p. 26)
   Mulaprakṛti is called the Veil of *Parabrahm*, or as *Transactions* puts it, 'In all cosmogonies the first differentiation was considered feminine. It is Mulaprakriti which conceals or veils Parabrahm; Sephira the *light* that emanates first from Ain-Soph; and in Hesiod it is Gaea who springs from Chaos . . .' (p. 2.)
283. This is the *mahāmāyā* of Indian philosophy – the great world illusion which hides the face of Reality.
284. This would correspond to Aditi in Indian mythology.
285. Unmanifested Logos.
286. 'Aether: With the ancients the divine luminiferous substance which pervades the whole universe, the "garment" of the Supreme Deity . . .' (*Glo.*, 'Aether', and see note 165.)
287. 'Akasa: The subtle, supersensuous spiritual essence which pervades all space; the primordial substance erroneously identified with Ether. But it is to Ether what Spirit is to Matter, or *Ātma* to *kama-rupa*. It is, in fact, the Universal Space in which lies inherent the eternal Ideation of the Universe in its ever-changing aspects on the planes of matter and objectivity, and from which radiates the *First Logos*, or expressed thought. This is why it is stated in the *Puranas* that Akasa has but one attribute, namely sound, for sound is but the translated symbol of *Logos* – "Speech" in its mystic sense.' (*Glo.*, 'Akasa'.)

288. *John* I:1.
289. The magical moments before nightfall and before dawn are called *saṇdhyās* by Hindus, a word which literally means 'twilight' but which is used in a more mystic context to refer to crucial and critical moments that distinguish one phase from another (night and day, dawn from night), when, as it were, cosmic energies trembled in the balance. At the cosmic level, there is a similar *saṅdhyā* before the dawn of manifestation.
290. 'Desire first arose in It . . .' says the *Ṛg Veda* Hymn of Creation. Desire here is love, compassion, creative energy.
291. The Many are an illusion – so we are told by Plato and the Upaniṣads. The World of Becoming, of *māyā* is only an image, at best, of the true reality.
292. *Ānanda*, 'joy, bliss', is regarded as one of the three eternal attributes of *Ātman* in Indian thought.
293. This is a reference to higher versus lower *eros* in Plato, or higher versus lower *kāma* in Indian philosophy. The lower is but a shadow, a distortion, perhaps an inversion, of its higher counterpart,
294. This 'Fall of the soul' in Plato and Plotinus results from drinking the waters of Lethe or forgetfulness. The condition of the soul is worsened by its gravitation towards earthly passions which further obscure its knowledge of its own divinity. 'Our birth is but a sleep and a forgetting.' (Wordsworth, 'Ode: Intimations of Immortality'.) In the Upaniṣads and Śaṅkara also, the soul forgets its true nature. *Avidyā*, 'nescience', is the source of all our difficulties and sorrows.
295. Plato in *Phaedrus* makes the soul see the vision of Beauty from afar and so it longs to move towards it.
296. The astral realm – mid-way between the material and the spiritual.
297. Giving in to the gravitational pull of *kāma* – passion – draws the human soul further and further away from its spiritual parent and towards the path of death and destruction, since the soul can only truly live (spiritually) so long as it keeps unbroken its connection with its divine Self. H.P. Blavatasky says that the noetic can only function when *kāma* is paralyzed. ('Psychic and Noetic Action', *Lucifer*, October 1890.)
298. This is *Fohat* which 'is the "bridge" by which the "Ideas" existing in the "Divine Thought" are impressed on Cosmic substance as the "laws of Nature". Fohat is thus the dynamic energy of Cosmic Ideation; or, regarded from the other side, it is the intelligent medium, the guiding power of all manifestation, the "Thought Divine" transmitted and made manifest through the Dhyan Chohans, the Architects of the visible World.' (*S.D.* I, p. 16.)
299. 'Light is Life and both are electricity.' (*I.U.* I, p. 258.) This Light or Life or dynamic cosmic energy of the cosmos is the fount of every form of energy. 'Fohat, then, is the personified electric vital power, the transcendental binding Unity of all Cosmic Energies, on the unseen as on the manifested planes, the action of which resembles – on an immense scale – that of a living Force created by WILL . . .' (*S.D.* I, p. 111.)
300. The Absolute may be symbolized or conceptualized by the human mind as Unconditioned Consciousness (cf. *S.D.*, I, p. 16) and thus may be called the root of all consciousness. The generator of the subjective side of nature is referred to as *Mahat* or Cosmic Mind. Mind in this sense is the possibility of consciousness on all planes of being throughout eternity. Its human expression is *manas*, the principle of self-consciousness in man. It is suggestive to note the resemblance between the Eastern term *manas* and the Celtic term for its parent principle.
301. *Prakṛti* or root substance, primordial matter in Indian thought. Mother-matter

718 Notes and Commentary to pages 159–161

or *mūlaprakṛti* in the Hindu system, the universal substance-principle that is the source of all objective form throughout the cosmos. It is homogenous substance, the essence of the chaotic reflection we call matter.

302. In Buddhist thought compassion is symbolized by Kwan-Yin, analogous to the Great Mother and related to the *yin* of Chinese thought.
303. In Buddhist thought, ultimately compassion and justice are one. Compassion is 'the Law of LAWS'. (*Voice*, pp. 75–6.)
304. The earliest races of mankind were of one thought, one speech, one mind, and therefore united in vision. 'The whole human race was at that time of "one language and one lip".' (*S.D.* II, p. 198.) The language refers also to a true ability to communicate with each other because of their purity of mind and childlike simplicity of heart. The allegory of the Tower of Babel shows the decline of this paradisaic sense of oneness.
305. This truth was enunciated by the earliest Vedic seers and by many sages of other cultures. One of the great *Ṛg Veda* hymns declares, 'They call it Indra, Mitra, Varuna and Agni, or the heavenly bird Garutmant (the Sun). The sages call the One Being in many ways; they call it Agni, Yama, Matariśvan.' (*Ṛg Veda* I, 164, 46.)
306. 'The documents were concealed, it is true, but the knowledge itself and its actual existence had never been made a secret of by the Hierophants of the Temple, wherein MYSTERIES have ever been made a discipline and stimulus to virtue. This is very old news, and was repeatedly made known by the great adepts, from Pythagoras and Plato down to the Neoplatonists.' (*S.D.* I, xxxv.)
307. The mystic invocation of the triple worlds is made at the beginning of all *mantras* and prayers – *Oṃ! bhūr, bhuvaḥ, svar*. For its mystical significance, see *B.U.*, 5.5.3–4, 6.3.6 and 6.4.25. It is from these syllables that the sacred OM issues forth. (See *Ch. U.*, 2.23.2, 3.15.3–7 and 4.17.3–6; *Tai U.*, 1.5. The mystical correspondences to the three worlds are given in *Tai U.*, 1.7; and *Mai. U.*, 6.5–6.
308. 'Note well, "Christos" with the Gnostics meant the impersonal principal, the Atman of the Universe, and the Atma within every man's soul – not Jesus.' (*S.D.* I, p. 132 fn.) The word 'Christos' was also used by ancient mystics to refer to the Logos from which radiated the streams of energy which created the universe. ' . . . the *logos* is Christos, that principle of our inner nature which develops in us into the Spiritual Ego – the Higher-Self – being formed of the indissoluble union of *Buddhi* (the sixth) and the spiritual efflorescence of *Manas*, the fifth principle. "The Logos is passive Wisdom in Heaven and Conscious, Self-Active Wisdom on Earth." It is the Marriage of "Heavenly man" with the "Virgin of the World" – Nature, as described in *Pymander*; the result of which is their progeny – immortal man. It is this which is called in St. John's Revelation the marriage of the lamb with his bride.' (*S.D.* II, pp. 230–1.) A.E. must mean, then, by the imagination, that divine creative thought of the Logos which shapes the universe.
309. In connection with the mystery of the Sabbath, H.P. Blavatsky declares that 'Paul, an Initiate, knew it well . . .' (*S.D.* I, p. 240.)
310. A general fourfold classification of states of being echoed in philosophical systems Eastern and Western. (Cf. the four *avasthas* mentioned earlier and the four elements of the alchemists.)
311. The universe is a plenum inhabited by beings of every grade of matter arranged in descending hierarchies radiating from the Central Spiritual Sun. They are the agglomeration of intelligent forces which comprise the manifold arrangements of matter and energy in space. The seer, by detaching himself from the earthly senses, can penetrate the inner realms of nature where these beings have their existence. (Cf. *S.D.* I, p. 641.)

Notes and Commentary to pages 161–164

312. Gazing intently into a deep, still pool of water or into a candle flame are devices sometimes used to aid the individual to go into a trance in which things not of this world may be seen. Water is universally regarded as the symbol of the psychic or astral plane (both in its higher as well as its lower aspects) and also the symbol of the great unconscious, the Great Mother.
313. These two colours seem to recur in the visions of mystics of every culture.
314. This may be the discarding of elementals of a negative kind which descend into the lower astral, while those which we purify by our thoughts rise upward to higher realms.
315. '7', the mystic number, occurs frequently in A.E.'s writings as it does in the teachings of mystics of ancient times.
316. Hierarchies in the formless worlds.
317. This is a reference to initiation rites.
318. Land of the Eternal, of Immortality, the plane of divine consciousness, called Ildathach in Celtic mythology.
319. 'But we say that this sun they have been examining is not the real one, nor any sun at all, but is only an appearance, a mere reflection to us of part of the true sun.' ('Our Sun and the True Sun', *The Path*, February 1890.)

> With a golden vessel
> The Real's face is covered o'er
> That do thou, O Pushan, uncover
> Unto the Eternal Real.
> (*Mai. U.*, 6.35)

320. 'This fire is the higher Self, the Spiritual Ego, or that which is eternally reincarnating under the influence of its lower personal Selves . . .' (*S.D.* II, p. 109.) Commenting upon John the Baptist's statement (*Matthew* III.2) that Jesus will baptize with the Holy Ghost and with fire, we are told that '. . . the wisdom which Jesus, an Initiate of the higher mysteries, would reveal to them, was of a higher character, for it was the "FIRE" Wisdom of the true gnosis or the *real spiritual* enlightenment.' (*S.D.* II, p. 566.) ' . . . it is termed by Theurgists and Occultists to this day "the living Fire"; and there is not a Hindu who practises at dawn a certain kind of meditation but knows its effects.' (*S.D.* I, p. 338.) '. . . there is "a fire that gives knowledge of the future".' (*S.D.* I, p. 339.) No wonder that the Being from the Land of Immortal Youth spoke of the fire ever living in his heart. For those who have attained to eternal life in consciousness, this fire is ever living and the spiritual sun is radiant; in the hearts of ordinary humanity it burns, but is only dimly seen, as through smoke and mist, far away.
321. 'A Defence of Poetry' and other writings.
322. Spiritual light, the Golden Age, as in Shelley's 'Hellas'.
323. 'The ever unknowable and incognizable *Karana* alone, the *Causeless* Cause of all causes, should have its shrine and altar on the holy and untrodden ground of our heart – invisible, intangible, unmentioned, save through "the still small voice" of our spiritual consciousness. Those who worship before it, ought to do so in the silence and the sanctified solitude of their Souls: making their spirit the sole mediator between them and the *Universal Spirit*, their good actions the only priests, and their sinful intentions the only visible and objective sacrificial victims to the *Presence*.' (*S.D.* I, p. 280.) (Cf. Wordsworth – 'that unseen Presence' in *The Prelude*.)
324. Cf. Wordsworth, *The Prelude*.
325. This sense of the personal self dissolving into a greater reality is felt by all mystics. In the highest sense this is, ultimately, the experience that must be *continuously* undergone by the individual in his journey back to the spiritual

source. Of it *The Secret Doctrine* says, 'For, with every effort of will toward purification and unity with that "Self-god", one of the lower rays breaks and the spiritual entity of man is drawn higher and ever higher to the ray that supersedes the first, until, from ray to ray, the inner man is drawn into the one and highest beam of the Parent-SUN.' (*S.D.* I, pp. 638–9.)
326. A familiar image in Sufi mystical writings.
327. The oracles at Delphi and elsewhere – the sibyls or pythonesses inhaled the fumes of bay leaves, verbena and other herbs in order to go into their oracular trances.
328. A.E. recognizes (as did Francis Thompson in 'The Hound of Heaven') that this type of Nature mysticism is not, perhaps, the highest kind of mystical experience that man may achieve.
329. The *Nirmāṇakāyas* who watch over the fate of large groups of humanity.
330. *Nirmāṇakāyas* may choose certain individuals whom they overbrood and inspire so that these may become the leaders of men. ' . . . instead of going into selfish bliss, he chooses a life of self-sacrifice, an existence which ends only with the life-cycle, in order to be enabled to help mankind in an invisible, yet most effective manner. . . . Thus a *Nirmāṇakāya* is not, as popularly believed, the body "in which a Buddha or a Bodhisattva appears on earth", but verily one, who, . . . an adept or a yogi during life, has since become a member of that invisible Host which ever protects and watches over Humanity within Karmic limits. Mistaken often for a "Spirit", a Deva, God himself, etc., a *Nirmāṇakāya* is ever a protecting, compassionate, verily a *guardian* angel, to him who becomes worthy of his help.' (*Glo.*, '*Nirmāṇakāya*'.)
331. Cf. Thompson, 'In No Strange Land'.
332. Cf. Plato – *Phaedrus, Symposium* and elsewhere. Plotinus – ' . . . the beauty, then, of bodily forms comes about in this way – from communion with the intelligible realm. . . . the beauties of the realm of sense which . . . have invaded matter, there to adorn and to ravish wherever they are perceived. But there are beauties more lofty than these, imperceptible to sense, that the soul without aid of sense perceives and proclaims. To perceive them we must go higher . . . It is impossible to talk about the "lustre" of right living and of learning and of the like if one has never cared for such things, never beheld "the face of justice" and temperance and seen it to be "beyond the beauty of evening or morning star". Seeing of this sort is done only with the eye of the soul.' (*Enneads* I, 6, 1 [O'Brien, pp. 36–7].)
333. 'The WISE ONES tarry not in pleasure-grounds of senses.' (*Voice*, p. 7.) The visions A.E. speaks of are not of the highest realm, but it is tempting to get caught up in them instead of moving on to higher planes.
334. The Holy Ghost.
335. This is the Christos, Logos, *Īśvara*, the 'Ego which is seated in the hearts of all beings', as the *Bhagavad Gītā* puts it. (See note 6.)
336. It is the higher vision that sanctifies and illuminates the hitherto mundane realm. This penetrating radiant insight that 'the Heart of things is sweet' (*The Light of Asia*) is not attainable at the level of the earlier Nature mysticism. This is similar to the 'honey-doctrine' of the *Bṛhadāraṇyaka Upaniṣad* (2.5).
337. All the mystics (St. John of the Cross; the author of *The Cloud of Unknowing*; Śaṅkara) have proclaimed that the fleeting pleasures of the sense world pale into insignificance beside the glorious treasures of the divine world.
338. Browning in 'Paracelsus' speaks of 'the imprisoned splendour', and exclaims

'There is an inmost centre in us all,
Where Truth abides in fulness; and around
Wall upon wall, the gross flesh hems it in,

Notes and Commentary to page 166

This perfect, clear perception – which is Truth.'
'All is impermanent . . . a form of clay material upon the lower surface.' (*Voice*, p. 63.)

339. Reminiscent of *The Voice of the Silence* (p. 79): 'Behold, the mellow light that floods the Eastern sky. In signs of praise both heaven and earth unite. And from the four-fold manifested Powers a chant of love ariseth, both from the flaming Fire and flowing Water, and from sweet-smelling Earth and rushing Wind.

'Hark! . . . from the deep unfathomable vortex of that golden light in which the Victor bathes, ALL NATURE'S wordless voice in thousand tones ariseth to proclaim:

'JOY UNTO YE, O MEN OF MYALBA.
'A PILGRIM HATH RETURNED BACK "FROM THE OTHER SHORE".'
'A NEW ARHAN IS BORN.' The moment of spiritual birth of a Bodhisattva is a moment when all Nature thrills with a sense of the oneness that is its true being.

340. True enlightenment is rising above the conventional notions of good and evil, beneficent and dreadful, etc., to a transcendental realm of Beauty, Truth and Goodness. This is an idea much emphasized in Taoism as well as in Mahāyāna Buddhism, where the Bodhisattva no longer sees even *Nirvāna* and *Saṁsāra* as separate.

341. See Edwin Arnold, *The Light of Asia*, VIII.

> Before beginning, and without an end,
>   As space eternal and as surety sure,
> Is fixed a Power divine which moves to good,
>   Only its laws endure.
>
> This is its touch upon the blossomed rose,
>   The fashion of its hand shaped lotus-leaves;
> In dark soil and the silence of the seeds
>   The robe of Spring it weaves;
>
> That is its painting on the glorious clouds,
>   And these its emeralds on the peacock's train;
> It hath its stations in the stars; its slaves
>   In lightning, wind, and rain.
>
> Out of the dark it wrought the heart of man,
>   Out of dull shells the pheasant's pencilled neck:
> Ever at toil, it brings to loveliness
>   All ancient wrath and wreck.
>
>   . . . .
>
> The ordered music of the marching orbs
>   It makes in viewless canopy of sky;
> In deep abyss of earth it hides up gold,
>   Sards, sapphires, lazuli.
>
> Ever and ever bringing secrets forth,
>   It sitteth in the green of forest-glades
> Nursing strange seedlings at the cedar's root,
>   Devising leaves, blooms, blades.
>
> It slayeth and it saveth, nowise moved
>   Except unto the working out of doom;

Its threads are Love and Life; and Death and Pain
   The shuttles of its loom.
It maketh and unmaketh, mending all;
   What it hath wrought is better than hath been;
Slow grows the splendid pattern that it plans
   Its wistful hands between.

THE SPEECH OF THE GODS

1. First appeared in *The Theosophist*, December 1887.
2. From the metaphysical viewpoint this may be shown as the gradual and successive emanations by hierarchies of divine beings who mystically give of their essence to man. The descending arc of the cycle (known as involution) is thus the 'formation' of man, if it may be so called, and his potencies, through a progressive particularization of the vehicles of the spirit. The upward arc is the unfoldment, the active manifestation of these powers embedded in the forms. To say, therefore, that some of man's powers belong to the downward and some to the upward swing of evolution is simply to divide them according to our limited understanding.
3. A.E. is not using the word 'Aryan' in its usual ethnic sense but in the special theosophical connotation of a 'race' which signifies a long period in man's psycho-spiritual evolution. The term 'Aryan' literally means 'noble'. In describing the Aryan language as 'man's inheritance from the planetary spirit', A.E. is probably referring to the teaching about the lighting up of the unmanifest spark of mind in man by Promethean hierarchies who taught early humanity the art and science of language. While this primordial event is not related directly to the Fifth Race, it is said that all subsequent spiritual teachers of humanity are in a line of mystical descent from the earliest divine instructors, and so also all root languages must ultimately stem from the original gift of these teachers.
4. All powers in man and the universe are but derivations of the one supernal energy or *śakti*, referred to in *The Secret Doctrine* I, pp. 292–3, where the six primary forces in nature, variations of the one force, are named. These energies are mystically correlated with sounds, colours and forms – all of these being but different rates of vibrations, at diverse levels, of the one energy.
5. According to the Sāṁkhya philosophy in India, the whole of the manifested universe is produced by the interplay of the three primary *guṇas* or qualities or attributes of the primordial substance. Each of the three qualities is represented by a colour, and the ceaselessly changing combinations of the *guṇas* produce what we call colour, sound and sensible qualities.
6. In the Sanskrit alphabet the consonants are methodically arranged according to phonetic values connected with their physiological origin, e.g., gutturals, palatals, linguals, dentals and labials.
7. Hindu tradition regards the three syllables of the sacred AUM as corresponding (among myriad other correspondences) with the trinity of Brahmā, Viṣṇu and Śiva. Since Śiva is the destroyer (as also the regenerator), it is fitting that he should be represented by the letter M, since, as A.E. shows here and elsewhere, this is the sound of closure, ending, death and universal dissolution. (See notes on AUM in *C.O.V.*, note 213.)

Notes and Commentary to pages 169–174   723

8. To the traditional four elements of Western thought, Indian philosophy adds a fifth – *ākaśa* or ether, whose attribute is sound.
9. *Parabrahm* or *Brahman* is, in Indian thought, the Absolute, the highest unconditioned, eternal, limitless and totally indescribable Reality. The use of this term which means literally 'beyond *Brahm*', signifying the Unknowable or Absolute, should be clarified here. It is utterly devoid of attributes and thus stands solely as the Absolute Negation of all manifestation. To say that *Parabrahm* creates is somewhat misleading as this would ascribe some kind of causal relationship between It and the cosmos which it definitely cannot have. However, one aspect of *Parabrahm* is *mūlaprakṛti* or 'root-substance', which is the true progenitor of ideation and form at the dawn of cosmic manifestation.
10. The word *Brahman* comes from the Sanskrit root *bṛh*, 'to expand'. All manifestation, the whole universe, comes from the expansion (mystically and metaphysically speaking, of course, since there is nowhere where *Brahman* is not) of *Parabrahm*. The first emanation from It is the Word variously called the Logos, the *Verbum* and *Brahma-Vāc*.
11. The Sāṁkhya has a complex schema in which the first subtle element to emerge is *ākaśā*, or ether, and from it successively come the other four. A.E.'s order of elements is not, however, that of the Sāṁkhyans, but based upon a brief verse in the *Taittīrīya Upaniṣad*.
12. The earth represents the greatest possible diversification of forms or particulars, the furthermost development of heterogeneity away from the homogeneity of the formless spirit. In this cycle the arc can swing no lower, all possibilities of emanation have been exhausted, and there can only be a swing upward.
13. As A.E. explains in *The Candle of Vision*, following ancient Indian mysticism, A is the first sound the human voice can utter when the mouth is opened. Many alphabets begin with the sound A – the Sanskrit *akāra*, the Greek *alpha*, and so on. The succession of sounds that follows in A.E.'s account seems to have no other source than his own intuitions. We know of no other parallel succession or list of correspondences which might be regarded as a possible source.
14. This is from the *Taittīrīya Upaniṣad*, 2.1 [Hume, p. 283].
15. Ouranos (Uranus) was the ancient Greek god of the sky, and this name is related to the Sanskrit 'Varuṇa', who was also the Vedic god of the deep blue sky.
16. Closely related to the Sanskrit root *jña*, 'to know' (also pronounced *gña*), from which, in turn, are derived terms such as 'gnosis'.
17. See *C.O.V.*, note 164, on the correspondence between sounds and colours.

THE ELEMENT LANGUAGE

1. First appeared in *The Irish Theosophist*, May-September 1893.
2. Perhaps A.E. is referring to *Senzar*. 'Tradition says, that it [the "very old Book" of mysteries] was taken down in *Senzar*, the secret sacerdotal tongue, from the words of the Divine Beings, who dictated it to the sons of Light, in Central Asia, at the very beginning of the 5th (our) race; for there was a time when its language (the *Sen-zar*) was known to the Initiates of every nation . . .' (*S.D.* I, p. xliii) Cf. *The Candle of Vision* for a complementary account of the divine origins of language. A.E. draws heavily upon the cosmological framework of *The Secret Doctrine* to support his conclusions, especially with regard to the teaching on Rounds and Races. Each Root Race of our Round

existed in a state of matter corresponding to the stage of evolution it had reached. It evolved a type of language appropriate to it ranging from the chant to formal grammar.

3. H.P. Blavatsky suggests that the key of analogy and correspondence is the Ariadne's thread which will guide us through the maze of the mysteries of the universe.
4. Whether we call it the Universal Life, Light, Cosmic Electricity or *Fohat*, there is one Force of which colour, sound, form, etc. are but manifestations of varying degrees and at diverse levels. ' "The abodes of Fohat are many", it is said.' (*S.D.* I, p. 204.) *The Secret Doctrine* quotes the mysterious Commentaries on the *Stanzas of Dzyān* – 'The agitation of the *Fohatic* Forces at the two cold ends (North and South Poles) of the Earth which resulted in a multicoloured radiance at night, have in them several of the properties of Akasa (Ether) *colour* and sound as well.' (*S.D.* I, p. 205.) And again the *Viṣṇu Purāṇa* corroborates this – 'Sound is the characteristic of Akasa (Ether): it generates air, the property of which is Touch; which (by friction) becomes productive of Colour and Light.' (*S.D.* I, p. 205.)
5. 'MANTRIKA-SAKTI. The force or power of letters, speech or music. The *Mantra Shastra* has for its subject-matter this force in all its manifestations . . . The influence of melody is one of its ordinary manifestations. The power of the ineffable name is the crown of this Sakti.' (*S.D.* I, p. 293.)
6. It is interesting to note that in the earliest mystical literature of India, the Vedas, supreme importance is given to song and chant, and all the Vedas are meant to be chanted. Indeed, one of the four Vedas is the *Sāma Veda*, *sāma* meaning 'song'.
7. Absolute consciousness in its highest sense. It is the root of all ideation and all subjectivity in relation to matter and the objective world. It is the power of self-reference, the eye through which, as Shelley said, the universe 'beholds itself and knows itself divine'. All creative activity is derivative from it.
8. Krishna in the *Bhagavad Gītā*, ch. X.42, p. 76.
9. These are the three primordial qualities of *sattva*, *rajas*, and *tamas*.
10. *Gītā*, ch. VII.8–9, p. 54.
11. 'The period of a mundane revolution, generally a cycle of time, but usually, it represents a "day" and "night" of Brahmā, a period of 4,320,000,000 years.' (*Glo.*, 'Kalpa'.)
12. 'A period of manifestation, as opposed to Pralaya (dissolution or rest), applied to various cycles, especially to a Day of Brahmā, 4,320,000,000 Solar years – and to the reign of one Manu – 308,448,000. (See Vol. II of *The Secret Doctrine*, p. 68 *et. seq.*) *Lit.*, Manuantara – "between Manus".' (*Glo.*, 'Manvantara'.)
13. 'Purānas (Sk.). *Lit.*, "ancient". A collection of symbolical and allegorical writings – eighteen in number now – supposed to have been composed by Vyasa, the author of the *Mahābhārata*.' (*Glo.*, 'Purānas'.)
14. The Upaniṣads constitute the final portion of the Vedic literature of India, and are also known as Vedānta (*Veda anta*, meaning 'the end of the Vedas' or 'the goal or final essence of the Vedas'). They are part of the *jñāna-kānda* – that section of the Vedas which is called 'the pórtion of knowledge'. There were originally over two hundred Upaniṣads, of which a little over a hundred are still extant. They are perhaps the most mystical texts in Indian religious literature and were written on the basis of the inward-turning experience of many ancient seers, known and unknown. The Upaniṣads, written in varying styles and form – dialogues, poetry, myth, allegory, discussions, philosophical discourses – are the outpourings of many generations of wise men who, turning inward into the depths of the consciousness, experienced directly the blazing illumination of

Notes and Commentary to pages 177–180 725

ultimate truth. Their expression of this experience has given us some of the most profound and beautiful literature to be found in the history of mysticism.
15. 'Tantra (Sk.). *Lit.*, "rule or ritual". Certain mystical and magical works, whose chief peculiarity is the worship of the *female* power, personified in Sakti.' (*Glo.*, 'Tantra'.)
16. The order of emanation of the elements is (with a slight variation) that given in the *Taittirīya Upaniṣad*.
17. *Puruṣa* is the person, the real self or spirit, often contrasted in Indian philosophy with *prakṛti*, matter or substance.
18. Many schools of Indian mysticism and occult philosophy hold that *cakras* (literally circles or wheels) are the centres of psycho-spiritual force or energy in the individual. They are often symbolized as lotuses which open out as the mystic or yogi gains control over himself and develops powers, allowing the mysterious energy to flow freely through him.
19. Part of the doctrine of *cakra* described above.
20. See *C.O.V.*, note 185, on the doctrine of the correlation of colours and sounds. 'Every person has about him a fluid, or plane, or sphere, or energy, whichever you please to call it, in which are constantly found elementals that partake of his nature. That is, they are tinted with his colour and impressed by his character.' ('Conversations on Occultism', *The Path*, September 1888.)
21. 'Astral Body, or Astral "Double". The ethereal counterpart or shadow of man or animal. The *Linga Śarira*, the "Doppelgänger". The reader must not confuse it with the ASTRAL SOUL, another name for the lower Manas or Kāma-Manas so-called, the reflection of the HIGHER EGO.' (*Glo.*, 'Astral Body'.) The astral body is the basis or design for the physical body, and the vehicle for the higher principles in man.
22. The Sanskrit word comes from the root *man*, 'to think, to will'. In the theosophical classification *manas* is the real thinker, the divine Ego, which sends its projected ray into incarnation. Thus there are two aspects of *manas* – the higher, possessing the power of understanding archetypal forms and universal ideas, and capable of focussing these through the concentrated power of meditation; the lower *manas* is that which becomes a fragmented consciousness in the phenomenal world and is caught up in the desires of the egotistic nature.
23. A.E.'s remarks about the three-syllabled AUM and its significance are commented upon elsewhere.
24. R, H, L and Y are all classified in the system of the Devanāgarī (Sanskrit) script as semi-vowels and would, therefore, be naturally close to the vowels.
25. *Gītā*, ch.X. 33, p. 75
26. *Ṛg Veda*, X. 129, 'Hymn of Creation'.
27. *The Book of Dzyān* is an archaic philosophical and mystical text which 'is utterly unknown to our Philologists', says H.P. Blavatsky (*S.D.* I, p. xxii). H.P. Blavatsky's monumental work is based upon and expands a few stanzas from the Book, together with its Commentaries.
28. The sequence described by A.E. in these paragraphs is briefly summed up in *The Secret Doctrine* in the following words: 'In the "beginning", that which is called in mystic phraseology "Cosmic *Desire*" evolves into absolute Light. Now light without any shadow would be absolute light – in other words, absolute darkness – as physical science seeks to prove. That shadow appears under the form of primordial matter, allegorized – if one likes – in the shape of the Spirit of Creative Fire or Heat. If, rejecting the poetical form and allegory, science chooses to see in this the primordial Fire-Mist, it is welcome to do so.' (*S.D.* I, p. 201.)

29. This is the duality inherent in what is sometimes called the 'Mother-Father.' Similar terms and concepts are found in a number of ancient cosmogonies. *The Secret Doctrine* says that once 'we pass in thought from this (to us) Absolute Negation, duality supervenes in the contrast of Spirit (or consciousness) and Matter, Subject and Object.' (*S.D.* I, p. 15.) From the great androgynous deity (as many mythologies portray the Mother-Father) arise the dualities without which there can be no manifested universe. 'The "Manifested Universe", therefore, is pervaded by duality, which is, as it were, the very essence of its EX-istence as "manifestation".' (*S.D.* I, p. 15.) As the *Bhagavad Gītā* puts it, 'These two, *light* and *darkness*, are the world's eternal ways.' (*Gītā*, ch. VIII. 26, p. 62.)

30. The series of steps referred to here is explained in great detail in the two volumes of *The Secret Doctrine*. It is briefly put by saying that the Gods (divine monads or spirits) have to pass through states which may be called 'Inmetallization, Inherbation, Inzoonization and finally Incarnation'. (*S.D.* I, p. 188.)

31. See notes to AUM in *The Candle of Vision* for the significance of the letter M. (*C.O.V.*, note 213.)

32. *Nirvāṇa*, literally meaning 'to blow out' desire and craving, is the term used by Buddha to refer to the ultimate state of enlightenment and egolessness. It is often described in negative language as the unborn, uncreated, unbecome, etc., because of its ineffability, but Buddha specifically forbade his disciples to think of it as annihilation. There are passages in Buddhist texts which also describe it as absolute peace, absolute joy and absolute compassion.

33. The atrophy of the power of intuitive speech would coincide with the loss or atrophy of the Third Eye of wisdom and intuition.

34. Several of these are, in fact, Sanskrit verb roots, e.g., *ad*, 'to eat', and *dā*, 'to give'.

35. This (or sounds very like it) is the root of words meaning 'to die', or 'death', in many languages (French *mort*, English 'mortal') and in Sanskrit the verb for 'die' is *mṛ*.

36. Repeated references to this doctrine are made by H.P. Blavatsky in *The Secret Doctrine* and elsewhere. Taking the example of the Hebrew Yodh or Jod, which is 'the number-letter 10, male and female' (*S.D.* I, p. 347) and 'is the symbolical letter of Kether and the essence and germ of the Holy Name' (*S.D.* I, p. 394), we begin to understand the symbolism of Yahweh. Further correlations of Jehovah with the formula $21 + 501 + 21 = 543$ tell us still more about the Old Testament deity, as well as hinting at the relation between Moses and Jehovah (*S.D.* II, p. 468). So also Viṣṇu, Śiva and other Hindu gods reveal their natures through mystical numerology.

37. In some schools of Indian philosophical thought, the Absolute *Brahman* or *Parabrahm* is conceived of under two aspects – the totally non-manifest, attributeless, non-relational and indescribable *nirguṇa brahman*, and the *saguṇa brahman* which may be thought of as the source of the universe. In turn, the latter may also be viewed as *Īśvara*, the Supreme Lord and Creator, whose nature and energies assume a triple aspect which is the trinity of Brahmā, Viṣṇu and Śiva. A.E. here prefers to use the name for the earlier, Vedic form of Śiva, i.e., Rudra.

38. Traditionally, the term *brahman* is said to come from the Sanskrit root *bṛh*, 'to expand'.

39. Connected with the Sanskrit root *viś*, 'to pervade', and *viṣ*, 'to act', 'to work', 'to rule'.

40. Usually, Rudra is said to be derived from the verbal root *rud*, 'to roar'. Rudra is

the Roarer, 'he who terrifies because of his destructive powers' (often associated with Agni, the god of Fire). Śiva is the destroyer and regenerator mystically as well as otherwise.
41. See *C.O.V.*, note 213.
42. A sacred Sanskrit formula or incantation that oftens ends a sacred text. 'Om' is AUM which has been referred to earlier and which is an untranslatable word; 'tat' means 'this' or 'that', and 'sat' is truth, Reality, Being. Although there are many possible interpretations of this sentence, we may say it means roughly, 'Om, all this is verily the ultimate Reality.'
43. The Absolute is 'devoid of all attributes and is essentially without any relation to manifested, finite Being. It is "Be-ness" rather than Being (in Sanskrit, *Sat*), and is beyond all thought or speculation.' (*S.D.* I, p. 14.)
44. A *loka* is a plane of consciousness, level of being or world of knowledge in Indian philosophy. The formula 'Om! *bhūr, bhuvaḥ, svar*' or '*Om! Bhūr! Bhuvas! Suvar!*' is a mystic utterance intoned as an opening invocation to the triple worlds (see *C.O.V.*, note 307) before chanting any important sacred verse. The three words following 'Om' are the designations of the three worlds – earthly, intermediate and divine – which in a mystical sense constitute the manifested universe. The crucial importance of this invocation can be seen from the fact that the Upaniṣads repeatedly offer symbolic meanings and correspondences for these three terms. See for example *B.U.*, 5.5.4. 'The head of the person who is here in the right eye is *Bhūr* – there is one head, this is one syllable. *Bhuvar* is the arms – there are two arms, these are two syllables. *Svar* is the feet – there are two feet, these are two syllables (*su-ar*). The mystic name *(upaniṣad)* therefore is "I" (*ahan*). He slays (*han*) evil, he leaves it behind (*hā*) who knows this.' Offering a different meaning, the *Chāndogya Upaniṣad* tells us, 'Prajāpati brooded upon the worlds. From them, when they had been brooded upon, issued forth the threefold knowledge. He brooded upon this. From it, when it had been brooded upon, issued forth these syllables: *bhūr, bhuvaḥ, svar*.

'He brooded upon them. From them, when they had been brooded upon, issued forth the syllable *Om*. As all leaves are held together by a spike, so all speech is held together by *Om*. Verily, *Om* is the world-all. Verily, *Om* is this world-all.' (*Chāndogya Up.*, 2.24.2–3 [*Ibid.*, p. 201].) The *Taittirīya Upaniṣad*, on the other hand, affirms that, mystically, *bhur* is Agni (fire); *bhuvas*, Vayu (wind); *suvar* is Aditya (the Sun), the fourth mystical term, *mahas*, being the Moon; it goes on to give further mystic correspondences with the principal divisions of the Vedas and with the different kinds of spiritual breaths. (See *Taittirīya Up.*, 1.5.1.) The *Maitri Upaniṣad* (6.5–6) offers still further inward meanings. The *Theosophical Glossary* says, in exploring a term from another tradition: 'Vyahritis (Slav.). *Lit.*, "fiery", *words lit by and born of fires*. The three mystical, creative words, said by Manu to have been milked by the Prajāpati from the *Vedas*: *bhūr* from the *Ṛg Veda*; *bhuvaḥ* from the *Yajur-Veda*; and *swar* from the *Sāma-Veda* (*Manu* II.76). All three are said to possess creative powers. The *Satapatha Brāhmaṇa* explains that they are "the three luminous essences" extracted from the *Vedas* by Prajāpati ("lords of creation", progenitors), through heat. "He (Brahmā) uttered the word *bhūr*, and it became the earth; *bhuvaḥ*, and it became the firmament; and *swar*, which became heaven." *Mahar* is the fourth "luminous essence", and was taken from the *Atharva-Veda*. But, as this word is purely *mantric* and magical, it is one, so to say, kept apart.' (*Glo.*, 'Vyahritis'.)
45. 'Pranic' means having to do with *prāṇa*, life-energy at all levels, cosmic as well as individual. *Prāṇa* also means 'breath'.

46. The term 'astral' refers to that plane or ethereal substance, more subtle than the physical but nevertheless 'material' rather than 'spiritual' (if such a dichotomy must be made). It is highly plastic and impressionable and the 'astral light' by which we are surrounded and permeated in the mundane world easily takes the impress and colour of our very thought and emotion. One of the lower vestures of the soul is also made of this substance.
47. Devachan is the state of rest and assimilation the soul experiences between births.
48. 'The Northern Buddhists, and all Chinamen, in fact, find in the deep roar of some of the great and sacred rivers the key-note of Nature . . . It is a well-known fact in Physical Science, as well as in Occultism, that the aggregate sound of Nature – such as is heard in the roar of great rivers, the noise produced by the waving tops of trees in large forests, or that of a city heard at a distance – is a definite single tone of quite an appreciable pitch. This is shown by physicists and musicians. Thus Professor Rice (*Chinese Music*) shows that the Chinese recognized the fact thousands of years ago by saying that "the waters of the Hoang-ho rushing by, intoned the *kung*", called "the great tone" in Chinese music; and he shows this tone corresponding with the F, "considered by modern physicists to be the actual tonic of Nature".' Professor B. Silliman mentions it, too, in his *Principles of Physics*, saying that "this tone is held to be the middle F of the piano; which may, therefore, be considered the key-note of Nature".' (*Voice*, p. 55 fn.)
49. *John* I.1.
50. *The Voice of the Silence* says, 'But, O Disciple, unless the flesh is passive, head cool, the Soul as firm and pure as flaming diamond, the radiance will not reach the *chamber*, its sunlight will not warm the heart, nor will the mystic sounds of the akasic heights reach the ear, however eager, at the initial stage.' (*Voice*, p. 19.)
51. *Yajña* is the Sanskrit term for 'sacrifice' but must be understood to extend far above and beyond the limited notion of a physical sacrifice. It is a mystical creative act, and the Vedas considered the whole universe to be the product of a divine sacrifice, while the Upaniṣads dwell on the idea of the symbolic meaning of *yajña* in the spiritual life of an individual.
52. A.E. is quoting a highly mysterious and occult passage from the *Maitri Upaniṣad* (6.28).
53. As Śaṅkara picturesquely puts it, 'A sickness is not cured . . .' (*The Crest Jewel of Discrimination*, p. 43.)

REVIEW OF *LYRICS*

1. First appeared in *The Irish Theosophist*, June 1895, as an unsigned review thought to be written by A.E.

REVIEW OF *FROM THE UPANISHADS*

1. First appeared in *The Irish Theosophist*, February 1896, as an unsigned review generally attributed to A.E.

WORKS AND DAYS

1. First appeared in *The Irish Theosophist*, June 1896.
2. The symbol of the chariot is central to the depiction of the cosmos given in the Upaniṣads. The 'fire' that drives its wheels is the Spiritual Sun or *Ātman*.
3. The Light of the Logos which diffuses itself into myriad rays of creative energy at the dawn of manifestation.
4. The divine monad or universal self-consciousness.
5. See 'The Element Language', notes 11-12.
6. Cf. *Bhagavad Gītā*, ch. VIII.24–5, pp. 61–2.
7. Sacred *mantram* found in the *Māṇḍukya Upaniṣad* and echoed by Śaṅkara.
8. Sacred Lodge of Masters and Adepts.

THE HOUR OF TWILIGHT (A)

1. First appeared in *The Irish Theosophist*, February-March 1893.
2. The twilight hour, the critical time between day and night, one of those mystical moments in the day, called *sandhyā* by the Indians, when the air is full of magical vibrations, is considered a most appropriate and auspicious time for reflection upon the deepest truths.
3. A reference to the old Indian legend of the beautiful maiden, Śakuntala, daughter of the sage Viśvāmitra, who lived in a forest with her foster-father, the sage Kaṇva, and surrounded by a few female companions. She was wooed, wedded and abandoned by the King Duṣyanta, bore him a son, and was later re-united with her husband. The poet Kālidasa has immortalized the story in his play called the *Abhijñāna-Śakuntala*.
4. All mystics agree that a mystical experience leaves behind a subtle effect, an indescribable influence, a sort of indefinable aroma that permeates the individual's subsequent life.
5. 'Devachan (Sk.). The "dwelling of the gods". A state intermediate between two earth-lives, into which the EGO (Atma-Buddhi-Manas, or the Trinity made One) enters, after its separation from kāma rupa, and the disintegration of the lower principles on earth.' (*Glo.*, 'Devachan.') Only the highest and most unselfish thoughts and aspirations of the previous life surround the soul in Devachan.
6. The universe is said to consist of seven great planes of being which may be called 'worlds'. (See, e.g., *S.D.* I, p. 200, diagram.) The withdrawal of these into the homogeneity of the One is the final dissolution of the universe at the beginning of what the Hindus call *pralaya* or the Night of Brahmā, which will eventually be followed once again by a Day of Brahmā.
7. The manifested universe is sometimes described as consisting of seven rays emitted by the One Spiritual Sun. At the onset of *pralaya*, the seven rays are withdrawn. Here is what *The Secret Doctrine* says – 'The Cosmic or Universal *Pralaya* comes only at the end of one hundred years of Brahmā; when the Universal dissolution is said to take place. Then the *Avyaya*, say the exoteric scriptures, the eternal life symbolized by Viṣṇu, assuming the character of Rudra, the *Destroyer*, enters into the *Seven* Rays of the Sun and drinks up all the waters of the Universe.' (*S.D.* II, p. 69 fn.)
8. This is a correct inference A.E. makes from the general doctrine of the soul's rest in Devachan. It is said that this state serves to enable the soul to assimilate

thoroughly those noble ideas and aspirations which it was unable to do in the rush and frenzy of incarnated life. The more an individual advances, however, upon the spiritual path, the more he can (and must) absorb and assimilate, through the conscious and continuous raising of the consciousness, that which is valuable in his life experiences. Thus he performs while still on earth his task of gleaning of eternal truths separated from the chaff of empty trivia. This is the process of gaining conscious immortality, of living a conscious life in the spirit, as H.P. Blavatsky called it. For such an individual, who is steadily rising above the falsities of the world, the illusions (for so they are, however noble) of Devachan become necessary.

9. This is a reference to the central message of the *Bhagavad Gītā*, which stresses 'the renunciation of the fruits of action'. 'Let, then, the motive for action be in the action itself, and not in the event. Do not be incited to actions by the hope of their reward, nor let thy life be spent in inaction.' (*Gītā* ch. II.47, p. 16.)
10. The highest ideal in Mahāyāna Buddhism as in Theosophy is that of the *Bodhisattva* – the individual who, having gained, through countless lives of unremitting effort, the right to enter into the peace and bliss of *Nirvāṇa*, renounces it, in order to return to earth to help suffering humanity. This is called making the Great Sacrifice. (*S.D.* I, p. 208.)
11. The *sandhyās* are those times when the mind should turn as naturally as flowers towards the sun to meditation on divine ideas. A.E. rightly remarks that no idea could be nobler or more ennobling than that of the compassionate *Bodhisattva*. To meditate on the *Bodhisattvas* is to draw oneself nearer to them even for a short space of time, and to become infused with their compassionate wisdom.

THE HOUR OF TWILIGHT (B)

1. First appeared in *The Irish Theosophist*, March 1893.
2. Mystical devotional texts continually refer to the Master seated in the heart of the spiritual aspirant. The devotee endeavours to make the Master a living power in his life.

THE SECRET OF POWER

1. First appeared in *The Irish Theosophist*, May 1893.
2. One who has concentrated his entire being in his lower self, that portion of his thinking principle which rules over his animal nature. He is an embodiment of absolute selfishness, possessing great power over matter, and the polar opposite of the good adept, who has purified the animal nature thoroughly and assimilated his entire being to his spiritual principles. The evil adept has cut the cord between himself and his higher principles and is thereby doomed by the Law to eventual annihilation.
3. This is the vision of the white adept, characterized by the mystic colours of blue and gold. His appeal is not to passion or self-gratification but to the self-validating nature of 'the Good' or Higher Self of which he is the embodiment.

4. The unmanifest refers to that portion of every man which is always beyond formulation and analysis. It can never be exhausted or corrupted by the world because it never enters into experience. Thus it is the true and final refuge of the soul and its abiding strength.

A PRIESTESS OF THE WOODS

1. First appeared in *The Irish Theosophist*, July 1893.
2. Points of semi-intelligent life which inhabit the four elements. Also called elementals.
3. Knowledge of and command over the elements was the natural inheritance of Third and Fourth Root Race man. Before man lost his visionary capacity with the fall of Atlantis, acquaintance with the invisible forces behind visible nature was common. These finer forces are called elementals in the theosophical lexicon. They are aggregates of intelligences behind natural phenomena and are subordinate to the higher cognitive capacities of man. Some aspects of their nature are described here. However, it is worthwhile to point out that they are capable of causing great havoc unless controlled by a disciplined mind and benevolent will. (Cf. *Glo.*, 'Elementals'.)
4. The stranger's speech here alludes to a major distinction often drawn in theosophical philosophy between the elemental world and the divine world. They are opposed in nature, as the elemental world is soulless and mindless, allied to form and matter; the divine world represents the perfection of soul and mind and is allied to the formless freedom of unfettered spiritual consciousness. The former is the world of demons and sorcerers, the latter the world of enlightened men.

A TRAGEDY IN THE TEMPLE

1. First appeared in *The Irish Theosophist*, September 1893.
2. Lilith is a symbolic expression of the aggressive and delusive aspects of *māyā* (or illusion considered philosophically) cast as the female seducer. Lilith is, however, more than an invitation to transgress moral restraints. She represents the temptation to be drawn away from the spiritual life altogether in order to pursue transfinite beauty for oneself alone. Thus her radiant and alluring appearance belies her intentions which are solely malevolent. Her equivalents in world mythology are numerous, ranging from Circe to the contemporary *femme fatale*. In Hindu terms she might be considered the consort of Māra, 'the great tempter' who seeks to divert spiritual aspirants with the lure of psychic and sensual pleasures. This is delusive and the psychological counterpart of illusion or *māyā*. (Cf. 'The Cave of Lilith'.)

THE MEDITATION OF ANANDA

1. First appeared in *The Irish Theosophist*, November 1893, under the title 'The Meditation of Parvati'. The text is the final version published in *Imaginations and Reveries*, 1915.
2. *Lit.* 'place', meaning the various planes of being in the cosmos from the material to the purely spiritual.
3. The words of the great spiritual teacher Gautama Buddha in the *Visuddimagga* by Buddhaghosa.
4. Cf. 'Imagination' in *The Candle of Vision*, for a description of the manifold potency of the spiritual imagination. The protean power of love is of such a divine character that in an intense moment of pure selflessness and devotion, one can rise above the limitations of personal time and space and experience events in a rarefied realm which is archetypal in nature, reflecting the inmost secrets of the soul. Keats referred to this power as 'negative capability', the potential to think and feel as another without any thought of self.
5. The divine prototype or Dhyāni Buddha that overbroods the incarnation of each individual.

A TALK BY THE EUPHRATES

1. First appeared in *The Irish Theosophist*, December 1893.

THE CAVE OF LILITH

1. First appeared in *The Irish Theosophist*, February 1894. The text is that of A.E.'s final version included in *Imaginations and Reveries*, 1915.
2. One of the chief powers of mind is to create thought-forms which have an abiding life if they are sustained by repeated attention. At lower levels of ideation these are known as *kāma rūpas* or astral demons which are created by and prey upon *kamic* or passional energies.
3. Lilith seems to be a personification and elaboration of Māra, 'The Great Ensnarer' referred to in *The Voice of the Silence*.

A STRANGE AWAKENING

1. First appeared in *The Irish Theosophist*, March-June 1894. The text is that of A.E.'s final version included in *Imaginations and Reveries*, 1915.
2. This is the higher counterpart of that aspect of the feminine depicted in 'The Cave of Lilith' and 'The Tragedy in the Temple'. The divine feminine archetype represented by Sophia or Celestial Wisdom is allied with the principle of *buddhi* in man. Its human reflection in time is Aphrodite or Venus, the goddess who serves as the bridge or barrier to higher truths. The critical factor seems to be the relative level of materialization of the idea of the feminine. In this story Olive Rayne exercises a genuinely spiritualizing influence but it becomes distorted by the protagonist's desire for personal appropriation.

THE MIDNIGHT BLOSSOM

1. First appeared in *The Irish Theosophist*, July 1894. The text is that of the final version included in *Imaginations and Reveries*, 1915.
2. *The Voice of the Silence*, p. 42.
3. One of three major deities in the Hindu pantheon who along with Brahmā and Viṣṇu constitute the Trimūrti, the three-faced Logos of creation, preservation and regeneration. As the god that embodies the collective forces of destruction and re-creation, he is often depicted as the god of wrath and retribution. However, this portrait is complementary to his role as the regenerator.
4. The god who rules the forces of creation in the cosmos. First member of Hindu Trimūrti, signifying expansive creative activity which arouses the universe to life after a period of non-being. Brahmā is thus allied with the first Logos and all creative forces in the universe.
5. Mystic sounds heard by the yogi at incipient stages of meditation.
6. The *Bodhisattvas*, those mighty men of meditation who, through their self-devised efforts, having conquered every vice and limitation of matter, rise above this plane of illusion to that celestial abode from which they oversee the struggle of other beings who aspire to follow the same path.
7. The 'shining ones' or lesser gods of the Hindu pantheon.

THE INTERPRETERS

1. First published by Macmillan and Co., 1923.
2. Cf. *C.O.V.*, note 17.
3. This particular aspect of the political allegory draws upon prevailing accounts of the ancient civilization of Atlantis. Airships were a fundamental feature of Atlantean superiority over nature. Many other qualities cultivated by that race of sorcerers directly parallel the characteristics of the despotic government described here. Accounts of flying-ships in ancient times are also found in the *Mahābhārata*. (Cf. *S.D.* II, pp. 426-7.)
4. The entire allegory of *The Interpreters* could be seen as a commentary upon the decline of the Mysteries in Ireland. For further understanding of A.E.'s thought concerning the Irish people see below 'The Awakening of the Fires' and 'Priest or Hero?', pp. 366–79.
5. The fifth cosmic principle called *ākāśa* by the Hindus and the *Mysterium Magnum* by medieval alchemists. It is matter in an undifferentiated state, being the seminal form as well as the vitalizing energy of the visible world.
6. Cf. *Bhagavad Gītā*, ch. XI, for Arjuna's vision of Krishna as the repository of all forms.
7. A.E. draws upon the figure of the Demiurge to serve as a divine prototype for the character of Culain. There is also a significant Masonic influence evident. The Masons established a philosophical tradition based upon the operations of the Divine Builders called 'Cosmocratores' who served as the architects of cosmic evolution. The Demiurge is a generic term for these builders. (Cf. Plato, *Timaeus*.)
8. The allusion here is to the archetypal struggle between good and evil that has both psychological and political ramifications. Its character is essentially outlined in the Promethean myth and explained further in A.E.'s article entitled 'The Awakening of the Fires'. It is the war between Spirit and matter deciding the ultimate fate of the human soul.

9. According to Theosophical teaching, each great historical epoch is marked by the emergence of a great civilization which most fully expresses the activity of the Universal Logos in time. The rise and fall of these civilizations is termed the progression of subraces, seven of which constitute an entire Root Race which in turn is one-seventh part of a much longer cycle called a Round. All of these divisions mark the periodic manifestation of a guiding intelligence or Oversoul which falls into time for the sake of the growth of the whole.
10. Reference is made here to the noetic realm of divine archetypes which exist prior to any sentient manifestation of form as explained in Plato's *Timaeus*. The Demiurge or Grand Architect of the Universe looks to this realm for those patterns which he will impress upon chaotic matter. (Cf. *Timaeus*, 28A-29D.)
11. See 'Retrospect' in *The Candle of Vision*, for an autobiographical account of a parallel mystical experience which occurred in A.E.'s youth. Much of Lavelle's character is drawn directly from precepts of *The Candle of Vision*. He speaks for the poetic and visionary side of the author.
12. Direct incarnations of the World Soul or Logos, called King-Initiates in ancient times, who brought divine wisdom to the pioneering peoples of this Root Race. (Cf. *S.D.* II, p. 365.)
13. The fundamental idea being expressed is that strong ideational currents must of necessity ally themselves with specific forces as a means of expression. Thought and energy are but complementary aspects of a unified field of activity which describes noetic functions. Thus higher thought is the true sovereign in the world, material nature being but a secondary effect. (Cf. *Ocean*, p. 102.)
14. A.E.'s description of the powers of the imagination is worked out most completely in *The Candle of Vision* ('Have Imaginations Body?') and *The Hero in Man*. The idea expressed here is that each human being is a generator of numerous electro-magnetic forces which bind with thought-forms of a similar type. This relationship is one of mutual attraction and is the basis for assigning karmic responsibility to all one's thoughts. The more universal and benevolent our thoughts, the more we can attract beings of a sympathetic nature who may take shape in terms of our actions in the world.
15. Cf. 'Meditation' in *The Candle of Vision*.
16. Heyt generally articulates the position of Thrasymachus in Plato's *Republic*. However, his argument becomes much more complex as his portion of the dialogue evolves. His standpoint is reminiscent of Zeus' in Aeschylus' *Prometheus Bound* or the Grand Inquisitor's in Dostoevsky's *Brothers Karamazov*.
17. An aspect of *ākāśa*; the *prima materia*; Adamic earth of the alchemists.
18. Theosophically, natural law is the activity of gods or spiritual intelligences in organizing chaotic matter. Such an idea was commonly expressed by Romantic writers like Wordsworth and Shelley but overlaid in the race-mind by the axioms of materialistic science. Heyt's position is a perverse combination of conflicting notions, which are essentially Atlantean in character, that is, the use of spiritual knowledge and power for material and despotic ends. It is an *inversion* of true Demiurgic activity.
19. The highest spiritual powers are beyond the reach of sorcerers, as they radiate directly from the Spiritual Sun and remain undefiled by matter. This is superior nature, the world of primary emanations called Dhyāni Buddhas. Inferior nature is composed of secondary and tertiary emanations or material energies. (Cf. *Tr.*, pp. 50-1.)
20. See The Myth of Er, *Republic*, bk. X.
21. Cf. *The Candle of Vision*, note 115.
22. Considered as the chief sin among the Buddhists, called 'the dire heresy of separateness'.

Notes and Commentary to pages 284–302

23. Compassion is depicted in the mystical text of *The Voice of the Silence* as the very highest of states or feelings. It is written that compassion is the 'Law of LAWS'. (Cf. *Voice*, pp. 75–6.)
24. All manifestation of life on the physical plane is the result of the outbreathing of the One Life or Spirit. Therefore, characteristics of culture, race and individuals proceed from the activities of forces both prior and causal to their physical expression. The eighth Proposition of Oriental Psychology as recorded by H.P. Blavatsky states: 'Races of men differ in spiritual gifts as in colour, stature, or any other external quality: among some people seership naturally prevails, among others mediumship.'
25. The deep mystery of the War in Heaven, the struggle between the forces of light and darkness, is treated extensively by H.P. Blavatsky in *The Secret Doctrine*, vol. II. The true conflict was not between good and evil *per se* as recounted in Christian theology, but, as is intimated here, was between the creators and those who refused to create man. It is a question of self-evolution. The so-called 'dark' forces allied to the unknown god sacrificed their own essence by incarnating into grossly limited human forms and raising them to the level of self-conscious godhood. They are the Fire-bearers or *prometheoi* of every cosmogony. They are classed as rebels by the priestly caste of every nation because they offered the opportunity for enlightenment to all souls instead of guarding the fire for the benefit of a privileged class alone. They are the true saviours of humanity. (Cf. *S.D.* I, pp. 193-4.)
26. The only deity Theosophy acknowledges is the unknown, incognizable god that manifests as a trinity under the aspects of spirit, energy and matter. This is the first fundamental proposition of Theosophy and the core of its philosophy. This triad is the very highest Self in the cosmos and ultimately inseparable from the human soul or monad which is its reflection in the microcosm.
27. Indian sages such as Patañjali teach that one can come to command the six *śakti* powers which are inherent in the fifth cosmic principle or *akāśa*. These powers enable a yogi to control the seminal forces of creation in the cosmos connected with heat, light, sound and cognition. The queen of the powers is *Kriyāśakti*, whereby a yogi may actually precipitate an objective image from his deep meditation.
28. Archetypal or Heavenly Man; Adam Kadmon.
29. By definition, the Absolute can never be other than what it is.
30. Theosophy teaches that the difference between the human and the divine worlds is one of degree and not of kind. The only temple Theosophy would approve is that which is dedicated to the unknown God. (See *Selections*, p. 47.)
31. A term used to describe the nature of the Holy Ghost in Christian theology. It corresponds to *Vāc* or the Great Breath in Eastern thought. The alternating activity of breathing has been depicted as reflecting the cosmic process of creation and dissolution. Out-breathing on a cosmic scale, therefore, signifies the re-awakening and radiation of hosts of creative forces. In this sense, the Word or *Verbum* and Holy Breath are equivalent terms. (Cf. *S.D.* I, pp. 42-3.)
32. A fundamental idea in theosophical thought, most cogently expressed in Patañjali's *Yoga Sūtras*; namely, that realization comes from dwelling upon the thing to be realized. Thought is, by its very nature, a transforming power. Thought-energies, divine or demonic, must react upon us in the manner in which we direct them.
33. Secrecy is the *sine qua non* of the occult life; the reason simply being that one's spiritual energies must be protected from the confused vibrations of the external world if the individual is to remain strong. Diffusion of energy by

means of superfluous speech is inimical to the development of a strong will and disciplined imagination.
34. See *The Hero in Man* for a further amplification of this theme. It depicts the awakened soul as a strong resonant centre of spiritual force invisibly influencing the lives of all with whom the individual comes in contact.
35. Man is composed of forty-nine fires representing his seven principles and their seven sub-principles. By concentration and will he can awaken these fires which express themselves as heightened faculties of knowledge, power and compassion. However, the impulse which ignites these fires must descend from above. The lower fires can never light up higher spiritual faculties. Therefore, the man who wishes to light up his entire nature must start with the very highest. Such a truth was echoed by the Initiate Jesus, when he said, 'Search ye after the kingdom of Heaven and all else will be given unto you.' (Cf. *S.D.* I, pp. 291 and 520–1 for an explanation of the forty-nine fires.)
36. Cf. 'The Many-Coloured Land' in *The Candle of Vision*.
37. Patterns and modes of thought and action residing in Plato's noetic realm. (See note 10 for a more complete definition.)
38. A restatement of A.E.'s formulation of the laws of karmic connection termed in other places the law of spiritual gravitation. H.P. Blavatsky describes the *kuṇḍalinī śakti* along similar lines. She defines it as a power which adjusts the external to the internal and *vice versa*. This is a mysterious process which is at the very centre of the teaching regarding *karma*. From the perspective of the soul, notions of inner and outer are wholly illusory. Therefore, the higher we reach in consciousness, the clearer we see the world transfigured by Spirit and the nearer we come to transcending the false dichotomy between subject and object. Yet this too is strictly regulated by karmic merit.
39. The spectator and source of all forms in the cosmos, visible and invisible.
40. *Matthew* V.48.
41. The alchemical justification of the total purification of the inner nature demanded in the spiritual life is touched upon here. Every attempt to heed the whisperings of the Spiritual Soul cleanses and clarifies the subtle elements which constitute our inner nature and replaces tainted life-atoms with those which more luminously reflect the brilliance of the Spiritual Sun. Transformation of elements in one's subtler bodies is a direct result of spiritual striving.
42. Associated with the *kāma* or desire principle of brute animal energy. To prepare for Initiation the aspirant must destroy this principle utterly past all re-animation. The soul then lives in a higher body refined of all earthly passions and impurities. (Cf. *Glo.*, 'Kama'.)
43. Based on one of the most ancient legends in Celtic mythology concerning the existence of a Holy Well in which swam the sacred salmon who fed upon the nuts of knowledge dropped by the Hazel Tree which threw its shade over the well. Violating an ancient law, the great god Dagda's wife approached the sacred spot and thereupon the well burst, siring a stream down which the salmon fled. The holy place was destroyed. However, it is said that the wise warrior, King Finn MacCool, later caught one of these fish downstream and upon eating it achieved the omniscience of a god.
44. Fabled land of divine peace and beauty located in central Greece according to the sages and poets of that ancient civilization. The god Hermes was reported to have been born in a cave in this region.

AT THE DAWN OF THE KALIYUGA

1. First appeared in *The Irish Theosophist*, October 1893.

'GO OUT IN THOUGHT'

1. First appeared in *The Internationalist*, February 1898. This unsigned essay is probably by A.E.

THE HERO IN MAN

1. First appeared in *The Irish Theosophist*, March and July 1897, *The Internationalist*, November 1897. Collected in pamphlet form, 1909, the text of which is reprinted here.
2. The Father is a metaphorical term for the First Logos, the spirit that moved upon the waters at the dawn of creation.
3. Christ-soul is equivalent to the Universal Spirit or *Ātman*.
4. Cf. *C.O.V.*, note 245, for an explanation of the law of spiritual gravitation. In mysticism it is known as the law of affinities based upon the Pythagorean science of harmonics and substantiated by the experiments of Franz Mesmer in 'animal magnetism'. The central thesis of this essay rests upon the reality of these laws operating in invisible nature.
5. From the *Visuddimagga* of Buddhaghosa. (Cf. 'The Meditation of Ananda', note 3.)
6. The master of realised adeptship. See note 4 in 'The Mystic Nights' Entertainment'.
7. The human race is commonly depicted in mystical literature as a great host of monadic light points proceeding as a collective radiation from a parent source; the Central Spiritual Sun.
8. Cf. *C.O.V.*, note 3.
9. *Luke* XXIII. 34.
10. In Sanskrit this chain of intelligences from the very highest beings to the sub-kingdoms of nature is referred to as the *Guruparampara*. All parts of manifestation are internally bound together by sympathetic ties of love, reverence and devotion.
11. In Tibetan Buddhism it is taught that an individual Dhyāni Buddha overbroods the incarnation of each soul, presiding in silence over its cosmic pilgrimage. This is the celestial prototype of man to which the soul must aspire if it is to achieve final emancipation. (Cf. *S.D.* I, p. 639.)
12. This is a veiled reference to the great sacrifice performed by all true teachers. It is said that after conquering all the illusions of earth life, they voluntarily choose to return to the world, accepting the mantle of suffering in order to show others the way to the freedom and wisdom they have achieved.

THE LEGENDS OF ANCIENT EIRE

1. First appeared in *The Irish Theosophist*, March-April 1895.
2. The spiritual soul and divine prototype that overbroods the incarnation of every man.
3. Known as Adam Kadmon in Kabbalistic literature. (See *C.O.V.*, note 115.)
4. *The Voice of the Silence*, p. 9.
5. Translated 'Abode of the Gods', it is the region that harbours souls between incarnations. It allows the most exalted thoughts from the previous life to be imagined and lived out in their fullest actuality. Adepts regard this state as illusory as they have overcome the need to incarnate involuntarily. For the uninitiated, however, Devachan bestows the peace and refreshment necessary to the soul before it resumes its earthly pilgrimage.
6. Great mystic and seer born in Germany in the sixteenth century. Boehme worked tirelessly to revive a more universal and esoteric conception of Christianity which was more consonant with the ancient teachings regarding the nature of man. Assailed by ecclesiastical authorities most of his life, he managed to avoid persecution and published a great number of philosophical and mystical texts which inspired and influenced later thinkers from Hegel to Schopenhauer.
7. Referring to the Third Eye or Eye of Wisdom which receded beneath the skull during the Fourth Race because of great abuses of spiritual powers by men. It remained active only in the wise and pure. The pineal gland is said to be its physiological equivalent in the physical brain.
8. Called *kuṇḍalinī* in the East. (Cf. *C.O.V.*, note 96.)
9. By this term is meant *kāma* or animal soul, the engine of passions that drives animal man. It is a reservoir of brute force which is consubstantial with the lower elements of nature. An Adept is one who has subdued these irrational passions utterly and consequently reduced his *kāma* to a cypher.

THE MOUNTAINS

1. First published in *The Irish Theosophist*, May 1896.

ON AN IRISH HILL

1. First appeared in *The Kilkenny Moderator* 1896. The text is that of A.E.'s final version included in *Imaginations and Reveries*, 1915.
2. A.E.'s poem 'The Nuts of Knowledge'.
3. In Celtic lore, Connla was the son of the great King Conn. Like the British Arthur, Conn was wooed by a goddess and borne away in a boat of glass to the earthly paradise beyond the sea.
4. The refrain from W.B. Yeats's 'The Stolen Child'.
5. Famous son of Lir, the Gaelic Poseidon, Manannan was reputed to have a boat called the wave-sweeper which propelled and guided itself wherever its owner wished. He was a mighty sea-god.
6. The crowning glory of the Gaelic pantheon; its sun-god is equivalent to Apollo in Greek mythology.
7. A.E.'s poem 'A Call of the Sidhe'.

THE AWAKENING OF THE FIRES

1. First appeared in *The Irish Theosophist*, January-February 1897. The text is that of A.E.'s final version printed as a pamphlet under the title *The Future of Ireland and the Awakening of the Fires*, 1897.
2. A.E.'s poem 'Breaghy'.
3. Ancient name for Ireland, derived from Eriu, one of the great queens of primeval Celtic lore.
4. Chief Druid and Magus of the tribe of Milesians who are reputed to be the first Gaelic people to enter Ireland. Amergin's song, recited as he first stepped on Irish shores, is recounted in the book of Taliesin and is considered to be the oldest record of identifiably Irish literature known. It is a Dionysian affirmation of the unity between the magic of nature and the deeds of man.
5. A.E. is drawing upon the imagery of the 'White Island', the permanent abode of the world's perfected men. (Cf. 'The Legends of Ancient Eire'.)

PRIEST OR HERO?

1. First appeared in *The Irish Theosophist*, April-May 1897. The text is that of A.E.'s final version printed as a pamphlet under the title *Ideals in Ireland: Priest or Hero?*, 1897.
2. Greatest warrior hero of Gaels and Celts. He possessed the combined qualities of Heracles and Achilles of the Greeks. Invincible in battle and yet 'to early death and sorrows doomed beyond the lot of normal man', his life was a series of wonderful exploits and labours. His father was the sun-god Lugh and the legend of his life is surrounded by many solar symbols. He was chief among the tribe of heroes referred to here, commonly known as 'the Champions of the Red Branch'.
3. According to Irish legend a noble band of warriors arose under the direction of Finn MacCool to protect the native people from the incursions of foreign tribes. Finn had two great sons, Fergus and Ossian (Oisin). In his youth Ossian was enticed by a beautiful maiden to leave his homeland and embark upon a journey which lasted over 300 years. Upon his return, he found that the tribe of Finn called Fennians had disappeared from the land and their descendants had been converted to Christianity by Patrick. The collection of tales and heroic exploits of the Fennians are known as Ossianic ballads. The conversations between Ossian and Patrick are generally called 'Dialogues of Ossian and Patrick', being a collection of popular ballads and folk-lore on the meeting of these symbolic and historical personages.
4. Goddess of fire and the hearth and especially poetry, which the Gaels deemed an incorporeal and supersensual form of flame. She is custodian of the flame of ancient Druid wisdom in the period of obscuration.

CHIVALRY

1. First appeared in *The Irish Theosophist*, October 1897; generally attributed to A.E.
2. Most noble and virtuous race of warriors in all Celtic mythology.

IN THE SHADOW OF THE GODS

1. First appeared in *The Internationalist*, March 1898.
2. Jehovah, the anthropomorphic conception of deity that A.E. sees as contrary to the true religious spirit.
3. Cf. 'The Many-Coloured Land' in *The Candle of Vision*.

AN IRISH MYSTIC'S TESTIMONY

1. From *The Fairy Faith in Celtic Countries*, by W.Y. Evans-Wentz (London: Oxford University Press, 1911; Gerrards Cross: Colin Smythe, 1977 and Atlantic Highlands, Humanities Press, 1978); Interview with A.E. For proof that A.E. was Evans-Wentz's anonymous informant, see Alan Denson, ed., *Letters from AE* (London, New York, Toronto: Abelard Schuman, 1961), p. 222.
2. Celtic Otherworld, called Tir-na-noge, the dwelling place of supernatural beings called the Sidhe.
3. Seership is the activation of the faculty of spiritual sight connected with the higher intuition. Mediumship is the surrender of any consciously directed power or thought to the will of external forces which impress themselves upon the pliant mind of the medium. Seership is the exaltation of the highest powers latent in every man. Mediumship is complete abdication of that birthright to the chaotic forces below man.
4. Cf. *C.O.V.*, note 127.
5. See *The Secret Doctrine* II, pp. 166-8, for an explanation of modes of reproduction in early races of men.
6. Cf. the writings of Paracelsus and Jacob Boehme for extensive discussions and explanations of the operations of elemental forces.

FACE TO FACE WITH NATURE

1. This review of Franz Hartmann's *Among the Gnomes* appeared in *Ourselves*, May 1896.

SONG AND ITS FOUNTAINS

1. First published by Macmillan and Co., 1932.
2. Meditation and trance involve sinking into the unconscious where the germs of past *karma* lie hidden. These germs are called *skandhas* which bear the impress of all past *karma* in seed form. In Patañjali's *Yoga Sūtras* the disciple is directed to burn out such seeds past all re-animation. (See *Key*, pp. 154-6.)
3. *The Secret Doctrine* depicts the adjustment of internal to external relations as a pimary characteristic of the *kuṇḍalini śakti* – one of the soul-powers of the Adept. (See *S.D.* I, p. 293.)

Notes and Commentary to pages 391–394   741

4. The seed of enlightenment is called *Bodhicitta* in Buddhist thought. The spiritual life could be seen as the nurturing of this seed to full flower.
5. This type of meditation, emphasized in Pythagorean and Buddhist traditions, is practised to free oneself from the hold of the past and its memories. Such self-examination is helpful in developing a detachment from the personal ego and its reactions to events. Through the endeavour to study the past in a spirit of balanced dispassion, the sense of perspective made possible by distance in time can liberate the mind from its self-created limitations.
6. The bud is the soul's primordial awareness of its divine nature before it becomes fragmented and lost amidst the confusion of incarnated existence.
7. Under the Law of Karma, the recognition of the root cause of error is the first step towards final emancipation of the mind.
8. The mystic power to see one's past lives is regarded, in Buddhist texts, as a definite stage in the meditator's path – one of the *jñānas*. It is one of the powers attained by the Buddha before he reached the highest enlightenment under the Bodhi Tree. 'Both I and thou have passed through many births, O harasser of thy foes! Mine are known unto me, but thou knowest not of thine.' (*Gītā*, ch. IV.5, p. 31.)
9. This is what the Hindus called the *sūtrātman*, the 'thread-soul'. It is depicted in ancient texts as a series of pearls strung on a golden thread. (See *S.D.* II, p. 79.) Throughout this work, A.E. uses 'psyche' in a specialized sense which the reader should note. Generally speaking, psyche refers to the inner sidereal man which is both the invisible double of the physical man and the essence of his passional nature. The term *psychic* is often used to describe the carnal and egotistic part of man's nature, opposed to his noetic self which is wholly spiritual. However, psyche here is used in a loftier sense to denote the true individuality which stands behind the mask of personal name and form. The psyche in this sense is the universal man imprisoned in the chrysalis of the physical body and confined to space and time. The personal man can only be redeemed by indissolubly allying itself with the divine destiny of the higher individuality or true psyche.
10. This word probably acted like a *mantra* on A.E.'s consciousness. W.Q. Judge remarks that sometimes the commonest words in English contain a mantramic power of sound. 'A mantram is a collection of words which, when sounded in speech, induce certain vibrations not only in the air, but also in the finer ether, thereby producing certain effects.' ('Conversations on Occultism', *The Path*, August 1888.)
11. Jesus used the phrase 'children of light'. (*John* XII. 36) (See also *Ephesians* V.8.)
12. 'O Arjuna! Be free from the "pairs of opposites" and constant in the quality of *Sattva*.' (*Gītā*, ch. II.45, p. 16.) The wise man 'is contented with whatever he receives fortuitously, is free from the influence of "the pairs of opposites".' (*Gītā*, ch. IV.22, p.33.)
13. See *Candle of Vision*, note 17.
14. Plotinus, placing Beauty in the realm of the Intelligible, points to the Good, which for him, as for Plato, is the ultimate One. 'Thus, in sum, one would say that the first hypostasis is Beauty. But, if one would divide up the intelligibles, one would distinguish Beauty, which is the place of Ideas, from the Good that lies beyond the beautiful and is its "source and principle".' (*Enneads* I, 6, 9 [O'Brien, p. 43].)
15. The being within, often described by the Upaniṣads as 'the Person the measure of a thumb', is often mentioned in the Upaniṣads. (Cf. *Kath. U.*, 4.12–13, 6.17 an *Mai. U.*, 6.38.) The inner self or psyche referred to here is what is called the

Higher Ego in Theosophy. The Higher Ego is composed of man's three higher principles: *Ātman* and *buddhi* (the Spiritual Self) wedded to *manas*, the principle of self-conscious intellection. Manas or mind is dual by nature and may ally itself with the Spiritual Soul or *buddhi* above it or the animal soul (*kāma*) below it. Manas, tied to its inferior egoistic nature, creates a series of ephemeral, elemental personalities above which the Higher Ego or thread-soul (*sūtrātman*), as it is called, remains undiminished throughout an innumerable series of incarnations.

16. One of the meanings of the term 'yoga' is 'union' (from *yuj* = yoke, unite). Through it we are enjoined to achieve union with our inmost immortal Self.
17. Our 'destiny is guided either by the heavenly voice of the invisible *prototype* outside of us, or by our more intimate *astral*, or inner man, who is but too often the evil genius of the embodied entity called man. Both these lead on the outward man, but one of them must prevail; . . .' (*S.D.* I, p. 639) '. . . the *rays* of the eternal divine Mind, considered as individual entities, assume a two-fold attribute which is (a) their *essential* inherent characteristic, heaven-aspiring mind (higher *Manas*), and (b) the human quality of thinking, or animal cogitation, rationalized owing to the superiority of the human brain, the *Kāma*-tending or lower Manas. One gravitates toward Buddhi, the other, tending downward, to the seat of passions and animal desires.' (*Key*, p. 184) Plotinus, explaining the descent of the soul as well as its longing to return to its true home, remarks, 'Souls of necessity lead a double life, partly in the intelligible realm and partly in that of sense . . .' (*Enneads* IV, 8, 4 [O'Brien p. 66].)
18. The rose has often occupied the same place in Western mystical symbology that the lotus retains in Eastern symbolism. Hence its choice as one of the chief symbols of the Rosicrucians. The opening of the rose, therefore, symbolizes the opening of divine wisdom within the soul, the rebirth of the spirit.
19. Francis Thompson in 'The Hound of Heaven', Browning and others. Such 'meetings with the soul' are also a frequent theme in Sufi poetry.
20. See Keats – 'Sleep and Poetry'.
21. Our past desires, thoughts and deeds create the ties that drag the soul back into incarnation. (See also Plato – The Myth of Er, *Republic*, bk. X.) The *Muṇḍaka Upaniṣad* points to the connection between desire and rebirth: 'He who in fancy forms desires, because of his desires is born again here and there.' (*Muṇ. U.*, 3.2.2.)
22. A Gnostic term meaning the ontological fullness of the invisible cosmos, i.e., that into which the Logos reflects all in the universe.
23. See *The Ocean of Theosophy*, pp. 86-7, where W.Q. Judge gives examples of child prodigies (Mozart, Napoleon, etc.) bringing back knowledge of past lives. Heredity and cultural environment seem to have little to do with the enormous differences of character and ability that we find in human beings. '. . . all these differences, such as those shown by babes from birth, by adults as character comes forth more and more, and by nations in their history, are due to long experience gained during many lives on earth, are the outcome of the soul's own evolution.' (*Ocean*, p. 81.) 'Individuals and nations in definite streams return in regularly recurring periods to the earth, and thus bring back to the globe the arts, the civilization, the very persons who once were on it at work.' (*Ocean*, p. 119.)
24. The 'mystery of the Ego' is a term used in *The Key to Theosophy* (pp. 177–80) to describe the unfathomable nature of the spiritual individuality. Since it is at root one with absoluteness, its essential nature can never be fully comprehended and will remain a mystery.

Notes and Commentary to pages 398–404   743

25. The spiritual atom is the divine imperishable spark in each man. Subsequent to each incarnation it refines and polishes experiences garnered in the previous life and carries forward that essential knowledge in order to arrive at spiritual wisdom after a long series of rebirths. (See *Enneads* IV, 8; VI, 9 [O'Brien] and *S.D.* I, p. 148.)
26. The reference here is to the fundamental cleavage in man's nature, the polar orientation of his thinking principle or *manas*. The lower mind gravitates naturally towards form and fragments itself amidst a sea of chaotic sensations, whereas the higher *manas* aspires to fusion with the Spiritual Soul or *buddhi*. Redemption of the lower *manas* or *persona* can only be accomplished by a complete turning around of its nature, so that it seeks union with its divine parent.
27. See *C.O.V.*, note 211.
28. H.P. Blavatsky uses the phrase 'plastic potency' in her article 'Dialogue Between Two Editors'. (*Lucifer*, December 1888.) The matter appropriate to the plane on which the psyche functions is much more subtle than ours, capable of reflecting the impress of thought more vividly.
29. A.E. seems here to intuit the true nature of the creative genius as having its roots in the divine immortal soul, rather than in that which we usually call 'mind'.
30. See *C.O.V.*, note 194, on the occult power of speech and sound.
31. An ancient symbol for the diastolic and systolic motions of nature; the outgoing and inward turning aspects of Spirit. Aspiration and inspiration are aspects of one ceaseless process throughout the cosmos. 'The One breathed, breathless.' (*Rg Veda*.) The sacred *Brahman* is identified with breath in the Upanishads.
32. The highest meditation is closely related to inward sacrifice, *yajña*. (See *Ch. U.*, 8.5, and 3.16; and *Mun. U.*, 1.2.7–11; also *Śv. U.*, 2.6.) The *Bhagavad Gītā*, too, speaks of *yajña yoga* or devotion by means of sacrificial action.
33. All creativity, all 'magical powers' or 'supernatural gifts' are but the expression of the power of the One Spirit manifesting in different ways and diverse forms. They are spoken of as *śaktis*, the six primary forces in nature. (See *S.D.* I, p. 292.)
34. All of these powers and aptitudes may be grouped under *Mantrikā-śakti* or power over sound. This is the incarnation of *Vāc*, the Holy Breath, the *Verbum*. It is one of the six yogic powers mastered by those who have thoroughly fused their individual consciousness with Cosmic Mind.
35. Śankara implies (in his commentary on the *Māṇḍukya Upaniṣad*) that the four states of consciousness (*jāgrat, svapna, suṣupti* and *turīya*) are not separate but interpenetrate one another, so that in each state the other three inhere as well.
36. The higher always begets the lower. Thus lower *manas* is but a fugitive ray of higher *manas* just as the physical brain is but the instrument of lower *manas* on the plane of physical sensation. Experiences in the higher mind will be distorted when channelled through a lesser vehicle which is inherently incapable of being a pure transmitter of higher vibrations.
37. This refers to a great mystic utterance of Plotinus, the consummation of the profoundest of meditations. '. . . the flight of the alone to the Alone'. (*Enneads* VI, 9, 11 [O'Brien, p. 88].)
38. Plotinus has much to say on this in *Enneads* IV, 3 and in IV, 8. 'Souls do not descend freely nor are they sent. At least their willingness is not a free choice. They move towards bodies indeliberately, as if by instinct, as one is drawn without reflection towards marriage or sometimes towards achieving of great

deeds.' (*Enneads* IV, 3, 14 [O'Brien, p. 142].) Continuing his own account of the mystery of the descent of the soul, Plotinus points out that '... our souls, charged with the managing of bodies less perfect than they, had to penetrate into them if they were to manage them truly.' (*Enneads* IV , 8, 1 [O'Brien, p. 63]) More enigmatically, he adds that although the souls dwell originally in the sunlit world of the Intelligible, '. . . There comes a point at which they come down from this state, cosmic in its dimensions, to one of individuality. They wish to be independent. They are tired, you might say, of living with someone else. Each steps down into its own individuality.' (*Enneads* IV, 8, 1 [O'Brien, p. 66].)

39. 'And in the fifth, O slayer of thy thoughts, all these again have to be killed beyond reanimation.' (*Voice*, p. 20.) This points to the self-perpetuating nature of lower thought forms. They must be destroyed utterly or they will surely resurface.

40. These entities are said to be nourished by the effluvia of carnal thoughts and emanations. Paracelsus explained that intensely sensuous thoughts and images released a type of fluid into the sidereal atmosphere from which were hatched hideous demonic beings. These incubi and succubi went about influencing passive individuals to repeat such thoughts, thus perpetuating their kind. Such is the dynamic power of thought that although desires may disappear from this plane, they may be reborn in more devious forms on other planes.

41. The *loka* or place referred to here is the post-mortem state of Devachan. It is a condition of rest and assimilation for the soul between incarnations. Only the highest thoughts and aspirations of that being comes into a subjective flowering during this idyllic, dream-like state. (See *Ocean*, p. 109.)

42. A broad characterization of the state of repose called Devachan, lit. 'abode of the gods'. It is the after-death state into which the soul enters after shedding its mortal coil and the desire (or *kāmic*) body in *kāma loka*. Devachan is a place of peace where the soul retires to rest between incarnations so as to purify and assimilate the knowledge acquired during the previous life. All wholesome thoughts and noble desires achieve their mental consummation. This plane is allied with dream and trance states, and is similar to the heaven world in A.E.'s terminology.

43. See note 49 in *C.O.V.* on 'tablet of nature'.

44. The 'ancestral memories' would be akin to what Plato calls 'recollection' connected with the pre-existence of the soul (cf. *Phaedo*) and to soul-memories from past lives in Theosophical literature (see *Key*, pp. 124-6); while the 'transient fusions' would be due to the rising of consciousness to the plane which transcends the egotistic separation of personalities. Both the 'memories' and the 'fusions' have to do with the consciousness of the timeless, Universal Self.

45. Cf. note 59 in *C.O.V.* for etymology of *deva*.

46. Cf *C.O.V.*, note 20.

47. An *Avatar* is an incarnation of the divine principle of the cosmos, symbolized by Viṣṇu. (Cf. *C.O.V.*, note 161.)

48. It is sometimes dangerous for a person in a deep state of meditative trance to be brought back suddenly into the waking state. The descent from higher to lower planes of consciousness must always be gradual, and even continuous in order to allow the assimilation of the intuition of the trance and its smooth linkage with the mundane world, creating that continuity of consciousness which is the essence of the spiritual life.

49. A.E. is referring to the elemental points of life that make up the kingdoms of nature. 'Existing . . . in all parts of the globe and the solar system, are the

Notes and Commentary to pages 409–414 745

elementals or nature forces. They are innumerable, and their divisions are almost infinite, as they are, in a sense, the nerves of nature. Each class has its own work just as has every natural element or thing.' See W.Q. Judge (*Ocean*, p. 104).

50. According to Theosophical teaching, we are bound to all beings in the cosmos by invisible but very real magnetic ties – part of a great universal chain of being. Related to this is the idea of the sacred *Guruparaṁpara* chain, extending from the highest beings to the lowest. As W.Q. Judge explains the concept, 'a long chain of influence extends from the highest spiritual guide who may belong to any man, down through vast numbers of spiritual chiefs, ending at last in the mere teacher of our youth. Or, to restate it in modern reversion of thought, a chain extends up from our teacher or preceptors to the highest spiritual chief in whose ray or descending line one may happen to be. And it makes no difference whatever, in this occult relation, that neither pupil nor final guide may be aware, or admit, that this is the case.' (*W.Q.J. Letters*, pp. 42-3. Cf. also *The Hero in Man*.)
51. See note on *Nirmāṇakāyic* influence on Shakespeare in *Echoes from the Orient*, p. 6.
52. H.P. Blavatsky refers to Balzac as 'the unconscious occultist of French literature'. (*Tr.*, p. 110.)
53. The emancipated *manas* is wedded to its spiritual progenitor *buddhi*. Such a state is anticipated by *Manas-Taijasī* – the radiant or ecstatic mind.
54. Aspect of Buddhist meditation and one of the *jhānas*. Buddha is said to have attained to this state as he sat under the Bodhi Tree.
55. The purpose of such recollection is to enable the individual to trace events and tendencies in the present life back to their original causes in past lives so that such traits may be eliminated and the old chain of causation broken.
56. The soul is not created at a point in time after which it continues to live forever, but is *truly* eternal, never having had a beginning, as it has no end. 'I myself never was not', says Krishna in *Bhagavad Gītā*, ch. II.12, p. 11.
57. Since the object of the Law of Karma and Reincarnation is to provide opportunities to learn for the pilgrim soul, there is no need to have the memory of every detail of past personal lives, any more than we need to remember every trivial detail of our childhood to know that there are important areas in which our infancy has influenced our adult personalities. We need only recollect the impersonal spiritual insights gained in past lives.
58. We are warned by many mystics and spiritual teachers not to rush into the spiritual life unprepared for the ordeals and trials. We may be wiser to wait. ' . . . thou of timid heart, be warned in time: remain content with the "Eye Doctrine" of the Law. Hope still. For if the "Secret Path" is unattainable this "day", it is within thy reach "to-morrow".' (*Voice*, p. 37.)
59. There comes a stage in the life of the spiritual aspirant when he must finally come face to face with his dark past, his shadow, which may take an actual form that ancient myths have symbolized as monsters, evil creatures of the night and so on. See W.Q. Judge's article 'The Dweller on the Threshold', *The Path*, December 1888. (See also modern allegories relating to this, e.g. Ursula Le Guin's *The Wizard of Earthsea*.)
60. The great world-illusion. (See *C.O.V.*, note 283.)
61. It is the human mind that creates illusions; *māyā* does not have an objective ontological status. (See Śaṅkara, especially the famous example of the serpent and the rope.)
62. The lower, discursive mind – lower *manas*.
63. Theosophy makes a firm distinction between soul-wisdom (intuition) and

head-learning (cerebration). They are as diametrically opposed as higher and lower *manas*; the first being the true knowledge of the internal relations of things, the second being cleverness in the organization of external relationships. The second is a useful analytic tool when guided by the higher reason yet perverse if used as a means of manipulation by the lower ego.

64. Many mystics know that wisdom is born out of the purificatory fire of suffering. Shelley writes that poets 'are cradled into poetry by wrong, They learn in suffering what they teach in song.'

65. The highest *Parabrahm* is neither spirit nor matter, but that out of which both spring. 'Spirit (or Consciousness) and Matter are, however, to be regarded, not as independent realities, but as the two facets or aspects of the Absolute (Parabrahm), which constitute the basis of conditioned Being whether subjective or objective.' (*S.D.* I, p. 15.) That which is beyond duality may also be called 'that infinite Ocean of Light, whose one pole is pure *Spirit* lost in the absoluteness of Non-Being, and the other, the *matter* in which it condenses . . .' (*S.D.* I, p. 481.)

66. The consummation of the journey on the path is described here in terms of the merging of the individual triad composed of man's three higher principles with its divine root, the Cosmic Triad, the synthesis of primordial ideation, substance and energy. In Pythagorean terms this is the creation of the Tetraktys, the reuniting of soul with spirit within the perfected man.

67. See *Māṇḍukya Upaniṣad* and the commentaries on it by Gauḍapāda and Śaṅkara.

68. *Bṛhadāraṇyaka Upaniṣad*, 4.3.11. In Charles Johnston's translation of this passage, the same phrase is used – 'the gold-gleaming Genius, swan of everlasting' – to describe the Spirit of man. (*Selections*, p. 13.) The whole poem is an expression of the ideas of this section of the *Bṛhadāraṇyaka Upaniṣad*.

69. This implies the four *avasthas* or planes of action of the soul from the dark state of sensory awareness to absolute illumination and omniscience in *turīya*. Each plane has its correspondence in other realms, for example:

jāgrat	equivalent to earth life	waking state
svapna	equivalent to *kāma loka*; mid-world	dream state
suṣupti	equivalent to *Devachan*; heaven-world	high psychic; deep sleep
turīya	transcendental world	enlightenment

70. The psyche loses the full consciousness of divine realms not only when it falls into incarnation but when it sinks from the visions of deep sleep or pure trance into the world of mundane, waking consciousness. As the ninth century Sufi mystic Ziyad B. al-Arabi expresses it, 'When he awakes from the vision, he loses what he has found, but his knowledge remains with him, and for a long time his spirit enjoys that . . .'

71. (See *B.U.*, 4.3.10.) A.E., is quoting from a translation almost identical with that of Charles Johnston's with the exception of a few words.

72. *Fohat*; supreme cosmic energy when transmitted through the human being is called Will. 'The perfection of will-force is referred to as Itchasakti.' (See *S.D.* I, pp. 292 and 339.)

73. The original reference is to the descent of the Holy Ghost on the Apostles on the Day of Pentecost. (*Acts* 2, especially vs. 3.) But A.E. uses it as an image for the descent of divine inspiration.

74. Medieval alchemists comprehended the natural order of things as the visible expression of internal psycho-spiritual forces which work in and through matter. They claimed that by applying the universal axioms of analogy and

correspondence, one could read in the external form of an object a sidereal signature which would reveal its inner nature and potency. The specific medicinal uses to which certain herbs were put is a good example of the benevolent aims of this lost science.

75. The Transfiguration of Jesus, when he appeared to his disciples in an illuminated body, with Moses and Elijah on either side of him. (*Luke*, ch. 9.) As a symbol the Mount of Transfiguration bears many characteristics ascribed to Mount Meru in Hindu mythology. Meru is the abode of Viṣṇu and the *fons et origo* of all wisdom and knowledge. It is the umbilicus of the world stretching from earth to heaven. On the human level, the symbol here seems to be closely related to the Third Eye, the Eye of Śiva represented physiologically by the pineal gland. It is said that the awakened eye can at a glance pierce to the core of any object or arouse any latent energy to life.

76. In the theosophical scheme, primordial substance or *mūlaprakṛti* (root-matter) is regarded as an aspect of Absolute Consciousness. At that level it is consubstantial with Cosmic Mind or *Mahat* which is the source of ceaseless ideation throughout the life of the cosmos. As thought always requires a vehicle or form for expression, so Cosmic Mind must always be radiated through the Substance-Principle and its infinite modifications.

77. Symbol of *buddhic* principle or Wisdom NATURE. (See Sayce, *Religion of Egypt and Babylonians*, p. 426.)

78. The state of *turīya*. (See note 69 above.)

79. The *Kaṭha Upaniṣad* (2.23) says, 'This Soul (*Ātman*) is not to be obtained by instruction, nor by Intellect, nor by much learning. He is to be obtained by the one whom he chooses; to such a one that Soul (*Ātman*) reveals his own person (*tanum svam*).' (The same verse recurs in the *Muṇḍaka Up.*, 3.2.3.)

80. The *Bhāgavata Purāṇa*.

81. In the *Bhāgavata Purāṇa* and *Gītā Govinda*.

82. According to the Hindus, the development of the life of the individual occurs in seven stages of approximately seven years in duration, each period signifying the incarnation or awakening of one of man's seven principles. This process begins with the formation of the body at birth continuing through to full spiritual maturity by the fiftieth year. It is at age seven that the mental principle is aroused and the I-making or egoic faculty consolidated. This faculty then represents the specific centre of action around which develop the characteristics of the *persona*.

83. Man is a direct and undifferentiated ray of Absolute Light, or the Central Spiritual Sun. In a natural state his vestures are unblemished and transmit the fullest radiance of light that his vehicles permit. However, due to association with matter and the exercise of the animal will, his nature impedes and refracts rather than propagates that light. The perfection of virtues can efface such opaque points just as the pursuit of vice will dilate them. Such opacities in one's psycho-physical constitution are recognized by trained seers.

84. The original reference is to Jacob's dream of the ladder to heaven in *Genesis* 28:12. In mystical poetry, we have a symbolic reference in Francis Thompson's 'In No Strange Land' to Jacob's ladder 'pitched betwixt Heaven and Charing Cross' – a saving vision which comes to the despairing soul when it cries aloud to Heaven in the dark. In *The Voice of the Silence* there is a reference to 'the ladder of the mystic sounds'. (p. 11.)

85. 'Behold! thou hast become the Light, thou hast become the Sound, thou art thy Master and thy God.' (*Voice*, p. 23.)

86. The spiritual sight possessed by the sage, who can discern the divine presence in all beings, even those in the most squalid state and destitute condition. Having

acquired mastery of both the eye of time and the eye of eternity, he witnesses simultaneously the divine root of all beings and its ceaseless modifications in manifest life.

87. 'The last series of powerful and deeply imprinted thoughts are those which give colour and trend to the whole life in *Devachan*.' (*Ocean*, p. 113.) Reference is made here to the death review which is regarded as a sacred activity. At death, the soul or Higher Ego is released from the prison-house of the body (as Plato wrote) and is reunited with its immortal parent. Before it retires from incarnation, however, it has the opportunity to review all experiences in the previous life and assimilate the essential wisdom from them that will enable it to progress further in future births. The death review is the summing-up and assessment of each life as well as the genesis of the next.

88. 'Builders of the universe,' the 'world architects', or the Creative Forces personified. (*Glo.*, 'Cosmocratores'.)

89. Christ and Prometheus are in every heart. According to *The Secret Doctrine* Christ and Prometheus represent the higher principles in man, Christ being the spiritual soul (*buddhi*) and Prometheus the divine intelligence (*manas*). Their sacrificial task, recounted in gospel and myth, was to effect the liberation of those beings caught in self-delusion.

90. In 'A Defence of Poetry' Shelley remarks that poets are 'the hierophants of an unapprehended inspiration'.

91. Eastern mystics have stressed that Truth is not to be found in verbal or conceptual formulations but in states of being. States of knowledge are *identical with* states of reality (or being). Śaṅkara says, 'A sickness is not cured by saying the word "medicine". You must take the medicine. Liberation does not come by merely saying the word "Brahman". Brahman must be actually experienced.' (*The Crest Jewel of Discrimination*, p. 43.)

92. A description of mankind as it was in the Third Root Race prior to the emergence of the Atlantean race. H.P. Blavatsky writes in *The Secret Doctrine* that the chief characteristic of this race was its unqualified devotion to spiritual teachers and the 'god within'. They were marked by a natural spirituality that was diminished by the arousal of the animal energies and impure desires which afflicted the Fourth Root Race called the Atlantean civilization.

93. *Dharma* = duty, law, virtue, right. (*Dharma*, from *dhṛ* = to uphold, bear, support.) The *Bhagavad Gītā* especially warns us not to take on the duty of another. (See *Gītā* III, p. 35.) The Great Law, as also the Buddhist Canon. The harmonious principle that adjusts internal qualities to external relations, individual needs to social roles.

94. 'The "Soul of the World", the same as the *alaya* of the Northern Buddhists; the divine essence which permeates, animates and informs all, from the smallest atom of matter to man and god.' (*Glo.*, 'Anima Mundi'.)

95. The Myth of Er in *The Republic*, bk. X.

96. The spiritual law referred to here is conceived differently in a variety of religious and philosophical traditions yet is similar in its function in the life of the individual. It is commonly known as the voice of conscience, yet it is seen by Plato as an overbrooding Daemon benevolently guiding the soul, or by Plotinus as a tutelary spirit. In the East, it is known as a spiritual intelligence which is the soul's true parent and progenitor linked to *buddhi* or divine discernment.

97. Plato's Allegory of the Cave – since Plato (*Phaedo*) calls the body the 'prison' of the soul, while Plotinus uses terms such as 'cave', 'grotto' and 'tomb'. (*Enneads* IV, 8, 3 [O'Brien, p. 65].)

98. Legendary king of the Tuatha de Danann who possessed a magical sword that made him invincible in battle.

99. Literally tribes of the goddess Dana. One of the divine prehistoric peoples of Ireland, skilled in Magic and all the arts, also powerful warriors.
100. A race of powerful and cruel demons continually fighting against the gods. The Tuatha de Danann were the children of light shepherded by the race of gods that first descended on ancient Ireland. They were opposed by the Fomorians whose name means literally 'from under the sea'. They were dark, chthonic forces, peoples of monstrous shape and titanic size. They warred continuously with the Tuatha de Danann for control of the Celtic nation. This struggle generated much of the heroic mythology which is so predominant in Celtic lore. It is a common theme in the mythology of many nations and resembles the battles between the gods and giants in pre-Homeric Greece. In the theosophical scheme it is a mirroring of the archetypal struggle between light and darkness that occurred in the transition between the Fourth and Fifth Root Races, culminating in the destruction of the Atlantean race of sorcerers.
101. This is Odin, who hung for nine days and nights upon the World Tree while pierced with a spear. He hung there as a sacrifice, 'myself given to myself'. He fasted and endured great suffering so that he might lift the runes which could bring secret knowledge to men.
102. Paul, I *Corinthians* XIII. 12.
103. A.E. often uses this metaphor to speak of the return of the consciousness of the soul to the highest spiritual state. (See *S.D.* I, pp. 638–9.)
104. Cf. *C.O.V.* note 3.
105. The blessed light referred to here is that of the *buddhi*, the sixth principle in man, which is the luminous reflection of *Ātman* or pure spirit. It is not to be considered solely as a spiritual entity but also a plane of radiant homogeneous matter in which enlightened individuals live and have their being. Our pure spiritual aspirations enable us to touch that transcendental plane and open channels to the mighty beings who exist in that state for the sake of evolving humanity.
106. This type of vision is referred to only rarely and reverently in mystical literature. It is one which a mystic may experience but once in an entire lifetime of contemplation. It may be called *samādhi, manteia* or *ecstasis*, yet little can be said of a state which is a total negation of the conditionality of common experience. It is complete union with Absolute Consciousness beyond any conception of an experiencing self.
107. The human psyche has a dual orientation, one divine, the other demonic, the struggle between these two deciding the fate of the soul. (See *Mun. U.*, 2.2.8 and *Mai. U.*, 7.11; also note 17.)
108. In the same sense that the eye cannot see itself except as a reflection, at the core of every man's consciousness, there is an abiding witness, *Īśvara*, who sees and comprehends all experiences generated by the human ego but remains totally unaffected by them. This is the absolute centre from which all the spreading circles of man's action emanate. The witness, *Īśvara*, creates but is wholly unfettered by its creations. This is the basis of the Theosophical teaching regarding the ultimate freedom of man.
109. The state called *samādhi* referred to earlier; the culmination of rigorous spiritual training over many lives, experienced only by the highest yogis. After initiation, it is the constant vision of the Adept.
110. The ultimate aim of Cosmic Evolution is to realize the highest ideal of compassion. Pure spirit is motivated primarily by the desire to redeem all conditioned being and loses itself in matter for this purpose. The result of this process is the creation of beings who are emancipated from the necessity of rebirth, yet willing to sacrifice personal bliss for the salvation of those who yet

live in ignorance and darkness.
111. This state of illusion is called *Mahāmāyā* or 'great illusion'. It is such because it is composed of elements of the astral world, a region which is inherently more unstable and variegated because less conditioned than the physical world. The forces that swirl about the astral realm can, owing to the plasticity of that medium, assume more colourful and pleasing shapes to deceive the unwary. It is the plane of great delusion as opposed to mere illusion because intrinsic to its nature is the power to deceive the Pilgrim with the simulacra of knowledge.
112. Mystics of every tradition have pointed to the inability of language to convey adequately spiritual truths or inner states of awareness. Most would agree that 'the mind is the great slayer of the Real'. However, Buddha taught that the mind and language can be redeemed if made to serve a higher purpose. Thought and speech may be sanctified, as A.E. claimed. The words of a compassionate and enlightened individual can be powerful instruments in the service of all mankind.
113. The chief distinction made here is between high psychic and full noetic or spiritual states of vision. The high psychic experience can be very pleasing and positive, even bestowing true knowledge, but it is not beyond the circumference of the ego and may in a moment of inattention propel one on an infernal odyssey through the inflamed passions of the lower nature. The true spiritual vision, however, does not carry with it this danger as it is formless and hence out of direct relation with the phenomenal world.

JAGRATA, SVAPNA AND SUSHUPTI

1. First appeared in *The Irish Theosophist*, January 1893.
2. The supreme *Brahman* is meant here.
3. In Indian mystical thought, these three states are both transcended by and included in the indescribable fourth state called *turīya*, referred to in the Upaniṣads and identified by the *Māṇḍukya Upaniṣad* especially with *Brahman*.
4. Rāja-Yoga or the 'royal' or 'kingly' discipline is that taught by the great master of meditation, Patañjali, in his *Yoga Sūtras*. It is contrasted with Haṭha Yoga, which concentrates on psycho-physical means and on correspondingly lower states of consciousness. The Rāja-Yogi is distinguishable by his concern with wholly inward methods of bringing about changes of consciousness, his insistence on the development of a pure selfless motive rooted in a transcendence of the separative ego, and his strict adherence to a life of ascetic virtue.
5. The three states of consciousness are not merely to be experienced in waking, dreaming and deep sleep – rather these are the primary psycho-physical states in which three types of consciousness are experienced. There are times when our consciousness may be of the turbulent and chaotic sort typical of the dream state; or we may sink in moments of meditation into those serene depths of awareness, untroubled by frenzied sense images, which correspond to the deep sleep state. Śankara suggests in his commentary on the *Māṇḍukya Upaniṣad* that each state is contained in the other three. (Cf. *C.O.V.*, note 109.)
6. Karma (literally meaning 'action') is the term used in Indian thought for the causal law of action and re-action at all levels of being. If the universe is governed by law, then law must operate everywhere in the cosmos – not merely every point in three-dimensional space' but every point in 'metaphysical space', i.e., on all planes of reality. The universe consists of a vast ladder of levels of

energy or planes of consciousness – a continuous and subtle gradation of planes shading into one another rather than discrete rungs – from the highest homogeneous and Universal Spirit down to the multitude of material forms. The human mind sometimes divides up this vast array of gradations into broad categories corresponding to the moral, mental, psychological and physical areas of human life. However we categorize them, law must reign supreme at all these levels. Generating motives, entertaining ideas, having feelings and attitudes – all these are as much a development of different energies as engaging in activity on the bodily plane. The whole concept of action, therefore, becomes enlarged, enhanced in subtlety and enriched in complexity in the Indian philosophical scheme. This multi-dimensional conception of action is crucial in grasping the Law of Karma. Thoughts and motives as well as physical actions have a corresponding reaction, which must come back to the individual who, as the causal agent, is the focal point of the generation of energy. Everything at all levels of our nature has consequences which come back to us, life after life, in the external circumstances of our birth as also in the psycho-mental characteristics that we have at birth. The doctrine of Karma is inextricably linked with the theory of reincarnation.

7. Strictly, we do not generate karma in the dreaming and deep sleep states, unless we are speaking of these as merely representative of certain kinds of consciousness experienced even while awake (see note 5 above). In the dream state we reap the effects of our experiences – or rather, of our reactions to experiences during the waking state. While our experience in the deep sleep state is not directly affected by the activities of the waking consciousness, our ability to remember the profound dreamless state is dependent upon the quality of the waking consciousness. To the extent that, as A.E. says, our experiences in either of these states directly or indirectly affect our later waking consciousness, they may, perhaps, be said to have a causal function.

8. We do, of course, remember some of our dreams, but it is far more difficult to remember the experiences of *suṣupti*. The consciousness, which cannot completely leap over any plane, must pass through *svapna*, an illusory region of chaotic and distorted images, not only on its way from *jāgrat* to *suṣupti*, but also back from *suṣupti* to *jāgrat*. Passing through the disturbing turbulence of *svapna*, the calmness and continuity of the consciousness becomes fragmented and lost. Only that individual can pass undisturbed through the *svapna* state who has mastered the art of continuity of consciousness in waking life.

9. 'There is no purifier in this world to be compared to spiritual knowledge; and he who is perfected in devotion findeth spiritual knowledge springing up spontaneously in himself in the progress of time.' (*Gītā*, ch. IV.38, p. 36.)

CONCENTRATION

1. First appeared in *The Irish Theosophist*, January 1893.
2. 'They consider the Fourth [*turīya*] to be that which is not conscious of the internal world, nor conscious of the external world, nor conscious of both the worlds, nor a mass of consciousness, nor simple consciousness, nor unconsciousness; which is unseen, beyond empirical dealings, beyond the grasp (of the organs of action), uninferable, unthinkable; indescribable; whose valid

proof consists in the single belief in the Self; in which all phenomena cease; and which is unchanging, auspicious, and non-dual. That is the Self, and that is to be known.' (Mān. U., 7 [tr. Swāmi Gambhīrānanda].)

3. Śaṅkara, commenting on an important verse in the Māṇḍukya Upaniṣad, affirms this very point about the turīya state as identical with the innermost Self. 'As the nature of the rope is realised by the negation of the (illusory) appearances of the snake etc., so also it is intended to establish the very Self, which subsists in the three states, as turīya. This is done in the same way as (the great Vedic statement) "Thou art that".'

4. The 'Divine Song' or the spiritual teaching given by Krishna to the warrior prince Arjuna on the battlefield of Kurukṣetra. The Bhagavad Gītā, which constitutes a very small portion of the Mahābhārata, is one of the central texts of Indian philosophic thought.

5. See 'Jagrata, Svapna and Sushupti', note 4.

6. Spiritual liberation or freedom, enlightenment or mokṣa.

7. These are the three qualities of prakṛti or primordial matter (and all its products) spoken of in Sāṁkhya philosophy. The Bhagavad Gītā makes repeated references to rising above or being free of these three qualities of manifest and changeable nature so that one may rise to the changeless Puruṣa or pure spirit. Tamas is the lowest of the three attributes and is the quality of darkness, ignorance, inertia, mass. Rajas is dynamism, energy; and sattva is knowledge, virtue, light. Says Krishna in the Bhagavad Gītā, 'All actions are effected by the qualities of nature. The man deluded by ignorance thinks, "I am the actor". But he, O strong-armed one! who is acquainted with the nature of the two distinctions of cause and effect, knowing that the qualities act only in the qualities, and that the Self is distinct from them, is not attached in action.' (Gita, ch. III.28, p. 26.)

8. 'Philosopher's Stone. Called also the "Powder of Projection". It is the Magnum Opus of the Alchemists, . . . a substance possessing the power of transmuting the baser metals into pure gold. Mystically, however, the Philosopher's Stone symbolises the transmutation of the lower animal nature of man into the highest and divine.' (Glo., 'Philosopher's Stone'.) A.E. is stressing that all such concepts are to be interpreted symbolically and metaphysically rather than literally. A pure motive is the truest touchstone, whereby the change to be brought about is an inward one. (See C.O.V., note 45.)

9. The Indian mystics held that as the individual progresses on the spiritual path, the vestures of the soul (kośas or śarīras) begin to undergo subtle changes, each becoming more luminous and ethereal. The consciousness abides more and more in higher vestures until, reaching the pure, bodiless Self, the most radiant vesture (Śaṅkara's ānandamayakośa) shines forth in the reflected glory of that Self.

10. 'I am, O Arjuna, the seed of all existing things, and there is not anything, whether animate or inanimate which is without me.' (Gītā, ch. X.39, p. 76.)

11. A.E. is here quoting from W.Q. Judge's rendition of the Bhagavad Gītā, ch. XIV.19, p. 103. 'When the wise man perceiveth that the only agents of action are these qualities, and comprehends that which is superior to the qualities, he attains to my state. And when the embodied self surpasseth these three qualities of goodness, action, and indifference – which are coexistent with the body it is released from rebirth and death, old age and pain, and drinketh of the water of immortality.'

COMFORT

1. First appeared in *The Irish Theosophist*, May 1894.
2. Theosophy teaches the identity of all souls in the Oversoul or *Ātman:* sparks from a parent flame.
3. The cyclic pilgrimage is a fundamental proposition of theosophical philosophy. (See *S.D.* I, p. 17.)

REVIEW OF *THE TREASURE OF THE HUMBLE*

1. First appeared in *The Irish Theosophist*, May 1897. This unsigned review is probably by A.E.

AN EASTERN CANDLE OF VISION

1. First appeared in *Spiritualism: Its present day meaning,* a symposium edited by Huntley Carter, London: Fisher Unwin, 1920.
2. [Note in original publication.] Mr. Russell refers to one of the highly elaborate systems of self-culture through concentration. The philosophic *Sūtras* of Patañjali are short sentences used for the purpose of instructing pupils into the theory and practice of Yoga.

THE CITY WITHOUT WALLS

1. First published in the 2nd edition of *City Without Walls* edited by Margaret Cushing Osgood, London: Jonathan Cape, 1932.

THE MASK OF APOLLO

1. First appeared in *The Irish Theosophist,* April 1893. The text here is that of A.E.'s final version included in *Imaginations* and *Reveries*, 1915.

THE STORY OF A STAR

1. First appeared in *The Irish Theosophist,* August 1894. The text is that of A.E.'s final version included in *Imaginations and Reveries*, 1915.
2. The Sanskrit term *māyā*, meaning illusion, is a central philosophic concept in much of Indian thought. *Māyā* is not only the great world illusion, but also signifies creative power. As illusion, e.g., in Śaṅkara's philosophy, it means the

superimposition of false attributes onto a subject that does not possess them. For instance, to imagine that the world of differentiations is real, that it has an ultimate and absolute truth, is to be under the sway of *māyā*. This does not mean, however, that the world is *totally* unreal, i.e., non-existent or an ideational subjective projection of a mind or minds. Śaṅkara explains this in the famous example of the serpent and the rope. But it is to attribute ultimate reality and permanence to something which is not changeless and therefore cannot be absolutely real. Only *Brahman*, the one, limitless, indefinable Absolute is absolutely real, but we superimpose the world on it and get trapped in an illusion of our own making. *Māyā*, therefore, has no *ontological* status, but is an epistemological and psychological factor to be reckoned with. As 'creative power' it is the magic power by which *Īśvara* creates the universe. The very deployment of this power creates the conditions in which any individual consciousness can mistake the manifested world for the Unmanifest and thus become subject to illusion. The two primary meanings of *māyā* are therefore not unrelated.
3. A brotherhood of Chaldean wise men and Kabbalists in the ancient Near East. An account of some of their practices and teachings is given in *The Life of Apollonius of Tyana*. They represent a major tributary of the Wisdom Religion.
4. Allusion to what is called the Third Eye in ancient philosophy; that faculty of spiritual sight which gradually opens with the ascent of the soul heavenward. (Cf. *C.O.V.*, note 70.)

A DOOMED CITY

1. First appeared in *The Irish Theosophist,* September 1894.
2. The civilization of the Fourth Root Race was said to be ruled by a race of giants and sorcerers who exercised a nearly inconceivable power over nature. Its fall coincided with the emergence of the Fifth Race, the Aryan, which is repaying the terrible karma accrued during that period.
3. A.E. alludes to the passing of epochs from the Third in which men were naturally reverent and spiritual to the Fourth in which man became predatory and demonic. The crucial evolutionary change which foreshadowed this fall into matter was the closing of the Wisdom Eye or Third Eye which damaged the connection between the human intelligence and its divine parent.

THE MYSTIC NIGHTS' ENTERTAINMENT

1. First appeared in *The Irish Theosophist,* October 1894 to January 1895.
2. This is a depiction of life in the hall of learning, the astral world, associated with the *svapna* state. It is the realm of *Mahāmāyā*, the Great Illusion, through which the probationer must pass in order to be tested and merit the wisdom which lies in the halls beyond.
3. Many Eastern schools of philosophy including the Taraka Raja Yoga and the Vedānta schools define man's nature in terms of sheaths or vestures. Called *kośas* or *upādhis* they are considered to encase the true man, the indestructible monadic essence. They exist principally to enable that soul to experience and thus comprehend life on all planes of manifestation. The closer the sheath to the soul,

the more refined, universal and cosmic is its constitution.
4. The association of the Tree of Life with the Adept is common in many religious and mythological traditions. It signifies the full flowering of metaphysical knowledge and power at the human level. The specific reference of the 'Tree of Life' is Biblical and has its true origin in the Kabbalistic Sephirothal tree composed of ten powers or qualities, three cosmic and seven human.
5. There is no mental action without corresponding effects in subtler realms.
6. Refers to *suṣupti* state or deep sleep where the soul retires to its pre-genetic state and enjoys a temporary loosening of its terrestrial ties.
7. 'He is, as said, the "Nameless One" who has so many names, and yet whose names and whose very nature are unknown. He is *the* "Initiator", called the "GREAT SACRIFICE". For, sitting at the threshold of LIGHT, he looks into it from within the circle of Darkness, which he will not cross; nor will he quit his post till the last day of this life-cycle.' (*S.D.* I, p. 208.)
8. A.E. may have intended to continue this story, for *The Irish Theosophist* has *To be continued*, but no further instalment appeared.

THE ENCHANTMENT OF CUCHULLAIN

1. First appeared in *The Irish Theosophist*, November 1895. Aretas was the pseudonym of James Morgan Pryse (1859–1942). According to a letter from A.E. to W.B. Yeats (*Letters from AE*, edited by Alan Denson, p. 16), only the first chapter was by him – 'This is mine. Pryse will do the rest.'

THE CHILDHOOD OF APOLLO

1. First appeared in *The Irish Theosophist*, November 1896. The text is that of A.E.'s final version included in *Imaginations and Reveries*, 1915.
2. Readers of Plato will here recognize Diotima from the *Symposium*. Socrates recounts that she was the personage who led him to the vision of the true form of Love or Divine Eros.

THE FOUNTAINS OF YOUTH

1. First appeared in *The Irish Theosophist*, September 1897.
2. The land of bliss and forgetfulness roughly corresponding to the after-death state of Devachan.
3. Queen of Connaught and wife of Ailell. She figures prominently in the story of the heroes of Ulster called the 'Irish *Iliad*'. She is the prototype of the Faery Queen and Queen Mab, both figures which recur regularly in English and Irish literature.
4. The many-coloured lands. (Cf. *C.O.V.*, 'The Many-Coloured Land'.)
5. A.E. here cites some of the most famous personages in the Celtic pantheon. Taken together, they represent an aggregate of divine forces and powers which prepared the way for the evolution of the human races on earth.
6. Cf. 'On an Irish Hill'. Irish equivalent to Delphi.

A DREAM OF ANGUS OGE

1. First appeared in *The Internationalist*, October 1897. The text was not changed when A.E. included it in *Imaginations and Reveries*, 1915.
2. Angus seems to be the equivalent of Eros in the Greek pantheon. He was a son of one of the greatest of the gods, Dagda, known as the fire god. Angus is the eternally youthful exponent of love and beauty. He possessed a golden harp which like that of Orpheus could cause all who heard its notes to follow him. He is the divine beauty hidden in earthly guise which leads men to discover their own relation to Deity.

RELIGION AND LOVE

1. First appeared in *Dana*, June 1904. The text is that of A.E.'s final version included in *Imaginations and Reveries*, 1915.
2. See *C.O.V.*, note 3.
3. *Mahat*, principle of cosmic ideation.
4. See canto XXX of 'Purgatorio' in *The Divine Comedy*.
5. William Butler Yeats.
6. A term used by H.P. Blavatsky to describe the intellection of the higher mind.
7. See cantos III and V of 'Inferno' in *The Divine Comedy*.

THE AVATARS

1. First published by Macmillan and Co., 1933. James Stephens's copy is inscribed to him by A.E. who made some slight deletions, totalling about fifteen words, to improve the flow of some of the conversations. These words have been marked by square brackets.
2. This refers to the fabled power of sorcerers who can malevolently influence action at a distance. Balor was a leader of the Fomorians, a dark race who sought to overcome the Tuatha de Danann. The power of his eye was so awesome that he could only open it during battle.
3. A.E. compresses here in a sentence an entire dialectic of the visionary experience, outlining the gradual transformations in consciousness one undergoes in passing from fantasy to true knowledge. Each state is a discrete level of consciousness characterized by its approximation to the world of realities or noumenal essences lying at the summit of the mystic's journey.
4. A critical distinction is made here between imagination and seership. It is roughly equivalent to the difference between a mystic and a sage. The issue is fundamentally one of control. The mystic is *granted* visions. He actively seeks them but they seem to occur apart from his will. The sage, on the other hand, is in the perpetual presence of the Real and can at will transfer the seat of his consciousness to any level of reality. Such a man has total control of all his vestures continually.
5. One of the most celebrated themes in Indian literature, the archetypal love between Krishna and his consort Rādhā. Hindus regard Krishna as the highest incarnation of the divine Logos and Rādhā as his potency in matter (*śakti*).
6. Cf. *Song and Its Fountains*, which traces dream and vision back to their divine root.

Notes and Commentary to pages 541–557

7. The distinction between reality and symbol is a difficult one. *The Secret Doctrine* states that symbols are the alpha and omega of philosophic thought. They are crucial links between noumenal realities and their phenomenal reflections in the world. They point the searcher to discoveries of higher truths yet at some stage the maps must be discarded as the aspirant approaches *metanoia*.
8. This is a somewhat specialized definition of an avatar. According to the Hindus, avatars were divine incarnations who further the enlightenment and salvation of the human race. They take birth in accordance with cyclic law at pivotal points in the evolution of humanity when spiritual leadership is most needed. Avatars of the kind depicted by A.E. are kingly souls and instruments of divine destiny, the indispensable means by which great karmic effects are precipitated. They are not necessarily the luminous self-conscious agents of Universal Mind. The great philosopher Śaṅkara said of these high beings that they might appear 'now as a Madman, now a Sage, now a glorious great king, now a humble wanderer . . . ever rejoicing in the highest bliss.'
9. The central fountain is the hidden heart of the universe composed of the sages of all ages who serve as the indissoluble link between the human and the divine worlds.
10. The defining characteristic of the Iron Age is the eclipsing of intuition or spiritual intelligence. It is marked intellectually by the exaggeration of head-learning or analytical reasoning and socially by role confusion. Therefore a declining age cannot be judged by external criteria.
11. Every human emanation impresses itself upon matter at the level of subtlety appropriate to its emanation. This receptacle is the plastic medium of the astral light which retains for varying periods of time the thought-energies poured into it by human consciousness. If the emanations are diseased, the astral light radiates these thoughts back as the demonic beings and noxious forces which afflict so many people. However, the true cause for these poisonous creations must lie within man himself.
12. Men are divided according to psycho-spiritual affinities which determine their patterns of grouping in incarnation. Genetic factors as well as temporal and spatial relationships are merely reflections of these laws. By altering one's psycho-tropisms one may enter into a new class of beings that share such affinities. (See 'Ten Propositions of Oriental Psychology', *I.U.* II, pp. 587–90.)
13. Theosophy teaches that a fraternity of divine teachers or Bodhisattvas, men who have risen above this plane of illusion and voluntarily return to light the path beyond it, has existed from the earliest incarnations of men on this planetary chain. It is from their sacred tribe that heroes, saints and sages have come to teach men.
14. It is thought in the East that a true avatar manifests but a portion of himself, his spiritual self held back to overbrood and guide the work of its reflected ray. The archetype of this is Krishna who said in the *Bhagavad Gītā*, 'I established this whole universe with a single portion of myself, and remain separate'. (*Gītā*, ch. X. 42, p. 76.)
15. In trance states mystics often refer to sound and vision as interchangeable powers, twin offspring of a common parent – the vibratory force of the Logos.
16. Called the Hindu Olympus (see *Glo.*, 'Meru'); the major peak in the spiritual topography of the earth. The blessed abode of the gods who extend a benevolent hand over slumbering earth. Geographically, it is an unknown mountain north of the Himalayas.
17. The Edenic myth is a faint echo of those palmy days of the Third Root Race when mankind was innocent of the knowledge of selfish desire and naturally disposed to express its love of the gods and sages who walked freely among

them. It is said that spirits were close to the earth then and all manner of invisible beings communicated joyfully with men. According to theosophical chronology, this race flourished over one million years ago. (See *S.D.* I, p. 439 fn.)
18. Spoken of at length in *The Candle of Vision* in the chapter entitled 'Many-Coloured Land'.
19. Lao Tzu defines the sage as one who is totally unmoved, yet leaves nothing undone (see *Tao-Te-Ching*, vs. 37 and vs. 63). The core of this paradox is obliquely referred to here. Our failure to compehend the intrinsic power of self-ideation to alter events independent of the limitations of time and space is responsible for our misconception of the mission of a great teacher or avatar. He can at will place the seat of his consciousness on any plane and thereby effect crucial changes for the benefit of mankind.
20. *Genesis* XXXII. 24–30.
21. According to the Theosophical teaching regarding Rounds and Races, the embryo forms of humanity of the sixth sub-race of the Fifth Root Race are now being created. Although the full flowering of the sixth sub-race is thousands of years hence, the incipient signs of its emergence can be seen in the revival of interest in divine wisdom.
22. *John* I.5.
23. Cf. *Song and Its Fountains* for a detailed description of the origin of the Beautiful.
24. The inner architecture of nature is depicted here in terms of the hierarchies of divine beings who radiate directly from the Universal Self or $\bar{A}tman$. These beings are the aggregate of intelligences which constitute the seven creative rays emanating from the Spiritual Sun. They represent the true differentiation of cosmic substance, the heterogeneity of earth-life being but a gross reflection of it.
25. Cf. *C.O.V.*, note 12. See also Glossary of Terms and Names.
26. According to *The Secret Doctrine,* this quality was innate in the pre-Atlantean races. It is said that their religion was of the heart and their temples built within the precincts of the soul. Outward expressions of love flowed from an inner allegiance to the overbrooding divine intelligence. (*S.D.* I, p. 210.)
27. The law of karmic affinities whereby internal states of consciousness are adjusted to external conditions. Accordingly, those of like mind and kindred spirit are brought together under the aegis of this law in order that spiritual development may be accelerated. The disciples who congregate around a spiritual teacher are drawn by magnetic attraction since the greater light attracts the lesser.
28. All true culture is the outgrowth of spiritual development and not the imposition of collective external forces upon the psyche of man. It is no more or less than a mirroring of inner states of awareness and soul-qualities. The birth of a new culture must be accompanied by a rebirth in spirit. Nothing can exist that has not been internally thought and felt.
29. These three qualities are in reference to the men and women of the new age, foreshadowing the characteristics that will mark the mature individual of the Aquarian Age. Aquarius is the personage who symbolizes a high development of manasic or ideational faculties combined with the power of compassionate application of ideas in the world. Overarching these potent gifts is an elegance of manner and lightness of heart which make his actions effortless and natural. A.E. has intimated those qualities which will signal the development of future humanity.
30. Ancient Finnish epic retelling the creation myth.
31. Cf. *Song and Its Fountains*, note 9.

Notes and Commentary to pages 573–581   759

32. The notion of truth here is radically different from its common use. According to the tenets of materialistic science, truth is what in thought conforms precisely to the external world. Truth is thus no more than that which can be embodied in words or precepts. A.E. alludes to the Platonic definition of truth as a non-relative state of absolute awareness in which subject and object, seer and seen, are fused. This is what Plato terms *noesis*. It is essentially inarticulate and non-communicable save to those who have undergone the rigorous discipline to reach that state themselves. (See Plato, *Republic*, bk. VI.)
33. The will is termed a colourless, dimensionless power that represents 'the force of spirit in action'. (See *Ocean*, p. 15.) The will is the nascent energy locked within all of man's principles providing the critical link between consciousness and matter. The application of will is thus the true agent behind all change. As will is no principle because of its universal nature, it can be said to be a direct radiation of the *Ātman* or One Life which energizes all things.
34. See Hume's translation of the Upaniṣads.
35. Every great teacher has pointed to the superhuman discipline that the path to spiritual enlightenment demands. Every nerve must be strained to exert a strong will over one's irrational tendencies. Every thought and feeling inconsistent with the final goal draws one back in evolution and retards one's progress. The devotees of divine wisdom must adhere to a moral posture which is far stricter than that of the ordinary man. At each stage of spiritual development faculties are awakened and powers aroused which animate each thought with many times its former force. Without the restraint exerted by an inflexible will, the most trivial desire may unleash a chain of destructive effects.
36. In Eastern philosophy, 'illusion'; the attribute of all that is not the Absolute.
37. The writings of Plato and Gandhi attest to the seemingly capricious nature of the indwelling god or daemon. In the case of both Gandhi and Socrates the inner oracle could be relied upon to speak truly but not always to speak. The inner voice is an expression of the *buddhic* principle in the shape of a presiding spirit who watches and oversees the destiny of the individual. His capacity to counsel the ego is strictly a function of karmic merit.
38. The character of Aoife is one of A.E.'s most notable creations. She has no speaking part so we can only judge her character in terms of her impact on those around her. She is allied with all the ennobling figures of the past who displayed the characteristics of the awakened potency associated with the *buddhic* principle. She is reminiscent of the fabled goddesses and heroines of universal mythology and Shakespeare's plays as well as historical personages such as the Neo-Platonist adept Hypatia.
39. These observations on the struggle between spiritual and material values in the collective life of man carry the force of a fulfilled prophecy. It is only in the last quarter of this century that we are privileged to see the premonitory rumblings of a spiritual renaissance which will lay the foundation of a new civilization. This is the culmination of a movement initiated by the Tibetan adept Tsong-ka-pa in the fourteenth century. His plan was to initiate a spiritual impulsion during the last quarter of each century to prepare the way of the re-establishment of the mystery schools and sacred colleges.
40. Indian sages commonly portray the senses as five 'liars' which ceaselessly contrive to confuse and delude the mind into mistaking the unreal for the 'real'. Plato suggested that the senses under the chaste control of the philosophic mind may be perpetual witnesses to the presence of 'the Beautiful' in the world. (See *Phaedrus*.)
41. This manner of communication was common to men and women of the Third Root Race. It is said that they had no need for language as their thoughts were

immediately intelligible to all. (Cf. *Tr.*, p. 45.)
42. Avatars have always issued cautionary warnings to the idle and curious speculators of every age. They have always attempted to disabuse men of the notion that the teacher can be known or defined in terms of external characteristics. A true teacher is, more than any other man, able to define himself and self-consciously choose the nature of the vestures through which he will work to perform his mission in the world. Since the true scope of his work can never be fully revealed, one has no criterion by which to judge the means he adopts as they are uniquely fitted to serve a benevolent end only he himself fully comprehends. (See *Gītā*, ch. XI, p. 85.)
43. Highly developed beings, mystics and adepts of every race and tradition live in a spiritual community based upon a solidarity of ideation. They exist on a continent of thought that operates according to its own laws. As they have their being on a more rarefied and homogeneous plane of substance, they are not subject to the material impediments that hamper others. Hence their communication occurs along channels of thought and is instantaneous. (Cf. *Ocean*, pp. 139–40.)
44. The imagination is the king-faculty. (Cf. *Ocean*, p. 139.) It is the power to give shape to the archetypal patterns which exist in germinal form in the *ākāśa* or Divine Mind. Thus, on the cosmic level it is the process by which Spirit organizes matter according to its own image. On the microcosmic level, it represents the causal agency which shapes the course of man's intellectual development. The more one can tap and control this visionary power, the more one can instantiate higher intuitions in his own life. This is a prelude to attaining the power of *Kriyāśakti* which is the crowning achievement of the path of creative imagination. *Kriyāśakti* is the capacity to precipitate objects in space at will by the sheer power of ideation. (Cf. *S.D.* II, p. 298.)
45. The Kabbalistic term for the aggregate of creative forces that constitute the invisible cosmos. They are the builders or architects who operate at seminal levels to fashion nature in harmony with Divine Law. Although they operate at a macrocosmic level, a portion of their intelligence and power is the birthright of every human soul. It is said that these transcendental forces can be tapped through concentrated discipline and right motive. (Cf. *S.D.* I, p. 42.)
46. Speech is a powerful creative potency that can either be therapeutic or lethal depending upon use. As it operates by means of sound, it is directly allied with the divine astral or *ākāśa*, the major characteristic of which is inaudible sound or vibration. A.E. indicates in various places that thoughtless speech or chatter is the way by which the innate spiritual energies of men are diffused and depleted in daily life.
47. Theosophy teaches that each man carries the fullness of god within him either in a latent or manifest state, while orthodox Christianity teaches that God is wholly distinct from and not to be mingled with man. Theosophically, higher beings are our elder brothers, siblings of the same parentage who have progressed farther in evolution but are yet likened to us by degrees of development and are not separate in kind.
48. The approach to spiritual life of Michael Gregors grows out of a mystical and philosophical tradition which scorns images or verisimilitudes as deceptions of and deviations from the goal of absolute wisdom. Those of this tradition hold that complete truth rests in the universal vision that has no shape or hue owing to its abstract nature.
49. Man is the microcosm of the macrocosm and therefore allied with every atom in space visible and invisible. Each of his actions interpenetrates the whole and produces either disharmony for which he is accountable or harmony by which he

Notes and Commentary to pages 594–600   761

is emancipated from the chains of karmic effects.
50. The Myth of Er, *Republic*, bk. X.
51. The Prometheus myth is an allegory of the descent of numberless beings called Manasaputras or Prometheoi who endowed men with the power of self-conscious thought and divine ideation by sacrificing of their own fiery essence to human embodiment. (Cf. *S.D.* II, p. 421.)
52. *Rubaiyat* of Omar Khayyam, stanza LXXIX (Fitzgerald tr., 4th ed.).
53. The doctrine of karma is a complex teaching which fuses ideas of freedom and determinism into a single uniform pattern of human evolution. It teaches that man is in essence free as a ray of absolute consciousness, yet is compelled to win or earn his freedom through the experience of unfreedom or conditionality in the manifest cosmos. To the extent to which he identifies with manifest particulars, to that extent is he karmically bound by them, but to the extent to which he works with and attempts to transmute them is he emancipated from them. As Spinoza stressed, 'Freedom is the recognition of necessity.' It is only by working with the great law of universal harmony instead of cultivating an idea of personal salvation that man can regain his primordial freedom. This is the third fundamental principle of Theosophy. (Cf. *S.D.* I, pp. 17–18.)
54. Manus were the direct incarnations of the Mānasaputras or Mānusha, as they are called. They are embodiments of divine intelligences who instruct men in ways of life that are most pleasing to the soul and most beneficial to the whole nature. Thus they are in a sense lawgivers but of a very high order as they reflect in their work the inner architecture of Cosmic Mind. They instruct mankind in patterns of conduct that will best conform to noetic models and assure the greatest harmony between all segments of his nature. They are 'Thought Divine' personified. (Cf. *S.D.* I, pp. 63 and 235 fn.)
55. An example of this type of ideation was mentioned in an earlier note (note 43 above) and it was by no means an isolated instance of the scope of an adept's work. One of the great mysteries the initiate is able to unravel is the true nature of time. Thus he operates in a manner independent of normal conceptions of temporality and duration, which are themselves illusory creations. The adept's work coincides with the sidereal clock which measures the greater and lesser karmic cycles of the earth. Timing and precision are most critical to him as they regulate the impact of his efforts. As he is not impeded by the productions of time, namely, form, name, or physical body, he can act according to the patterns of eternity. For the adept, time as we know it is an illusion. According to Patañjali, the man of meditation comes to master the ultimate divisions of time. (Cf. *Yoga Aphorisms*.)
56. See opening stanzas of the *Ṛg Veda*.
57. *Bhagavad Gītā*, ch. IV, vs. 6.
58. Cf. note 42 above, discussing the dual nature of avatars' incarnations.
59. The yoga of right thought or imagining is convincingly developed here. Even though the mind is the great deceiver, it is also the instrument by which man can achieve final liberation from his illusions. This path is termed *jñāna* yoga in the East. It describes the conceptual topography traversed by the mystic-philosopher as he attempts to supplant each mental image or picture with one that is a closer approximation of Absolute Truth. This journey may culminate either in a final fusion of the individual with the Universal Mind or satisfaction with a partial image of the whole which will contain a certain element of illusion. Any state less than total emancipation from limited notions of the real will guarantee incarnation into a set of material conditions commensurate with the individual's awareness. Thus the chief determinant of change in a man's destiny is the growth or regression of his mental concepts. (Cf. *Theosophy*, vol. 43, p. 307.)

60. Cf. *Light on the Path.*
61. This high theme is echoed throughout mystic tradition as the key to fruitful meditation. It is a practice that can be beneficial to all. Its importance derives from Patañjali's axiom that realization flows from meditating upon the thing to be realized.
62. Spirit has manifold voices. Its clearest representation on earth is the Brotherhood of Bodhisattvas who protect the purity of the single spiritual vibration of the *Word* amidst the cacophony of the world.
63. Some traditions in the East have developed an entire metaphysic based on sound alone, considered as root vibration at the cosmic level condensing by degrees into every form and relation on the human level. The primary sound or vibration is called *Śabda Brahman* from which all thought and form is produced.
64. The spiritual training offered in Theosophical teachings is compatible with a psychology of transmutation as opposed to negation. On the path of negation, the aspirant tries to cut himself off from every thought, feeling or deed which will bind him to further action. He seeks Nirvāṇa or complete isolation from any sense of conditionality. The man who practises transmutation, on the other hand, attempts to bind himself to a compassionate ideal whereby he preserves the knowledge gained through experience in order to develop skills in action to help other beings as yet trapped in those experiences. Through the fire of devotion to this ideal, he is able to awaken the spiritual element in all his activities and thus immeasurably extend his usefulness to others.
65. The 'leaders' of the world are the spiritual teachers or Buddhas.
66. A.E. uses the journalist to demonstrate how esoteric wisdom, the work of avatars, is subject to misinterpretation and inversion by the exoteric world and hence the necessity of mystery schools and vows of silence. Jesus alluded to this phenomenon when he cautioned 'Let not thy left hand know what thy right hand is doing.' That is, keep the sacred and profane separate lest one pollute the other. Theosophy refers to inversion in consciousness as the result of ahaṁkāric speech or thought. *Ahaṁkāra* is the bridge between the lower mind and the higher. If the passage between the two is uncontrolled, the tendency is for the lower to appropriate the higher, an example of which would be the personalizing of the concept of Deity. Spiritual materialism is another name for this phenomenon. (Cf. *Glo.*, 'Ahaṅkāra'.)
67. Krishna states in the *Bhagavad Gītā*, 'Light and Darkness are the world's eternal ways.' (p. 62.) The conditions surrounding the spiritual teacher reflect this universal law to a greater degree of intensity than is normally manifest. This is because the avatar radiates spiritual energy indifferently, quickening the growth of high souls and wicked ones in the same manner that the sun warms the households of all men equally.
68. See Lao-Tzu, *Tao-Te-Ching.*
69. See Plato's *Republic,* bk. X.
70. Theosophy teaches that the human being is composed of superior and inferior intelligences which allow the individual to fuse the polar forces of spirit and matter, macrocosm and microcosm together as a synthetic reflection of Absolute Truth. It is only when the lower portion of the soul is infected with the principle of desire or *kāma* that it can be inimical to the spiritual intelligence. The thinking principle is intrinsically a synthesizing power as it simultaneously functions in abstract and concrete worlds. It is when identity is consolidated in the lower portion and the higher obscured that apparently irresolvable contradictions and conflicts arise.
71. *Popul Vuh,* ancient esoteric text of the Mayas and Quiches.
72. The true test of spiritual progress has always been a deepening kinship with all

humanity and the whole of nature. True spiritual growth is toward the universal and compassionate and away from the personal and selfish.

THE ASCENDING CYCLE

1. First appeared in *The Irish Theosophist*, November 1893.
2. (See *The Secret Doctrine*.) This is a brief summary of the elaborate scheme presented in *The Secret Doctrine*. It is a system of epicycles within greater cycles and spirals of progress, all being subordinated to Spirit's great journey into and out of matter. The aim is self-consciousness in Spirit. Within the course of evolution, the path of progress is adjusted by Karma which binds together the events of each epoch and period. Experiences undergone in one cycle will be recapitulated in a condensed form in the next, assuring a continuity of knowledge acquired. Thus mankind will, after experiencing the apex of physical development (which is the nadir of the spiritual), reascend to the semi-divine state enjoyed prior to the fall into matter. Yet the re-emergence on a higher plane of development will be merited by choices made in times of comparative darkness.
3. *S.D.* I, pp. 207–8.
4. *S.D.* I, p. 341.
5. See *C.O.V.*, note 17.
6. The *Voice of the Silence* uses the phrase, 'the delusion called "Great Heresy" ', and H.P. Blavatsky explains that the reference is to '*Attavada*, the heresy of the belief in Soul, or rather in the separateness of Soul or *Self* from the One Universal, Infinite SELF'. (*Voice*, p. 4, fn. 4.)
7. The Indian mystics regarded the whole of the manifested universe as the product of the outbreathing of Brahmā.
8. This is a profoundly mystical expression of the teaching about the progressive union of each incarnated human being with his own divine Self which, in turn, dissolves, like a momentarily radiated spark, back into the One Fire. This mysterious process is described in *The Secret Doctrine* – 'The closer the approach to one's *Prototype*, "in Heaven", the better for the mortal whose personality was chosen, by his own *personal* deity (the seventh principle), as its terrestrial abode. For, with every effort of will toward purification and unity with that "Self-god", one of the lower rays breaks and the spiritual entity of man is drawn higher and ever higher to the ray that supersedes the first, until, from ray to ray, the inner man is drawn into the one and highest beam of the Parent-SUN.' (*S.D.* I, pp. 638-9.)
9. This would be a return to the unity of thought, heart and speech, which characterized the early races of humanity. As A.E. points out, evolution moves in cycles or spirals, and the future races will re-enact the golden vibration of the early age.
10. See 'Objects of the Theosophical Society' in 'The Theosophical Society – Information for Enquirers', Appendix to *The Key to Theosophy*, p. 308.
11. The Third Race of Humanity was, according to Theosophical teaching, the first truly human race by virtue of having had the gift of self-conscious mind bestowed upon it by Promethean beings who sacrificed themselves in order to

redeem the then 'mindless' race. Infant humanity was also privileged to be taught the rudiments of philosophy, religion, the arts and the sciences by these perfected beings themselves and later by successive races of hierophants and initiates.

12. 'In the first or earlier portion of the existence of this third race, while it was yet in its state of purity, the "Sons of Wisdom", who, as will be seen, incarnated in this Third Race, produced by *kriyāśakti* a progeny called the "Sons of Ad" or "of the Fire-Mist", the "Sons of Will and Yoga", etc. They were a conscious production, as a portion of the race was already animated with the divine spark of spiritual, superior intelligence. It was not a Race, this progeny. It was at first a wondrous Being, called the "Initiator", and after him a group of semi-divine and semi-human beings. "*Set apart*" in Archaic *genesis* for certain purposes, they are those in whom are said to have incarnated the highest Dhyanis, "Munis and Rishis from previous Manvantaras" – *to form the nursery for future human adepts*, on this earth and during the present cycle. These "Sons of Will and Yoga" born, so to speak, in an immaculate way, remained, it is explained, entirely apart from the rest of mankind.

'The "BEING" just referred to, which has to remain nameless, is the *Tree* from which, in subsequent ages, all the great *historically* known Sages and Hierophants, such as the Rishi Kapila, Hermes, Enoch, Orpheus, etc., etc., have branched off. As objective *man*, he is the mysterious (to the profane – the ever invisible) yet ever present Personage about whom legends are rife in the East, especially among the Occultists and the students of the Sacred Science. It is he who changes form, yet remains ever the same. And it is he again who holds spiritual sway over the *initiated* Adepts throughout the whole world. He is, as said, the "Nameless One" who has so many names, and yet whose names and whose very nature are unknown. He is *the* "Initiator", called the "GREAT SACRIFICE".' (*S.D.* I, pp. 207-8.)

SHADOW AND SUBSTANCE

1. First appeared in *The Irish Theosophist*, January 1896.
2. The life of the Magi is that which A.E. elsewhere calls 'the path' leading to divine wisdom, sometimes called true 'magic'.
3. A.E. reminds us that we are but making endless excuses to cover up our delays and hesitations in beginning the spiritual life. To say that we are waiting for the appropriate gifts and necessary powers to develop is but to pretend, for there are no powers that we do not already innately possess. To the would-be disciple who begged for time to go first and bury his father before following him, Jesus said, 'Follow me; and let the dead bury their dead.' (*Matthew* VIII. 21-22.)
4. The spiritual path, as every great teacher warns us, is never easy – indeed, it is usually fraught with grave obstacles and intense suffering (as the prisoners in Plato's cave would find if they tried to walk out of it). Jesus said, 'Strait is the gate and narrow the way, which leadeth unto life.' (*Matthew* VII.14.) If we delay, however, we only store up further pain for ourselves, as Buddha taught. Suffering can be the great awakener. When, as all the mystics have remarked, one's whole life lies in ruins, one may be forced by the sheer intensity of suffering and the emptiness of old values, to turn towards the spiritual life.
5. The compassionate Titan, Prometheus, of Greek mythology may be identified symbolically with Lucifer, the Light-bringer and Son of the Morning, who, in later Christian myth, was equated with Satan, the Evil One. H.P. Blavatsky

points however, to the key to the true interpretation of the War in Heaven, the Fall of Lucifer and the 'Temptation' in the Garden of Eden. No doubt A.E. has the Theosophical interpretations in mind.
6. A.E. refers to the theme, later found in *The Candle of Vision* and elsewhere, of the duality in the being of man. The 'dust' and the 'opalescent airs' are reminiscent of the passage in which *The Voice of the Silence* speaks of the two aspects of man – 'All is impermanent in man except the pure bright essence of Alaya. Man is its crystal ray; a beam of light immaculate within, a form of clay material upon the lower surface.' (*Voice*, p. 63.)
7. These are the precise words used by W.Q. Judge in his translation of verse 18 of ch. IX of the *Bhagavad Gītā* – 'I am the goal, the Comforter, the Lord, the Witness, the resting-place, the asylum and the Friend.' (p. 66.)
8. An idea to be found in the *Upaniṣads*, Plato, Spinoza and many others – that true spiritual knowledge is *qualitatively* different from (and not merely quantitatively greater than) ordinary, empirical knowledge of the worldly kind (Plato's true knowledge vs. opinion and belief, Spinoza's *scientia intuitiva* vs. knowledge based on the imagination). Furthermore, levels of knowledge must be equivalent to states of inward being, so that to *know* more is to *be* more real in the spiritual sense. Such knowledge, being a complete portion of one's true nature, allows for no pretence and thus, in the truest sense we cannot communicate more than we know.
9. We are encouraged in Theosophy, and by ancient mystics who knew the profound truths that lay within the simplest of myths, to think of ourselves as being Prometheus, as being capable of bringing the divine fire down to the realm of our mortal nature.
10. 'Then from the heart that Power shall rise into the sixth, the middle region, the place between thine eyes, when it becomes the breath of the ONE-SOUL.' (*Voice*, p. 10.)
11. Since father and son or the first and the second Logos come from the One Unknown, the highest state of consciousness is where the mystic has risen even beyond the level of the Logos to that Darkness where there is no differentiation and which has no name.

THE RENEWAL OF YOUTH

1. The first versions appeared in *The Irish Theosophist*, August and October 1895 and June 1897, as 'The Age of the Spirit', 'Yes, and Hope' and 'Content'. The basic text used here is that published in *Imaginations and Reveries*. Those passages in square brackets appeared in *The Irish Theosophist* only, and were not subsequently reprinted. Slight changes in wording have been ignored. 'Yes, and Hope' ended with the words '. . . Gods as equals and companions'. The ending of Part II is extracted from 'Shadow and Substance', *The Irish Theosophist*, January 1896.
2. See *The Interpreters*, note 25.
3. Known as the Ancient Source in *The Secret Doctrine* – the ever-existent Universal Wisdom beyond cyclic change.
4. Echo of an archetypal theme in the evolution of mankind. Zeus represents those forces which seek to enslave man to the tyranny of lower material nature. Prometheus is the Greek equivalent of Lucifer, 'the light bringer' who sacrifices his celestial state for the sake of imparting the fires of spiritual will to man. A.E. has here changed the original version's 'Titan and Divinity' to 'Titan and Zeus'.

5. This expression is often used by H.P. Blavatsky of the divine, re-incarnating soul. (See, for example *Key*, p.167.)
6. It is the ephemeral *persona*, the separative, egotistic self which clings to the body and makes a false identification with the name. This identification with *nāma-rūpa*, name and form, is what prevents us from responding to the call of the higher voice.
7. W.Q. Judge often said that we should spend at least as much time on thinking, as on reading, otherwise we are liable to suffer from mental indigestion.
8. Description of Krishna in the *Bhagavad Gītā*, ch. IX, vs.18 (p. 66).
9. Esoteric commentary on the first five books of the Old Testament. In the first version A.E. used the words *Ātma*, *buddhi* and *manas* here. In the theosophical classification of the principles of human nature, *Ātma* is the divine spirit, *buddhi* is the intuitive soul and the clear reflector of the universal light of *Ātma*, and *manas* is the higher mind capable of understanding eternal ideas. The three-in-one constitute the immortal self.
10. In the first version, A.E. used the word *mānasa*, beings who have perfected themselves in the power of meditative thought, and impart the spark of their essence to those in whom the flame of self-conscious mind has not yet been aroused.
11. Sometimes spoken of by Indian mystics as the forty-nine Fires.
12. *Matthew* III. 3, and Psalm XXIV, 7.
13. Cf. *C.O.V.*, note 103.
14. Cf. *C.O.V.*, note 96, on the awakening of the *Kuṇḍalinī* power.
15. This is what the Upaniṣads call 'the Light in the head'.
16. Cf. *C.O.V.*, note 3, on the Great Mother.
17. Mystical texts, such as *Light on the Path*, speak of the courageous soul in man which does battle against egotism, greed, and selfishness, as 'the Warrior'.
18. The will is a force like a colourless fluid, which takes on the character of the motives which direct it. The spiritual will – one of the highest forces in the universe – is impelled by the altruistic motive of rendering service to all beings.
19. Cf. *C.O.V.*, pp. 147–48 for a detailed explanation of 'the fiery power'.
20. Central Spiritual Sun.
21. *The Voice of the Silence* speaks of the Three Halls (states of consciousness, planes of being) which lead to that which lies beyond them, 'the shoreless waters of Akshara, the indestructible Fount of Omniscience' (*turīya*). The earth is only a shadowy gateway to these, and *The Voice of the Silence* says, 'This earth, O ignorant Disciple, is but the dismal entrance leading to the twilight that precedes the valley of true light – that light which no wind can extinguish, that light which burns without a wick or fuel.' (*Voice*, pp. 4-5.)
22. *Luke* XV. 11–32.
23. 'Just as milliards of bright sparks dance on the waters of an ocean above which one and the same moon is shining, so our evanescent personalities – the illusive envelopes of the immortal MONAD-EGO – twinkle and dance on the waves of Maya. They last and appear, as the thousands of sparks produced by the moon-beams, only so long as the Queen of Night radiates her lustre on the running waters of life: the period of a Manvantara; and then they disappear, the beams – symbols of our eternal Spiritual Egos – alone surviving, re-merged in, and being, as they were before, one with the Mother-Source.' (*S.D.* I, p. 237.)
24. The unmanifested Logos.
25. That which is called the 'sacred white island' or 'the Islands of the Blest' in ancient traditions. The celestial abode of adepts and sages of every nation.
26. A reference to the Spiritual Sun.
27. 'The garden of Eden' stands for the primordial purity of the soul, the inward

golden age or 'paradise' from which the soul is an exile, but which it dimly remembers and to which it must one day return, after a journey fraught with pain and travail. The verse from *Ezekiel*, in saying '. . . every precious stone was thy covering . . .', perhaps implies that the soul has innate within it every precious gift and faculty, although these no longer shine forth because their lustre has been covered with the dust of the earth. (*Ezekiel* XXIII. 13)

28. Mystics throughout the ages have spoken, often in veiled metaphors and guarded tones, of the centre within the head which 'lights up' when the faculty of spiritual intuition is awakened. The Indian sages advise meditation on certain points in the face and head, but it is not the external or the physical organs that are meant. The ancient sages knew about mystical centres in the head which are connected with the awakening of divine insight. These, at the purely physiological level, may be *represented* by the organs spoken of by A.E. but cannot be *identified* with them. The spiritual may occasionally be symbolized by the physiological, but can never be reduced to it.

29. A.E. makes frequent reference to the 'centres' or *cakras* which are particularly potent points along the pathway of the electric, psycho-spiritual force called *kuṇḍalinī*.

30. *Ezekiel* XXVIII.17.

31. 'The rose must re-become the bud . . . The Pupil must regain *the child-state he has lost* ere the first sound can fall upon his ear.' (*Voice*, pp. 18 & 19.)

32. Theosophy teaches that the spiritual glory we shall attain when we have recovered our divine heritage and gone back to the world of the Spirit will be far brighter than that from which we fell; for the earlier glory was the glory of innocent but undeveloped childhood, but the later one will be what we have achieved through self-conscious effort, having faced evil and overcome it with knowledge, and thus all our powers and faculties will be developed. We must eat of the fruit of the Tree of knowledge of good and evil and leave the garden of Eden before we may taste the fruit of the Tree of eternal life.

SELF-RELIANCE

1. First appeared in *The Irish Theosophist*, May 1896.
2. That brotherhood of beings who have evolved beyond the need for bodily limitation but have voluntarily stopped short of total absorption in Absolute Being or Nirvāṇa in order to aid those trapped in earthly illusion.
3. Theosophically, Masters are the agents of the Law or Karma which can be said to be a direct emanation of the Absolute, itself coeval with Universal Mind. They do not adjust or determine the law but execute it precisely and compassionately. They thus form a crucial link between the highest imperatives of the Law and their reflections in the lower regions of the cosmos, i.e., those closest to the physical plane.

IRELAND BEHIND THE VEIL

1. First published in *Universal Brotherhood*, June 1897. Reprinted in *The Theosophical Path* (Point Loma, California) ed. Katherine Tingley, Vol. XXII, No. 3, March 1922, from which this text is reprinted.
2. William Larminie (1849?–1900), *West Irish Folk-Tales and Romances*, London 1893.

ON THE MARCH

1. First appeared in *The Internationalist*, November 1897.
2. See note 8 of *The Avatars* for a full account of A.E.'s understanding of this sacred term.
3. Reference is made to H.P. Blavatsky, founder of the Theosophical Society in 1875.
4. Reference is made to W.Q. Judge, president of the American Section of the Theosophical Society.

TRANSFORMATIONS

1. First appeared in *The Internationalist*, February 1889.
2. Literature on the mystical and spiritual life abounds in references to a return to the pure, clear consciousness of childhood. One of the primary symbols of Taoist mysticism is that of a new-born babe, to whom the sage is frequently compared, while *The Voice of the Silence* says, 'The Pupil must regain *the child-state he has lost* ere the first [mystic] sound can fall upon his ear.' (p. 19.) Jesus remarked of little children that 'of such is the kingdom of God' (*Luke*, XVIII.16.) When St. John of the Cross says that God instructs 'the soul that is empty and disencumbered' (*D.N.* I, ch. 12, p. 79) or when Richard of St. Victor points out that 'the essence of purgation is self-simplification', they are speaking of the same thing, as is the author of *The Cloud of Unknowing* by the statement, 'By "darkness" I mean "a lack of knowing".' (Ch.4, p. 58.) Even the 'proficients' of St. John necessarily 'experience God as little children'. (*D.N.* II, ch. 3, p. 97.)
3. Cf. *C.O.V.*, note 189.

THE CHRIST

1. First appeared in *The Path*, February 1911.
2. No individual, be he human or divine, can save any other. We bless or blight our own destiny, through our own deeds, our words, our very thoughts above all. No God, as Buddha warns us, can save or damn us. Buddha taught his followers:

> 'Pray not! the Darkness will not brighten! Ask
> Nought from the Silence, for it cannot speak!
> Vex not your mournful minds with pious pains!
> Ah! Brothers, Sisters! seek
> Nought from the helpless gods by gift and hymn.'
> (Edwin Arnold, *The Light of Asia*, bk. VIII)

> 'Each hath such lordship as the loftiest ones;
> Nay, for with Powers above, around, below,
> As with all flesh and whatsoever lives,
> Act maketh joy and woe.
> What hath been bringeth what shall be, and is,
> Worse – better – last for first and first for last;
> The Angels in the Heavens of Gladness reap
> Fruits of a holy past.'
> (*Ibid.*)

> 'Higher than Indra's ye may lift your lot,
> And sink it lower than the worm or gnat;
> The end of many myriad lives is this,
> The end of myriads that.'
>
> (*Ibid.*)

As we cannot bear the burden of such spiritual responsibility we rely upon the notion of a personal Creator, an external arbiter of our fate, and finally end up with the idea of a historical saviour in time. The idea of such a personage, says A.E., may temporarily assuage our spiritual fears, but does not accord with the facts of the spiritual life.

3. This is the Word that lies deep within the consciousness of every individual, the power of sound beyond all sounds and in the silence of the innermost soul. See *C.O.V.* note 213 on 'AUM'.
4. To make an idol is to externalize, to try, mistakenly, to limit the limitless within the confines of a form in time and space. To do this is to make oneself incapable of understanding the Idea which, in its fullness, must ever elude form and name.
5. As Jesus sorrowfully exclaimed, 'Except ye see signs and wonders, ye will not believe.' (*John* IV.48.) We are caught up in the illusion of the reality (and the sole reality) of the physical world, but the universal, eternal Spirit, as A.E. points out, cannot fully manifest through any one physical form with its historical and spatial limitations.
6. The doctrine of cycles (on all planes) and their return.
7. The teaching of the Christ within every human heart is a central tenet of Theosophical mysticism, as it was of many earlier mystics. 'The birth of Christ within the soul' was a constantly reiterated idea in Eckhart's sermons.
8. 'The general condition of men's minds and hearts will have been improved and purified by the spread of its teachings, and, as I have said, their prejudices and dogmatic illusions will have been, to some extent at least, removed. Not only so, but besides a large and accessible literature ready to men's hands, the next impulse will find a numerous and *united* body of people ready to welcome the new torch-bearer of Truth. He will find the minds of men prepared for his message, a language ready for him in which to clothe the new truths he brings an organization awaiting his arrival, which will remove the merely mechanical, material obstacles and difficulties from his path. Think how much one, to whom such an opportunity is given, could accomplish.' (*Key*, p. 307.) H.P. Blavatsky gives us the conditions under which the work of a spiritual teacher is made easier. This paragraph in A.E. seems to derive directly from such passages in Theosophical literature.

APPENDIX A:

THE THEOSOPHICAL MOVEMENT

1. 'Lodges of Magic' was the heading given to two letters to the Editor of *Lucifer* (H.P. Blavatsky), in the issues of 15 December 1888 and 15 January 1889, with Mme. Blavatsky's comments. They are probably by Russell.
2. 'A Word upon the Objects of the Theosophical Society' was published in *The Irish Theosophist*, 15 November 1892.
3. *To the Fellows of the Theosophical Society* was originally printed in 1894 on The Irish Theosophist Press, Dublin. It was reprinted in *The Theosophical*

Movement (Bombay) vol. VIII, 17 March 1938, pp. 66-68.
4. 'On the Spur of the Moment' was first published in *The Irish Theosophist*, 15 February 1895.
5. 'To the Editor of *Lucifer*' was published in its 15 March 1895 issue.
6. 'A Basis for Brotherhood' was published in *The Irish Theosophist*, 15 July 1895.
7. 'W.Q.J.' was published in *The Irish Theosophist*, 15 April 1896. W.Q. Judge had died on 21 March.
8. 'Stand and Serve' was published in *The Irish Theosophist*, 15 February 1897.
9. 'Word and Theory' was published in the *Ethical Echo*, September and November 1893. The text is printed from photocopies provided by courtesy of the Lilly Library, Indiana University, Bloomington, Indiana.

SELECT BIBLIOGRAPHY

Arnold, Sir Edwin. *The Light of Asia*. London, 1879, London: Routledge and Kegan Paul Ltd., 1959.
Bhagavad-Gītā. Translated by William Q. Judge. Los Angeles: The Theosophy Company, 1947.
The Bible. All references are from the King James Version.
Blavatsky, Helena Petrovna. *Isis Unveiled*. A photographic reproduction of the original edition, first published at New York City, 1877. Los Angeles: The Theosophy Company, 1968.
——. *The Secret Doctrine*. Facsimile of the original edition of 1888. Los Angeles: The Theosophy Company, 1974.
——. *Theosophical Glossary*. A photographic reproduction of the original edition, first issued at London, 1892. Los Angeles: The Theosophy Company, 1971.
——. *Transactions of the Blavatsky Lodge*. Reprinted verbatim from the original edition of 1890–91. Los Angeles: The Theosophy Company, 1923.
——. *The Voice of the Silence*. From *The Book of the Golden Precepts*. Translated and annotated by 'H.P.B.'. Los Angeles: The Theosophy Company, 1928.
Bose, Abinash Chandra. *Three Mystic Poets: A study of W.B. Yeats, A.E. and Rabindranath Tagore*, with Introduction by J.H. Cousins. Kolhapur, 1945, Folcroft, Pa.: Folcroft Press, 1970.
Burtt, E.A. *The Teachings of the Compassionate Buddha*. Edited with introduction and notes by E.A. Burtt. New York: New American Library, 1955.
The Cloud of Unknowing. Translated with Introduction by Clifton Wolfers. Baltimore, Md.: Penguin, 1961.
Collins, Mabel. *Light on the Path*. Written down by 'M.C.', with notes and comments by the author. Bombay: Theosophy Company (India), 1968.
Denson, Alan. *Printed Writings by George William Russell (A.E.)*. A bibliography with notes on his pictures and portraits. London, and Evanston, Ill. Northwestern University Press, 1961.
Dhammapada. Translated with notes by editors of Cunningham Press. Alhambra, Calif., 1955.
Eek, Sven, and de Zirkoff, Boris. *William Quan Judge, Theosophical Pioneer*. Wheaton, Ill.: The Theosophical Publishing House, 1969.
Figgis, Darrell. *A.E. George W. Russell: A Study of a Man and a Nation*. Dublin, 1915, New York: Kennikat Press, 1970.
Grant, Michael, and Hazel, John. *Gods and Mortals in Classical Mythology*. Springfield, Mass.: G. & C. Merriam Company, 1973.
Judge, William Quan. *Notes on the Bhagavad-Gita*. Los Angeles: The Magazine Theosophy, 1956.
Kain, Richard Morgan, and O'Brien, James H. *George Russell, (A.E.)*. Lewisburg, Pa.: Bucknell University Press, 1976.
Kingsland, William. *The Real H.P. Blavatsky: A Study in Theosophy and a Memoir of a Great Soul*. London: John M. Watkins, 1928.
Lucifer. Began publication in September 1887. Published by Madame H.P. Blavatsky. London.

Magee, William Kirkpatrick. *A Memoir of George William Russell*, by John Eglinton (pseud. of W.K. Magee) London: Macmillan and Co., 1937.
Monier-Williams, Sir Monier. *English-Sanskrit Dictionary*. Oxford: Clarendon Press, 1899.
Neff, Mary K. *Personal Memoirs of H.P. Blavatsky*. Wheaton, I11.: The Theosophical Publishing House, 1967.
Norton Anthology of Poetry. Revised edition. Edited by Allison, Barrows, Blake, Carr, Eastman and English. New York: W.W. Norton and Co., 1970.
Orage, A.R. *Readers and Writers 1917–1921*. Freeport, N.Y.: Books for Libraries Press, 1969.
Patañjali. *The Yoga Aphorisms*. An Interpretation by William Quan Judge. Los Angeles: The Theosophy Comany, 1967.
The Path. A theosophical journal. First appeared in 1886. Edited by W.Q. Judge. New York: The Aryan Press.
Plato. *Collected Dialogues*. Edited with introduction and prefatory notes by Edith Hamilton and Huntington Cairns. Princeton, N.J.: Princeton University Press, 1961.
Plotinus. *The Essential Plotinus*. Selected and newly translated with Introduction and commentary by Elmer O'Brien. New York: New American Library, 1964.
Russell, George William. *A.E.'s Letters to Mínanlábáin*. With Introduction by L.K. Porter. New York: The Macmillan Co., 1937.
——. *Letters from A.E.* Selected and edited by Alan Denson, with a Foreword by Monk Gibbon. London: Abelard-Schumann, 1961.
——. *Some Passages from the Letters of W.B. Yeats*. Dublin: Cuala Press, 1936; Shannon: Irish University Press, 1971.
——. *Collected Poems*. London: Macmillan and Co., 1913.
Sangharakshita, Bhikshu. *A Survey of Buddhism*. Bangalore, India: The Bangalore Printing and Publishing Co., 1957.
Sañkara. *Crest Jewel of Discrimination*. Tr. by Swami Prabhavananda and Christopher Isherwood. New York: Mentor, 1970.
Selections from The Upanishads and The Tao Te King. Translated by Charles Johnston (Upanishads) and Lionel Giles (Tao Te King). Alhambra, Calif.: The Cunningham Press, 1951.
Thompson, Francis. *Poems of Francis Thompson*. Edited with biographical and textual notes by Rev. Terence L. Connolly. London: D. Appleton-Century Co., 1941.
Shelley, P.B. *Poetical Works of Percy Bysshe Shelley*. London: Oxford University Press, 1905.
Squire, Charles. *Celtic Myth and Legend*. First published in 1905 under the title *The Mythology of the British Islands*. Hollywood, Calif.: Newcastle Publishing Co., 1975.
St. John of the Cross. *Complete Works*. Translated and edited by E. Allison Peers. Westminster, Md.: Newman Press, 1964.
Summerfield, Henry. *That Myriad-Minded Man: A biography of A.E.*. Gerrards Cross, Bucks: Colin Smythe Ltd., 1975, Totowa; N.J.: Rowman & Littlefield, 1976.
Theosophical Movement, The History of the. New York: E.P. Dutton & Co., 1925.
Upanishads. The thirteen principal Upanishads. Translated from the Sanskrit and with a commentary by Robert Ernest Hume. London: Oxford University Press, Second Edition Revised, 1931.

GLOSSARY OF TERMS AND NAMES

Adam Kadmon	archetypal man, heavenly man
Adept	lit., 'He who has attained'; a Master in the science of self-knowledge
Aditi	Vedic name for *mūlaprakṛti*, the Mother-Goddess
Aeon	emanations from the divine essence
Agni	the god of fire in the Vedas, oldest and most revered of Hindu gods
ahaṁkāra	self-consciousness or self-identity
Ah-hi	Dhyān-Chohans, Serpents of Wisdom
Ain Soph	Kabbalistic equivalent of Hindu Parabrahm, the One Reality
ākāśa	supersenuous essence pervading all space, universal creative potency
Alāya	universal soul; Tibetan term, identical with *ākāśa* mystically and *mūlaprakṛti* philosophically
alchemy	transmutation of the gross into the subtle
Amergin	first Druid to land on Irish soil; author of four poems said to be the oldest Irish literary record
Ancient of Days	Kabbalistic term for the primordial creator
Angus Oge	Gaelic eros, god of love and beauty; cosmic energy, *Fohat*
Anima Mundi	lit., 'Soul of the World', divine essence which permeates everything
antaḥkaraṇa	bridge between divine Soul and personal ego
Archaeus	Kabbalistic term for the oldest manifested deity
astral	substratum of physical matter; invisible counterpart of the human or animal form
astral light	subtle essence enveloping the earth; lowest plane of *ākāśa*
Aśvattha	the Bo-tree, the tree of knowledge
Ātman	supreme spirit, universal soul, seventh principle in the human constitution
AUM	the sacred syllable, eternal vibration
Avatár	direct incarnation of the Logos
Balor	chief among the race of sorcerers called the Fomors, he possessed the power to slay his enemies with a single glance
Bhagavad Gītā	lit., 'Song of God'; series of discourses between Krishna and his disciple Arjuna forming a portion of the Indian epic *Mahābhārata*
bodhicitta	lit., 'seed of enlightenment'; embryo of spiritual man
Bodhisattva	lit., 'he whose essence (*satva*) has become Wisdom (*Bodhi*)'; those who need but one more incarnation to become perfect Buddhas
Brahmā	male Logos and creator of the Hindu pantheon; first person of the Trimurti

Brigid	Gaelic goddess of fire, poetry and the hearth
buddhi	power of spiritual discrimination; moral perception; sixth principle in the human constitution
cakra	wheel or disk; circle of Viṣṇu
Caolte	One of the most mystic and supernatural of the Fenian warriors
Central Sun	One Reality; source of all life; universal spirit
chaos	the abyss, 'Great Deep'; undifferentiated matter
Conchobar	the legendary king of Ulster in its Golden Age
Connla	Irish king wooed by a goddess and borne away in a boat of glass to an earthly paradise beyond the sea
Cosmic Mind	universal creative spirit; intelligent soul of the cosmos; *Mahat*
Cosmocratores	world architects, or creative forces personified
Cuchullain, Cuculain	greatest champion of Red Branch cycle, solar symbol, descended from highest gods
Dagda	Gaelic god of the earth
Dana	mother of all the gods of the Celtic pantheon, the Tuatha de Danann who took their name from her; primordial substance, *mūlaprakṛti*
Day of Brahmā	period of manifestation during a *manvantara*; alternating with periods of rest called Brahmā's night
Demiurge	divine architect, Plato's 'second God'
deva	resplendent divinity, celestial being
Devachan	lit., 'dwelling of the Gods'; intermediate state between two earth-lives into which the Higher Self (*Ātma-Buddhi-Manas*) enters after its separation from the lower elements at death
dharma	duty, moral law; social and personal morality; natural law, natural obligation
dhāraṇā	state of uninterrupted meditation
dhyāna	lit., 'contemplation'; a state of abstraction far above the plane of sensuous perception
Dhyān Chohan	lit., 'the Lords of Light'; divine intelligences
divine darkness	unmanifest potency, pure potentiality
Dzyān	Tibetan term for divine wisdom
Earth Spirit	*Anima Mundi;* the earth and all its inhabitants represented as a single being informed by divine intelligence
elementals	spirits of the elements; creatures animating the kingdoms of earth, water, air and fire
Elohim	supernatural hosts of forces; the sevenfold power of the godhead
Eri	Celtic goddess and queen representing Ireland
Fenians	band of noble warriors loyal to Finn
Finn MacCool	demi-god and warrior hero of the Finn cycle, or age of heroes; Celtic equivalent to British King Arthur
Fire-Mist	*Ākāśa*; primordial form of *Fohat*
Fohat	the essence of cosmic force or electricity; primordial light
Fomorians	Gaelic deities of death, darkness and the sea; the chthonic powers
Golden Age	first of four *yugas*
Great Mother	radiant matter; supersensuous form of the Beautiful
Great Sacrifice	renunciation of Nirvāṇa for the sake of universal enlightenment

Glossary of Terms and Names

guṇas	qualities or attributes; the threefold division of qualities in Hindu thought; namely, *sattva, rajas* and *tamas*
Hazel	tree held sacred by ancient Druids; symbol of cosmic manifestation
hierophant	lit., 'one who explains sacred things'; discloser of sacred things; a chief among Initiates
holy breath	synthesis of the seven powers in man and the cosmos
Holy Well	sacred source of waters of wisdom; oracular sites visited by Druid priest for divine guidance
Hy-Breasail	lit., Breasail's Island; mythical land, representing the earth in a golden age
incubus	male elemental called forth from the astral light by human passion
Indra	Vedic deity, king of the sidereal gods
Isle of Immortals	permanent abode of White Adepts
Īśvara	the divine within each man, the true perceiver
jāgrat	waking state of consciousness
jīva	universal life; the divine monad, *Ātma-Buddhi*
jñāna	spiritual knowledge
Kabiri	ancient gods worshipped by the peoples of the Near East; at one time connected with all forms of fire
Kali Yuga	last of four great evolutionary ages; period of spiritual obscuration
kalpa	the period of a mundane revolution, representing a 'day' or 'night' of Brahmā
kāma	seat of animal passions and selfishness; fourth principle in the human constitution
kāma loka	semi-material and subjective state where disembodied entities or astral forms disintegrate after death
kāma rūpa	subjective form created through mental and physical desire, surviving the death of the body; vampire
karma	law of ethical causation and moral retribution; causality, action
kriyāśakti	power of ideation; creative potency of the yogi
kuṇḍalinī	yogic power developed by those of high spiritual attainment; activated *buddhi*
Kwan-Yin	the female Logos, called 'Mother of Compassion' by Chinese sages
Light of Lights	Central Spiritual Sun; *Ātman*
Lir	boundless space; parent source; first principle of Celtic cosmogony
Logoi	celestial agents of the Logos; the Builders, Dhyān Chohans, Archangels
Logos	outward expression of divine and hidden cause; operation of spiritual intelligence
Lugh	Gaelic Apollo; Celtic sun-god
magic	divine science; practical knowledge of the hidden mysteries of nature
Magus	sage, magician, a wise man of the Chaldeans
mahāmāyā	lit., Great Illusion; the illusion produced by manifestation
Mahat	first principle of universal intelligence and consciousness
Manannan	first offspring of Lir; *Mahat*, Cosmic Mind
manas	power of thought; seat of intelligence; fifth human principle
mantra	sacred verses used as incantations and charms

Descent of the Gods

Mantrikā śakti	the power of mystic words, sounds, numbers or letters in *mantras*
Manu	cosmically, the Logos or progenitor of mankind; in human evolution, the first legislator of an epoch, a semi-divine being
manvantara	period of manifestation
Master	*Mahātma*; highest form of Adeptship; one who has achieved total enlightenment
māyā	illusion; appearance; that which is opposed to reality
Meave (also Medh)	queen of Connaught, prominent figure in the 'Irish Iliad'
mediumship	state of passive absorption in which an individual is subject to astral forces beyond his direct control
Meru, Mount	Hindu 'Olympus' or abode of the gods
mūlaprakṛti	abstract, feminine principle; undifferentiated substance
Nirmāṇakāya	lit., a transformed 'body'; post-mortem state or condition entered into by adepts or yogis who have renounced Nirvāṇa for the sake of assisting other beings on the path to enlightenment
Nirvāṇa	state of absolute existence and absolute consciousness
noesis	the plane of higher manasic activity
Nuada	Gaelic Zeus and chief war god
Odin	Scandinavian equivalent to Hermes or Creative Wisdom
Ossian (Oisin)	son of Finn, epic poet and author of 'Ossianic Ballads', the tales of the great deeds of Finn and the Fenians
Oversoul	pure essence of the universal sixth principle – *Mahābuddhi*
Parabrahm	lit., 'beyond Brahmā'; the Absolute, secondless Reality; attributeless, impersonal principle
Paraclete	name for Holy Spirit in Christian trinity; light of the Logos
pitris	spiritual ancestors and creators of mankind
pleroma	a Gnostic term for the divine world; abode of the invisible gods
prakṛti	manifest Nature in general as opposed to *Puruṣa* or pure spirit
pralaya	period of obscuration or repose
prāṇa	animating principle of life; breath of life
psyche	lit., 'breath'; the terrestrial soul in man connected with the *kāma* principle attracted to the lower portion of *manas*
Purāṇas	lit., 'ancient', a collection of allegorical writings composed by the author of the *Mahābhārata*
Puruṣa	the spiritual Self
Rāja Yoga	system of developing spiritual powers through union with the Supreme Spirit; regulation and concentration of thought
Red Branch Heroes	gods and warriors comprising the second Gaelic cycle of heroes or Ulster cycle, sometimes termed the Irish *Iliad*
rishis (ṛsis)	sages, divine seers
rūpa	body; any form which is objective on its own plane
Śabda Brahman	unmanifested Logos; eternal vibration of *Brahman*
śakti	forces of nature synthesized; universal energy
samādhi	state of ecstatic and complete trance; highest state of yoga
sandhyā	lit., 'twilight'; period of transition between adjoining cycles
seership	the capacity to see formless spiritual essences; spiritual clairvoyance
Senzar	mystic name for the sacerdotal language of adepts

Glossary of Terms and Names

Sephiroth	the ten emanations of Deity in the Kabbala
Sidhe	fairies, numinous spirits inhabiting various Irish hills; hill sanctuaries inhabited by gods and fairies
Śiva	god of destruction and regeneration; patron of ascetics; third person of Trimūrti
Soma	name of the moon; juice of the plant used for trance purposes
sorcerer	master of infernal magic; evil magician
Spirit	homogeneous, universal consciousness
succubus	female elemental that preys on the passions of men
suṣupti	deep sleep state, corresponding to Devachan
sūtrātman	lit., 'the thread of spirit'; the immortal and reincarnating Ego; universal energy
svapna	dream state
tantras	lit., 'rules of rituals'; worship of cosmic forces
Tao	incomprehensible source of all things; the philosophy of Lao Tzu
tapas	moral fervour; purificatory action; austerities, penance
tejas tattva	radiant thought-body or *mānasa rūpa;* power of ideation
theurgy	communication with, and bringing down to earth, celestial spirits
Tir-na-noge	lit., 'land of the young', a mythic realm of perpetual peace, devachan
Tree of Life	universal symbol of the mystical forces in nature; symbol of the adept
triloka	the three worlds – Swarga, Bhūmi and Pātāla – corresponding to spiritual and psychic regions
Trimūrti	lit., 'three faces' or 'triple form'; Brahmā, Viṣṇu and Śiva of the Hindu pantheon
Tuatha de Danann	great pantheon of Celtic gods, the first order of Celtic cosmogony
turīya	fourth and highest state of consciousness; spiritual wakefulness
Vāc	mystic personification of speech; the female Logos
Verbum	Gnostic term for the ceaseless activity of the Logos
Viṣṇu	second person of the Hindu Trimūrti, the preserver and renovator
yajña	sacrifice; invisible fires extending from heaven to earth
yoga	spiritual discipline; union with the divine; skill in action
yuga	periods of manifestation, classified as Gold, Silver, Bronze and Iron Ages

TITLE INDEX

Analytic, 100
Ancient Intuitions, 142
Architecture of Dream, The, 123
Ascending Cycle, The, 616
At the Dawn of the Kaliyuga, 322
Avatars, The, 535
Awakening of the Fires, The, 354

Basis for Brotherhood, A, 668

Candle of Vision, The, 81
Cave of Lilith, The, 214
Celtic Imagination, The, 160
Celtic Cosmogony, 154
Childhood of Apollo, 515
Chivalry, 370
Comfort, 458
Concentration, 456

Doomed City, A, 476
Dream of Angus Oge, A, 523
Dreams, 118

Earth, 160
Earth Breath, The, 87
Eastern Candle of Vision, An, 462
Element Language, The, 174
Enchantment of Cuchullain, The, 490

Fountains of Youth, The, 518

'Go Out In Thought', 325

Have Imaginations Body?, 129

Hero in Man, The, 328
Hour of the Twilight, The, (A), 195
Hour of the Twilight, The, (B), 197

Ideals in Ireland: Priest or Hero?, 362
Imagination, 113
Interpreters, The, 243
In the Shadow of the Gods, 372
Intuition, 134
Ireland Behind the Veil, 635
Irish Mystic's Testimony, An, 377

Jagrata, Svapna and Sushupti, 454

Language of the Gods, The, 138
Legends of Ancient Eire, The, 341
Lodges of Magic, 653

Many-Coloured Land, The, 95
Mask of Apollo, The, 469
Meditation, 91
Meditation of Ananda, The, 210
Memory of Earth, The, 108
Memory of the Spirit, The, 149
Midnight Blossom, The, 236
Mingling of Natures, The, 104
Mountains, The, 348
Mystic Nights' Entertainment, The, 478

On an Irish Hill, 350
On the March, 641
On the Spur of the Moment, 664

Power, 146
Priestess of the Woods, A, 203
Priest or Hero?, 362

Religion and Love, 527
Renewal of Youth, The, 622
Retrospect, 83
Return, The, 677
Reviews
   Among the Gnomes, (Franz Hartmann), 383
   Christ Myth, The, (Dr. Arthur Drews), 648
   City Without Walls, The, (Margaret Cushing Osgood), 464
   From the Upanishads, (Charles Johnston), 189
   Lyrics, (R.H. Fitzpatrick), 187
   Treasure of the Humble, The, (Maurice Maeterlinck), 460

Secret of Power, The, 200
Self-Reliance, 632
Shadow and Substance, 619
Slave of the Lamp, The, 89
Song and its Fountains, 387
Speech of the Gods, The, 167
Stand and Serve, 672
Story of a Star, The, 472
Strange Awakening, A, 220

Talk by the Euphrates, A, 214
To the Editor of *Lucifer*, 667
To the Fellows of the Theosophical Society, 659
Tragedy in the Temple, A, 207
Transformations, 645

Word and Theory, 674
Word upon the Objects of the Theosophical Society, A, 657
Works and Days, 190
W.Q.J., 671